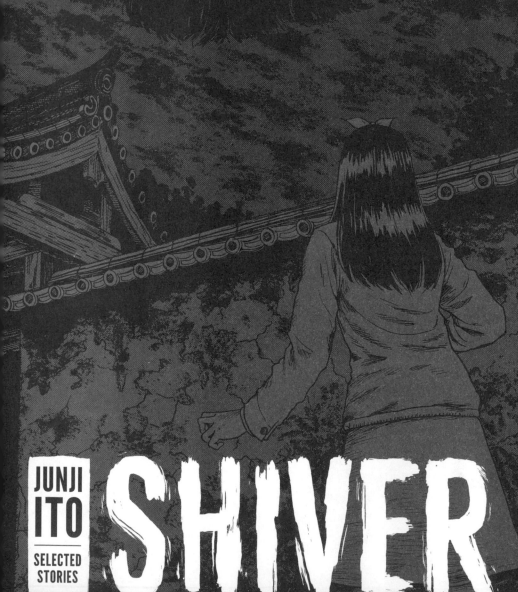

JUNJI
ITO

SELECTED
STORIES

SHIVER

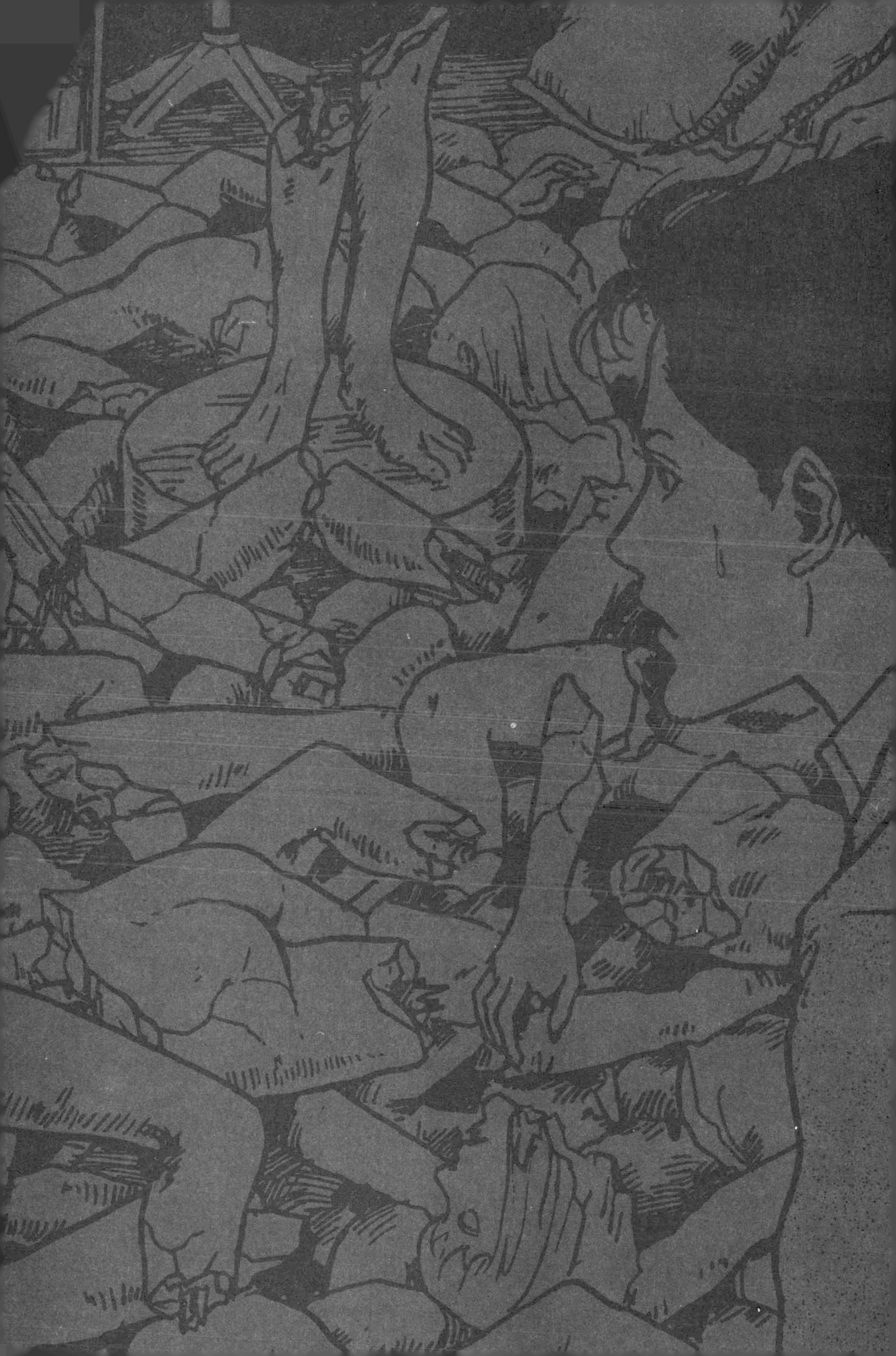

CONTENTS

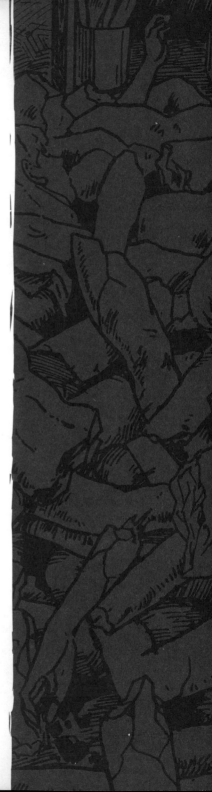

Used Record 5
COMMENTARY 39

Shiver 43
COMMENTARY 75

Fashion Model 77
COMMENTARY 109

Hanging Blimp 113
COMMENTARY 175

Marionette Mansion 179
COMMENTARY 239

Painter 241
COMMENTARY 281

The Long Dream 283
COMMENTARY 315

Honored Ancestors 317
COMMENTARY 349

Greased 351
COMMENTARY 383

PREVIOUSLY UNPUBLISHED NEW STORY

**Fashion Model:
Cursed Frame** 387

AFTERWORD 397

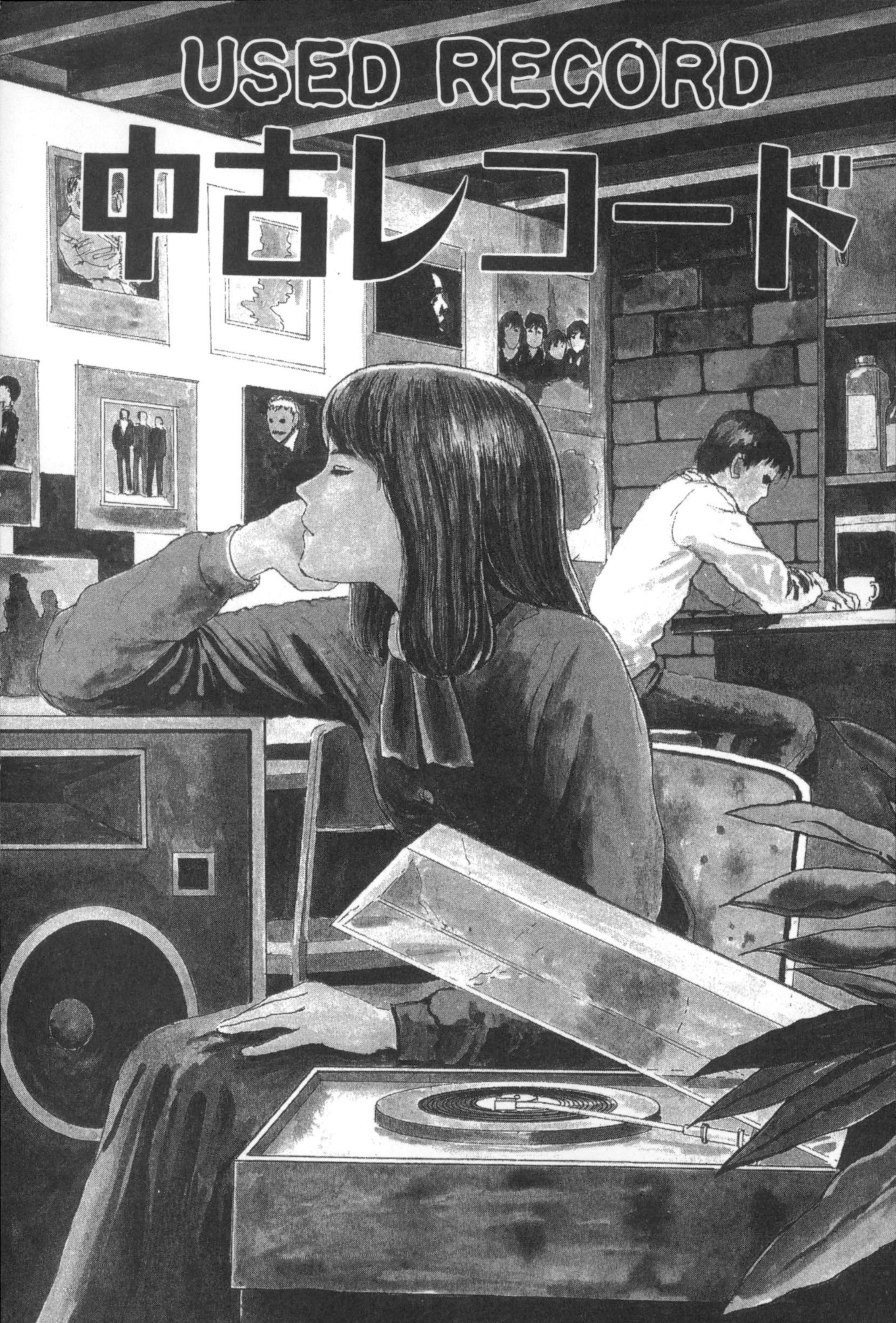
USED RECORD
中古レコード

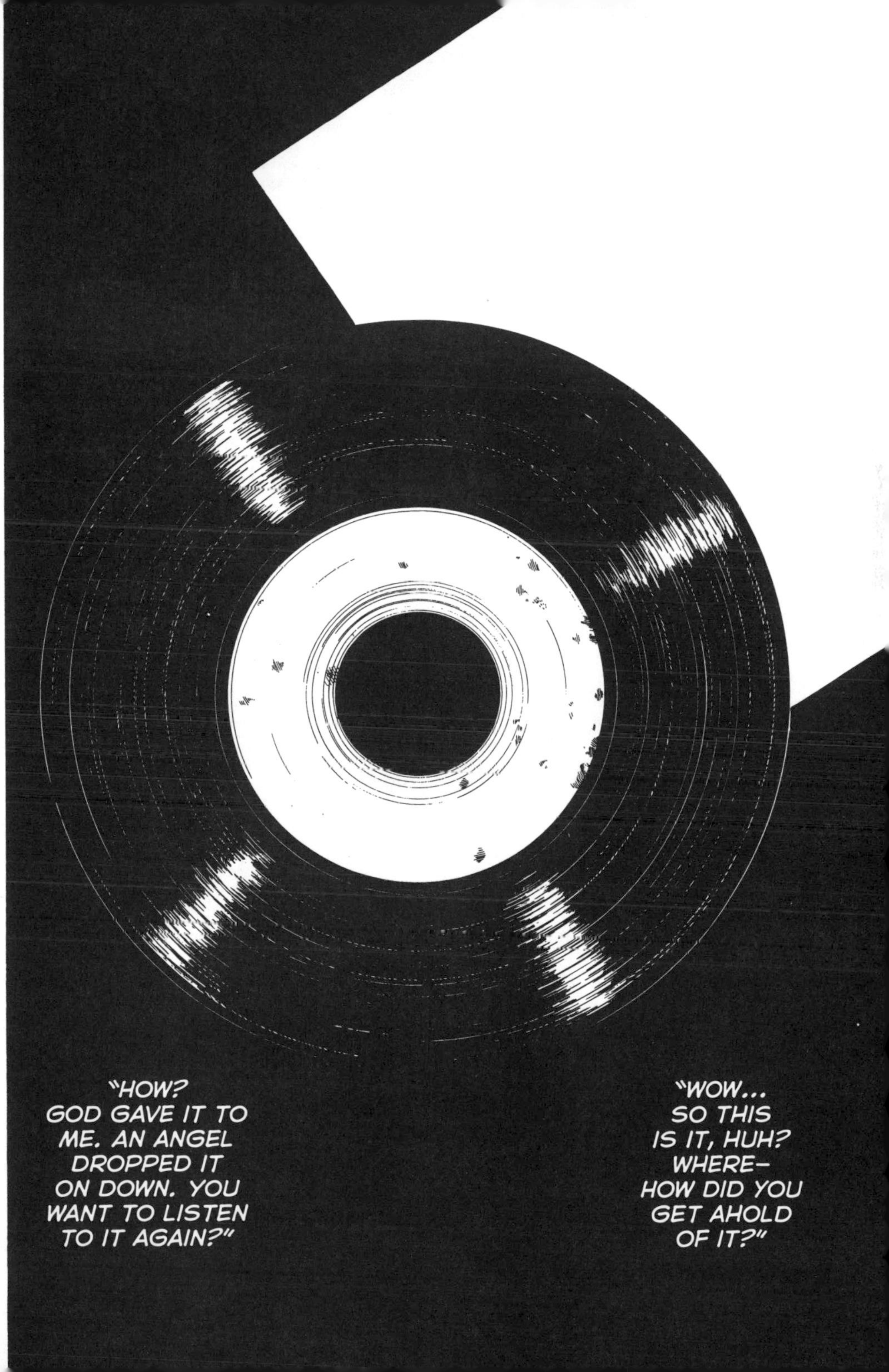
"WOW... SO THIS IS IT, HUH? WHERE— HOW DID YOU GET AHOLD OF IT?"
"HOW? GOD GAVE IT TO ME. AN ANGEL DROPPED IT ON DOWN. YOU WANT TO LISTEN TO IT AGAIN?"

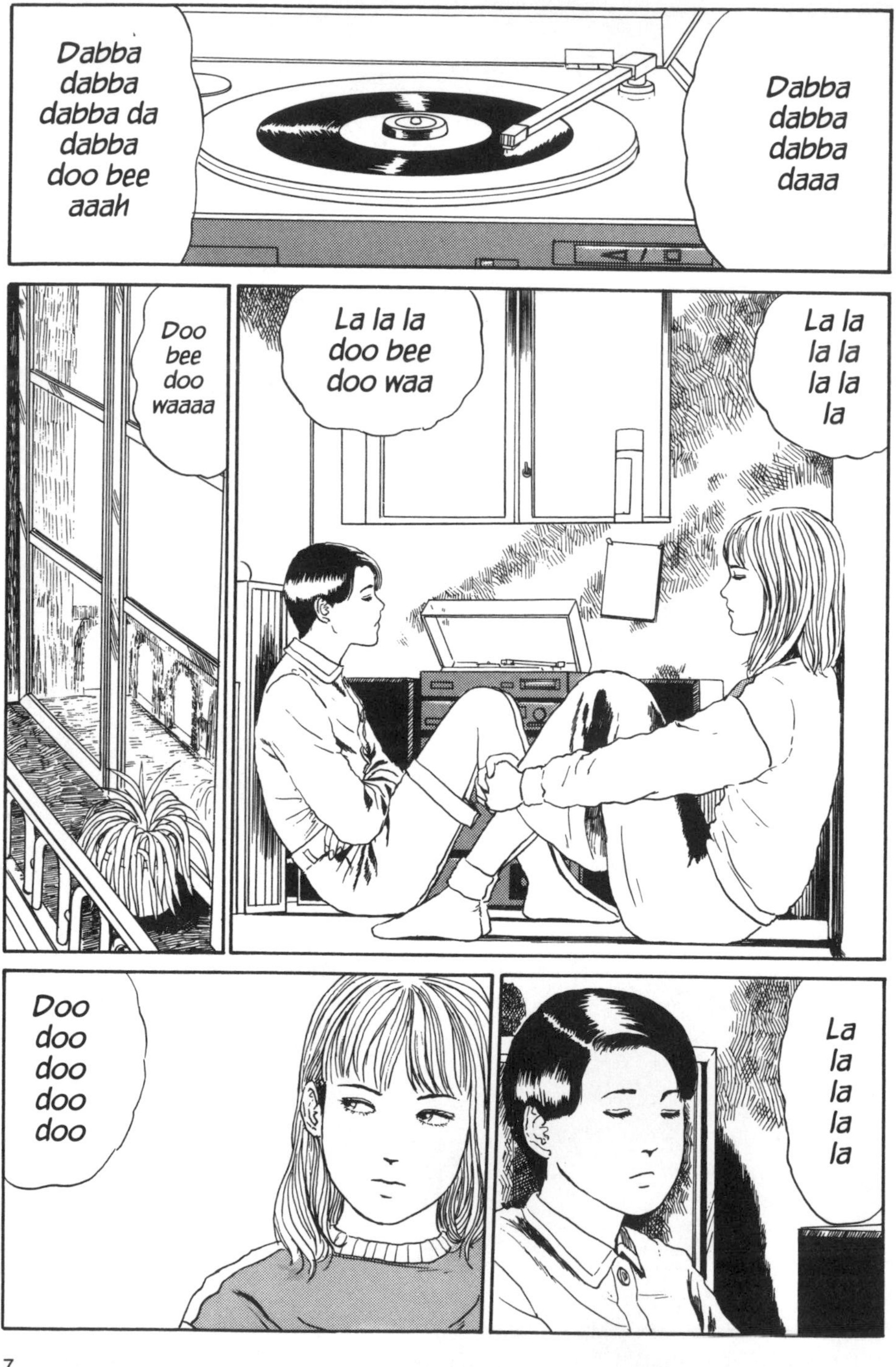
Dabba dabba dabba daaa
Dabba dabba dabba da dabba doo bee aaah
La la la la la la la
La la la doo bee doo waa
Doo bee doo waaaa
La la la la la
Doo doo doo doo doo

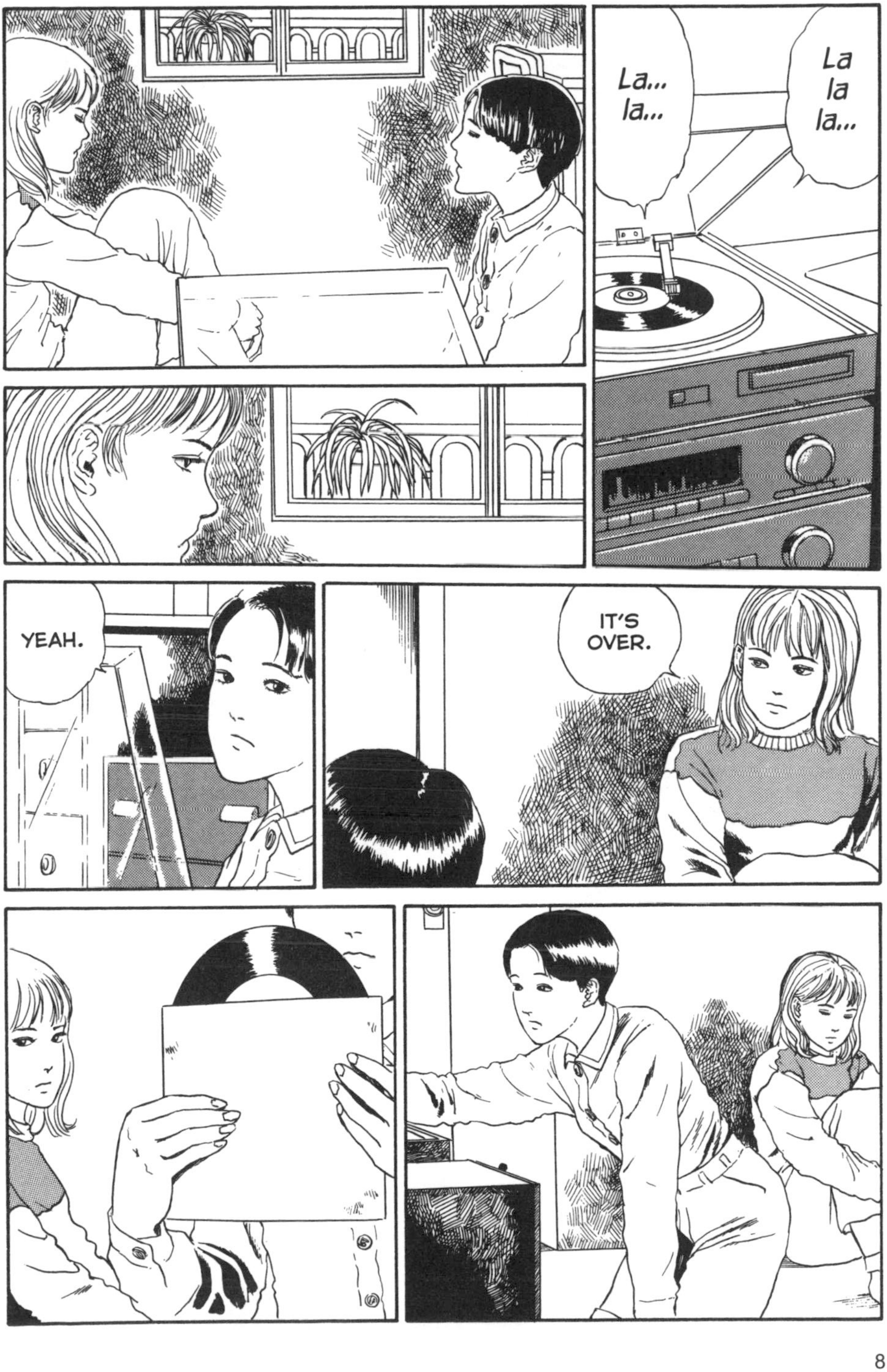
La la la...
La... la...
IT'S OVER.
YEAH.

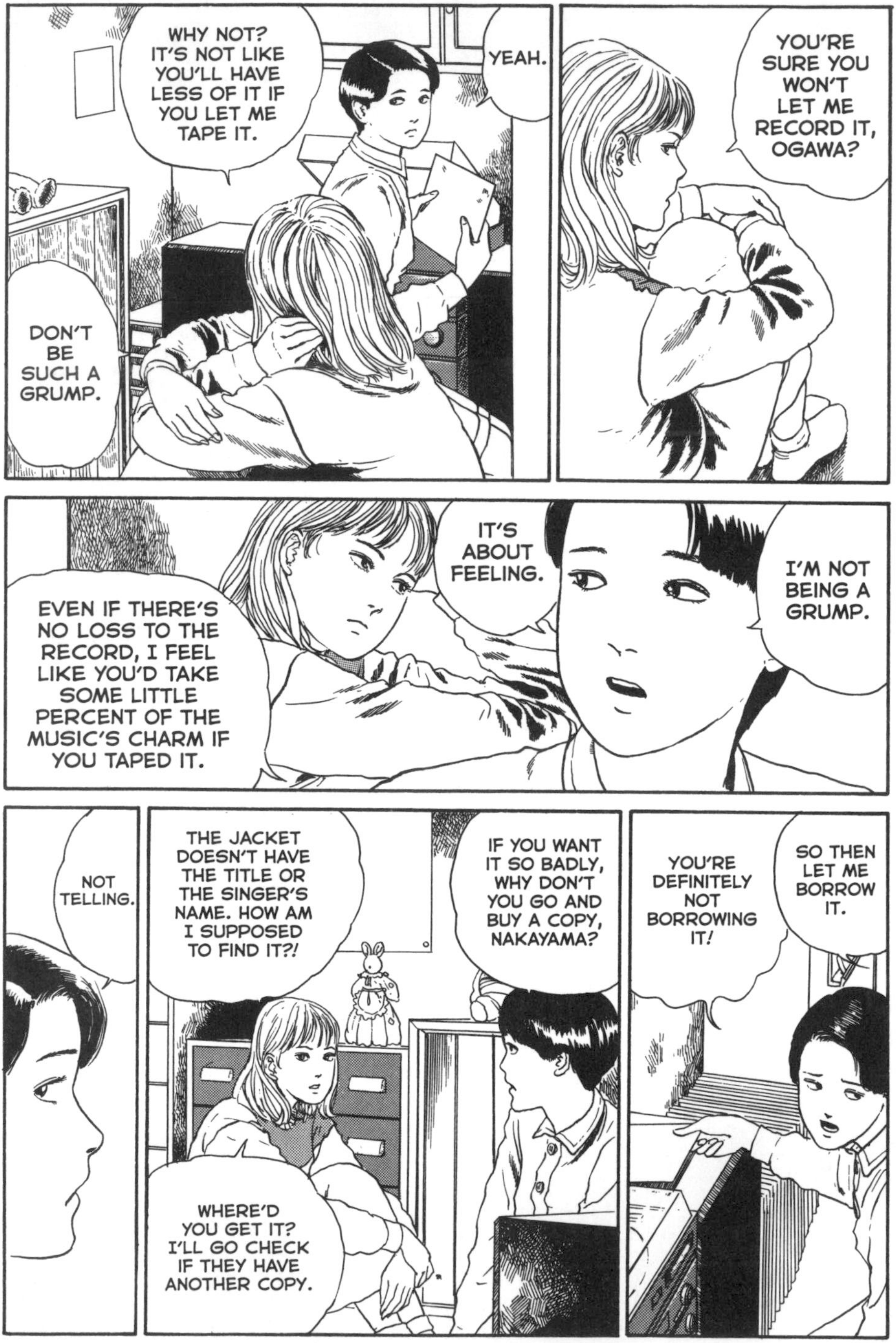
YOU'RE SURE YOU WON'T LET ME RECORD IT, OGAWA?
YEAH.
WHY NOT? IT'S NOT LIKE YOU'LL HAVE LESS OF IT IF YOU LET ME TAPE IT.
DON'T BE SUCH A GRUMP.
I'M NOT BEING A GRUMP.
IT'S ABOUT FEELING.
EVEN IF THERE'S NO LOSS TO THE RECORD, I FEEL LIKE YOU'D TAKE SOME LITTLE PERCENT OF THE MUSIC'S CHARM IF YOU TAPED IT.
SO THEN LET ME BORROW IT.
YOU'RE DEFINITELY NOT BORROWING IT!
IF YOU WANT IT SO BADLY, WHY DON'T YOU GO AND BUY A COPY, NAKAYAMA?
THE JACKET DOESN'T HAVE THE TITLE OR THE SINGER'S NAME. HOW AM I SUPPOSED TO FIND IT?!
WHERE'D YOU GET IT? I'LL GO CHECK IF THEY HAVE ANOTHER COPY.
NOT TELLING.

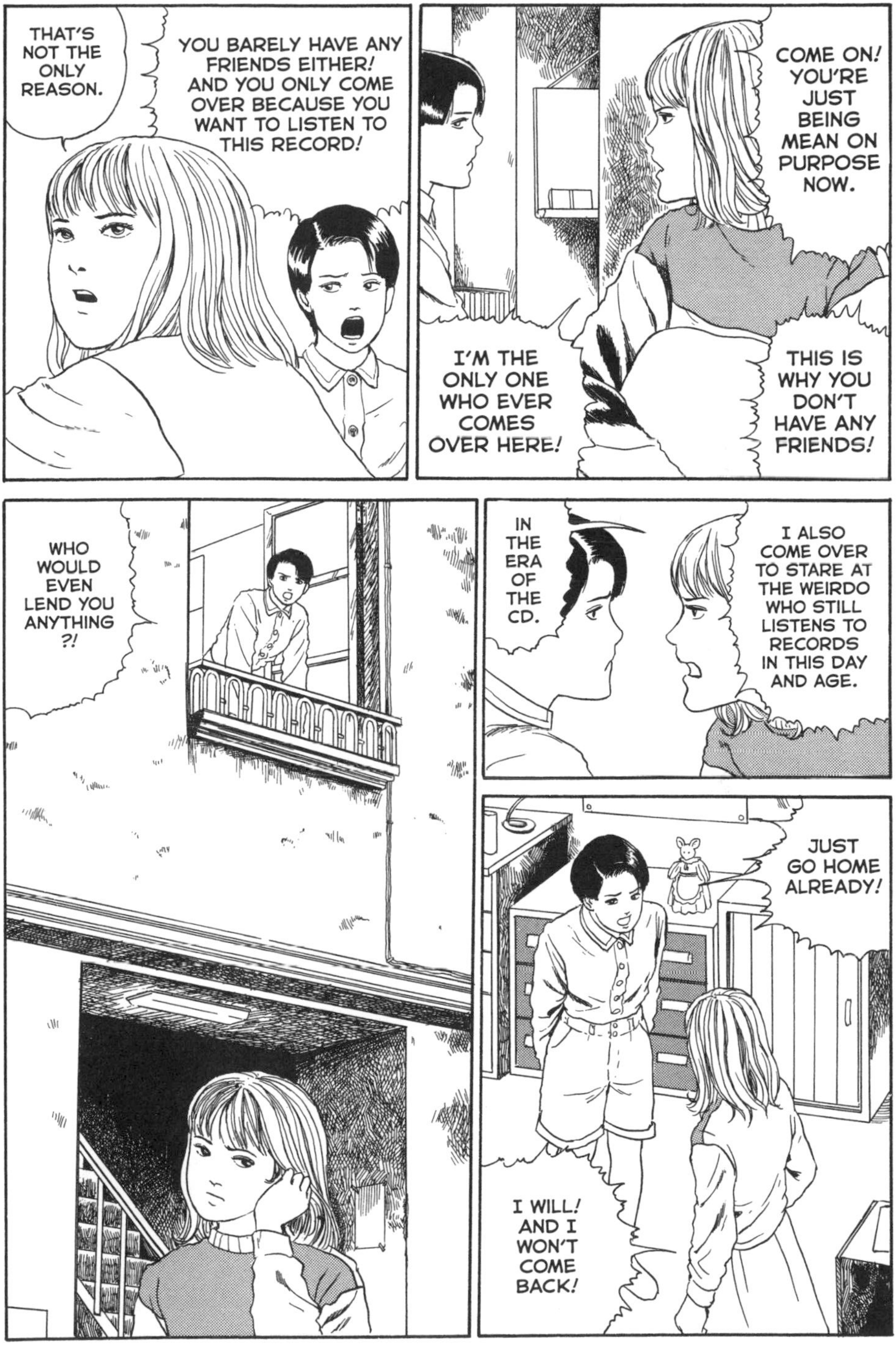
COME ON! YOU'RE JUST BEING MEAN ON PURPOSE NOW.
THIS IS WHY YOU DON'T HAVE ANY FRIENDS!
I'M THE ONLY ONE WHO EVER COMES OVER HERE!
YOU BARELY HAVE ANY FRIENDS EITHER! AND YOU ONLY COME OVER BECAUSE YOU WANT TO LISTEN TO THIS RECORD!
THAT'S NOT THE ONLY REASON.
I ALSO COME OVER TO STARE AT THE WEIRDO WHO STILL LISTENS TO RECORDS IN THIS DAY AND AGE.
IN THE ERA OF THE CD.
JUST GO HOME ALREADY!
I WILL! AND I WON'T COME BACK!
WHO WOULD EVEN LEND YOU ANYTHING?!

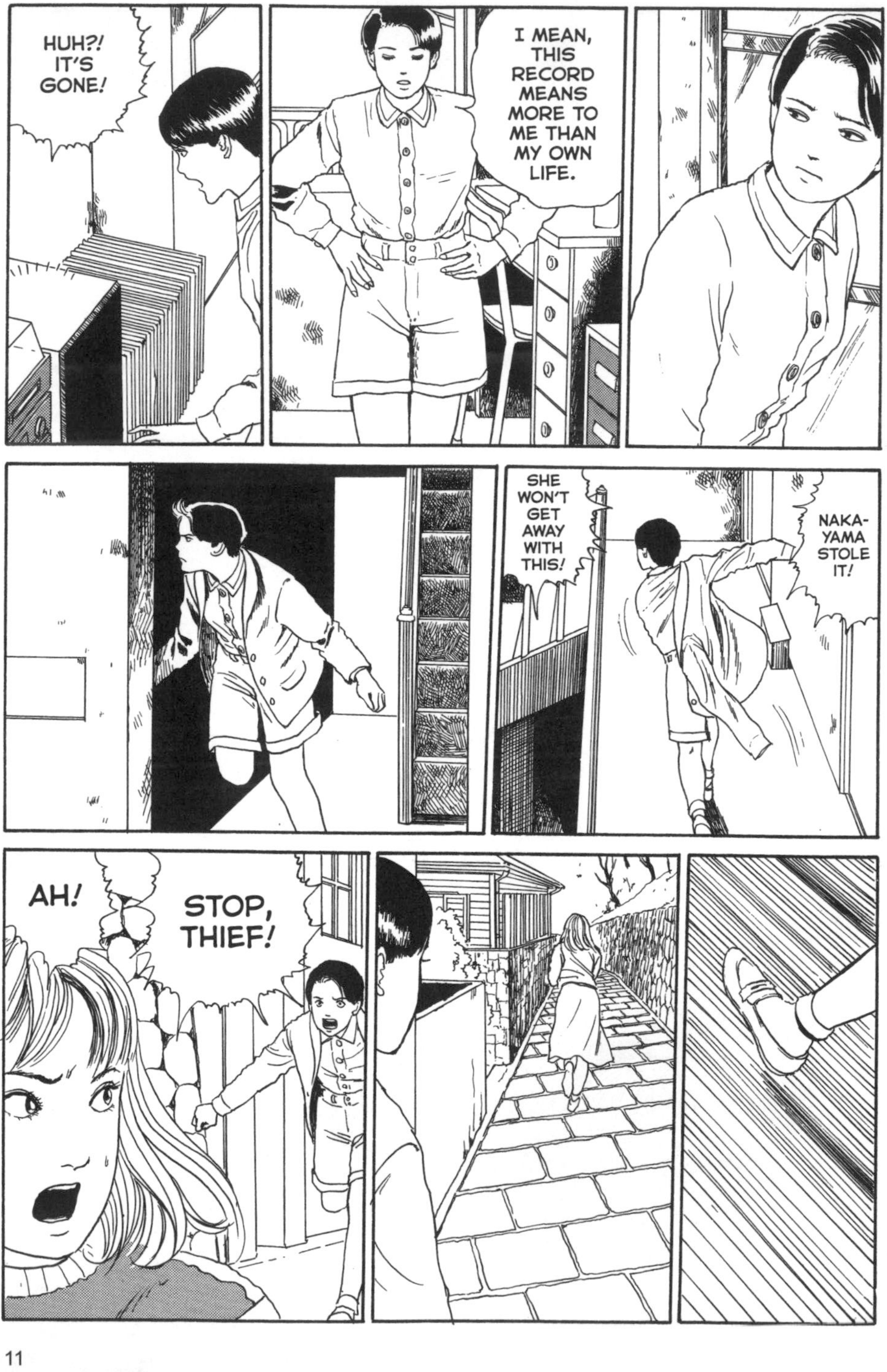
I MEAN, THIS RECORD MEANS MORE TO ME THAN MY OWN LIFE.
HUH?! IT'S GONE!
NAKA-YAMA STOLE IT!
SHE WON'T GET AWAY WITH THIS!
STOP, THIEF!
AH!

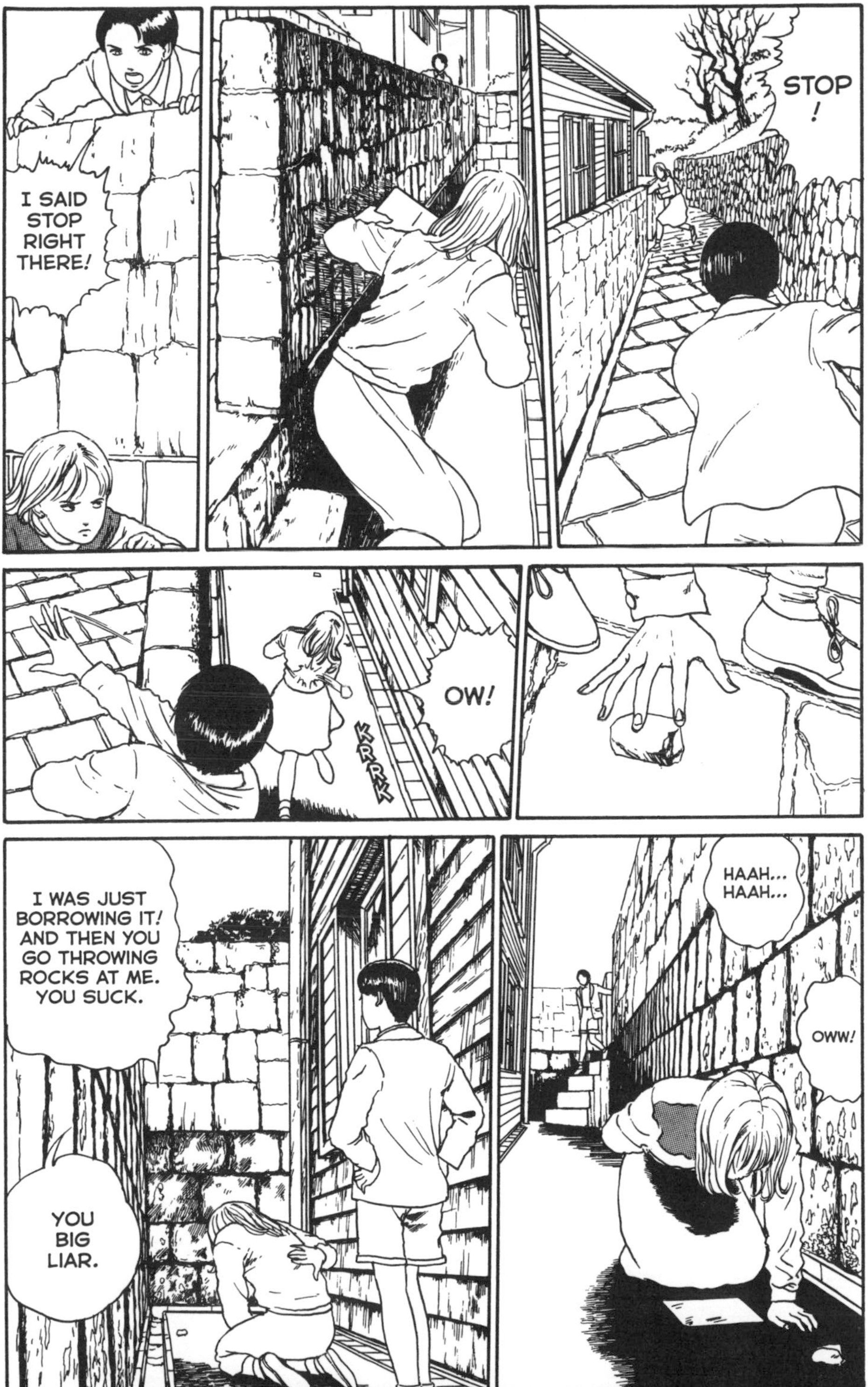
STOP!
I SAID STOP RIGHT THERE!
OW!
KRRRK
HAAH... HAAH...
OWW!
I WAS JUST BORROWING IT! AND THEN YOU GO THROWING ROCKS AT ME. YOU SUCK.
YOU BIG LIAR.

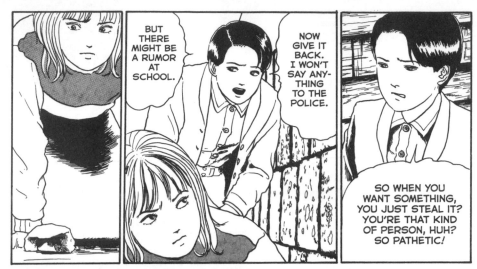

SO WHEN YOU WANT SOMETHING, YOU JUST STEAL IT? YOU'RE THAT KIND OF PERSON, HUH? SO PATHETIC!
NOW GIVE IT BACK. I WON'T SAY ANYTHING TO THE POLICE.
BUT THERE MIGHT BE A RUMOR AT SCHOOL.
NOW!! GIVE IT BACK, YOU THIEF!
NOW!
BASH

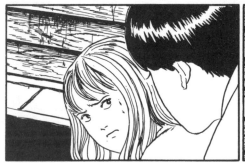

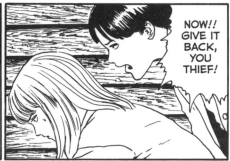

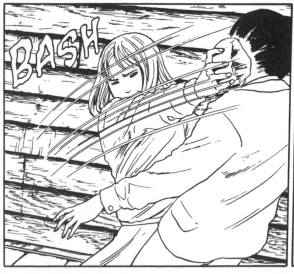

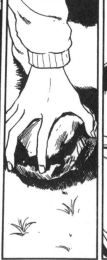

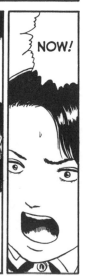

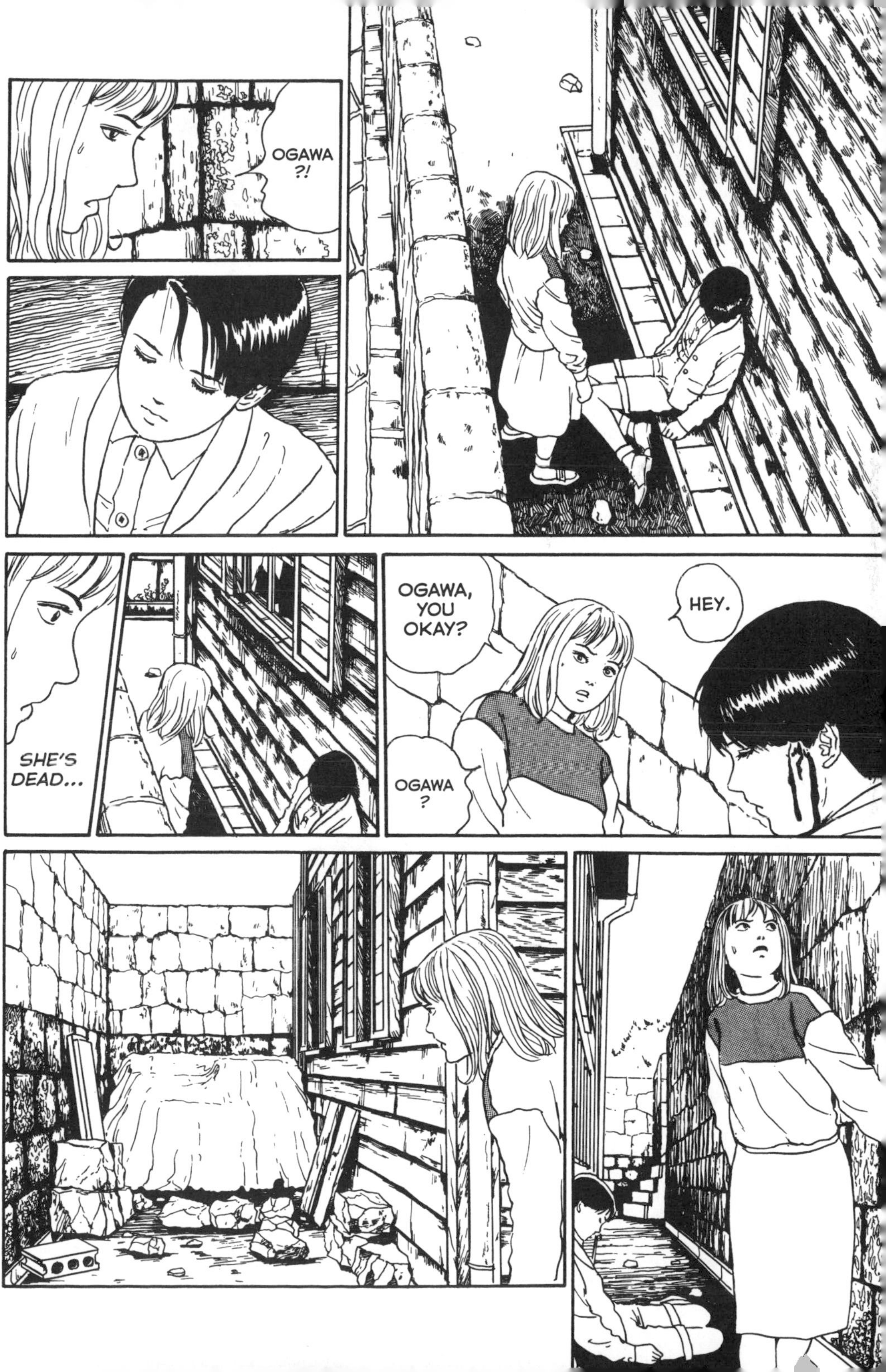
OGAWA ?!
HEY.
OGAWA, YOU OKAY?
OGAWA ?
SHE'S DEAD...

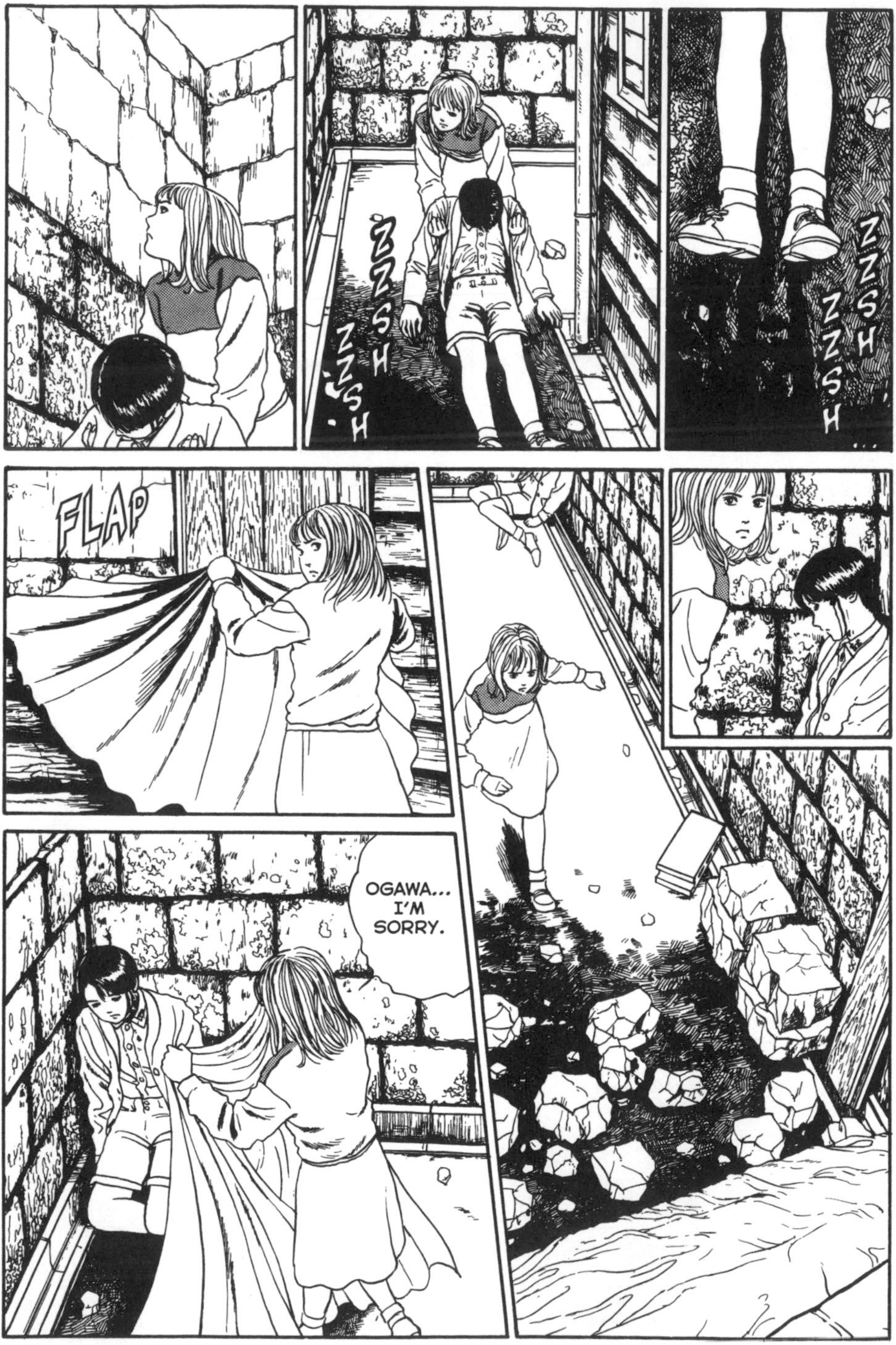
ZZSH
ZZSH
...
ZZSH
ZZSH
FLAP
OGAWA... I'M SORRY.

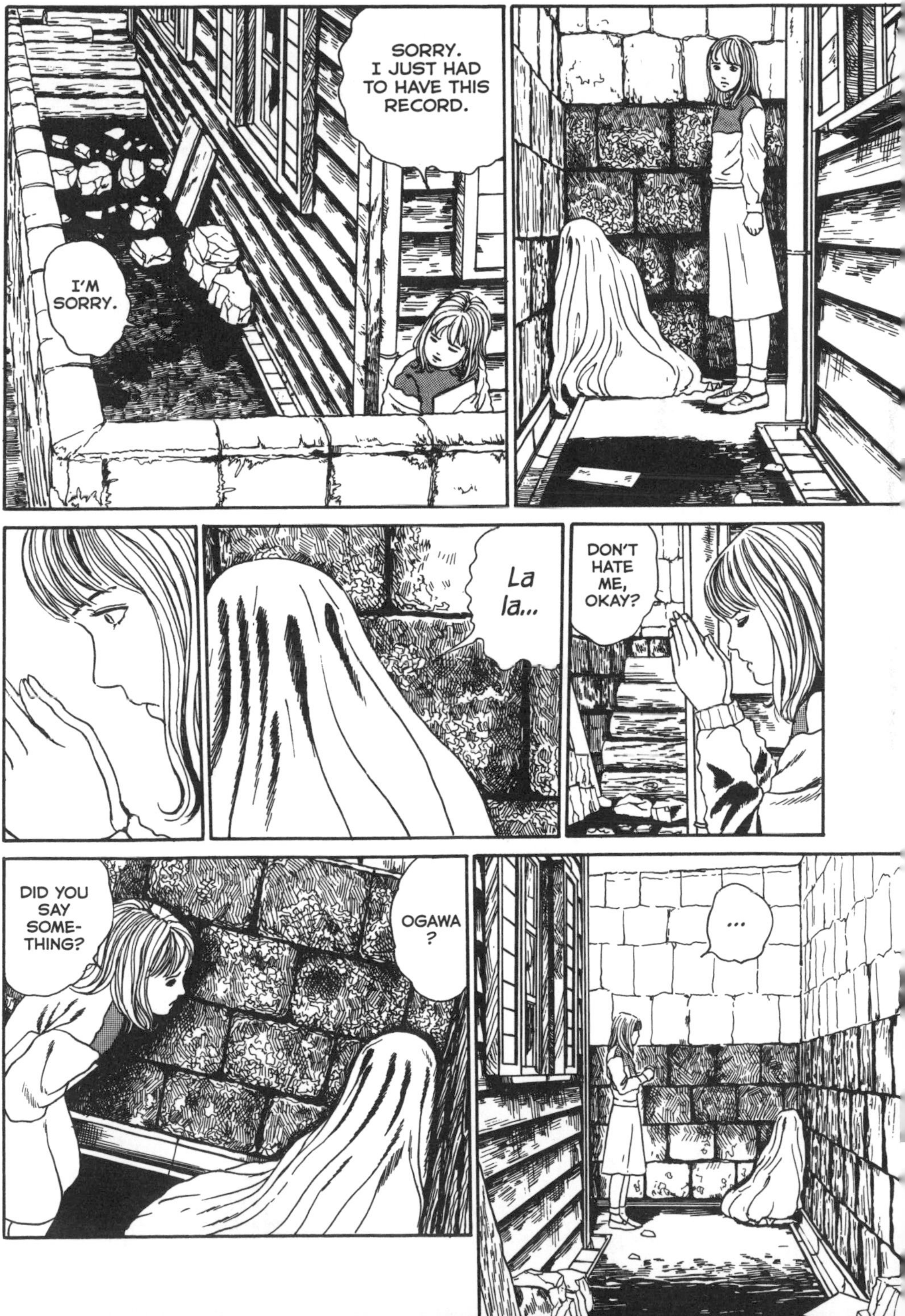
SORRY. I JUST HAD TO HAVE THIS RECORD.
I'M SORRY.
DON'T HATE ME, OKAY?
La la...
...
OGAWA?
DID YOU SAY SOMETHING?

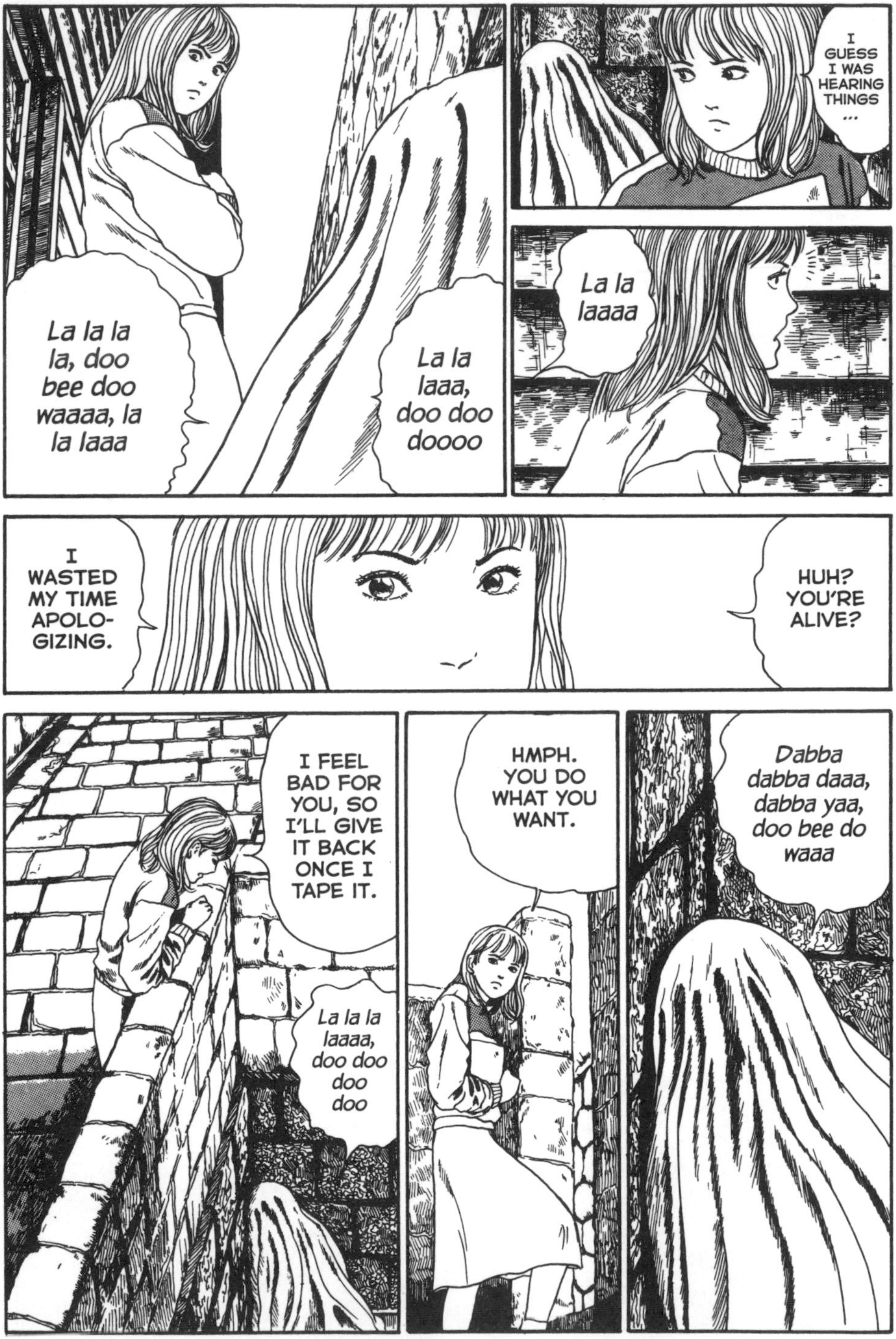
I GUESS I WAS HEARING THINGS ...
La la laaaa
La la laaa, doo doo doooo
La la la la, doo bee doo waaaa, la la laaa
HUH? YOU'RE ALIVE?
I WASTED MY TIME APOLOGIZING.
Dabba dabba daaa, dabba yaa, doo bee do waaa
HMPH. YOU DO WHAT YOU WANT.
I FEEL BAD FOR YOU, SO I'LL GIVE IT BACK ONCE I TAPE IT.
La la la laaaa, doo doo doo doo

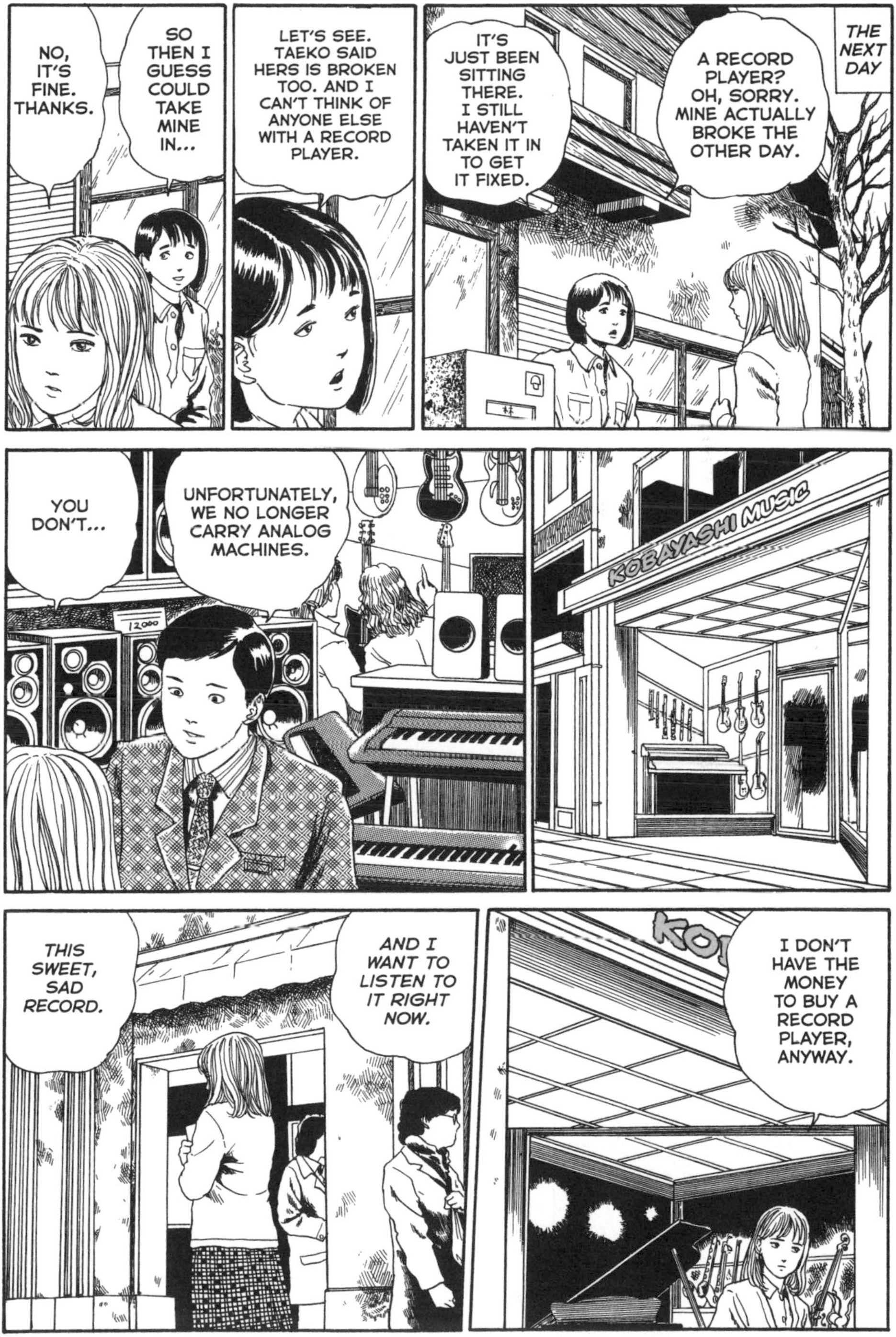
THE NEXT DAY
A RECORD PLAYER? OH, SORRY. MINE ACTUALLY BROKE THE OTHER DAY.
IT'S JUST BEEN SITTING THERE. I STILL HAVEN'T TAKEN IT IN TO GET IT FIXED.
LET'S SEE. TAEKO SAID HERS IS BROKEN TOO. AND I CAN'T THINK OF ANYONE ELSE WITH A RECORD PLAYER.
SO THEN I GUESS COULD TAKE MINE IN...
NO, IT'S FINE. THANKS.
KOBAYASHI MUSIC
UNFORTUNATELY, WE NO LONGER CARRY ANALOG MACHINES.
YOU DON'T...
12000
I DON'T HAVE THE MONEY TO BUY A RECORD PLAYER, ANYWAY.
AND I WANT TO LISTEN TO IT RIGHT NOW.
THIS SWEET, SAD RECORD.

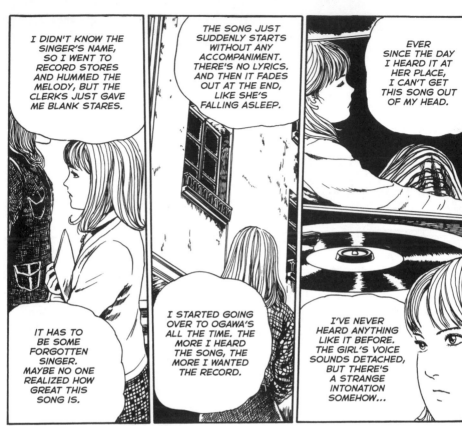

EVER SINCE THE DAY I HEARD IT AT HER PLACE, I CAN'T GET THIS SONG OUT OF MY HEAD.
I'VE NEVER HEARD ANYTHING LIKE IT BEFORE. THE GIRL'S VOICE SOUNDS DETACHED, BUT THERE'S A STRANGE INTONATION SOMEHOW...
THE SONG JUST SUDDENLY STARTS WITHOUT ANY ACCOMPANIMENT. THERE'S NO LYRICS. AND THEN IT FADES OUT AT THE END, LIKE SHE'S FALLING ASLEEP.
I STARTED GOING OVER TO OGAWA'S ALL THE TIME. THE MORE I HEARD THE SONG, THE MORE I WANTED THE RECORD.
I DIDN'T KNOW THE SINGER'S NAME, SO I WENT TO RECORD STORES AND HUMMED THE MELODY, BUT THE CLERKS JUST GAVE ME BLANK STARES.
IT HAS TO BE SOME FORGOTTEN SINGER. MAYBE NO ONE REALIZED HOW GREAT THIS SONG IS.
AND NOW I FINALLY HAVE THE RECORD...
...BUT NOW I DON'T HAVE ANYWHERE TO PLAY IT.
CHENG CHENG HA
USED AND IMPORTED RECORDS
10:00 ~21:00
TEL

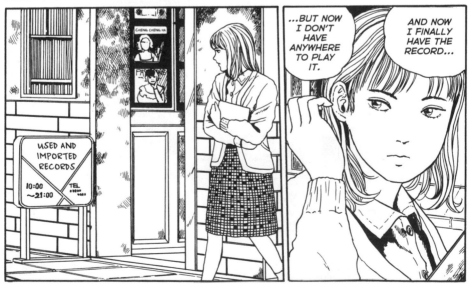

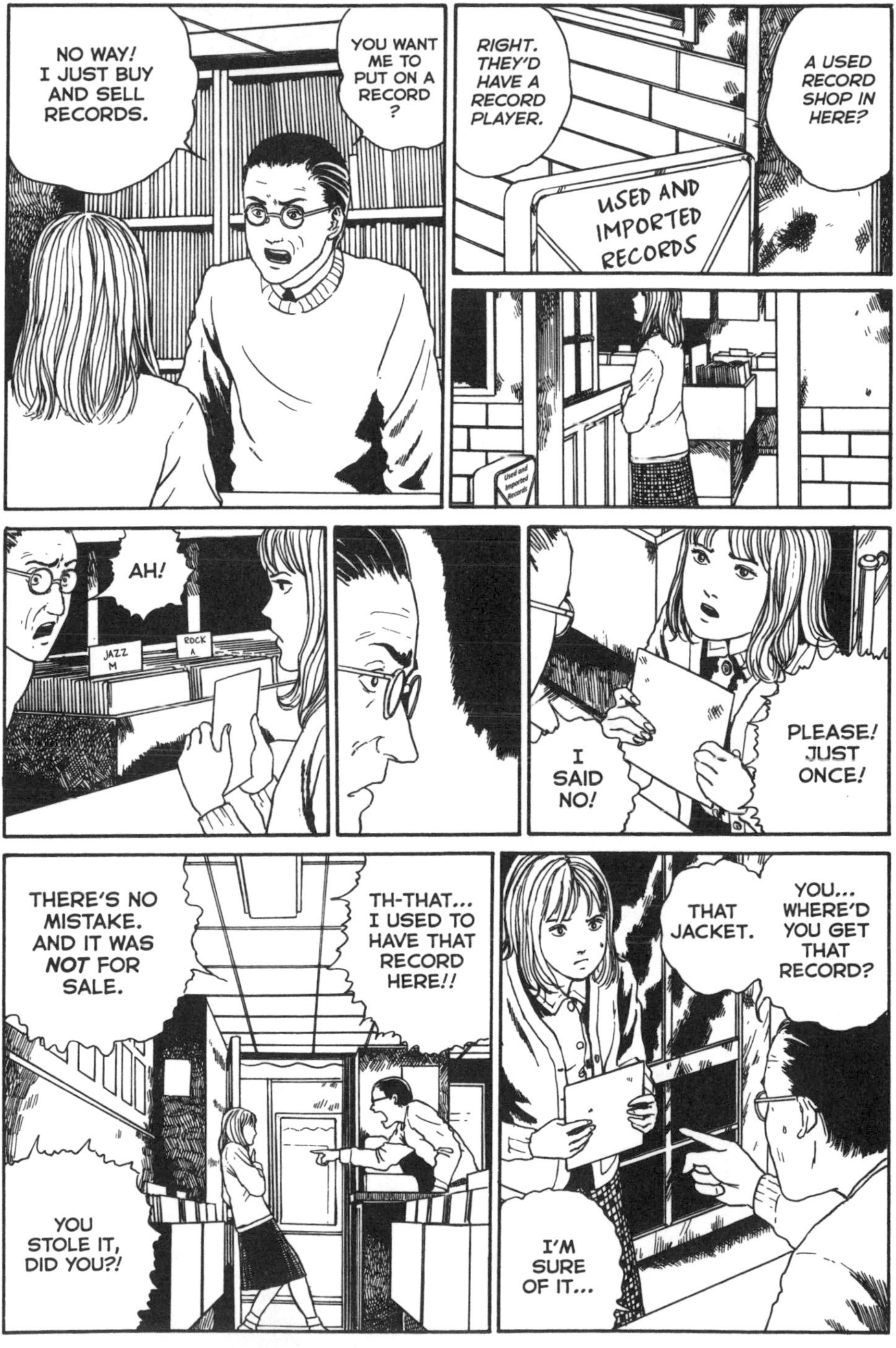
A USED RECORD SHOP IN HERE?
RIGHT. THEY'D HAVE A RECORD PLAYER.
USED AND IMPORTED RECORDS
YOU WANT ME TO PUT ON A RECORD?
NO WAY! I JUST BUY AND SELL RECORDS.
PLEASE! JUST ONCE!
I SAID NO!
AH!
JAZZ M
ROCK A
YOU... WHERE'D YOU GET THAT RECORD?
THAT JACKET.
I'M SURE OF IT...
TH-THAT... I USED TO HAVE THAT RECORD HERE!!
THERE'S NO MISTAKE. AND IT WAS NOT FOR SALE.
YOU STOLE IT, DID YOU?!

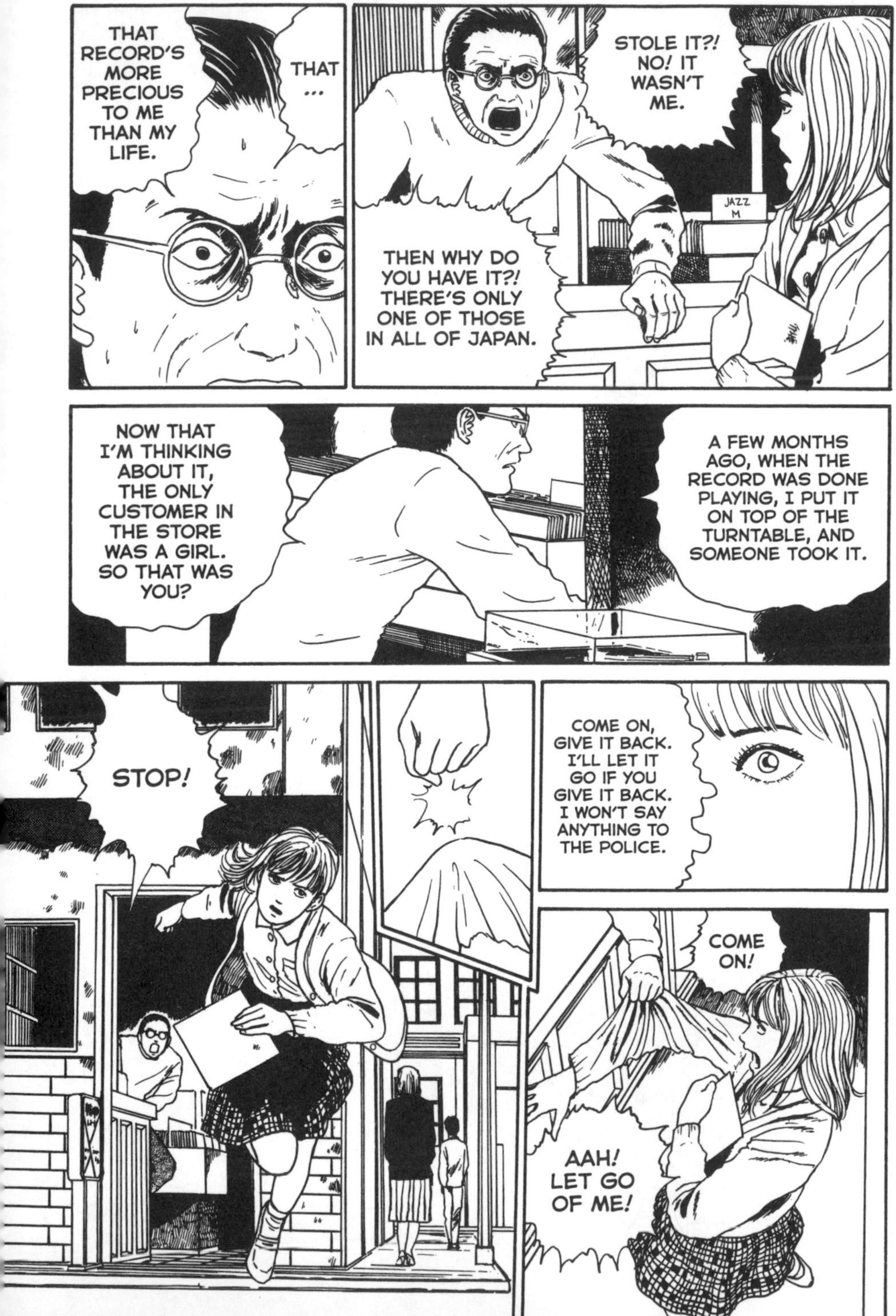
STOLE IT?! NO! IT WASN'T ME.
JAZZ M
THEN WHY DO YOU HAVE IT?! THERE'S ONLY ONE OF THOSE IN ALL OF JAPAN.
THAT ...
THAT RECORD'S MORE PRECIOUS TO ME THAN MY LIFE.
A FEW MONTHS AGO, WHEN THE RECORD WAS DONE PLAYING, I PUT IT ON TOP OF THE TURNTABLE, AND SOMEONE TOOK IT.
NOW THAT I'M THINKING ABOUT IT, THE ONLY CUSTOMER IN THE STORE WAS A GIRL. SO THAT WAS YOU?
COME ON, GIVE IT BACK. I'LL LET IT GO IF YOU GIVE IT BACK. I WON'T SAY ANYTHING TO THE POLICE.
COME ON!
AAH! LET GO OF ME!
STOP!

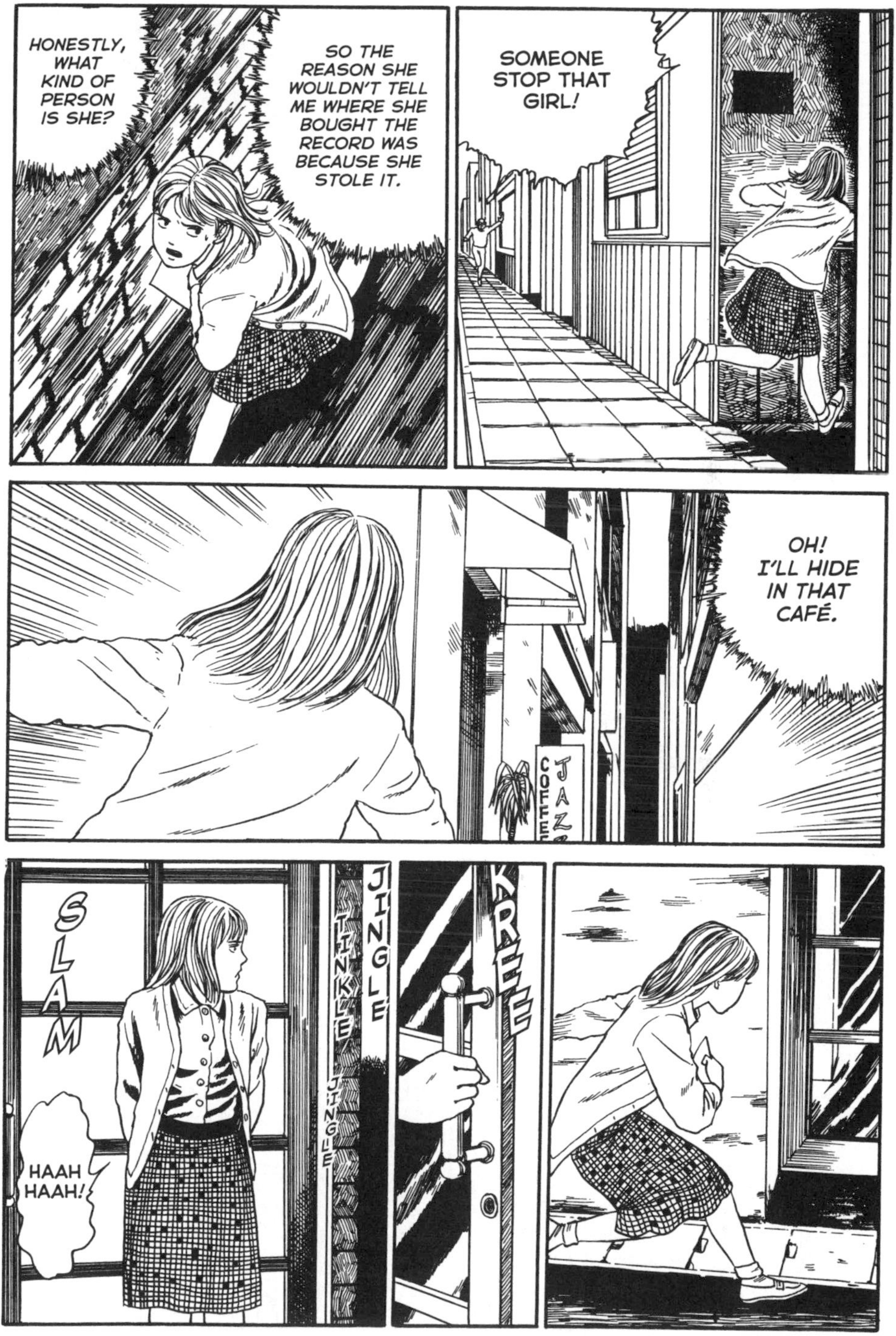
SOMEONE STOP THAT GIRL!
SO THE REASON SHE WOULDN'T TELL ME WHERE SHE BOUGHT THE RECORD WAS BECAUSE SHE STOLE IT.
HONESTLY, WHAT KIND OF PERSON IS SHE?
OH! I'LL HIDE IN THAT CAFÉ.
KREE
JINGLE
TINKLE
JINGLE
SLAM
HAAH HAAH!

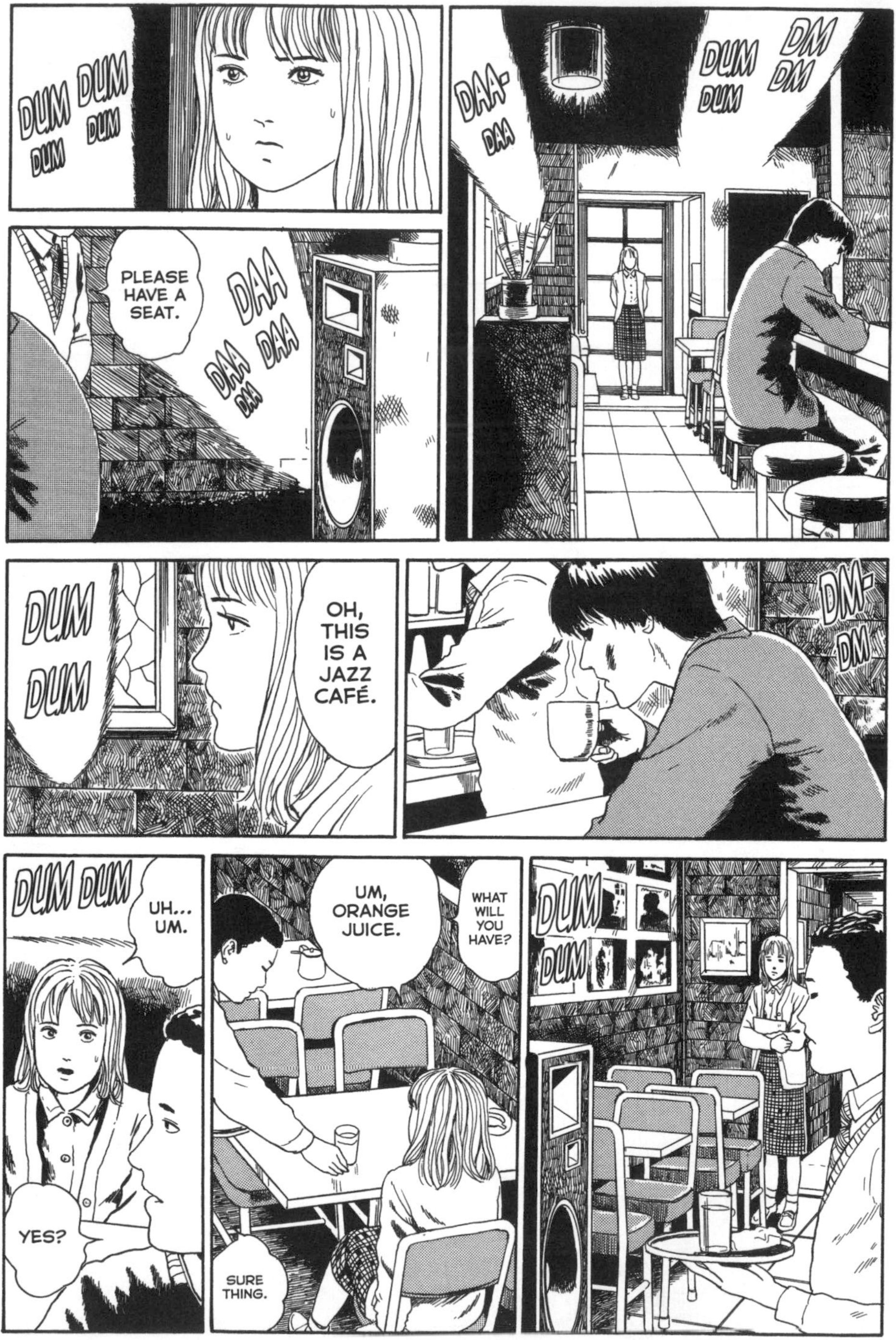
DM DM
DUM DUM DUM
DAA-DAA
DUM DUM DUM DUM
PLEASE HAVE A SEAT.
DAA DAA DAA DAA DAA
DM-DM
OH, THIS IS A JAZZ CAFÉ.
DUM DUM
DUM DUM
WHAT WILL YOU HAVE?
UM, ORANGE JUICE.
SURE THING.
DUM DUM
UH... UM.
YES?

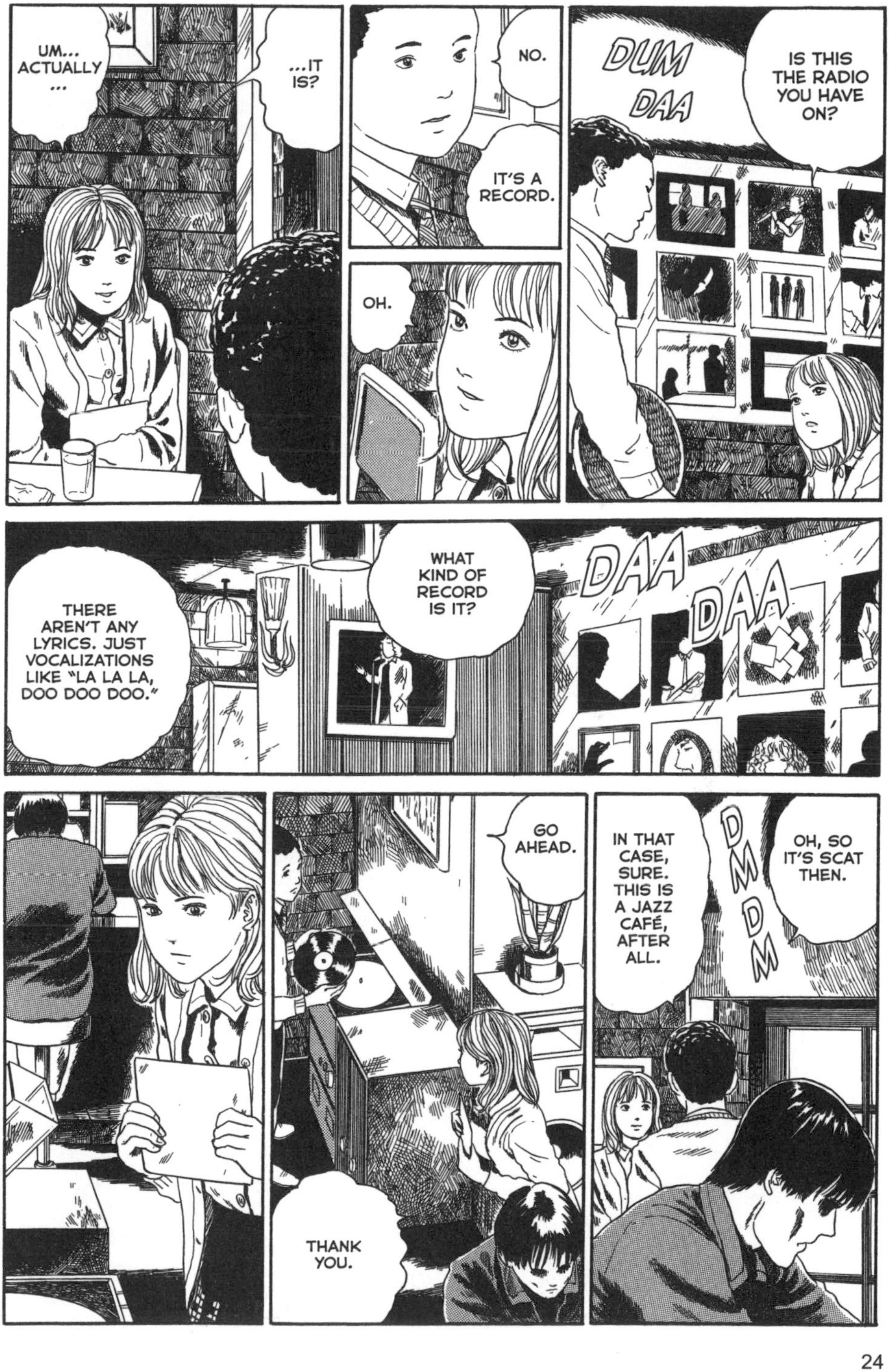
DUM DAA
IS THIS THE RADIO YOU HAVE ON?
NO.
IT'S A RECORD.
OH.
...IT IS?
UM... ACTUALLY ...
DAA DAA
WHAT KIND OF RECORD IS IT?
THERE AREN'T ANY LYRICS. JUST VOCALIZATIONS LIKE "LA LA LA, DOO DOO DOO."
OH, SO IT'S SCAT THEN.
DMDM
IN THAT CASE, SURE. THIS IS A JAZZ CAFÉ, AFTER ALL.
GO AHEAD.
THANK YOU.

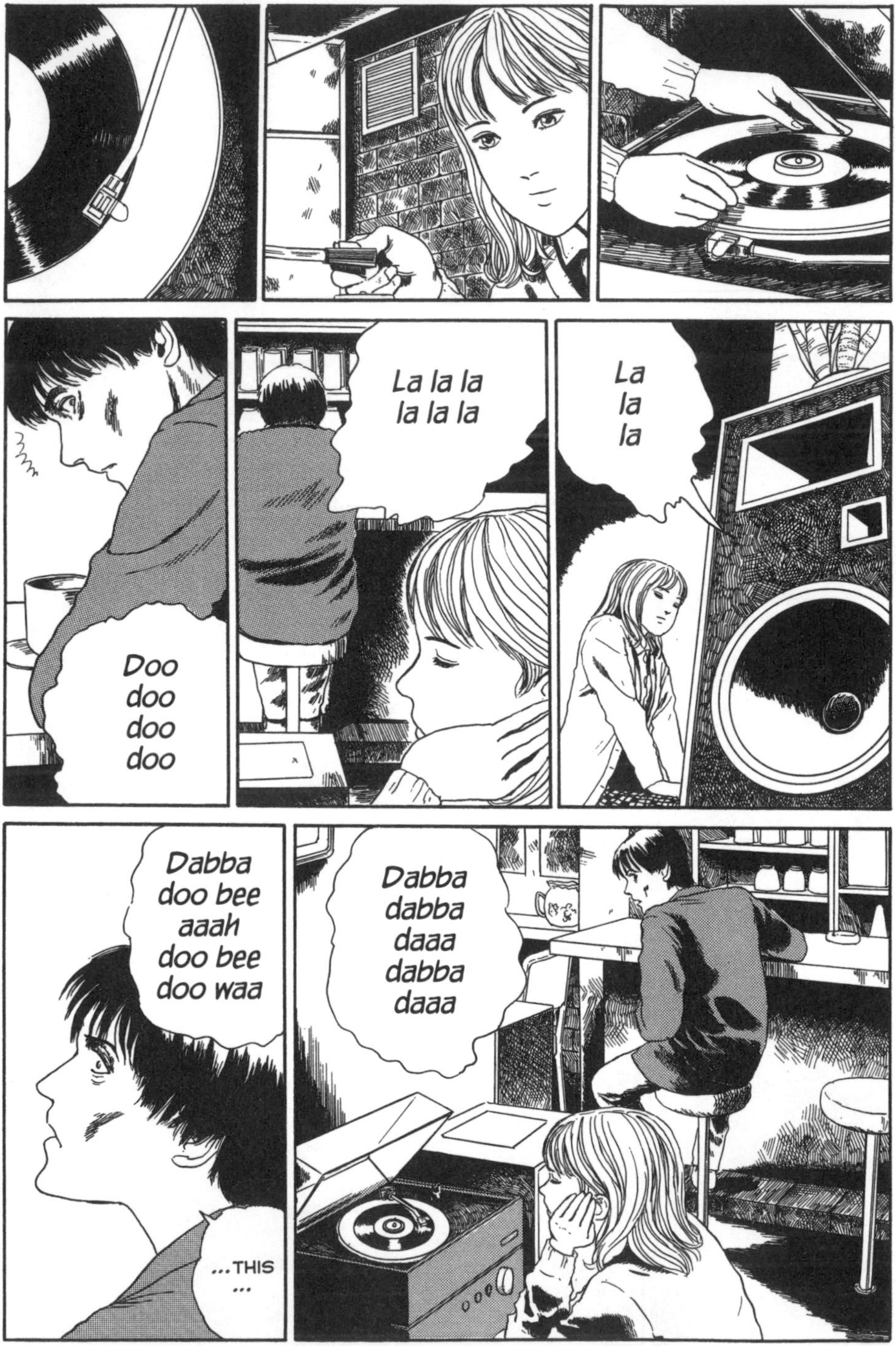
La la la
La la la la la la
Doo doo doo doo
Dabba dabba daaa dabba daaa
Dabba doo bee aaah doo bee doo waa
...THIS ...

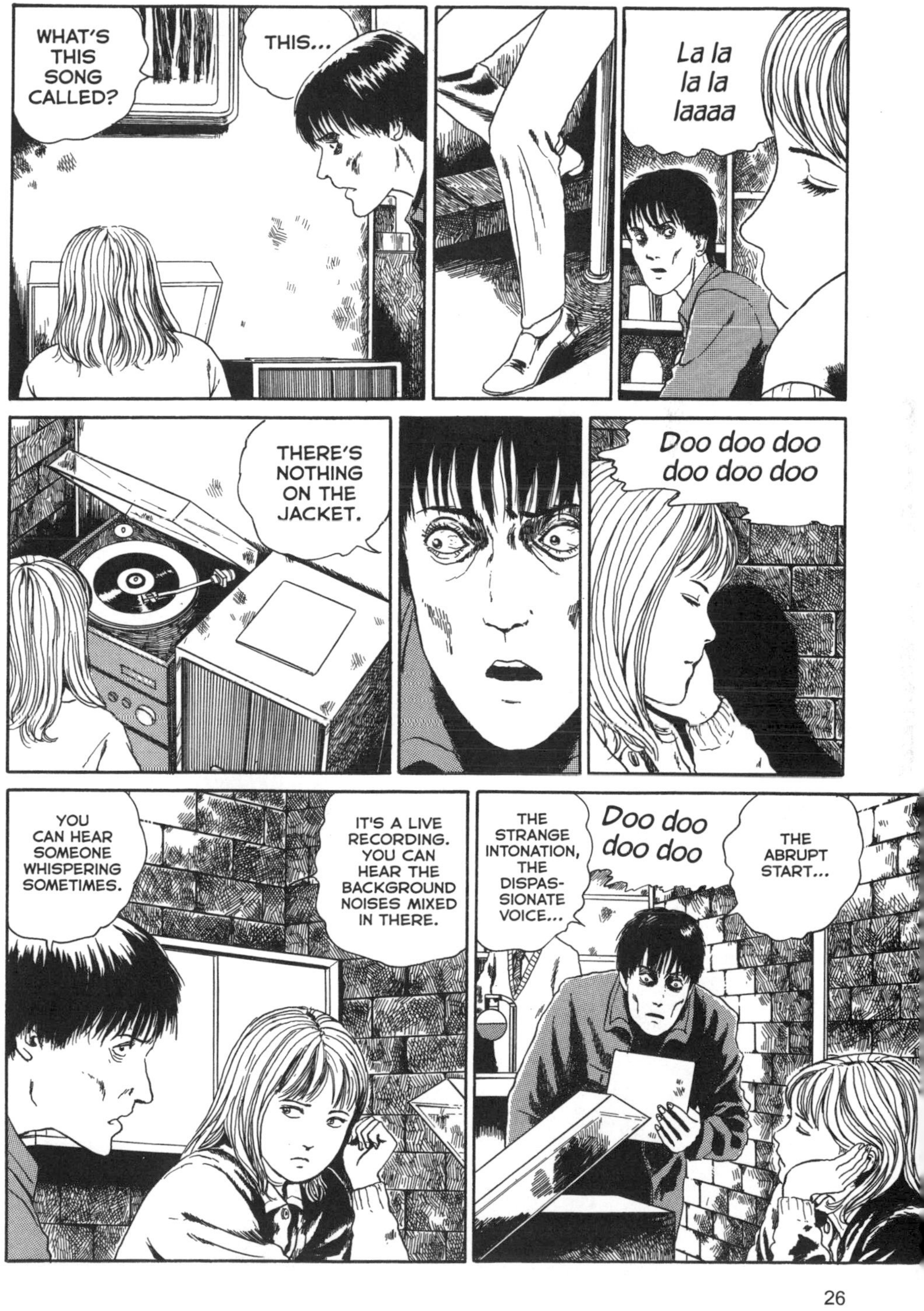
La la la la laaaa
THIS...
WHAT'S THIS SONG CALLED?
Doo doo doo doo doo doo
THERE'S NOTHING ON THE JACKET.
THE ABRUPT START...
Doo doo doo doo
THE STRANGE INTONATION, THE DISPAS- SIONATE VOICE...
IT'S A LIVE RECORDING. YOU CAN HEAR THE BACKGROUND NOISES MIXED IN THERE.
YOU CAN HEAR SOMEONE WHISPERING SOMETIMES.

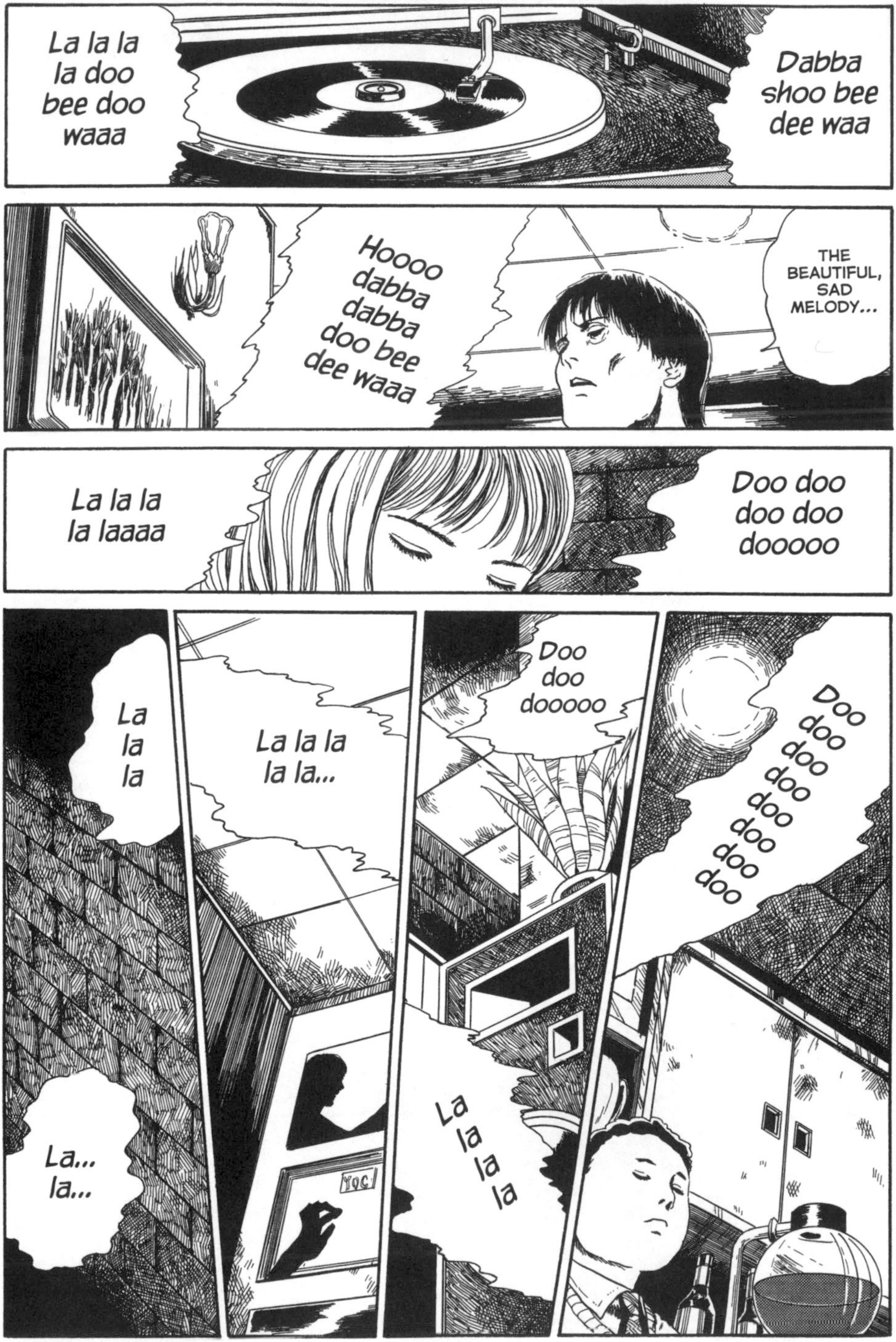

Dabba shoo bee dee waa
La la la la doo bee doo waaa
THE BEAUTIFUL, SAD MELODY...
Hoooo dabba dabba doo bee dee waaa
Doo doo doo doo dooooo
La la la la laaaa
Doo doo doo doo doo doo doo doo
Doo doo dooooo
La la la la
La la la la la...
La la la
La... la...

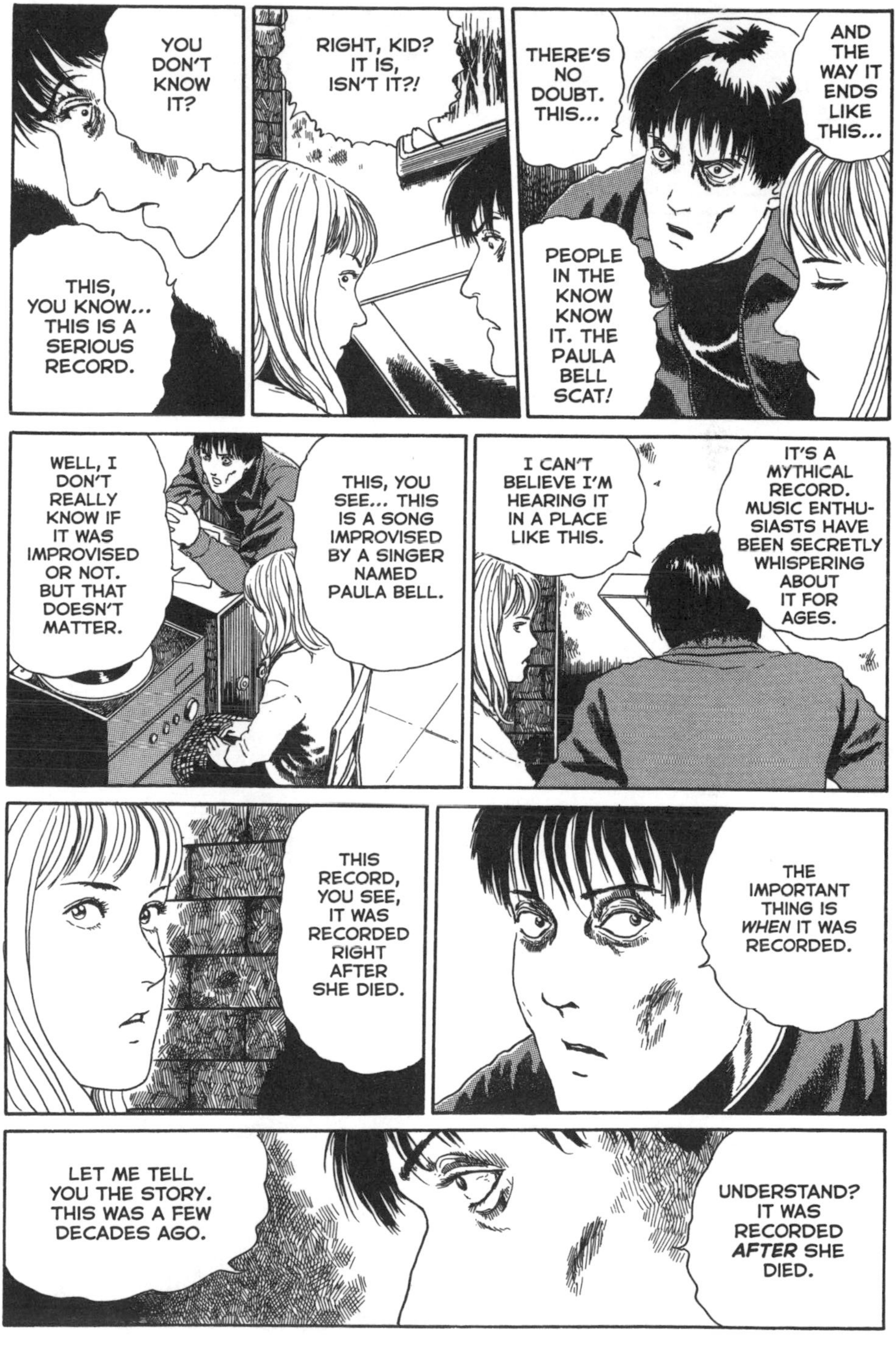
AND THE WAY IT ENDS LIKE THIS...
THERE'S NO DOUBT. THIS...
PEOPLE IN THE KNOW KNOW IT. THE PAULA BELL SCAT!
RIGHT, KID? IT IS, ISN'T IT?!
YOU DON'T KNOW IT?
THIS, YOU KNOW... THIS IS A SERIOUS RECORD.
IT'S A MYTHICAL RECORD. MUSIC ENTHUSIASTS HAVE BEEN SECRETLY WHISPERING ABOUT IT FOR AGES.
I CAN'T BELIEVE I'M HEARING IT IN A PLACE LIKE THIS.
THIS, YOU SEE... THIS IS A SONG IMPROVISED BY A SINGER NAMED PAULA BELL.
WELL, I DON'T REALLY KNOW IF IT WAS IMPROVISED OR NOT. BUT THAT DOESN'T MATTER.
THE IMPORTANT THING IS *WHEN* IT WAS RECORDED.
THIS RECORD, YOU SEE, IT WAS RECORDED RIGHT AFTER SHE DIED.
UNDERSTAND? IT WAS RECORDED ***AFTER*** SHE DIED.
LET ME TELL YOU THE STORY. THIS WAS A FEW DECADES AGO.

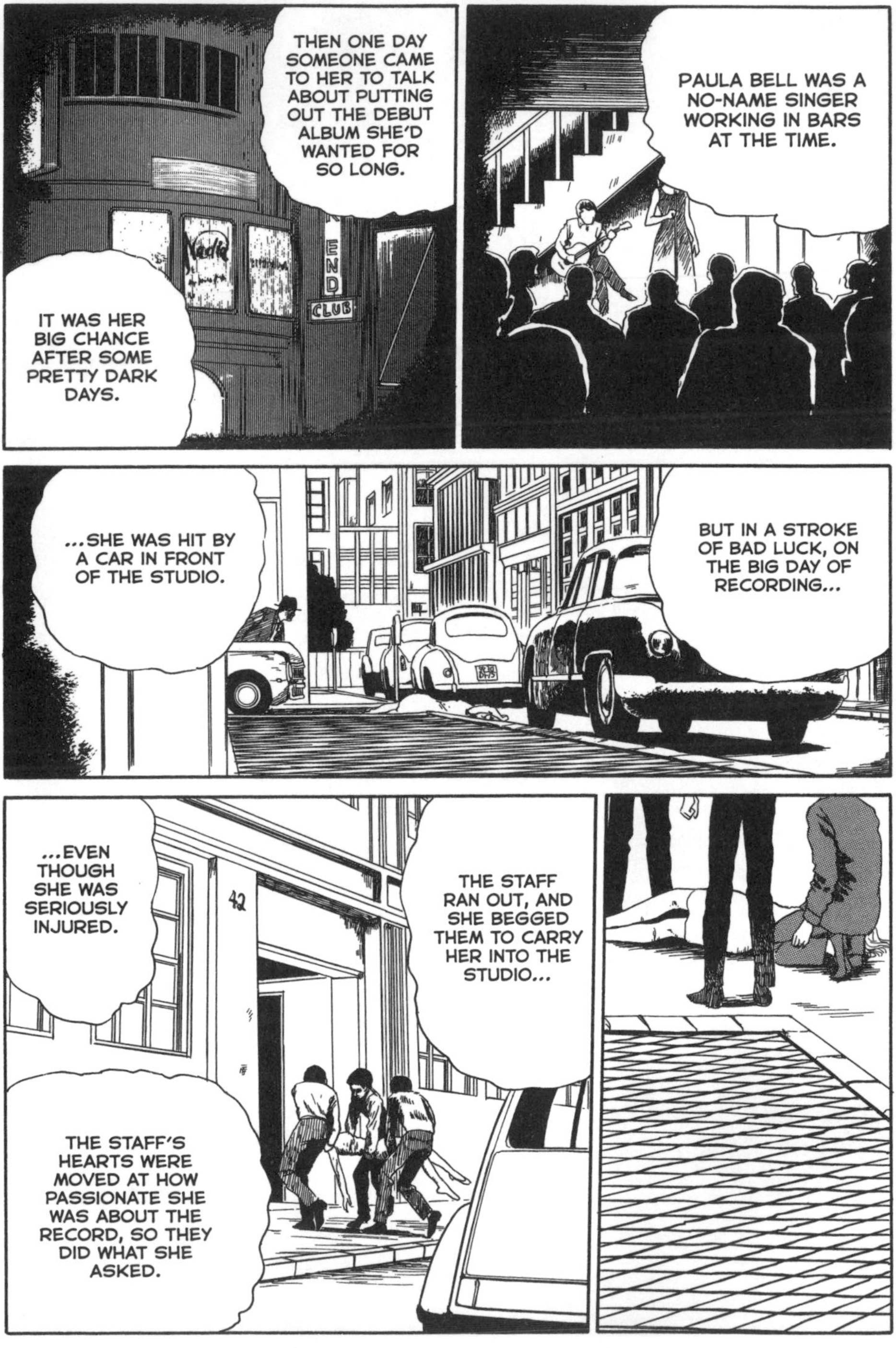
PAULA BELL WAS A NO-NAME SINGER WORKING IN BARS AT THE TIME.
THEN ONE DAY SOMEONE CAME TO HER TO TALK ABOUT PUTTING OUT THE DEBUT ALBUM SHE'D WANTED FOR SO LONG.
IT WAS HER BIG CHANCE AFTER SOME PRETTY DARK DAYS.
BUT IN A STROKE OF BAD LUCK, ON THE BIG DAY OF RECORDING...
...SHE WAS HIT BY A CAR IN FRONT OF THE STUDIO.
THE STAFF RAN OUT, AND SHE BEGGED THEM TO CARRY HER INTO THE STUDIO...
...EVEN THOUGH SHE WAS SERIOUSLY INJURED.
THE STAFF'S HEARTS WERE MOVED AT HOW PASSIONATE SHE WAS ABOUT THE RECORD, SO THEY DID WHAT SHE ASKED.

BUT ANYONE COULD SEE SHE WAS IN NO CONDITION TO SING.
SHE TOOK HER LAST BREATH AT THE FOOT OF THE MIC.
SUCH A TRAGIC DEATH, JUST WHEN SHE WAS ON THE VERGE OF MAKING HER DEBUT. AND THE WAY SHE CLUNG TO THIS WORLD...
SEVERAL OF THE STAFF MEMBERS CRIED, PERHAPS.
BUT THEN, A FEW MINUTES LATER...
...SHE STARTED TO SING.
EVERYONE THOUGHT SHE HAD COME BACK TO LIFE. BUT HER HEART STILL WASN'T BEATING.
AS THEY STOOD THERE, STUNNED. SHE SANG A SONG THEY'D NEVER HEARD BEFORE, NOT THE ONE SHE WAS SUPPOSED TO SING.
FINALLY, AS THOUGH HER STRENGTH WAS EXHAUSTED, HER VOICE GREW FAINTER...
THEY SAY SHE DIDN'T OPEN HER MOUTH AGAIN.

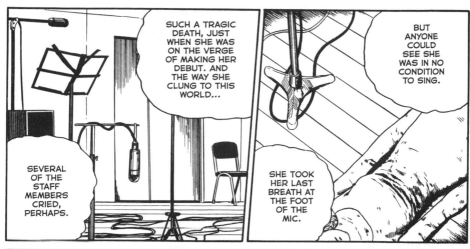

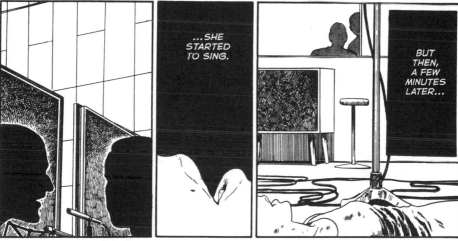

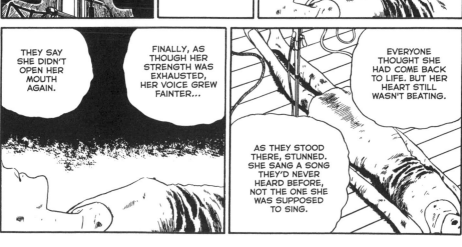

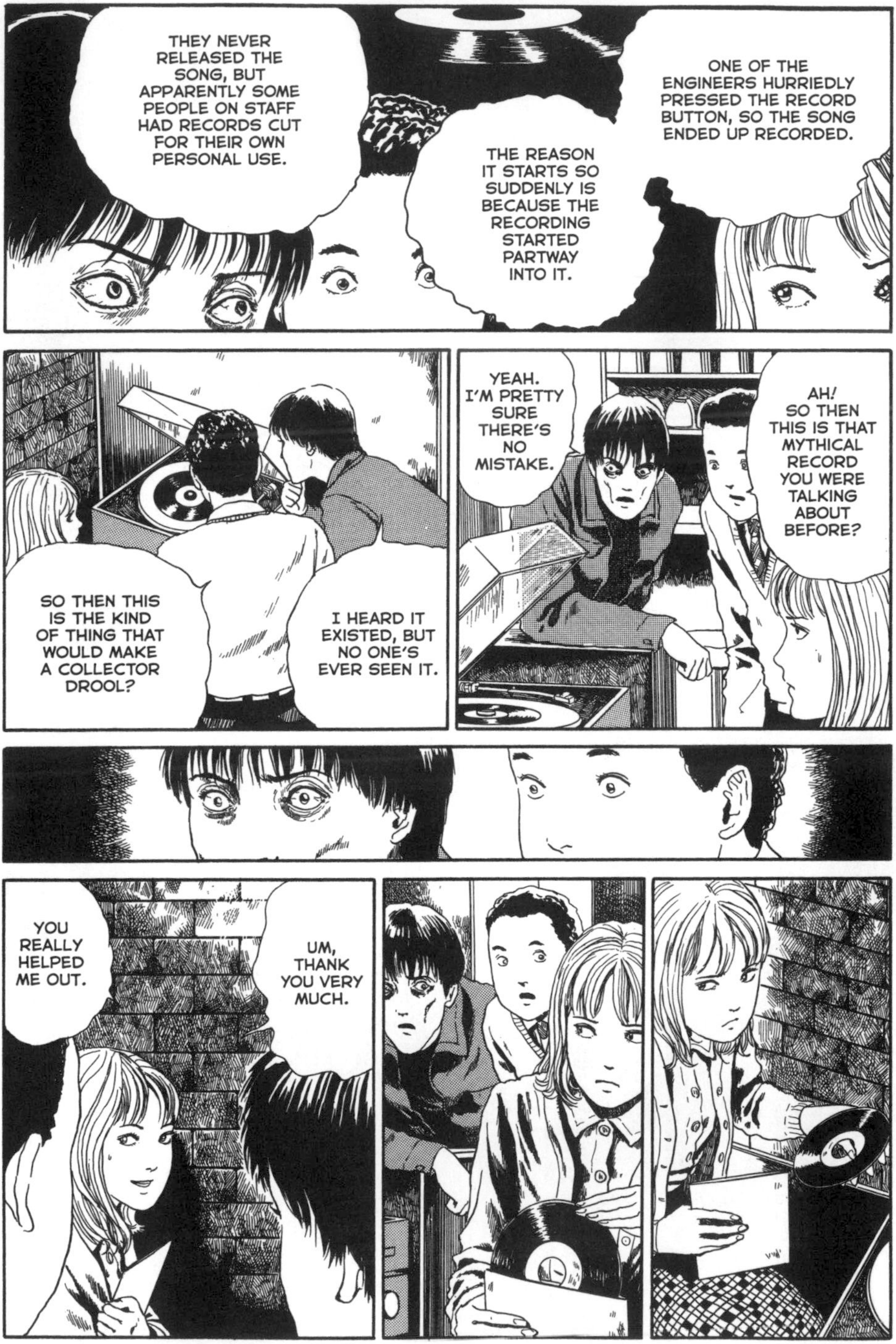
ONE OF THE ENGINEERS HURRIEDLY PRESSED THE RECORD BUTTON, SO THE SONG ENDED UP RECORDED.
THE REASON IT STARTS SO SUDDENLY IS BECAUSE THE RECORDING STARTED PARTWAY INTO IT.
THEY NEVER RELEASED THE SONG, BUT APPARENTLY SOME PEOPLE ON STAFF HAD RECORDS CUT FOR THEIR OWN PERSONAL USE.
AH! SO THEN THIS IS THAT MYTHICAL RECORD YOU WERE TALKING ABOUT BEFORE?
YEAH. I'M PRETTY SURE THERE'S NO MISTAKE.
I HEARD IT EXISTED, BUT NO ONE'S EVER SEEN IT.
SO THEN THIS IS THE KIND OF THING THAT WOULD MAKE A COLLECTOR DROOL?
UM, THANK YOU VERY MUCH.
YOU REALLY HELPED ME OUT.

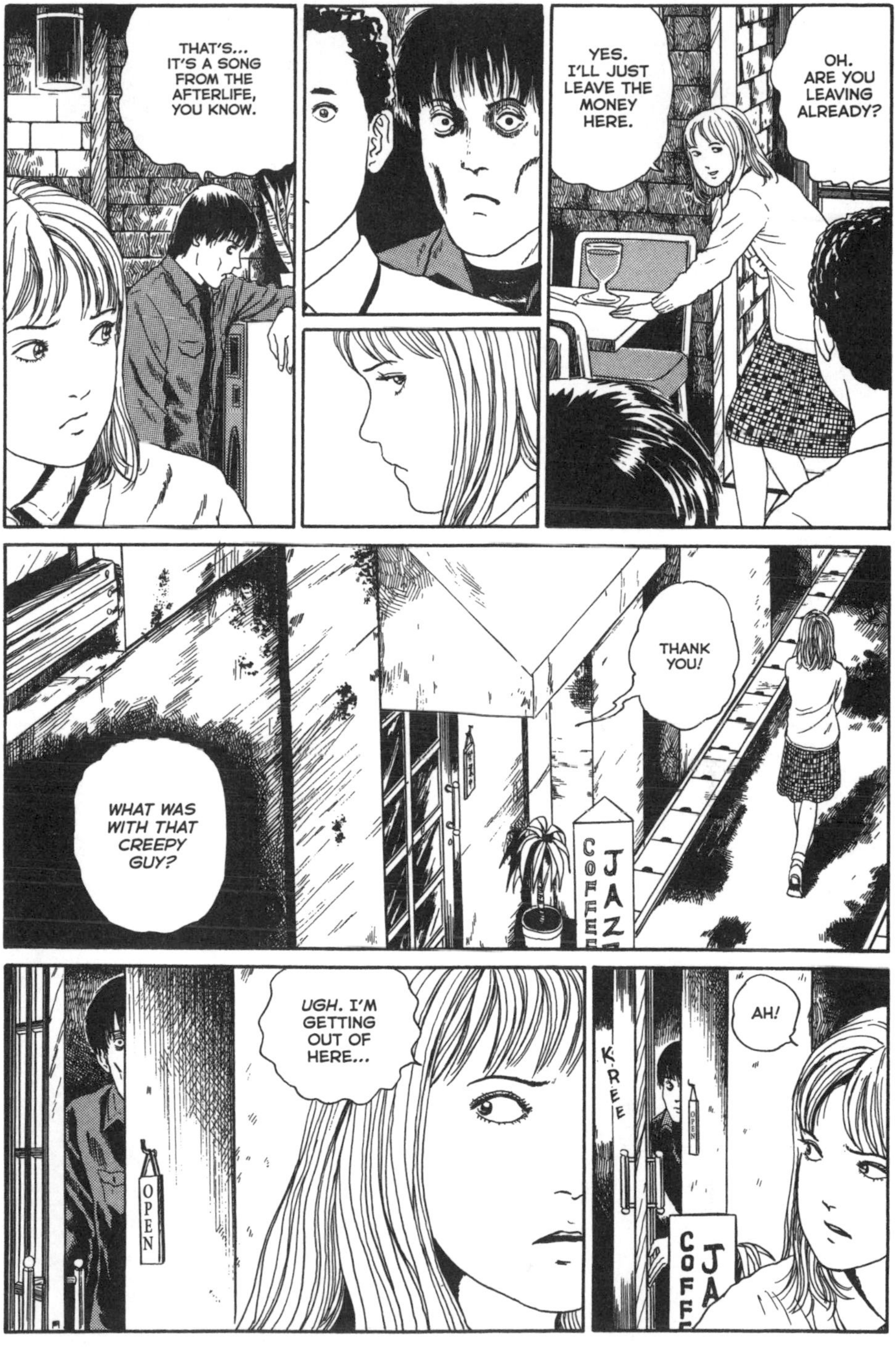
OH. ARE YOU LEAVING ALREADY?
YES. I'LL JUST LEAVE THE MONEY HERE.
THAT'S... IT'S A SONG FROM THE AFTERLIFE, YOU KNOW.
THANK YOU!
WHAT WAS WITH THAT CREEPY GUY?
AH!
UGH. I'M GETTING OUT OF HERE...
OPEN

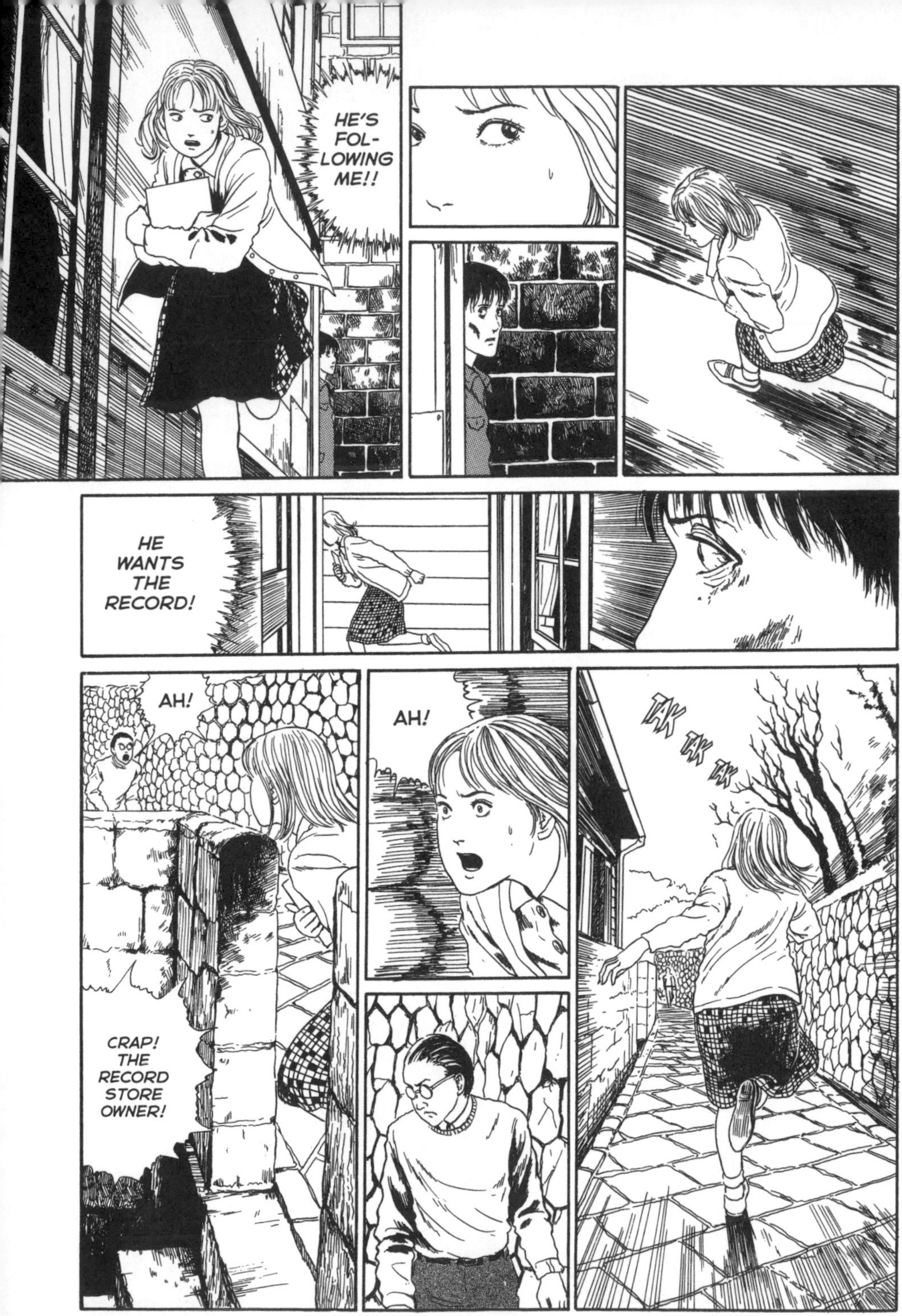
HE'S FOL-LOWING ME!!
HE WANTS THE RECORD!
TAK TAK TAK
AH!
AH!
CRAP! THE RECORD STORE OWNER!

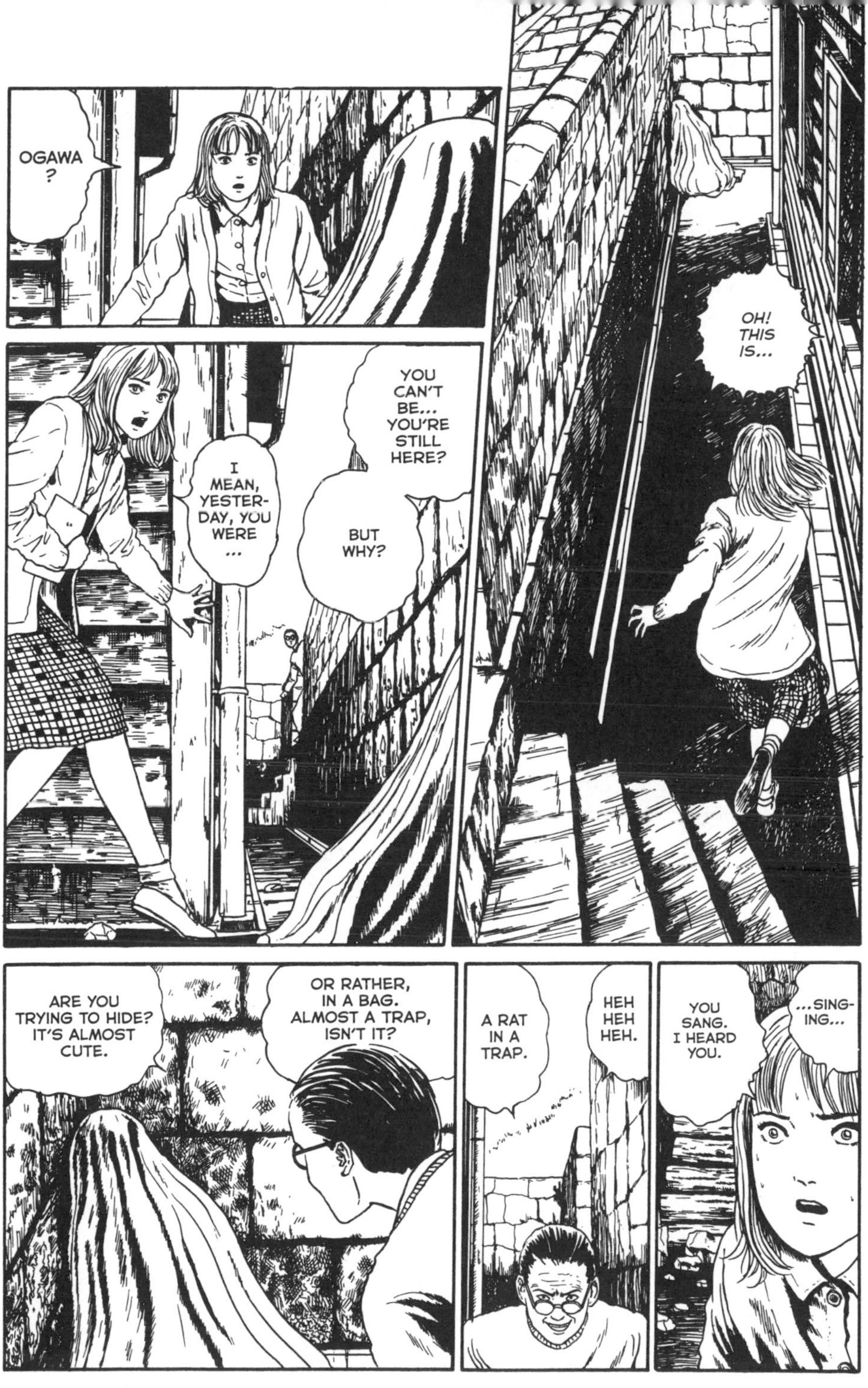
OH! THIS IS...
OGAWA ?
YOU CAN'T BE... YOU'RE STILL HERE?
BUT WHY?
I MEAN, YESTER-DAY, YOU WERE ...
...SING-ING...
YOU SANG. I HEARD YOU.
HEH HEH HEH.
A RAT IN A TRAP.
OR RATHER, IN A BAG. ALMOST A TRAP, ISN'T IT?
ARE YOU TRYING TO HIDE? IT'S ALMOST CUTE.

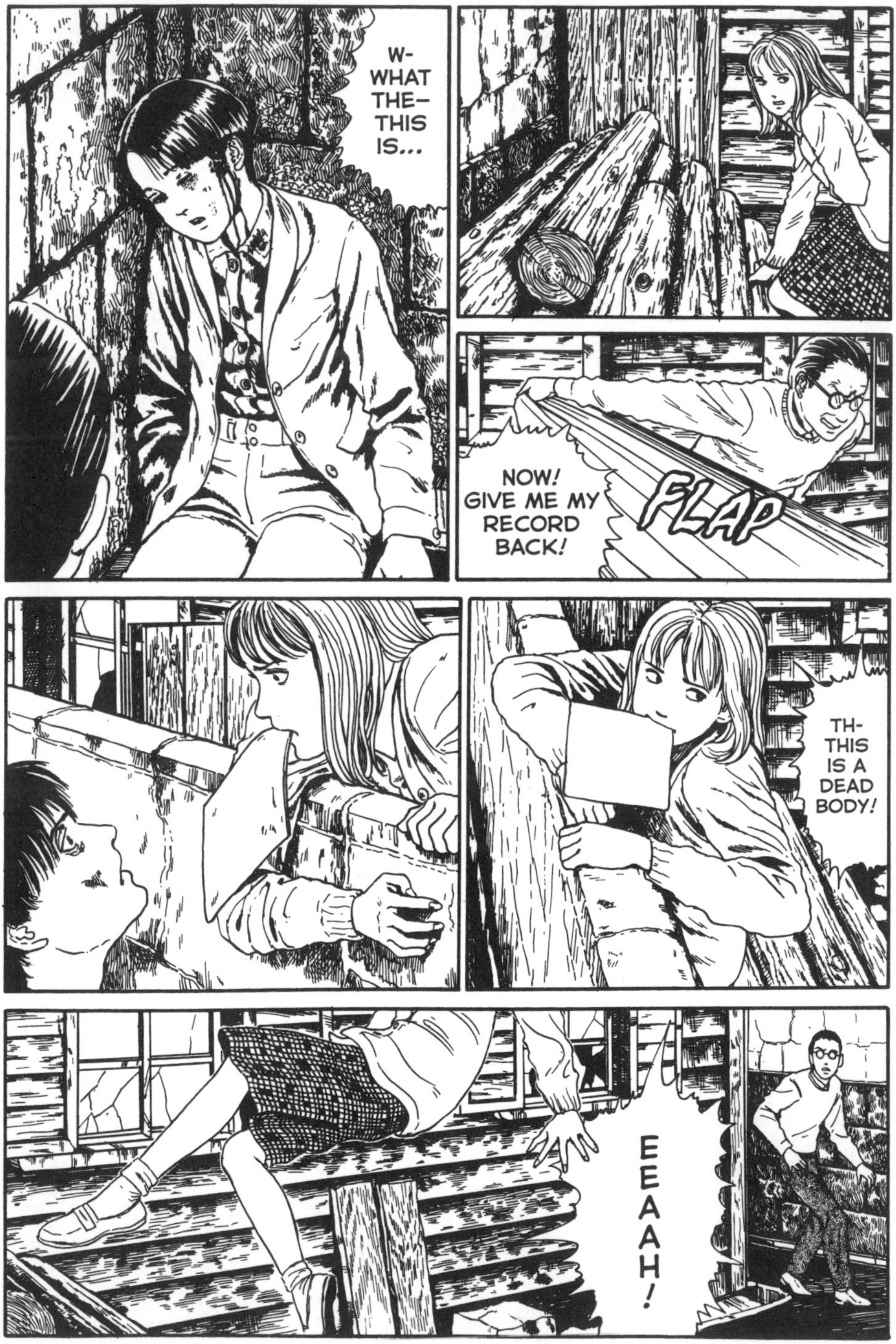
NOW! GIVE ME MY RECORD BACK!
FLAP
W- WHAT THE— THIS IS...
TH- THIS IS A DEAD BODY!
EEAAAH!

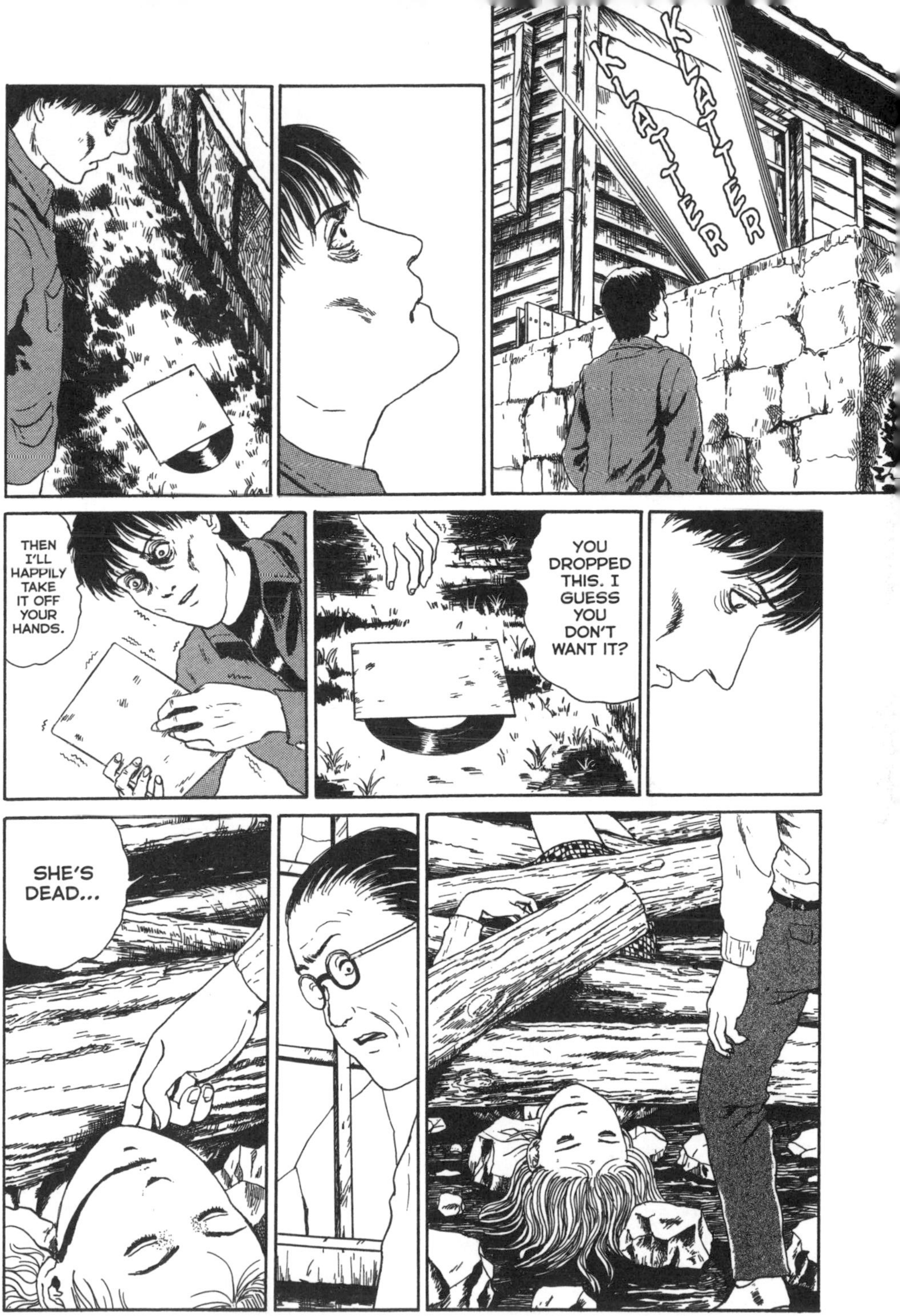
YOU DROPPED THIS. I GUESS YOU DON'T WANT IT?
THEN I'LL HAPPILY TAKE IT OFF YOUR HANDS.
SHE'S DEAD...

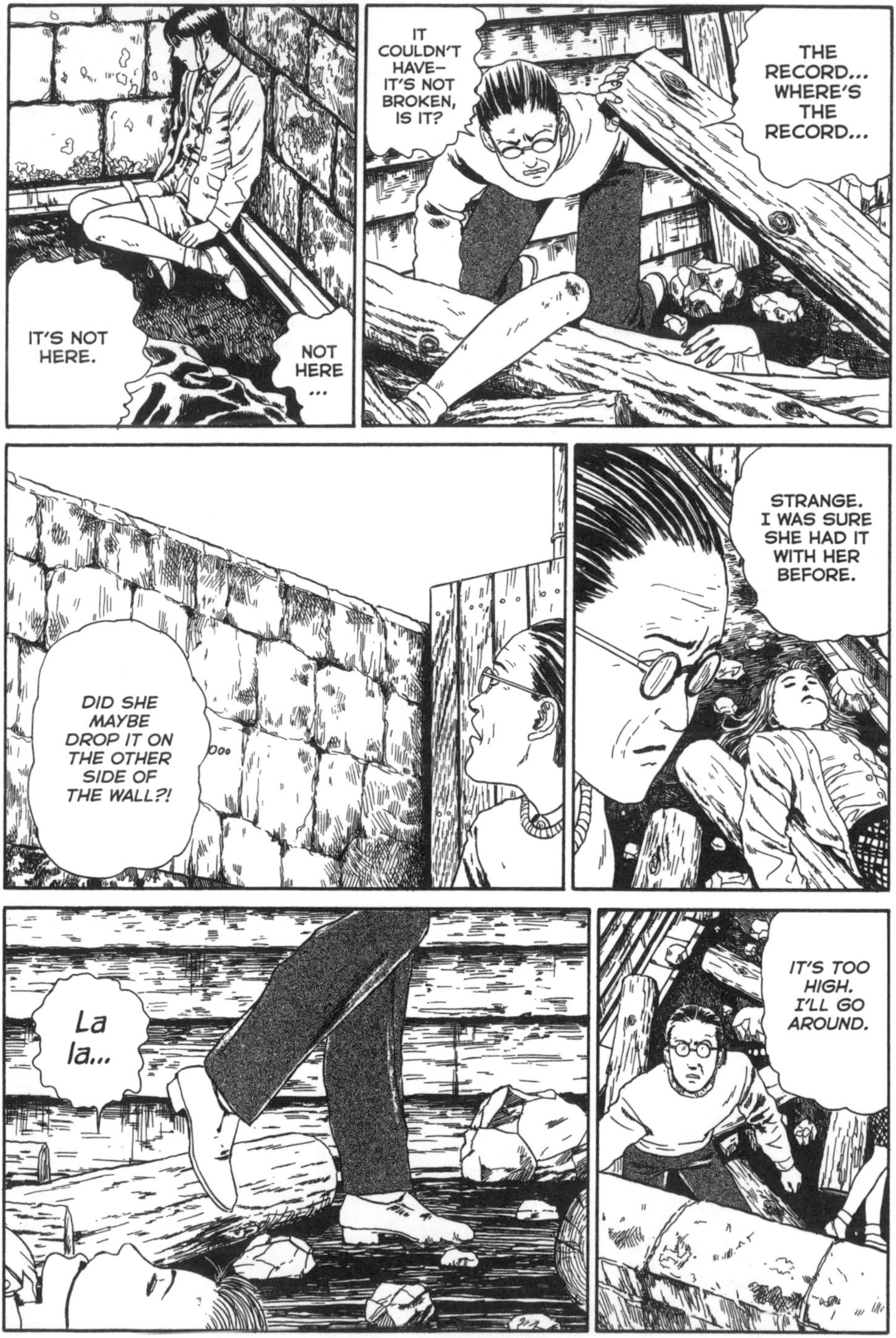
THE RECORD... WHERE'S THE RECORD...
IT COULDN'T HAVE— IT'S NOT BROKEN, IS IT?
NOT HERE ...
IT'S NOT HERE.
STRANGE. I WAS SURE SHE HAD IT WITH HER BEFORE.
DID SHE MAYBE DROP IT ON THE OTHER SIDE OF THE WALL?!
IT'S TOO HIGH. I'LL GO AROUND.
La la...

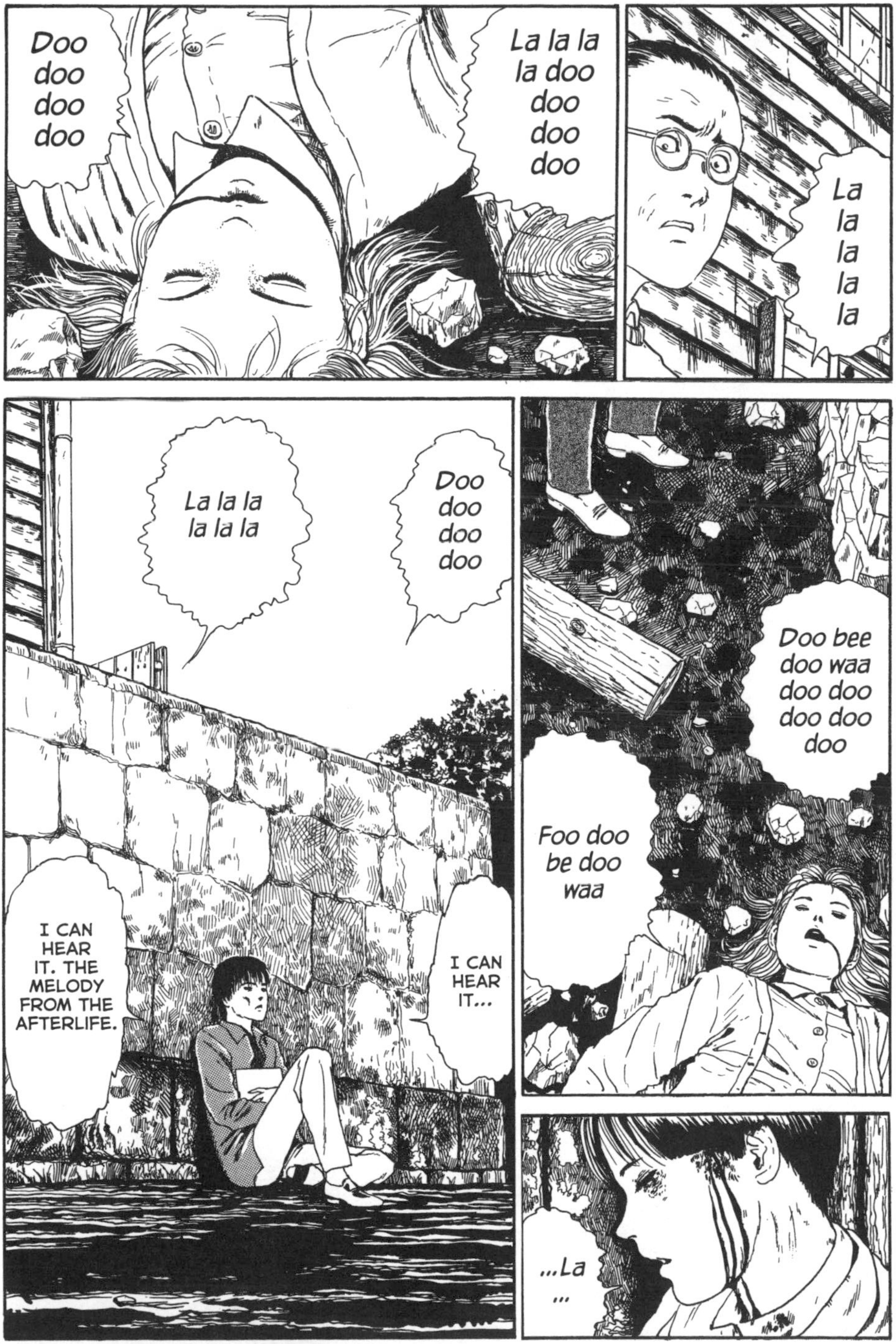
La la la la la
La la la la doo doo doo doo
Doo doo doo doo
Doo bee doo waa doo doo doo doo doo
Foo doo be doo waa
...La ...
Doo doo doo doo
La la la la la la
I CAN HEAR IT...
I CAN HEAR IT. THE MELODY FROM THE AFTERLIFE.

USED RECORD / END

USED RECORD

At the time, I lived in the Issha area of Meito Ward in Nagoya, and there was a little used record shop near Issha Station. (I don't know if it's still there now.) I was delighted to find an old record there of the Swingle Singers scat-singing Bach, and I wanted to try capturing the mood of a used record store like that in manga. As the next story in the series of one-shots I was doing for the monthly magazine *Halloween*, I still hadn't come up with a story when I drew the preview art. And then, right after that, I took another finished manga work to Tokyo, and I was discussing my next work with my editor Harada-san, when he jumped off from the used record store and made it a story about a Tokyo jazz café. He even said, "I've got a feeling this next story's going to be good."

I also decided to throw in the idea of a record of a singer immediately after she died, an idea I'd been cooking up for a while, so there's a combination of different elements in this story. The scat Paula Bell sings here is music that I imagine would surprise the Swingle Singers (the original members, though) up in Heaven.

SKETCH

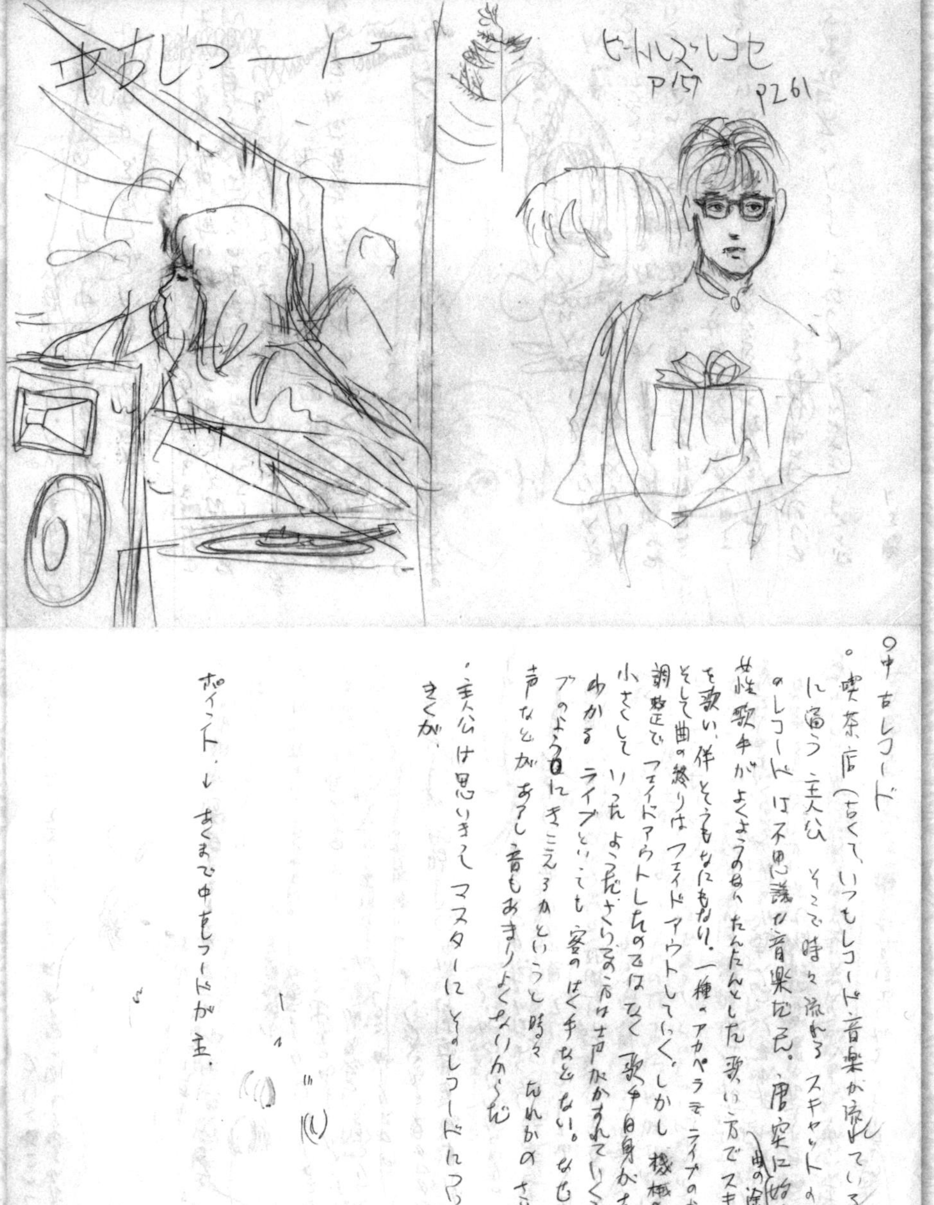
中古レコード
ビートルズレコード
P157
P261
○中古レコード
○喫茶店（古くて、いつもレコード音楽が流れている）に通う主人公 そこで時々流れるスキャットの独唱のレコードは不思議な音楽だった。唐突に始まり、（曲の途中から）女性歌手がよくようのない たんたんとした歌い方でスキャットを歌い、伴奏も何もなし。一種のアカペラでライブのようだ そして曲の終りはフェイドアウトしていく。しかし機械の調整でフェイドアウトしたのではなく 歌手自身が声を小さくしていったようだ。さらにその方は声がかすれていくのでわかる ライブといっても客のはく手などない。なぜライブのように聞こえるかというと時々だれかのささやき声などがあるし音もあまりよくないからだ
・主人公は思いきってマスターにそのレコードについてきくが、
ポイント↓ あくまで中古レコードが主。

Used Record

• *Protagonist who frequents a coffee shop (old, always records playing). Then there's this mysterious music, a solo scat record that they play sometimes. The song starts abruptly in the middle, the female singer scats in this dispassionate singing voice with no intonation, there's also no accompaniment. It's sort of like an a cappella concert. Then it fades out at the end of the song. But the fade-out's not from twisting knobs on the recording equipment; the voice of the singer itself seems to be getting quieter. You can tell because her voice gets hoarser toward the end. It's live, but there's no applause. It sounds like it's a live recording because from time to time, you can hear someone murmuring, and the sound isn't very good.*

• *The protagonist goes ahead and asks the coffee shop owner about the record, but,*

Point → In the end, the used record is the focus.

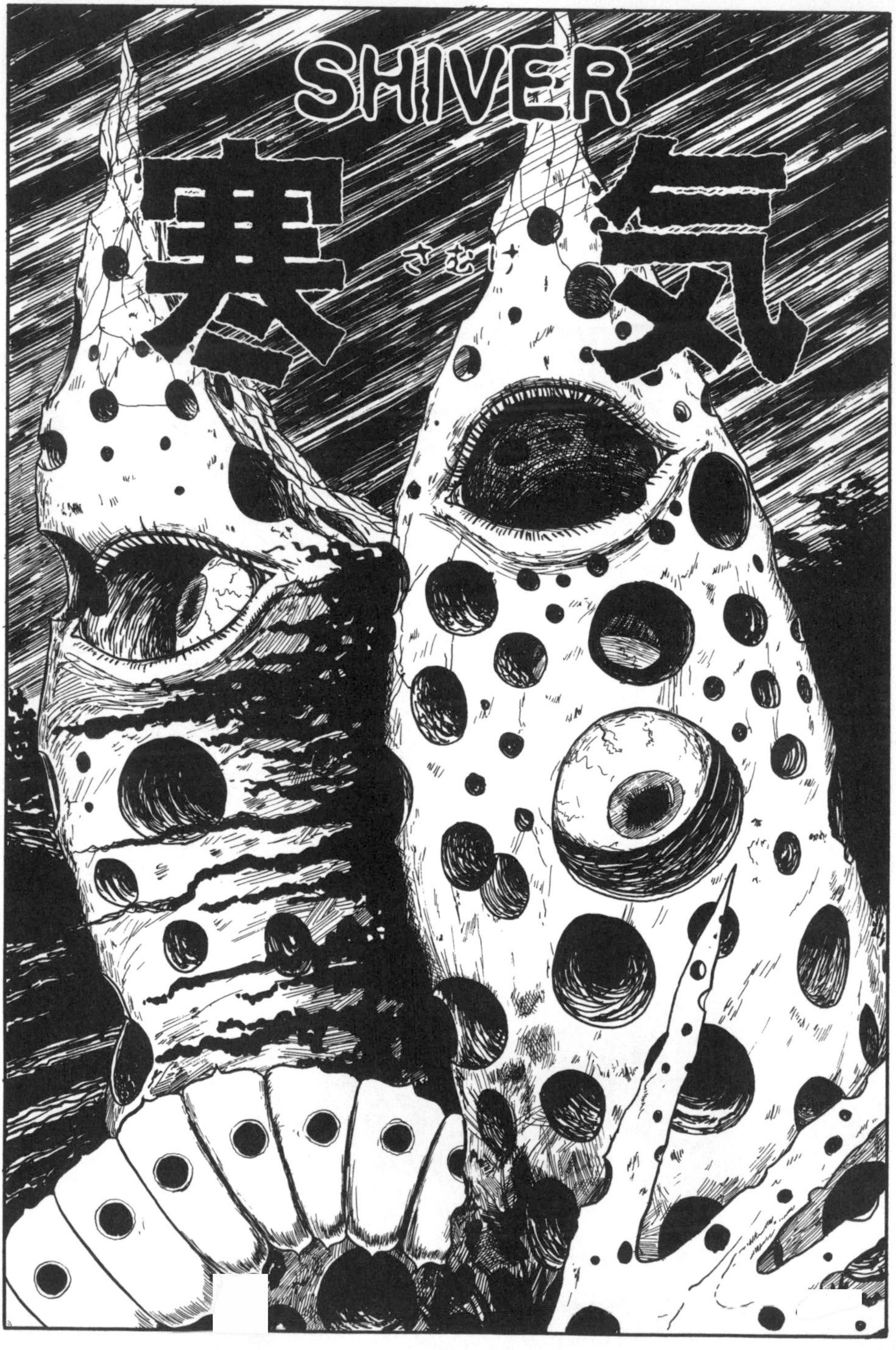
SHIVER
寒気
さむけ

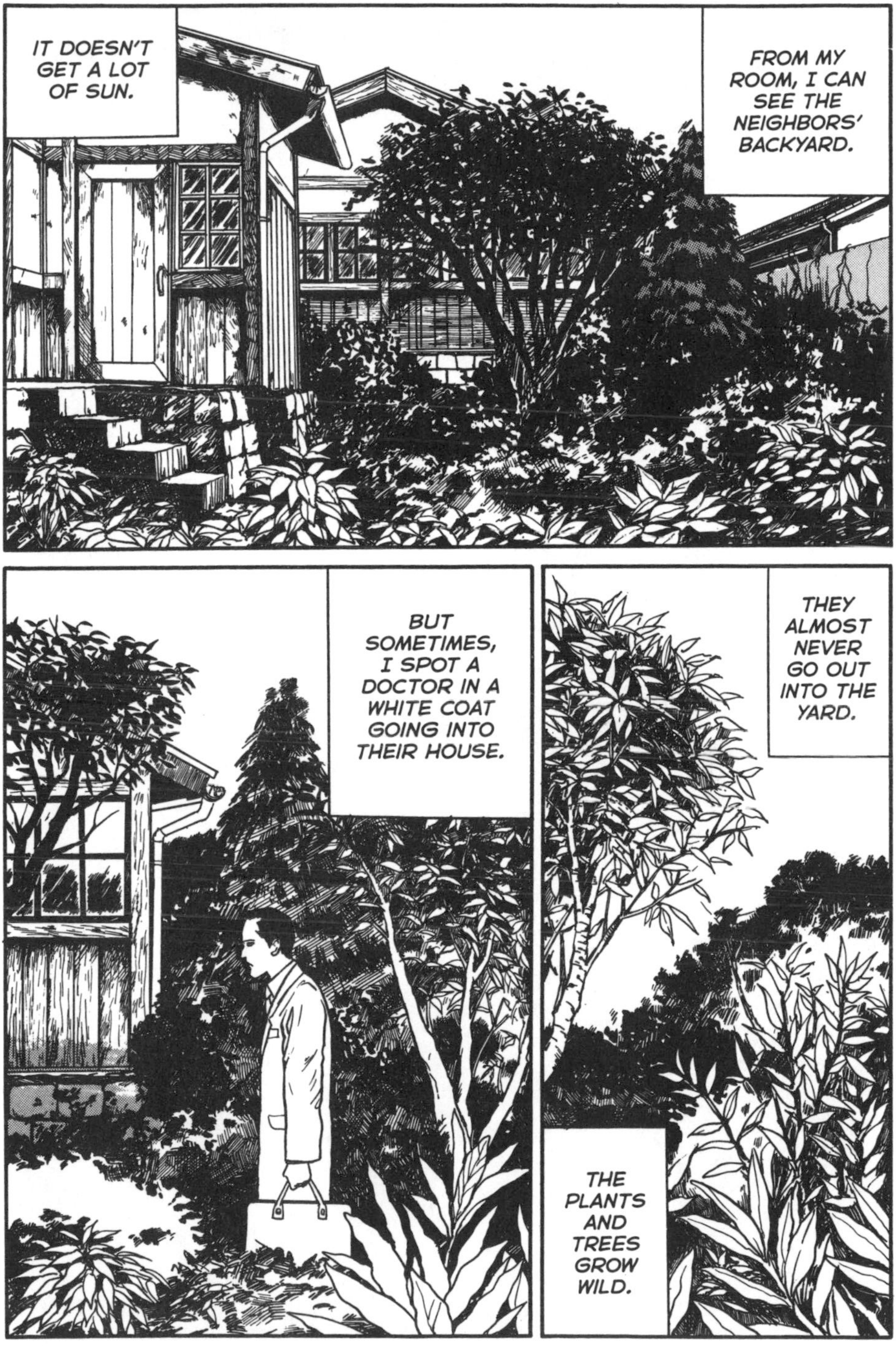
FROM MY ROOM, I CAN SEE THE NEIGHBORS' BACKYARD.
IT DOESN'T GET A LOT OF SUN.
THEY ALMOST NEVER GO OUT INTO THE YARD.
THE PLANTS AND TREES GROW WILD.
BUT SOMETIMES, I SPOT A DOCTOR IN A WHITE COAT GOING INTO THEIR HOUSE.

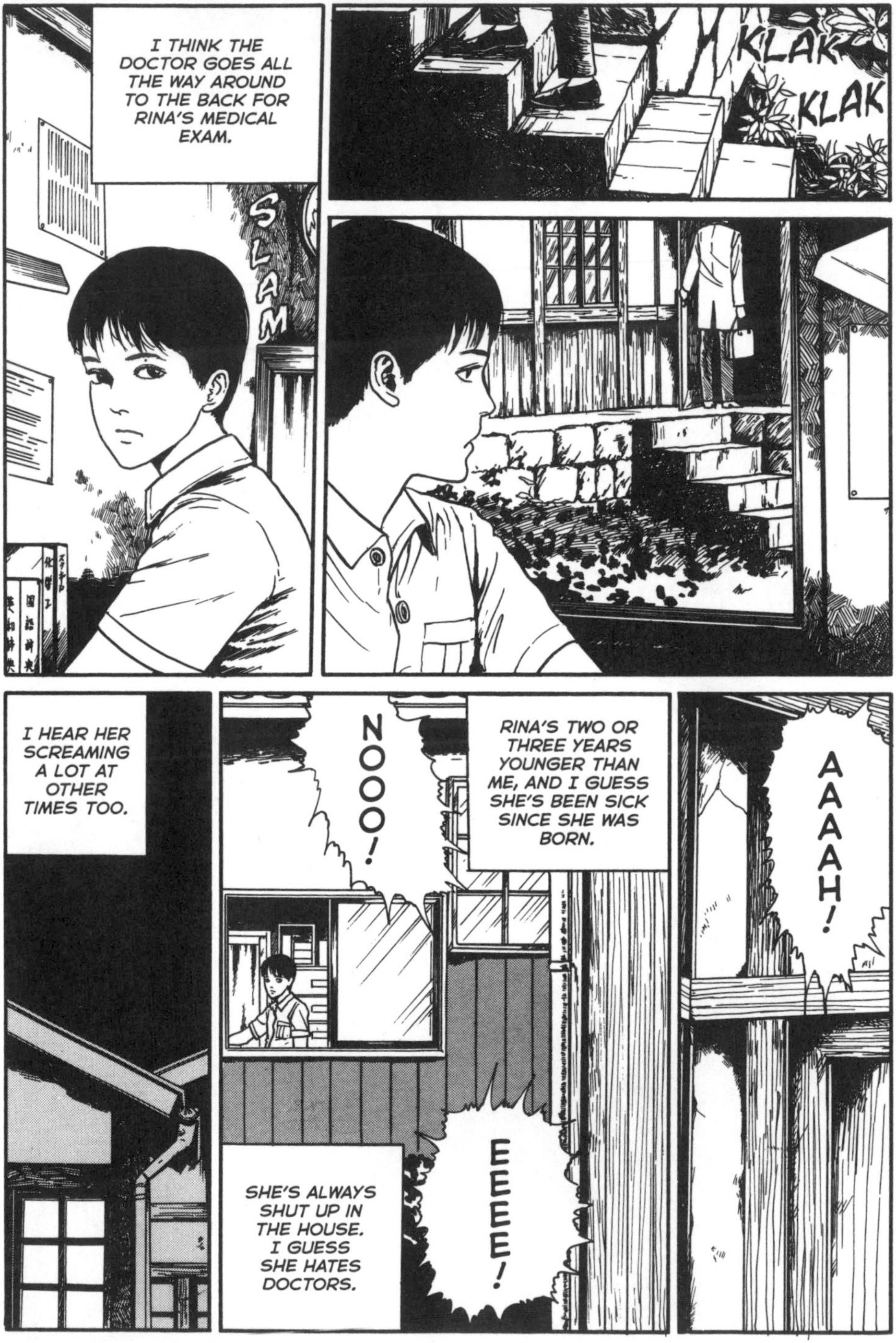
KLAK
KLAK
I THINK THE DOCTOR GOES ALL THE WAY AROUND TO THE BACK FOR RINA'S MEDICAL EXAM.
SLAM
AAAAH!
RINA'S TWO OR THREE YEARS YOUNGER THAN ME, AND I GUESS SHE'S BEEN SICK SINCE SHE WAS BORN.
NOOO!
EEEE!
SHE'S ALWAYS SHUT UP IN THE HOUSE. I GUESS SHE HATES DOCTORS.
I HEAR HER SCREAMING A LOT AT OTHER TIMES TOO.

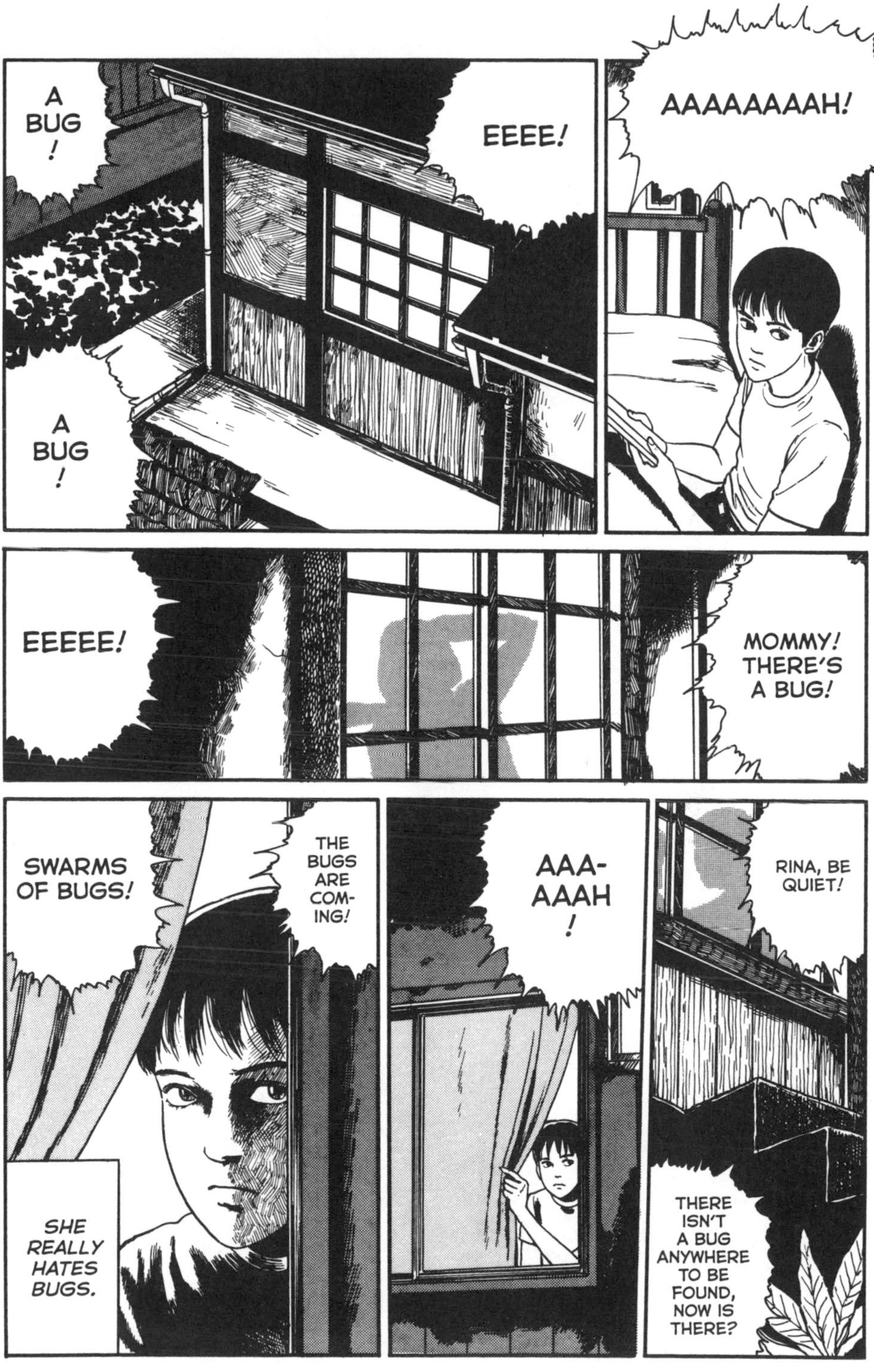
AAAAAAAAH!
EEEE!
A BUG!
A BUG!
MOMMY! THERE'S A BUG!
EEEEE!
RINA, BE QUIET!
THERE ISN'T A BUG ANYWHERE TO BE FOUND, NOW IS THERE?
AAA-AAAH!
THE BUGS ARE COMING!
SWARMS OF BUGS!
SHE REALLY HATES BUGS.

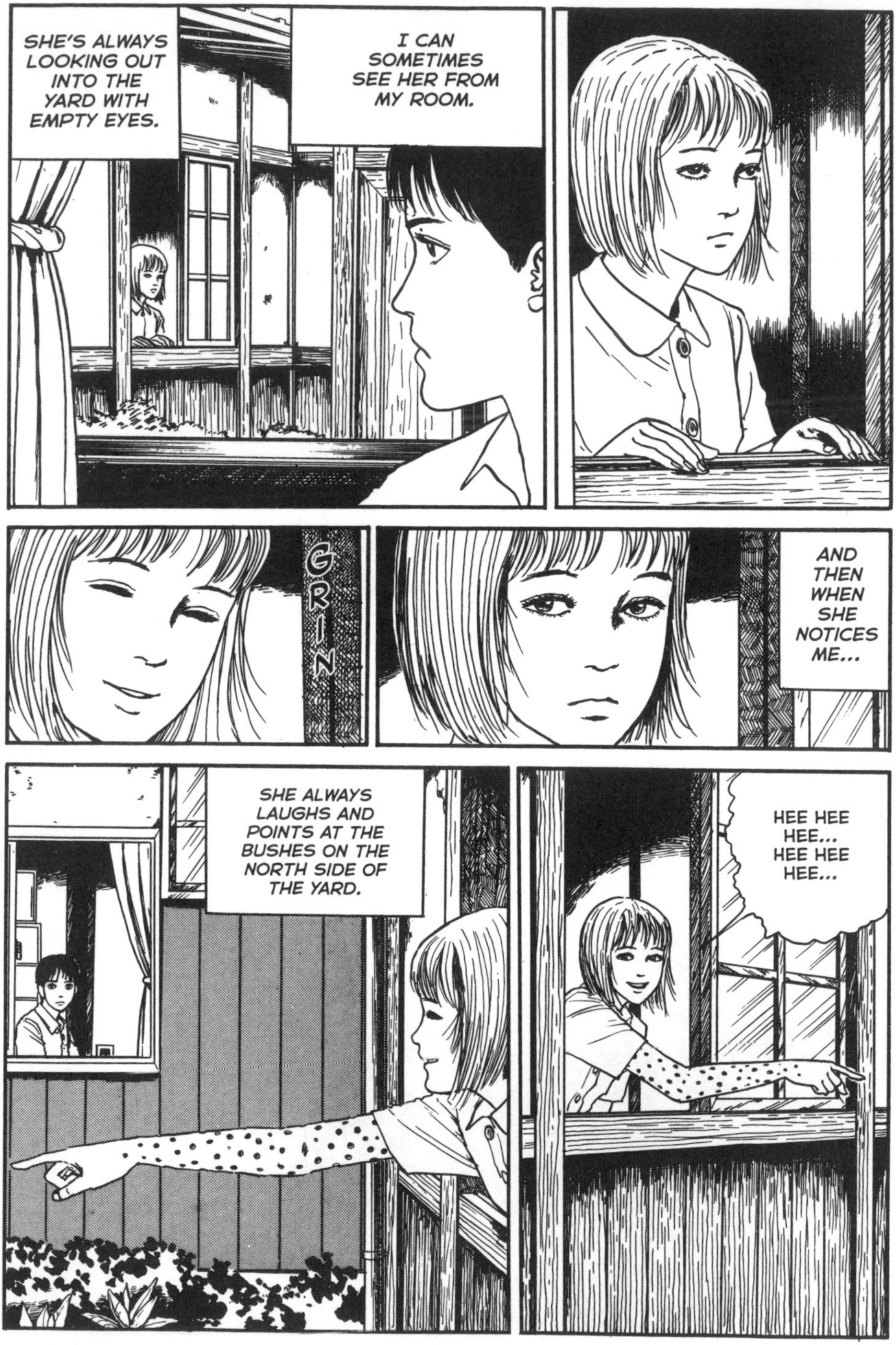
I CAN SOMETIMES SEE HER FROM MY ROOM.
SHE'S ALWAYS LOOKING OUT INTO THE YARD WITH EMPTY EYES.
AND THEN WHEN SHE NOTICES ME...
GRIN
HEE HEE HEE... HEE HEE HEE...
SHE ALWAYS LAUGHS AND POINTS AT THE BUSHES ON THE NORTH SIDE OF THE YARD.

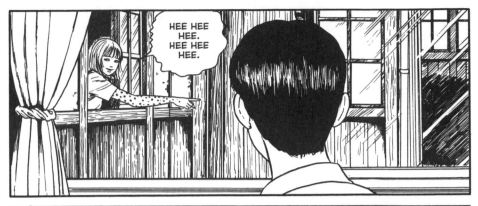

HEE HEE HEE. HEE HEE HEE.
HER ARM IS COVERED IN COUNTLESS HOLES...
A MEMORY CAME BACK TO LIFE IN MY HEAD.
OF THE DISTANT PAST...
A MEMORY THE COLOR OF LEAD.

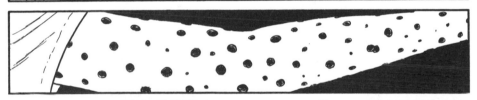

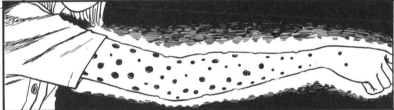

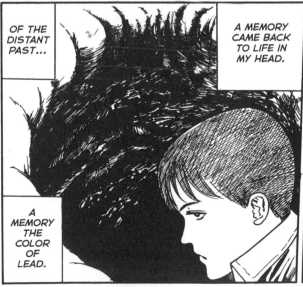

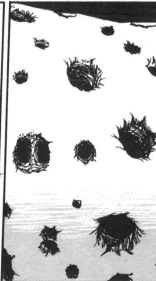

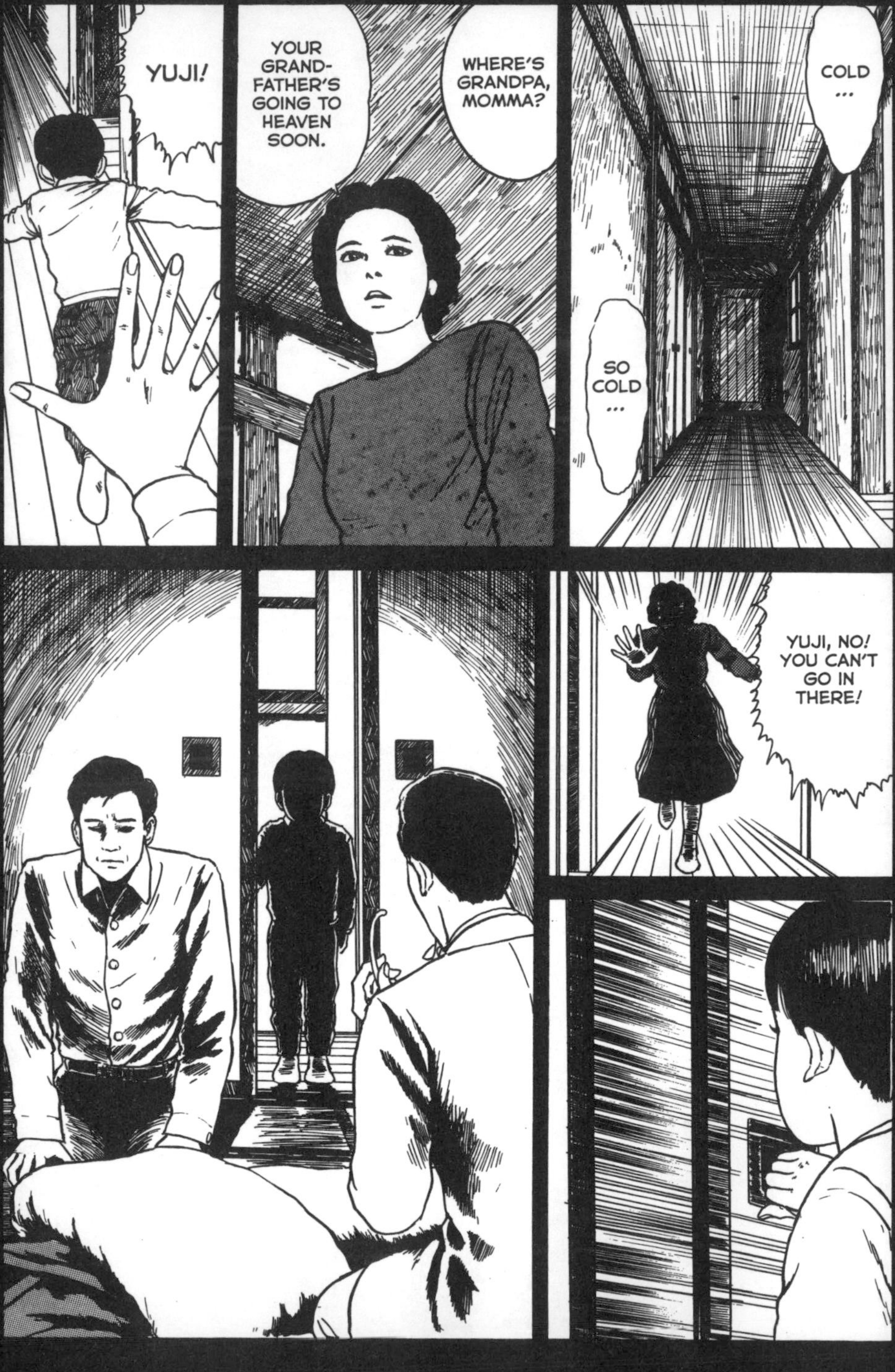
COLD ...
SO COLD ...
WHERE'S GRANDPA, MOMMA?
YOUR GRAND-FATHER'S GOING TO HEAVEN SOON.
YUJI!
YUJI, NO! YOU CAN'T GO IN THERE!

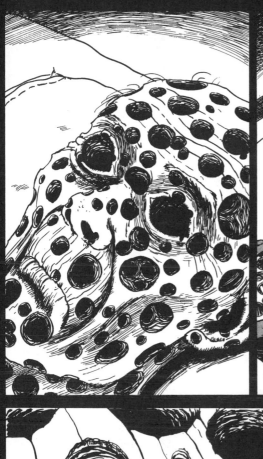

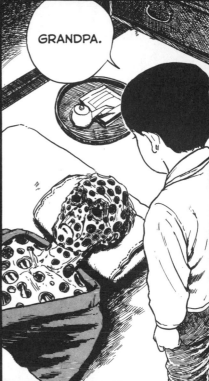

GRANDPA.

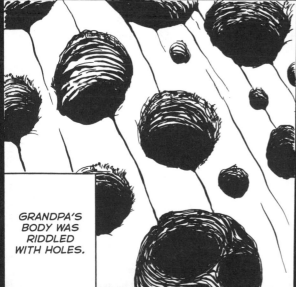

GRANDPA'S BODY WAS RIDDLED WITH HOLES.

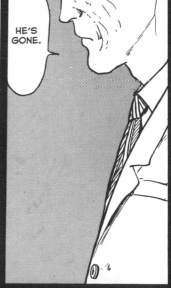

HE'S GONE.

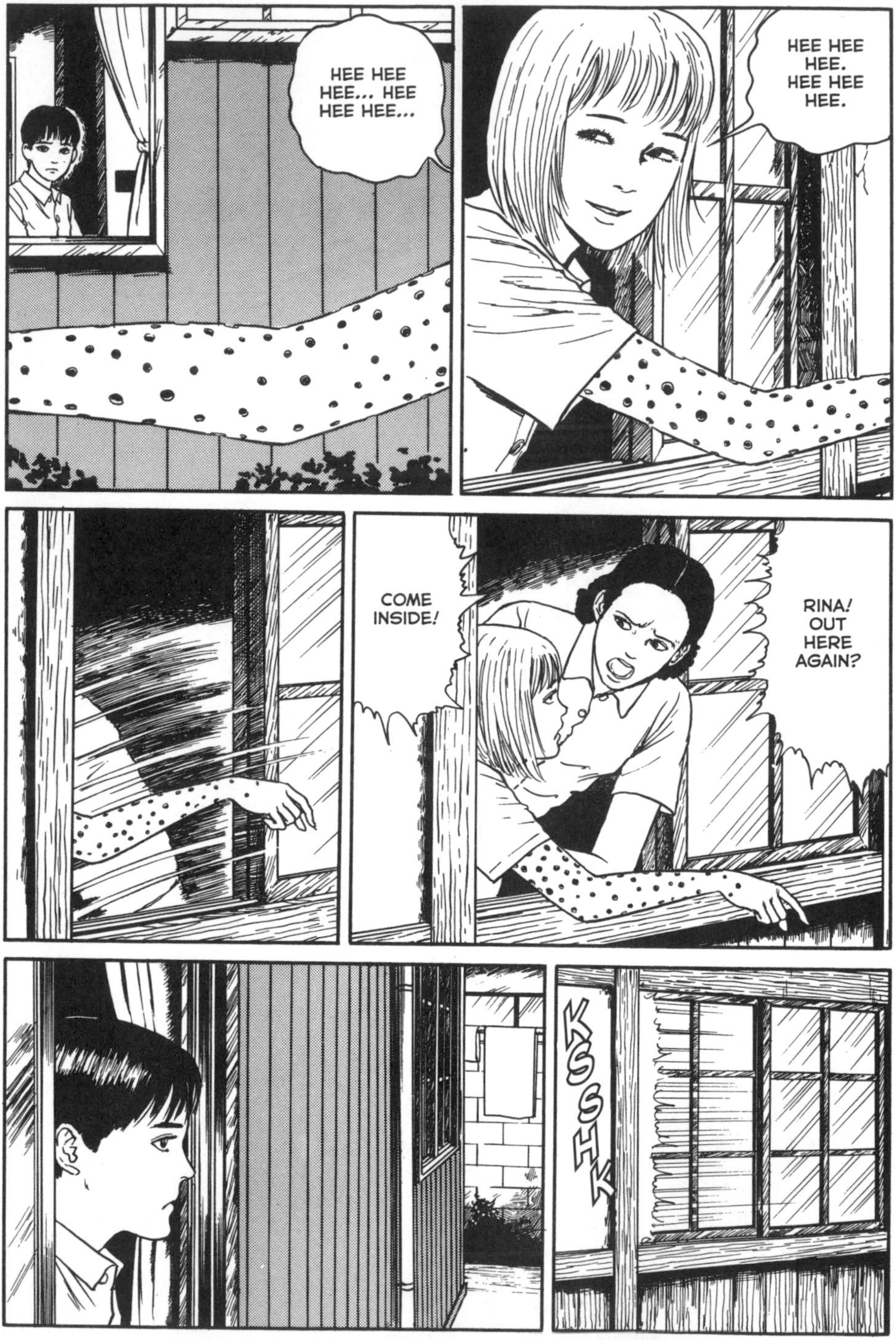
HEE HEE HEE. HEE HEE HEE.
HEE HEE HEE... HEE HEE HEE...
RINA! OUT HERE AGAIN?
COME INSIDE!
KSSHK

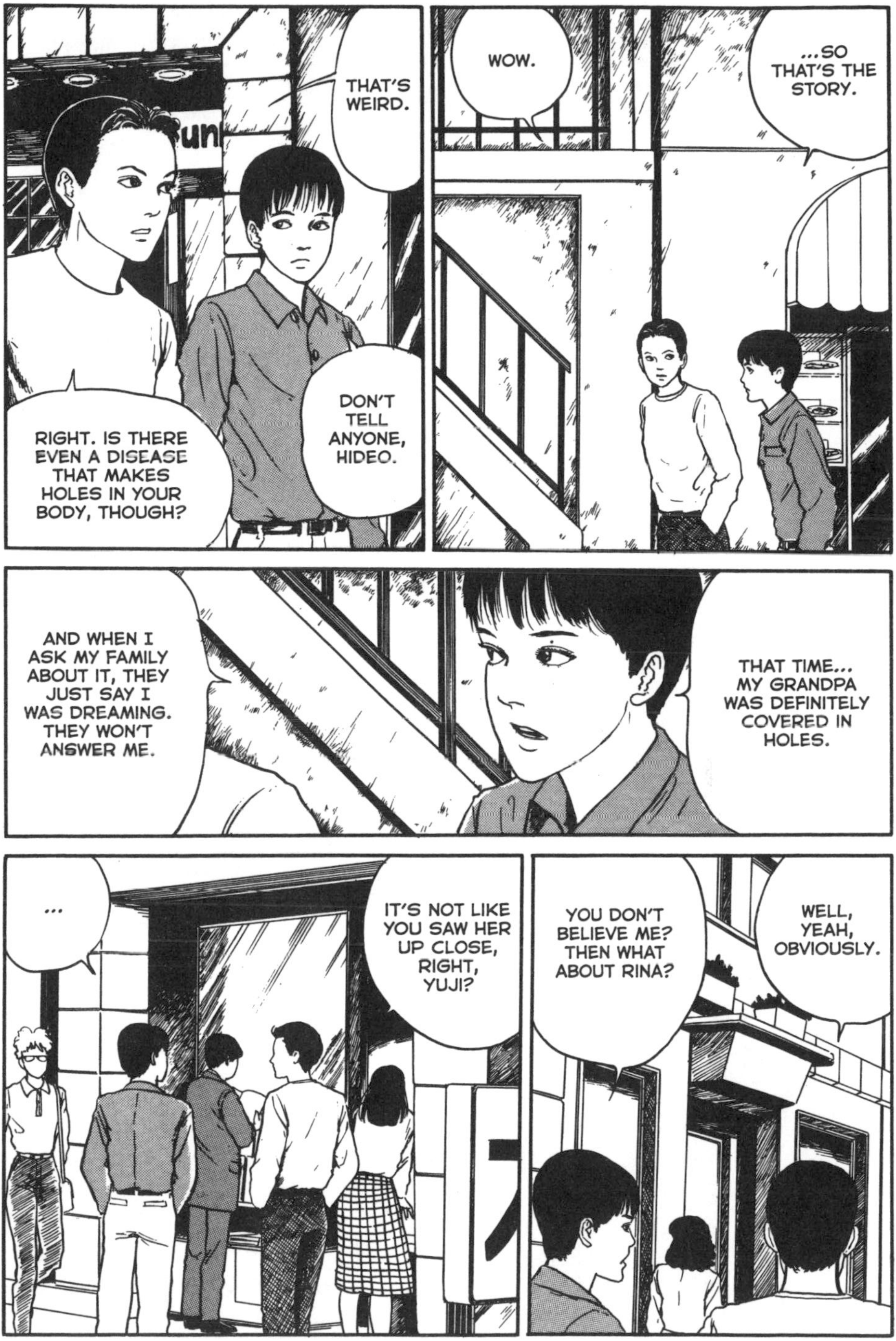
...SO THAT'S THE STORY.
WOW.
THAT'S WEIRD.
DON'T TELL ANYONE, HIDEO.
RIGHT. IS THERE EVEN A DISEASE THAT MAKES HOLES IN YOUR BODY, THOUGH?
THAT TIME... MY GRANDPA WAS DEFINITELY COVERED IN HOLES.
AND WHEN I ASK MY FAMILY ABOUT IT, THEY JUST SAY I WAS DREAMING. THEY WON'T ANSWER ME.
WELL, YEAH, OBVIOUSLY.
YOU DON'T BELIEVE ME? THEN WHAT ABOUT RINA?
IT'S NOT LIKE YOU SAW HER UP CLOSE, RIGHT, YUJI?
...

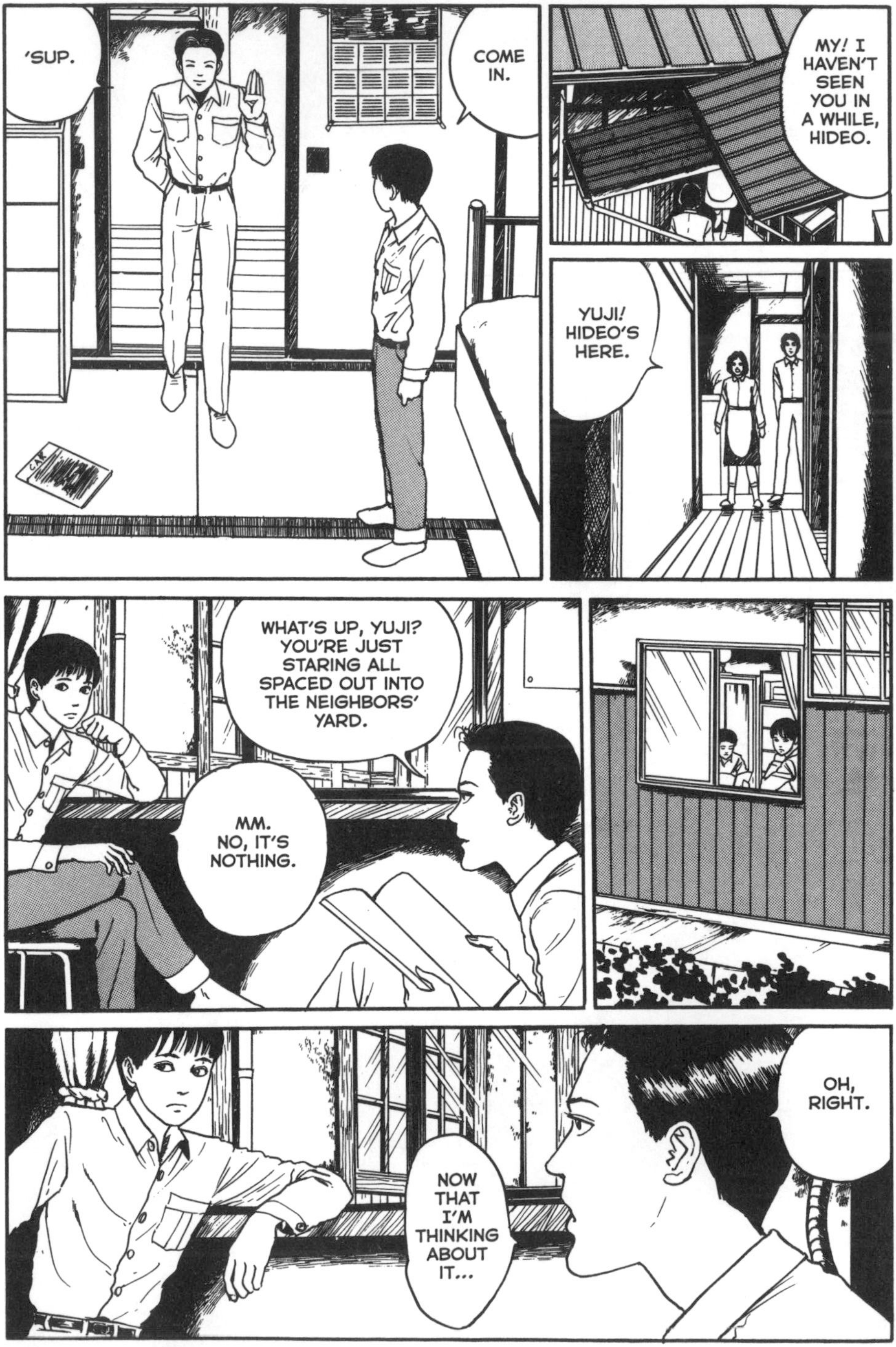
MY! I HAVEN'T SEEN YOU IN A WHILE, HIDEO.
YUJI! HIDEO'S HERE.
COME IN.
'SUP.
WHAT'S UP, YUJI? YOU'RE JUST STARING ALL SPACED OUT INTO THE NEIGHBORS' YARD.
MM. NO, IT'S NOTHING.
OH, RIGHT.
NOW THAT I'M THINKING ABOUT IT...

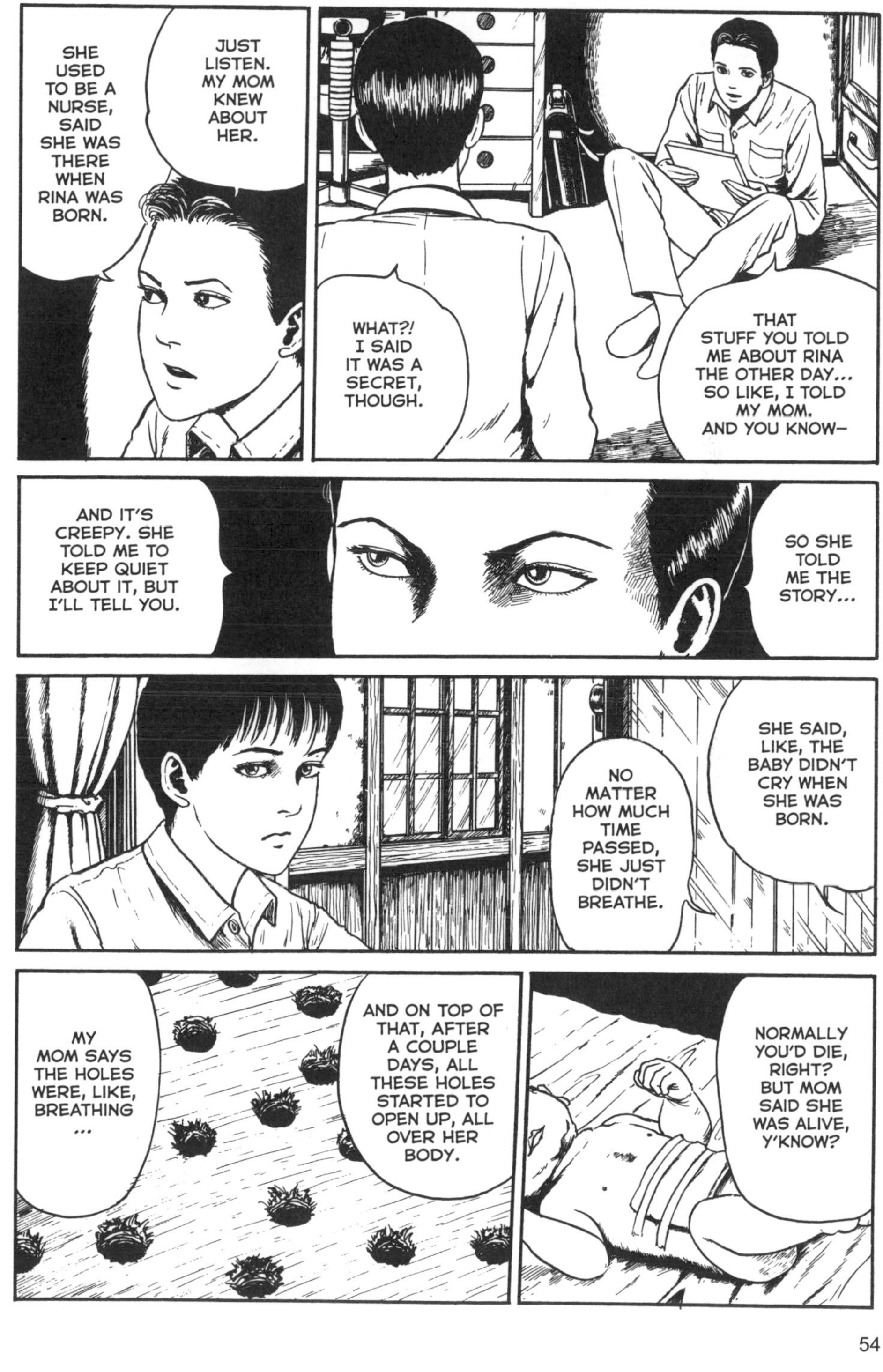
THAT STUFF YOU TOLD ME ABOUT RINA THE OTHER DAY... SO LIKE, I TOLD MY MOM. AND YOU KNOW–
WHAT?! I SAID IT WAS A SECRET, THOUGH.
JUST LISTEN. MY MOM KNEW ABOUT HER.
SHE USED TO BE A NURSE, SAID SHE WAS THERE WHEN RINA WAS BORN.
SO SHE TOLD ME THE STORY...
AND IT'S CREEPY. SHE TOLD ME TO KEEP QUIET ABOUT IT, BUT I'LL TELL YOU.
SHE SAID, LIKE, THE BABY DIDN'T CRY WHEN SHE WAS BORN.
NO MATTER HOW MUCH TIME PASSED, SHE JUST DIDN'T BREATHE.
NORMALLY YOU'D DIE, RIGHT? BUT MOM SAID SHE WAS ALIVE, Y'KNOW?
AND ON TOP OF THAT, AFTER A COUPLE DAYS, ALL THESE HOLES STARTED TO OPEN UP, ALL OVER HER BODY.
MY MOM SAYS THE HOLES WERE, LIKE, BREATHING ...

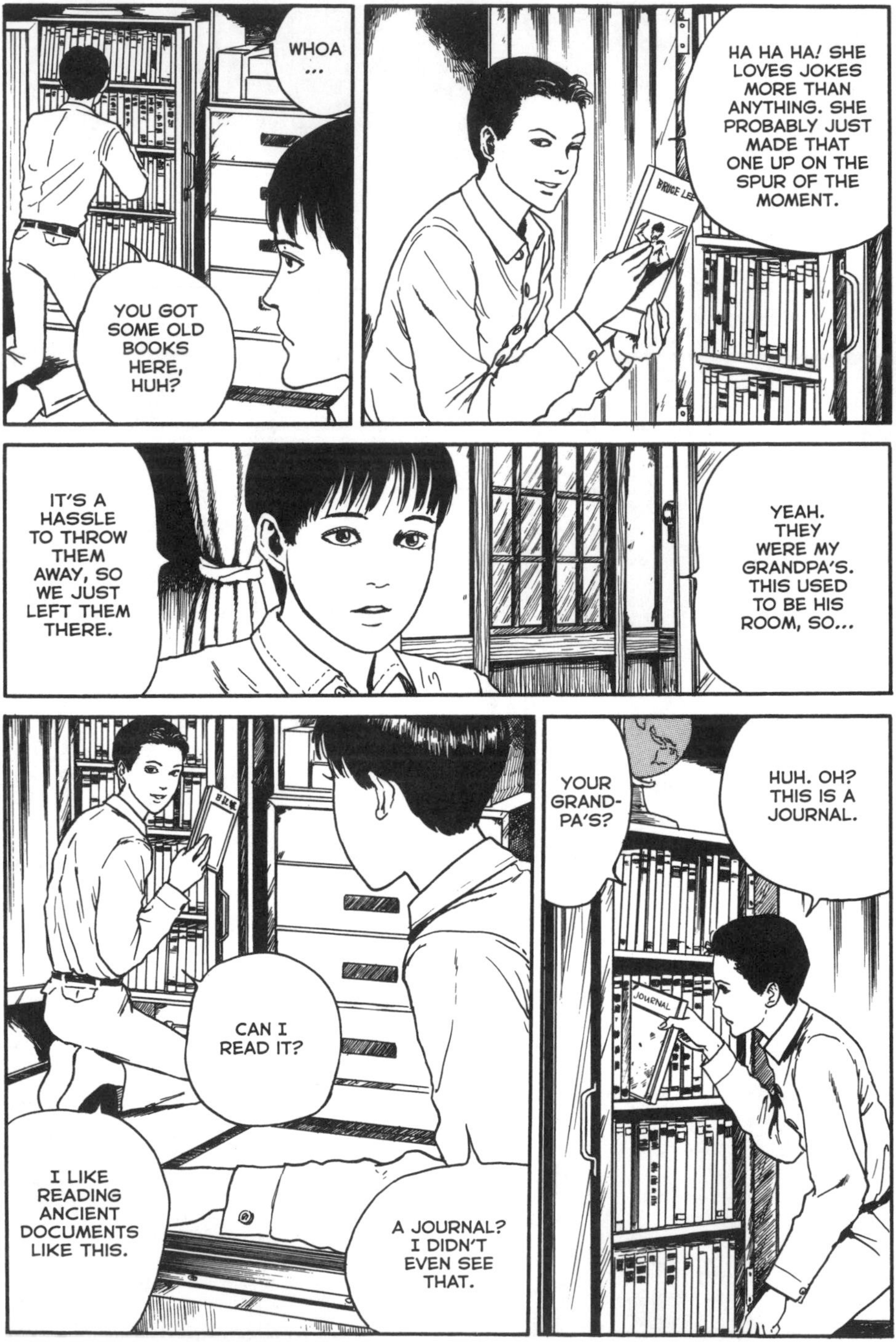
HA HA HA! SHE LOVES JOKES MORE THAN ANYTHING. SHE PROBABLY JUST MADE THAT ONE UP ON THE SPUR OF THE MOMENT.
BRUCE LEE
WHOA ...
YOU GOT SOME OLD BOOKS HERE, HUH?
YEAH. THEY WERE MY GRANDPA'S. THIS USED TO BE HIS ROOM, SO...
IT'S A HASSLE TO THROW THEM AWAY, SO WE JUST LEFT THEM THERE.
HUH. OH? THIS IS A JOURNAL.
YOUR GRANDPA'S?
JOURNAL
A JOURNAL? I DIDN'T EVEN SEE THAT.
I LIKE READING ANCIENT DOCUMENTS LIKE THIS.
CAN I READ IT?

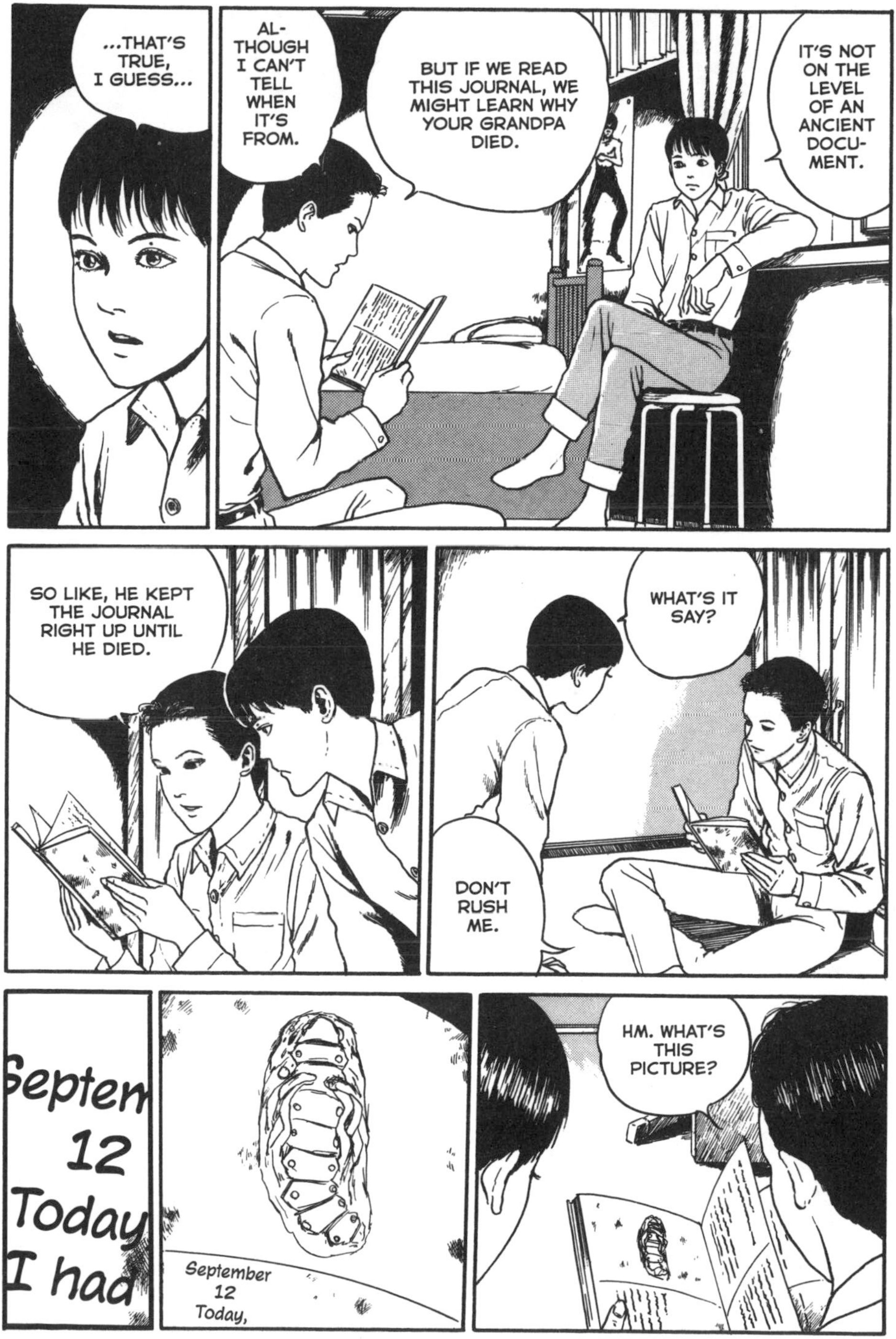
IT'S NOT ON THE LEVEL OF AN ANCIENT DOCUMENT.
BUT IF WE READ THIS JOURNAL, WE MIGHT LEARN WHY YOUR GRANDPA DIED.
AL-THOUGH I CAN'T TELL WHEN IT'S FROM.
...THAT'S TRUE, I GUESS...
WHAT'S IT SAY?
DON'T RUSH ME.
SO LIKE, HE KEPT THE JOURNAL RIGHT UP UNTIL HE DIED.
HM. WHAT'S THIS PICTURE?
September 12 Today,
Septem 12 Today I had

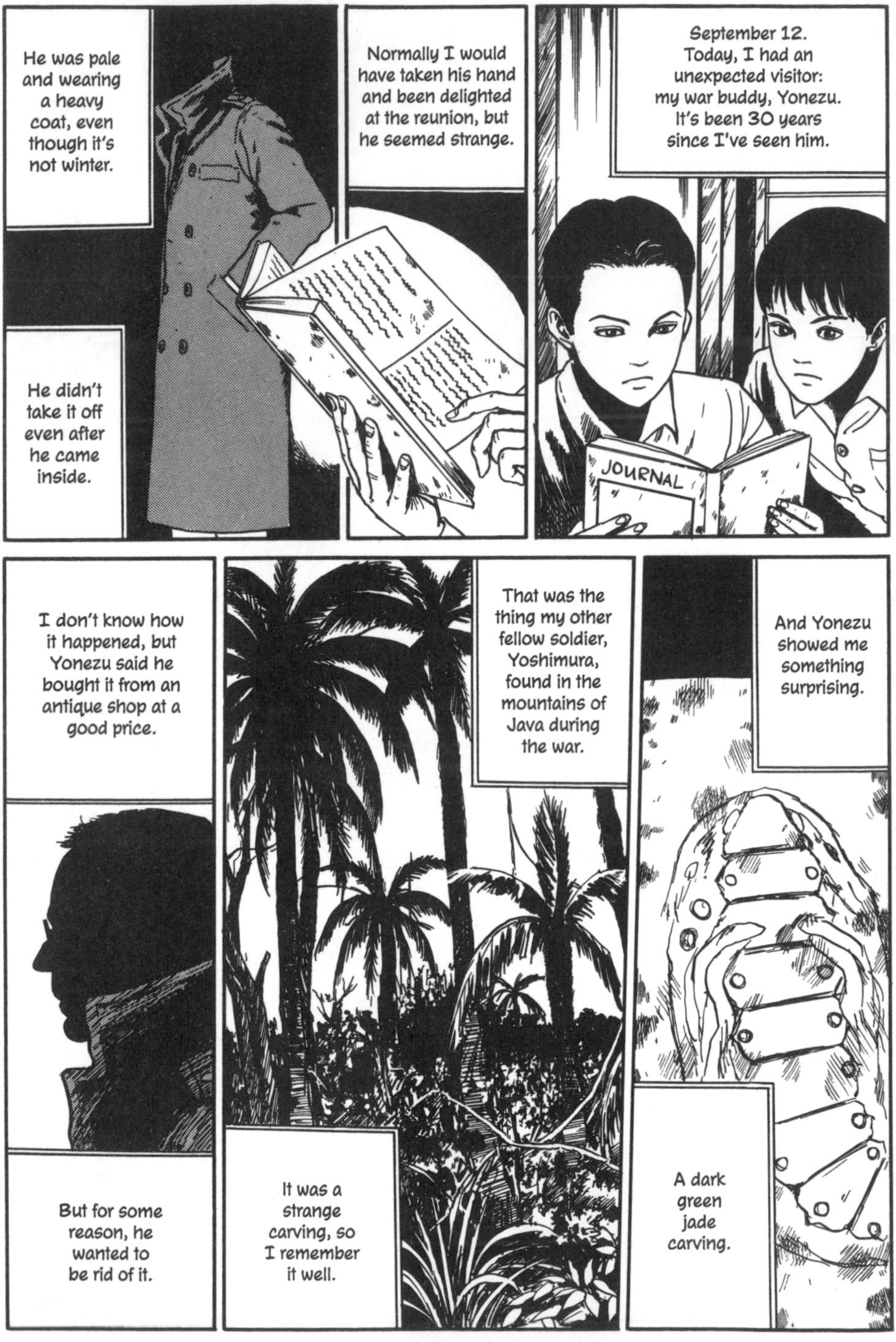
September 12. Today, I had an unexpected visitor: my war buddy, Yonezu. It's been 30 years since I've seen him.
JOURNAL
Normally I would have taken his hand and been delighted at the reunion, but he seemed strange.
He was pale and wearing a heavy coat, even though it's not winter.
He didn't take it off even after he came inside.
And Yonezu showed me something surprising.
A dark green jade carving.
That was the thing my other fellow soldier, Yoshimura, found in the mountains of Java during the war.
It was a strange carving, so I remember it well.
I don't know how it happened, but Yonezu said he bought it from an antique shop at a good price.
But for some reason, he wanted to be rid of it.

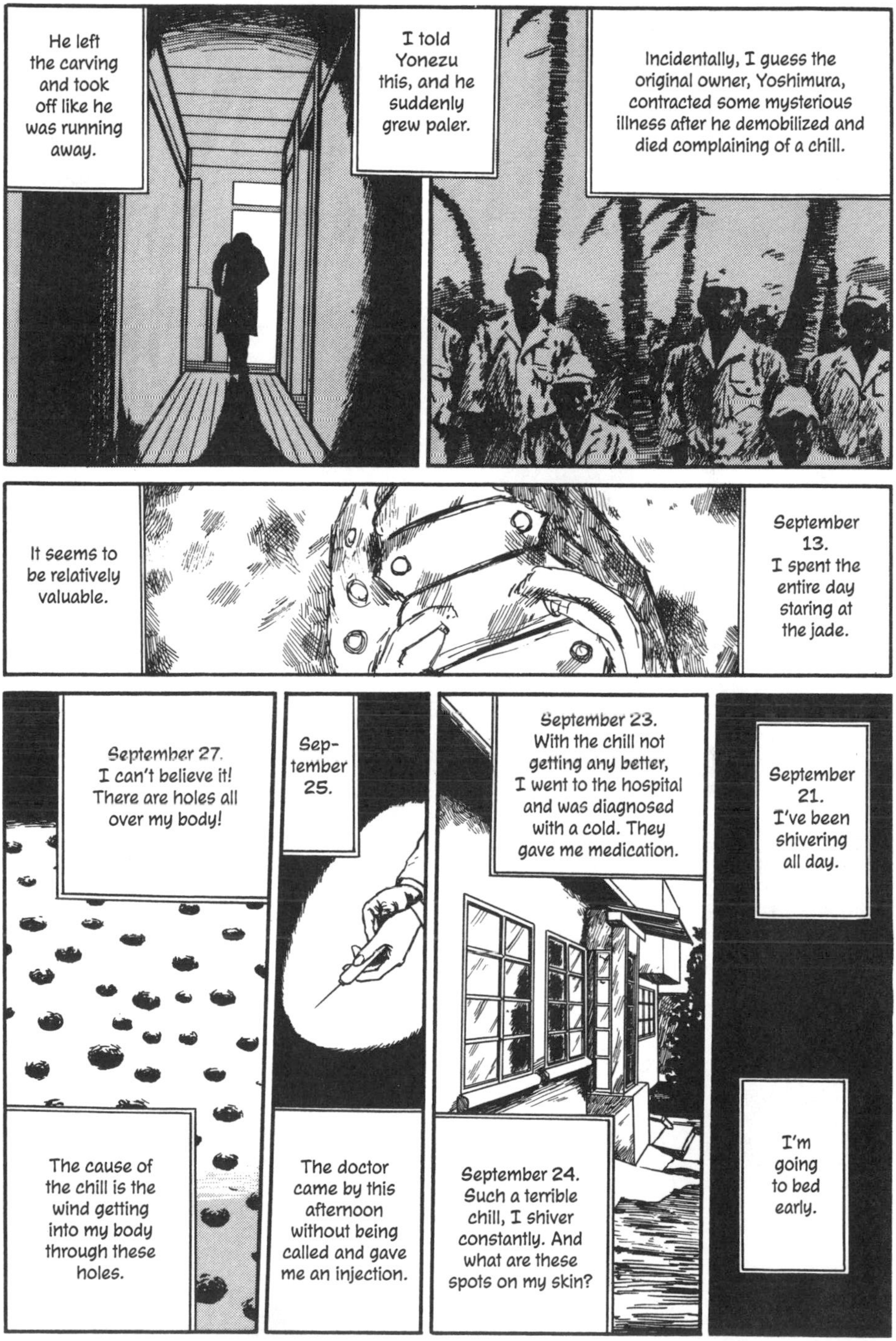

Incidentally, I guess the original owner, Yoshimura, contracted some mysterious illness after he demobilized and died complaining of a chill.
I told Yonezu this, and he suddenly grew paler.
He left the carving and took off like he was running away.
September 13. I spent the entire day staring at the jade.
It seems to be relatively valuable.
September 21. I've been shivering all day.
I'm going to bed early.
September 23. With the chill not getting any better, I went to the hospital and was diagnosed with a cold. They gave me medication.
September 24. Such a terrible chill, I shiver constantly. And what are these spots on my skin?
September 25.
The doctor came by this afternoon without being called and gave me an injection.
September 27. I can't believe it! There are holes all over my body!
The cause of the chill is the wind getting into my body through these holes.

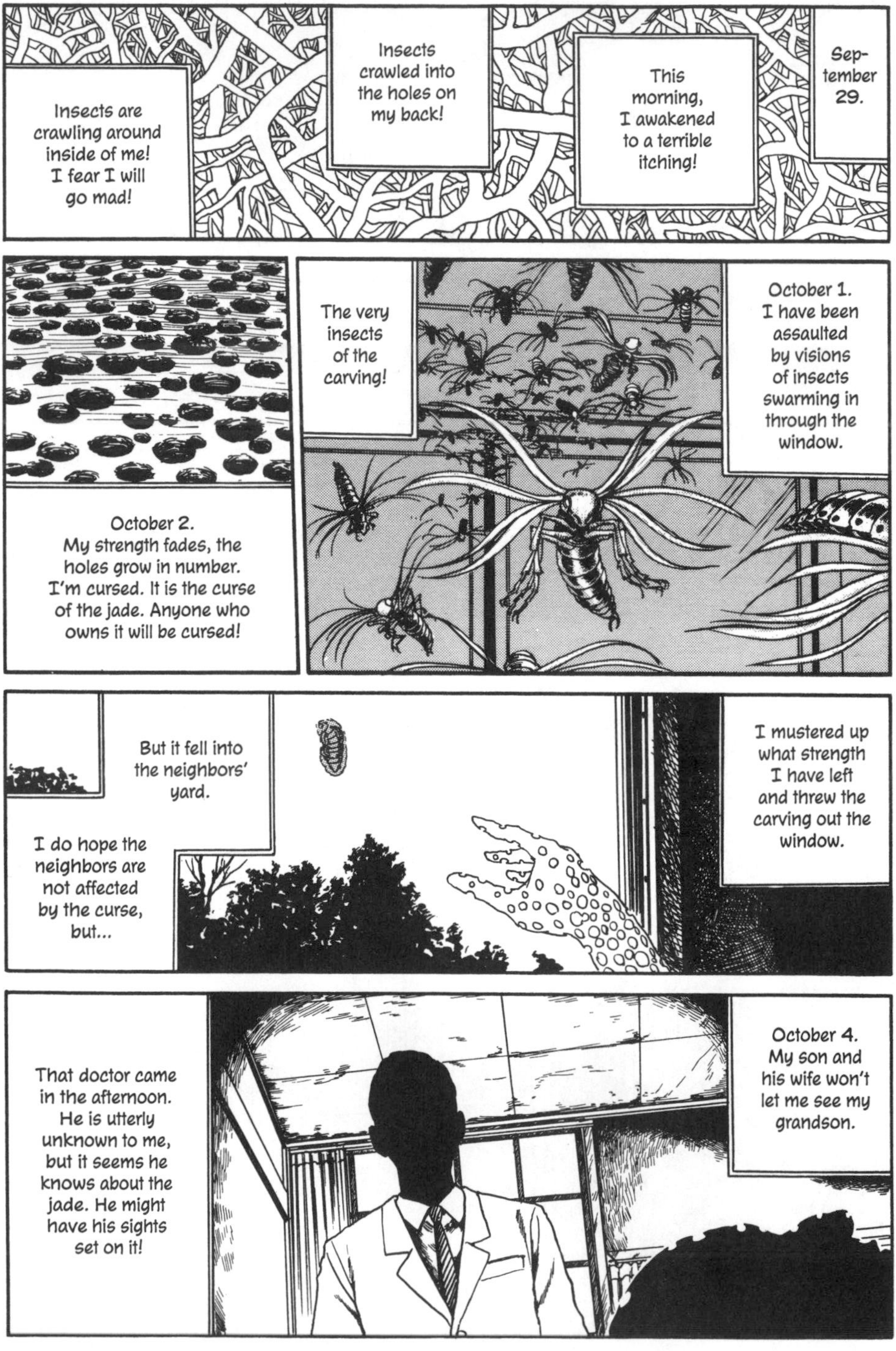
September 29.
This morning, I awakened to a terrible itching!
Insects crawled into the holes on my back!
Insects are crawling around inside of me! I fear I will go mad!
October 1. I have been assaulted by visions of insects swarming in through the window.
The very insects of the carving!
October 2. My strength fades, the holes grow in number. I'm cursed. It is the curse of the jade. Anyone who owns it will be cursed!
I mustered up what strength I have left and threw the carving out the window.
But it fell into the neighbors' yard.
I do hope the neighbors are not affected by the curse, but...
October 4. My son and his wife won't let me see my grandson.
That doctor came in the afternoon. He is utterly unknown to me, but it seems he knows about the jade. He might have his sights set on it!

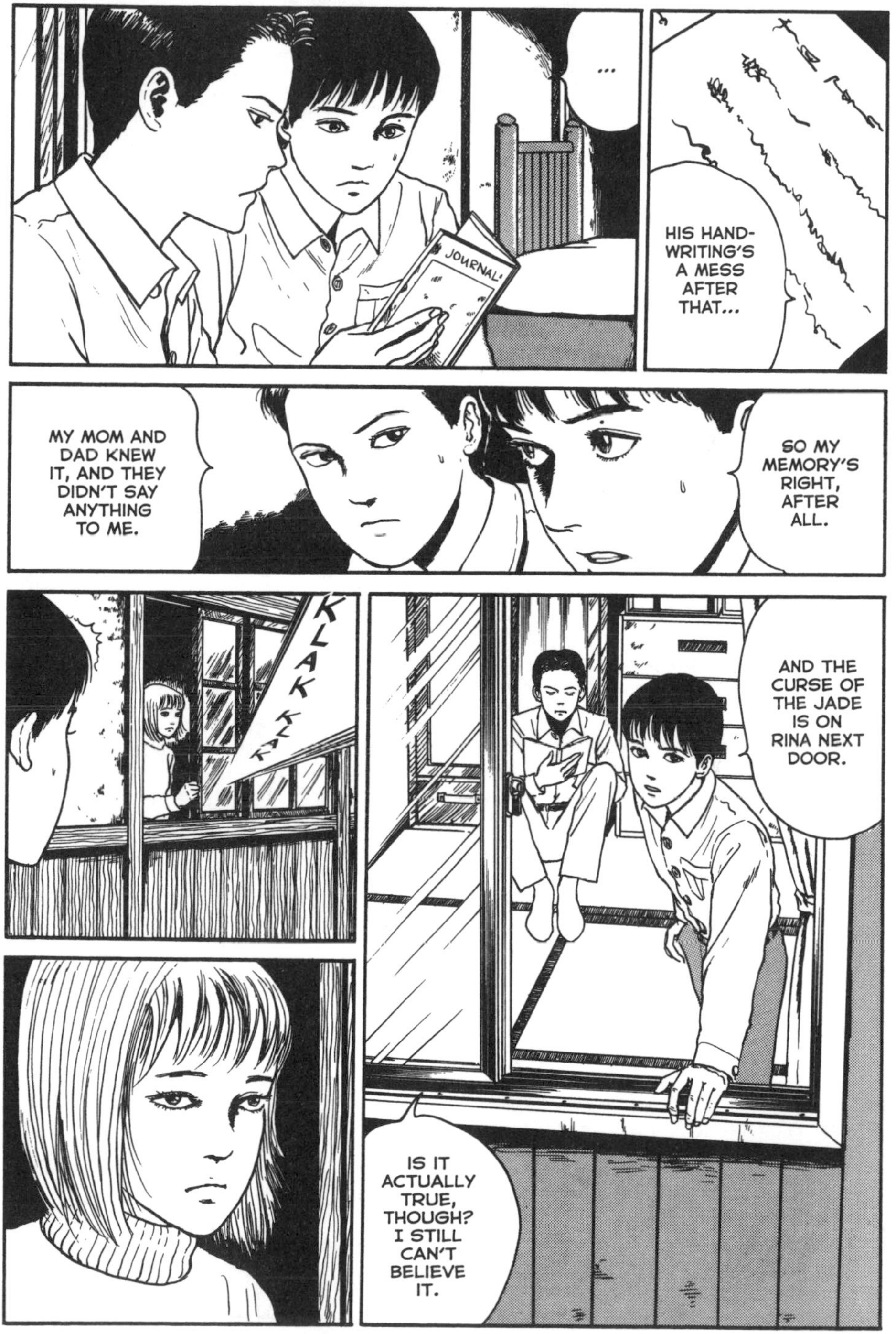
HIS HAND-WRITING'S A MESS AFTER THAT...
...
SO MY MEMORY'S RIGHT, AFTER ALL.
MY MOM AND DAD KNEW IT, AND THEY DIDN'T SAY ANYTHING TO ME.
AND THE CURSE OF THE JADE IS ON RINA NEXT DOOR.
IS IT ACTUALLY TRUE, THOUGH? I STILL CAN'T BELIEVE IT.
JOURNAL
KLAK KLAK

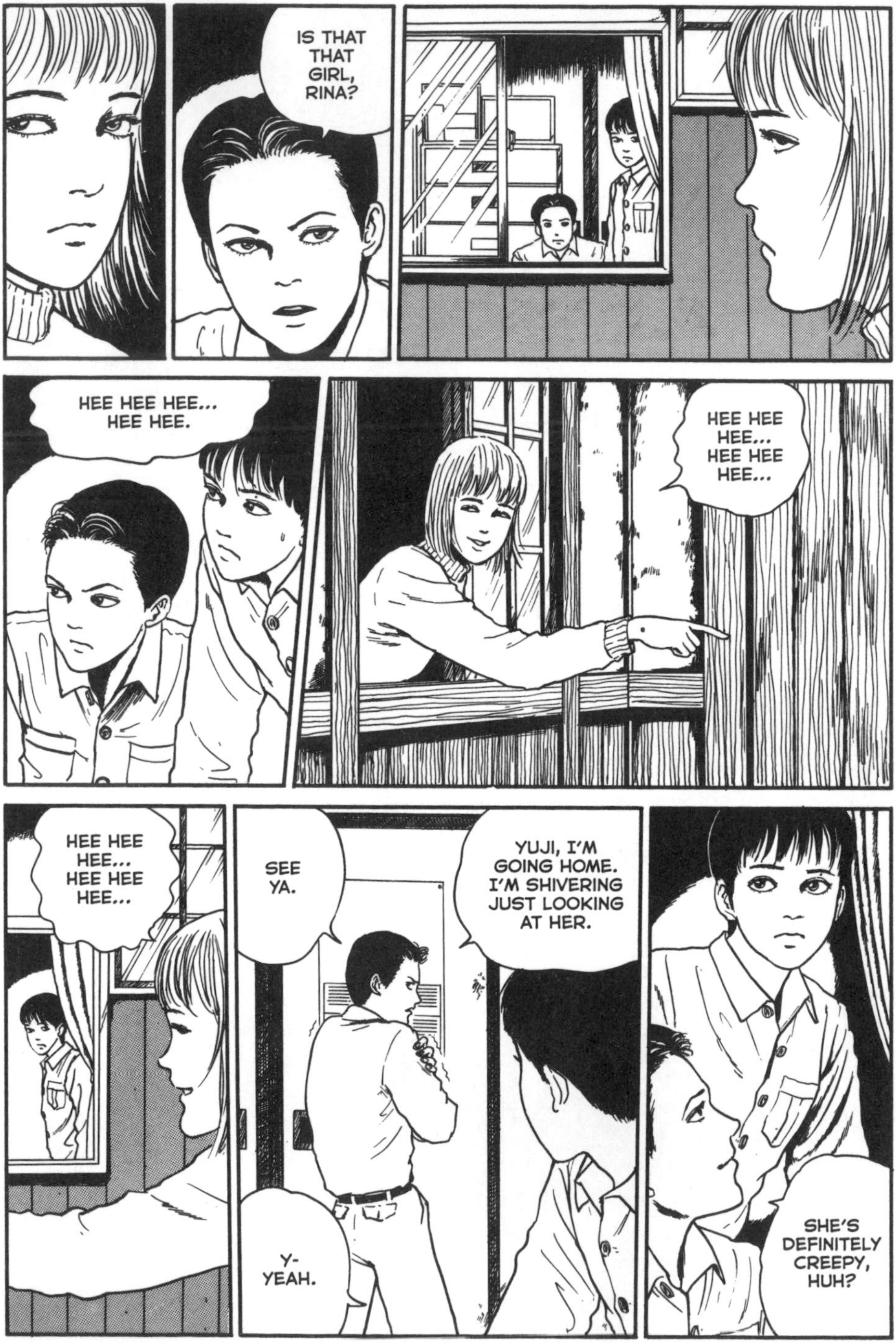
IS THAT THAT GIRL, RINA?
HEE HEE HEE... HEE HEE HEE...
HEE HEE HEE... HEE HEE.
SHE'S DEFINITELY CREEPY, HUH?
YUJI, I'M GOING HOME. I'M SHIVERING JUST LOOKING AT HER.
SEE YA.
Y-YEAH.
HEE HEE HEE... HEE HEE HEE...

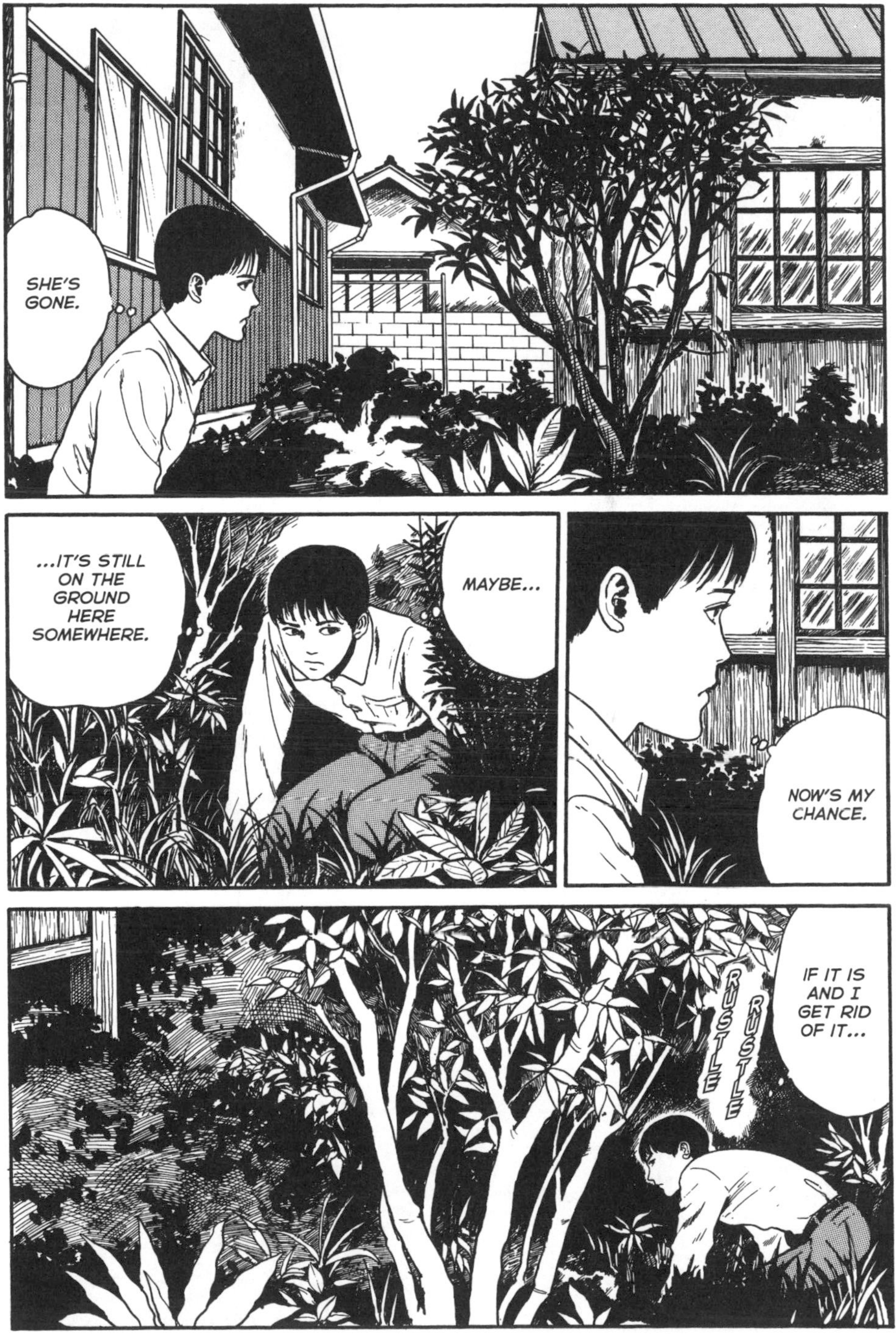
SHE'S GONE.
NOW'S MY CHANCE.
MAYBE...
...IT'S STILL ON THE GROUND HERE SOMEWHERE.
IF IT IS AND I GET RID OF IT...
RUSTLE
RUSTLE

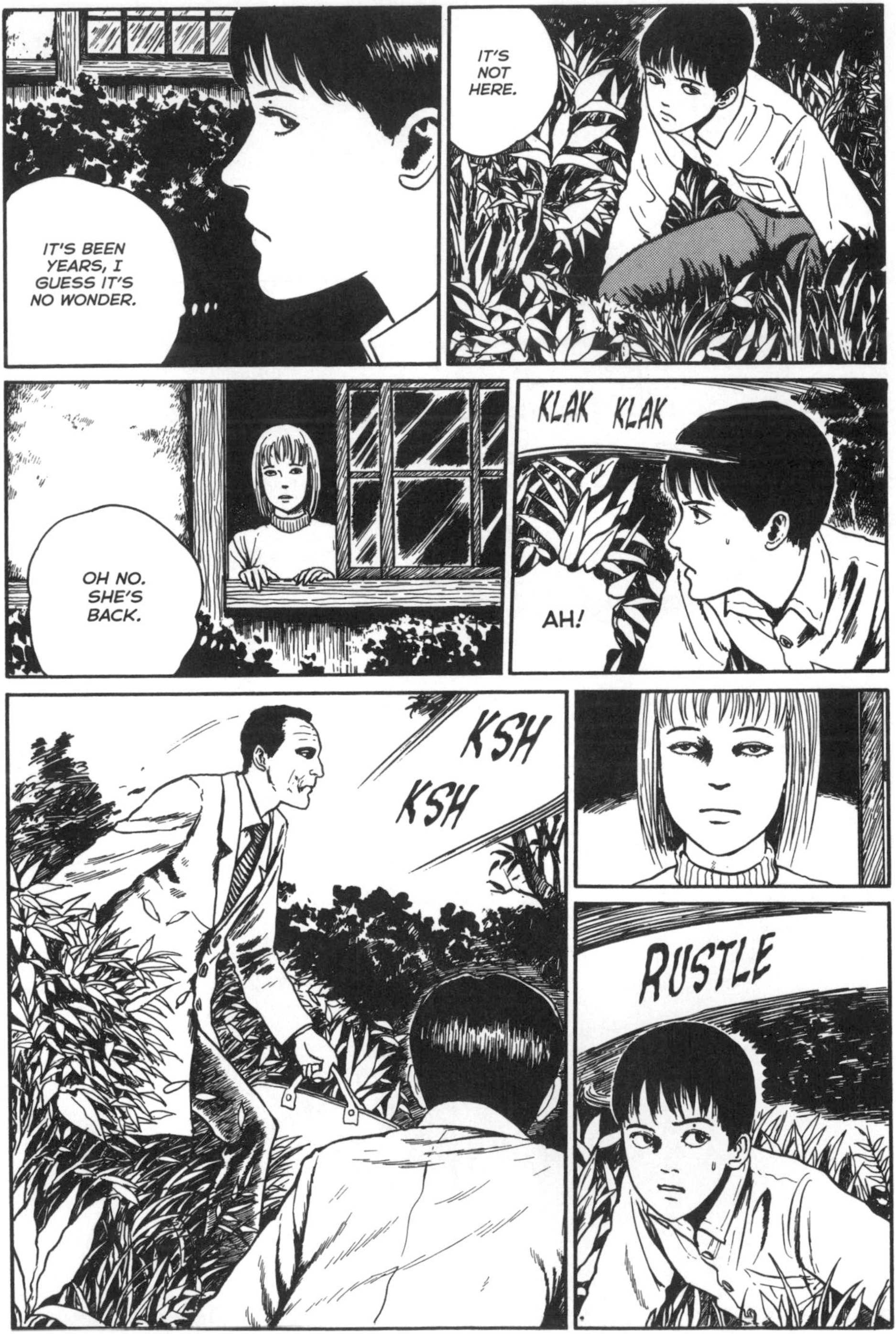
IT'S NOT HERE.
IT'S BEEN YEARS, I GUESS IT'S NO WONDER.
KLAK KLAK
AH!
OH NO. SHE'S BACK.
RUSTLE
KSH KSH

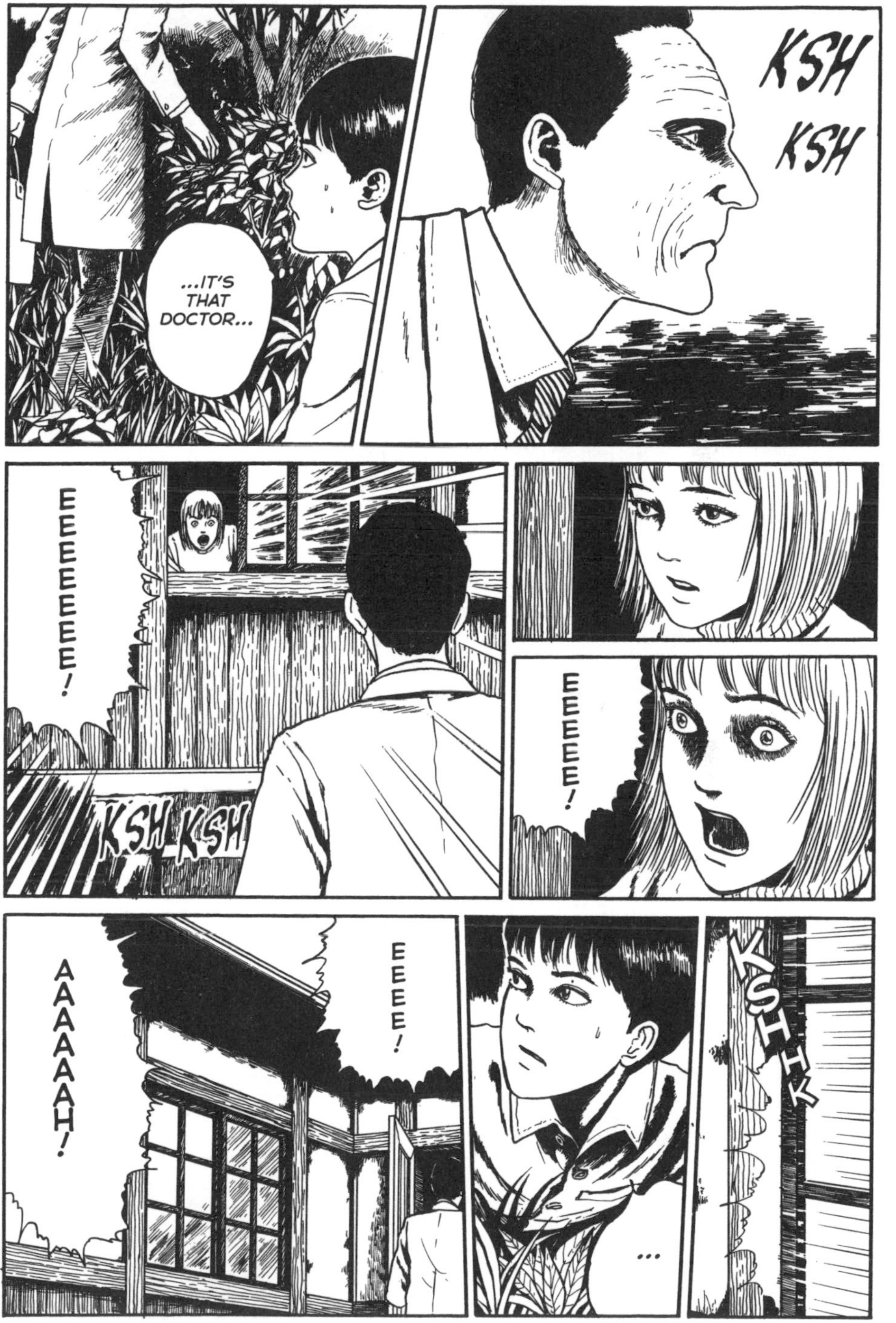
KSH
KSH
...IT'S THAT DOCTOR...
EEEEEE!
EEEEEEEEE!
KSH KSH
KSHHK
...
EEEE!
AAAAAAH!

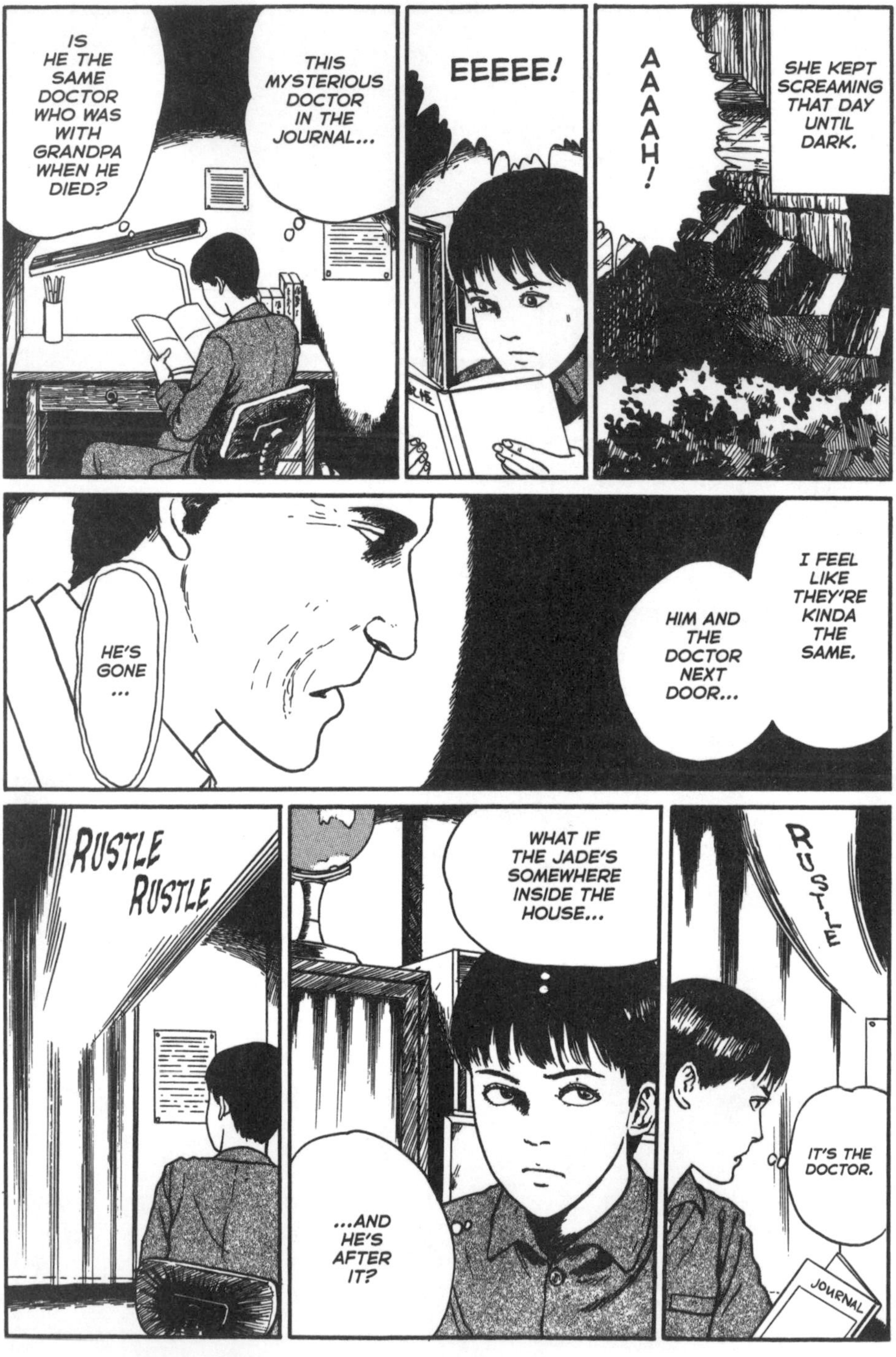
SHE KEPT SCREAMING THAT DAY UNTIL DARK.
AAAAH!
EEEEE!
THIS MYSTERIOUS DOCTOR IN THE JOURNAL...
IS HE THE SAME DOCTOR WHO WAS WITH GRANDPA WHEN HE DIED?
I FEEL LIKE THEY'RE KINDA THE SAME.
HIM AND THE DOCTOR NEXT DOOR...
HE'S GONE ...
RUSTLE
IT'S THE DOCTOR.
JOURNAL
WHAT IF THE JADE'S SOMEWHERE INSIDE THE HOUSE...
...AND HE'S AFTER IT?
RUSTLE RUSTLE

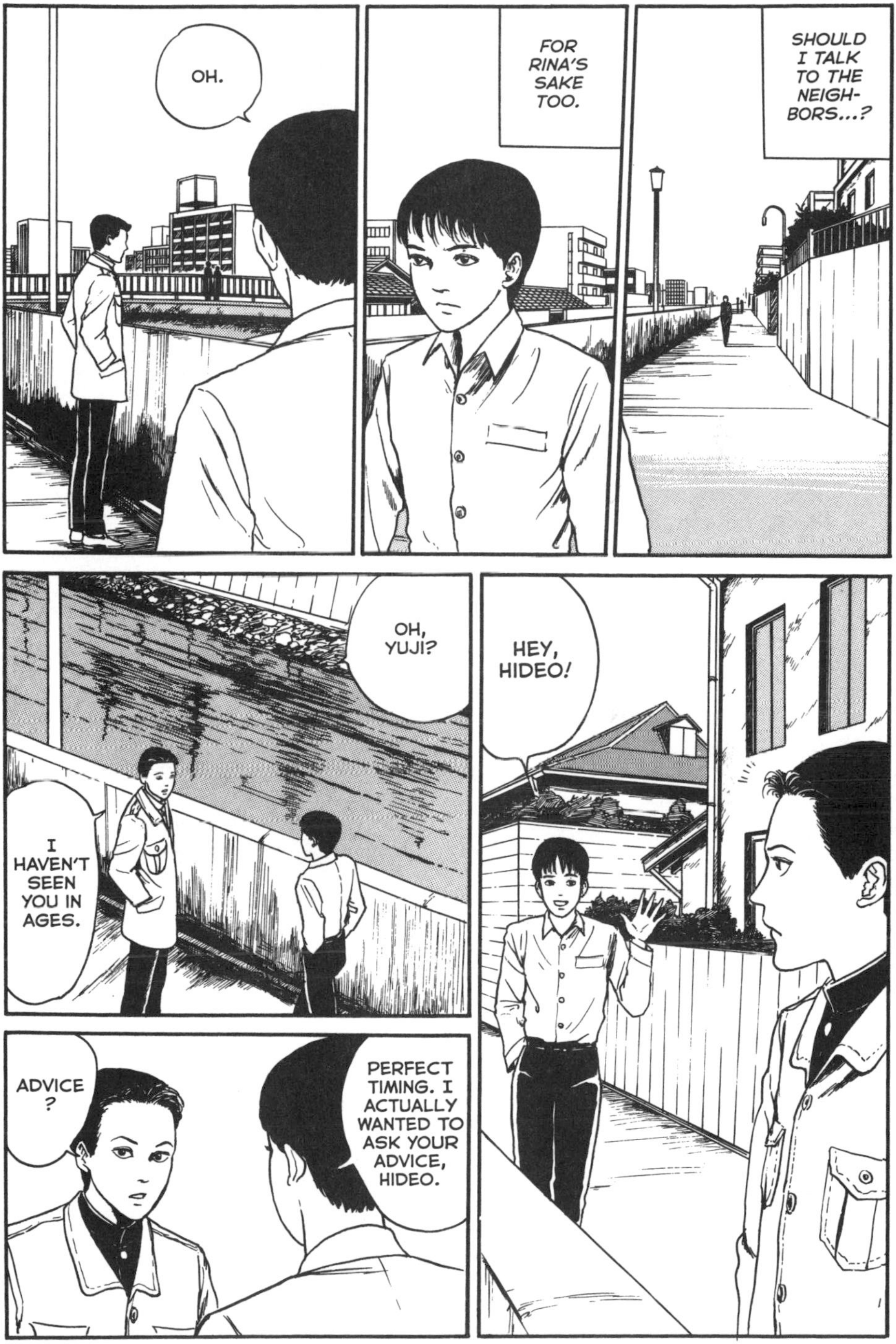
SHOULD I TALK TO THE NEIGHBORS...?
FOR RINA'S SAKE TOO.
OH.
HEY, HIDEO!
OH, YUJI?
I HAVEN'T SEEN YOU IN AGES.
PERFECT TIMING. I ACTUALLY WANTED TO ASK YOUR ADVICE, HIDEO.
ADVICE?

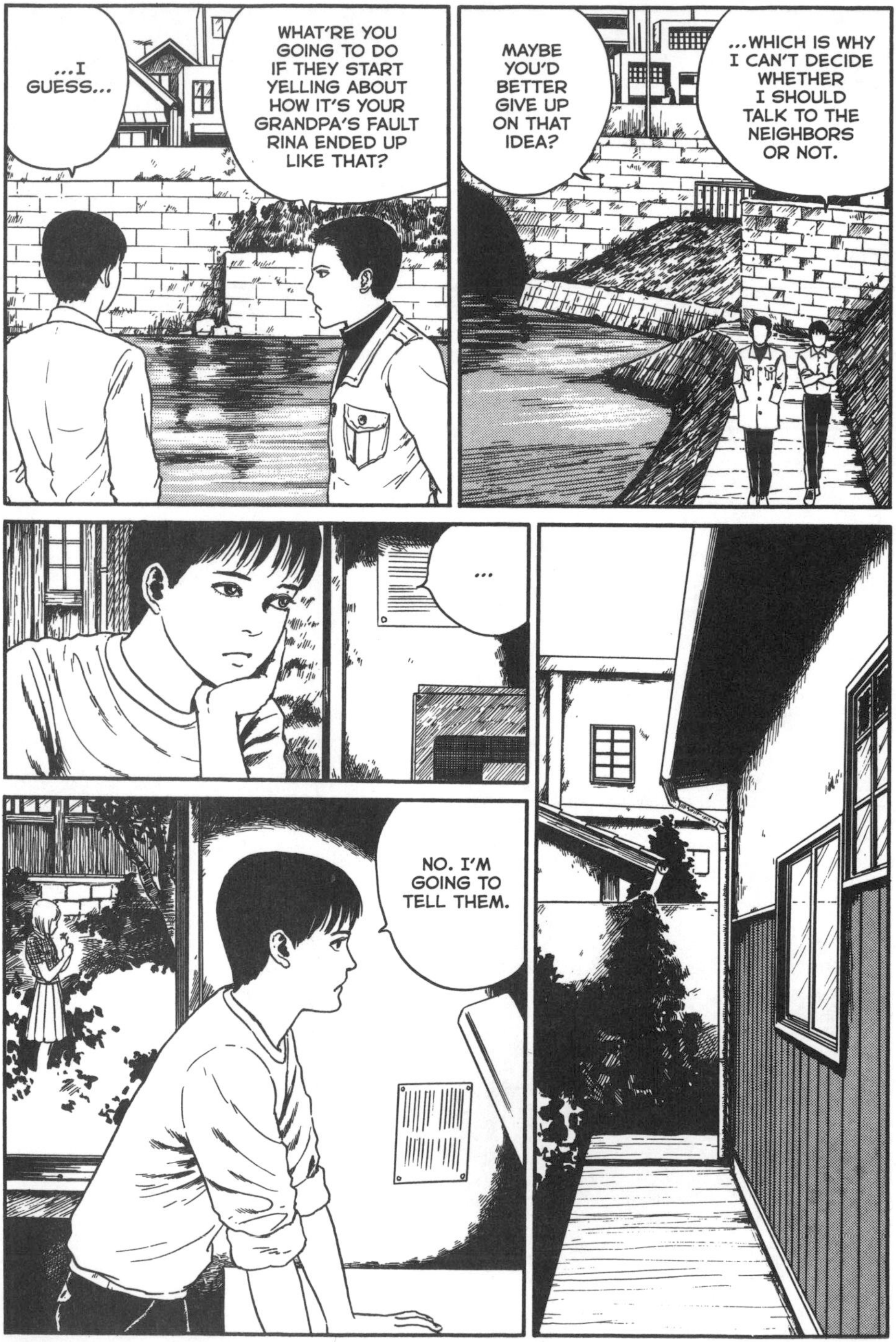
...WHICH IS WHY I CAN'T DECIDE WHETHER I SHOULD TALK TO THE NEIGHBORS OR NOT.
MAYBE YOU'D BETTER GIVE UP ON THAT IDEA?
WHAT'RE YOU GOING TO DO IF THEY START YELLING ABOUT HOW IT'S YOUR GRANDPA'S FAULT RINA ENDED UP LIKE THAT?
...I GUESS...
...
NO. I'M GOING TO TELL THEM.

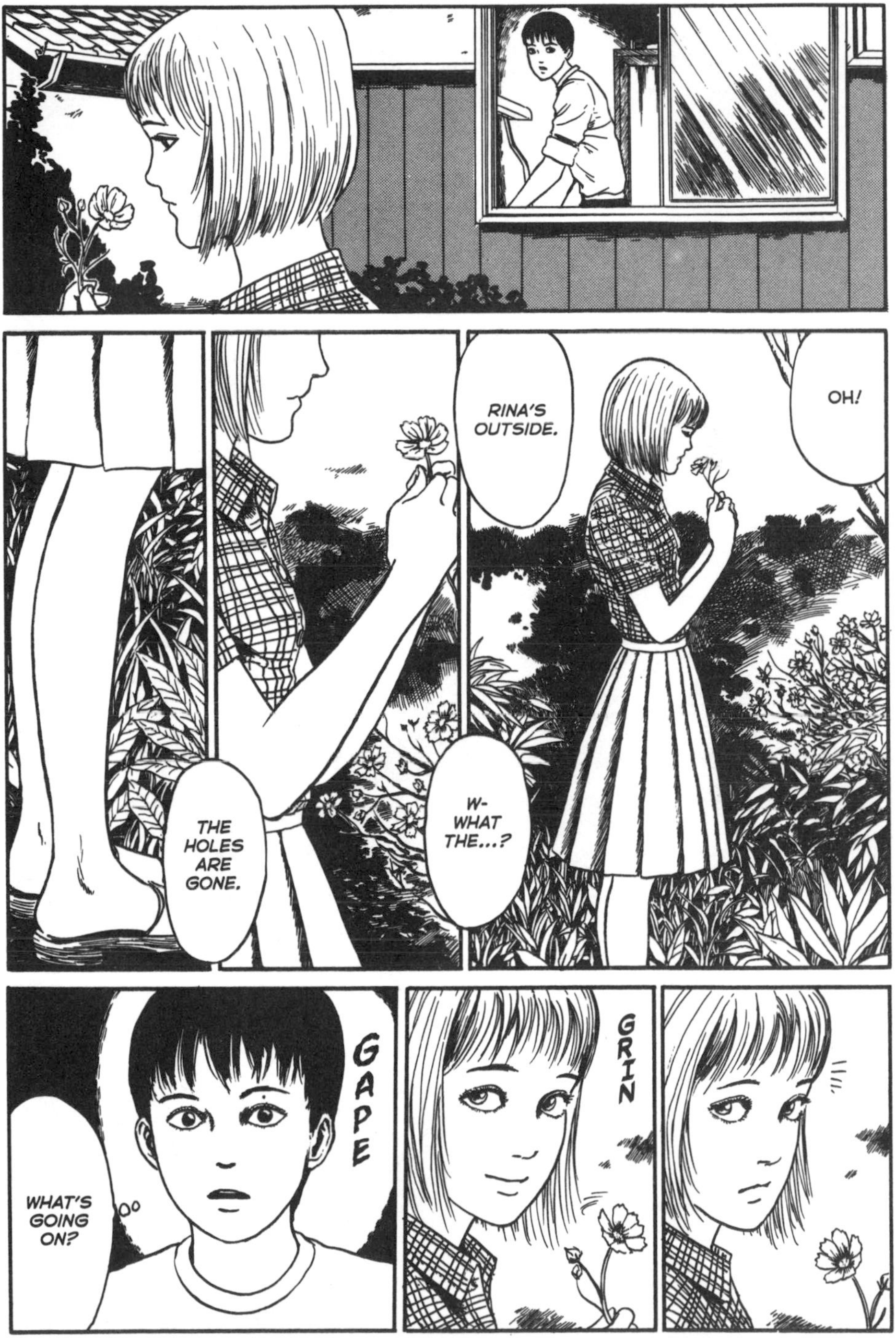
OH!
RINA'S OUTSIDE.
W- WHAT THE...?
THE HOLES ARE GONE.
GRIN
GAPE
WHAT'S GOING ON?

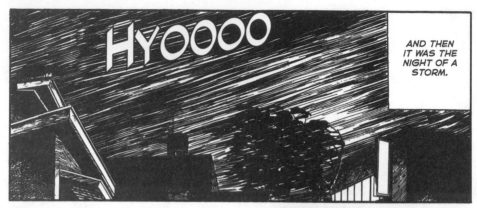

AND THEN IT WAS THE NIGHT OF A STORM.
HYOOOO
THE LARGE, POWERFUL TYPHOON NUMBER 21 IS CURRENT-LY AT THE SOUTHERN TIP OF THE KII PENINSULA.
THE MAXIMUM SPEED NEAR THE CENTER IS...
YUJI, THE WINDOW IN YOUR ROOM'S RATTLING LIKE CRAZY. GO CHECK ON IT?
IT IS... I'LL GO LOOK.
KLAK
KLAK
CHK
K KLAK
K KLAK
SHFF

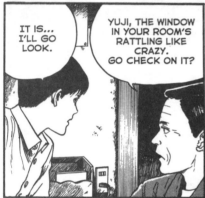

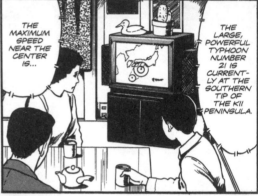

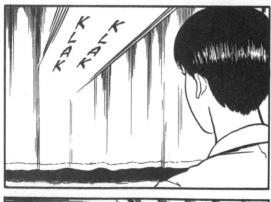

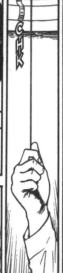

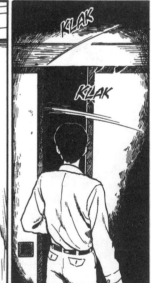

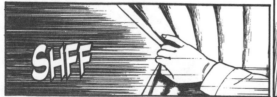

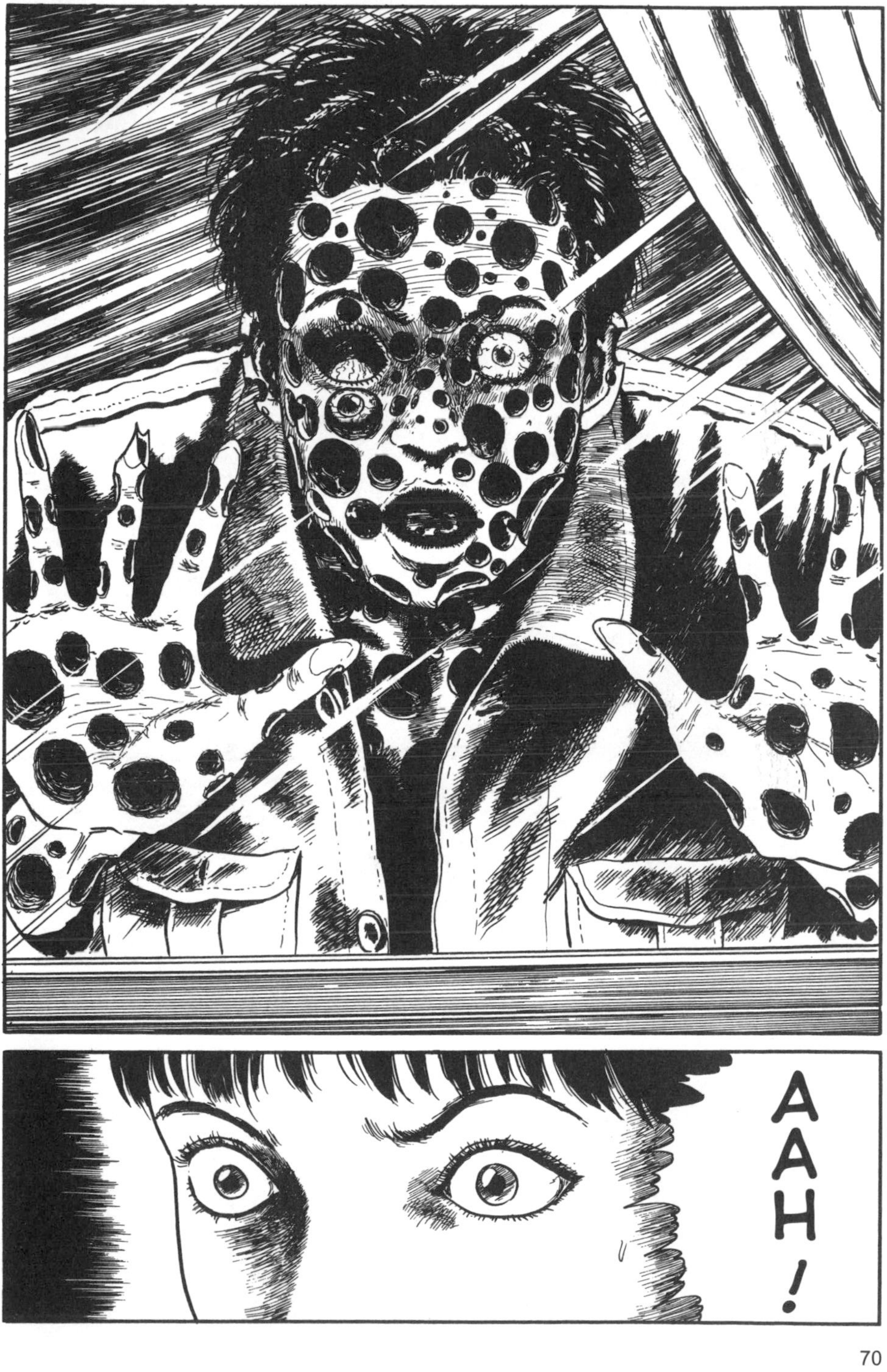
AAH!

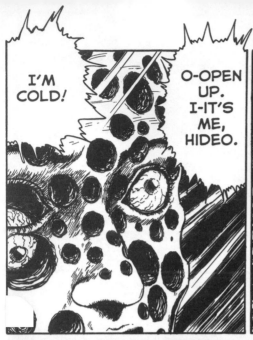

I'M COLD!

O-OPEN UP. I-IT'S ME, HIDEO.

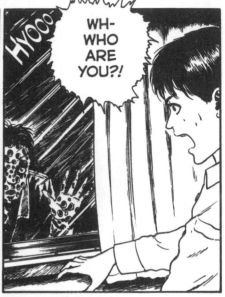

HYOOO-

WH-WHO ARE YOU?!

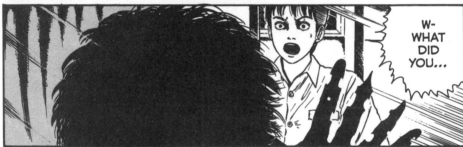

W-WHAT DID YOU...

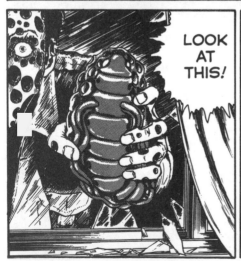

LOOK AT THIS!

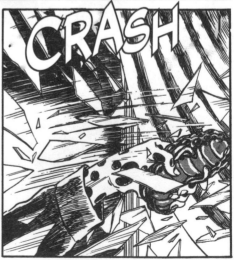

CRASH

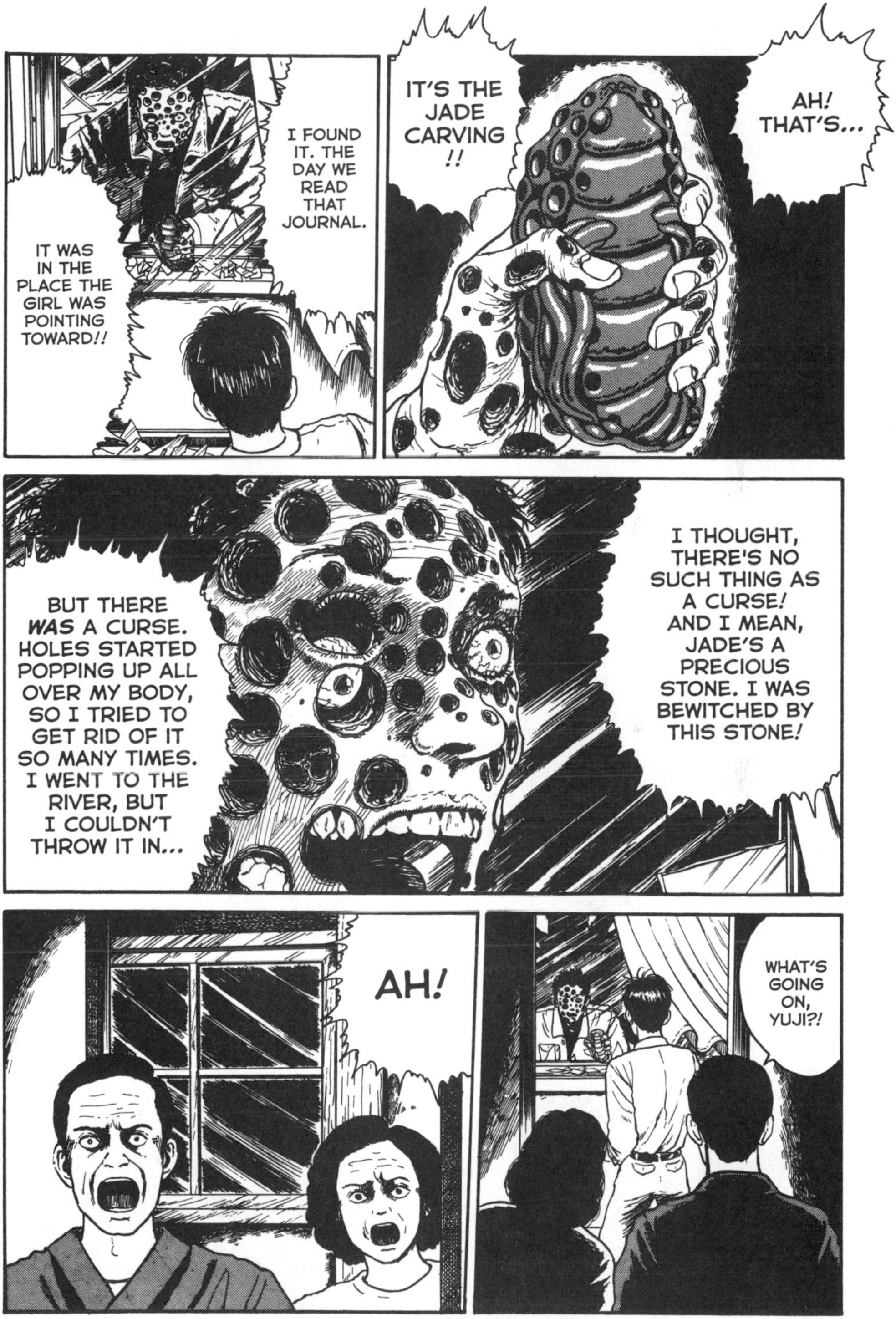
AH! THAT'S...
IT'S THE JADE CARVING!!
I FOUND IT. THE DAY WE READ THAT JOURNAL.
IT WAS IN THE PLACE THE GIRL WAS POINTING TOWARD!!
I THOUGHT, THERE'S NO SUCH THING AS A CURSE! AND I MEAN, JADE'S A PRECIOUS STONE. I WAS BEWITCHED BY THIS STONE!
BUT THERE *WAS* A CURSE. HOLES STARTED POPPING UP ALL OVER MY BODY, SO I TRIED TO GET RID OF IT SO MANY TIMES. I WENT TO THE RIVER, BUT I COULDN'T THROW IT IN...
WHAT'S GOING ON, YUJI?!
AH!

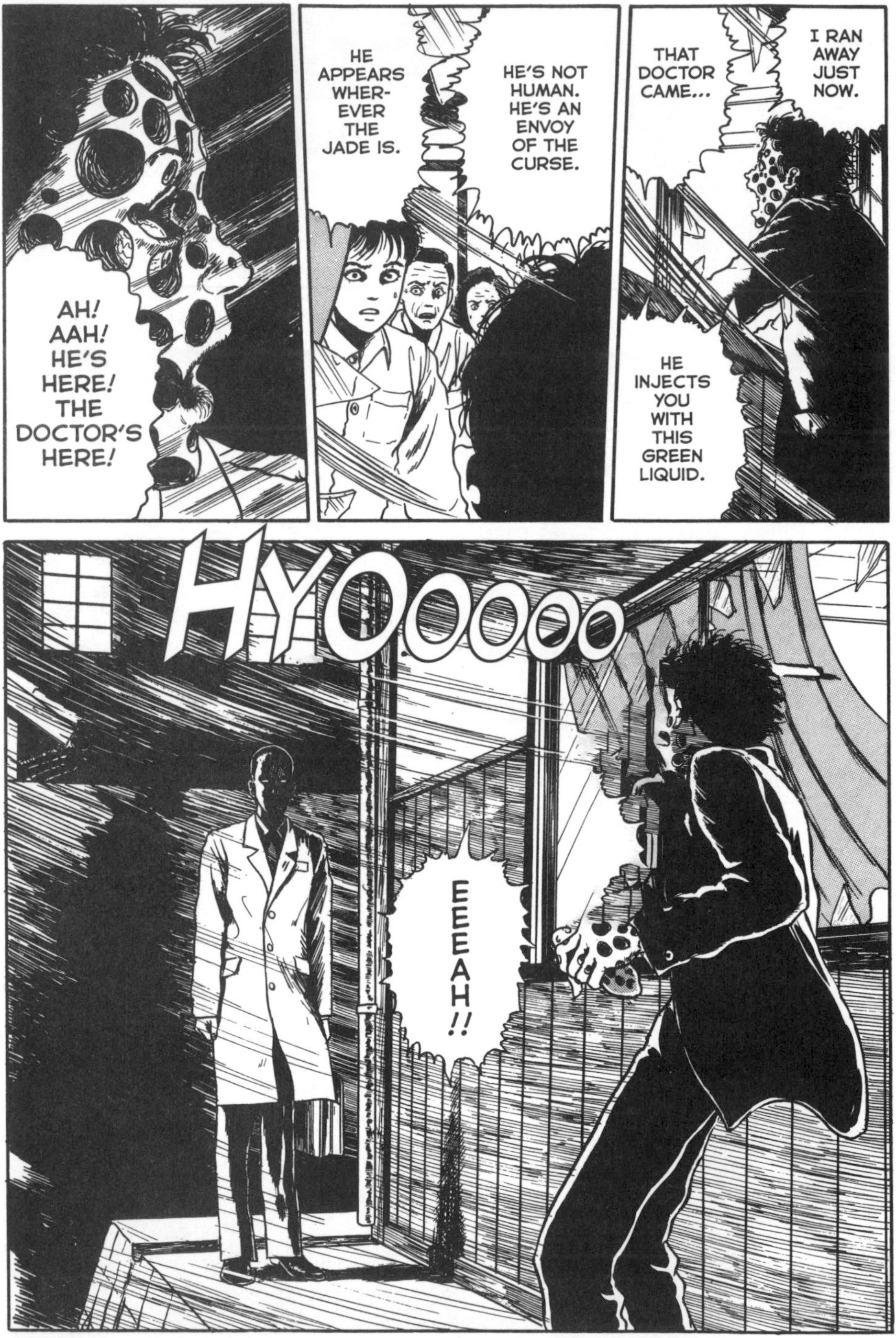
I RAN AWAY JUST NOW.
THAT DOCTOR CAME...
HE INJECTS YOU WITH THIS GREEN LIQUID.
HE'S NOT HUMAN. HE'S AN ENVOY OF THE CURSE.
HE APPEARS WHER-EVER THE JADE IS.
AH! AAH! HE'S HERE! THE DOCTOR'S HERE!
HYOOOOO
EEEEAH!!

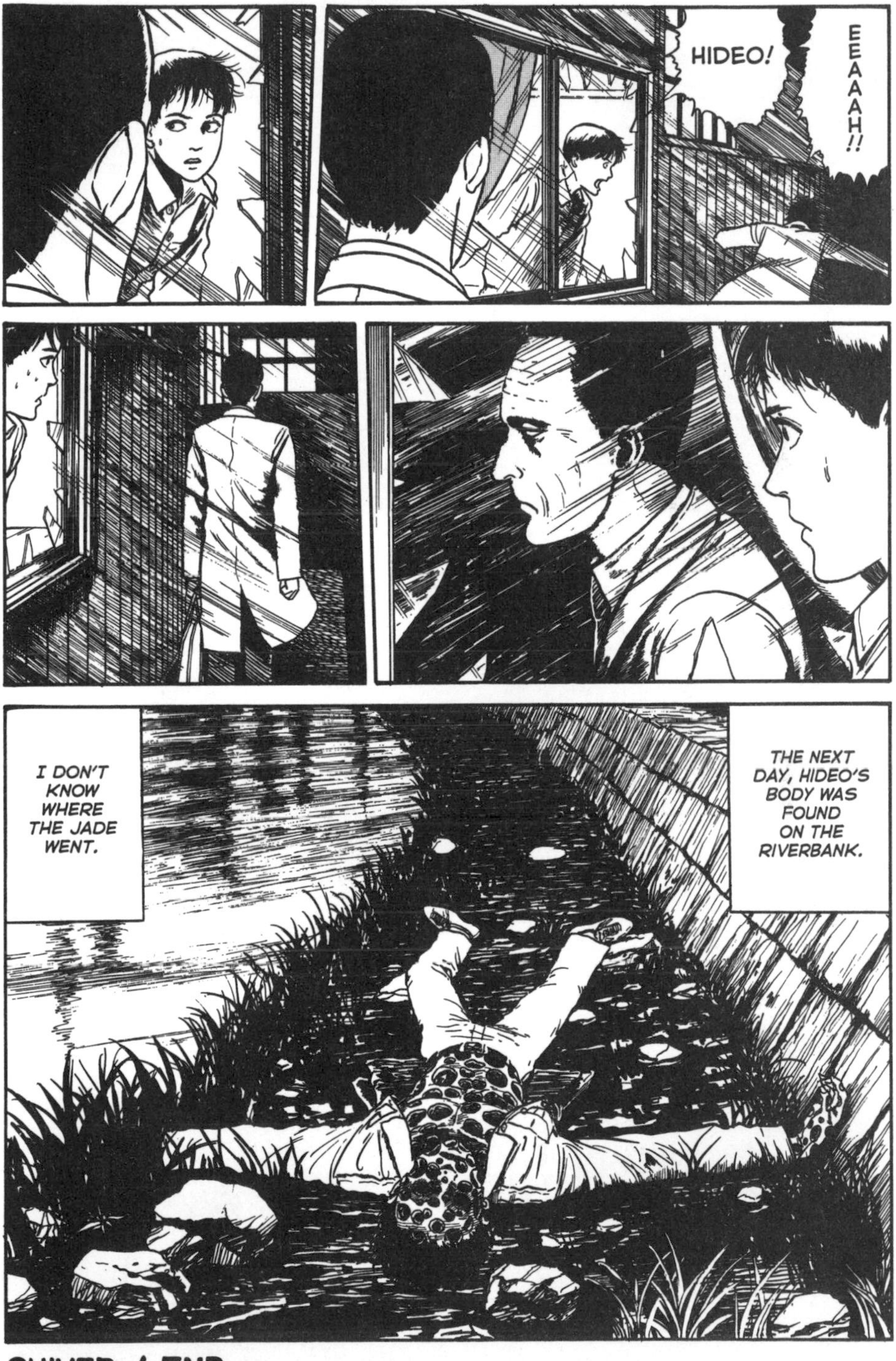
EEAAAAH!!
HIDEO!
THE NEXT DAY, HIDEO'S BODY WAS FOUND ON THE RIVERBANK.
I DON'T KNOW WHERE THE JADE WENT.

SHIVER / END

SHIVER

I was looking at an illustrated reference book on insects, and I learned that they have these holes on the sides of their abdomen for breathing, called spiracles, and I wondered if I couldn't use that in a manga. I changed it to people and developed the idea of holes in a person's body, holes through which they seemed to be breathing somehow. The neighbor's backyard in the story is based on the backyard of the people who lived next to my childhood home. The neighbors, Mr. and Mrs. Y, once ran a *ryokan* inn, but the couple were already quite elderly back then, and the house was no longer an inn, so the backyard was left unattended, with plants growing all over the place.

Mr. Y had shipped out during WWII, and when I was writing "The House with the Deserting Soldier," I actually talked with him about his experience as a soldier for reference. Given this, perhaps that's why I decided to incorporate WWII elements again here in the process of imagining Mr. Y's backyard.

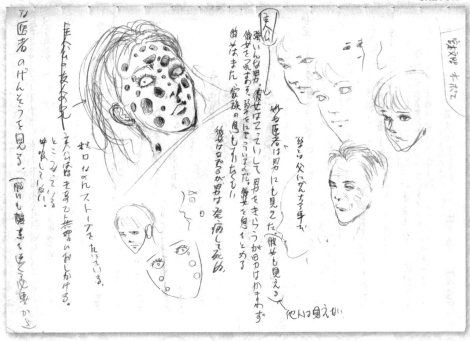

Fumiaki Miyamoto oboe

Weakness is related to the father.

The man can see the strange doctor. (She can see him too.) Other people can't.
*   Protagonist   aggressive man   She thoroughly detests him, but the man doesn't care; he drags her out of there. He stops her breathing. She doesn't want to breathe her family's breath either. She gets better, but the man falls ill and dies.*

↑
~~the brother of the protagonist's friend~~

It's only the beginning of fall, but they have the heat on. The protagonist likes her, so he forces his way in and she's like this. She's not breathing.

See a vision of the doctor. (Because the brain needs the delivery of oxygen.)

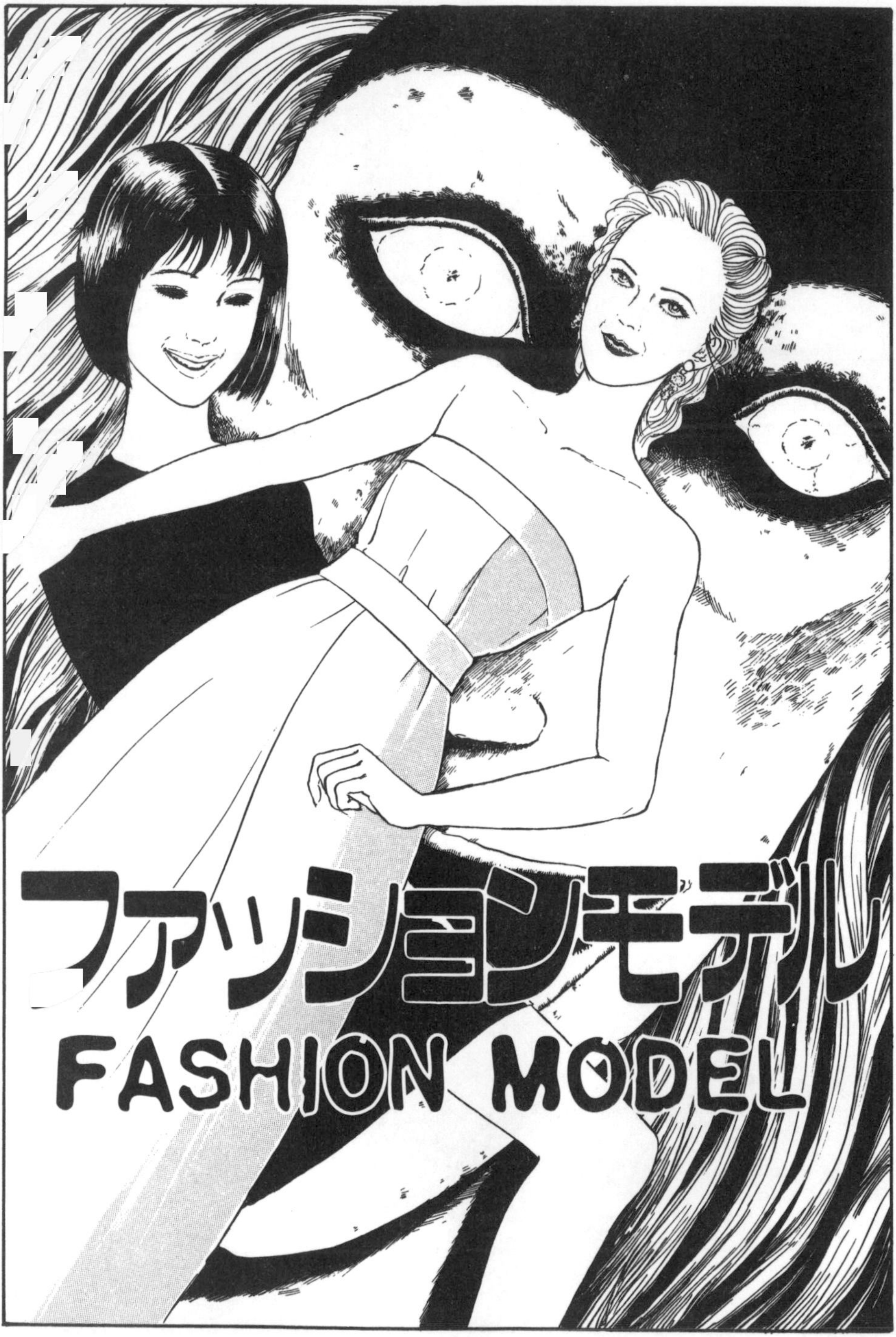
ファッションモデル
FASHION MODEL

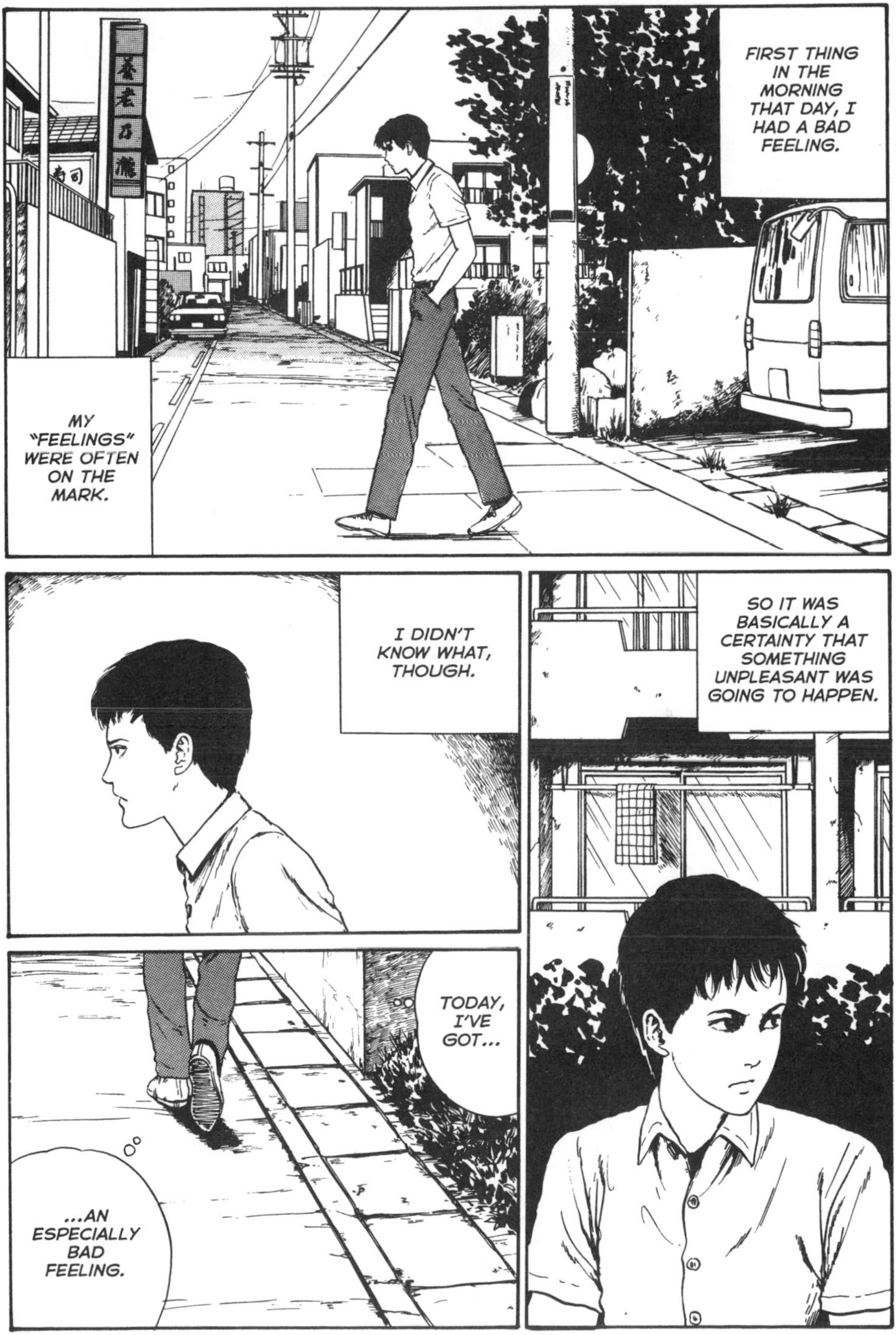
FIRST THING IN THE MORNING THAT DAY, I HAD A BAD FEELING.
MY "FEELINGS" WERE OFTEN ON THE MARK.
SO IT WAS BASICALLY A CERTAINTY THAT SOMETHING UNPLEASANT WAS GOING TO HAPPEN.
I DIDN'T KNOW WHAT, THOUGH.
TODAY, I'VE GOT...
...AN ESPECIALLY BAD FEELING.

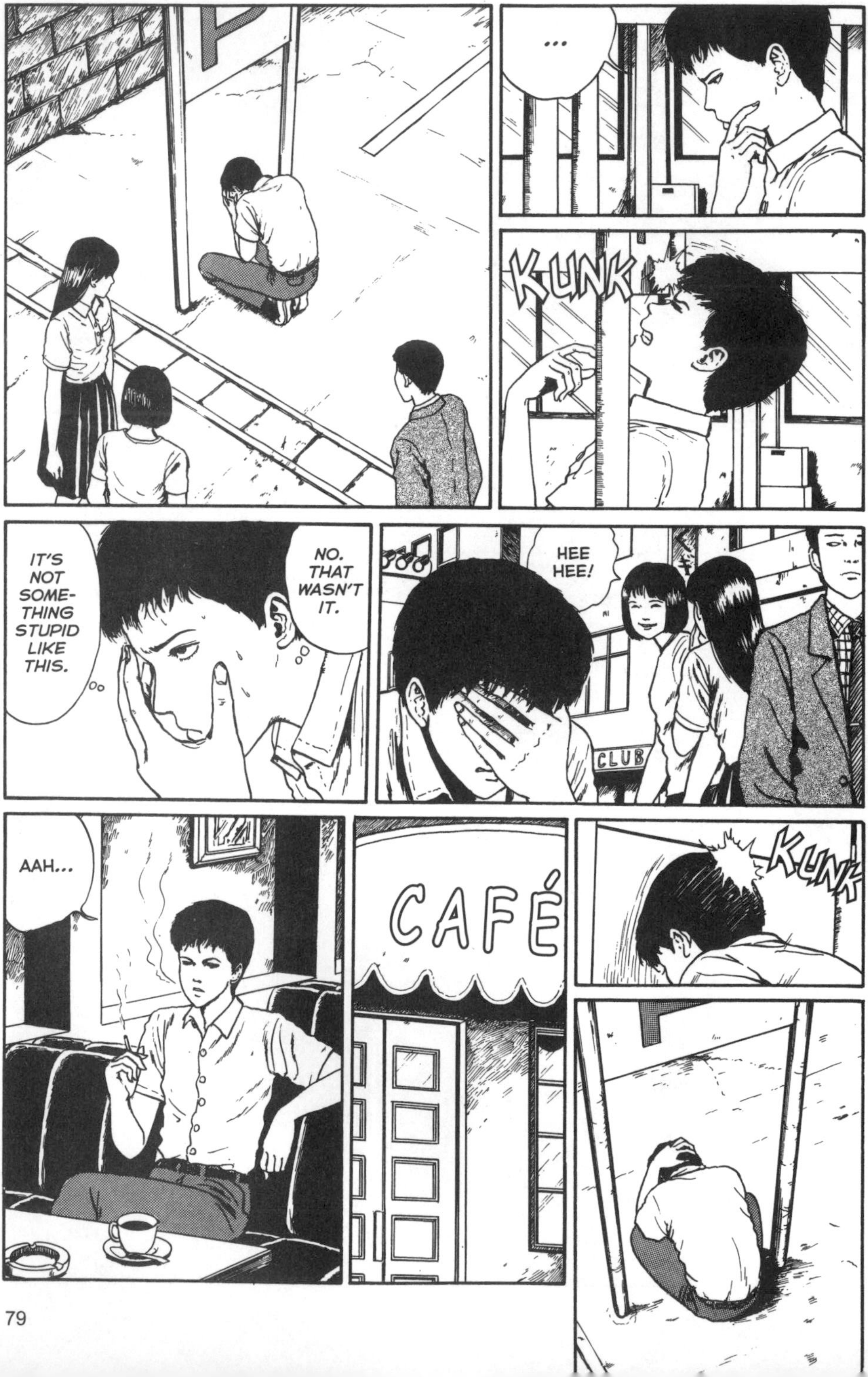
...
KUNK
HEE HEE!
CLUB
NO. THAT WASN'T IT.
IT'S NOT SOMETHING STUPID LIKE THIS.
KUNK
CAFÉ
AAH...

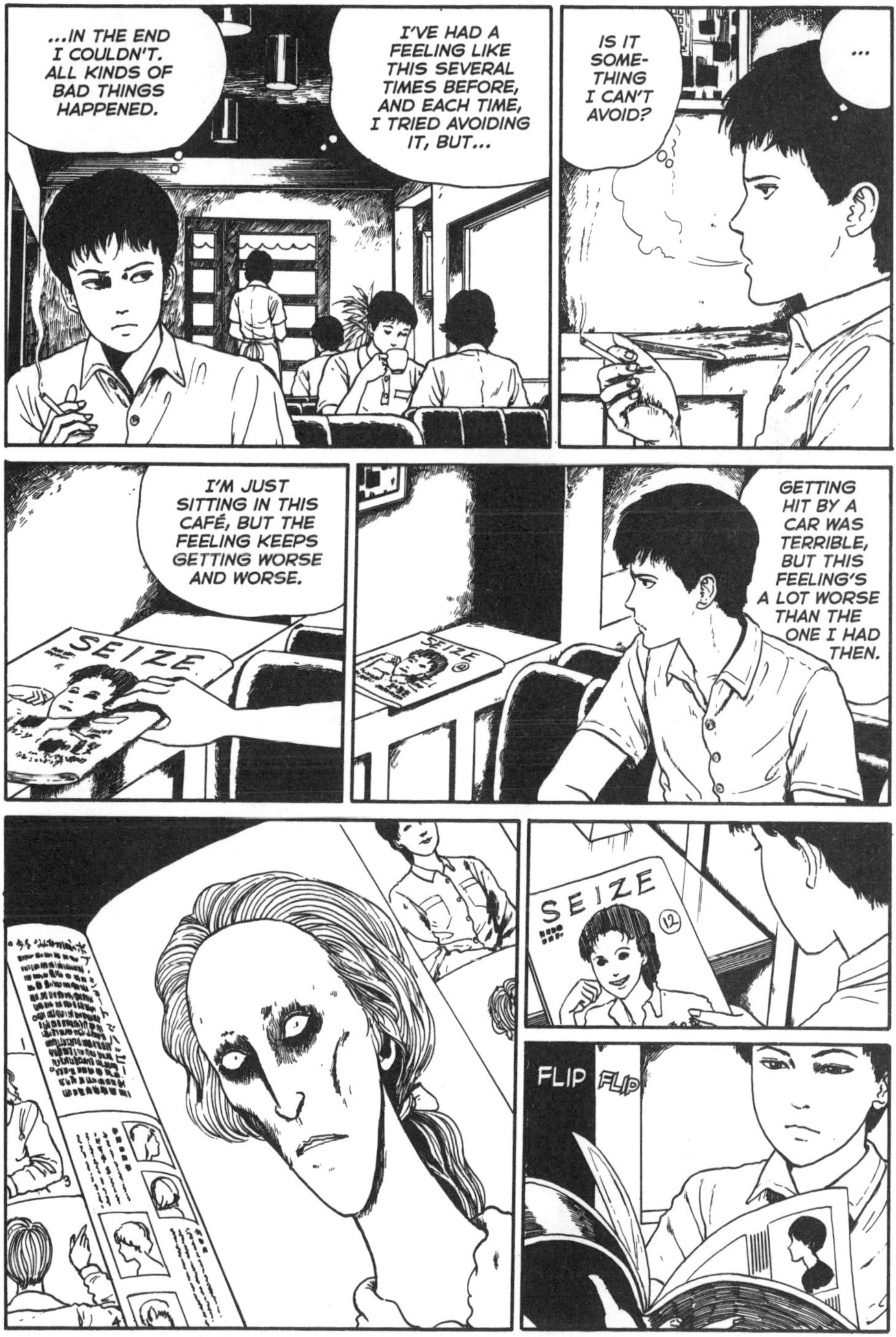
...
IS IT SOMETHING I CAN'T AVOID?
I'VE HAD A FEELING LIKE THIS SEVERAL TIMES BEFORE, AND EACH TIME, I TRIED AVOIDING IT, BUT...
...IN THE END I COULDN'T. ALL KINDS OF BAD THINGS HAPPENED.
GETTING HIT BY A CAR WAS TERRIBLE, BUT THIS FEELING'S A LOT WORSE THAN THE ONE I HAD THEN.
SEIZE
I'M JUST SITTING IN THIS CAFÉ, BUT THE FEELING KEEPS GETTING WORSE AND WORSE.
SEIZE
SEIZE
12
FLIP
FLIP

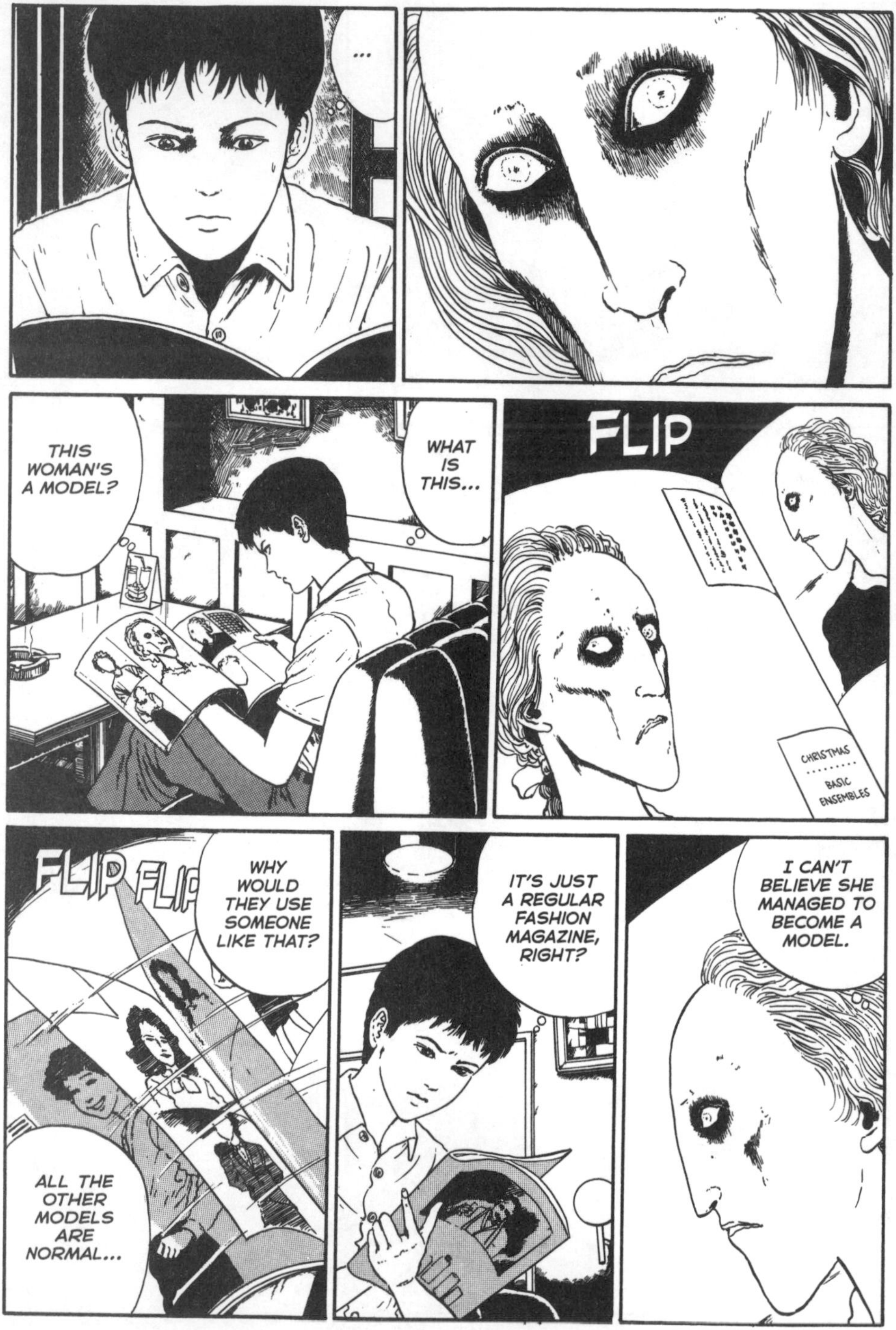
...
FLIP
CHRISTMAS
BASIC ENSEMBLES
WHAT IS THIS...
THIS WOMAN'S A MODEL?
I CAN'T BELIEVE SHE MANAGED TO BECOME A MODEL.
IT'S JUST A REGULAR FASHION MAGAZINE, RIGHT?
WHY WOULD THEY USE SOMEONE LIKE THAT?
FLIP FLIP
ALL THE OTHER MODELS ARE NORMAL...

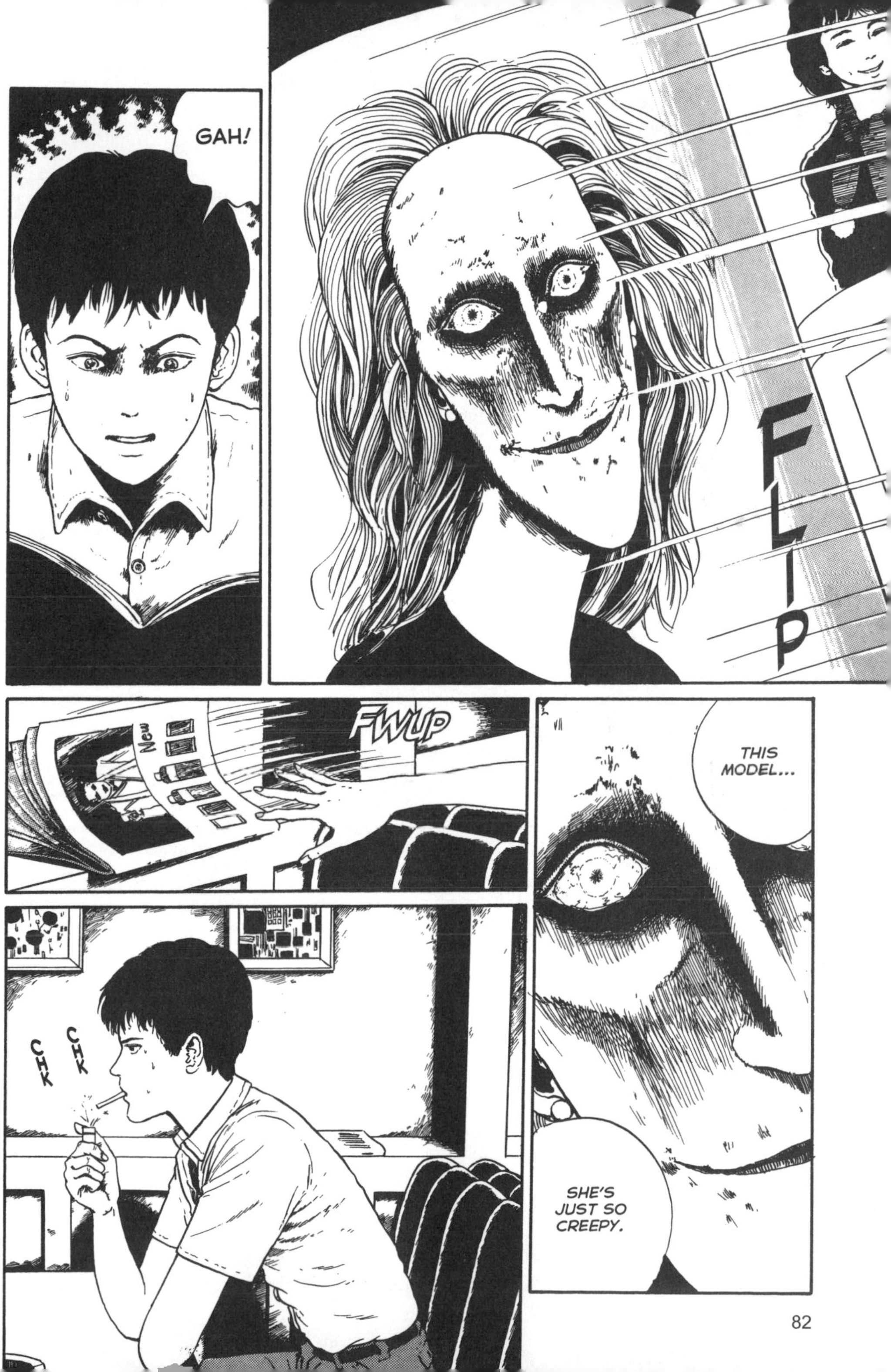
FLIP
GAH!
THIS MODEL...
SHE'S JUST SO CREEPY.
FWUP
New
CHK CHK

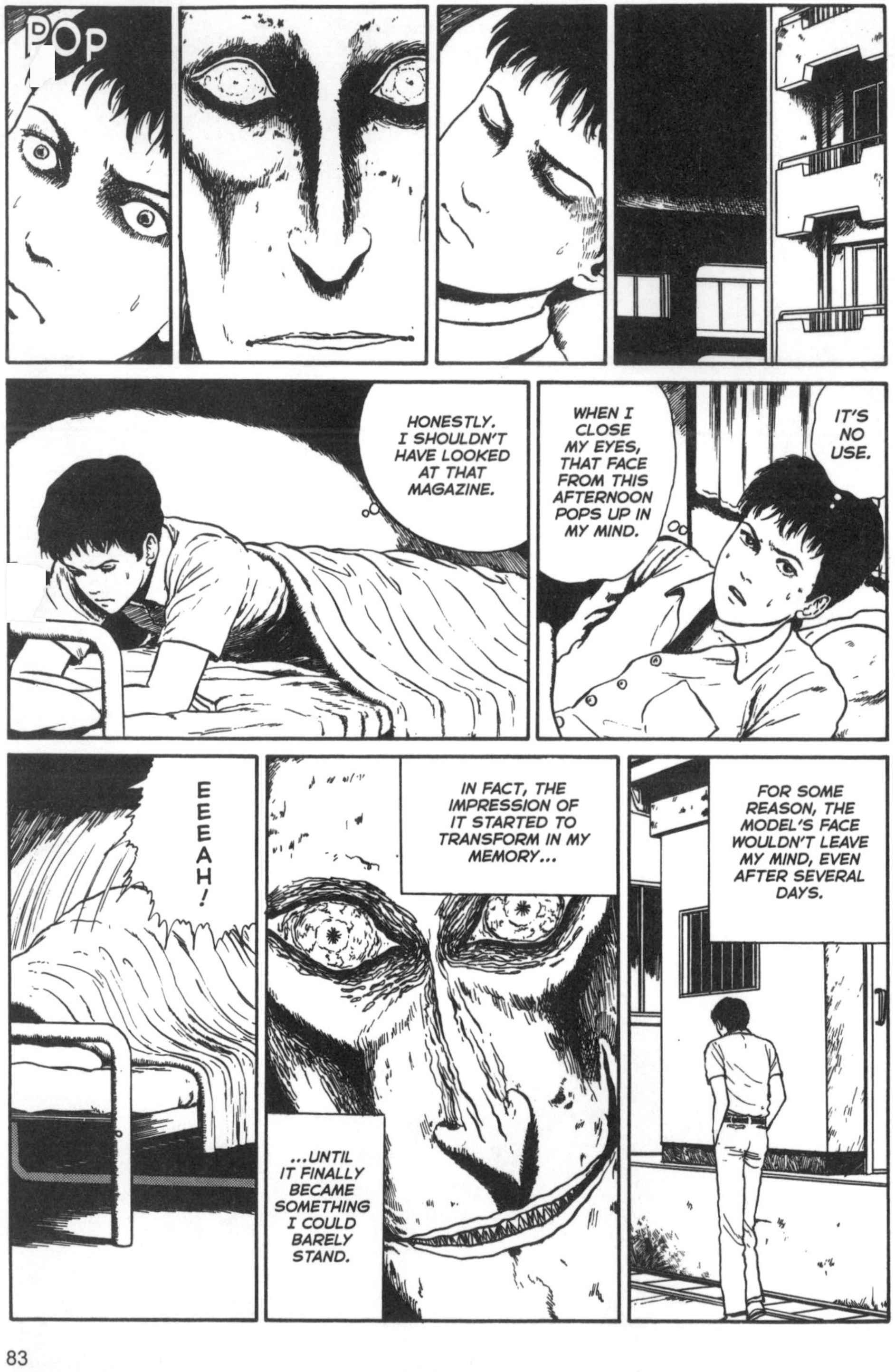
POP
IT'S NO USE.
WHEN I CLOSE MY EYES, THAT FACE FROM THIS AFTERNOON POPS UP IN MY MIND.
HONESTLY. I SHOULDN'T HAVE LOOKED AT THAT MAGAZINE.
FOR SOME REASON, THE MODEL'S FACE WOULDN'T LEAVE MY MIND, EVEN AFTER SEVERAL DAYS.
IN FACT, THE IMPRESSION OF IT STARTED TO TRANSFORM IN MY MEMORY...
...UNTIL IT FINALLY BECAME SOMETHING I COULD BARELY STAND.
EEEEAH!

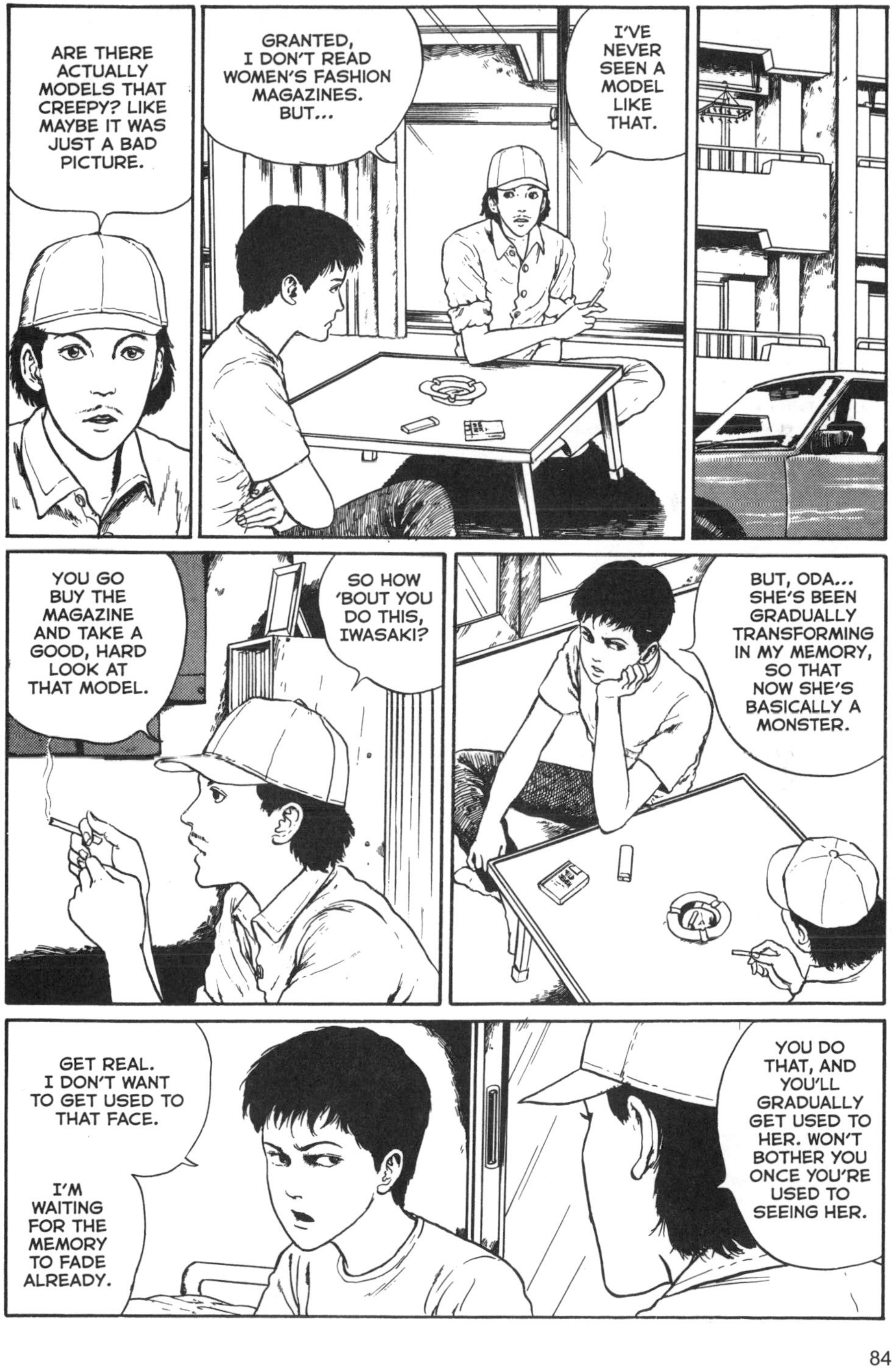
I'VE NEVER SEEN A MODEL LIKE THAT.
GRANTED, I DON'T READ WOMEN'S FASHION MAGAZINES. BUT...
ARE THERE ACTUALLY MODELS THAT CREEPY? LIKE MAYBE IT WAS JUST A BAD PICTURE.
BUT, ODA... SHE'S BEEN GRADUALLY TRANSFORMING IN MY MEMORY, SO THAT NOW SHE'S BASICALLY A MONSTER.
SO HOW 'BOUT YOU DO THIS, IWASAKI?
YOU GO BUY THE MAGAZINE AND TAKE A GOOD, HARD LOOK AT THAT MODEL.
YOU DO THAT, AND YOU'LL GRADUALLY GET USED TO HER. WON'T BOTHER YOU ONCE YOU'RE USED TO SEEING HER.
GET REAL. I DON'T WANT TO GET USED TO THAT FACE.
I'M WAITING FOR THE MEMORY TO FADE ALREADY.

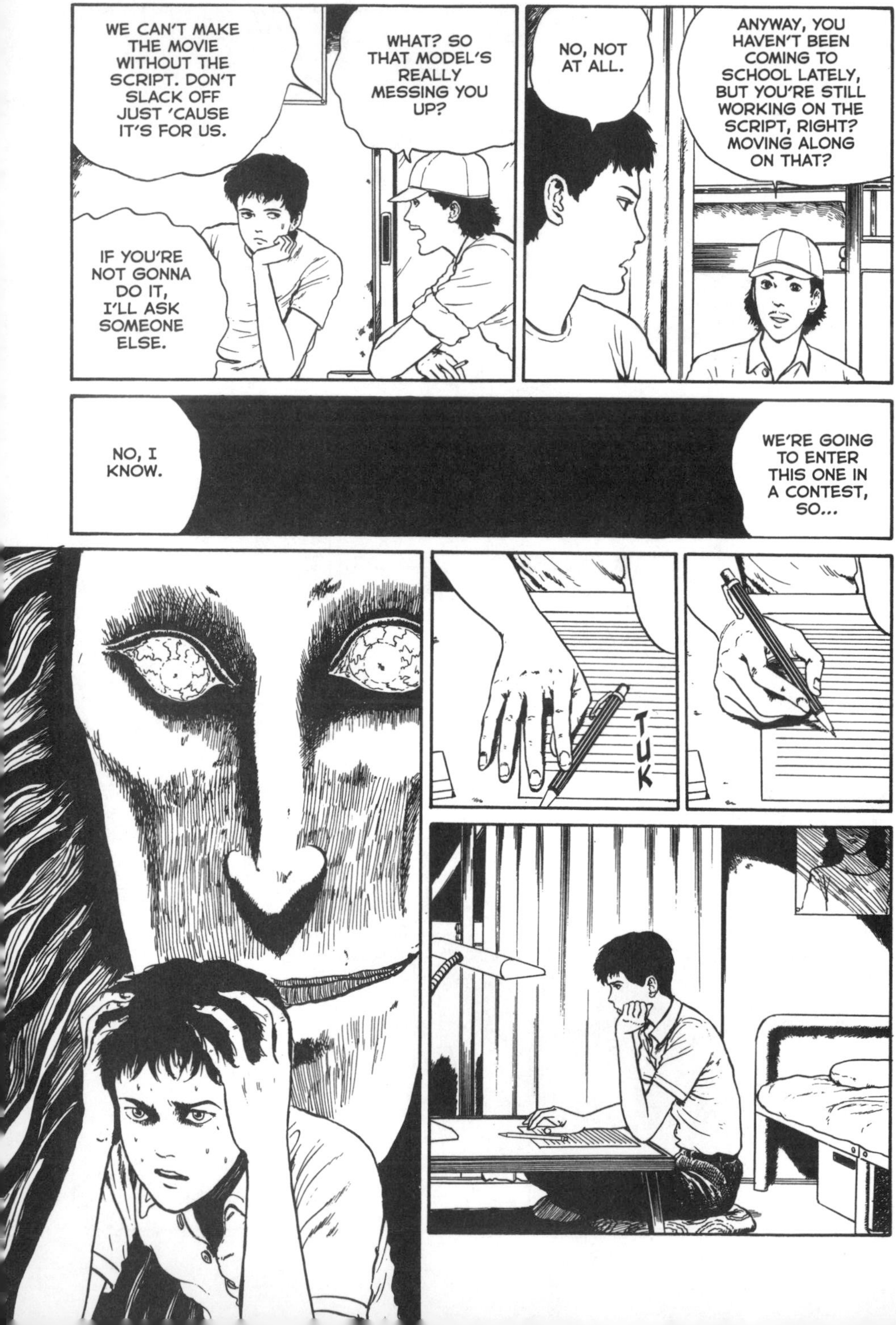
ANYWAY, YOU HAVEN'T BEEN COMING TO SCHOOL LATELY, BUT YOU'RE STILL WORKING ON THE SCRIPT, RIGHT? MOVING ALONG ON THAT?
NO, NOT AT ALL.
WHAT? SO THAT MODEL'S REALLY MESSING YOU UP?
WE CAN'T MAKE THE MOVIE WITHOUT THE SCRIPT. DON'T SLACK OFF JUST 'CAUSE IT'S FOR US.
IF YOU'RE NOT GONNA DO IT, I'LL ASK SOMEONE ELSE.
WE'RE GOING TO ENTER THIS ONE IN A CONTEST, SO...
NO, I KNOW.
TUK

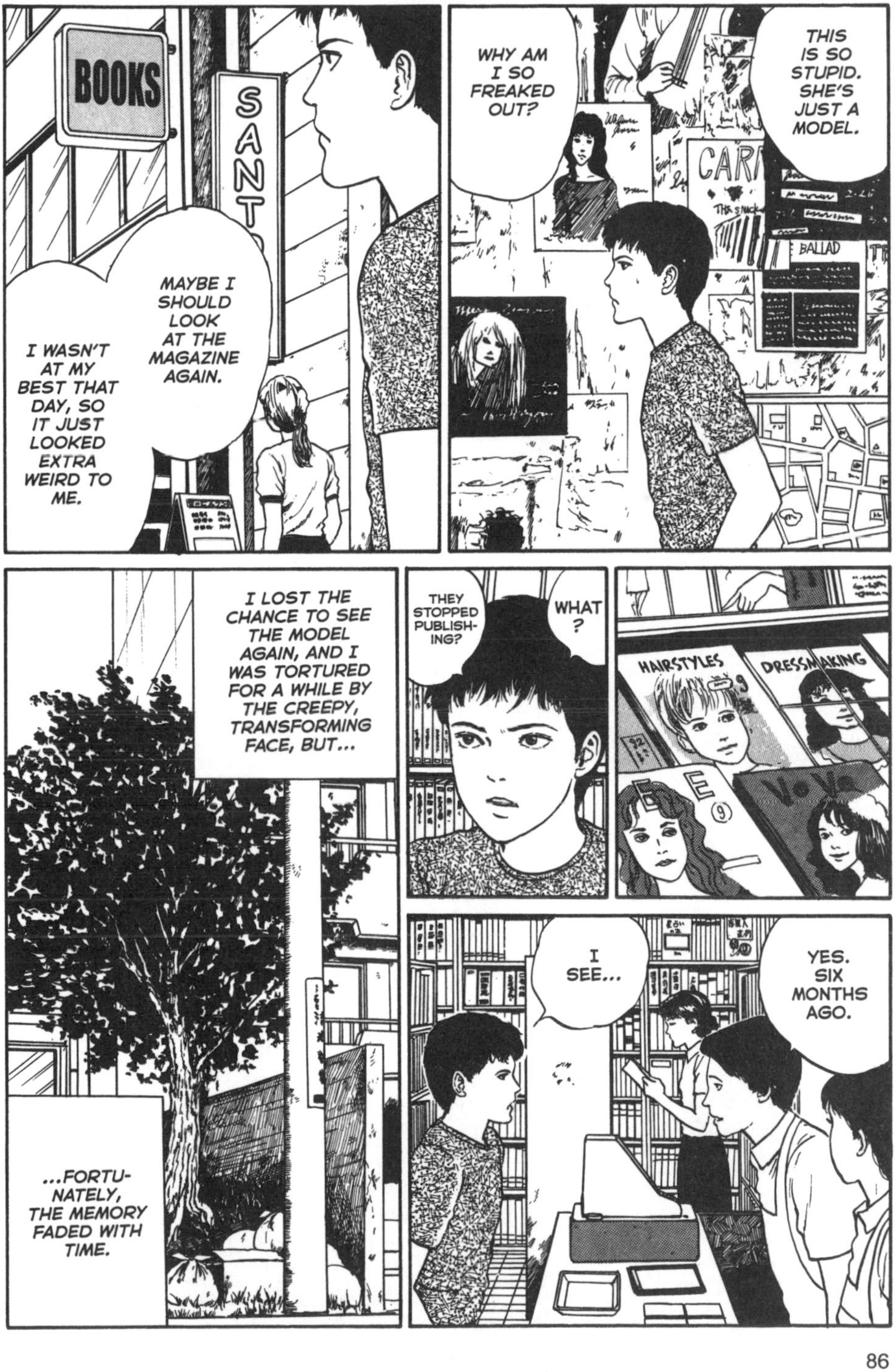
THIS IS SO STUPID. SHE'S JUST A MODEL.
WHY AM I SO FREAKED OUT?
BALLAD
BOOKS
MAYBE I SHOULD LOOK AT THE MAGAZINE AGAIN.
I WASN'T AT MY BEST THAT DAY, SO IT JUST LOOKED EXTRA WEIRD TO ME.
HAIRSTYLES
DRESSMAKING
WHAT?
THEY STOPPED PUBLISHING?
YES. SIX MONTHS AGO.
I SEE...
I LOST THE CHANCE TO SEE THE MODEL AGAIN, AND I WAS TORTURED FOR A WHILE BY THE CREEPY, TRANSFORMING FACE, BUT...
...FORTUNATELY, THE MEMORY FADED WITH TIME.

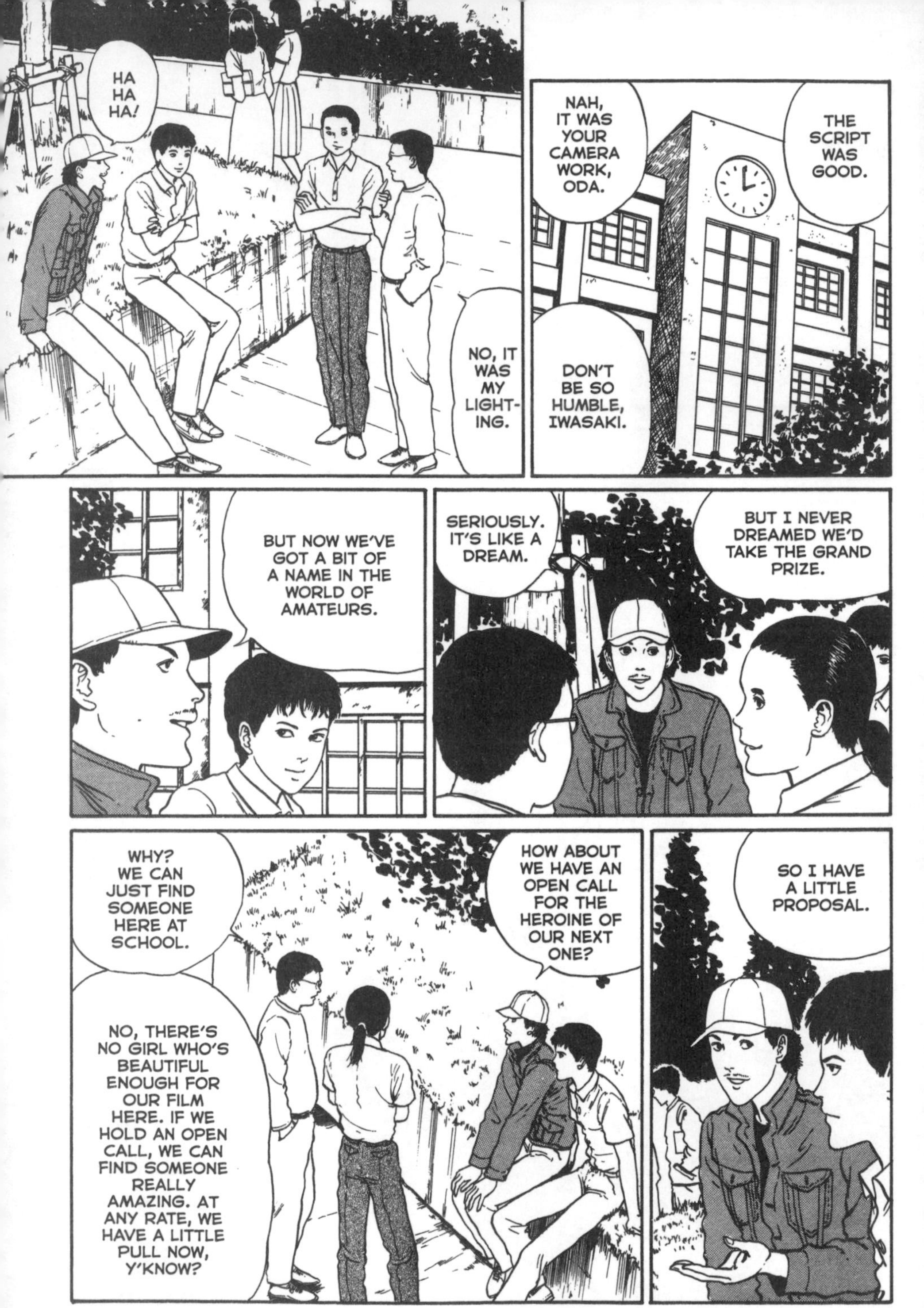
THE SCRIPT WAS GOOD.
NAH, IT WAS YOUR CAMERA WORK, ODA.
DON'T BE SO HUMBLE, IWASAKI.
NO, IT WAS MY LIGHT-ING.
HA HA HA!
BUT I NEVER DREAMED WE'D TAKE THE GRAND PRIZE.
SERIOUSLY. IT'S LIKE A DREAM.
BUT NOW WE'VE GOT A BIT OF A NAME IN THE WORLD OF AMATEURS.
SO I HAVE A LITTLE PROPOSAL.
HOW ABOUT WE HAVE AN OPEN CALL FOR THE HEROINE OF OUR NEXT ONE?
WHY? WE CAN JUST FIND SOMEONE HERE AT SCHOOL.
NO, THERE'S NO GIRL WHO'S BEAUTIFUL ENOUGH FOR OUR FILM HERE. IF WE HOLD AN OPEN CALL, WE CAN FIND SOMEONE REALLY AMAZING. AT ANY RATE, WE HAVE A LITTLE PULL NOW, Y'KNOW?

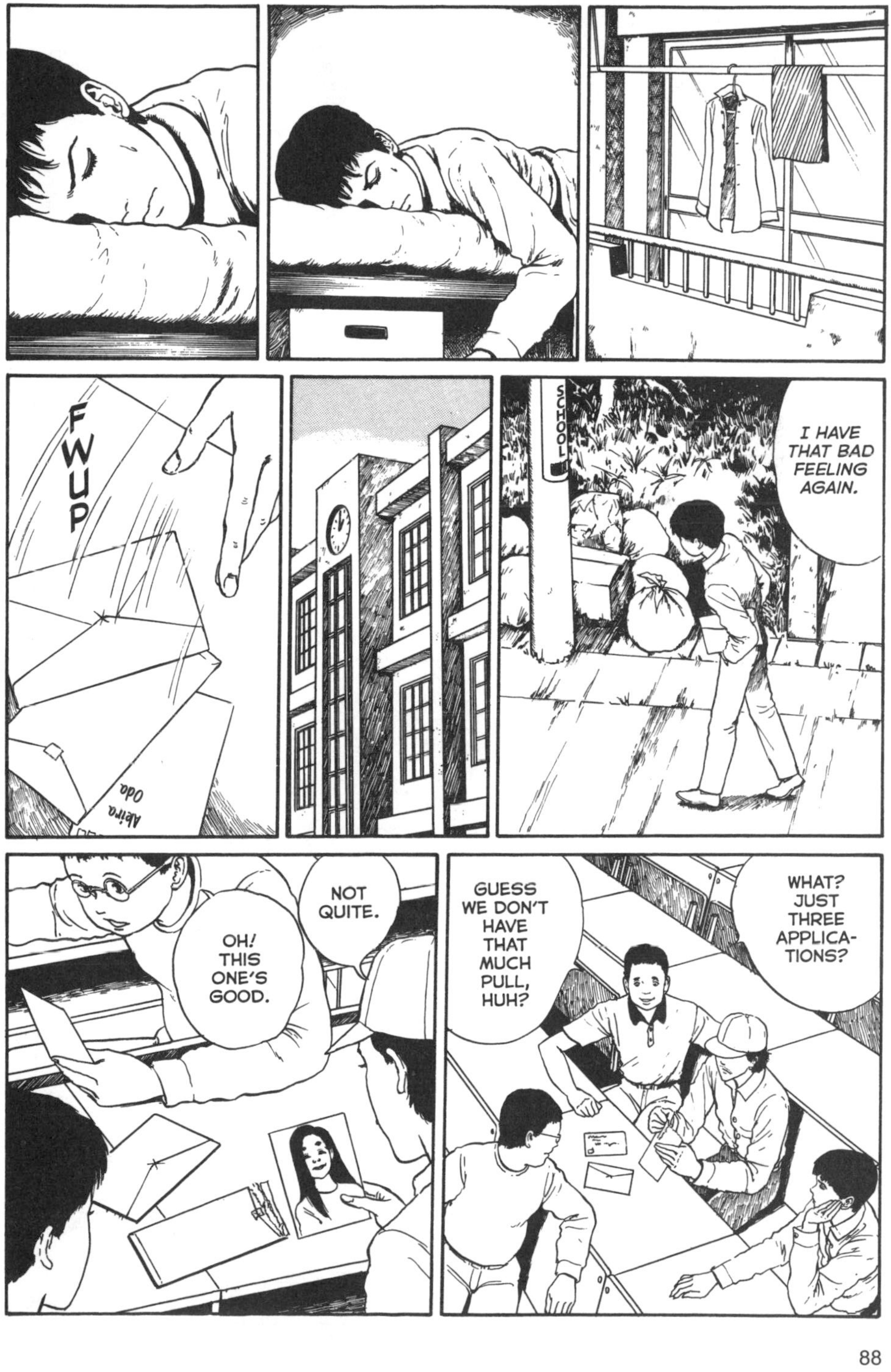
I HAVE THAT BAD FEELING AGAIN.
SCHOOL
FWUP
Akira Oda
WHAT? JUST THREE APPLICA-TIONS?
GUESS WE DON'T HAVE THAT MUCH PULL, HUH?
NOT QUITE.
OH! THIS ONE'S GOOD.

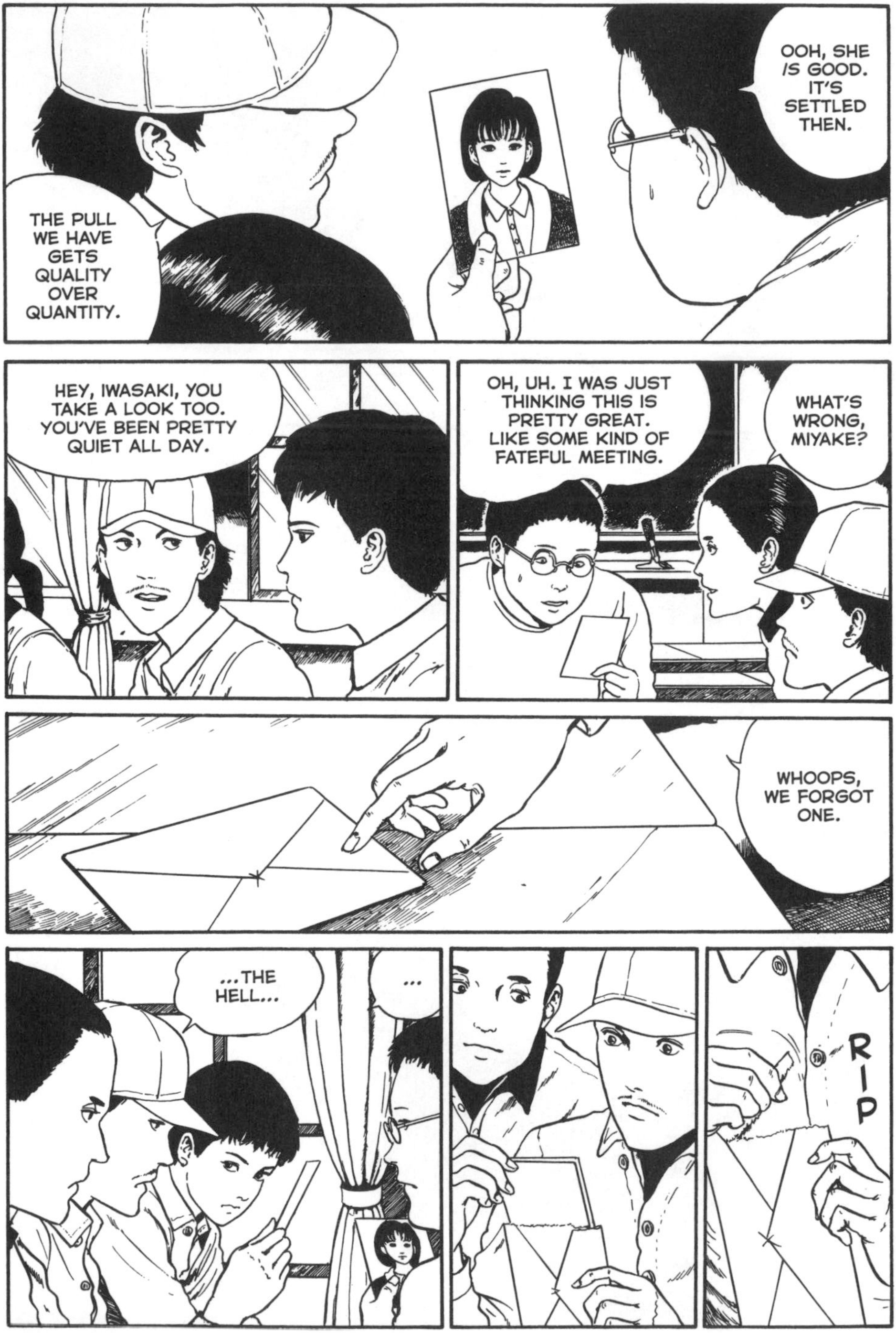
OOH, SHE IS GOOD. IT'S SETTLED THEN.
THE PULL WE HAVE GETS QUALITY OVER QUANTITY.
WHAT'S WRONG, MIYAKE?
OH, UH. I WAS JUST THINKING THIS IS PRETTY GREAT. LIKE SOME KIND OF FATEFUL MEETING.
HEY, IWASAKI, YOU TAKE A LOOK TOO. YOU'VE BEEN PRETTY QUIET ALL DAY.
WHOOPS, WE FORGOT ONE.
RIP
...
...THE HELL...

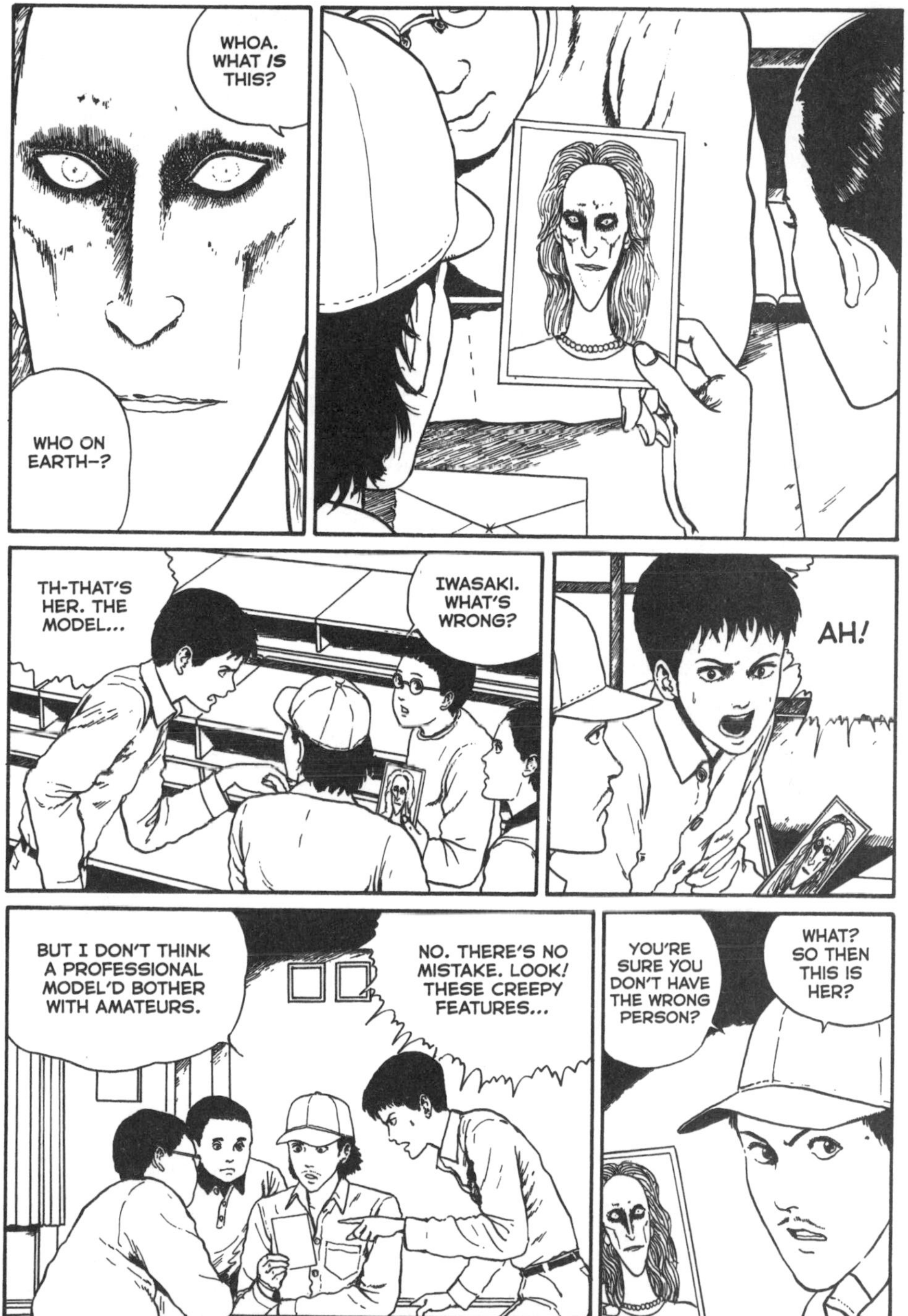
WHOA. WHAT *IS* THIS?
WHO ON EARTH–?
AH!
IWASAKI. WHAT'S WRONG?
TH-THAT'S HER. THE MODEL...
WHAT? SO THEN THIS IS HER?
YOU'RE SURE YOU DON'T HAVE THE WRONG PERSON?
NO. THERE'S NO MISTAKE. LOOK! THESE CREEPY FEATURES...
BUT I DON'T THINK A PROFESSIONAL MODEL'D BOTHER WITH AMATEURS.

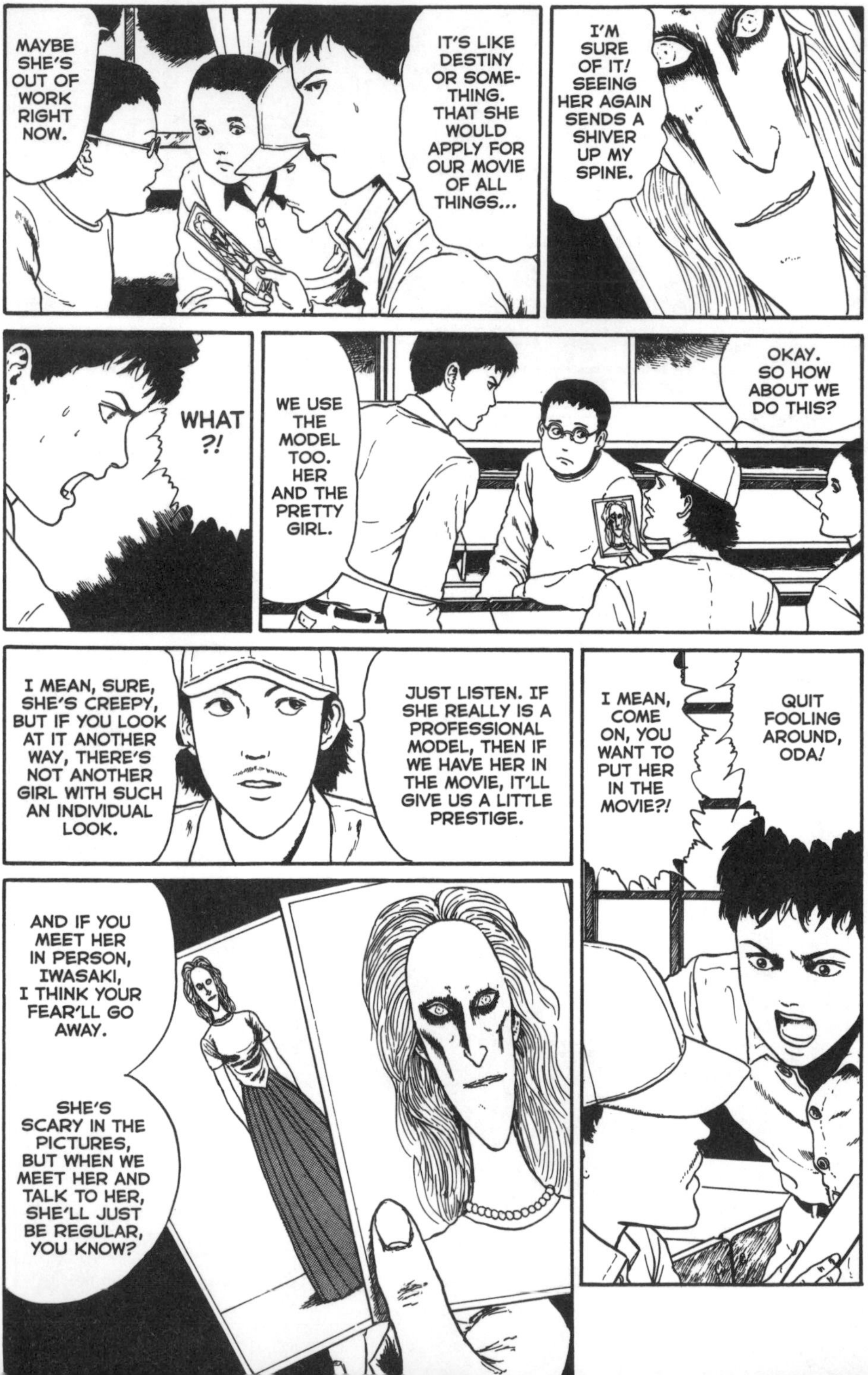
I'M SURE OF IT! SEEING HER AGAIN SENDS A SHIVER UP MY SPINE.
IT'S LIKE DESTINY OR SOME-THING. THAT SHE WOULD APPLY FOR OUR MOVIE OF ALL THINGS...
MAYBE SHE'S OUT OF WORK RIGHT NOW.
OKAY. SO HOW ABOUT WE DO THIS?
WE USE THE MODEL TOO. HER AND THE PRETTY GIRL.
WHAT?!
QUIT FOOLING AROUND, ODA!
I MEAN, COME ON, YOU WANT TO PUT HER IN THE MOVIE?!
JUST LISTEN. IF SHE REALLY IS A PROFESSIONAL MODEL, THEN IF WE HAVE HER IN THE MOVIE, IT'LL GIVE US A LITTLE PRESTIGE.
I MEAN, SURE, SHE'S CREEPY, BUT IF YOU LOOK AT IT ANOTHER WAY, THERE'S NOT ANOTHER GIRL WITH SUCH AN INDIVIDUAL LOOK.
AND IF YOU MEET HER IN PERSON, IWASAKI, I THINK YOUR FEAR'LL GO AWAY.
SHE'S SCARY IN THE PICTURES, BUT WHEN WE MEET HER AND TALK TO HER, SHE'LL JUST BE REGULAR, YOU KNOW?

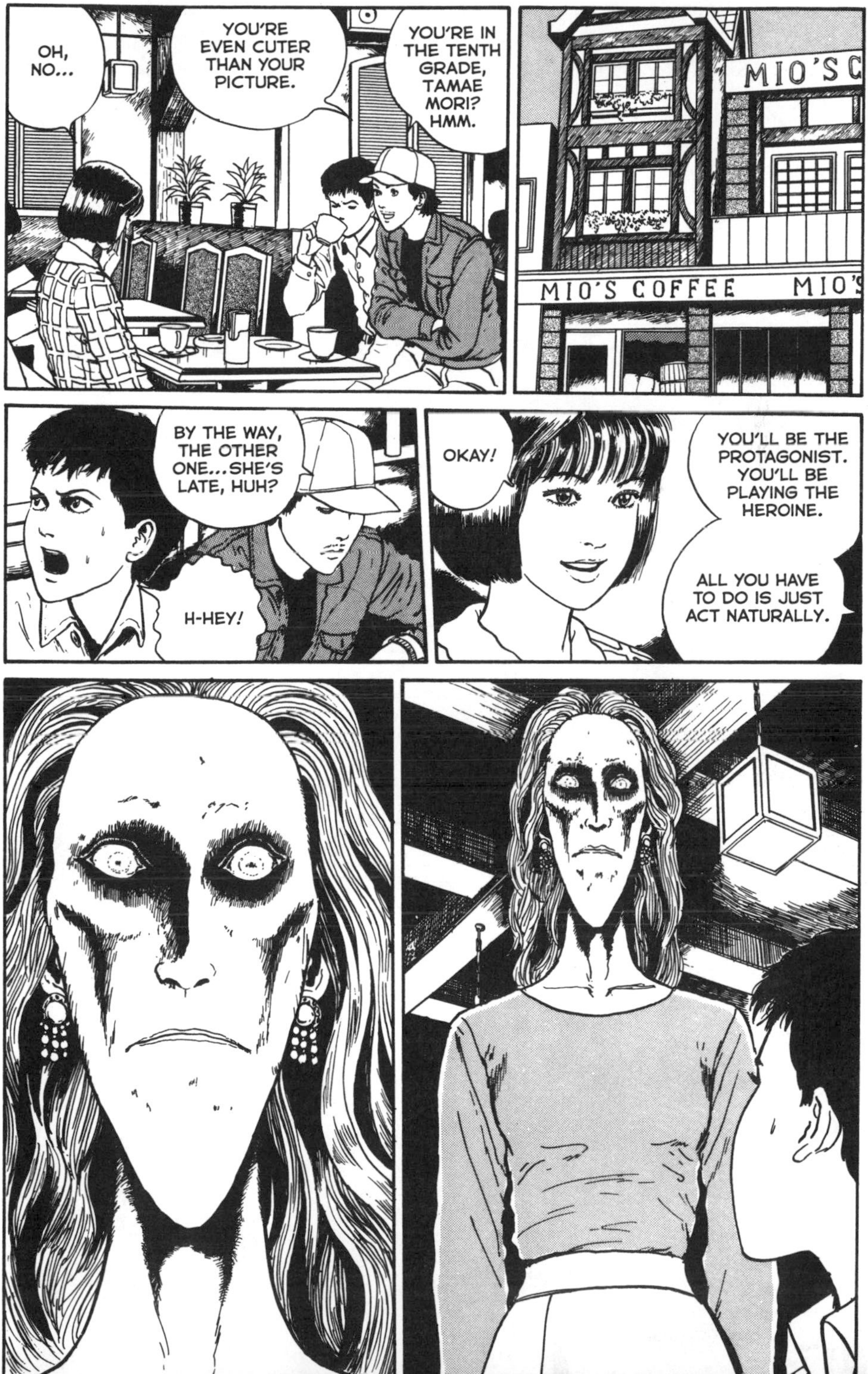
MIO'S C
MIO'S COFFEE
MIO'S
YOU'RE IN THE TENTH GRADE, TAMAE MORI? HMM.
YOU'RE EVEN CUTER THAN YOUR PICTURE.
OH, NO...
YOU'LL BE THE PROTAGONIST. YOU'LL BE PLAYING THE HEROINE.
OKAY!
ALL YOU HAVE TO DO IS JUST ACT NATURALLY.
BY THE WAY, THE OTHER ONE...SHE'S LATE, HUH?
H-HEY!

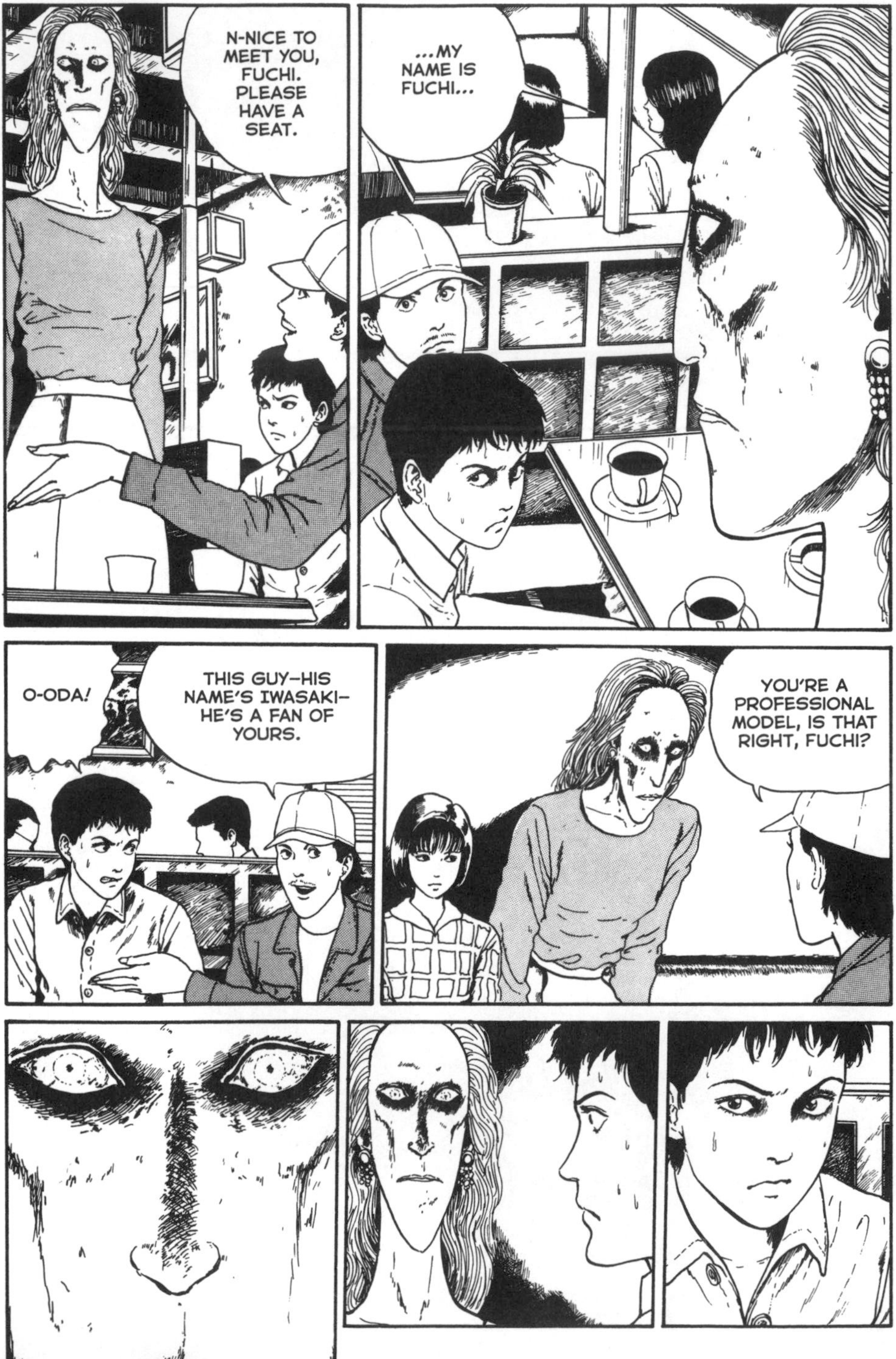
...MY NAME IS FUCHI...
N-NICE TO MEET YOU, FUCHI. PLEASE HAVE A SEAT.
YOU'RE A PROFESSIONAL MODEL, IS THAT RIGHT, FUCHI?
THIS GUY—HIS NAME'S IWASAKI—HE'S A FAN OF YOURS.
O-ODA!

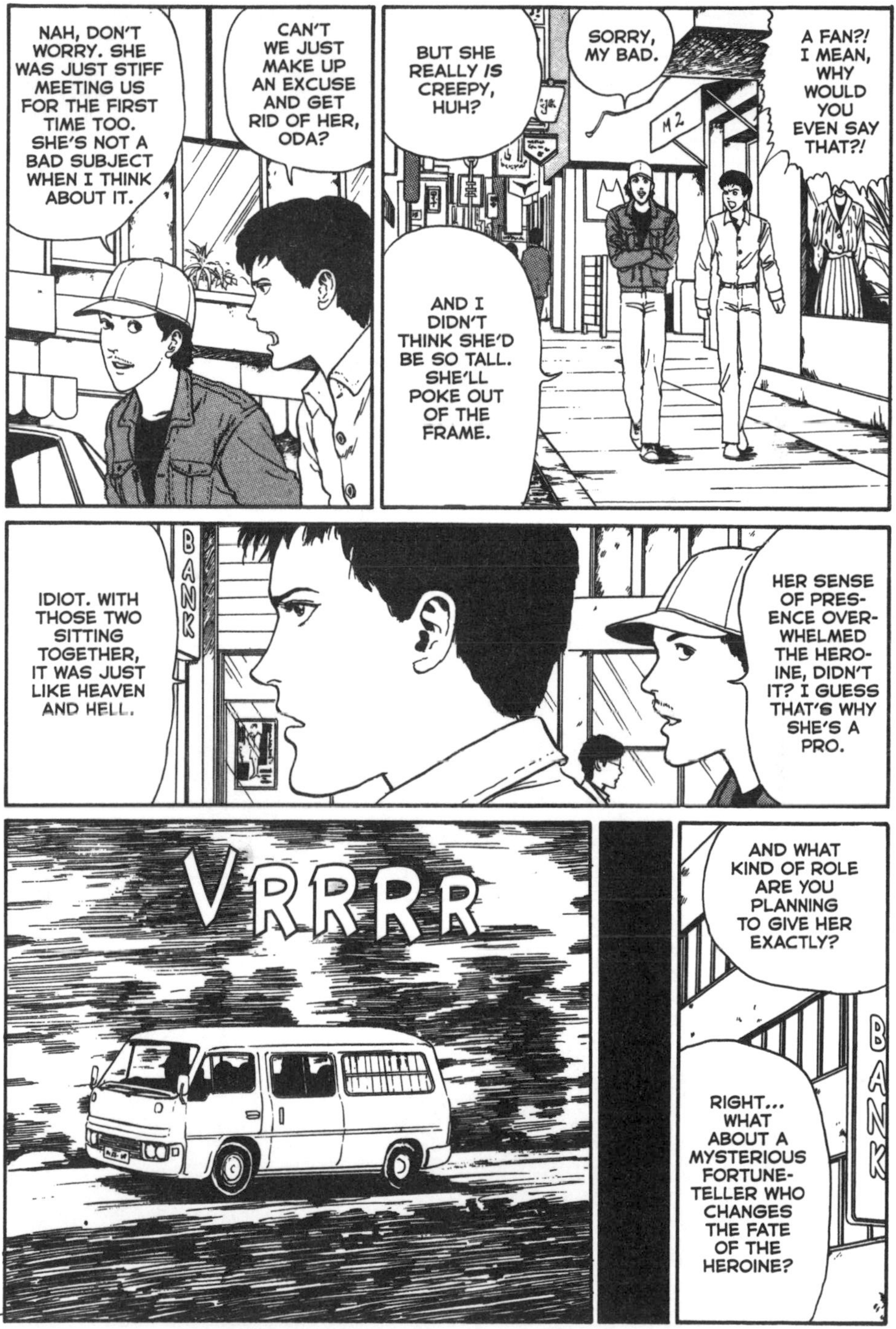

A FAN?! I MEAN, WHY WOULD YOU EVEN SAY THAT?!
SORRY, MY BAD.
BUT SHE REALLY *IS* CREEPY, HUH?
AND I DIDN'T THINK SHE'D BE SO TALL. SHE'LL POKE OUT OF THE FRAME.
CAN'T WE JUST MAKE UP AN EXCUSE AND GET RID OF HER, ODA?
NAH, DON'T WORRY. SHE WAS JUST STIFF MEETING US FOR THE FIRST TIME TOO. SHE'S NOT A BAD SUBJECT WHEN I THINK ABOUT IT.
HER SENSE OF PRESENCE OVERWHELMED THE HEROINE, DIDN'T IT? I GUESS THAT'S WHY SHE'S A PRO.
IDIOT. WITH THOSE TWO SITTING TOGETHER, IT WAS JUST LIKE HEAVEN AND HELL.
AND WHAT KIND OF ROLE ARE YOU PLANNING TO GIVE HER EXACTLY?
RIGHT... WHAT ABOUT A MYSTERIOUS FORTUNE-TELLER WHO CHANGES THE FATE OF THE HEROINE?
VRRRR

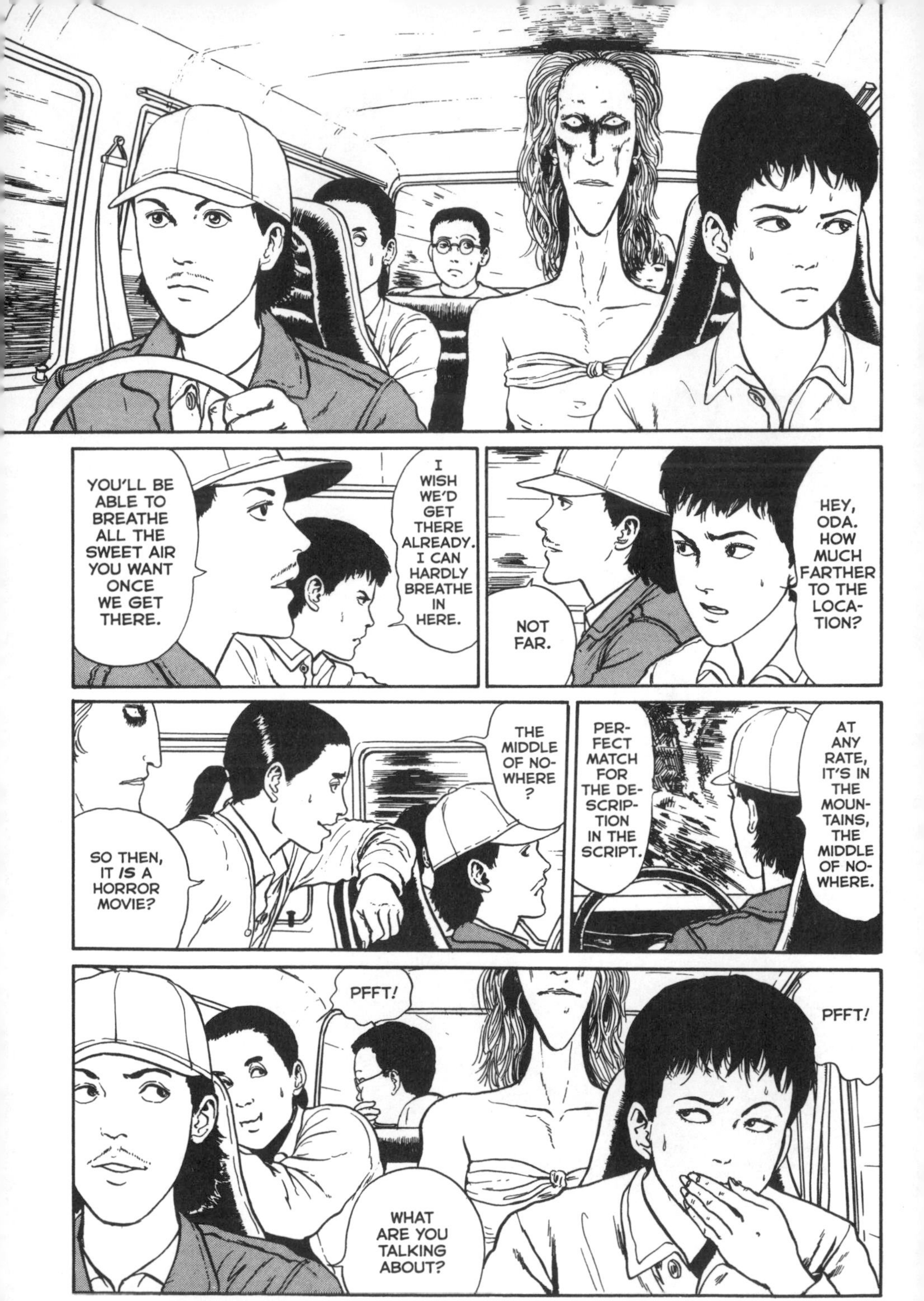
HEY, ODA. HOW MUCH FARTHER TO THE LOCATION?
NOT FAR.
I WISH WE'D GET THERE ALREADY. I CAN HARDLY BREATHE IN HERE.
YOU'LL BE ABLE TO BREATHE ALL THE SWEET AIR YOU WANT ONCE WE GET THERE.
AT ANY RATE, IT'S IN THE MOUNTAINS, THE MIDDLE OF NOWHERE.
PERFECT MATCH FOR THE DESCRIPTION IN THE SCRIPT.
THE MIDDLE OF NOWHERE?
SO THEN, IT *IS* A HORROR MOVIE?
PFFT!
PFFT!
WHAT ARE YOU TALKING ABOUT?

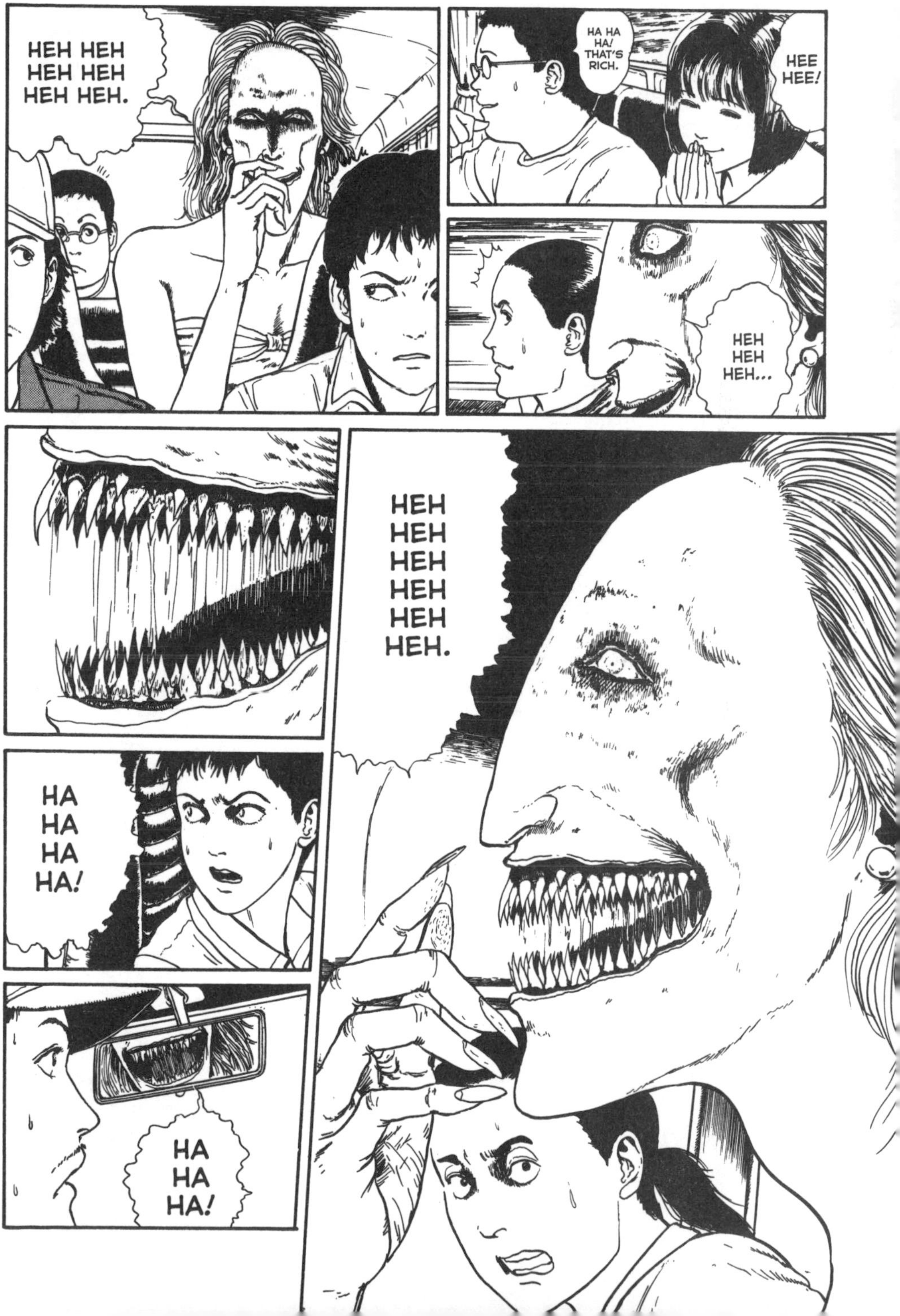
HEE HEE!
HA HA HA! THAT'S RICH.
HEH HEH HEH...
HEH HEH HEH HEH HEH HEH.
HEH HEH HEH HEH HEH HEH.
HA HA HA HA!
HA HA HA!

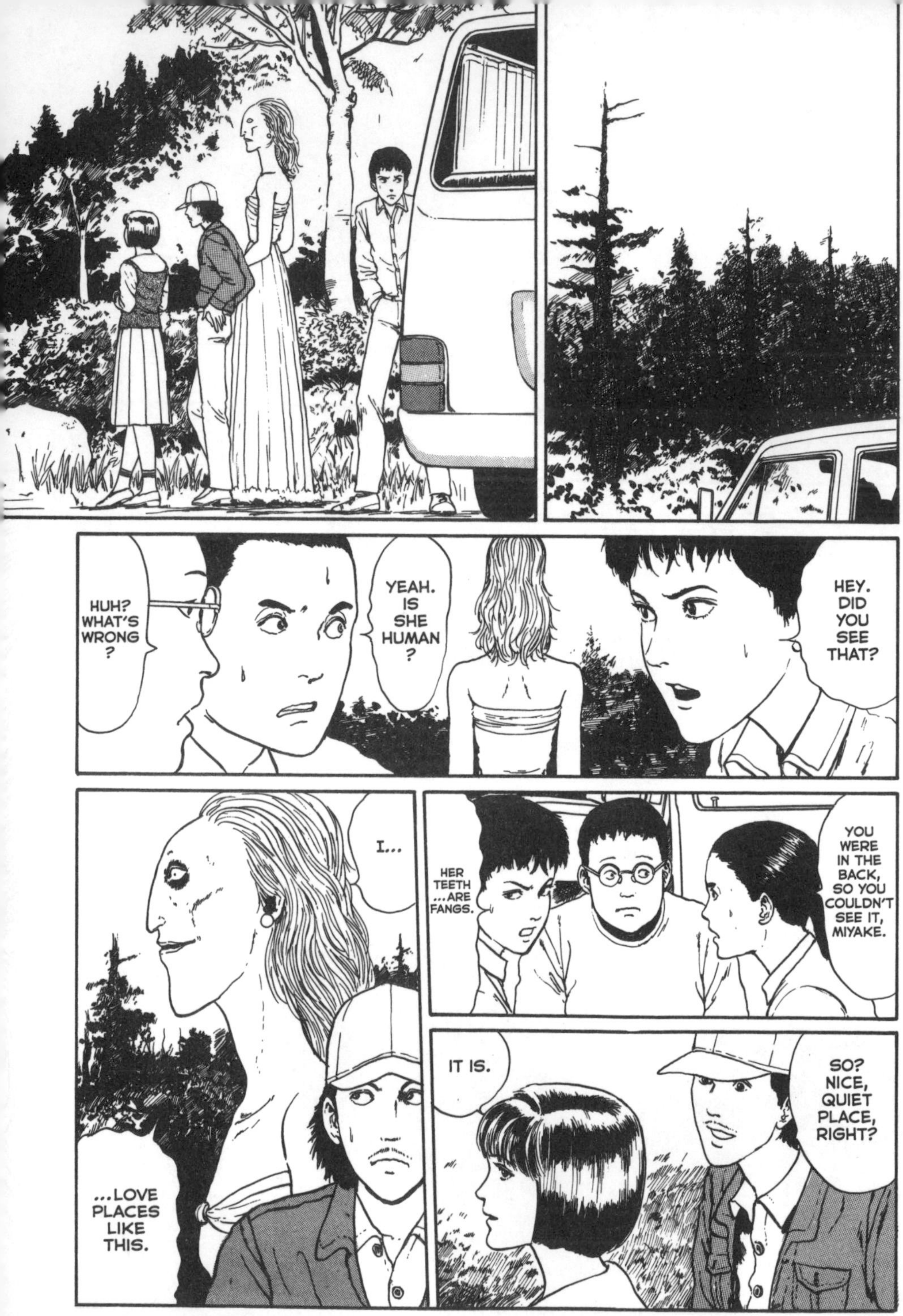
HEY. DID YOU SEE THAT?
YEAH. IS SHE HUMAN?
HUH? WHAT'S WRONG?
YOU WERE IN THE BACK, SO YOU COULDN'T SEE IT, MIYAKE.
HER TEETH ...ARE FANGS.
SO? NICE, QUIET PLACE, RIGHT?
IT IS.
I...
...LOVE PLACES LIKE THIS.

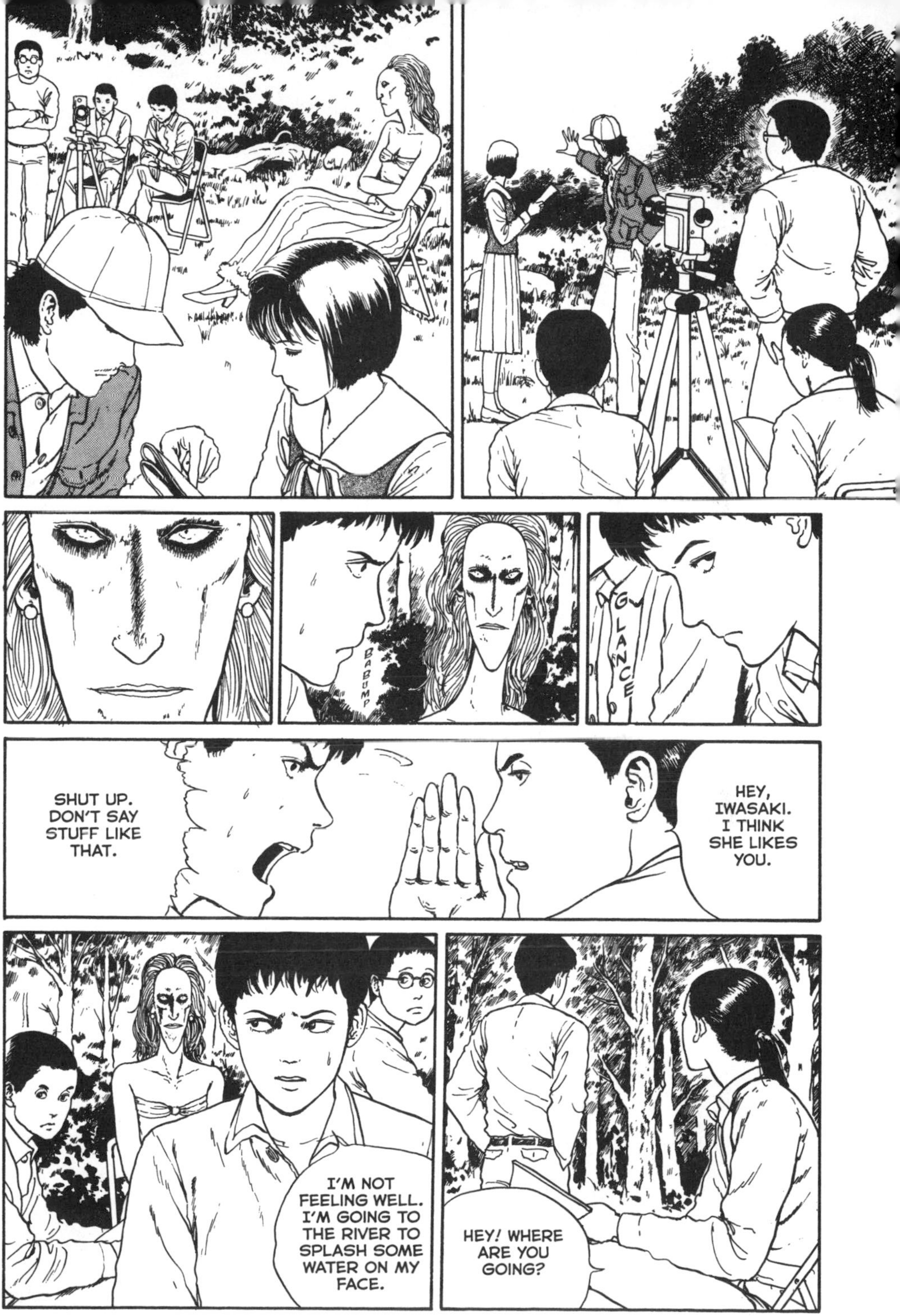
GLANCE
BABUMP
HEY, IWASAKI. I THINK SHE LIKES YOU.
SHUT UP. DON'T SAY STUFF LIKE THAT.
HEY! WHERE ARE YOU GOING?
I'M NOT FEELING WELL. I'M GOING TO THE RIVER TO SPLASH SOME WATER ON MY FACE.

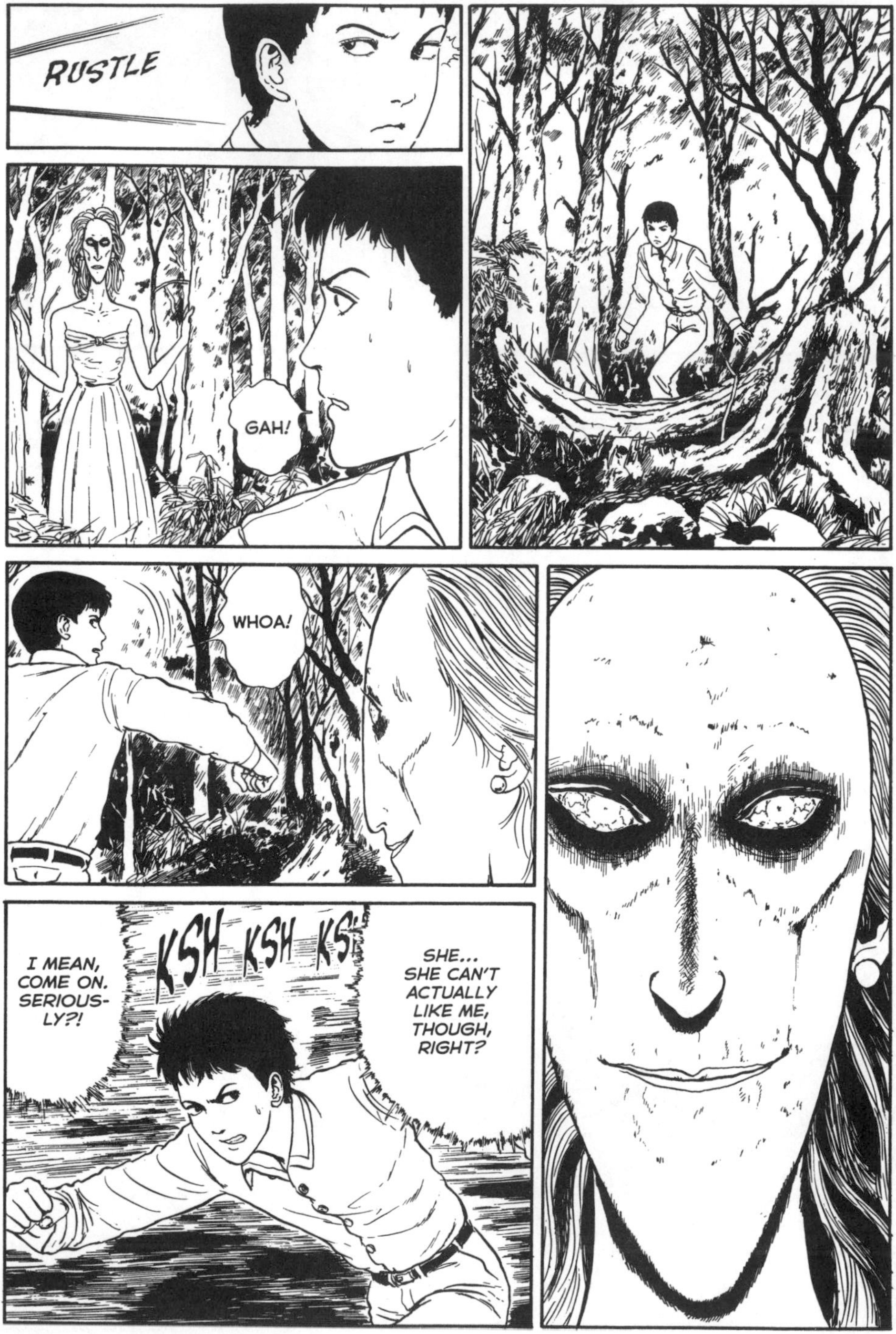
RUSTLE
GAH!
WHOA!
SHE... SHE CAN'T ACTUALLY LIKE ME, THOUGH, RIGHT?
KSH KSH KS
I MEAN, COME ON. SERIOUS-LY?!

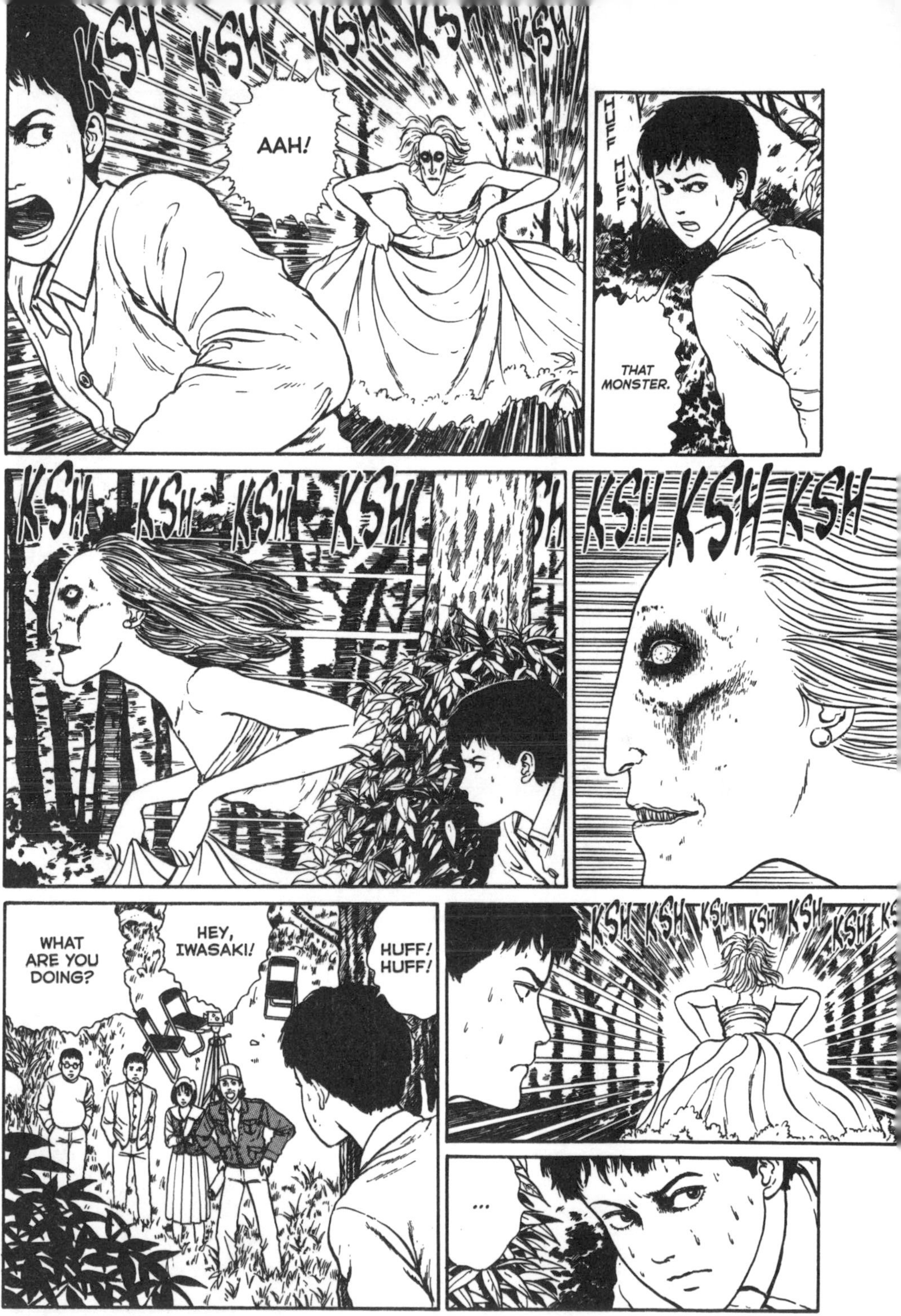
HUFF HUFF
THAT MONSTER.
KSH KSH KSH KSH KSH
AAH!
KSH KSH KSH
SH
KSH KSH KSH KSH
KSH KSH KSH KSH KSH KSH
...
HUFF! HUFF!
HEY, IWASAKI!
WHAT ARE YOU DOING?

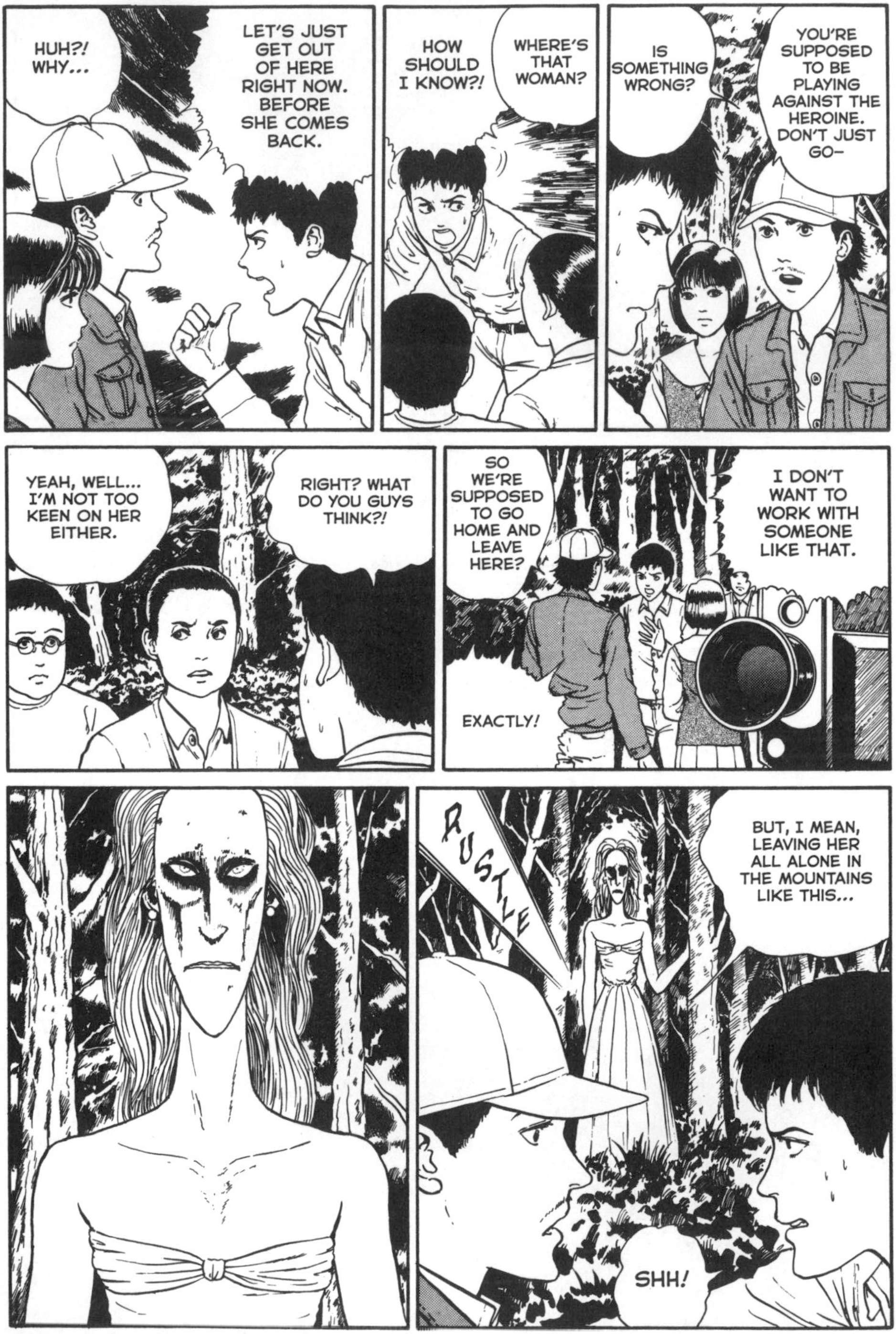
YOU'RE SUPPOSED TO BE PLAYING AGAINST THE HEROINE. DON'T JUST GO–
IS SOMETHING WRONG?
WHERE'S THAT WOMAN?
HOW SHOULD I KNOW?!
LET'S JUST GET OUT OF HERE RIGHT NOW. BEFORE SHE COMES BACK.
HUH?! WHY...
I DON'T WANT TO WORK WITH SOMEONE LIKE THAT.
SO WE'RE SUPPOSED TO GO HOME AND LEAVE HERE?
EXACTLY!
RIGHT? WHAT DO YOU GUYS THINK?!
YEAH, WELL... I'M NOT TOO KEEN ON HER EITHER.
BUT, I MEAN, LEAVING HER ALL ALONE IN THE MOUNTAINS LIKE THIS...
RUSTLE
SHH!

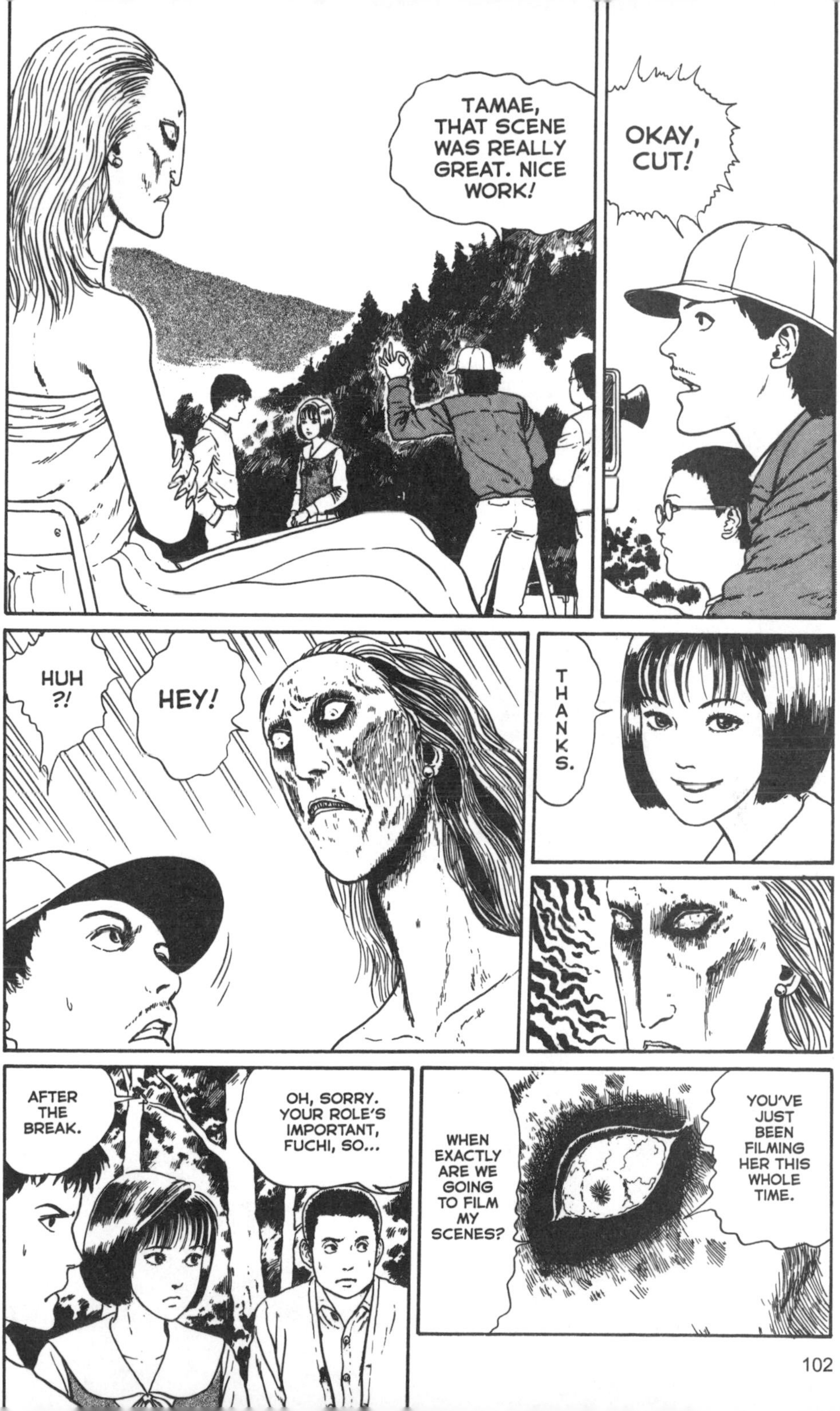
OKAY, CUT!
TAMAE, THAT SCENE WAS REALLY GREAT. NICE WORK!
THANKS.
HEY!
HUH?!
YOU'VE JUST BEEN FILMING HER THIS WHOLE TIME.
WHEN EXACTLY ARE WE GOING TO FILM MY SCENES?
OH, SORRY. YOUR ROLE'S IMPORTANT, FUCHI, SO...
AFTER THE BREAK.

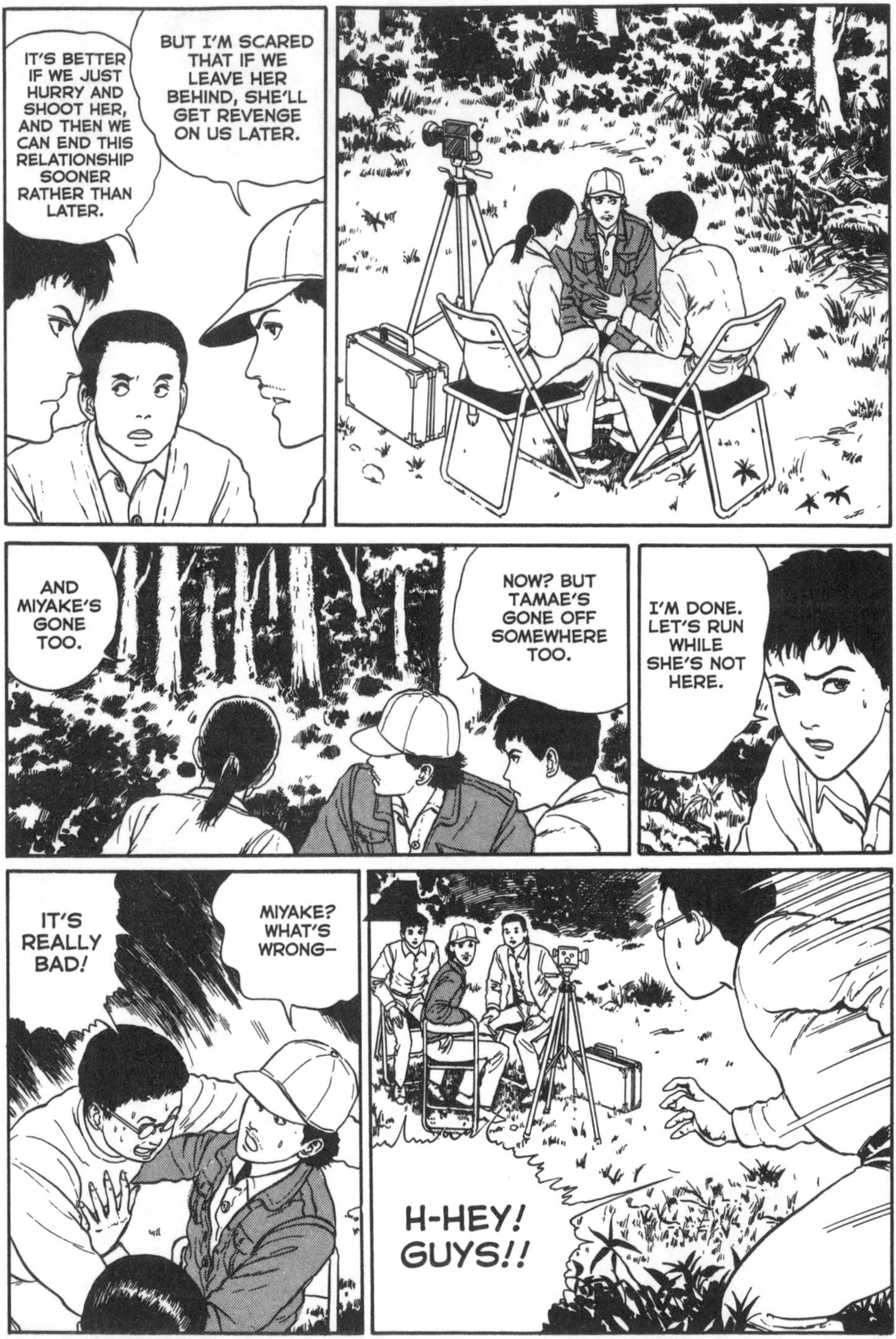
BUT I'M SCARED THAT IF WE LEAVE HER BEHIND, SHE'LL GET REVENGE ON US LATER.
IT'S BETTER IF WE JUST HURRY AND SHOOT HER, AND THEN WE CAN END THIS RELATIONSHIP SOONER RATHER THAN LATER.
I'M DONE. LET'S RUN WHILE SHE'S NOT HERE.
NOW? BUT TAMAE'S GONE OFF SOMEWHERE TOO.
AND MIYAKE'S GONE TOO.
H-HEY! GUYS!!
MIYAKE? WHAT'S WRONG–
IT'S REALLY BAD!

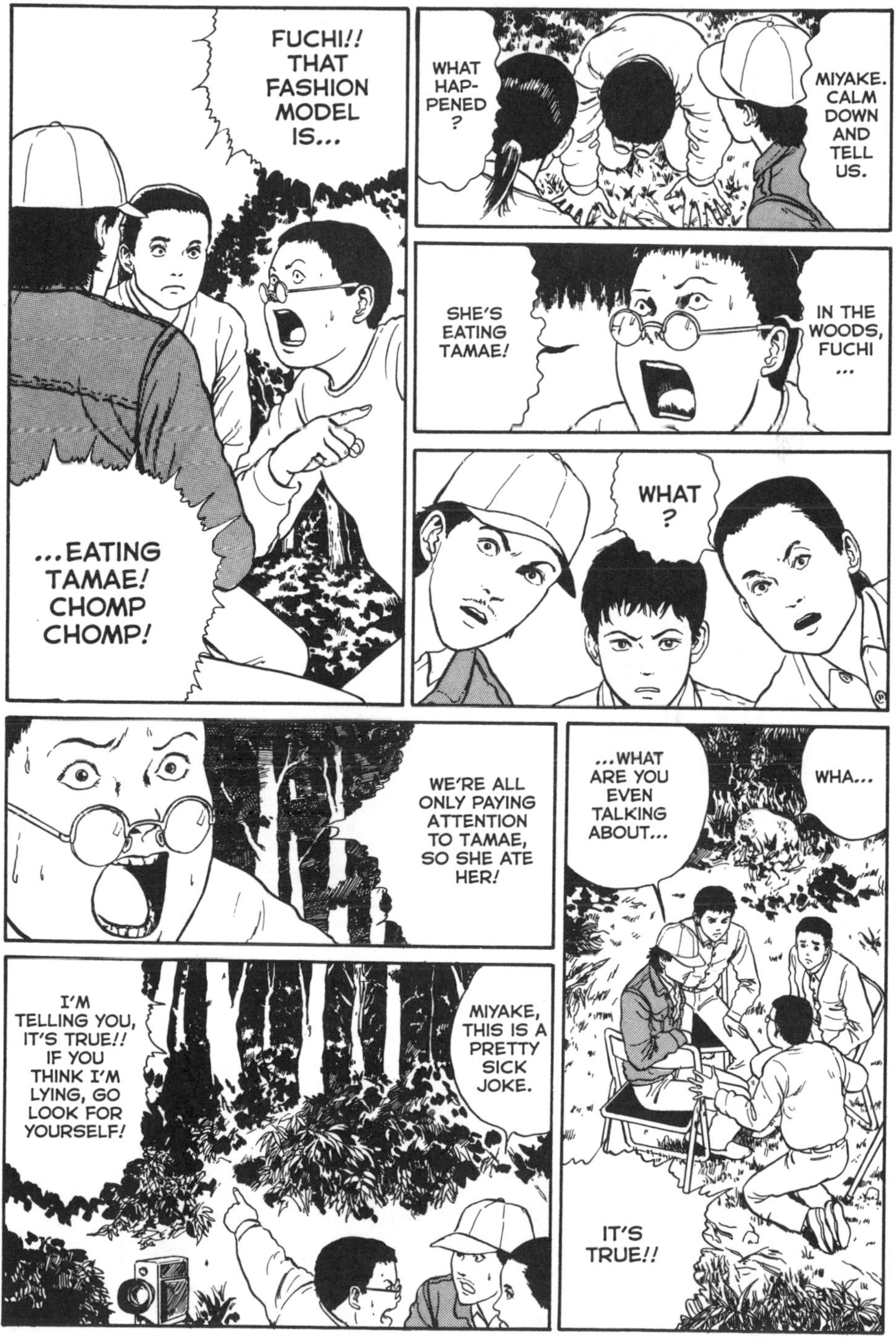
MIYAKE. CALM DOWN AND TELL US.
WHAT HAPPENED?
IN THE WOODS, FUCHI...
SHE'S EATING TAMAE!
WHAT?
FUCHI!! THAT FASHION MODEL IS...
...EATING TAMAE! CHOMP CHOMP!
WHA...
...WHAT ARE YOU EVEN TALKING ABOUT...
IT'S TRUE!!
WE'RE ALL ONLY PAYING ATTENTION TO TAMAE, SO SHE ATE HER!
MIYAKE, THIS IS A PRETTY SICK JOKE.
I'M TELLING YOU, IT'S TRUE!! IF YOU THINK I'M LYING, GO LOOK FOR YOURSELF!

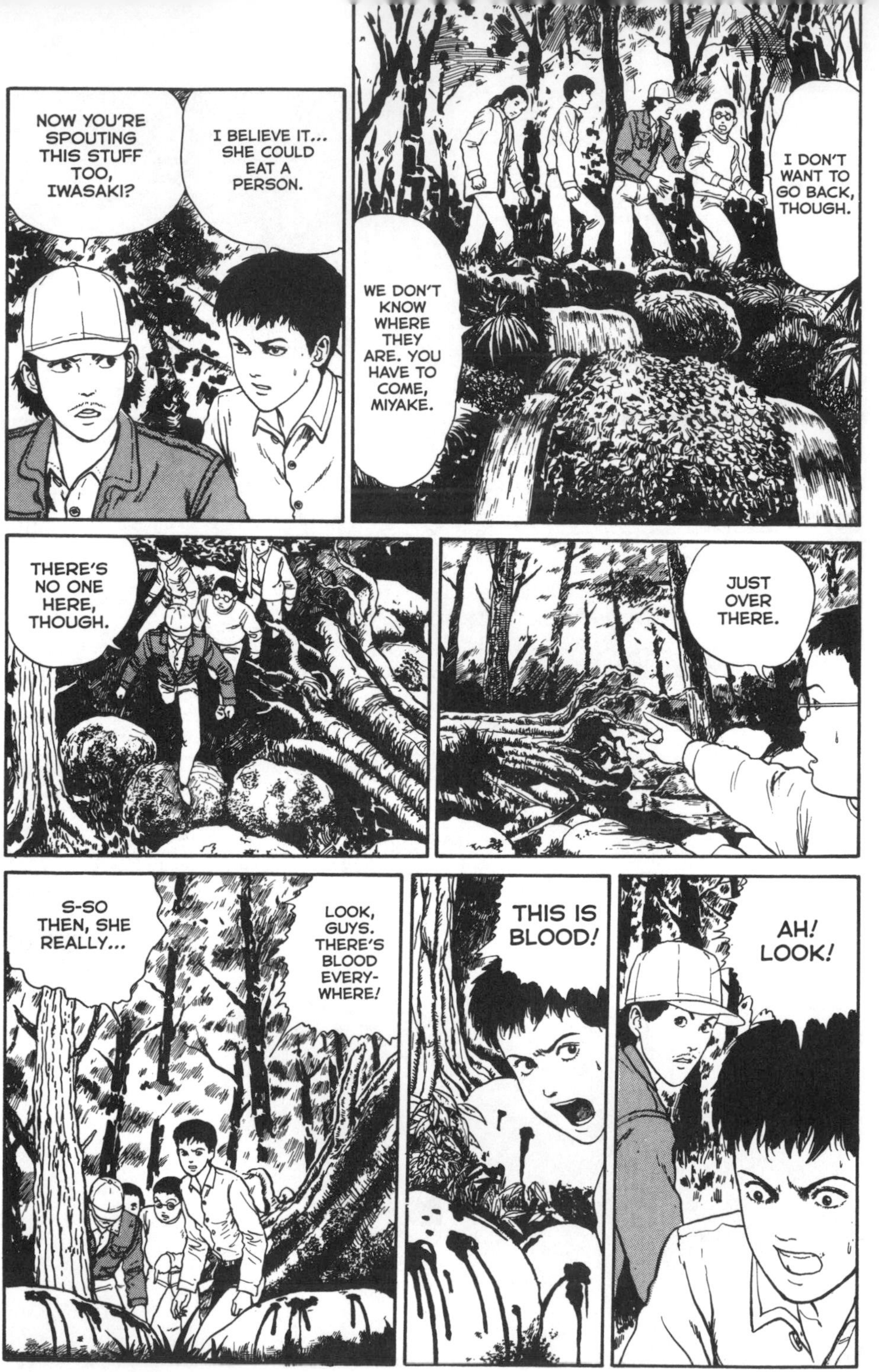
I DON'T WANT TO GO BACK, THOUGH.
WE DON'T KNOW WHERE THEY ARE. YOU HAVE TO COME, MIYAKE.
I BELIEVE IT... SHE COULD EAT A PERSON.
NOW YOU'RE SPOUTING THIS STUFF TOO, IWASAKI?
JUST OVER THERE.
THERE'S NO ONE HERE, THOUGH.
AH! LOOK!
THIS IS BLOOD!
LOOK, GUYS. THERE'S BLOOD EVERY-WHERE!
S-SO THEN, SHE REALLY...

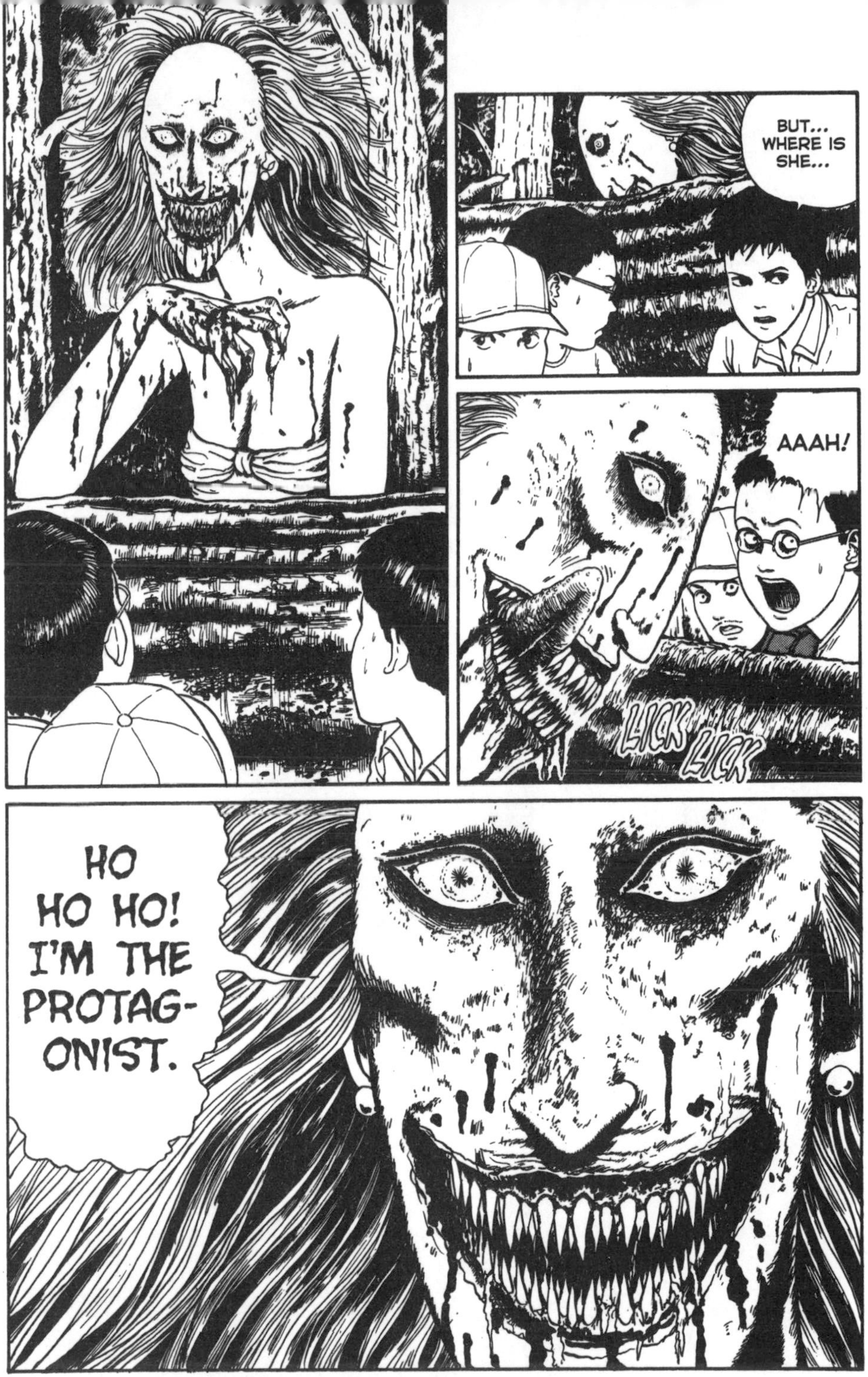
BUT... WHERE IS SHE...
AAAH!
LICK LICK
HO HO HO! I'M THE PROTAG-ONIST.

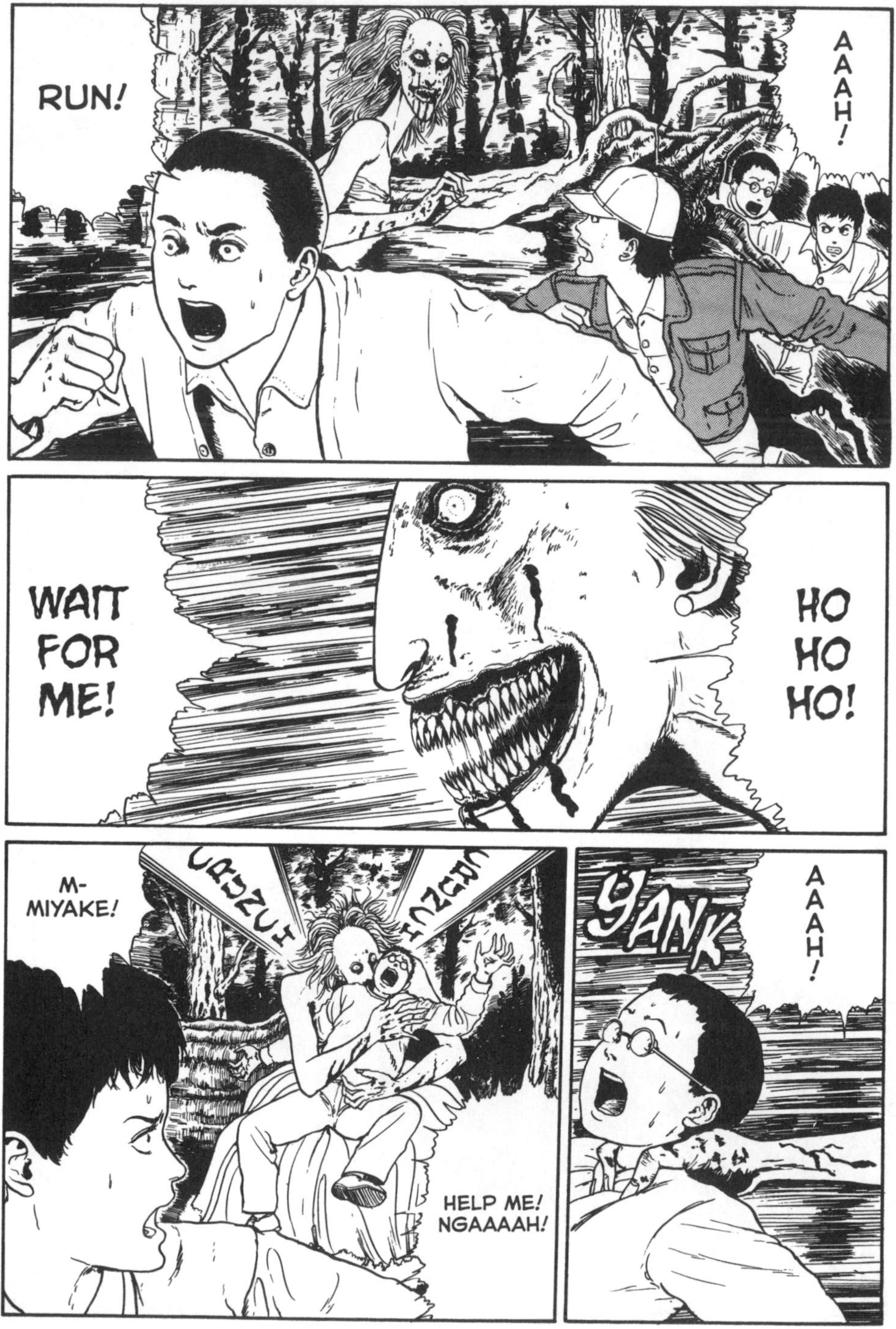
AAAH!
RUN!
HO HO HO!
WAIT FOR ME!
AAAH!
YANK
M-MIYAKE!
HELP ME! NGAAAAH!

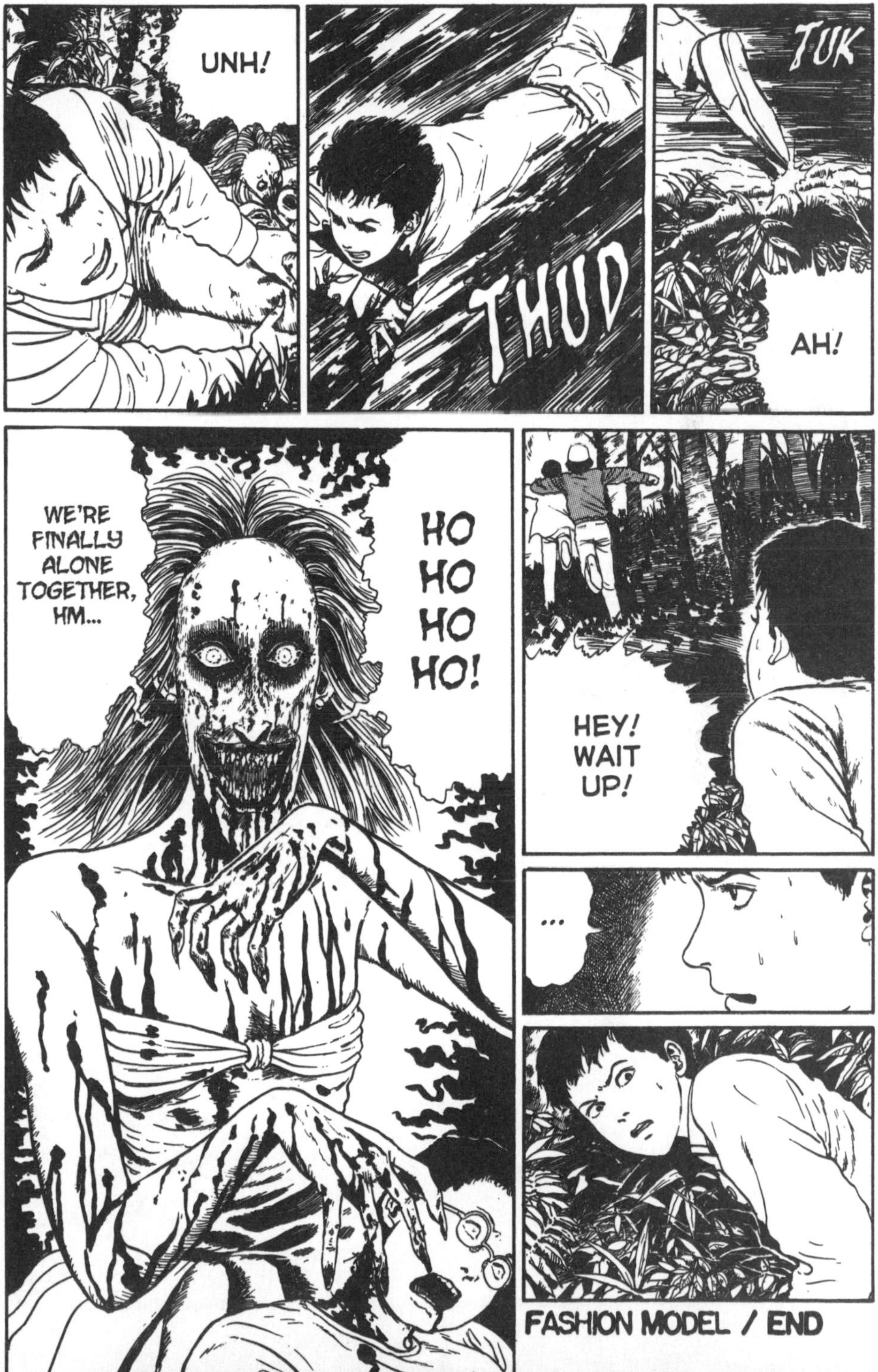
TUK
AH!
THUD
UNH!
HEY! WAIT UP!
...
HO HO HO HO HO!
WE'RE FINALLY ALONE TOGETHER, HM...

FASHION MODEL / END

FASHION MODEL

I often look at fashion magazines for manga reference, and I always notice just how many types of models there are. In this one magazine I happened to look at, there was a photo of a model who was pretty, but emitted this weird aura somehow (or at least, that's what I thought viewing her through my own subjective lens). So I came up with the idea of a fashion model who's actually a monster. Maybe I should have made her more attractive, but this is the face she ended up with.

I also thought of adding an element of the "shark woman" to this monster. But it just so happened that at the time, there was an incident where a shark attacked a fisherman in the Seto Inland Sea, and everyone was talking about that, so I locked that element away.

・その夜　絵が壁からぬけだして　あそぶようになった。

モデルの話

ヘアスタイルの本を見ていたら一人なんとも
不気味なモデルの写真。いびつな顔↓（夢にまで出てくる。
その後その雑誌は廃刊。そのモデルを見た事も
なかった

その後、自主映画を作ろうと出演者を雑誌の読者欄で
募集したら妙な写真が送られてくる。それはあのモデル
だった。「これ見たことある」といって仲間の一人がファッション誌でもってくる
その仲間はこれを見た時の異様な印象を話す。「そのあと廃刊になった」
仲間のうちの一人が冗談半分で会おうということになる
会うと思いの他巨大な女。
（仲間が本めいに個人的に会い、その妙な女をかんとくに会うよう手はいしてしまえ
A は冗談で
一度会ってみよう
と言ったんだ）
（主人公のかんとくもしてみる？）
。アマチュアでは知られた有名なかんとく
この女の恐怖。
この女は自分がたいへん魅力的だと思っているとか
って。しかし口びるが薄く、目はうつろで、どこを見て
いるのかわからないし歯は牛のようにとがって見える。
映画のヒロインのイメージにはほど遠いが本人はピッタリだと
思っているらしかった。
ふるまいがしばいがかっている
A が主人公なのでかんとくが、この女にほれているとウソ
をつく。女は本気にする

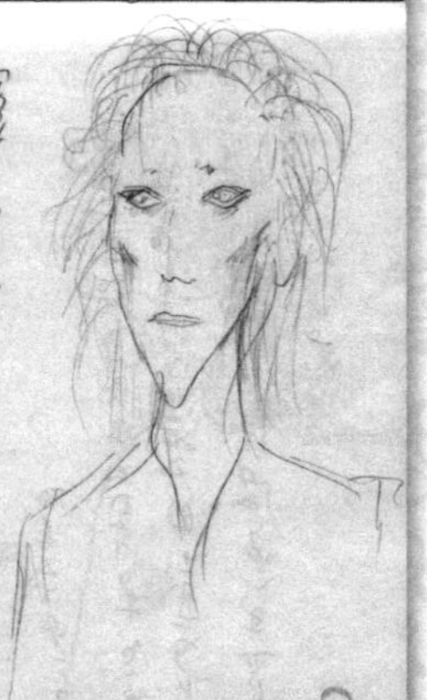

「この女…オレたちとタッチが違うな」
「あなたたち見る目がある…
先見性がある…
私みたいな女が
絶世の美女とみなされる
時代がやって来るわ。
私の中ではすでにそうなってるのよ」
そして不気味に笑う。

30.48
2.54
5フィート
11インチ
30.48
5
152.40
30.48
5
152.40
2.54
11
2.54
2.54
27.94
152.40
27.94
180.34

この女は妙なマネージャーがいる。ロケ地にあらわれる

「プロのモデルをやってた人がなぜこんなアマチュアのところへ？」
「別に理由はないわ」
しょうがないから彼女も出演させる事になる、
ロケ先でとんでもない事になる。
スタッフが「ホラー映画にしようか」などと言う。
ある場所でロケするが、仲間は彼女を無視して
撮えいをはじめる。気を悪くする。彼女はだまって
場所をうつすがおいかけてくる。
「あの女ウス気味悪いぞ……」
ロケのうちあわせの時間をうりを言っておりていくが
あとから追って現れる。
本命が彼女に殺される。
車で逃げる途中、前方に急に現れひき殺してしまう。
ワゴンの下に入って車が出せない
なんとか下の彼女をだそうとしたが出らない。

[Top page]
• That night, the painting stole away from the wall and seemed to be playing.

Story about a model
Flipping through a book of hairstyles, a picture of one seriously creepy model. Warped face → (He even dreams about it.)
The magazine quits publishing after that. He doesn't see the model anymore.

Later, when they're trying to making an independent film, they recruit performers in the reader column of a magazine, and a strange photo is sent to them. It's the model. "I've seen her before," one of the guys says and brings out a fashion magazine. This guy talks about the bizarre impression he got when he saw it. "The magazine folded after that." One of the guys half-jokes that they should meet her then.
When they do, the woman is surprisingly huge.
One of the guys meets the real star individually, and A arranges for the director and the others to meet this weird girl as a joke.
• Director known in the amateur world. He suggests they do a general casting call.
The terror of this woman.
The woman seems to think she's extremely attractive. But her lips are thin, her eyes are blank, so you never know where she's looking, and her teeth are tapered like fangs.
She's a far cry from a movie heroine, but she herself seems to believe she's perfect for the role.
She carries herself very theatrically.
A lies and says the director's in love with her. She takes him seriously.

[Bottom page]
"You all have eyes that can see.
You have real vision.
The time when a woman like me is deemed an unequalled beauty
is finally here.
It's already the truth in my heart."
And then she laughs creepily.

"That woman...She's got a different style."
The woman has a weird manager. He shows up at the shoot location.

"Why would a professional model be in this amateur thing?"
"No particular reason."

With no real choice left to them, they have her act in the film.
Things get pretty unhinged at the shoot.
The crew are talking like, "How about we turn it into a horror film?"

They go up to the shoot location, but the guys ignore her and start filming. She takes offense. They change locations without telling her, but she comes chasing after them. She kills the real star.

"That woman's creepy, man..."
They lie about the time to meet at the location, but she comes chasing up from behind.

As they're fleeing in the car, she suddenly appears before them, and they run her over, killing her. She goes under the van, and they can't pull out. They try to get her out from underneath, but they can't.

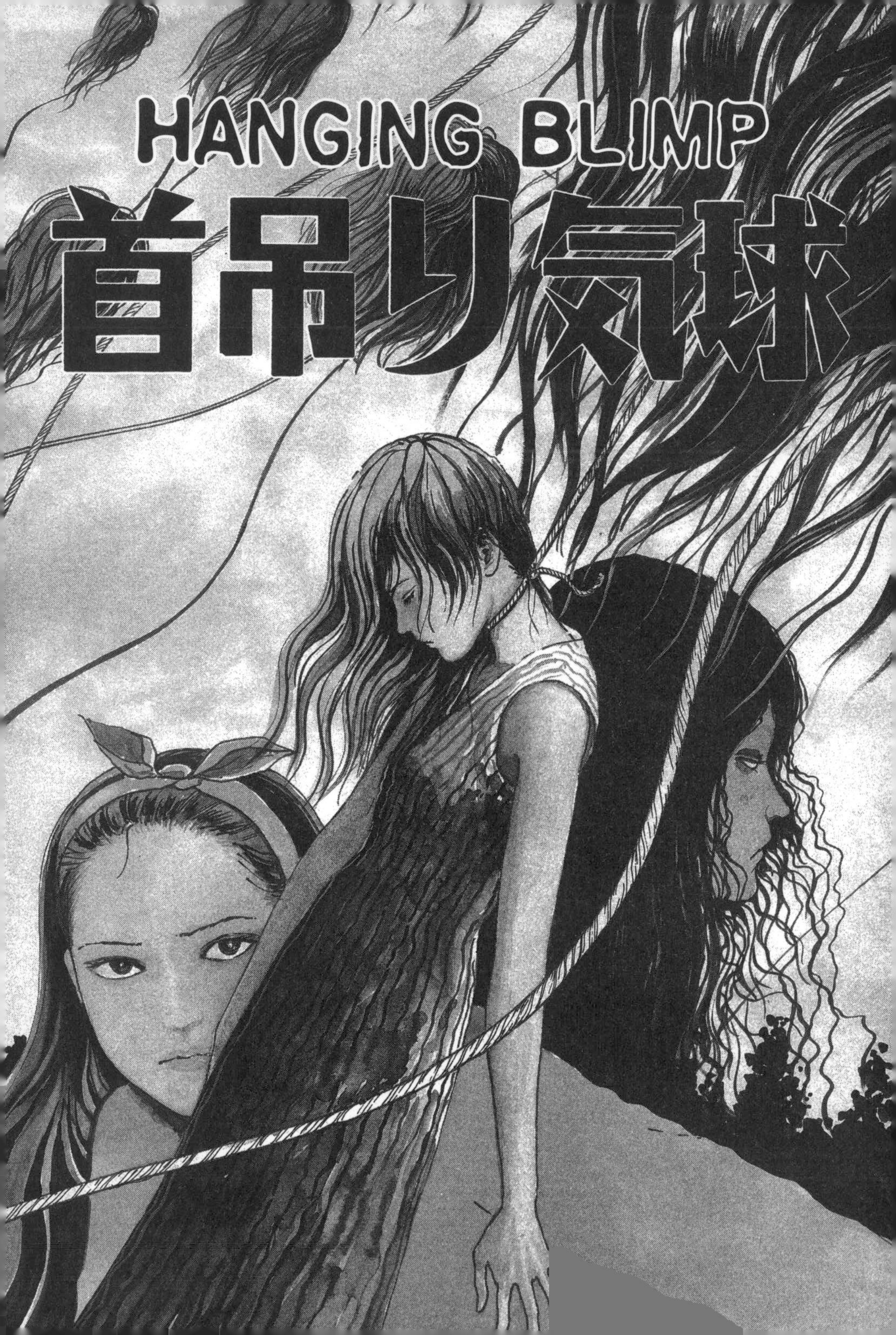
HANGING BLIMP
首吊り気球

KNOCK KNOCK
KNOCK KNOCK

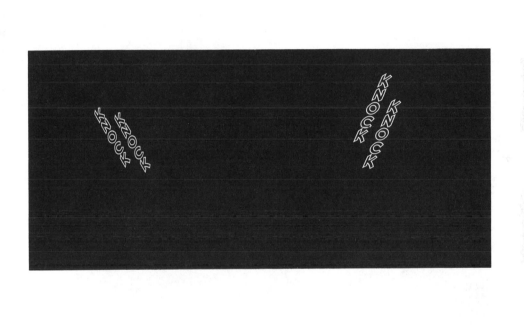

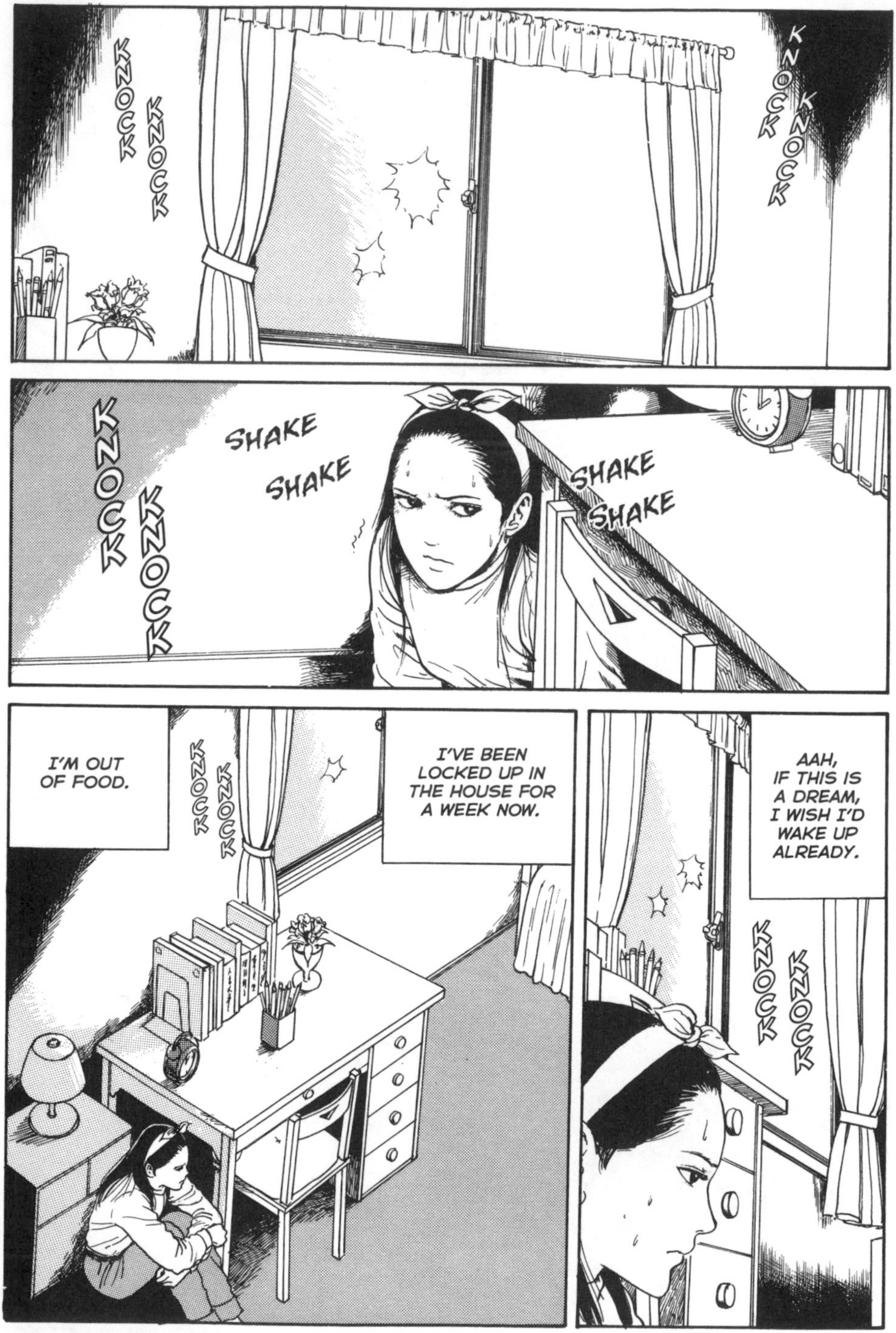
KNOCK KNOCK
KNOCK KNOCK
SHAKE SHAKE
SHAKE SHAKE
KNOCK KNOCK
AAH, IF THIS IS A DREAM, I WISH I'D WAKE UP ALREADY.
KNOCK KNOCK
I'VE BEEN LOCKED UP IN THE HOUSE FOR A WEEK NOW.
KNOCK KNOCK
I'M OUT OF FOOD.

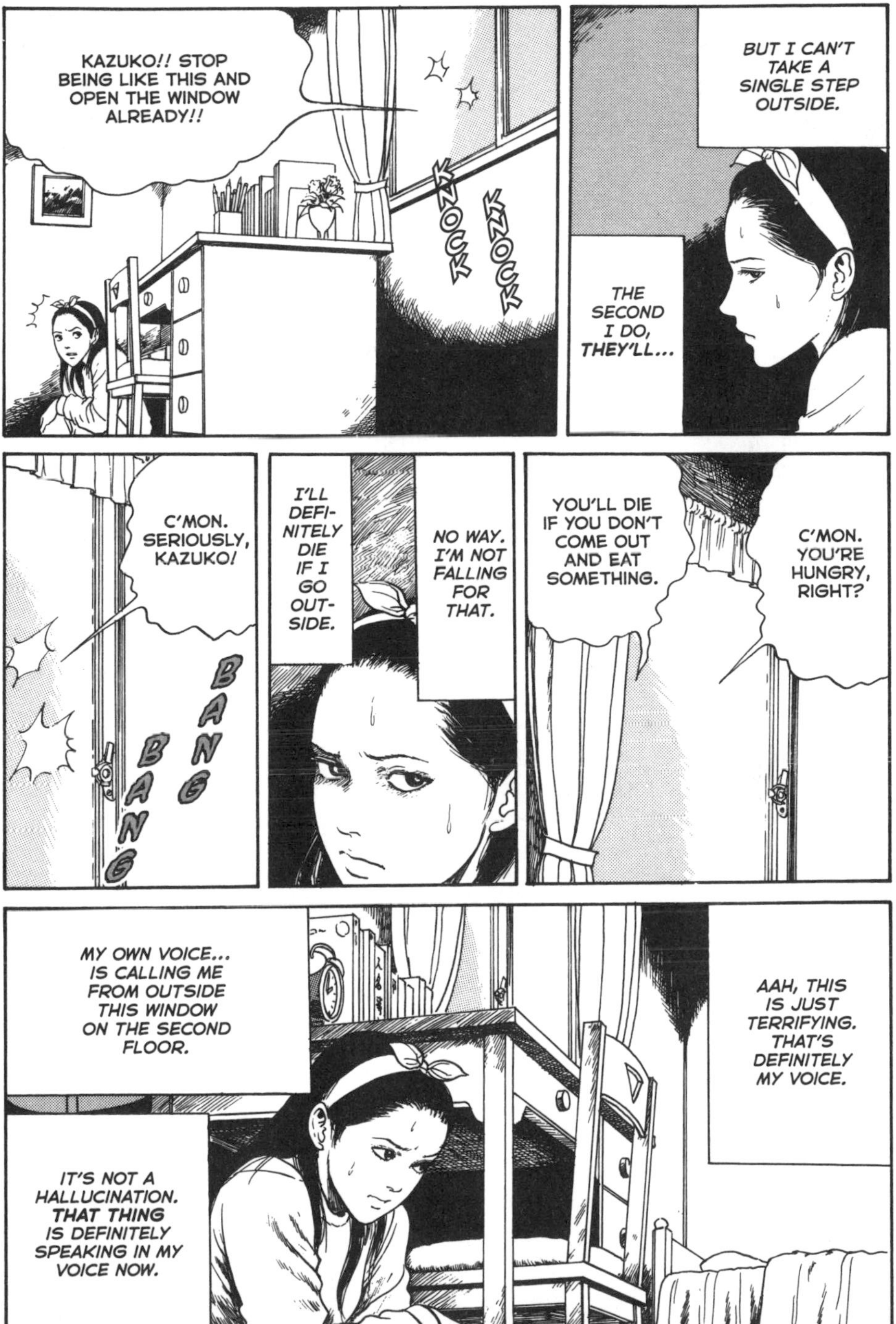
BUT I CAN'T TAKE A SINGLE STEP OUTSIDE.
THE SECOND I DO, THEY'LL...
KAZUKO!! STOP BEING LIKE THIS AND OPEN THE WINDOW ALREADY!!
KNOCK
KNOCK
C'MON. YOU'RE HUNGRY, RIGHT?
YOU'LL DIE IF YOU DON'T COME OUT AND EAT SOMETHING.
NO WAY. I'M NOT FALLING FOR THAT.
I'LL DEFINITELY DIE IF I GO OUTSIDE.
C'MON. SERIOUSLY, KAZUKO!
BANG
BANG
AAH, THIS IS JUST TERRIFYING. THAT'S DEFINITELY MY VOICE.
MY OWN VOICE... IS CALLING ME FROM OUTSIDE THIS WINDOW ON THE SECOND FLOOR.
IT'S NOT A HALLUCINATION. THAT THING IS DEFINITELY SPEAKING IN MY VOICE NOW.

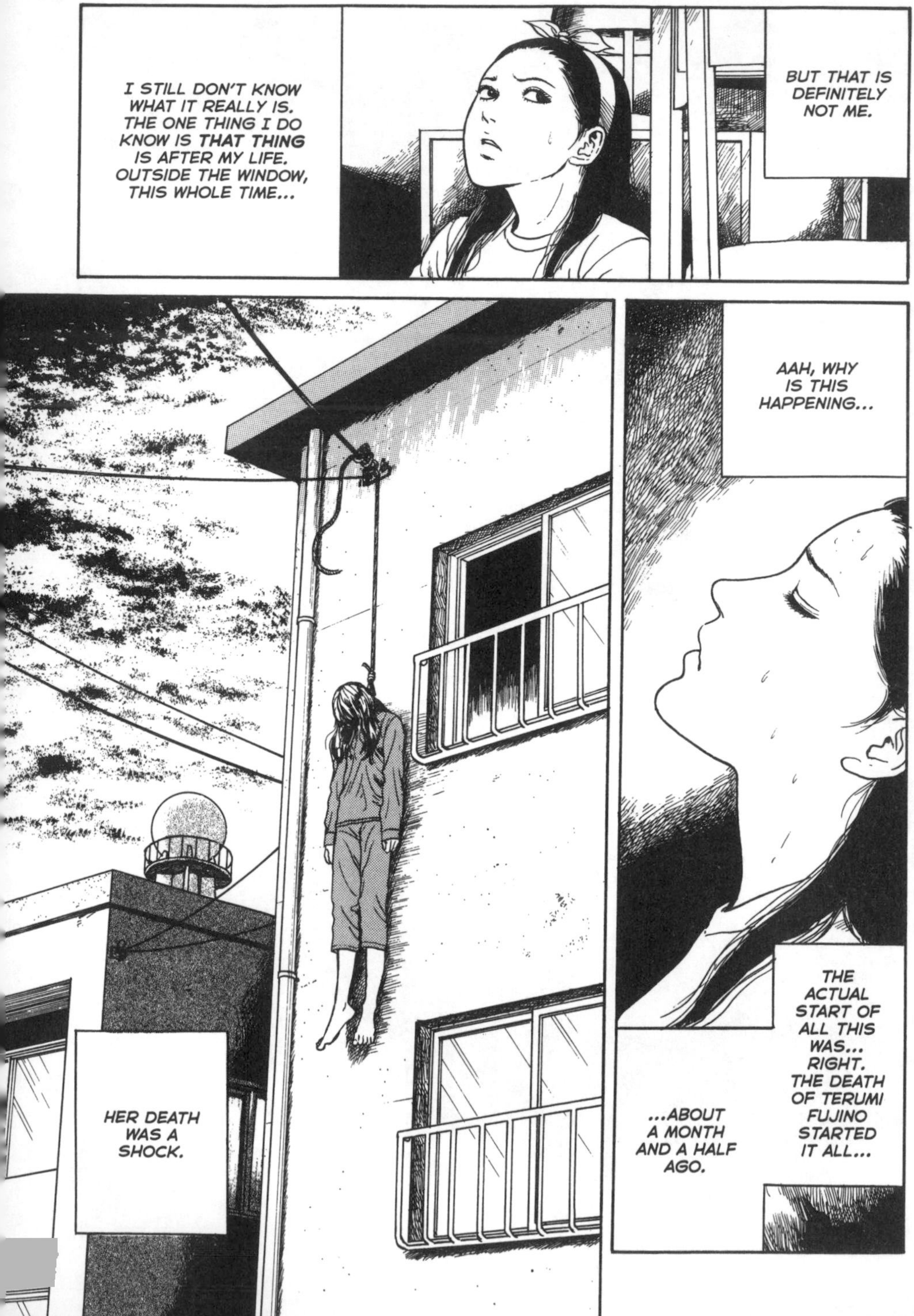
BUT THAT IS DEFINITELY NOT ME.
I STILL DON'T KNOW WHAT IT REALLY IS. THE ONE THING I DO KNOW IS **THAT THING** IS AFTER MY LIFE. OUTSIDE THE WINDOW, THIS WHOLE TIME...
AAH, WHY IS THIS HAPPENING...
THE ACTUAL START OF ALL THIS WAS... RIGHT. THE DEATH OF TERUMI FUJINO STARTED IT ALL...
...ABOUT A MONTH AND A HALF AGO.
HER DEATH WAS A SHOCK.

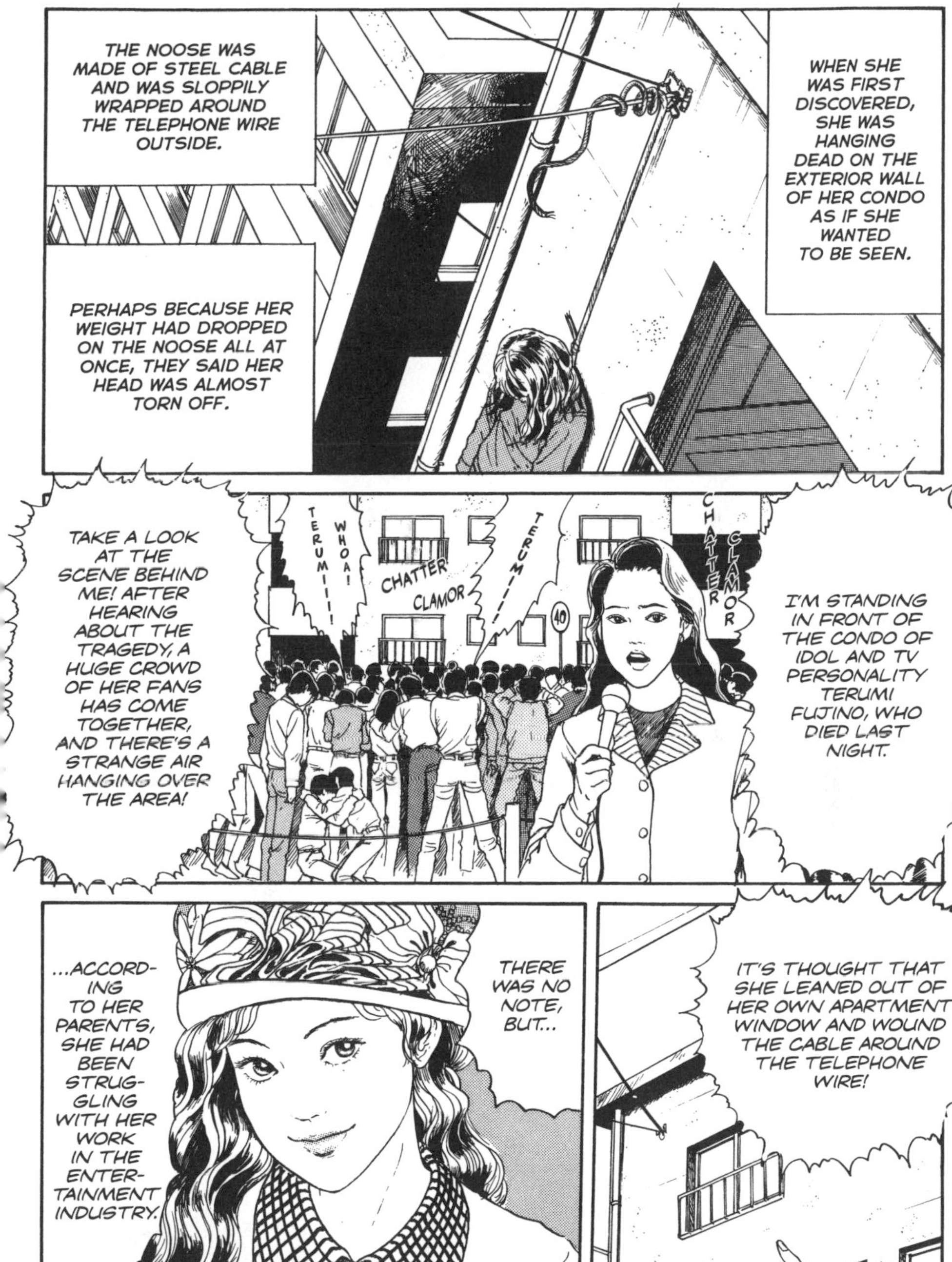
WHEN SHE WAS FIRST DISCOVERED, SHE WAS HANGING DEAD ON THE EXTERIOR WALL OF HER CONDO AS IF SHE WANTED TO BE SEEN.
THE NOOSE WAS MADE OF STEEL CABLE AND WAS SLOPPILY WRAPPED AROUND THE TELEPHONE WIRE OUTSIDE.
PERHAPS BECAUSE HER WEIGHT HAD DROPPED ON THE NOOSE ALL AT ONCE, THEY SAID HER HEAD WAS ALMOST TORN OFF.
I'M STANDING IN FRONT OF THE CONDO OF IDOL AND TV PERSONALITY TERUMI FUJINO, WHO DIED LAST NIGHT.
CHATTER
CLAMOR
TERUMI!!!
CHATTER
CLAMOR
WHOA!
TERUMI!!!
TAKE A LOOK AT THE SCENE BEHIND ME! AFTER HEARING ABOUT THE TRAGEDY, A HUGE CROWD OF HER FANS HAS COME TOGETHER, AND THERE'S A STRANGE AIR HANGING OVER THE AREA!
IT'S THOUGHT THAT SHE LEANED OUT OF HER OWN APARTMENT WINDOW AND WOUND THE CABLE AROUND THE TELEPHONE WIRE!
THERE WAS NO NOTE, BUT...
...ACCORDING TO HER PARENTS, SHE HAD BEEN STRUGGLING WITH HER WORK IN THE ENTERTAINMENT INDUSTRY.

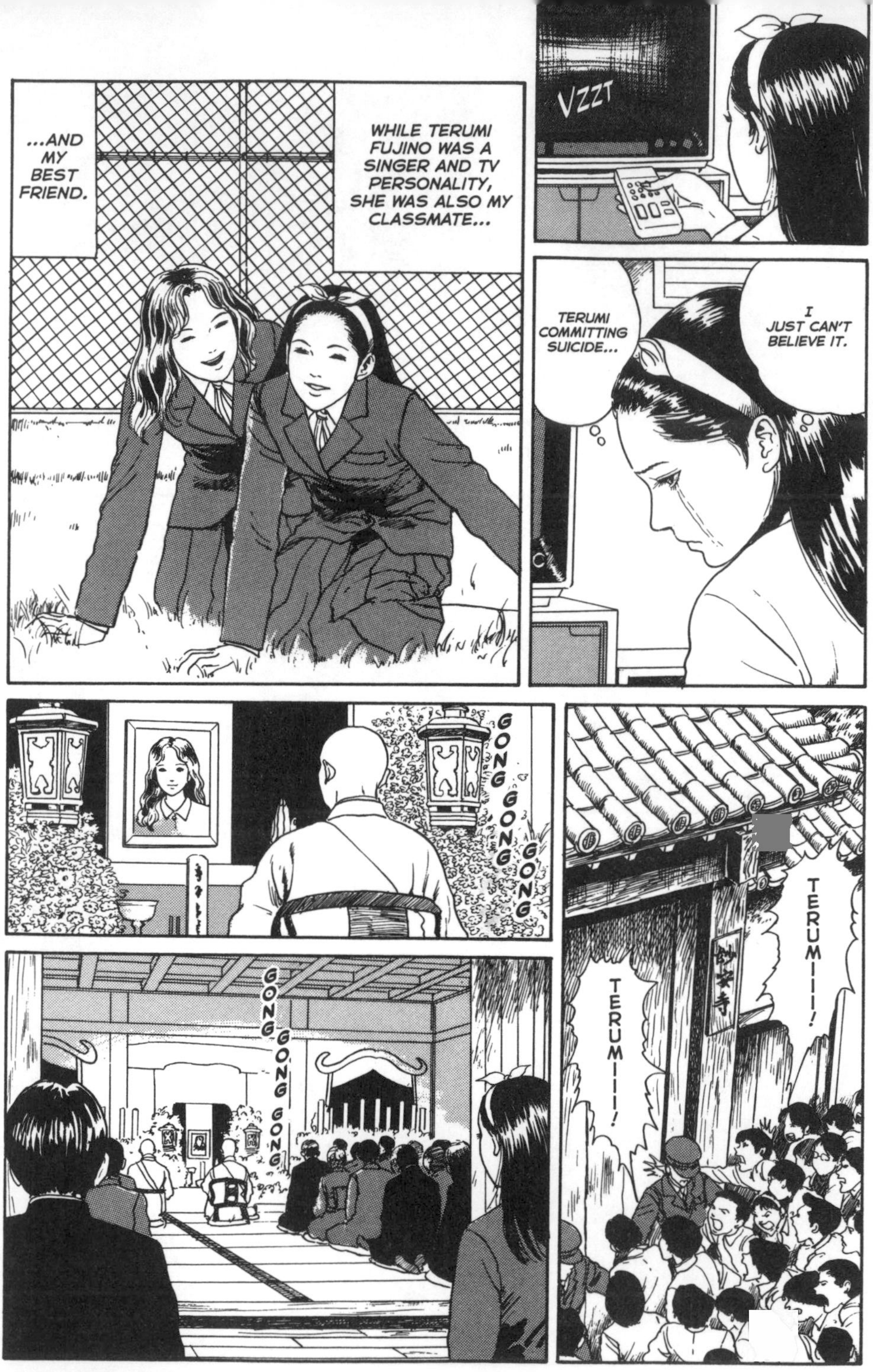
VZZT
I JUST CAN'T BELIEVE IT.
TERUMI COMMITTING SUICIDE...
WHILE TERUMI FUJINO WAS A SINGER AND TV PERSONALITY, SHE WAS ALSO MY CLASSMATE...
...AND MY BEST FRIEND.
TERUMI!!!!
TERUMI!!!!
GONG GONG GONG GONG
GONG GONG GONG

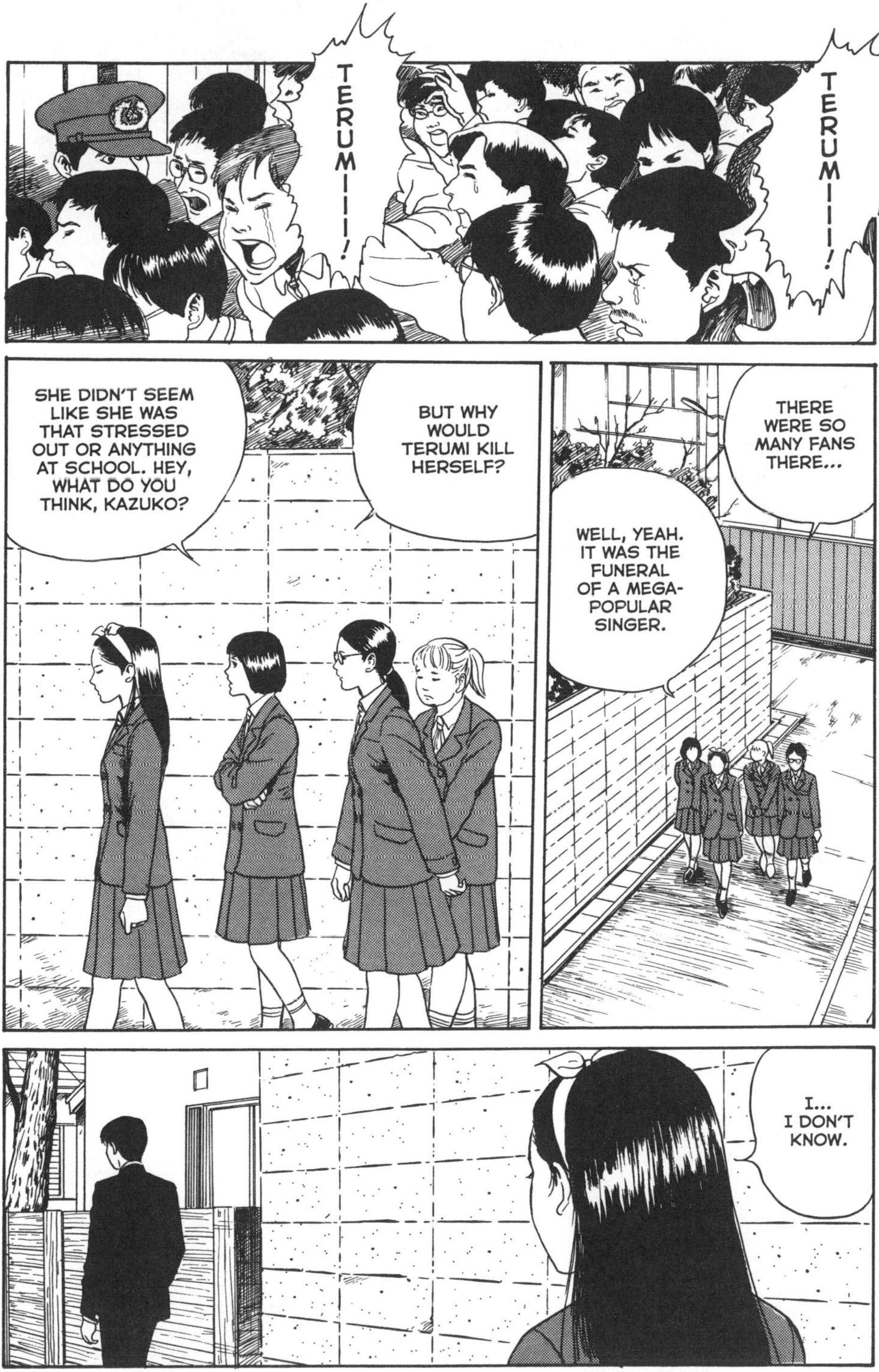
TERUMI!!!
TERUMI!!!
THERE WERE SO MANY FANS THERE...
WELL, YEAH. IT WAS THE FUNERAL OF A MEGA-POPULAR SINGER.
BUT WHY WOULD TERUMI KILL HERSELF?
SHE DIDN'T SEEM LIKE SHE WAS THAT STRESSED OUT OR ANYTHING AT SCHOOL. HEY, WHAT DO YOU THINK, KAZUKO?
I... I DON'T KNOW.

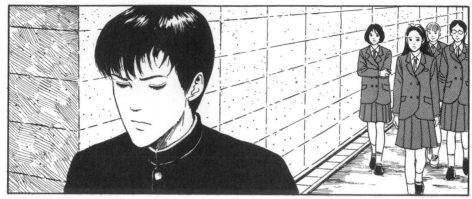

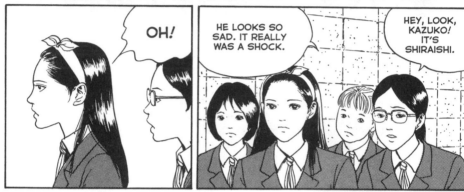

HEY, LOOK, KAZUKO! IT'S SHIRAISHI.
HE LOOKS SO SAD. IT REALLY WAS A SHOCK.
OH!

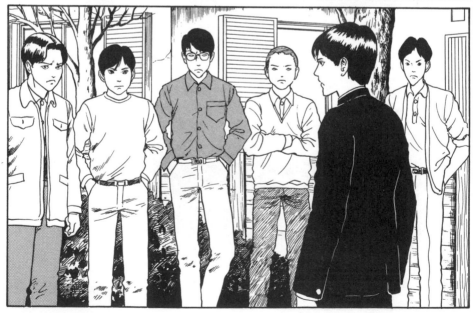

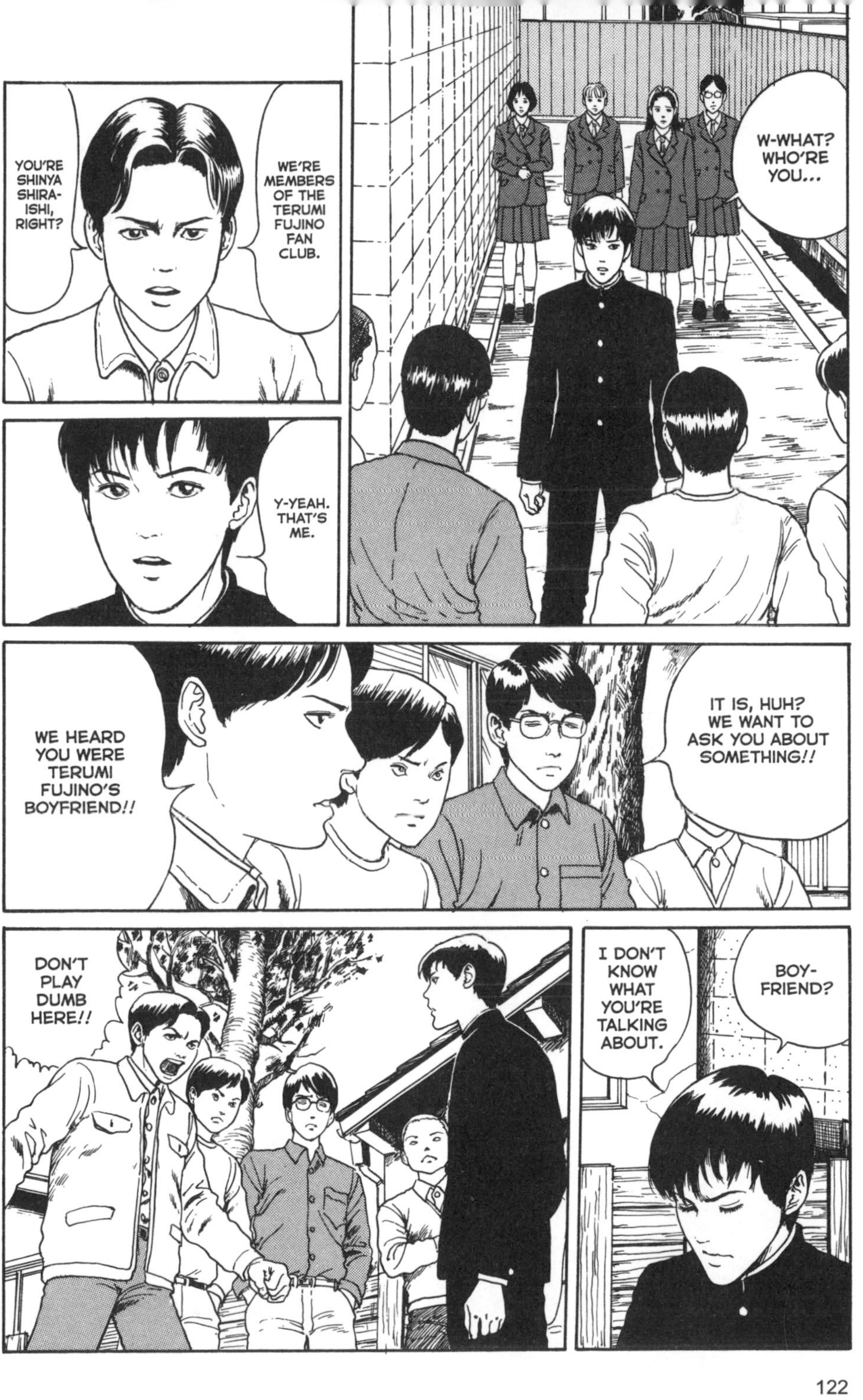
W-WHAT? WHO'RE YOU...
WE'RE MEMBERS OF THE TERUMI FUJINO FAN CLUB.
YOU'RE SHINYA SHIRAISHI, RIGHT?
Y-YEAH. THAT'S ME.
IT IS, HUH? WE WANT TO ASK YOU ABOUT SOMETHING!!
WE HEARD YOU WERE TERUMI FUJINO'S BOYFRIEND!!
BOY-FRIEND?
I DON'T KNOW WHAT YOU'RE TALKING ABOUT.
DON'T PLAY DUMB HERE!!

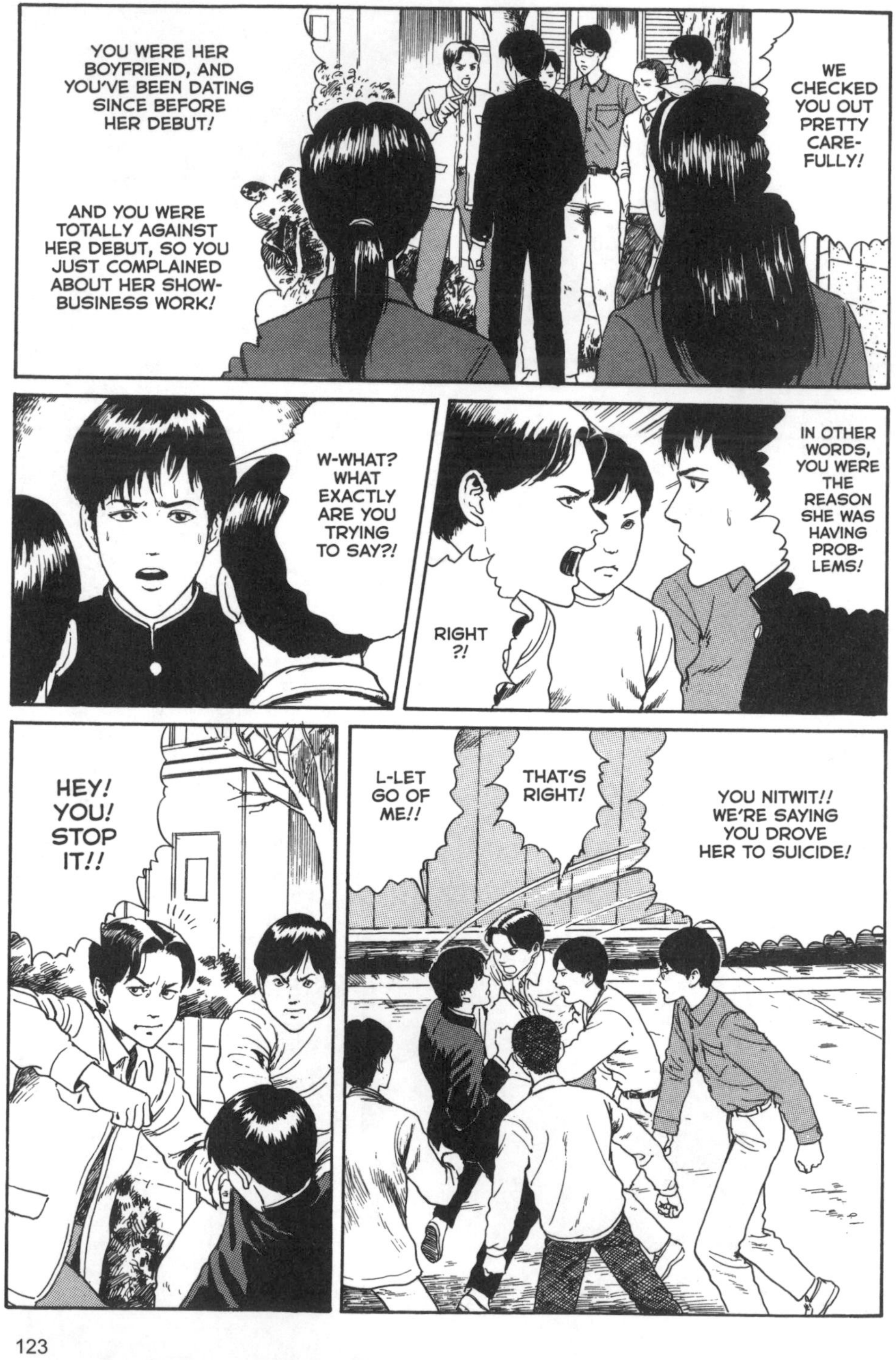
WE CHECKED YOU OUT PRETTY CARE-FULLY!
YOU WERE HER BOYFRIEND, AND YOU'VE BEEN DATING SINCE BEFORE HER DEBUT!
AND YOU WERE TOTALLY AGAINST HER DEBUT, SO YOU JUST COMPLAINED ABOUT HER SHOW-BUSINESS WORK!
IN OTHER WORDS, YOU WERE THE REASON SHE WAS HAVING PROB-LEMS!
RIGHT ?!
W-WHAT? WHAT EXACTLY ARE YOU TRYING TO SAY?!
YOU NITWIT!! WE'RE SAYING YOU DROVE HER TO SUICIDE!
THAT'S RIGHT!
L-LET GO OF ME!!
HEY! YOU! STOP IT!!

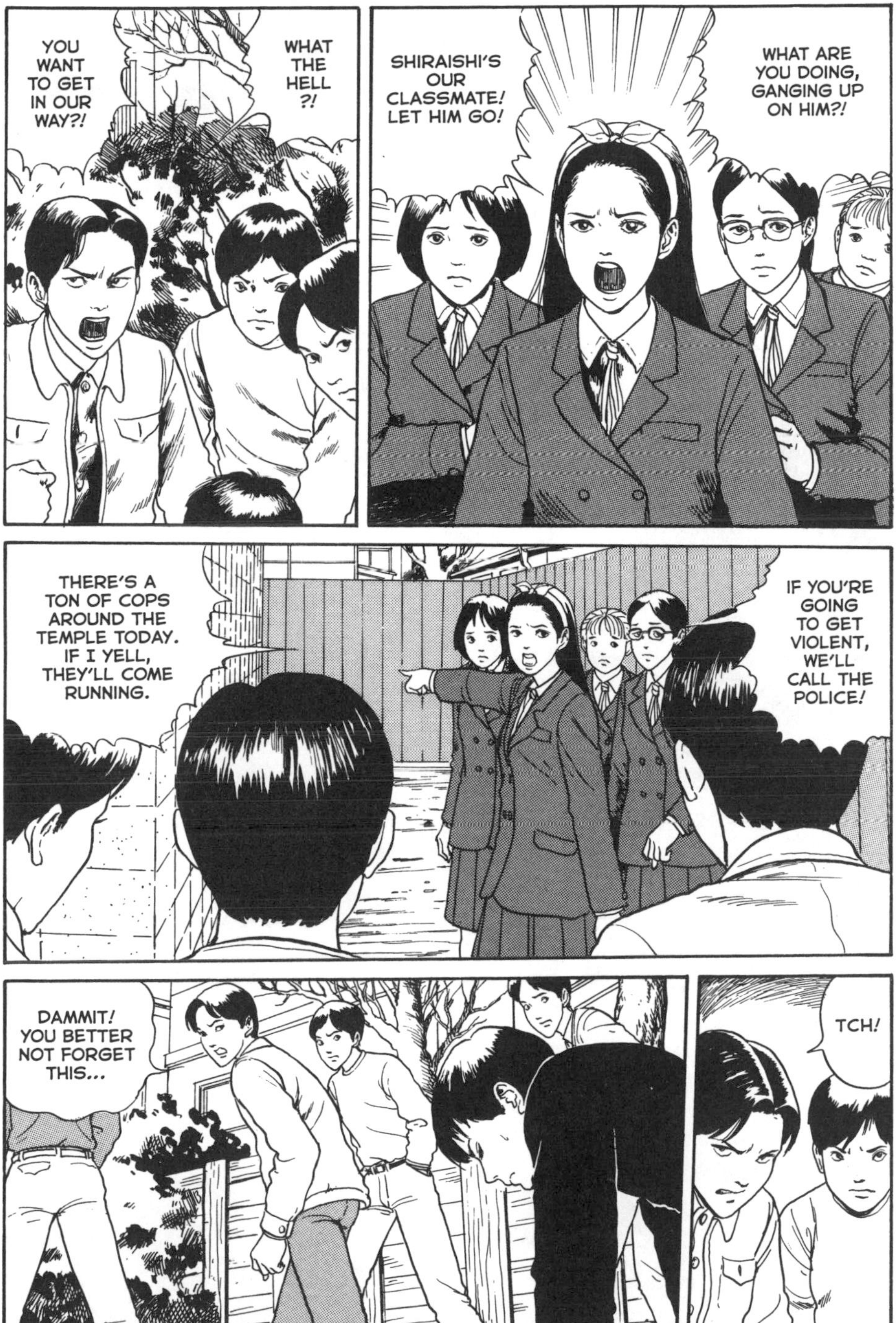
WHAT ARE YOU DOING, GANGING UP ON HIM?!
SHIRAISHI'S OUR CLASSMATE! LET HIM GO!
WHAT THE HELL ?!
YOU WANT TO GET IN OUR WAY?!
IF YOU'RE GOING TO GET VIOLENT, WE'LL CALL THE POLICE!
THERE'S A TON OF COPS AROUND THE TEMPLE TODAY. IF I YELL, THEY'LL COME RUNNING.
TCH!
DAMMIT! YOU BETTER NOT FORGET THIS...

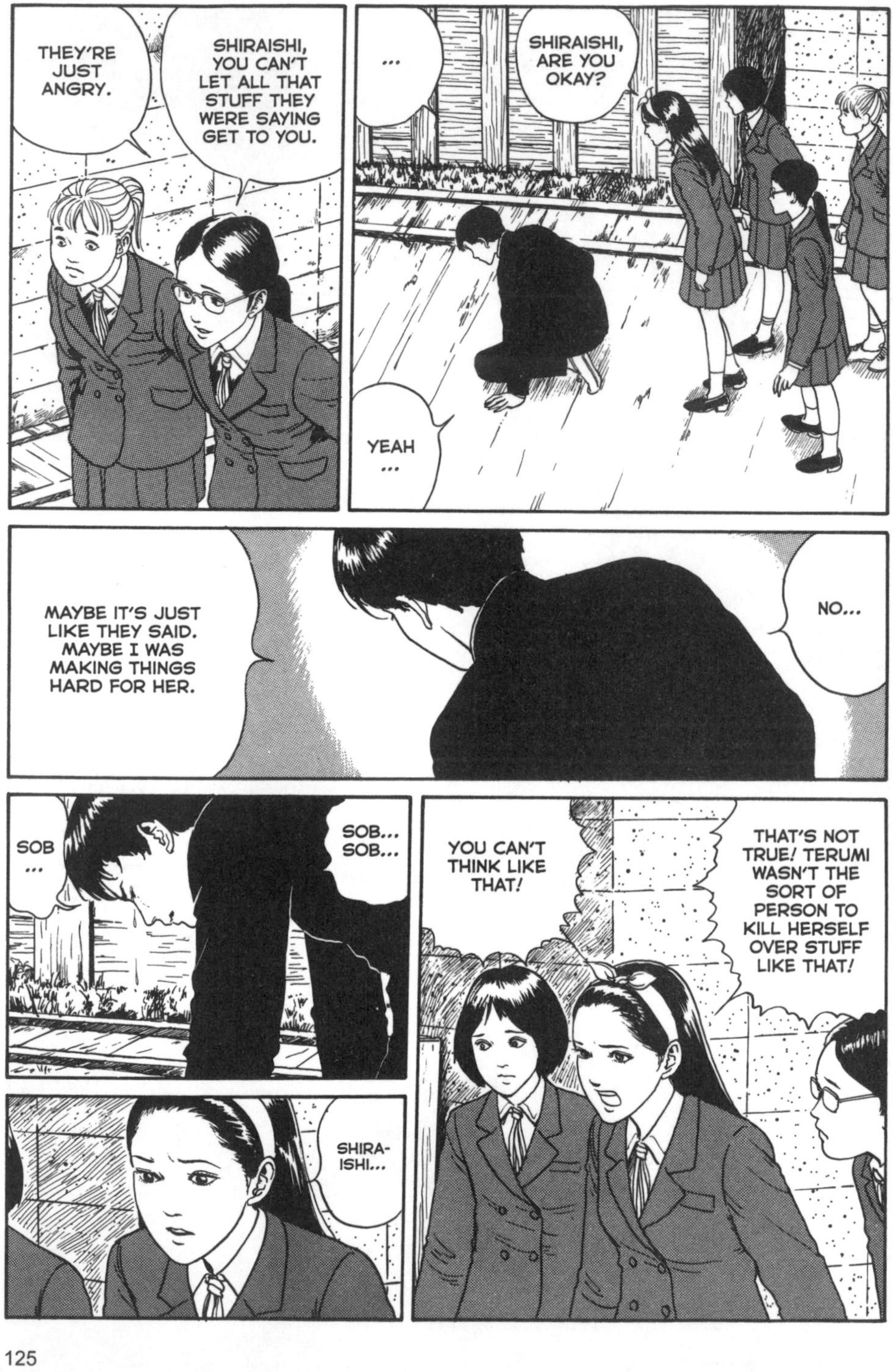
SHIRAISHI, ARE YOU OKAY?
...
YEAH ...
SHIRAISHI, YOU CAN'T LET ALL THAT STUFF THEY WERE SAYING GET TO YOU.
THEY'RE JUST ANGRY.
NO...
MAYBE IT'S JUST LIKE THEY SAID. MAYBE I WAS MAKING THINGS HARD FOR HER.
THAT'S NOT TRUE! TERUMI WASN'T THE SORT OF PERSON TO KILL HERSELF OVER STUFF LIKE THAT!
YOU CAN'T THINK LIKE THAT!
SOB... SOB...
SOB ...
SHIRA-ISHI...

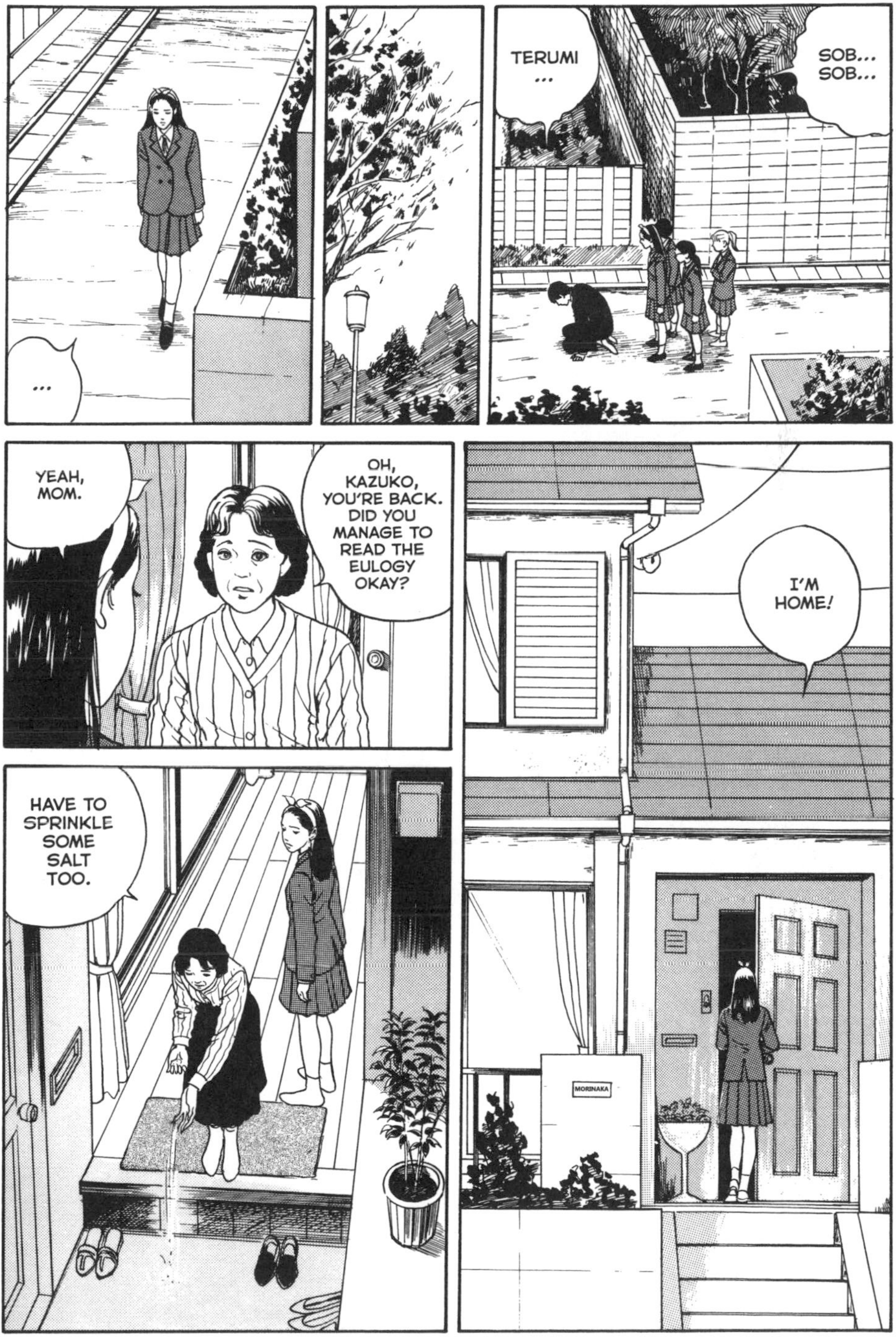
SOB... SOB...
TERUMI ...
...
I'M HOME!
OH, KAZUKO, YOU'RE BACK. DID YOU MANAGE TO READ THE EULOGY OKAY?
YEAH, MOM.
HAVE TO SPRINKLE SOME SALT TOO.
MORINAKA

Salt is sprinkled in the entryway after returning home from a funeral so that the spirit doesn't follow you inside.

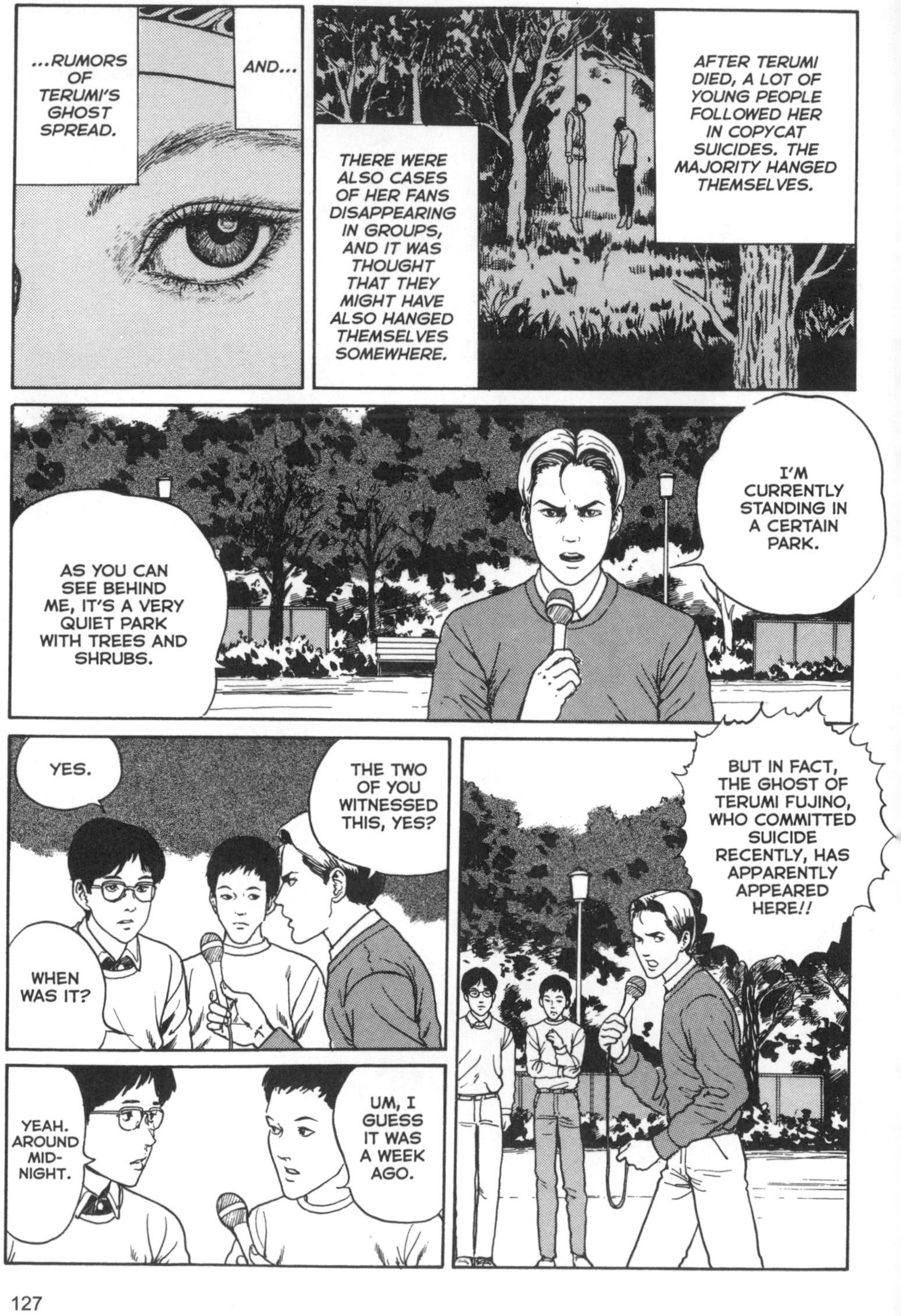
AFTER TERUMI DIED, A LOT OF YOUNG PEOPLE FOLLOWED HER IN COPYCAT SUICIDES. THE MAJORITY HANGED THEMSELVES.
THERE WERE ALSO CASES OF HER FANS DISAPPEARING IN GROUPS, AND IT WAS THOUGHT THAT THEY MIGHT HAVE ALSO HANGED THEMSELVES SOMEWHERE.
AND...
...RUMORS OF TERUMI'S GHOST SPREAD.
I'M CURRENTLY STANDING IN A CERTAIN PARK.
AS YOU CAN SEE BEHIND ME, IT'S A VERY QUIET PARK WITH TREES AND SHRUBS.
BUT IN FACT, THE GHOST OF TERUMI FUJINO, WHO COMMITTED SUICIDE RECENTLY, HAS APPARENTLY APPEARED HERE!!
THE TWO OF YOU WITNESSED THIS, YES?
YES.
WHEN WAS IT?
UM, I GUESS IT WAS A WEEK AGO.
YEAH. AROUND MID-NIGHT.

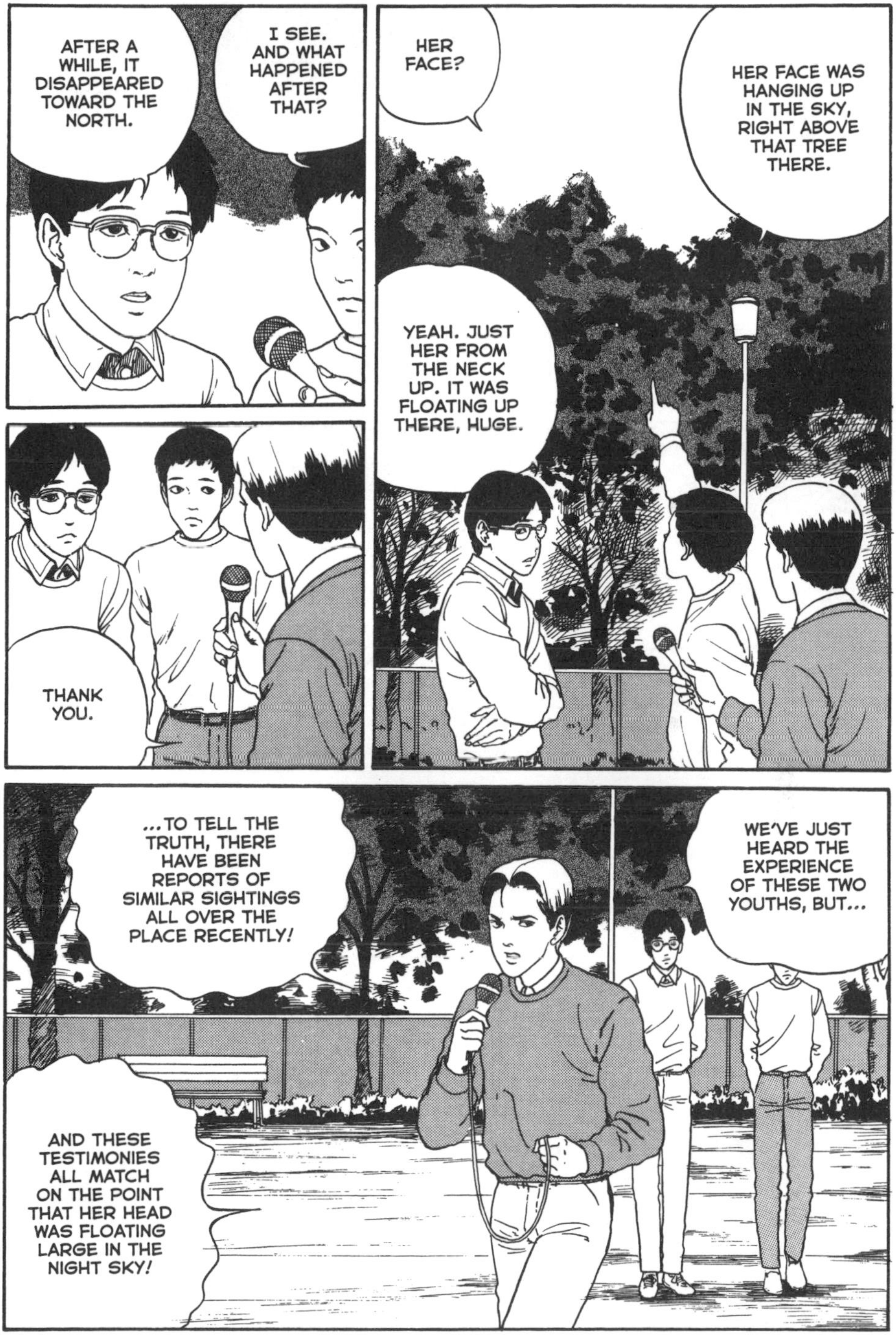
HER FACE WAS HANGING UP IN THE SKY, RIGHT ABOVE THAT TREE THERE.
HER FACE?
YEAH. JUST HER FROM THE NECK UP. IT WAS FLOATING UP THERE, HUGE.
I SEE. AND WHAT HAPPENED AFTER THAT?
AFTER A WHILE, IT DISAPPEARED TOWARD THE NORTH.
THANK YOU.
WE'VE JUST HEARD THE EXPERIENCE OF THESE TWO YOUTHS, BUT...
...TO TELL THE TRUTH, THERE HAVE BEEN REPORTS OF SIMILAR SIGHTINGS ALL OVER THE PLACE RECENTLY!
AND THESE TESTIMONIES ALL MATCH ON THE POINT THAT HER HEAD WAS FLOATING LARGE IN THE NIGHT SKY!

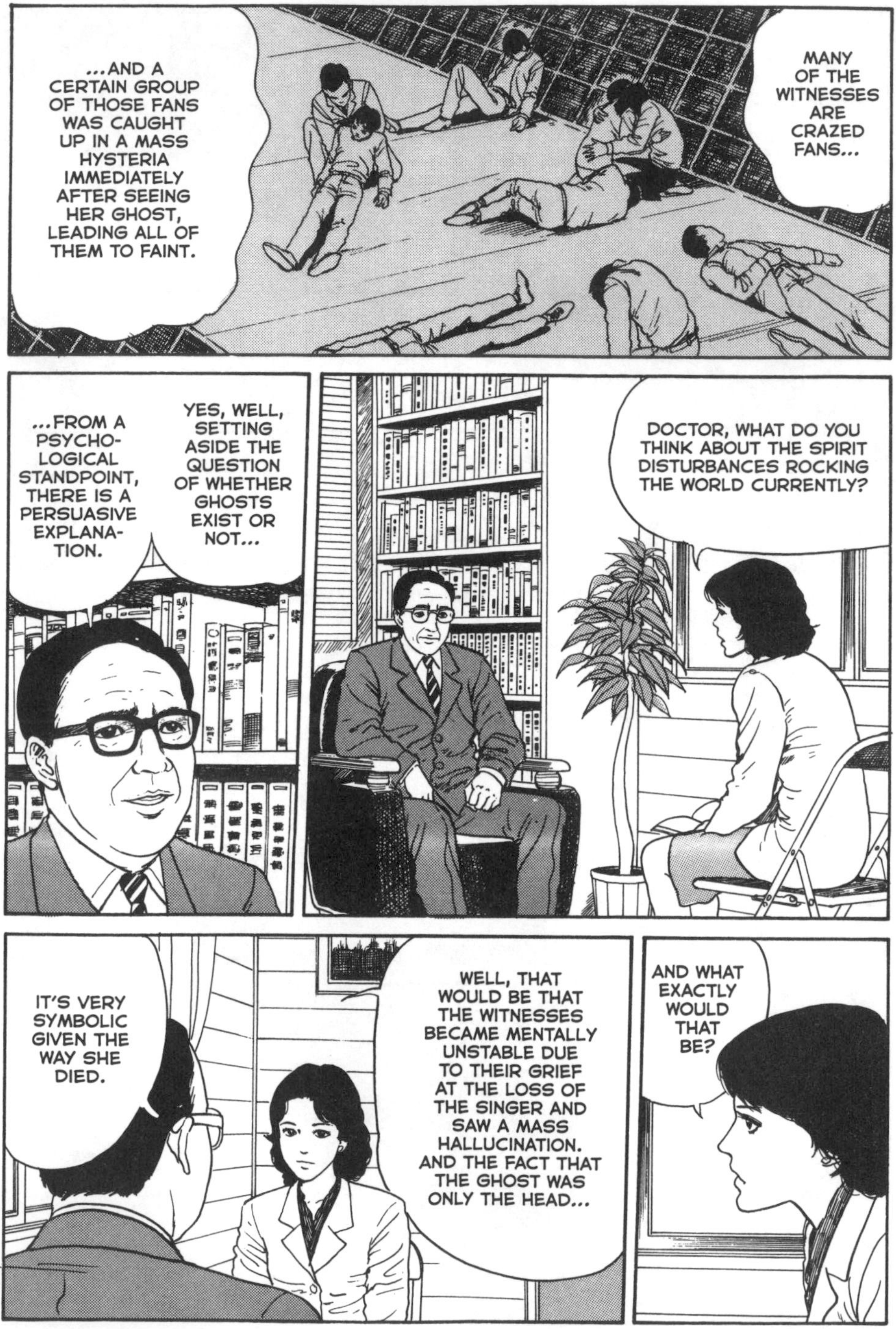
MANY OF THE WITNESSES ARE CRAZED FANS...
...AND A CERTAIN GROUP OF THOSE FANS WAS CAUGHT UP IN A MASS HYSTERIA IMMEDIATELY AFTER SEEING HER GHOST, LEADING ALL OF THEM TO FAINT.
DOCTOR, WHAT DO YOU THINK ABOUT THE SPIRIT DISTURBANCES ROCKING THE WORLD CURRENTLY?
YES, WELL, SETTING ASIDE THE QUESTION OF WHETHER GHOSTS EXIST OR NOT...
...FROM A PSYCHO-LOGICAL STANDPOINT, THERE IS A PERSUASIVE EXPLANA-TION.
AND WHAT EXACTLY WOULD THAT BE?
WELL, THAT WOULD BE THAT THE WITNESSES BECAME MENTALLY UNSTABLE DUE TO THEIR GRIEF AT THE LOSS OF THE SINGER AND SAW A MASS HALLUCINATION. AND THE FACT THAT THE GHOST WAS ONLY THE HEAD...
IT'S VERY SYMBOLIC GIVEN THE WAY SHE DIED.

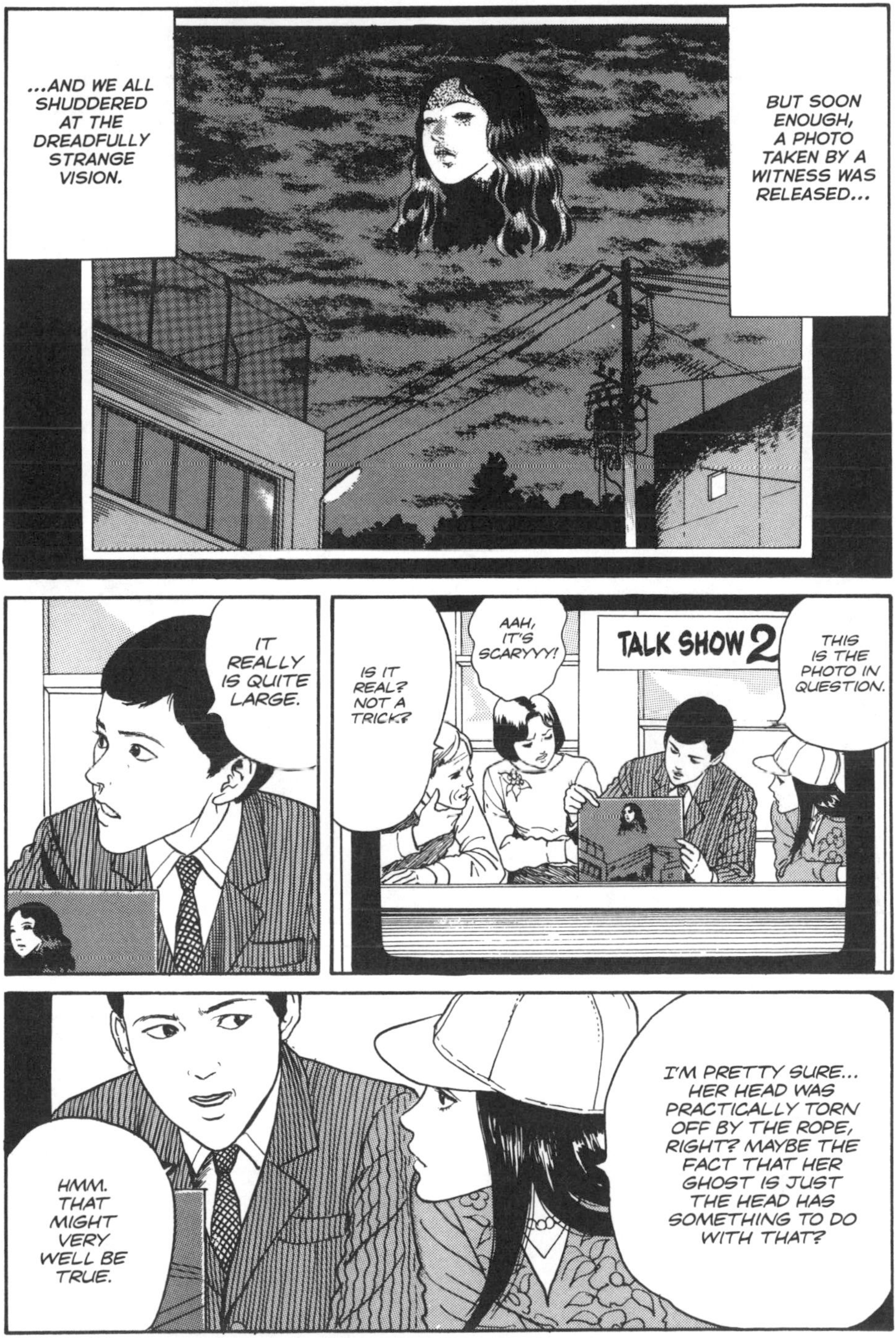
BUT SOON ENOUGH, A PHOTO TAKEN BY A WITNESS WAS RELEASED...
...AND WE ALL SHUDDERED AT THE DREADFULLY STRANGE VISION.
THIS IS THE PHOTO IN QUESTION.
TALK SHOW 2
AAH, IT'S SCARYYY!
IS IT REAL? NOT A TRICK?
IT REALLY IS QUITE LARGE.
I'M PRETTY SURE... HER HEAD WAS PRACTICALLY TORN OFF BY THE ROPE, RIGHT? MAYBE THE FACT THAT HER GHOST IS JUST THE HEAD HAS SOMETHING TO DO WITH THAT?
HMM. THAT MIGHT VERY WELL BE TRUE.

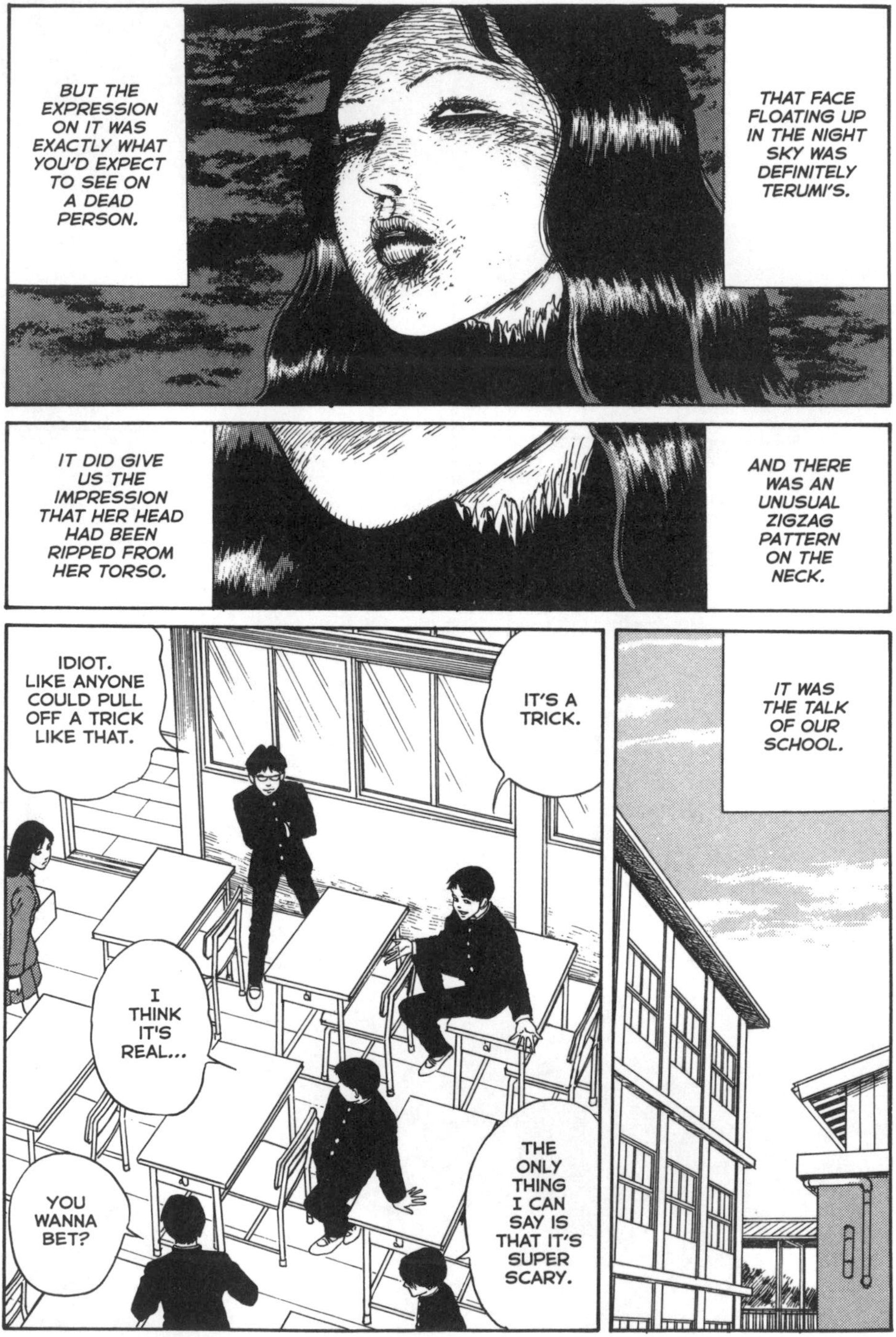
THAT FACE FLOATING UP IN THE NIGHT SKY WAS DEFINITELY TERUMI'S.
BUT THE EXPRESSION ON IT WAS EXACTLY WHAT YOU'D EXPECT TO SEE ON A DEAD PERSON.
AND THERE WAS AN UNUSUAL ZIGZAG PATTERN ON THE NECK.
IT DID GIVE US THE IMPRESSION THAT HER HEAD HAD BEEN RIPPED FROM HER TORSO.
IT WAS THE TALK OF OUR SCHOOL.
IT'S A TRICK.
IDIOT. LIKE ANYONE COULD PULL OFF A TRICK LIKE THAT.
I THINK IT'S REAL...
THE ONLY THING I CAN SAY IS THAT IT'S SUPER SCARY.
YOU WANNA BET?

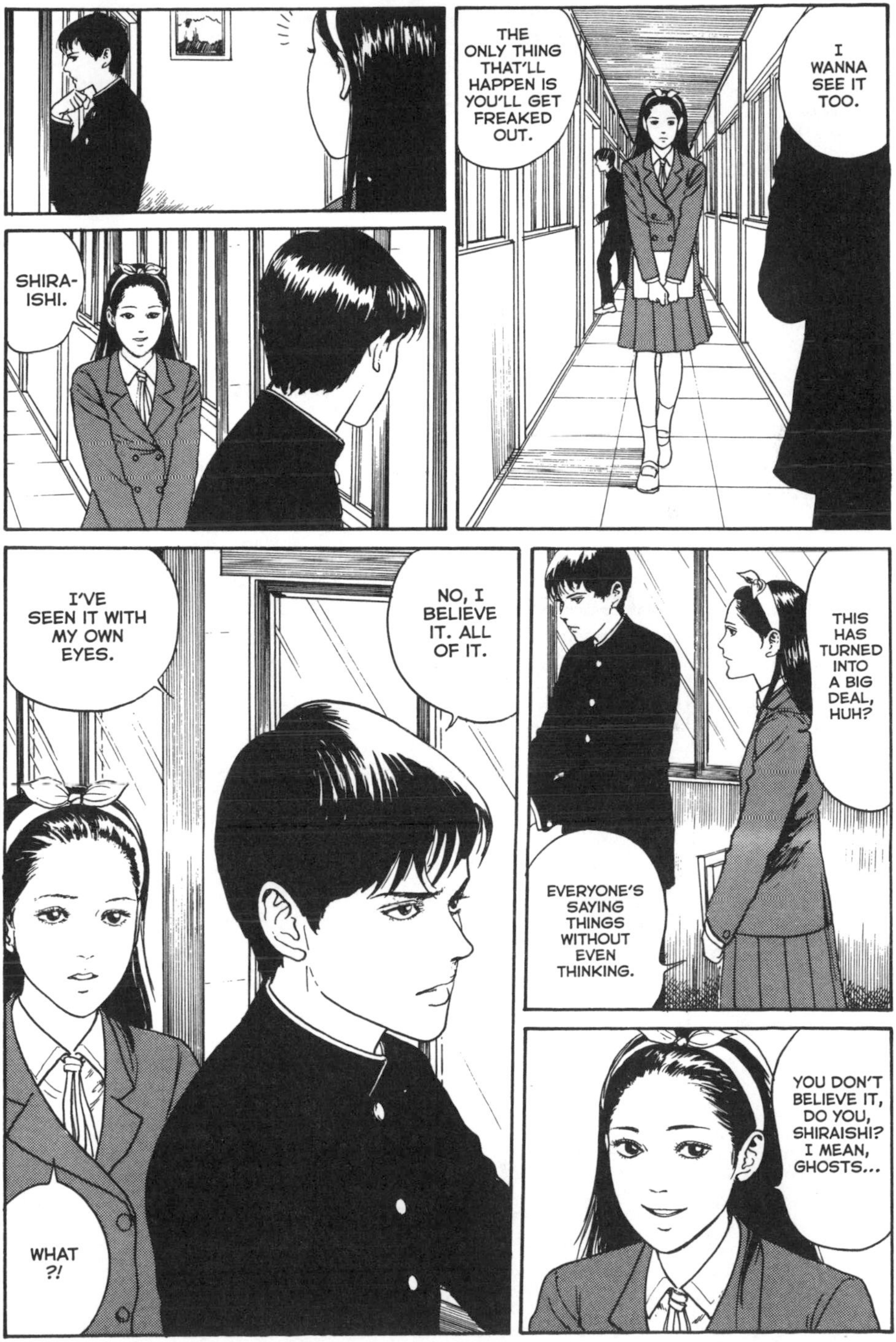
I WANNA SEE IT TOO.
THE ONLY THING THAT'LL HAPPEN IS YOU'LL GET FREAKED OUT.
SHIRA-ISHI.
THIS HAS TURNED INTO A BIG DEAL, HUH?
EVERYONE'S SAYING THINGS WITHOUT EVEN THINKING.
YOU DON'T BELIEVE IT, DO YOU, SHIRAISHI? I MEAN, GHOSTS...
NO, I BELIEVE IT. ALL OF IT.
I'VE SEEN IT WITH MY OWN EYES.
WHAT ?!

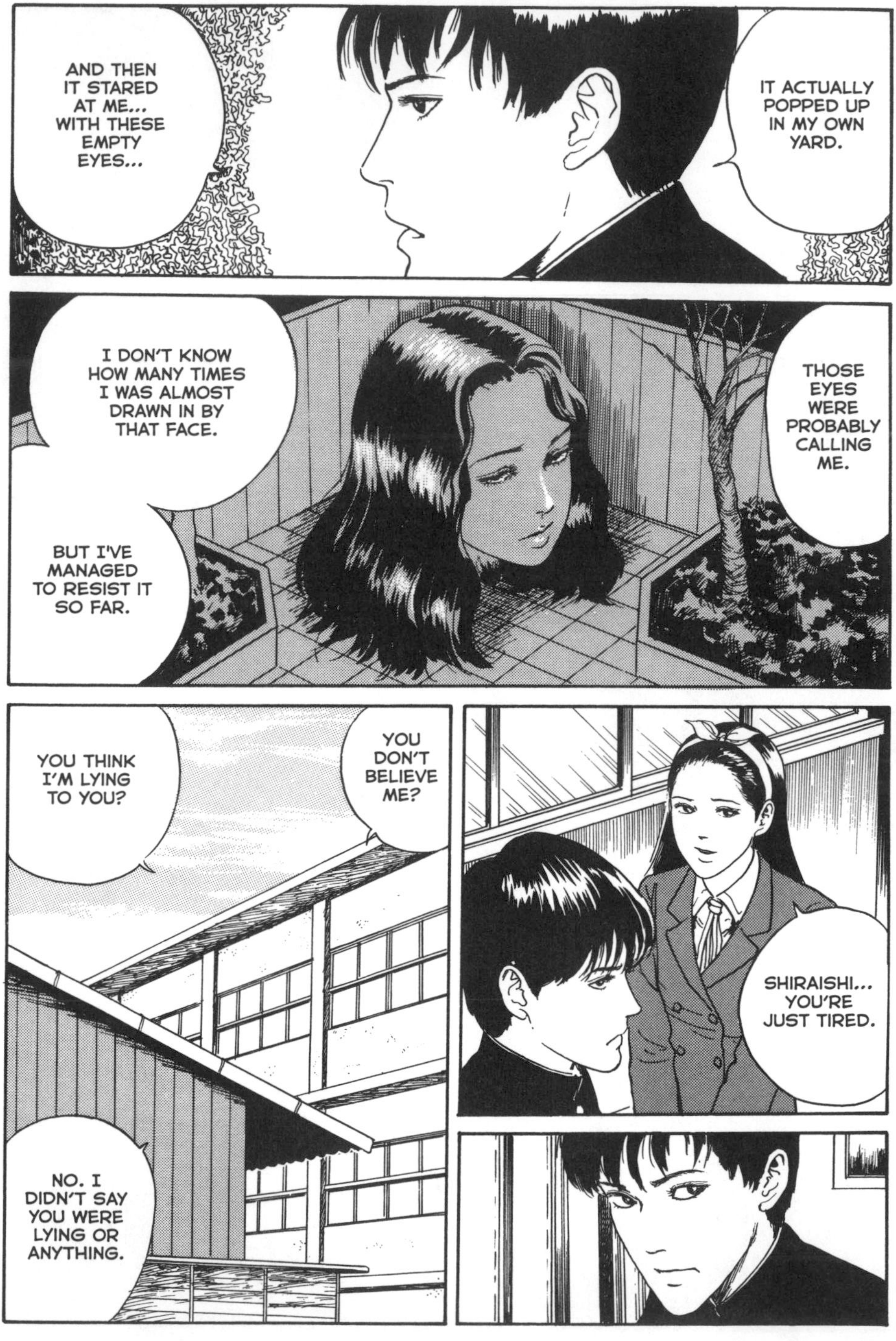
IT ACTUALLY POPPED UP IN MY OWN YARD.
AND THEN IT STARED AT ME... WITH THESE EMPTY EYES...
THOSE EYES WERE PROBABLY CALLING ME.
I DON'T KNOW HOW MANY TIMES I WAS ALMOST DRAWN IN BY THAT FACE.
BUT I'VE MANAGED TO RESIST IT SO FAR.
SHIRAISHI... YOU'RE JUST TIRED.
YOU DON'T BELIEVE ME?
YOU THINK I'M LYING TO YOU?
NO. I DIDN'T SAY YOU WERE LYING OR ANYTHING.

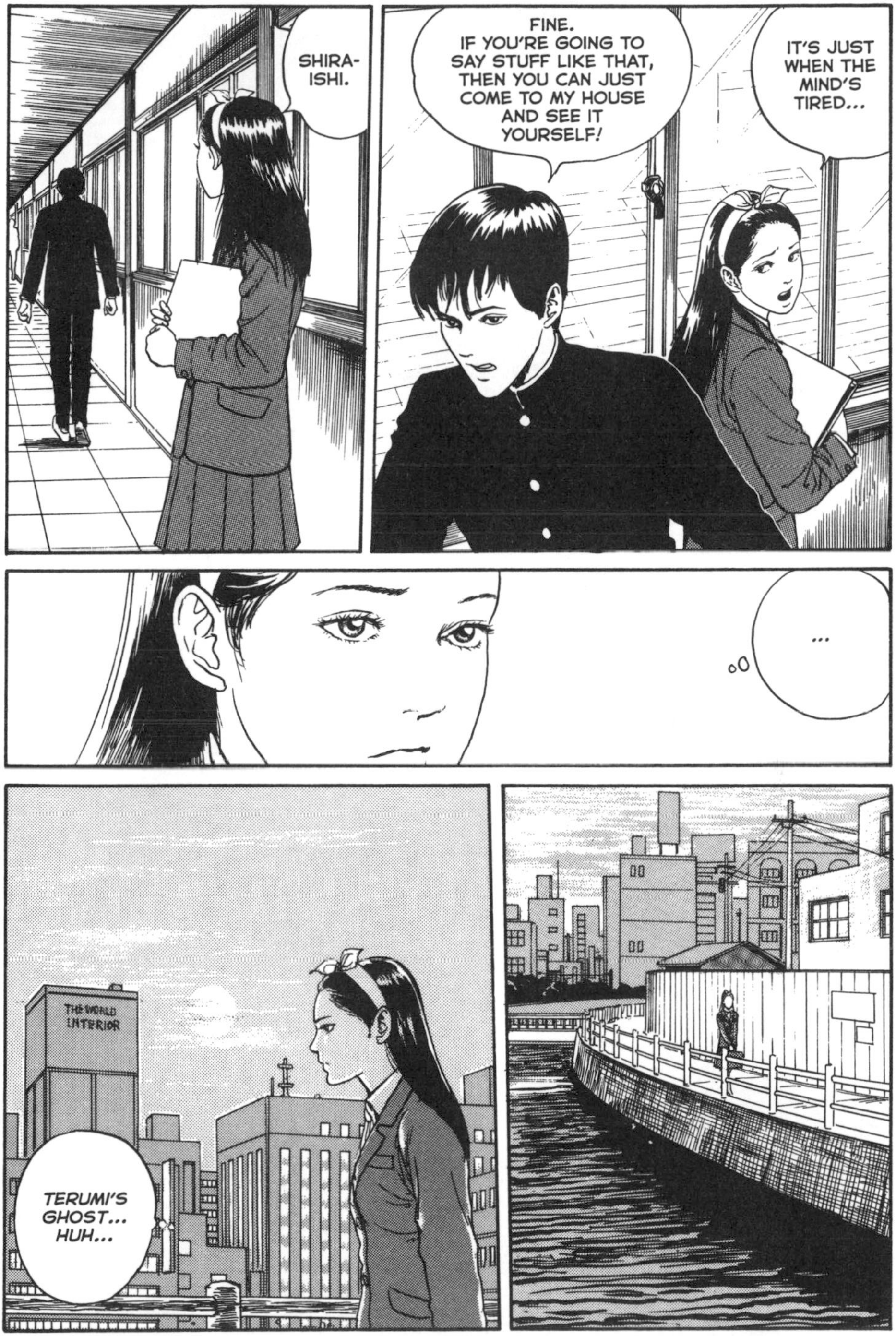
IT'S JUST WHEN THE MIND'S TIRED...
FINE. IF YOU'RE GOING TO SAY STUFF LIKE THAT, THEN YOU CAN JUST COME TO MY HOUSE AND SEE IT YOURSELF!
SHIRA-ISHI.
...
THE WORLD INTERIOR
TERUMI'S GHOST... HUH...

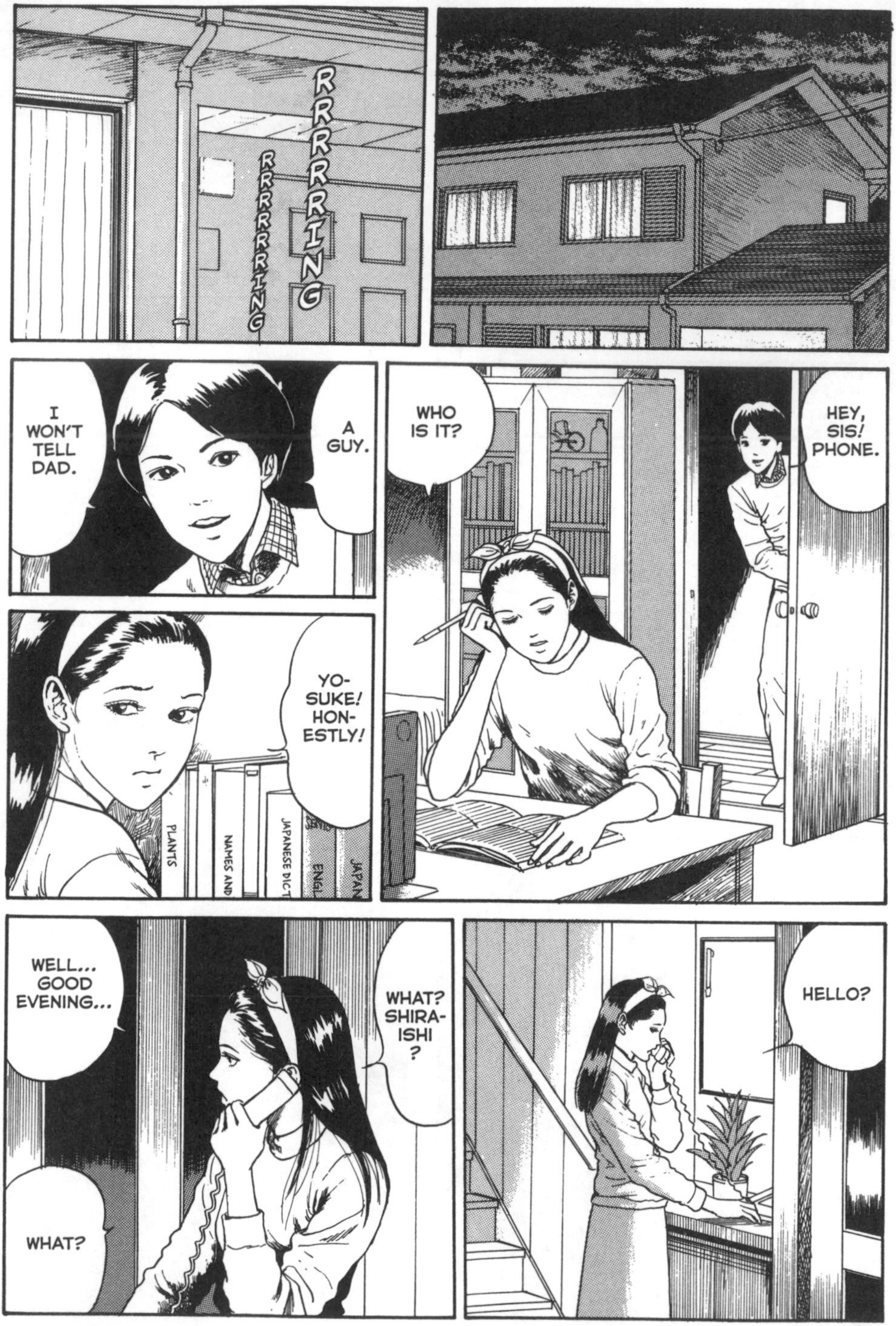
RRRRING
RRRRRRING
HEY, SIS! PHONE.
WHO IS IT?
A GUY.
I WON'T TELL DAD.
YO-SUKE! HON-ESTLY!
JAPANESE DICT
NAMES AND
PLANTS
HELLO?
WHAT? SHIRA-ISHI?
WELL... GOOD EVENING...
WHAT?

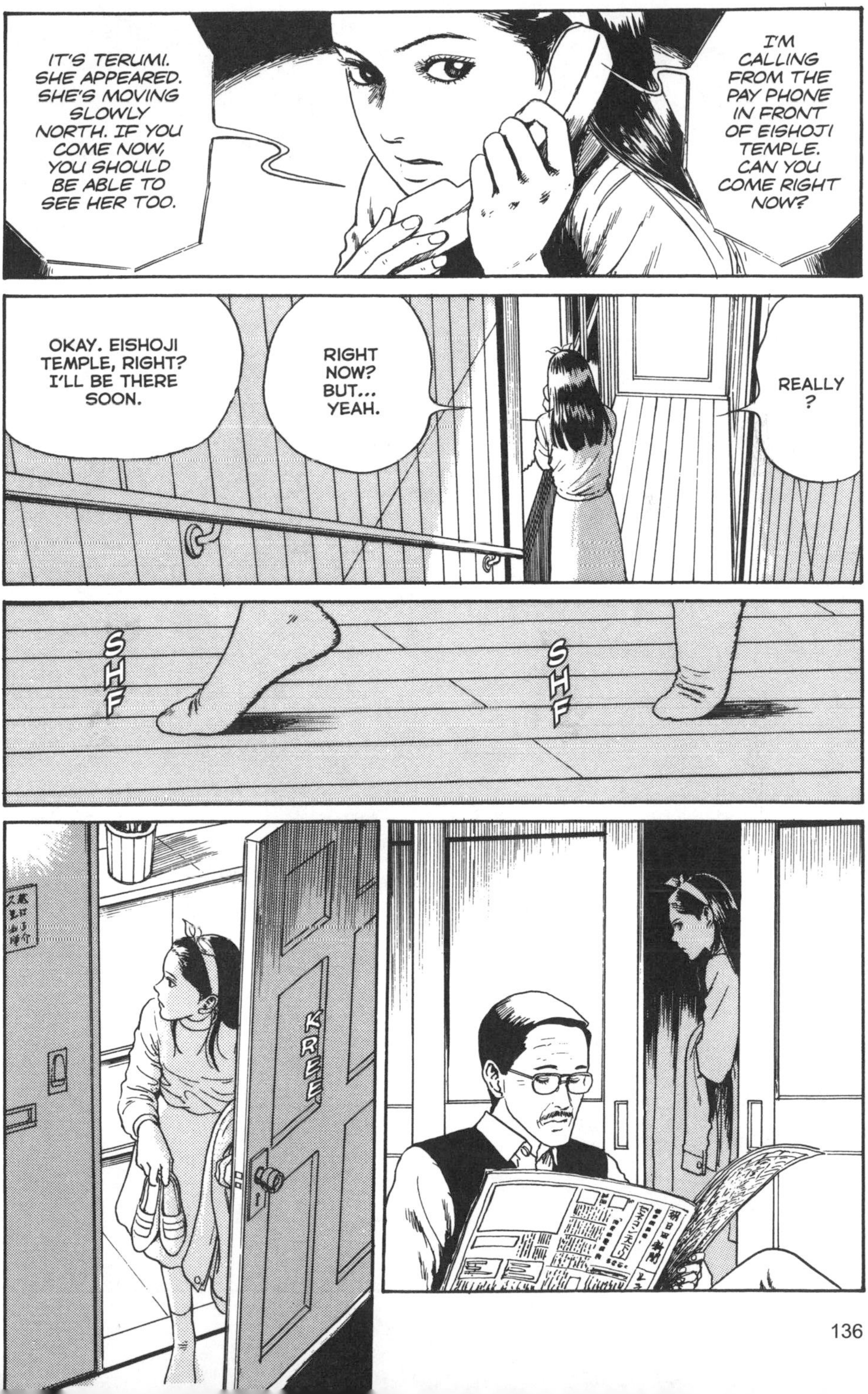
I'M CALLING FROM THE PAY PHONE IN FRONT OF EISHOJI TEMPLE. CAN YOU COME RIGHT NOW?
IT'S TERUMI. SHE APPEARED. SHE'S MOVING SLOWLY NORTH. IF YOU COME NOW, YOU SHOULD BE ABLE TO SEE HER TOO.
REALLY?
RIGHT NOW? BUT... YEAH.
OKAY. EISHOJI TEMPLE, RIGHT? I'LL BE THERE SOON.
SHF
SHF
KREE

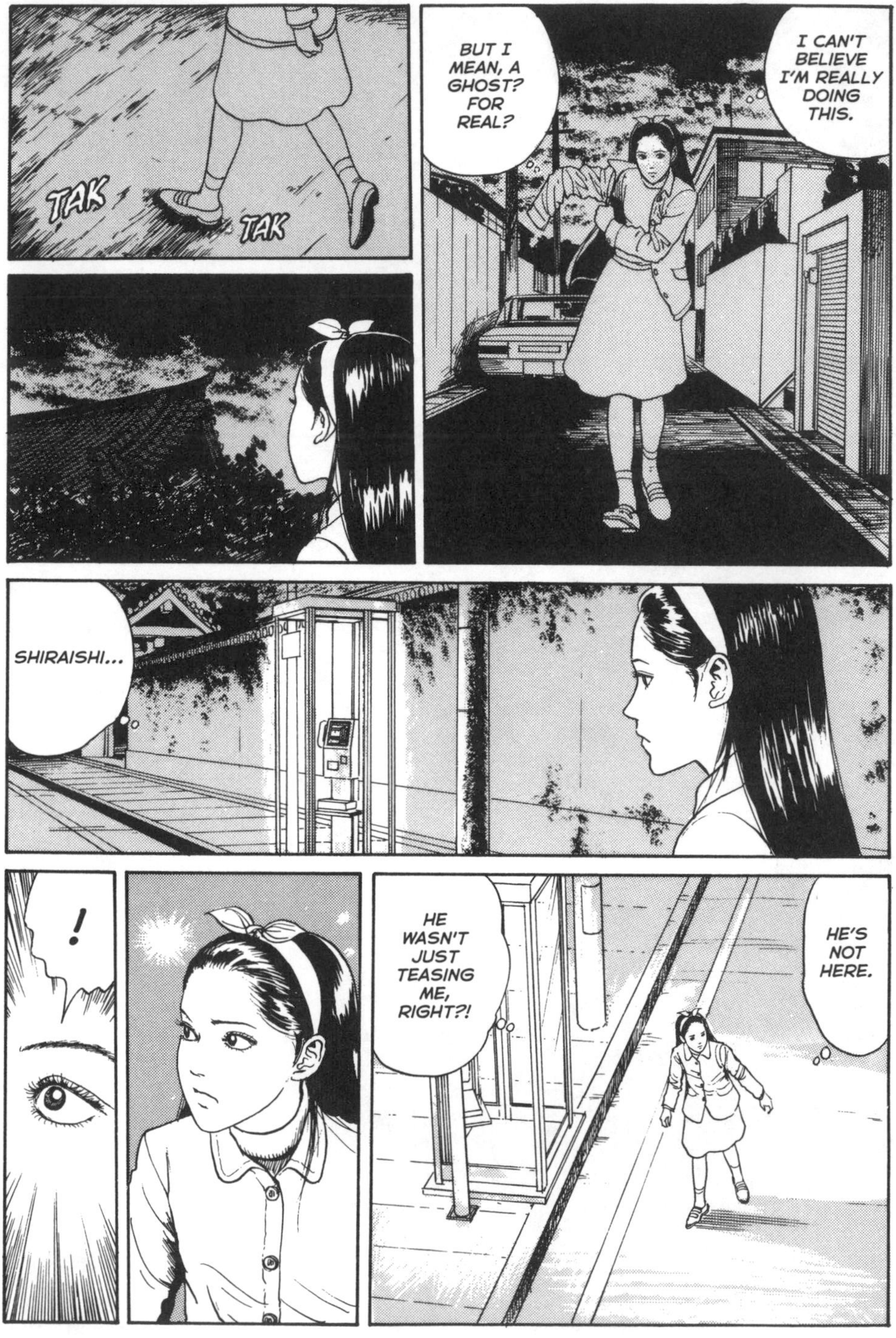
I CAN'T BELIEVE I'M REALLY DOING THIS.
BUT I MEAN, A GHOST? FOR REAL?
TAK
TAK
SHIRAISHI...
HE'S NOT HERE.
HE WASN'T JUST TEASING ME, RIGHT?!
!

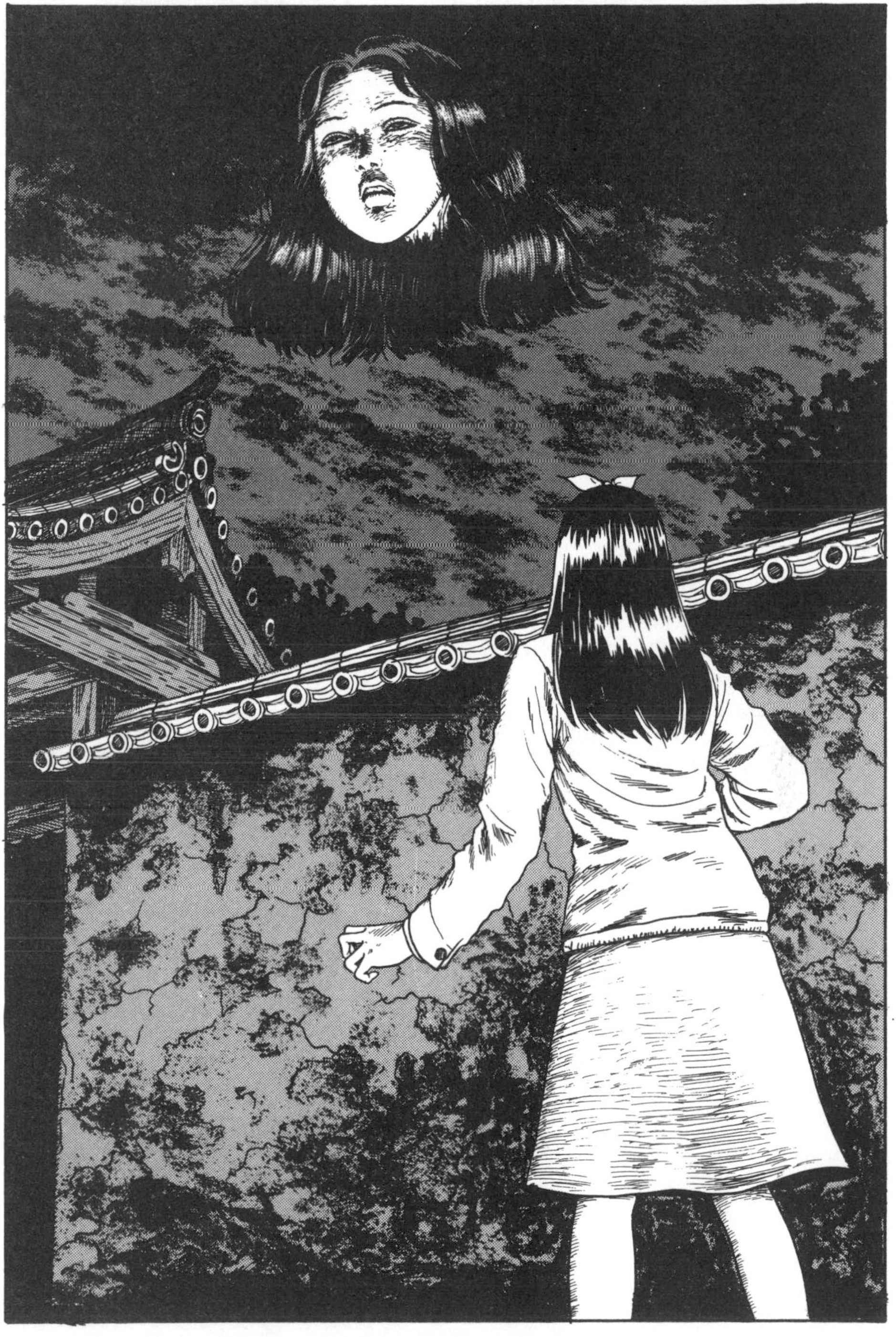

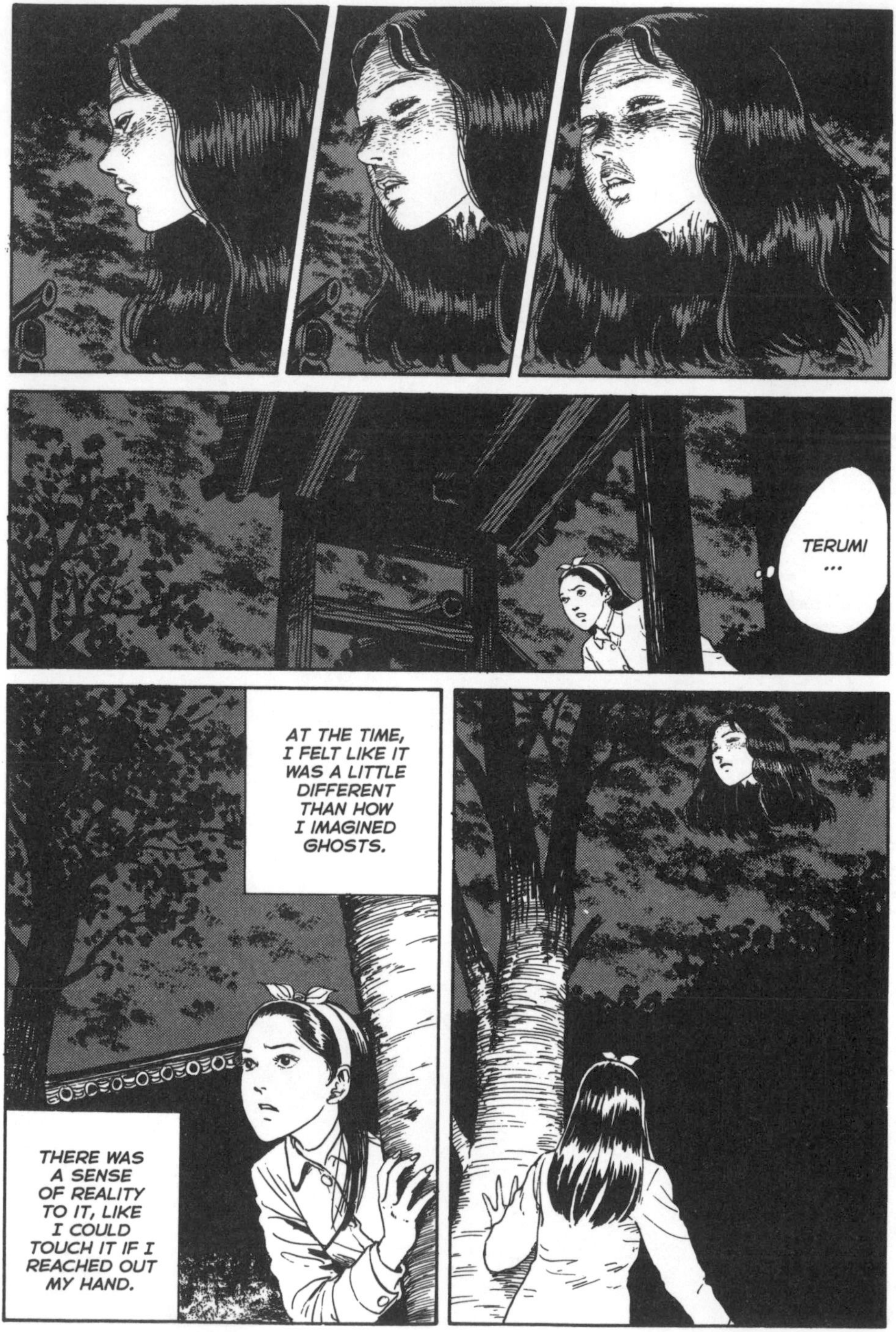
TERUMI ...
AT THE TIME, I FELT LIKE IT WAS A LITTLE DIFFERENT THAN HOW I IMAGINED GHOSTS.
THERE WAS A SENSE OF REALITY TO IT, LIKE I COULD TOUCH IT IF I REACHED OUT MY HAND.

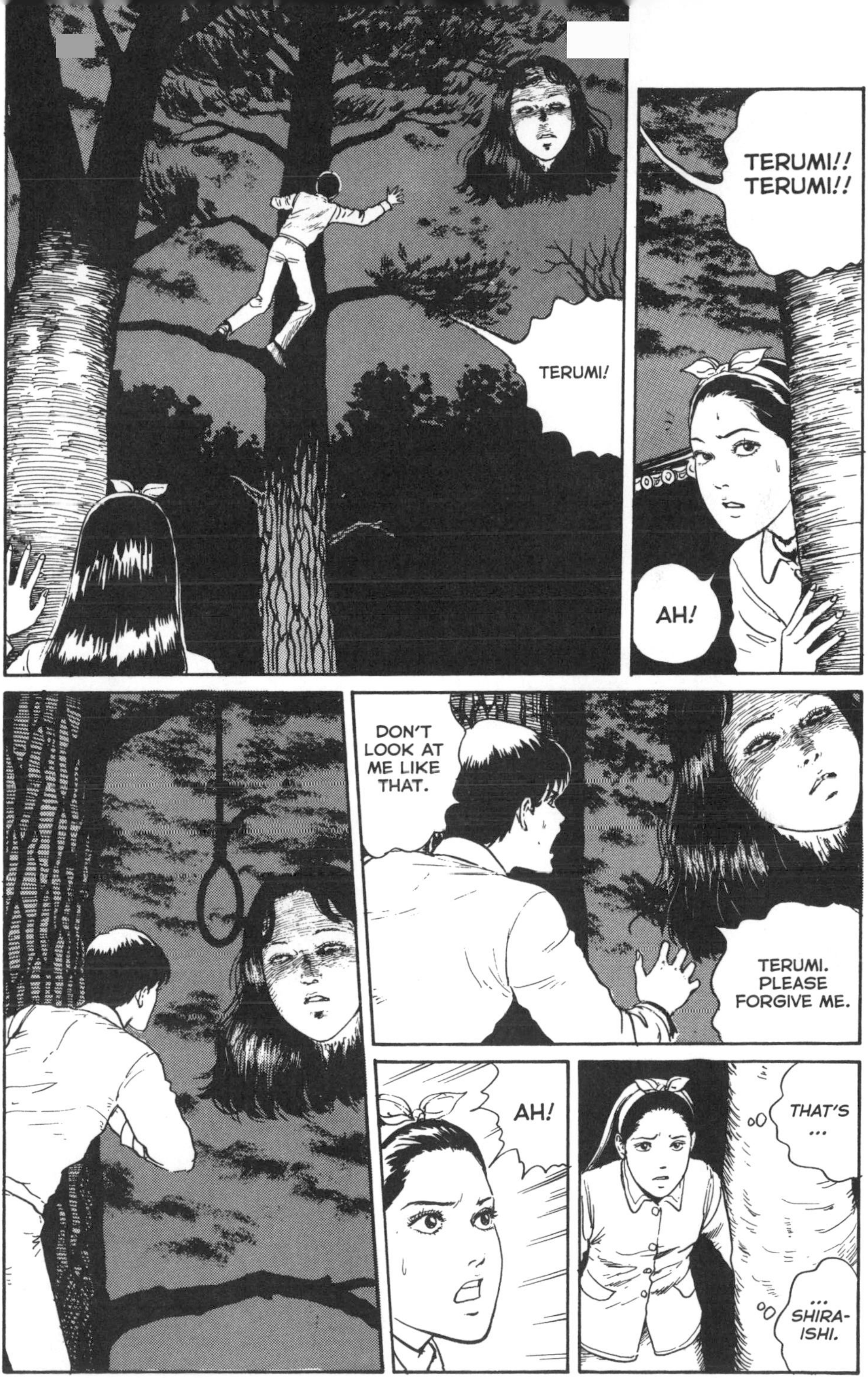

TERUMI!! TERUMI!!
AH!
TERUMI!
DON'T LOOK AT ME LIKE THAT.
TERUMI. PLEASE FORGIVE ME.
THAT'S ...
... SHIRA-ISHI.
AH!

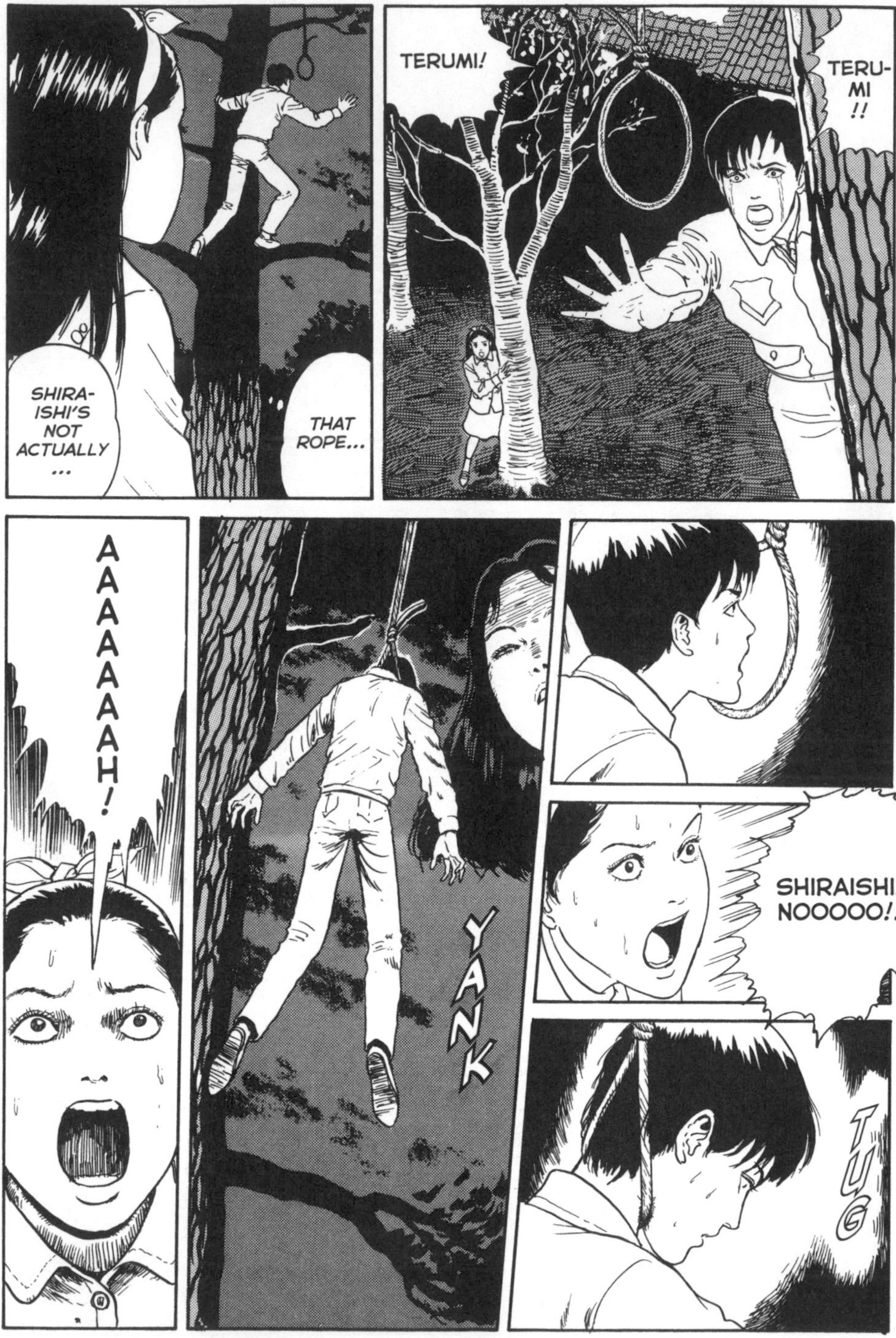
TERU-MI!!
TERUMI!
THAT ROPE...
SHIRA-ISHI'S NOT ACTUALLY ...
SHIRAISHI! NOOOOO!!
TUG
YANK
AAAAAAAAAH!

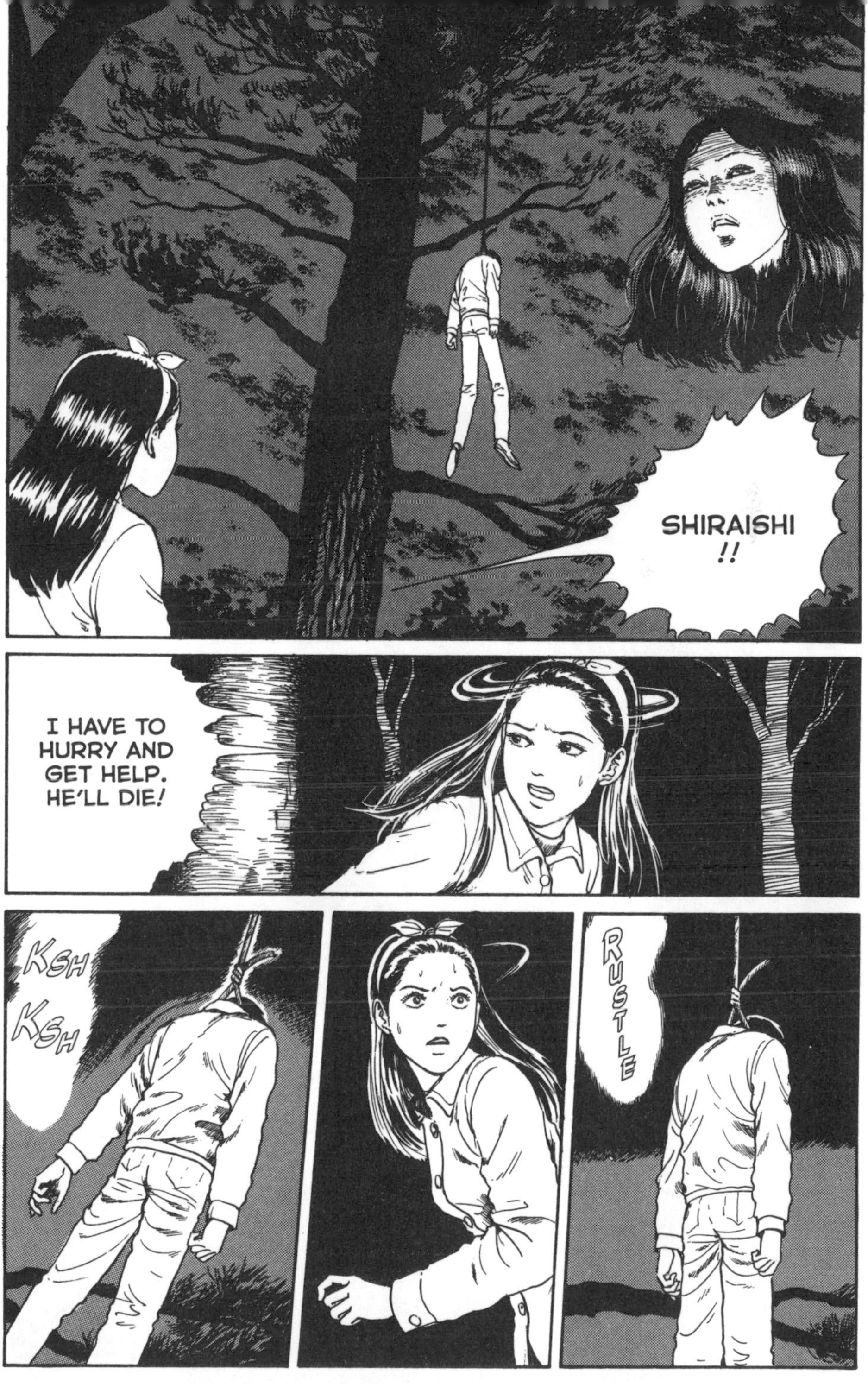
SHIRAISHI !!
I HAVE TO HURRY AND GET HELP. HE'LL DIE!
RUSTLE
KSH KSH

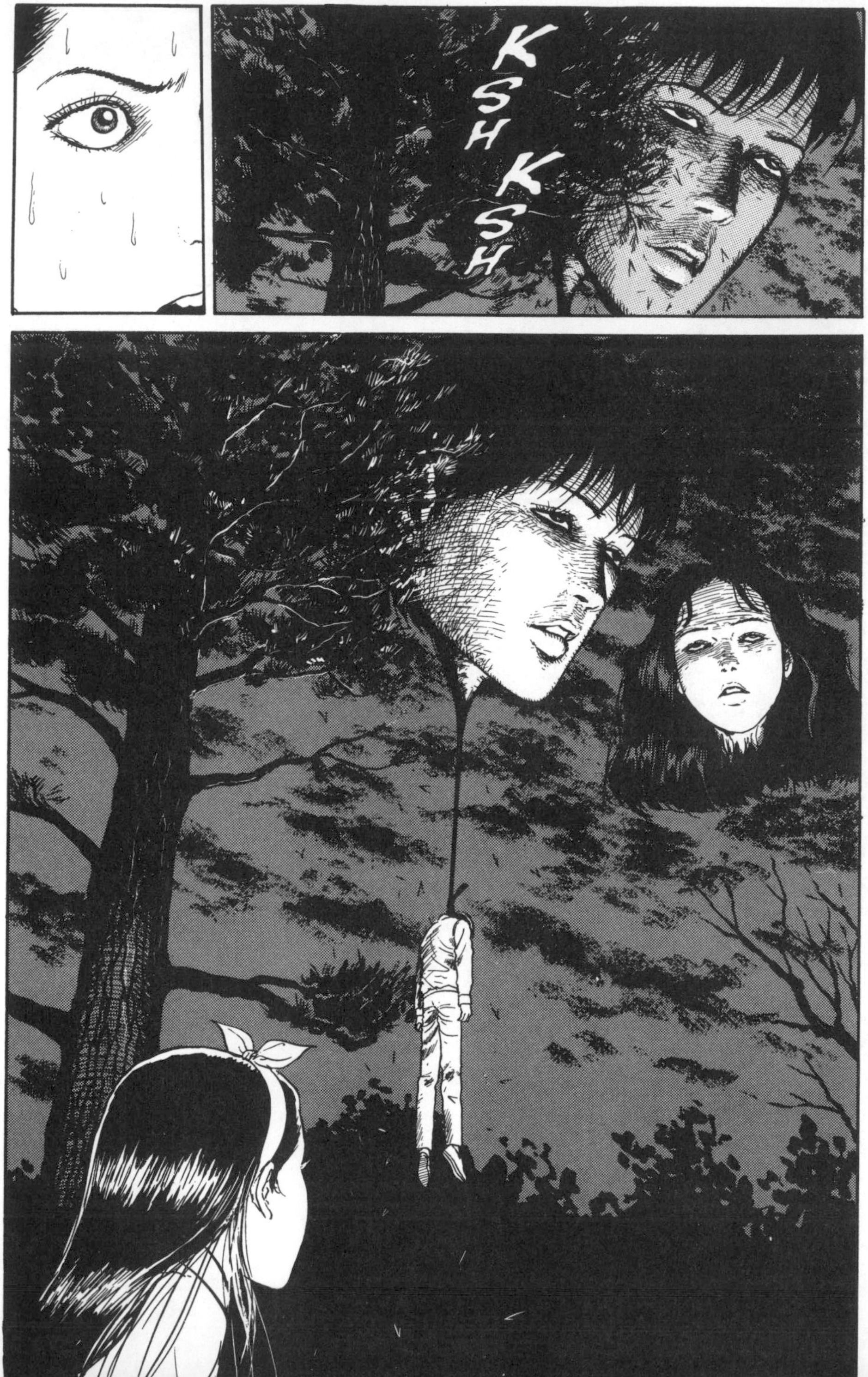
KSH KSH

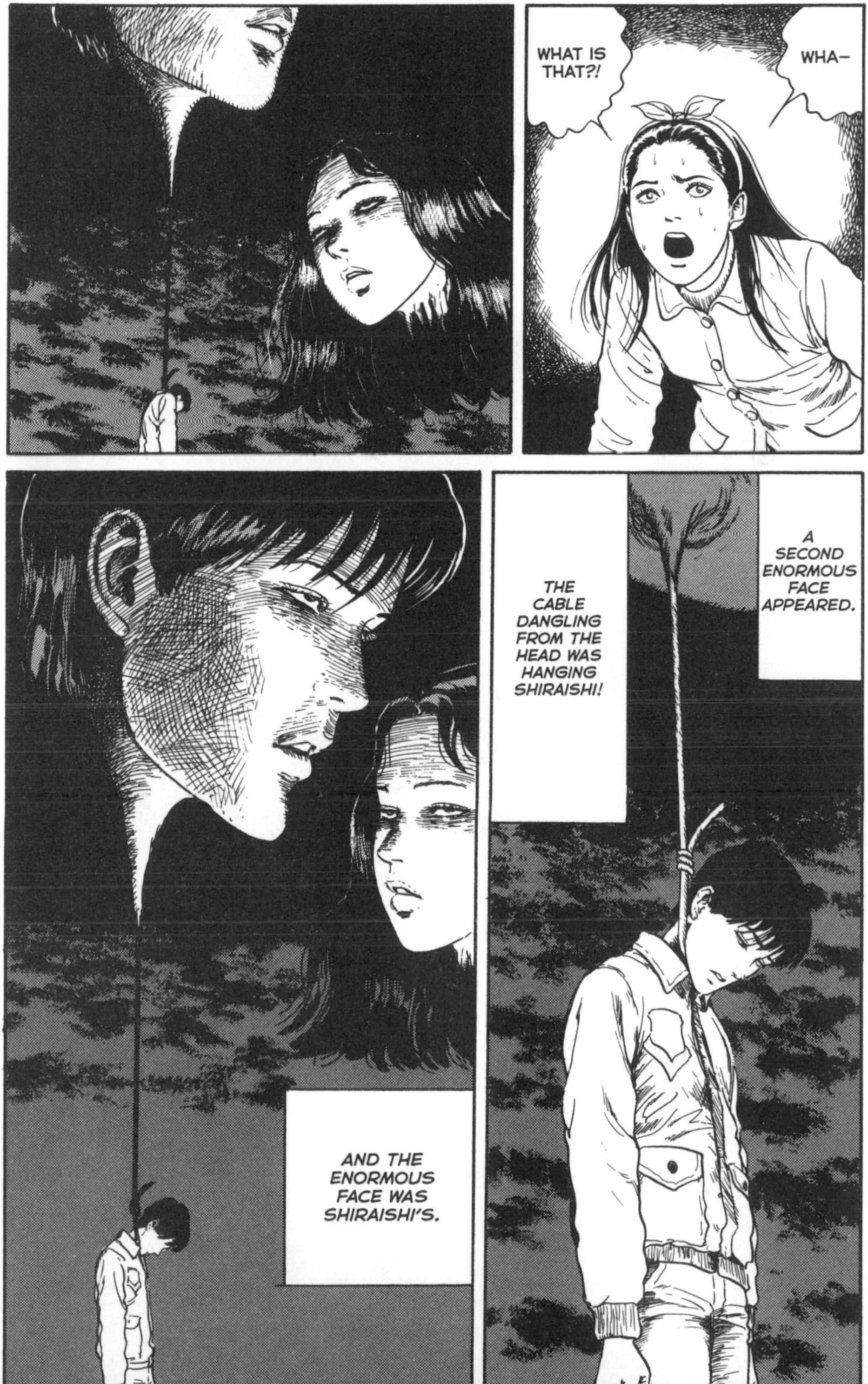
WHA—
WHAT IS THAT?!
A SECOND ENORMOUS FACE APPEARED.
THE CABLE DANGLING FROM THE HEAD WAS HANGING SHIRAISHI!
AND THE ENORMOUS FACE WAS SHIRAISHI'S.

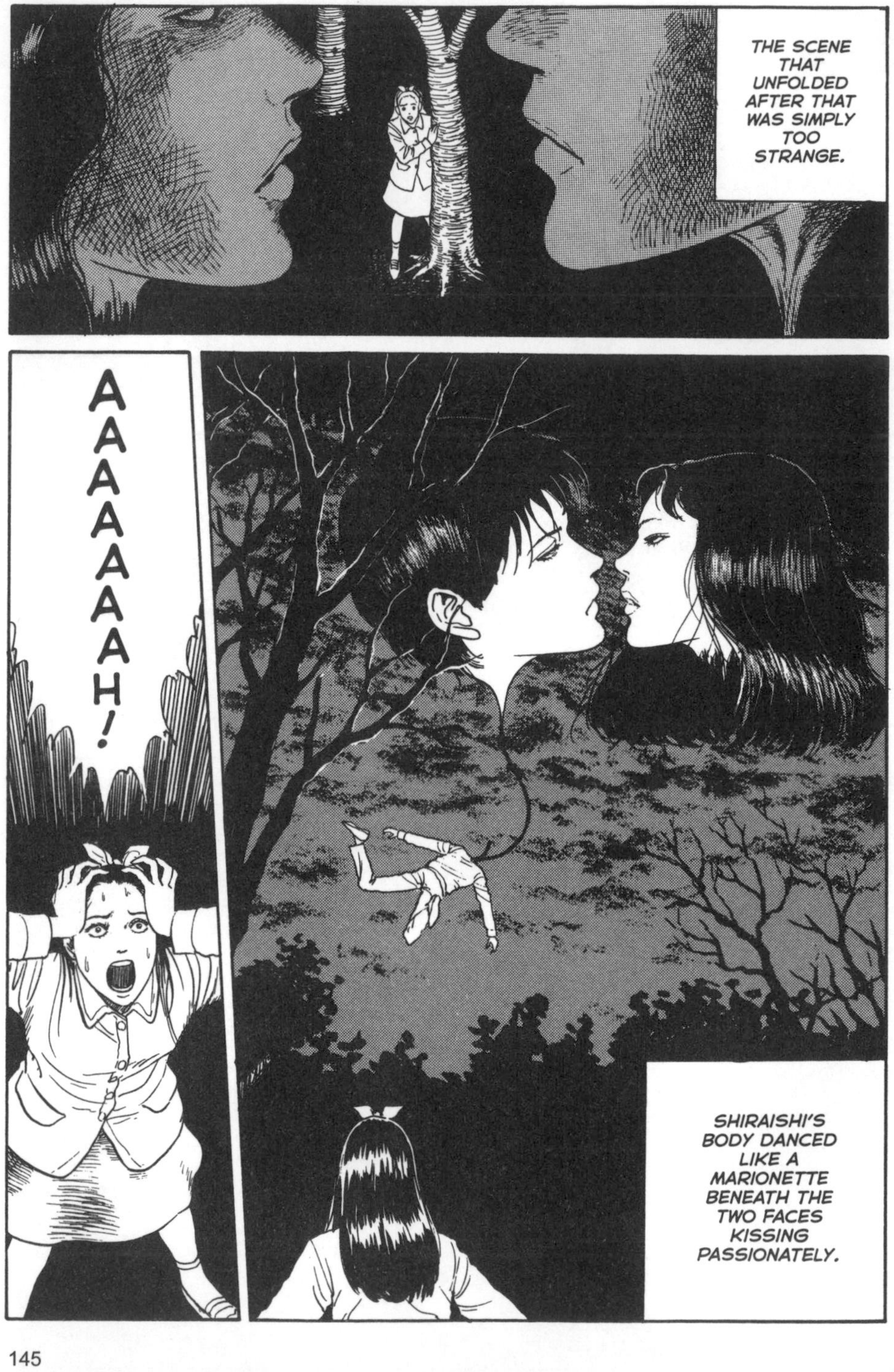
THE SCENE THAT UNFOLDED AFTER THAT WAS SIMPLY TOO STRANGE.
SHIRAISHI'S BODY DANCED LIKE A MARIONETTE BENEATH THE TWO FACES KISSING PASSIONATELY.
AAAAAAAAH!

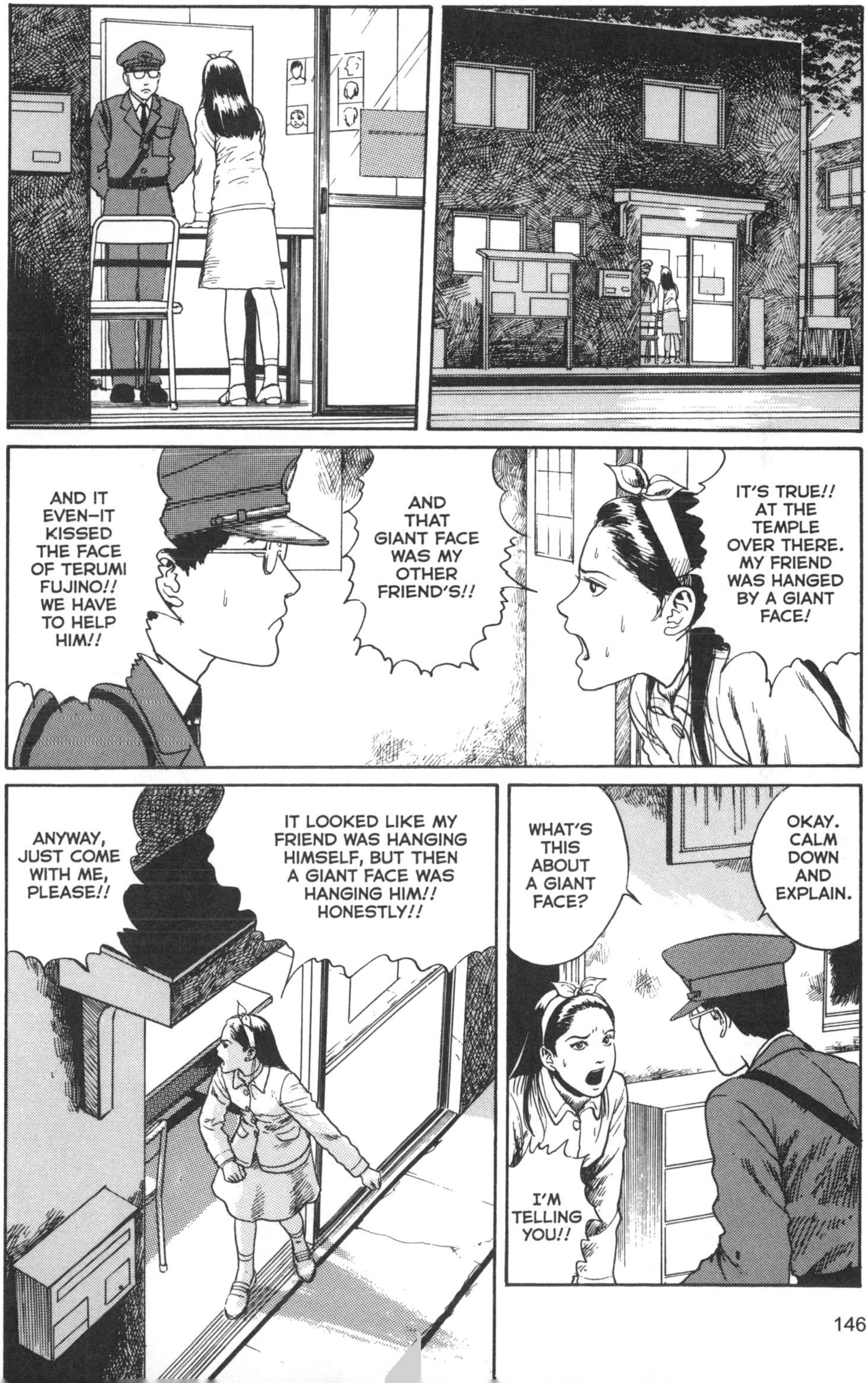
IT'S TRUE!! AT THE TEMPLE OVER THERE. MY FRIEND WAS HANGED BY A GIANT FACE!
AND THAT GIANT FACE WAS MY OTHER FRIEND'S!!
AND IT EVEN—IT KISSED THE FACE OF TERUMI FUJINO!! WE HAVE TO HELP HIM!!
OKAY. CALM DOWN AND EXPLAIN.
WHAT'S THIS ABOUT A GIANT FACE?
I'M TELLING YOU!!
IT LOOKED LIKE MY FRIEND WAS HANGING HIMSELF, BUT THEN A GIANT FACE WAS HANGING HIM!! HONESTLY!!
ANYWAY, JUST COME WITH ME, PLEASE!!

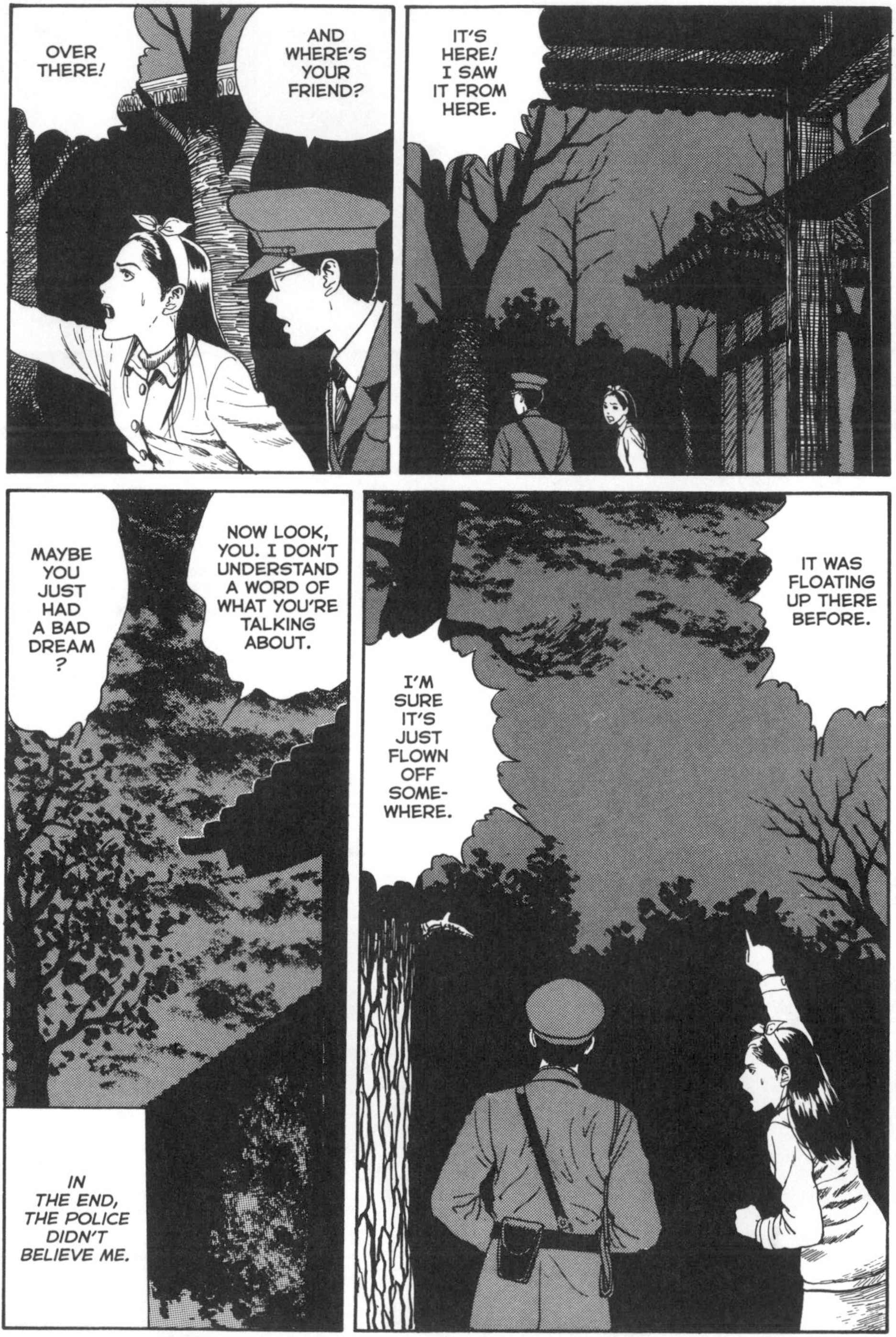
IT'S HERE! I SAW IT FROM HERE.
AND WHERE'S YOUR FRIEND?
OVER THERE!
IT WAS FLOATING UP THERE BEFORE.
I'M SURE IT'S JUST FLOWN OFF SOME-WHERE.
NOW LOOK, YOU. I DON'T UNDERSTAND A WORD OF WHAT YOU'RE TALKING ABOUT.
MAYBE YOU JUST HAD A BAD DREAM?
IN THE END, THE POLICE DIDN'T BELIEVE ME.

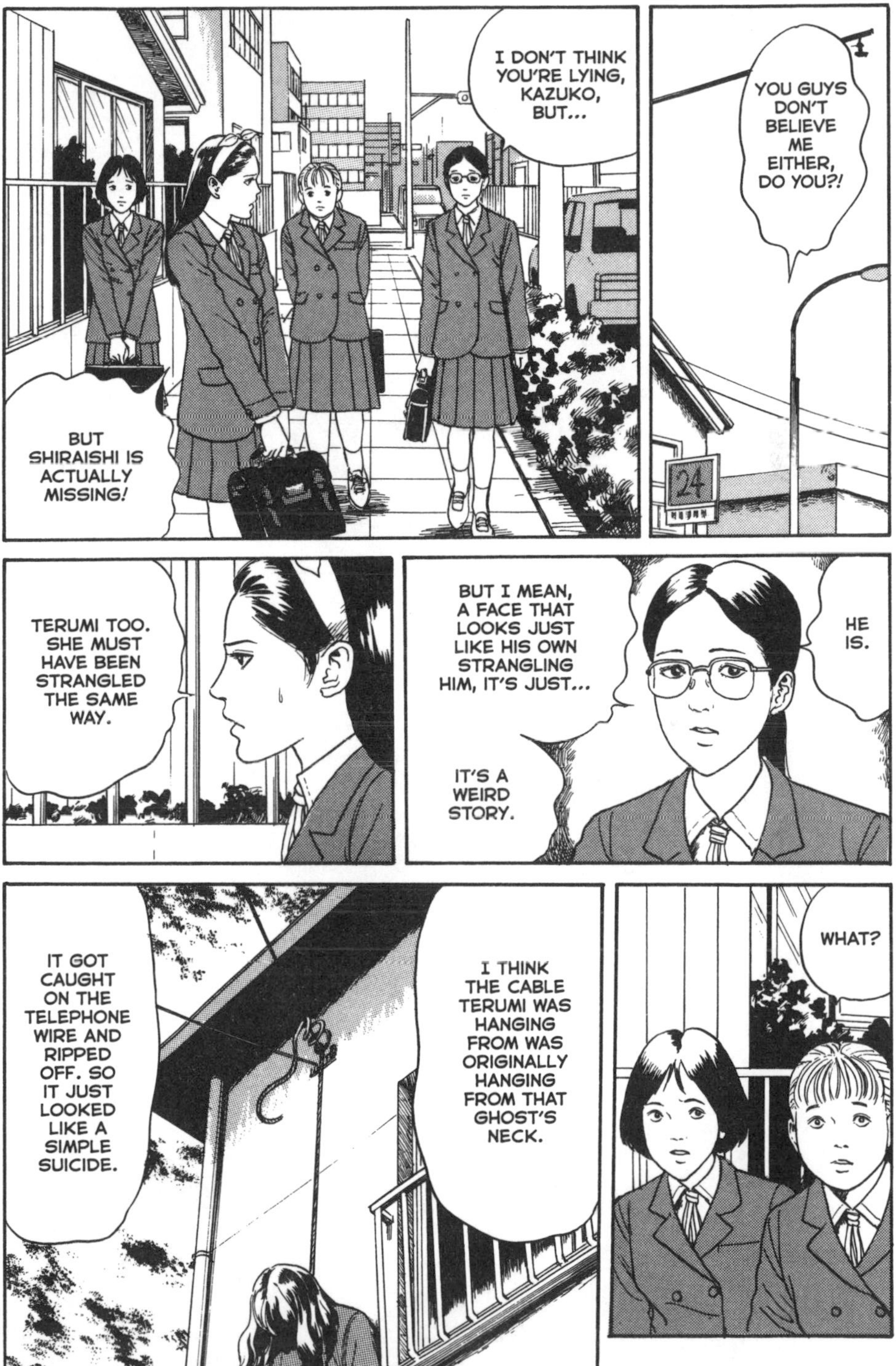
YOU GUYS DON'T BELIEVE ME EITHER, DO YOU?!
I DON'T THINK YOU'RE LYING, KAZUKO, BUT...
BUT SHIRAISHI IS ACTUALLY MISSING!
HE IS.
BUT I MEAN, A FACE THAT LOOKS JUST LIKE HIS OWN STRANGLING HIM, IT'S JUST...
IT'S A WEIRD STORY.
TERUMI TOO. SHE MUST HAVE BEEN STRANGLED THE SAME WAY.
WHAT?
I THINK THE CABLE TERUMI WAS HANGING FROM WAS ORIGINALLY HANGING FROM THAT GHOST'S NECK.
IT GOT CAUGHT ON THE TELEPHONE WIRE AND RIPPED OFF. SO IT JUST LOOKED LIKE A SIMPLE SUICIDE.

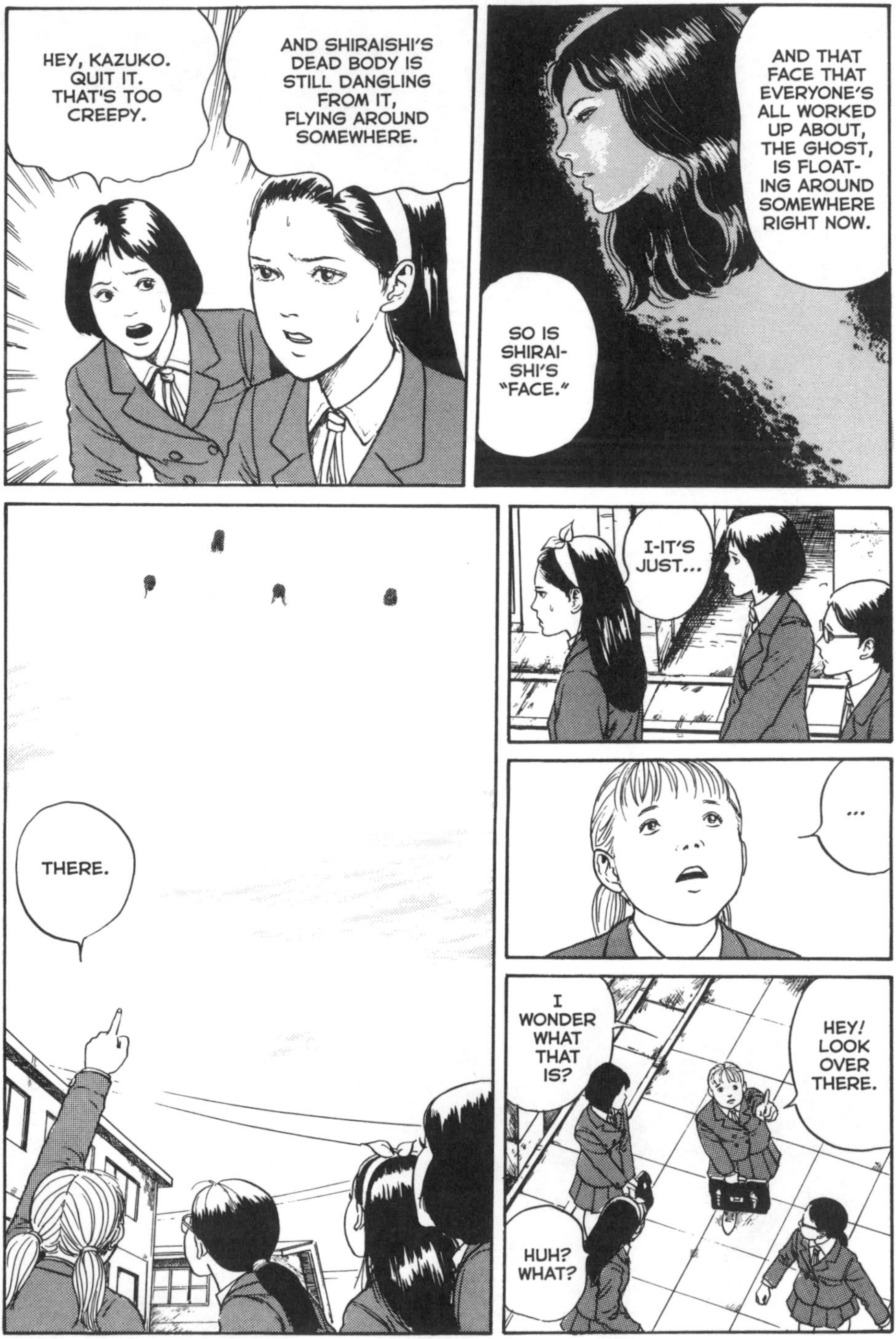
AND THAT FACE THAT EVERYONE'S ALL WORKED UP ABOUT, THE GHOST, IS FLOAT-ING AROUND SOMEWHERE RIGHT NOW.
SO IS SHIRAI-SHI'S "FACE."
AND SHIRAISHI'S DEAD BODY IS STILL DANGLING FROM IT, FLYING AROUND SOMEWHERE.
HEY, KAZUKO. QUIT IT. THAT'S TOO CREEPY.
I-IT'S JUST...
...
HEY! LOOK OVER THERE.
I WONDER WHAT THAT IS?
HUH? WHAT?
THERE.

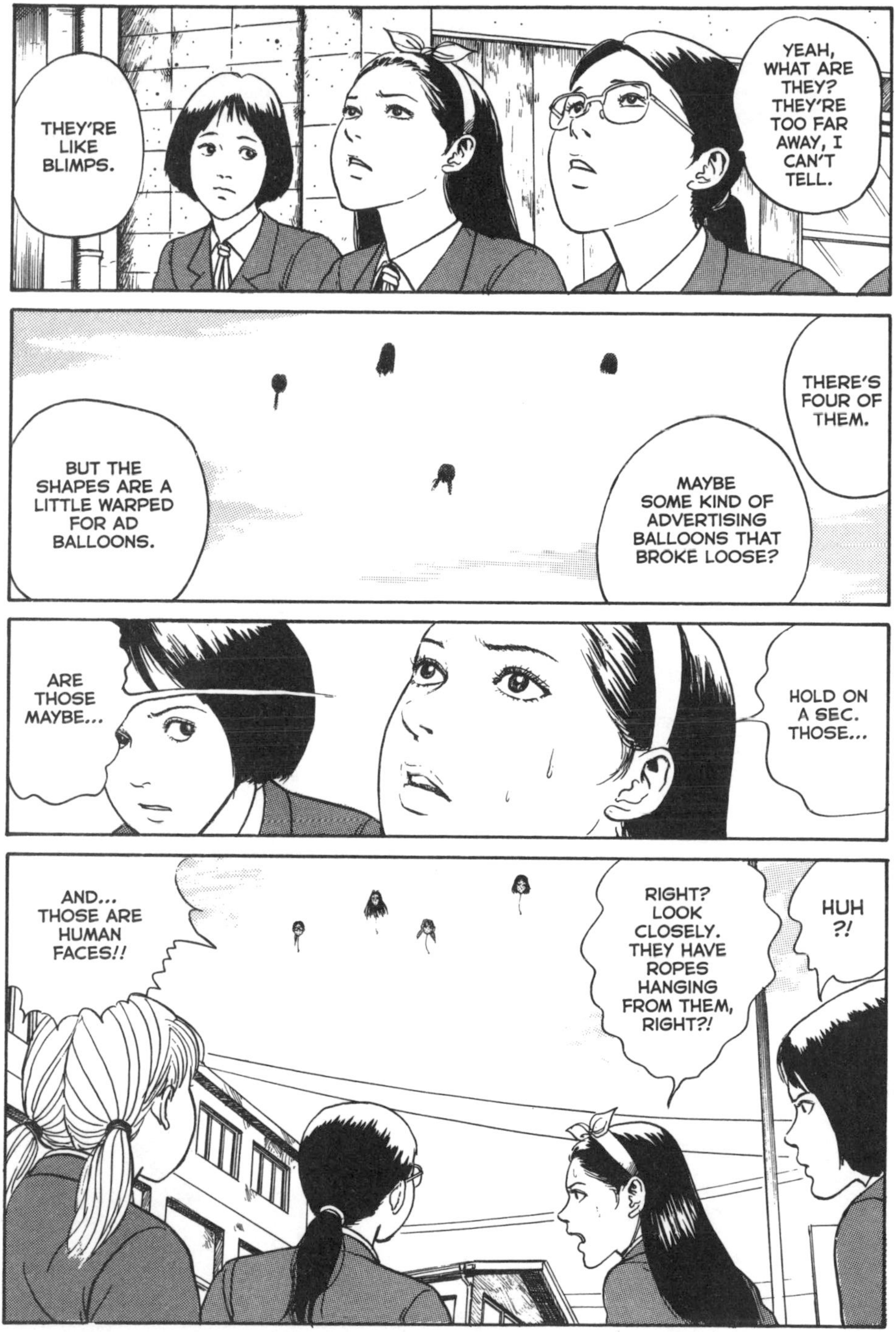
YEAH, WHAT ARE THEY? THEY'RE TOO FAR AWAY, I CAN'T TELL.
THEY'RE LIKE BLIMPS.
THERE'S FOUR OF THEM.
MAYBE SOME KIND OF ADVERTISING BALLOONS THAT BROKE LOOSE?
BUT THE SHAPES ARE A LITTLE WARPED FOR AD BALLOONS.
HOLD ON A SEC. THOSE...
ARE THOSE MAYBE...
HUH?!
RIGHT? LOOK CLOSELY. THEY HAVE ROPES HANGING FROM THEM, RIGHT?!
AND... THOSE ARE HUMAN FACES!!

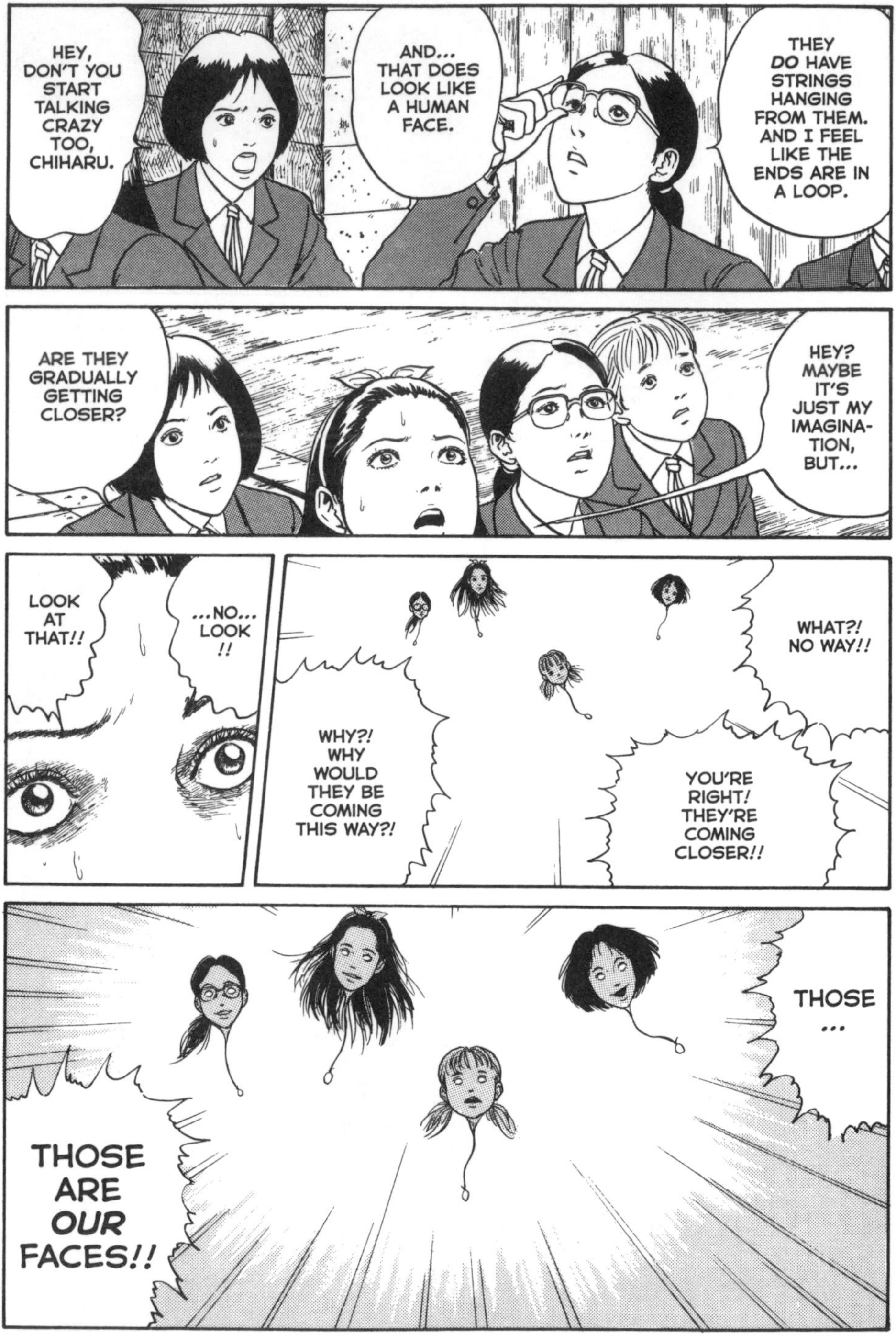
THEY *DO* HAVE STRINGS HANGING FROM THEM. AND I FEEL LIKE THE ENDS ARE IN A LOOP.
AND... THAT DOES LOOK LIKE A HUMAN FACE.
HEY, DON'T YOU START TALKING CRAZY TOO, CHIHARU.
HEY? MAYBE IT'S JUST MY IMAGINATION, BUT...
ARE THEY GRADUALLY GETTING CLOSER?
WHAT?! NO WAY!!
YOU'RE RIGHT! THEY'RE COMING CLOSER!!
WHY?! WHY WOULD THEY BE COMING THIS WAY?!
...NO... LOOK!!
LOOK AT THAT!!
THOSE...
THOSE ARE *OUR* FACES!!

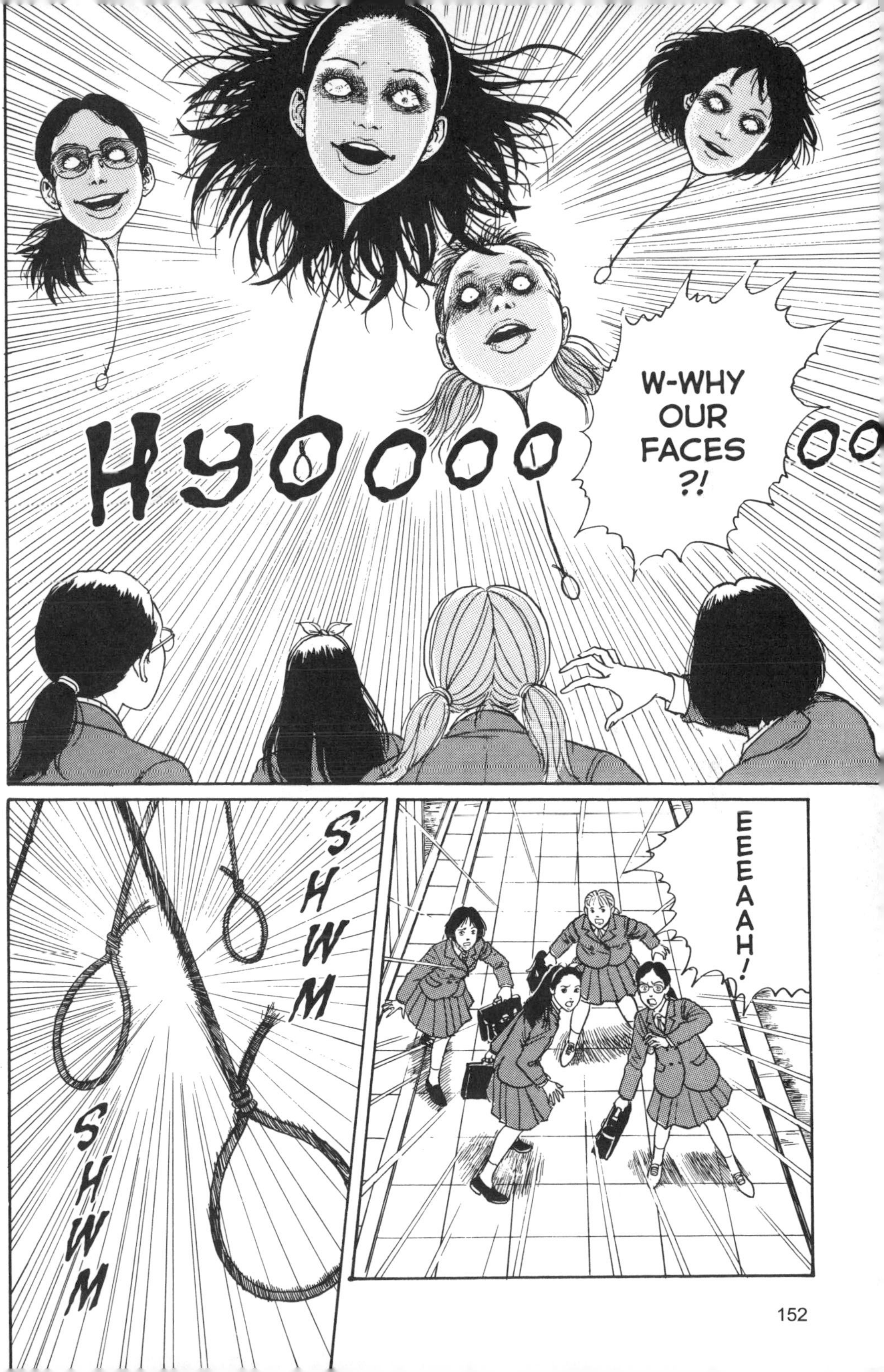
W-WHY OUR FACES ?!
HYOOOOOOO
EEEAAAH!
SHWM
SHWM

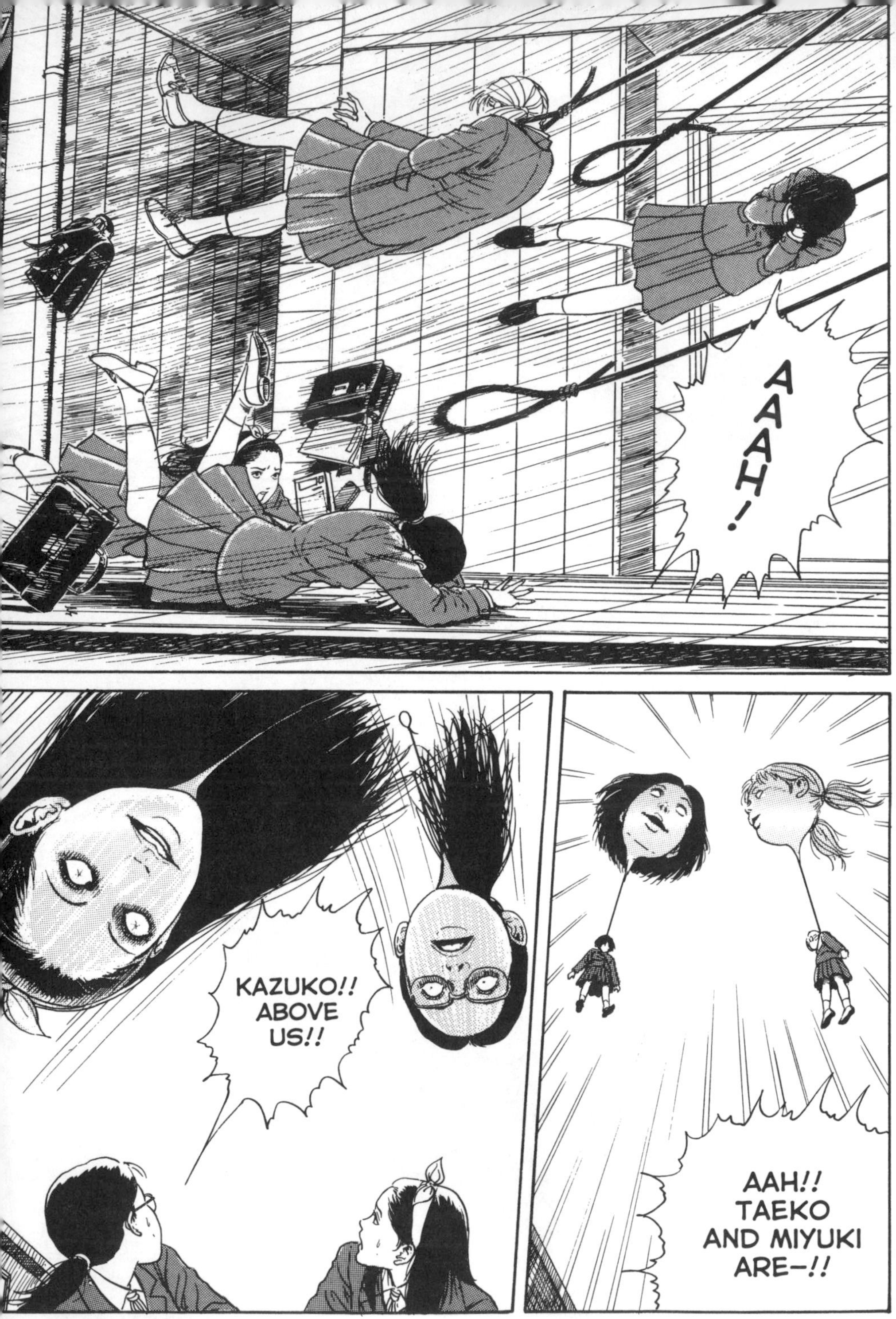
AAAH!
AAH!! TAEKO AND MIYUKI ARE–!!
KAZUKO!! ABOVE US!!

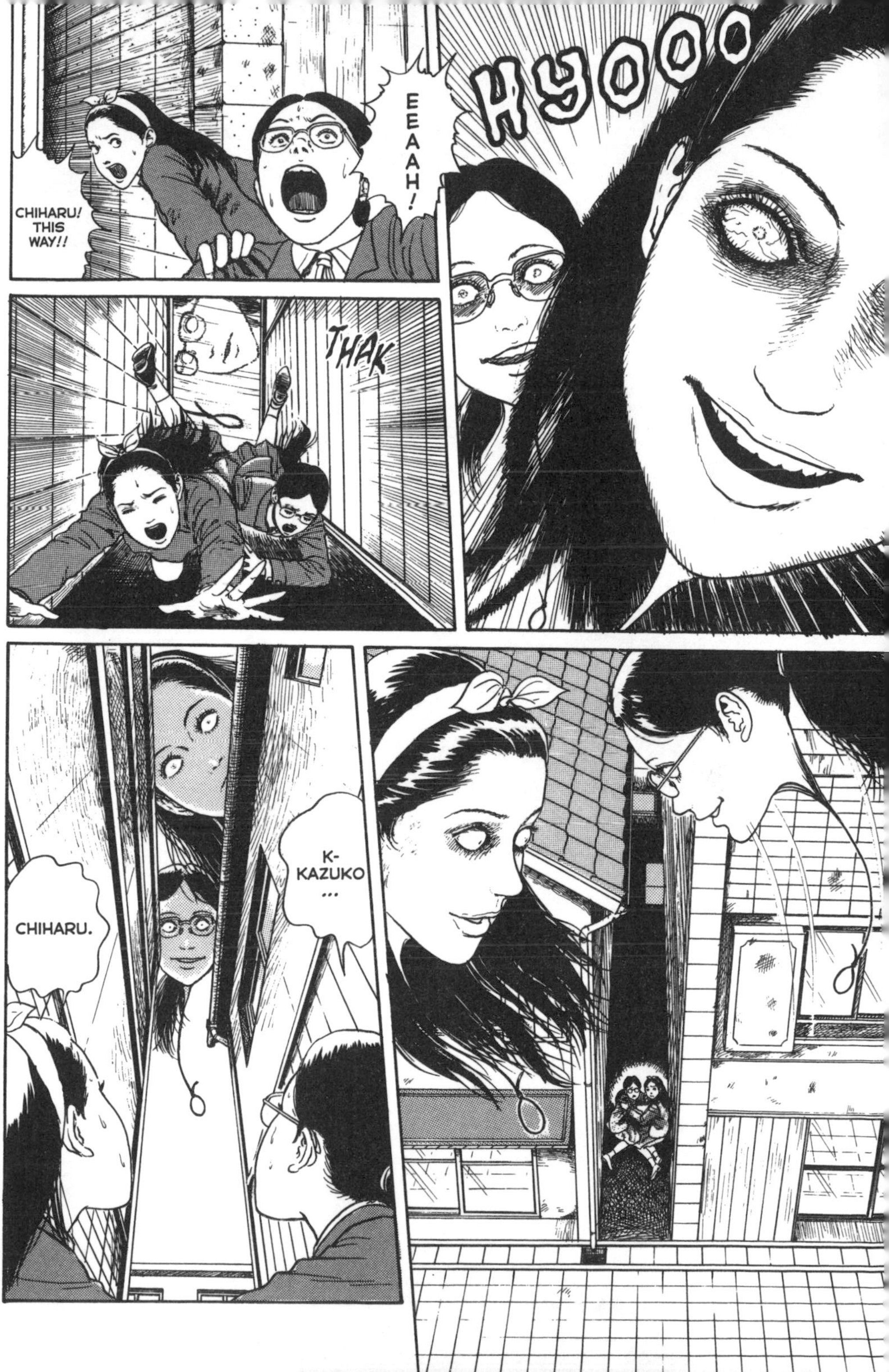
HYOOO
EEEAAH!
CHIHARU! THIS WAY!!
THAK
K-KAZUKO...
CHIHARU.

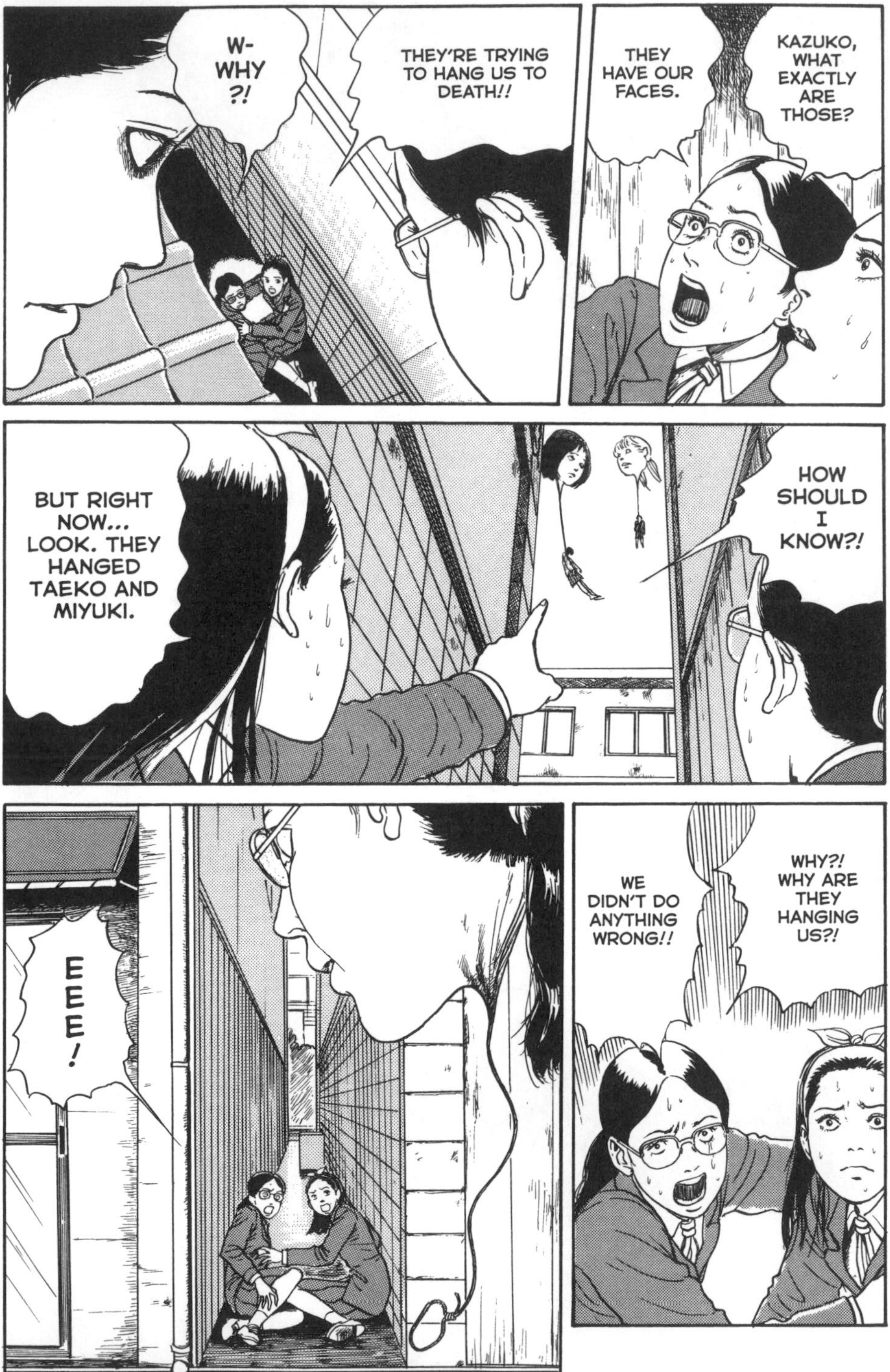
KAZUKO, WHAT EXACTLY ARE THOSE?
THEY HAVE OUR FACES.
THEY'RE TRYING TO HANG US TO DEATH!!
W-WHY?!
HOW SHOULD I KNOW?!
BUT RIGHT NOW... LOOK. THEY HANGED TAEKO AND MIYUKI.
WHY?! WHY ARE THEY HANGING US?!
WE DIDN'T DO ANYTHING WRONG!!
EEE!

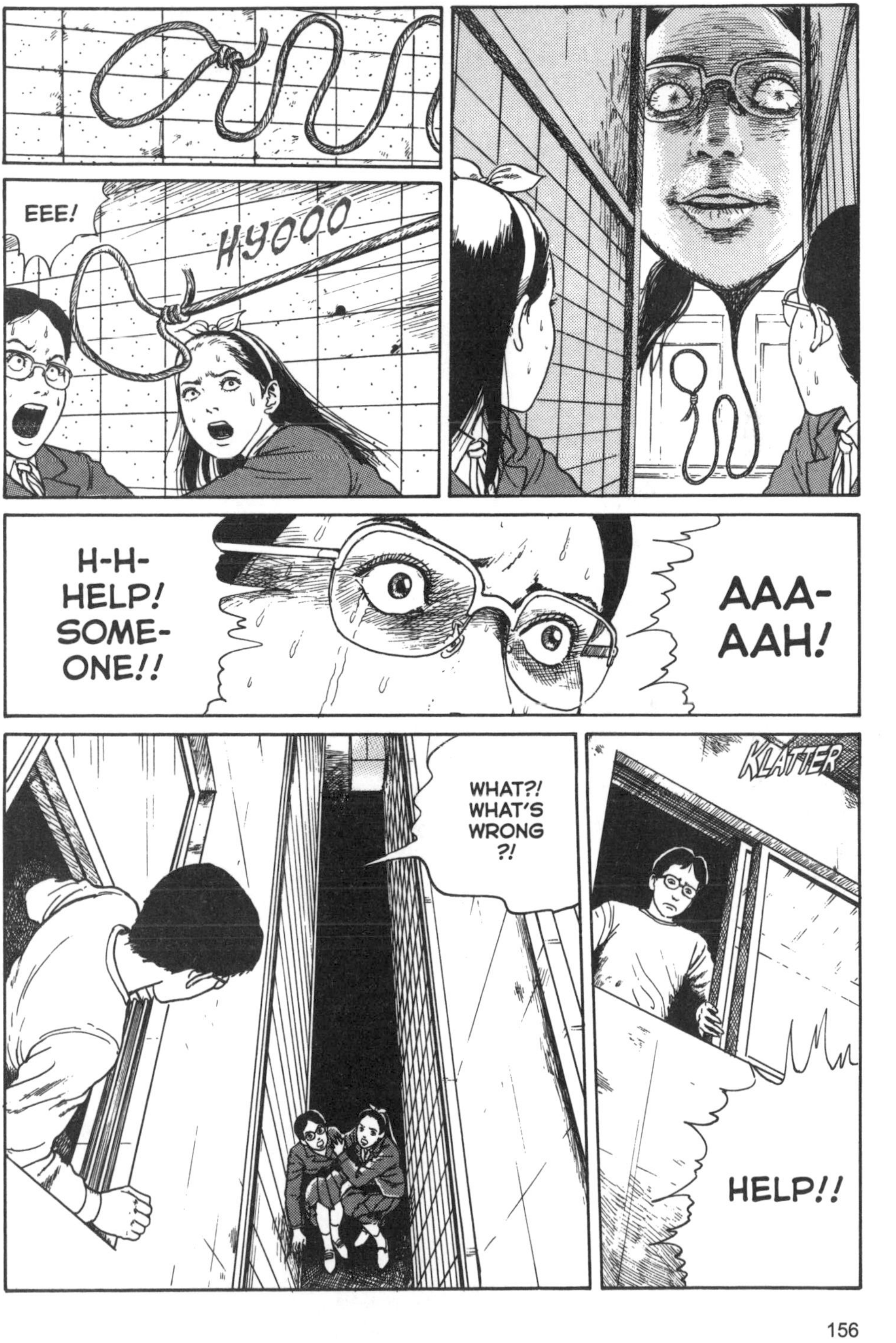
EEE!
HYOOO
AAA-AAH!
H-H-HELP! SOME-ONE!!
KLATTER
HELP!!
WHAT?! WHAT'S WRONG ?!

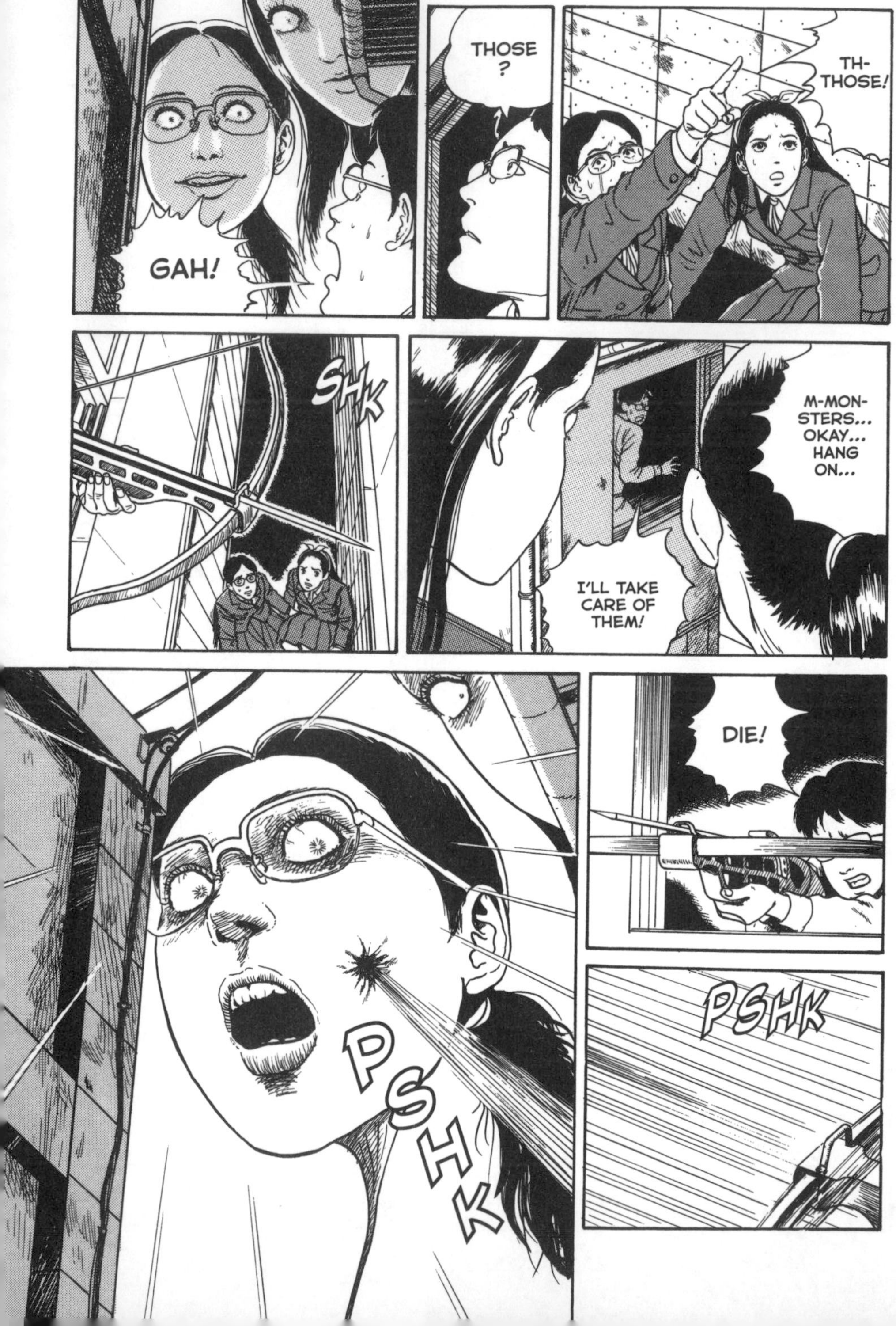
TH-
THOSE!
THOSE
?
GAH!
M-MON-
STERS...
OKAY...
HANG
ON...
I'LL TAKE
CARE OF
THEM!
SHK
DIE!
PSHK
PSHK

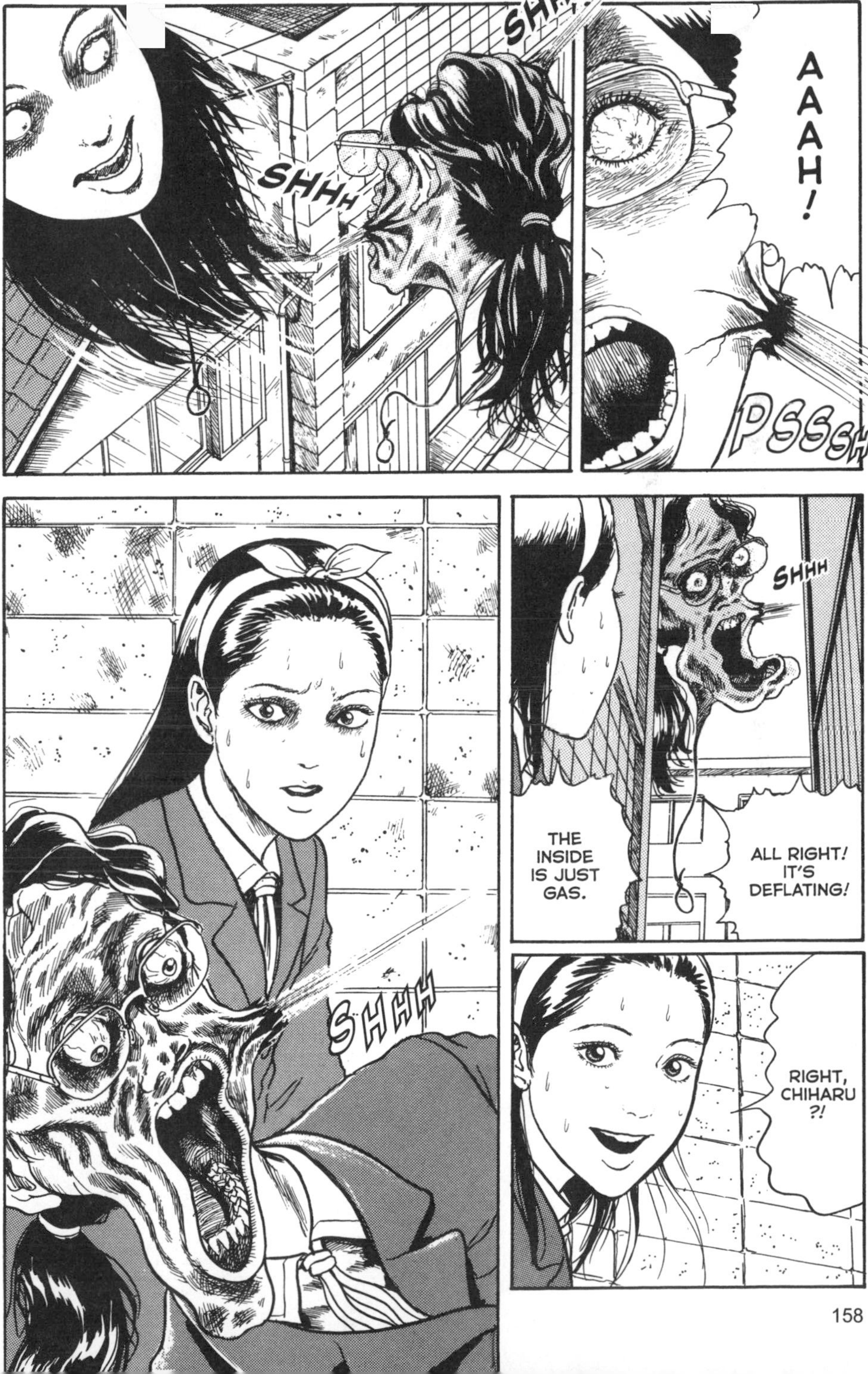
AAAH!
PSSSH
SHHH
SHHH
SHHH
ALL RIGHT! IT'S DEFLATING!
THE INSIDE IS JUST GAS.
RIGHT, CHIHARU ?!
SHHH

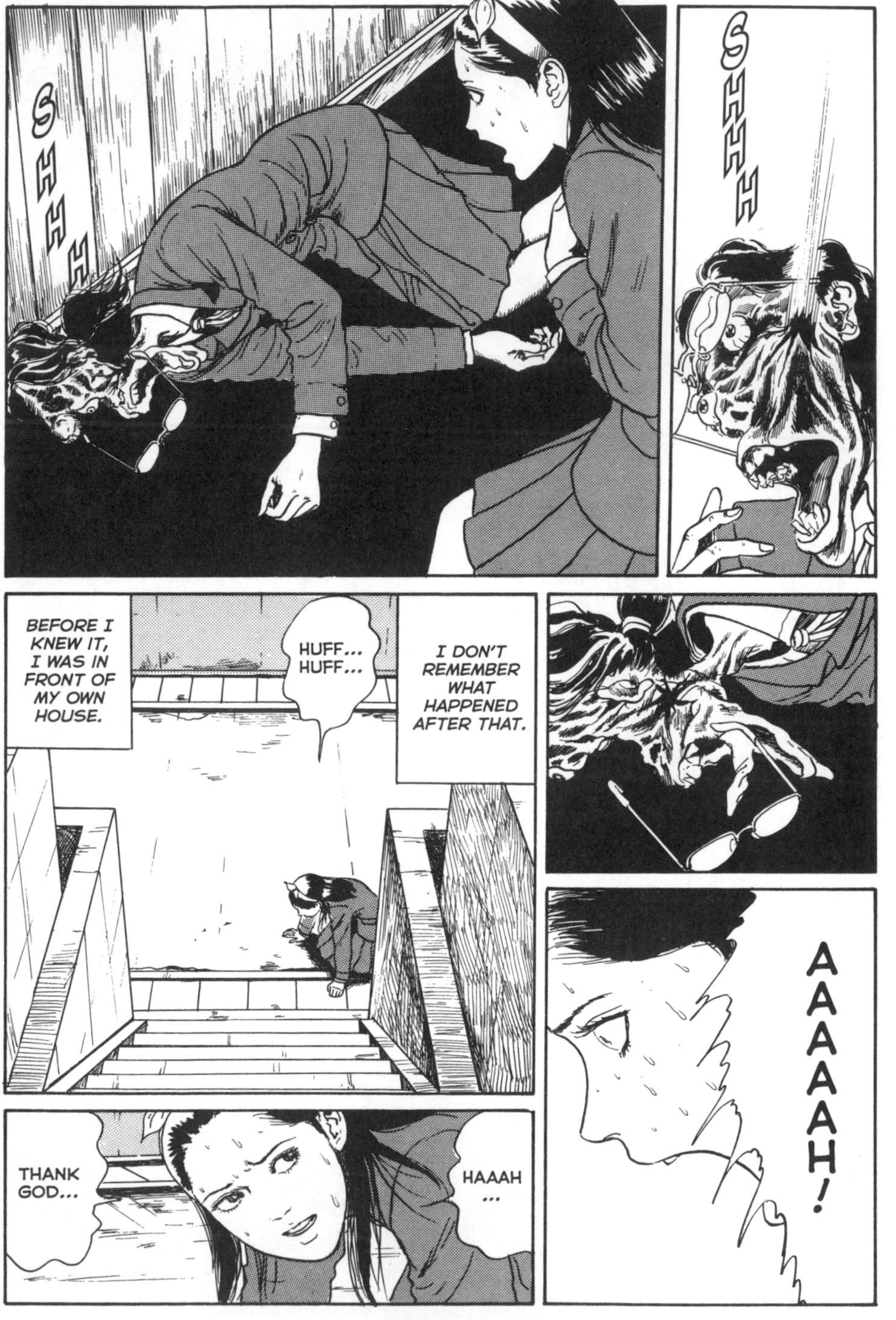
SHHHH
SHHHHH
AAAAAH!
I DON'T REMEMBER WHAT HAPPENED AFTER THAT.
HUFF... HUFF...
BEFORE I KNEW IT, I WAS IN FRONT OF MY OWN HOUSE.
HAAAH ...
THANK GOD...

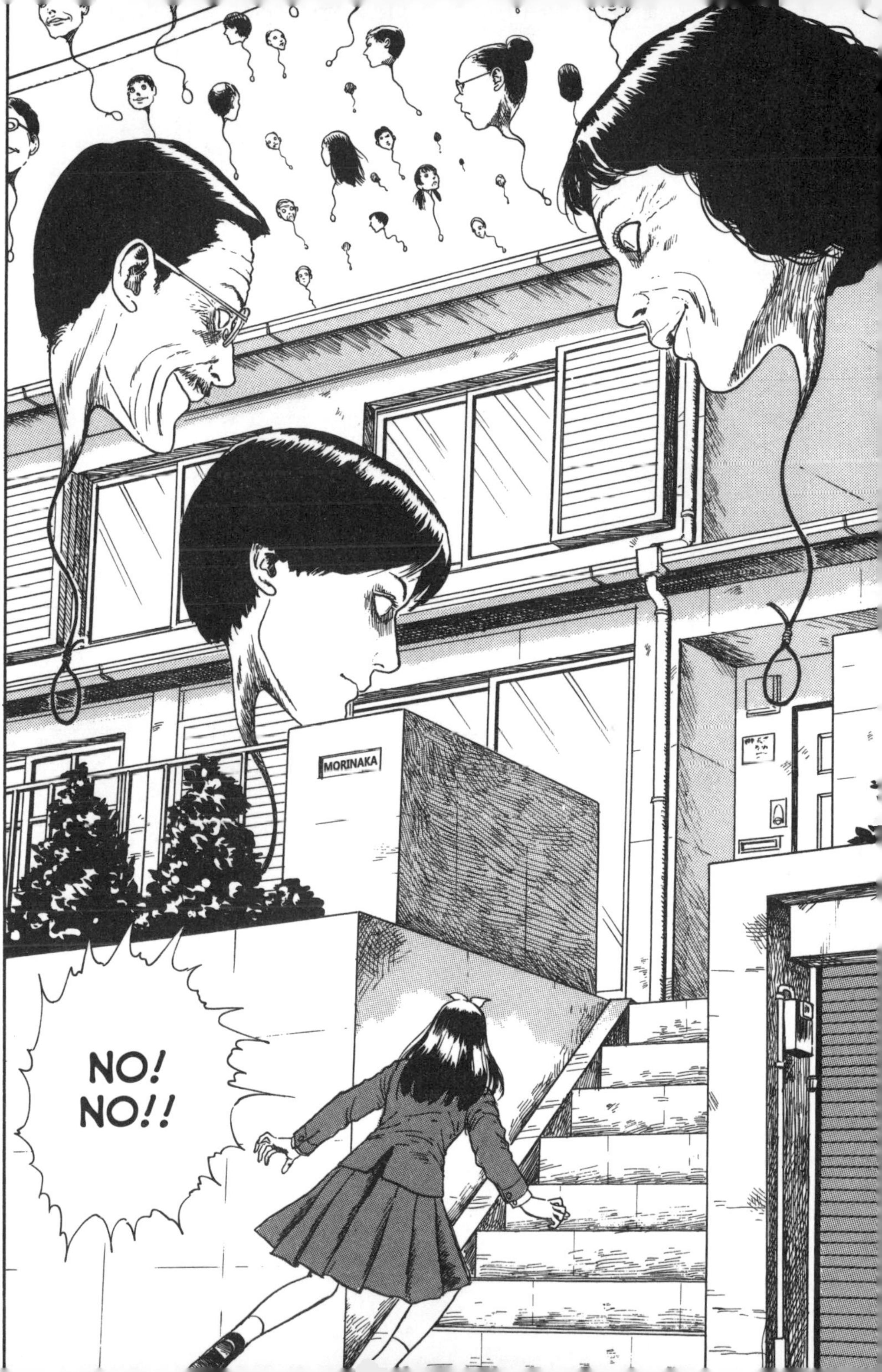
MORINAKA
NO! NO!!

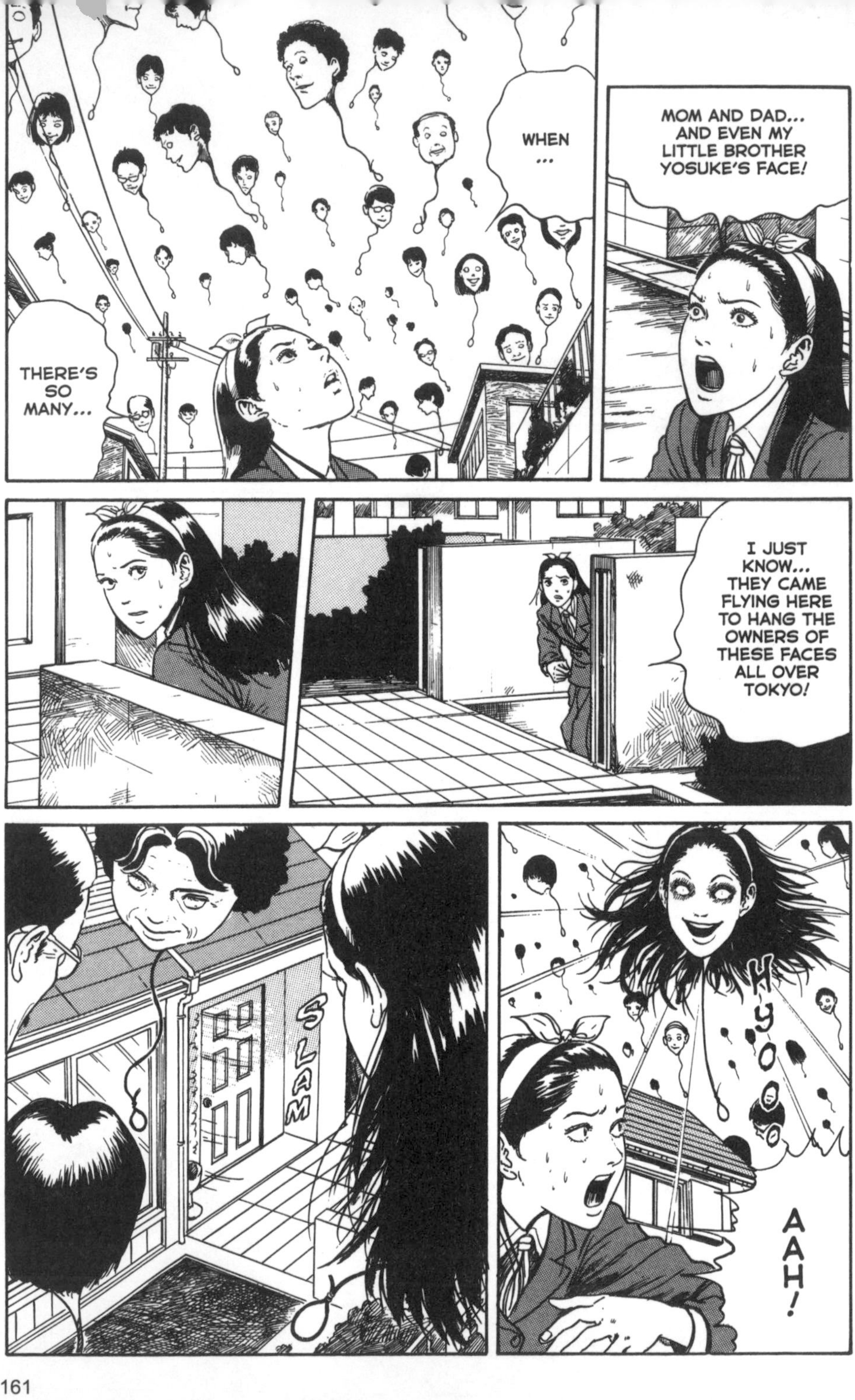
MOM AND DAD... AND EVEN MY LITTLE BROTHER YOSUKE'S FACE!
WHEN ...
THERE'S SO MANY...
I JUST KNOW... THEY CAME FLYING HERE TO HANG THE OWNERS OF THESE FACES ALL OVER TOKYO!
HYOOO
AAH!
SLAM

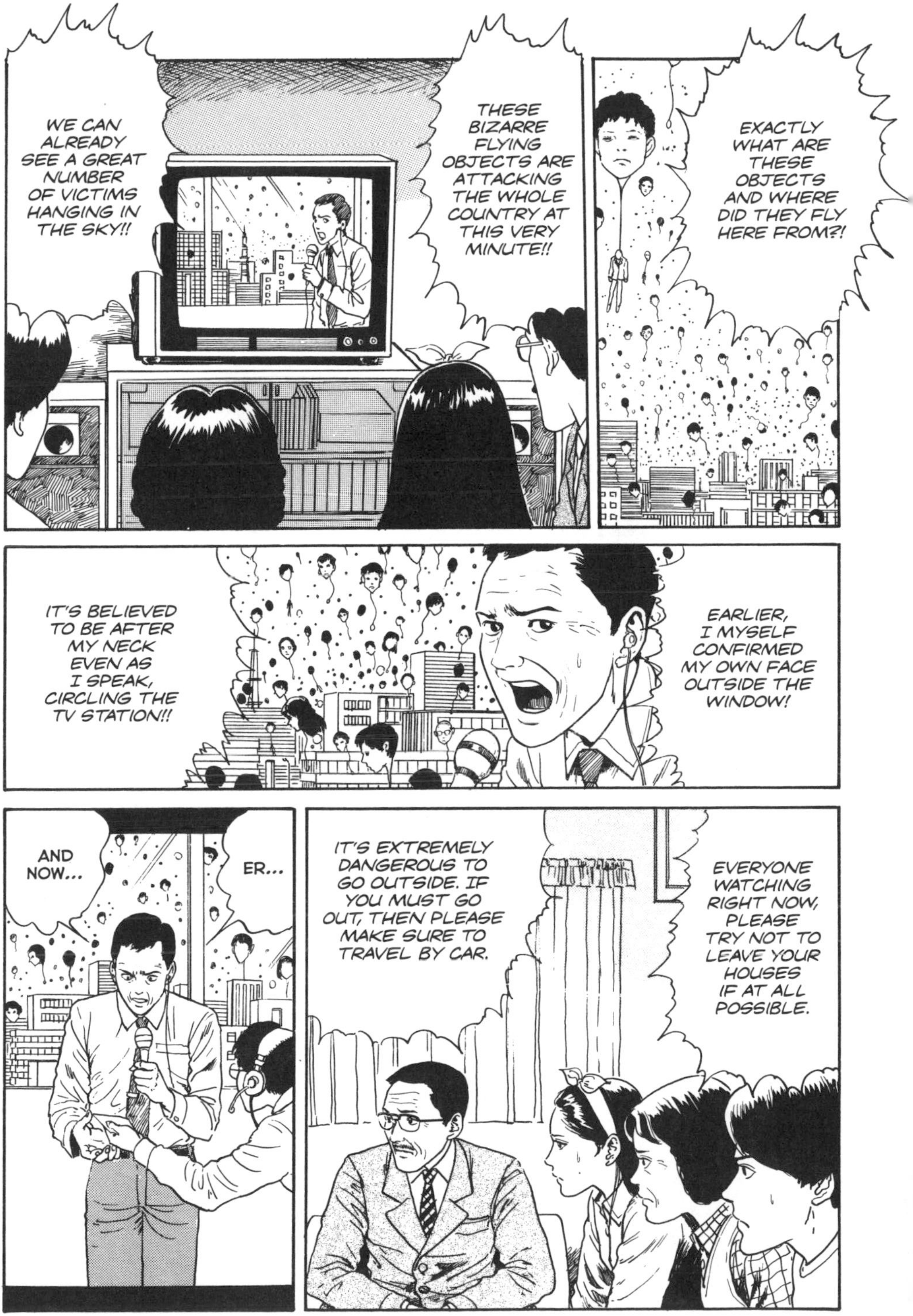
EXACTLY WHAT ARE THESE OBJECTS AND WHERE DID THEY FLY HERE FROM?!
THESE BIZARRE FLYING OBJECTS ARE ATTACKING THE WHOLE COUNTRY AT THIS VERY MINUTE!!
WE CAN ALREADY SEE A GREAT NUMBER OF VICTIMS HANGING IN THE SKY!!
EARLIER, I MYSELF CONFIRMED MY OWN FACE OUTSIDE THE WINDOW!
IT'S BELIEVED TO BE AFTER MY NECK EVEN AS I SPEAK, CIRCLING THE TV STATION!!
EVERYONE WATCHING RIGHT NOW, PLEASE TRY NOT TO LEAVE YOUR HOUSES IF AT ALL POSSIBLE.
IT'S EXTREMELY DANGEROUS TO GO OUTSIDE. IF YOU MUST GO OUT, THEN PLEASE MAKE SURE TO TRAVEL BY CAR.
ER...
AND NOW...

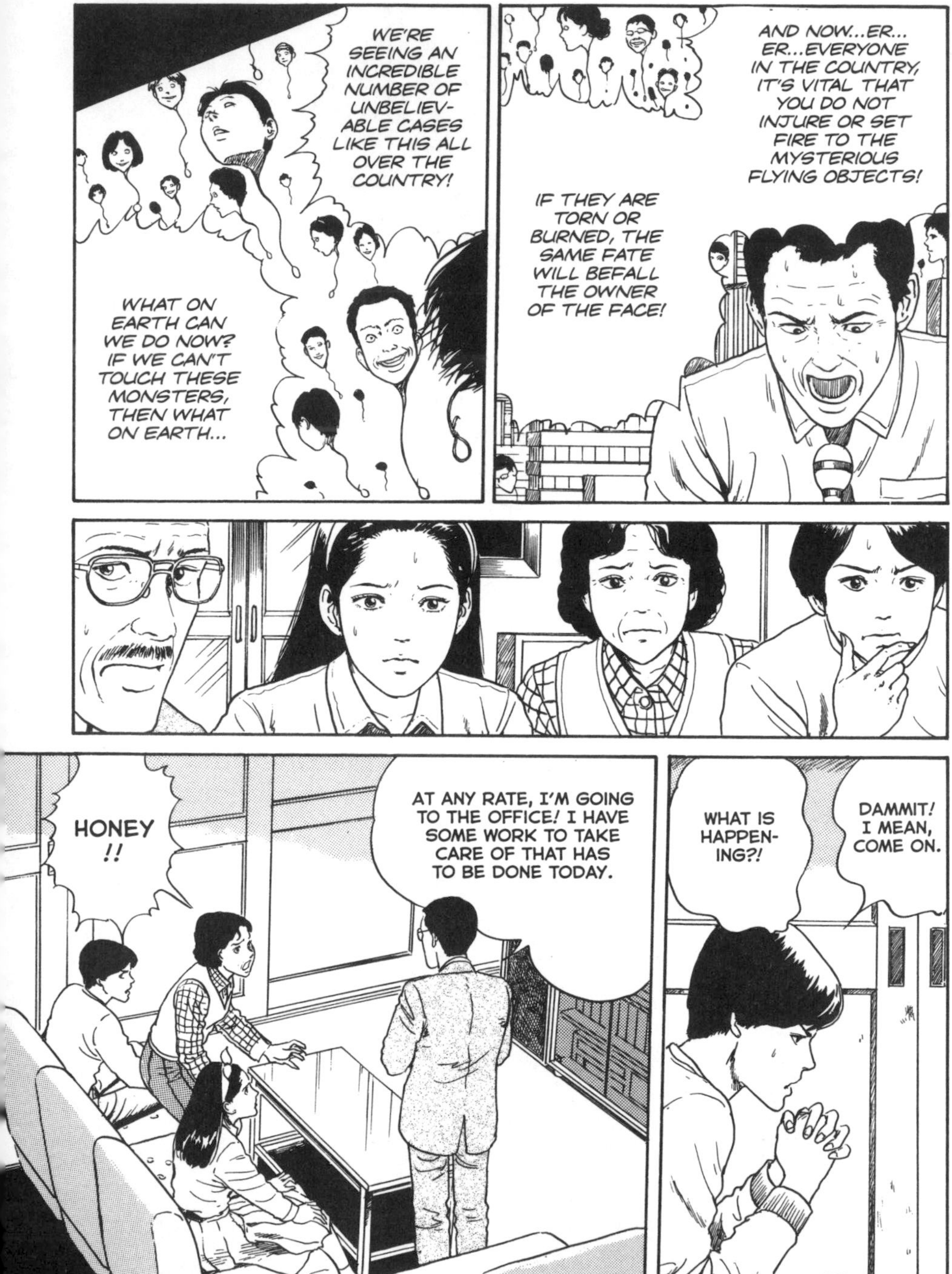
AND NOW...ER... ER...EVERYONE IN THE COUNTRY, IT'S VITAL THAT YOU DO NOT INJURE OR SET FIRE TO THE MYSTERIOUS FLYING OBJECTS!
IF THEY ARE TORN OR BURNED, THE SAME FATE WILL BEFALL THE OWNER OF THE FACE!
WE'RE SEEING AN INCREDIBLE NUMBER OF UNBELIEV-ABLE CASES LIKE THIS ALL OVER THE COUNTRY!
WHAT ON EARTH CAN WE DO NOW? IF WE CAN'T TOUCH THESE MONSTERS, THEN WHAT ON EARTH...
DAMMIT! I MEAN, COME ON.
WHAT IS HAPPEN-ING?!
AT ANY RATE, I'M GOING TO THE OFFICE! I HAVE SOME WORK TO TAKE CARE OF THAT HAS TO BE DONE TODAY.
HONEY !!

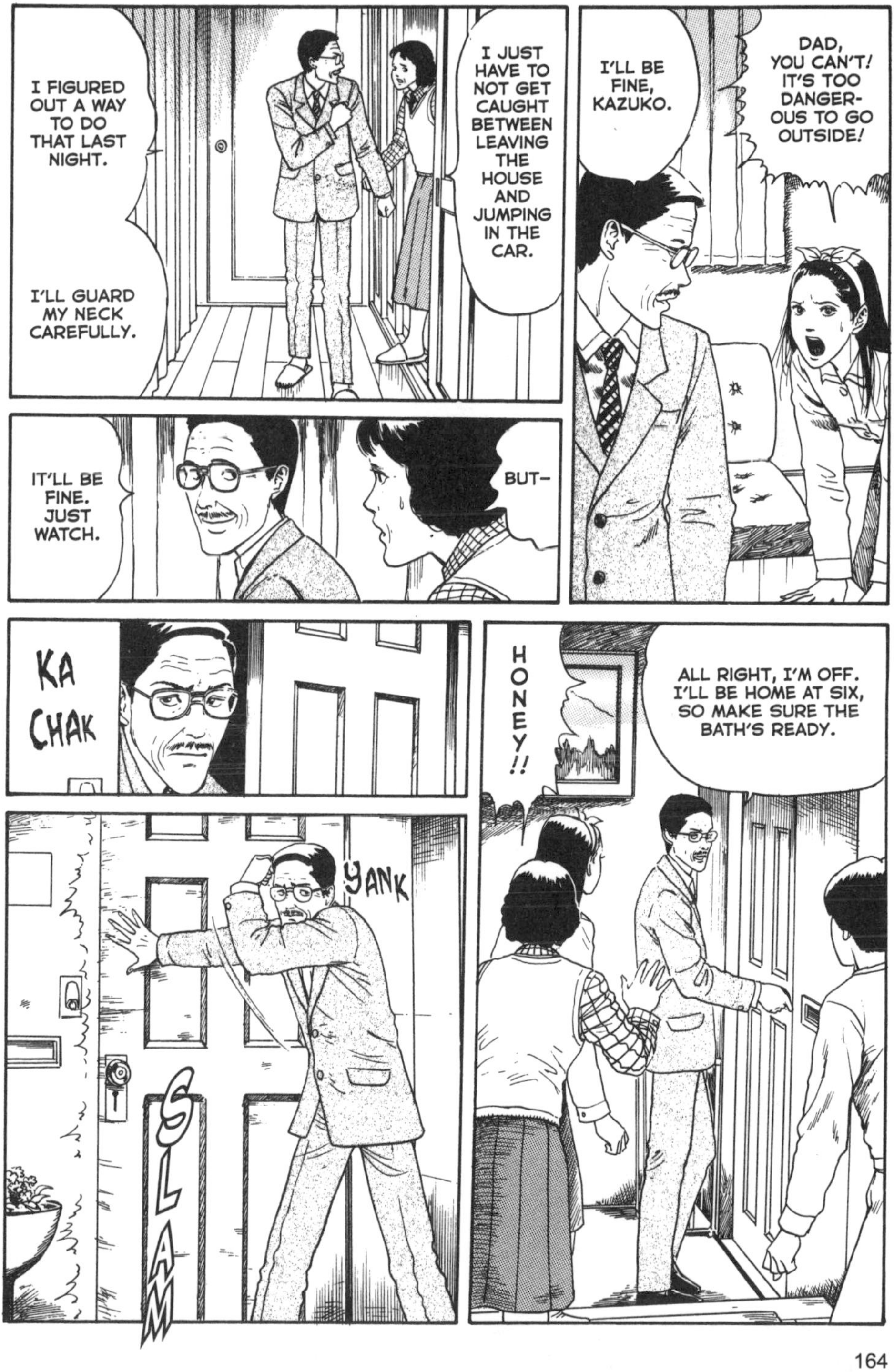
DAD, YOU CAN'T! IT'S TOO DANGEROUS TO GO OUTSIDE!
I'LL BE FINE, KAZUKO.
I JUST HAVE TO NOT GET CAUGHT BETWEEN LEAVING THE HOUSE AND JUMPING IN THE CAR.
I FIGURED OUT A WAY TO DO THAT LAST NIGHT.
I'LL GUARD MY NECK CAREFULLY.
BUT–
IT'LL BE FINE. JUST WATCH.
ALL RIGHT, I'M OFF. I'LL BE HOME AT SIX, SO MAKE SURE THE BATH'S READY.
HONEY!!
KA CHAK
YANK
SLAM

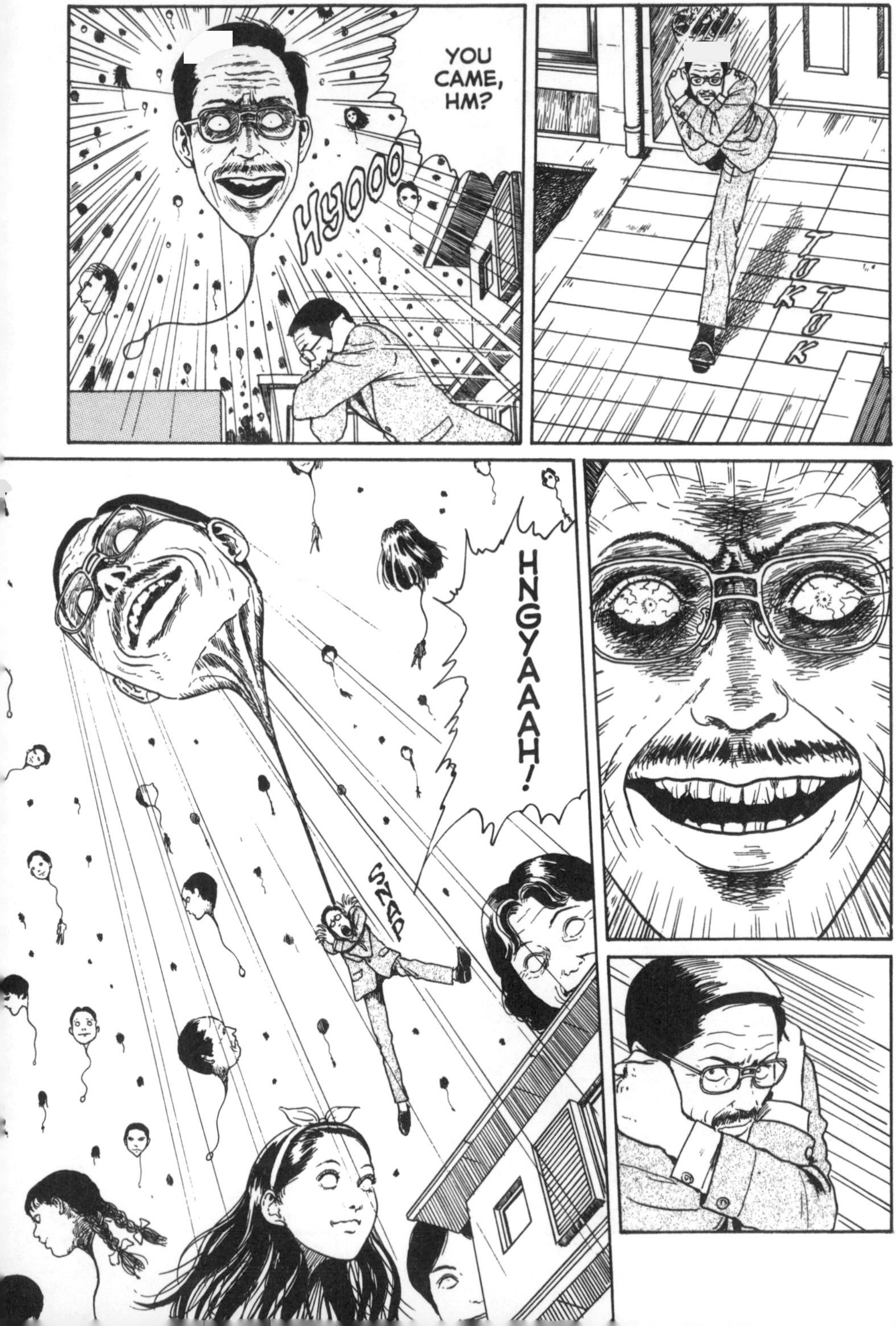
TUK TUK
YOU CAME, HM?
HYOOO
HNGYAAAH!

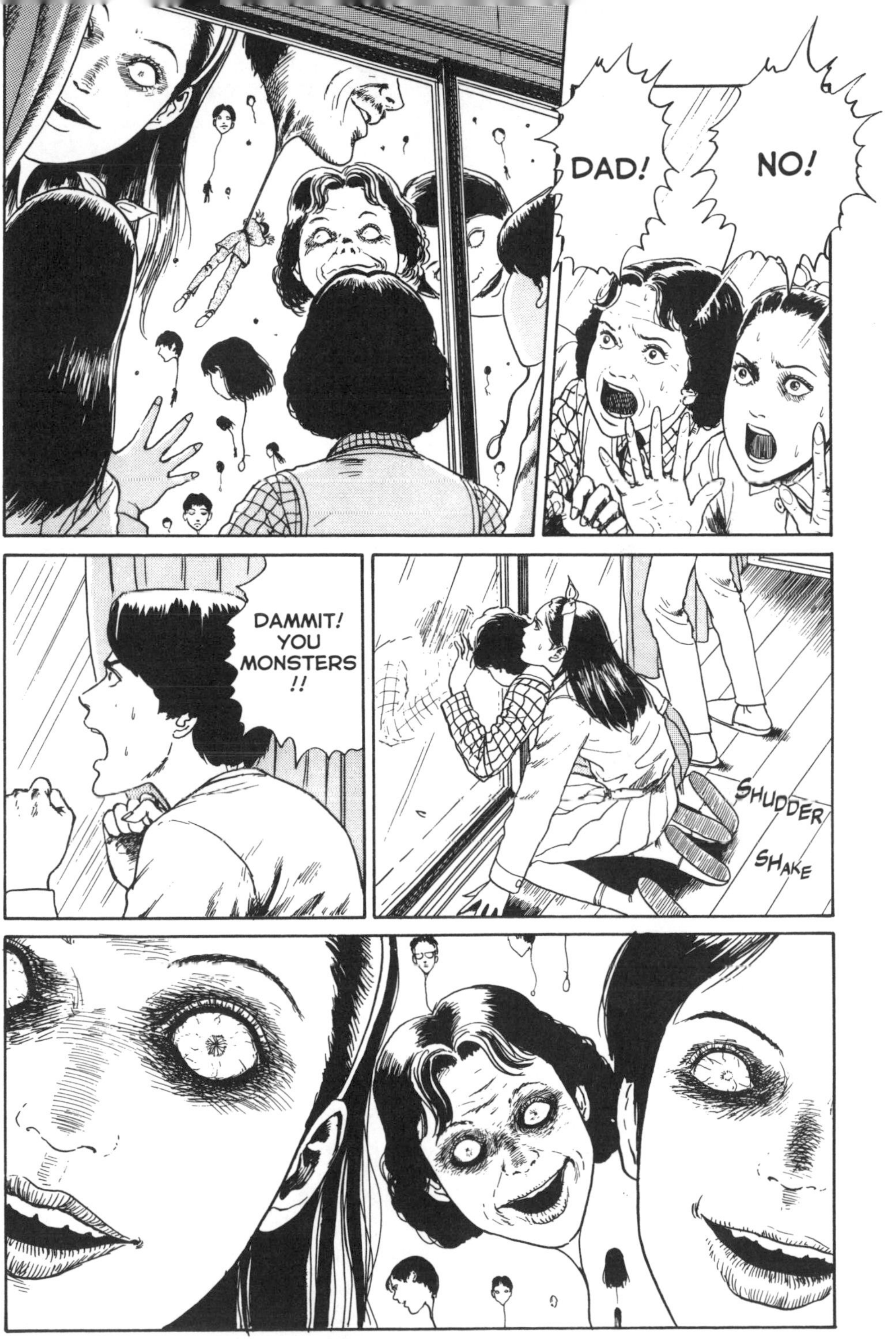
NO!
DAD!
SHUDDER
SHAKE
DAMMIT! YOU MONSTERS!!

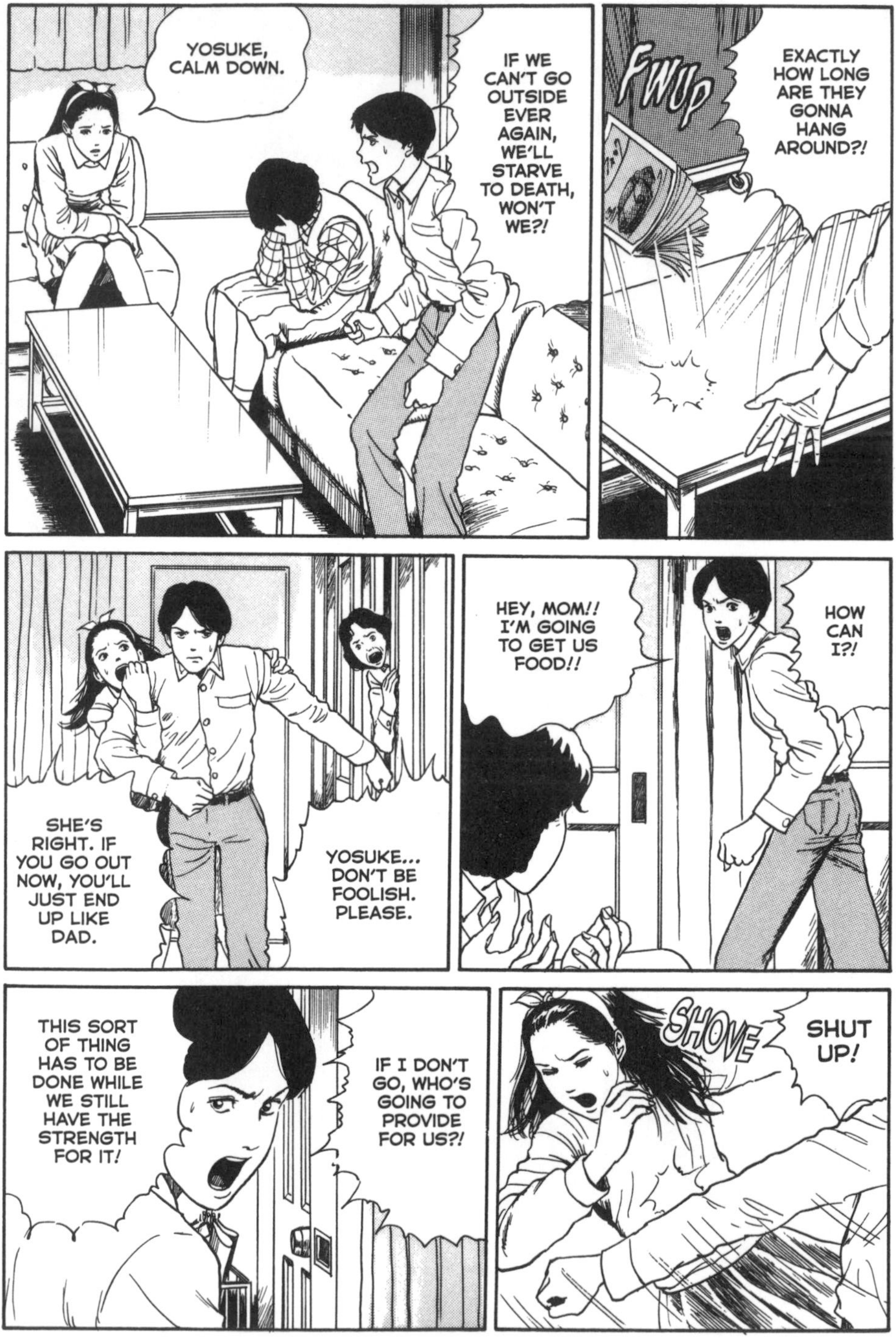
EXACTLY HOW LONG ARE THEY GONNA HANG AROUND?!
FWUP
IF WE CAN'T GO OUTSIDE EVER AGAIN, WE'LL STARVE TO DEATH, WON'T WE?!
YOSUKE, CALM DOWN.
HOW CAN I?!
HEY, MOM!! I'M GOING TO GET US FOOD!!
YOSUKE... DON'T BE FOOLISH. PLEASE.
SHE'S RIGHT. IF YOU GO OUT NOW, YOU'LL JUST END UP LIKE DAD.
SHUT UP!
SHOVE
IF I DON'T GO, WHO'S GOING TO PROVIDE FOR US?!
THIS SORT OF THING HAS TO BE DONE WHILE WE STILL HAVE THE STRENGTH FOR IT!

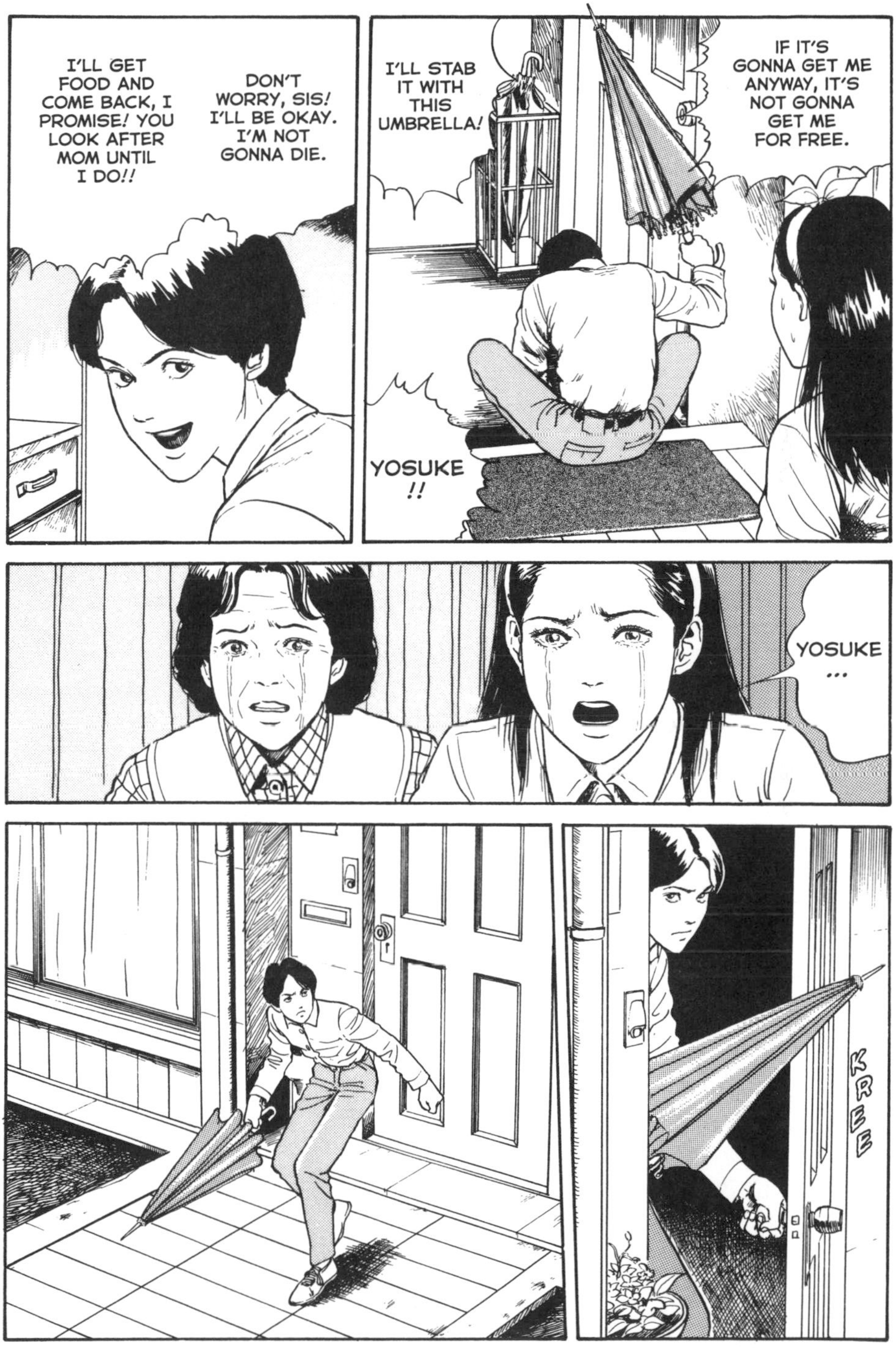
IF IT'S GONNA GET ME ANYWAY, IT'S NOT GONNA GET ME FOR FREE.
I'LL STAB IT WITH THIS UMBRELLA!
YOSUKE !!
DON'T WORRY, SIS! I'LL BE OKAY. I'M NOT GONNA DIE.
I'LL GET FOOD AND COME BACK, I PROMISE! YOU LOOK AFTER MOM UNTIL I DO!!
YOSUKE ...
KREE

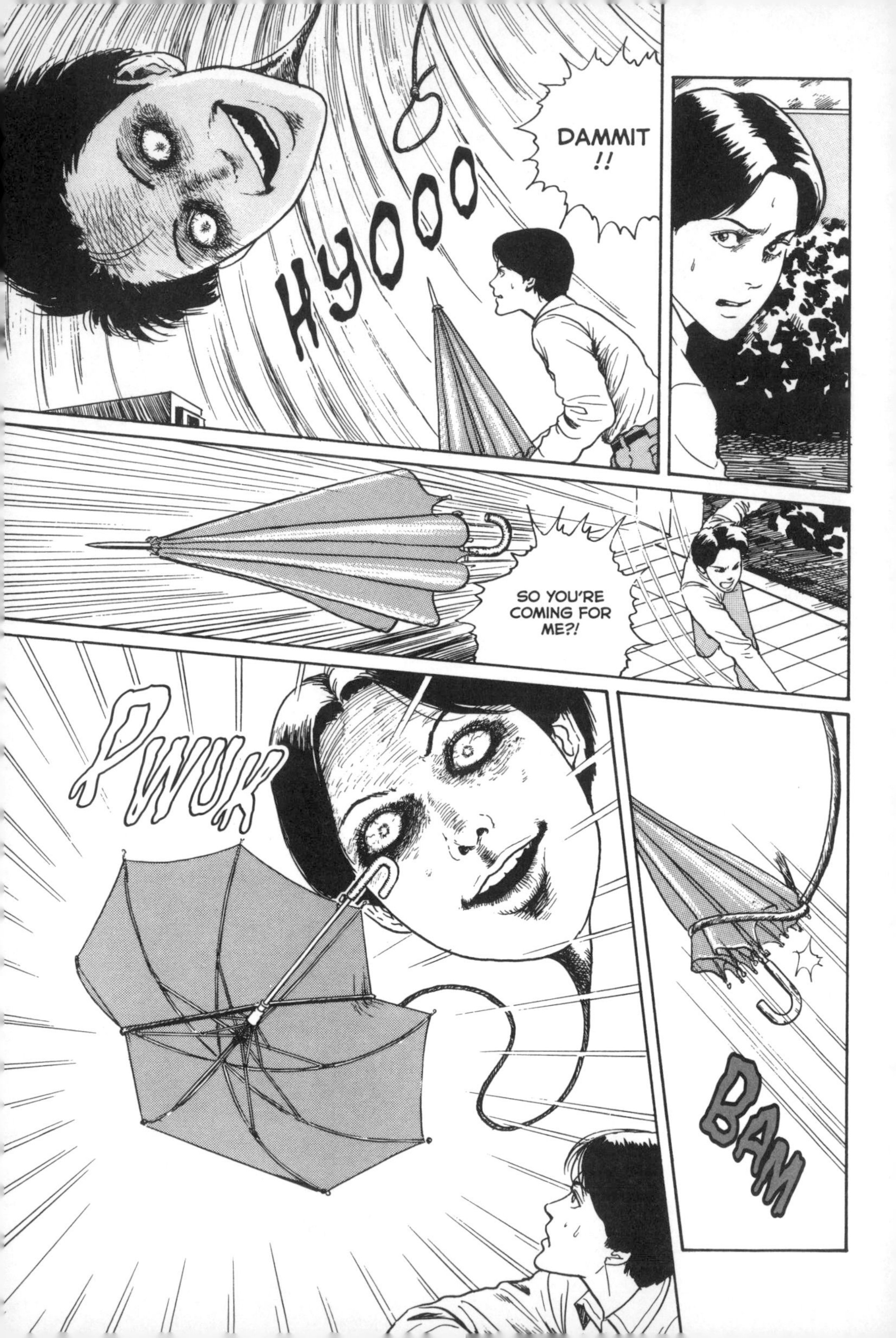
DAMMIT !!
HYOOO
SO YOU'RE COMING FOR ME?!
BAM
PWUK

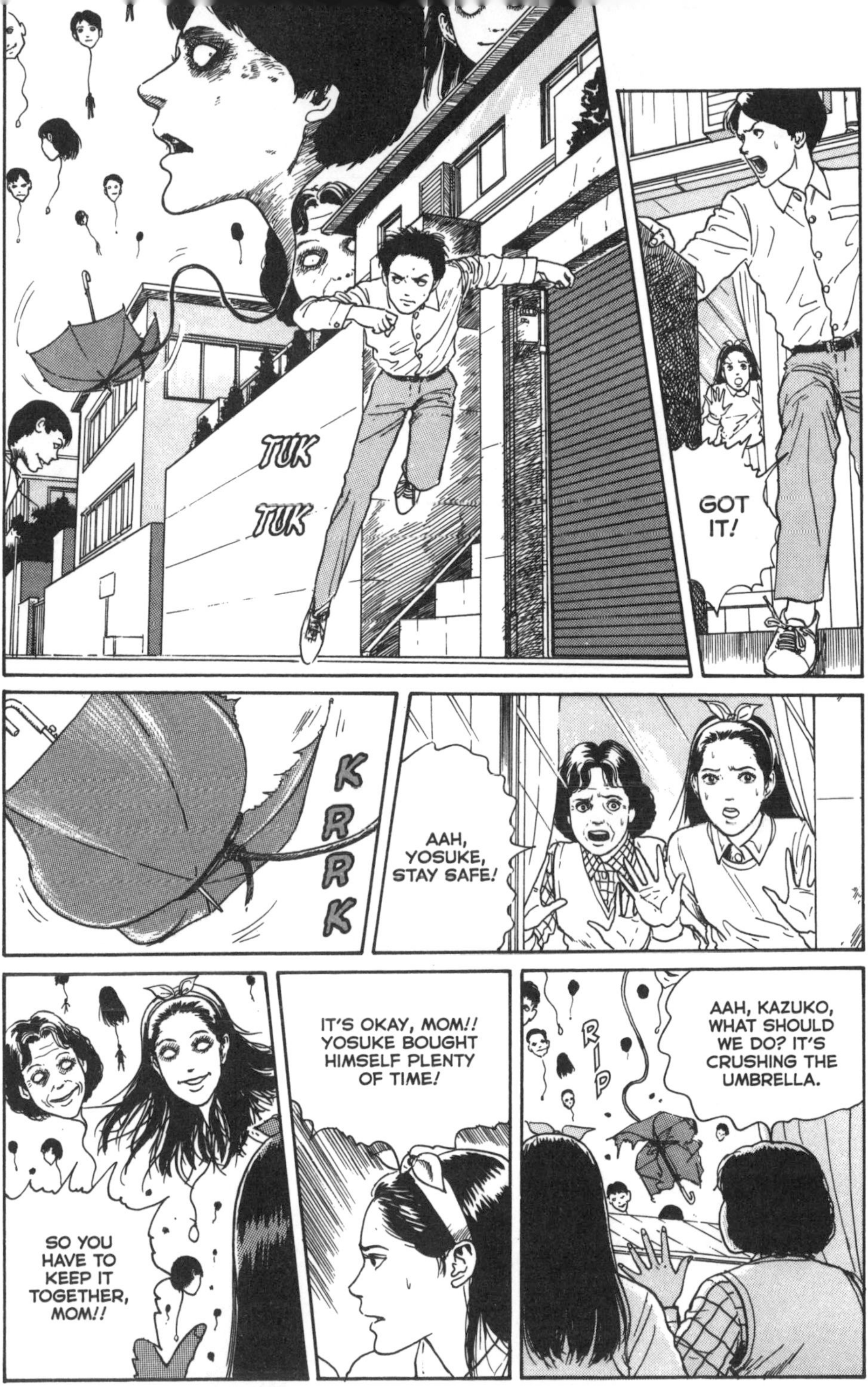
GOT IT!
TUK
TUK
AAH, YOSUKE, STAY SAFE!
KRRK
AAH, KAZUKO, WHAT SHOULD WE DO? IT'S CRUSHING THE UMBRELLA.
RIP
IT'S OKAY, MOM!! YOSUKE BOUGHT HIMSELF PLENTY OF TIME!
SO YOU HAVE TO KEEP IT TOGETHER, MOM!!

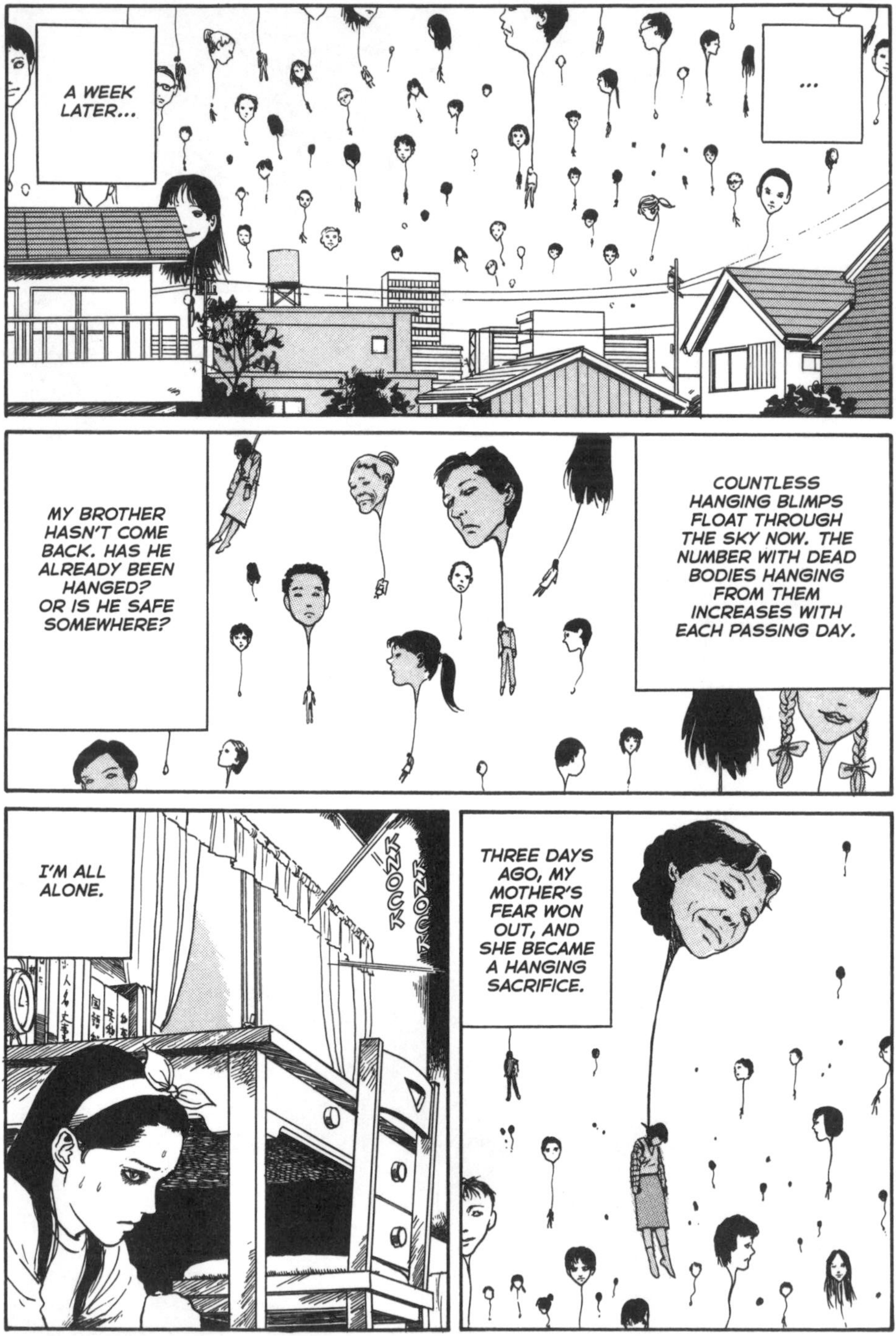
...
A WEEK LATER...
COUNTLESS HANGING BLIMPS FLOAT THROUGH THE SKY NOW. THE NUMBER WITH DEAD BODIES HANGING FROM THEM INCREASES WITH EACH PASSING DAY.
MY BROTHER HASN'T COME BACK. HAS HE ALREADY BEEN HANGED? OR IS HE SAFE SOMEWHERE?
THREE DAYS AGO, MY MOTHER'S FEAR WON OUT, AND SHE BECAME A HANGING SACRIFICE.
KNOCK
KNOCK
I'M ALL ALONE.

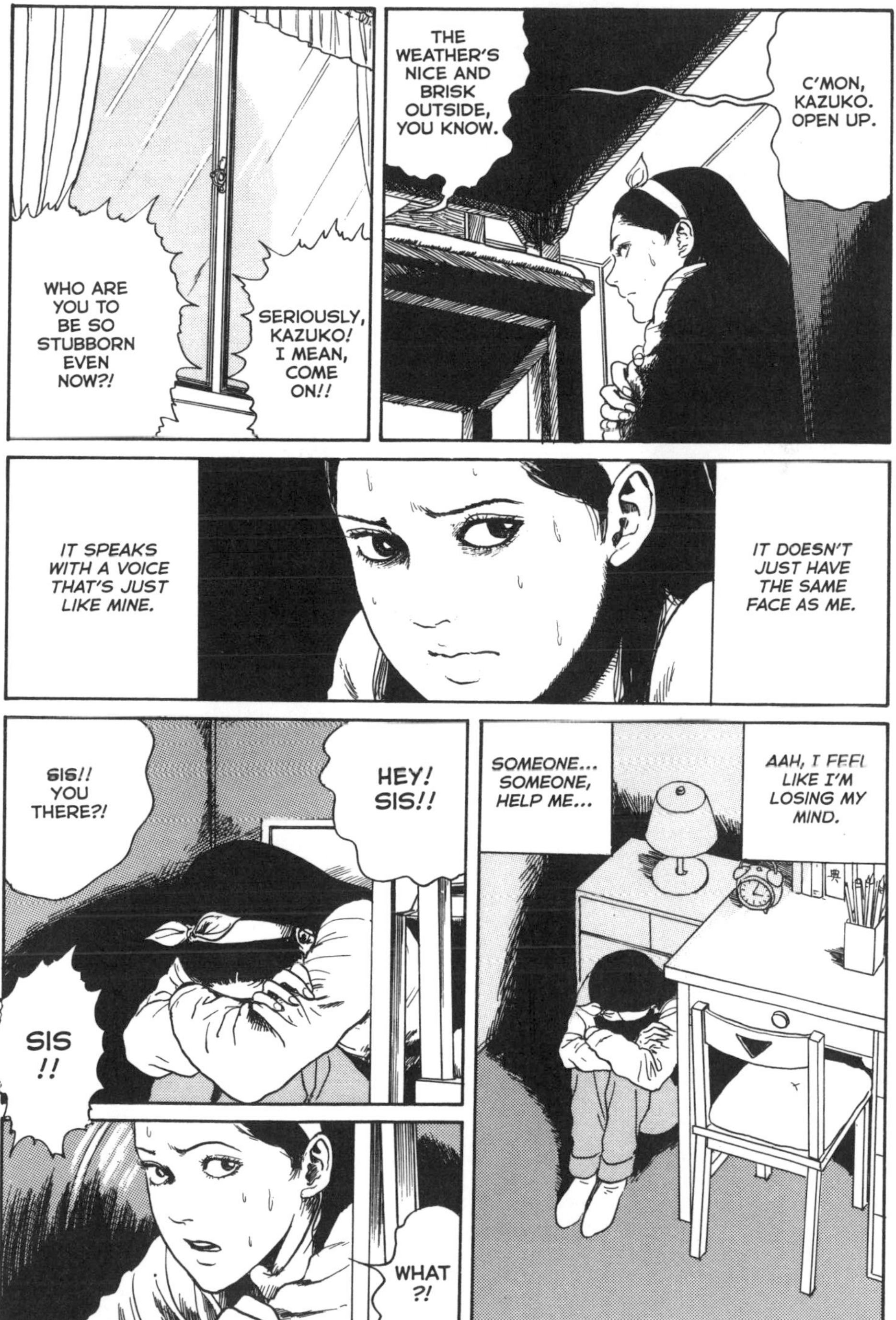
C'MON, KAZUKO. OPEN UP.
THE WEATHER'S NICE AND BRISK OUTSIDE, YOU KNOW.
SERIOUSLY, KAZUKO! I MEAN, COME ON!!
WHO ARE YOU TO BE SO STUBBORN EVEN NOW?!
IT DOESN'T JUST HAVE THE SAME FACE AS ME.
IT SPEAKS WITH A VOICE THAT'S JUST LIKE MINE.
AAH, I FEEL LIKE I'M LOSING MY MIND.
SOMEONE... SOMEONE, HELP ME...
HEY! SIS!!
SIS!! YOU THERE?!
SIS !!
WHAT ?!

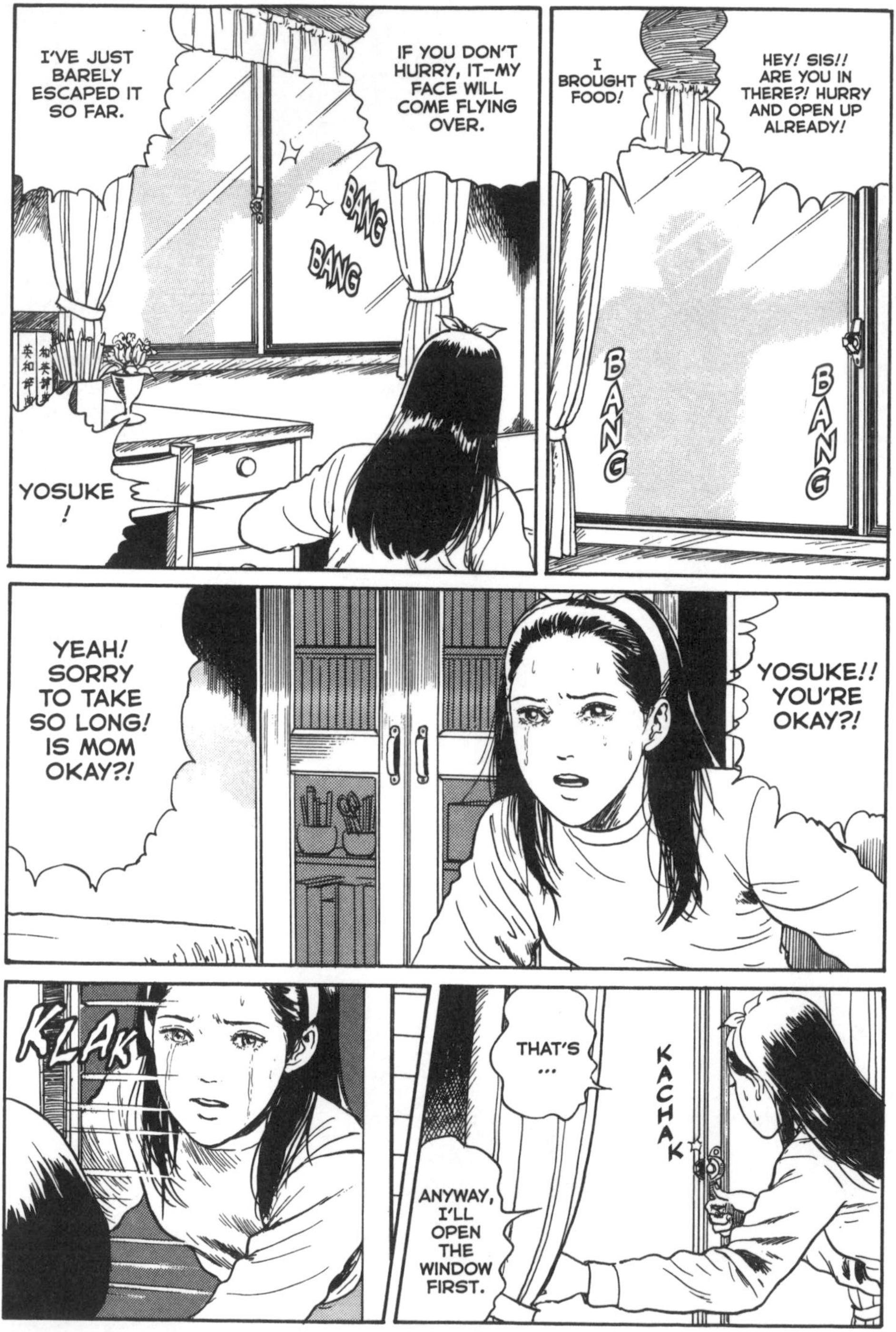
HEY! SIS!! ARE YOU IN THERE?! HURRY AND OPEN UP ALREADY!
I BROUGHT FOOD!
BANG
BANG
IF YOU DON'T HURRY, IT—MY FACE WILL COME FLYING OVER.
I'VE JUST BARELY ESCAPED IT SO FAR.
BANG
BANG
YOSUKE!
YOSUKE!! YOU'RE OKAY?!
YEAH! SORRY TO TAKE SO LONG! IS MOM OKAY?!
THAT'S ...
KACHAK
ANYWAY, I'LL OPEN THE WINDOW FIRST.
KLAK

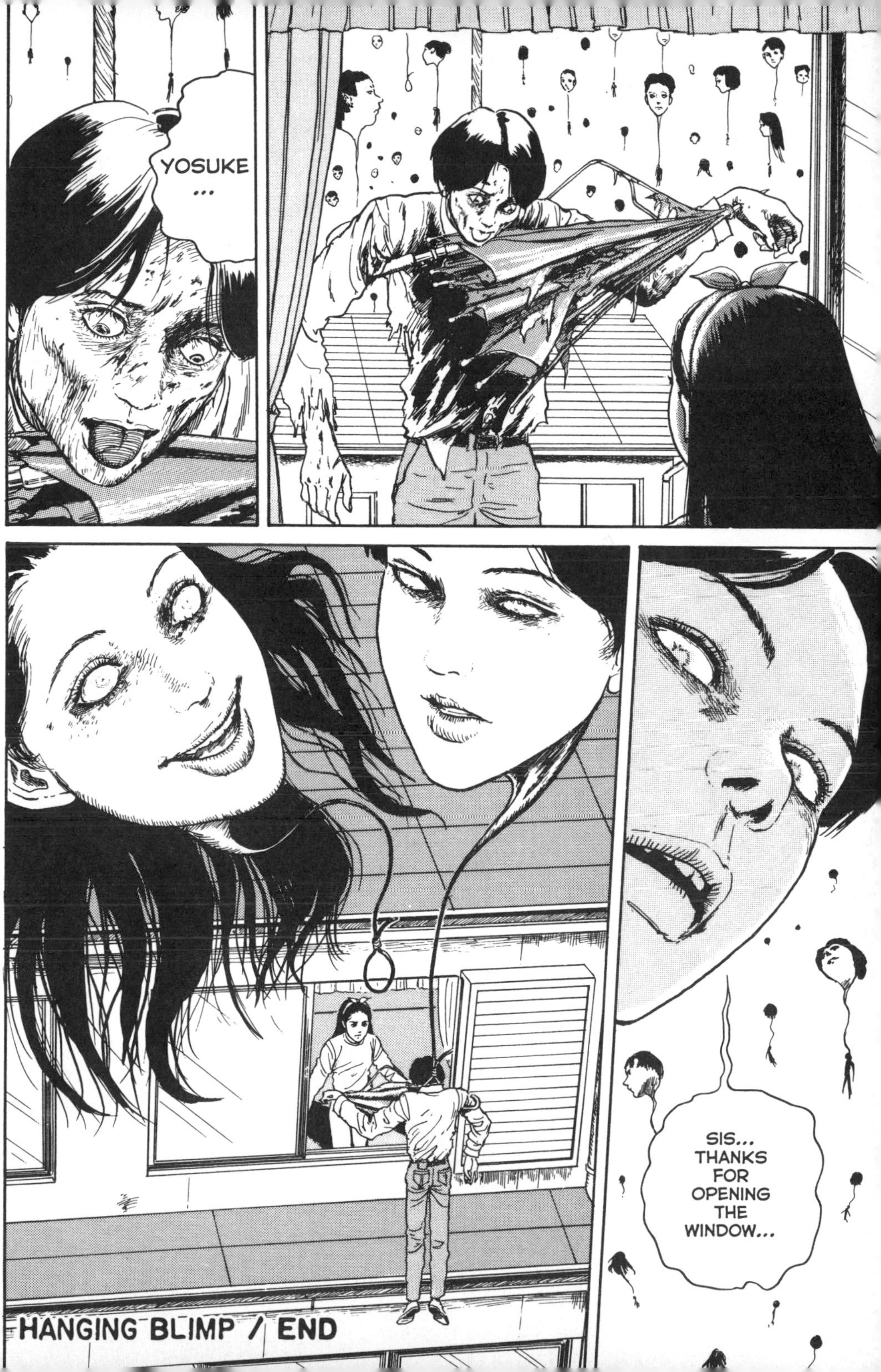
YOSUKE ...
SIS... THANKS FOR OPENING THE WINDOW...
HANGING BLIMP / END

HANGING BLIMP

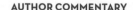

This is based on a dream I originally had when I was little. In the dream, I was somewhere like an airport when a clay figure of a woman's torso with a rope dangling from it came flying down and hanged me by the neck.

And then, after I became a manga artist, I came up with this image of a balloon that had a dead body hanging from it by the neck. When that balloon passed through the sky, something would happen in the town. I was going to draw it as an opener, this ominous harbinger. But I couldn't think of the thing that would happen, the key part. While I was thinking about this and that, I started imagining it would be more interesting to make it a story of blimps actively coming to hang people. But just regular blimps would be boring. So then I continued brainstorming and came up with the idea of a blimp with your face that flies around hunting you, and I drew it, excited the whole time.

For the "Hanging Blimp" included in this collection, I used pages I revised slightly when the story was published in an anthology with another publisher. It's just a few places, so if you're interested, please try and look for those differences.

。首吊り気球の死体は死んでいるが、動いて人々をおそう。
はじめ人々は首を吊られて死んでいるとは思わない。気球にぶらさがって
いるだけだと思う。そしてぶらさがりながら人々をおどかしているのかと思う
が、地上におろして調べてみると、気球からたれたロープは、その人の首
にまきついてくいこんでおり、(その人は死んでおり)
あきらかに首を吊って死んでいた。

。しだいに空に首吊り気球が大量にうかびあがる

これらの気球はなかなか回収できないため、空にただよい
つづける (数ヶ月)
これらは夜になると地上におりてきて、人々を恐怖させる

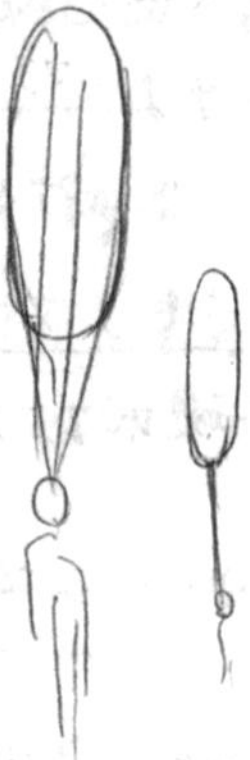

★この気球は人の顔をしていて、この顔にはモデル
がおり、それはごく一般の人の顔で その人を
見つけると この気球は首吊りをさせる。
つまり、自分の顔をした気球が空にあら
われると、それは自分を首吊りにするた
めに自分のところへ近づいてくるのだ
そして にげまどう当人の首にロープ
にかけ、つりあげてしまう。
なぜ自分にそっくりの気球があらわれ、
しかも自分を首吊りにしようとするのか
すべてが謎である。とにかく自分そっくり
の気球があらわれたら吊りあげられ
ないように逃げるしかないのだ
銃でうちおとそうとしたりやりでつこうとしても
だめだ (はじめのうちはうまくいったが…)

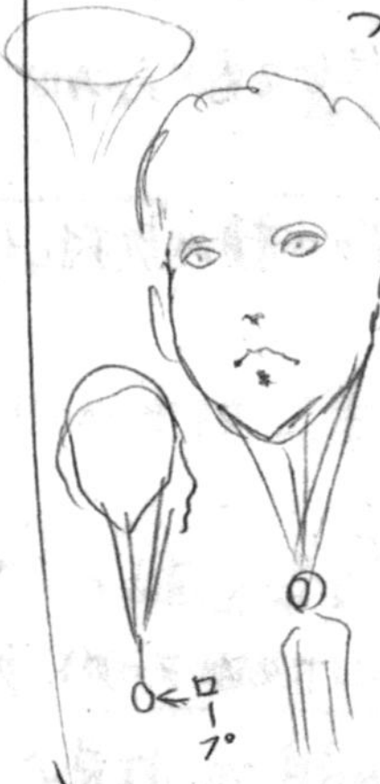
ロープ

• The bodies on the hanging blimps are dead, but they attack moving people.

In the beginning, people don't think the hanging people are dead. They think they're just being dangled from the blimps. They wonder if maybe they are threatening people while dangling like that, but after one crashes to the ground, they examine it and find that the person is dead. The rope they hang on from the blimp is wrapped around their neck and digging into their flesh, so it's clear they were hanged to death.

• Gradually, a great number of hanging blimps rise up into the sky.

Because the people can't really collect the blimps, many just continue to drift through the sky. When night falls, they come down to earth to terrorize people.

* These blimps have human faces, and these faces have models; they are the faces of regular people, and when a blimp finds the person with its face, it hangs them.

In other words, when a blimp with your own face appears in the sky, it approaches you so that it can hang you.

And then it tosses a rope around the person's neck as they try to run away and pulls them up to hang them.

Why do blimps appear that look just like people? And why are they trying to hang people? All of this is a mystery. At any rate, once a blimp that looks just like you appears, the only thing to do is run away so it doesn't hang you. It's also no use trying to shoot it down with a gun or pierce it with a lance. (In the beginning, they rupture, but...)

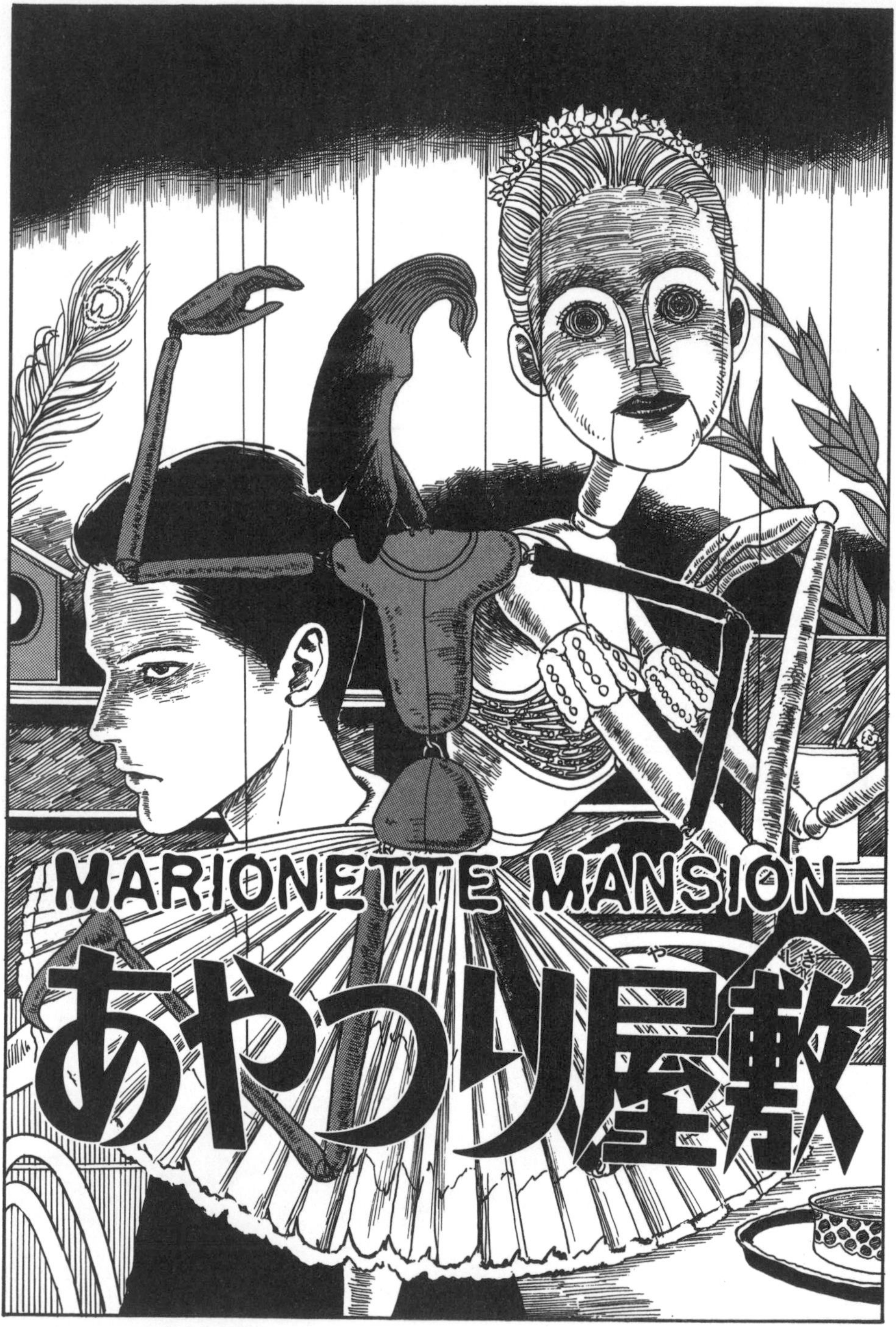
MARIONETTE MANSION
あやつり屋敷

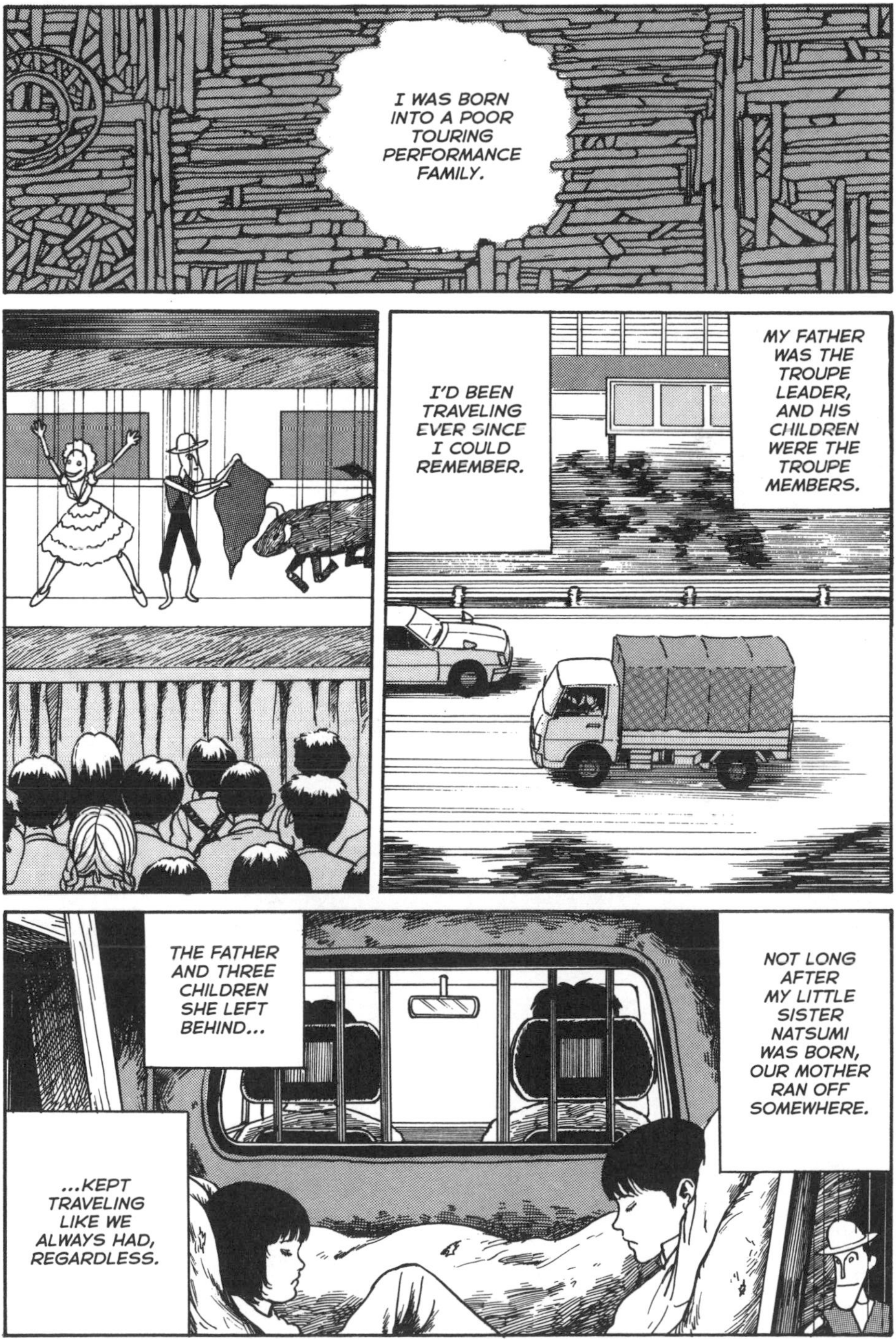
I WAS BORN INTO A POOR TOURING PERFORMANCE FAMILY.
MY FATHER WAS THE TROUPE LEADER, AND HIS CHILDREN WERE THE TROUPE MEMBERS.
I'D BEEN TRAVELING EVER SINCE I COULD REMEMBER.
NOT LONG AFTER MY LITTLE SISTER NATSUMI WAS BORN, OUR MOTHER RAN OFF SOMEWHERE.
THE FATHER AND THREE CHILDREN SHE LEFT BEHIND...
...KEPT TRAVELING LIKE WE ALWAYS HAD, REGARDLESS.

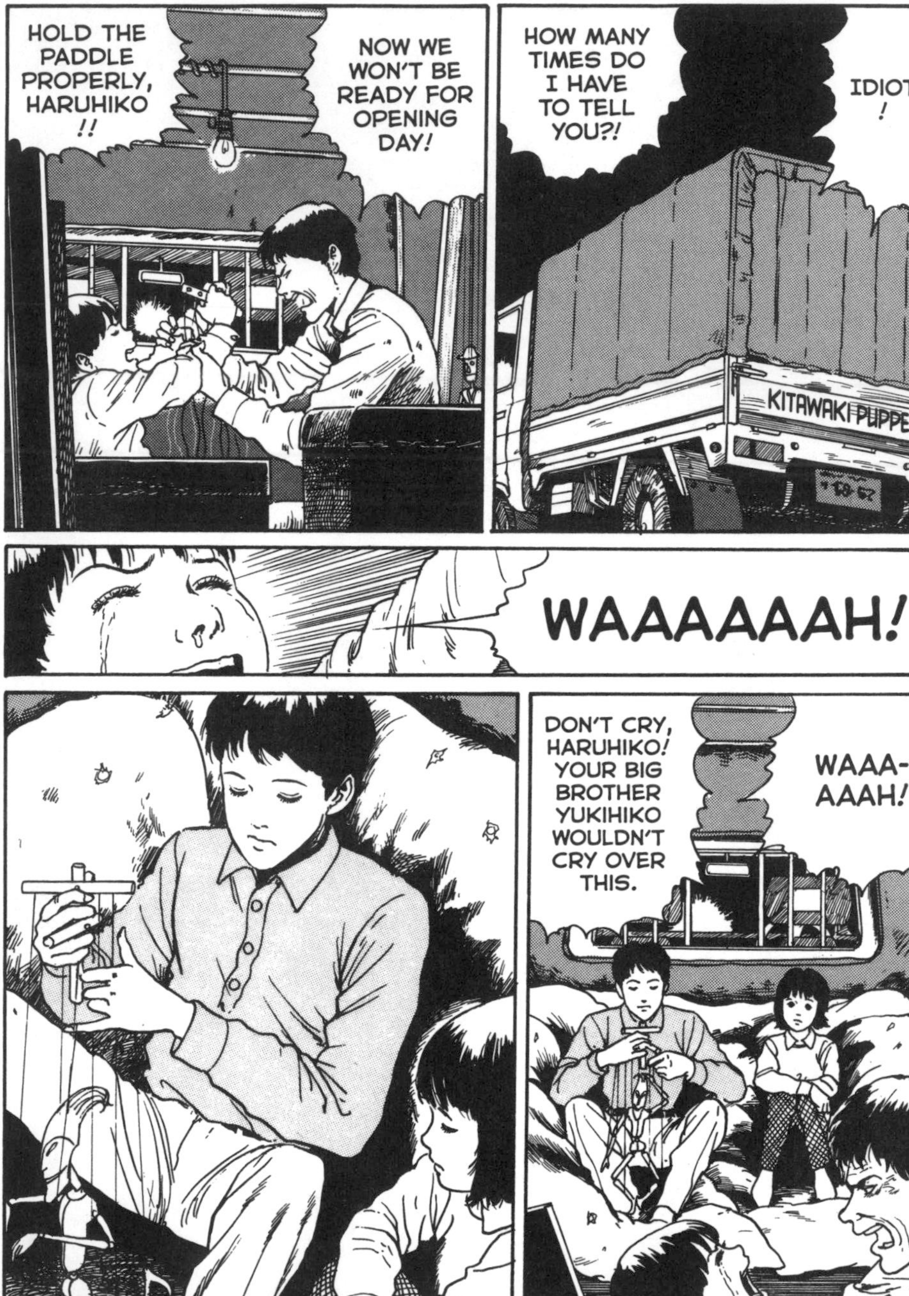
HOW MANY TIMES DO I HAVE TO TELL YOU?!
IDIOT!
KITAWAKI PUPPET
HOLD THE PADDLE PROPERLY, HARUHIKO!!
NOW WE WON'T BE READY FOR OPENING DAY!
WAAAAAAH!
DON'T CRY, HARUHIKO! YOUR BIG BROTHER YUKIHIKO WOULDN'T CRY OVER THIS.
WAAA-AAAH!

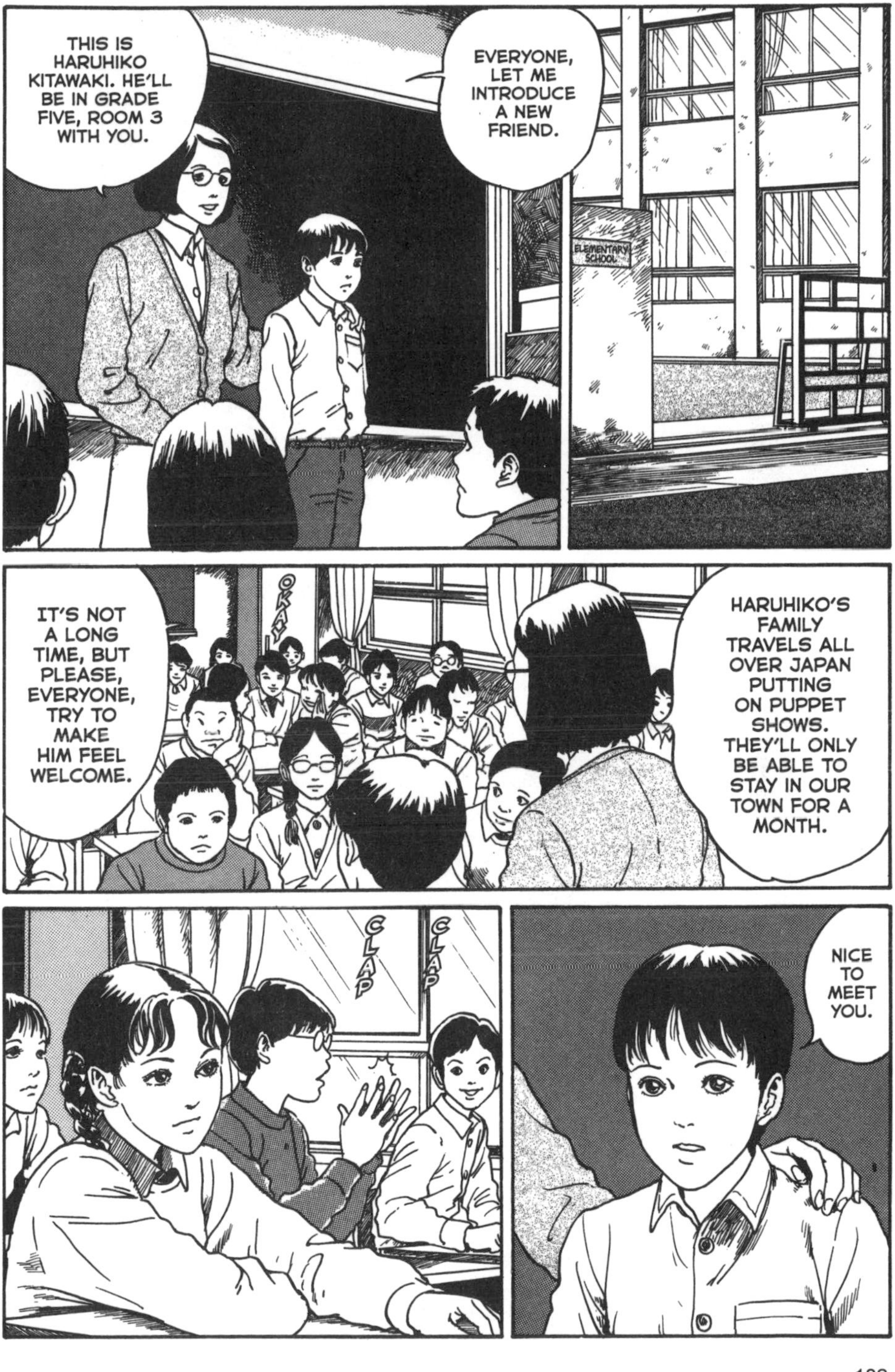
ELEMENTARY SCHOOL
EVERYONE, LET ME INTRODUCE A NEW FRIEND.
THIS IS HARUHIKO KITAWAKI. HE'LL BE IN GRADE FIVE, ROOM 3 WITH YOU.
HARUHIKO'S FAMILY TRAVELS ALL OVER JAPAN PUTTING ON PUPPET SHOWS. THEY'LL ONLY BE ABLE TO STAY IN OUR TOWN FOR A MONTH.
OKAY
IT'S NOT A LONG TIME, BUT PLEASE, EVERYONE, TRY TO MAKE HIM FEEL WELCOME.
NICE TO MEET YOU.
CLAP
CLAP

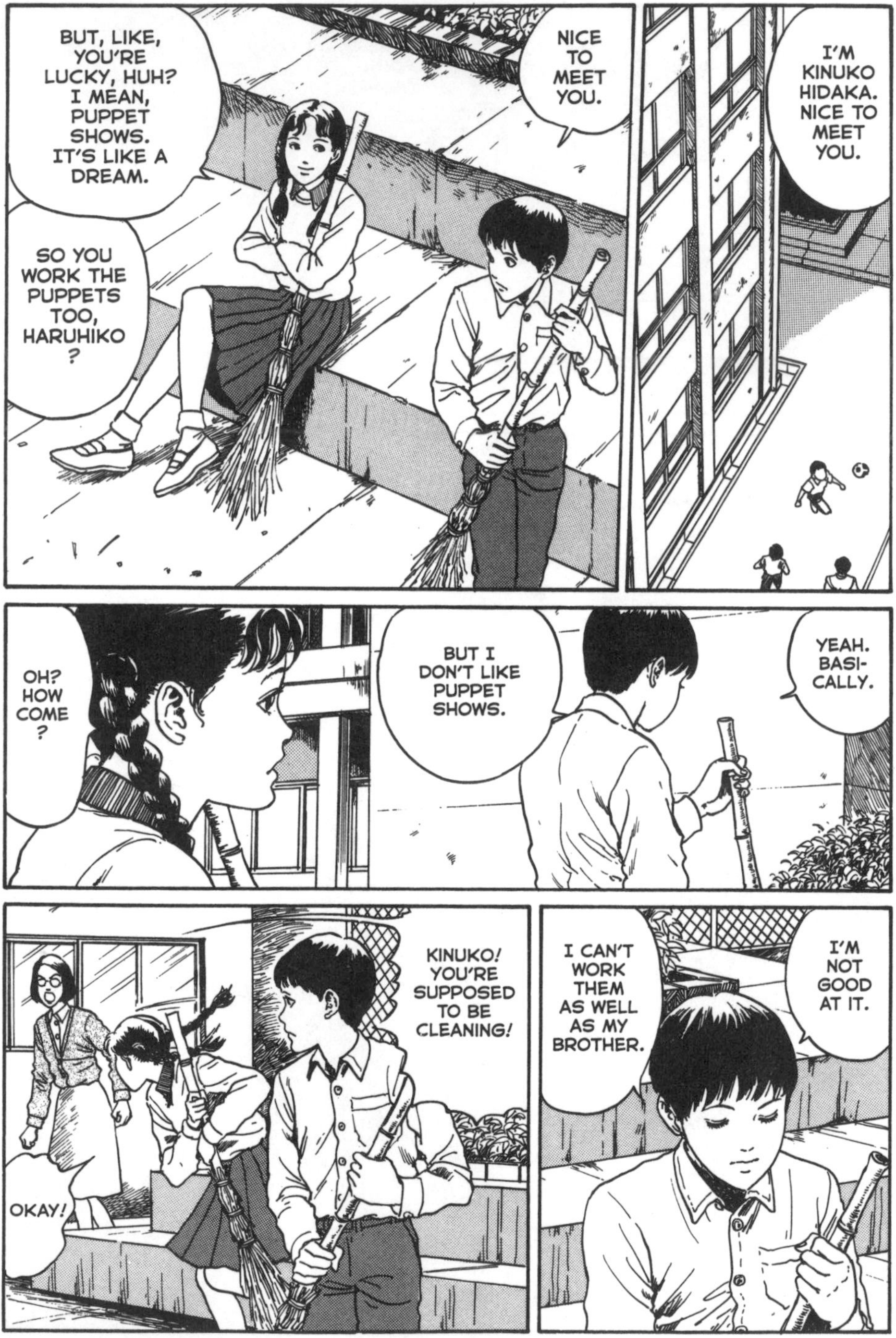
I'M KINUKO HIDAKA. NICE TO MEET YOU.
NICE TO MEET YOU.
BUT, LIKE, YOU'RE LUCKY, HUH? I MEAN, PUPPET SHOWS. IT'S LIKE A DREAM.
SO YOU WORK THE PUPPETS TOO, HARUHIKO?
YEAH. BASI-CALLY.
BUT I DON'T LIKE PUPPET SHOWS.
OH? HOW COME?
I'M NOT GOOD AT IT.
I CAN'T WORK THEM AS WELL AS MY BROTHER.
KINUKO! YOU'RE SUPPOSED TO BE CLEANING!
OKAY!

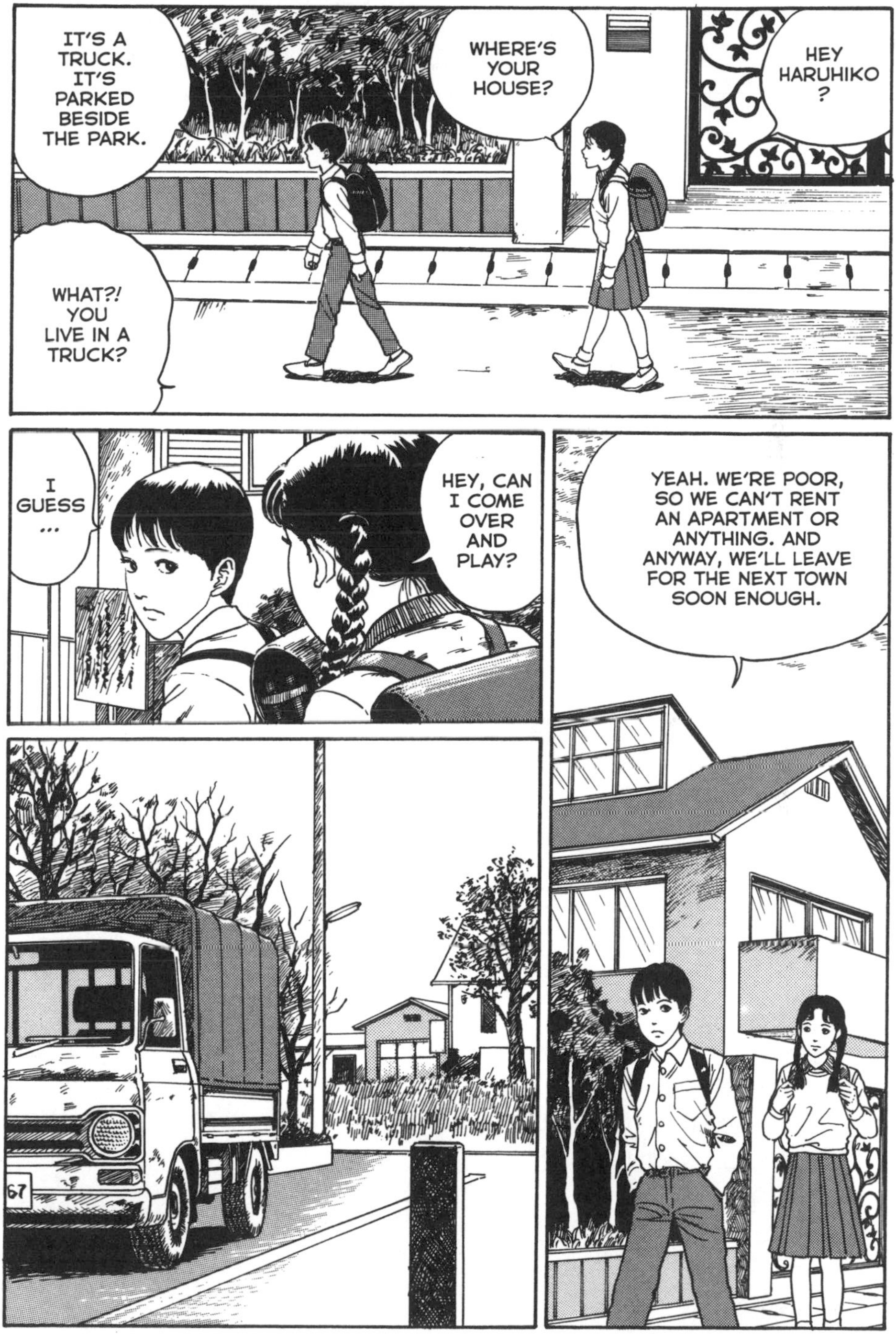
HEY HARUHIKO?
WHERE'S YOUR HOUSE?
IT'S A TRUCK. IT'S PARKED BESIDE THE PARK.
WHAT?! YOU LIVE IN A TRUCK?
YEAH. WE'RE POOR, SO WE CAN'T RENT AN APARTMENT OR ANYTHING. AND ANYWAY, WE'LL LEAVE FOR THE NEXT TOWN SOON ENOUGH.
HEY, CAN I COME OVER AND PLAY?
I GUESS...

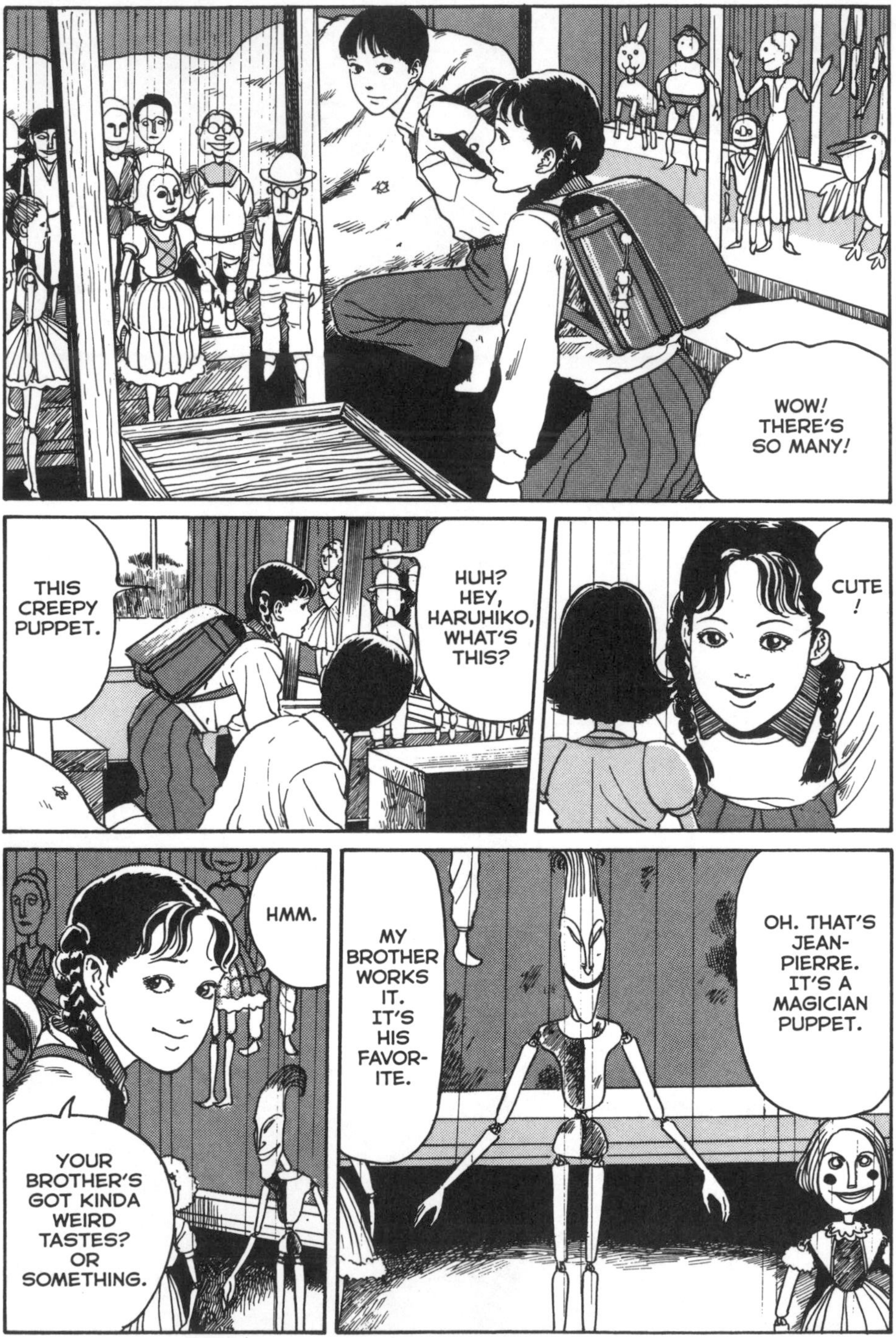
WOW! THERE'S SO MANY!
CUTE!
HUH? HEY, HARUHIKO, WHAT'S THIS?
THIS CREEPY PUPPET.
OH. THAT'S JEAN-PIERRE. IT'S A MAGICIAN PUPPET.
MY BROTHER WORKS IT. IT'S HIS FAVOR-ITE.
HMM.
YOUR BROTHER'S GOT KINDA WEIRD TASTES? OR SOMETHING.

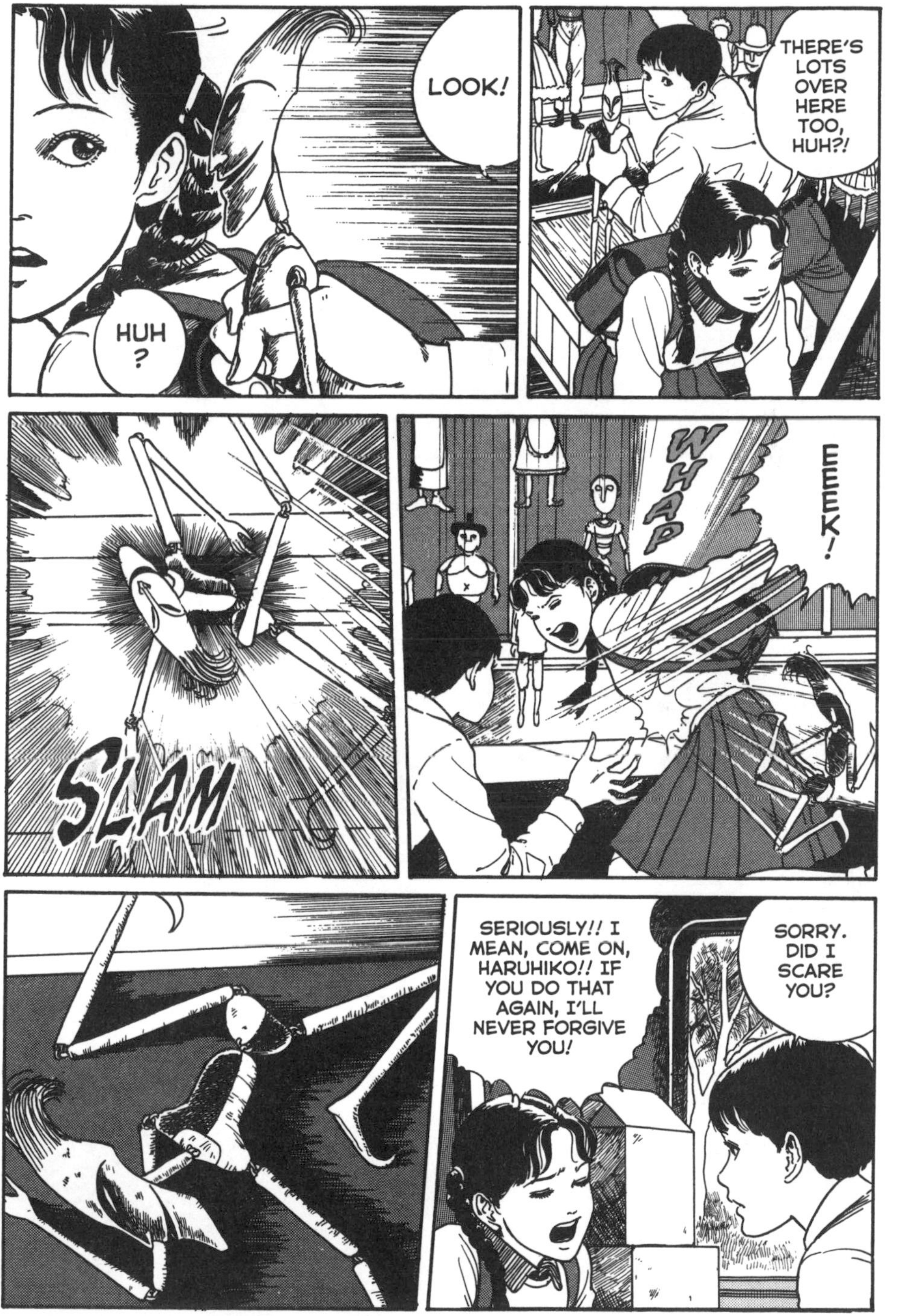
THERE'S LOTS OVER HERE TOO, HUH?!
LOOK!
HUH ?
EEEK!
WHAP
SLAM
SORRY. DID I SCARE YOU?
SERIOUSLY!! I MEAN, COME ON, HARUHIKO!! IF YOU DO THAT AGAIN, I'LL NEVER FORGIVE YOU!

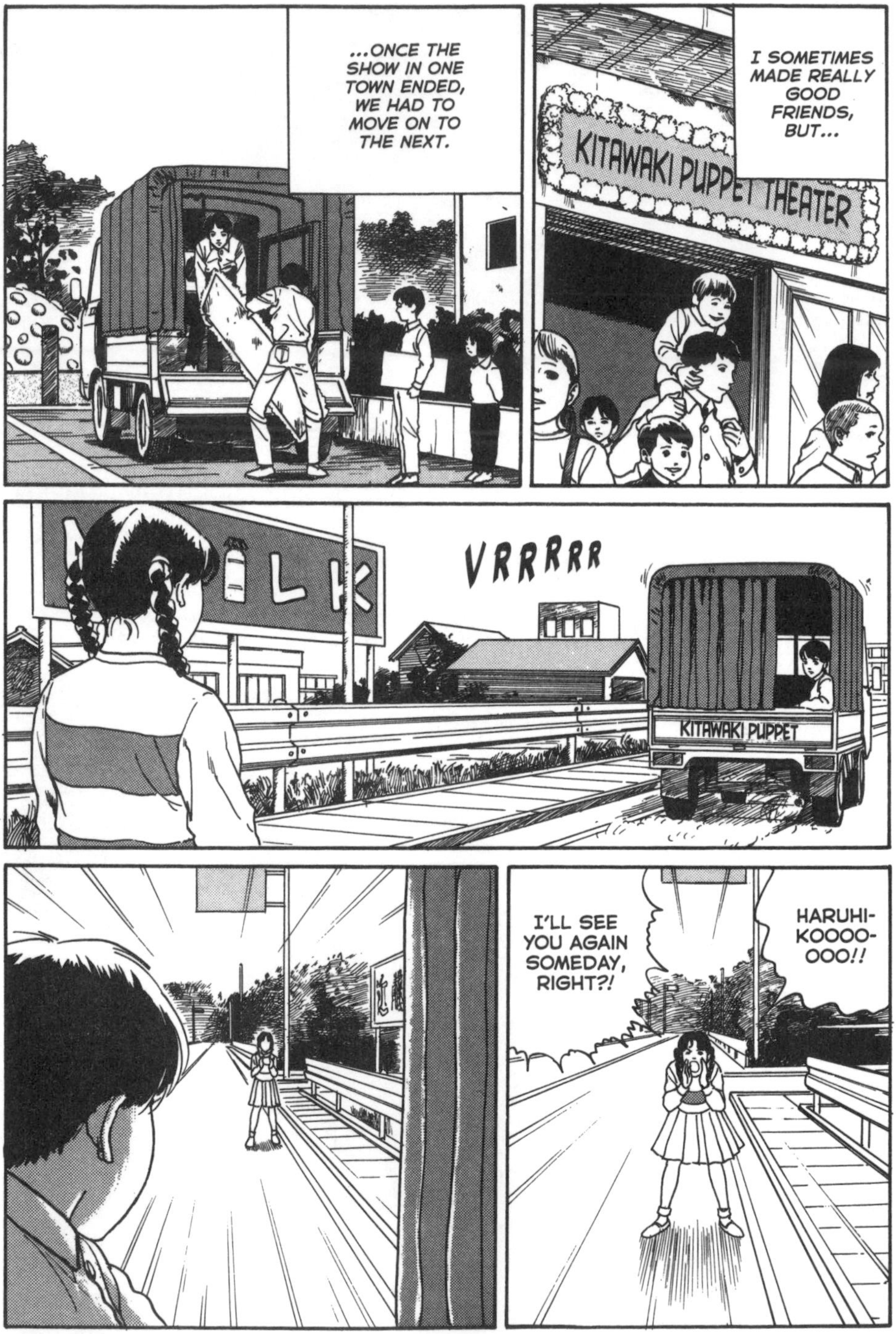
I SOMETIMES MADE REALLY GOOD FRIENDS, BUT...
KITAWAKI PUPPET THEATER
...ONCE THE SHOW IN ONE TOWN ENDED, WE HAD TO MOVE ON TO THE NEXT.
VRRRRR
KITAWAKI PUPPET
HARUHI-KOOOO-OOO!!
I'LL SEE YOU AGAIN SOMEDAY, RIGHT?!

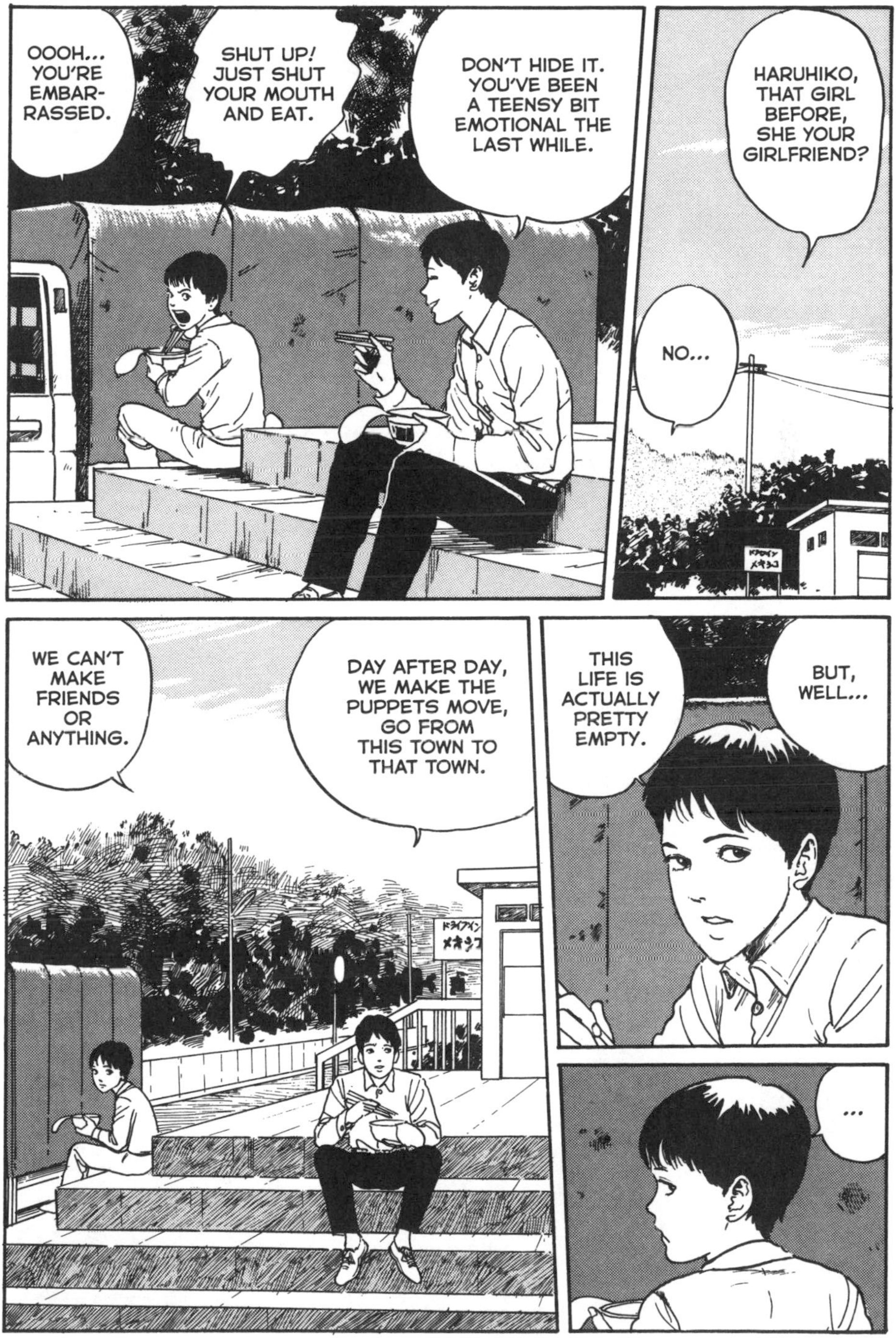
HARUHIKO, THAT GIRL BEFORE, SHE YOUR GIRLFRIEND?
NO...
DON'T HIDE IT. YOU'VE BEEN A TEENSY BIT EMOTIONAL THE LAST WHILE.
SHUT UP! JUST SHUT YOUR MOUTH AND EAT.
OOOH... YOU'RE EMBAR-RASSED.
BUT, WELL...
THIS LIFE IS ACTUALLY PRETTY EMPTY.
...
DAY AFTER DAY, WE MAKE THE PUPPETS MOVE, GO FROM THIS TOWN TO THAT TOWN.
WE CAN'T MAKE FRIENDS OR ANYTHING.

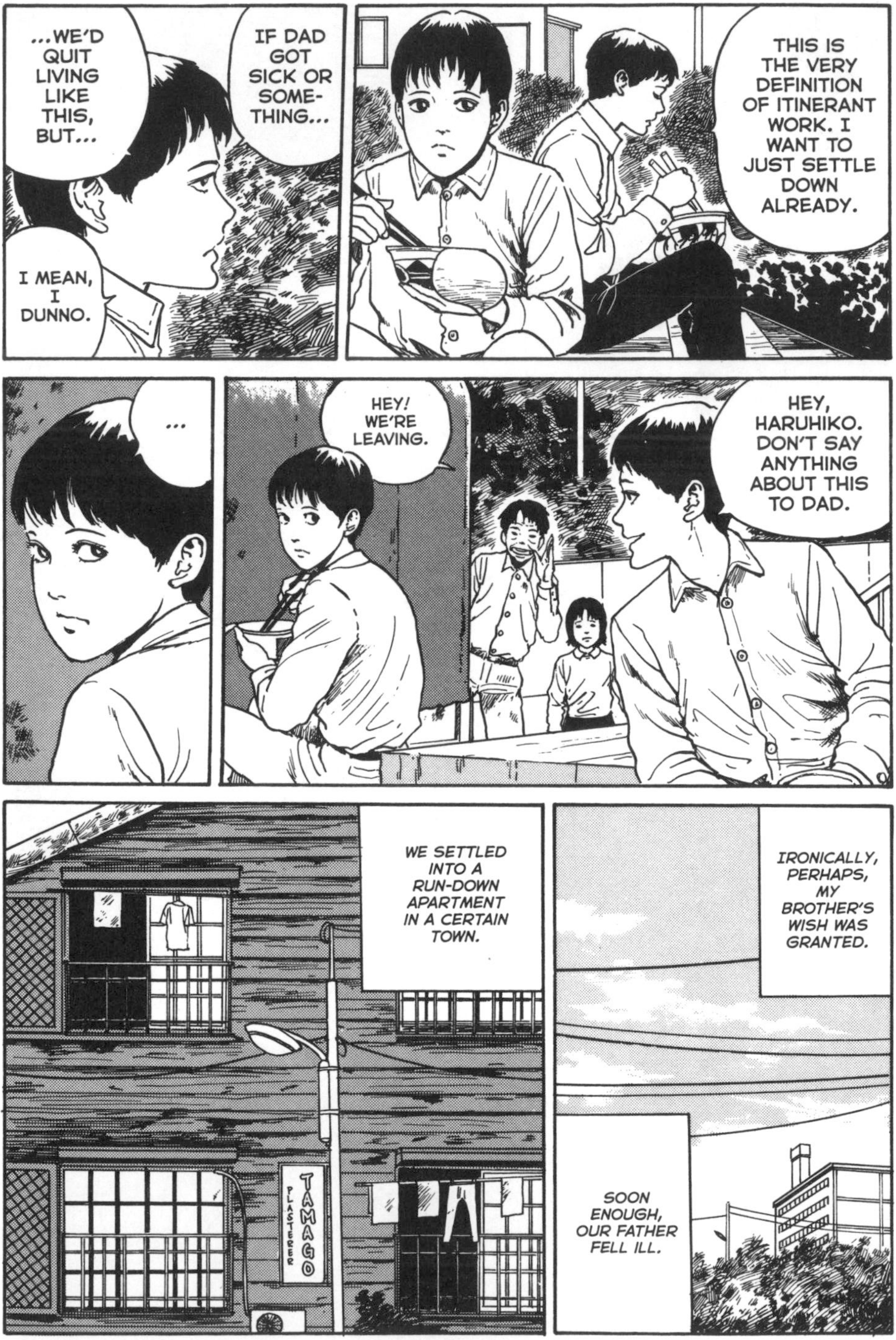
THIS IS THE VERY DEFINITION OF ITINERANT WORK. I WANT TO JUST SETTLE DOWN ALREADY.
IF DAD GOT SICK OR SOME-THING...
...WE'D QUIT LIVING LIKE THIS, BUT...
I MEAN, I DUNNO.
HEY, HARUHIKO. DON'T SAY ANYTHING ABOUT THIS TO DAD.
HEY! WE'RE LEAVING.
...
IRONICALLY, PERHAPS, MY BROTHER'S WISH WAS GRANTED.
SOON ENOUGH, OUR FATHER FELL ILL.
WE SETTLED INTO A RUN-DOWN APARTMENT IN A CERTAIN TOWN.
TAMAGO
PLASTERER

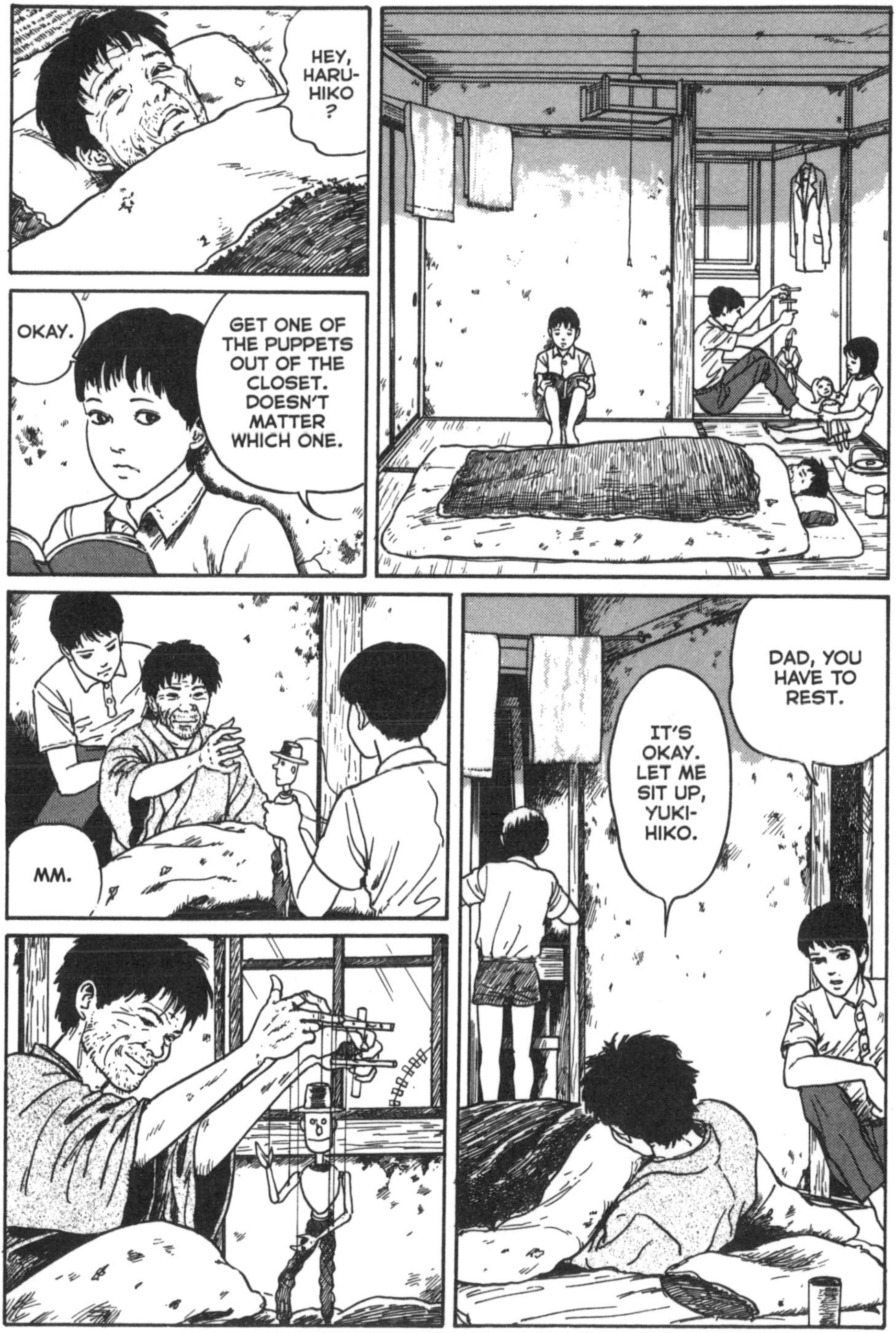
HEY, HARU-HIKO?
GET ONE OF THE PUPPETS OUT OF THE CLOSET. DOESN'T MATTER WHICH ONE.
OKAY.
DAD, YOU HAVE TO REST.
IT'S OKAY. LET ME SIT UP, YUKI-HIKO.
MM.

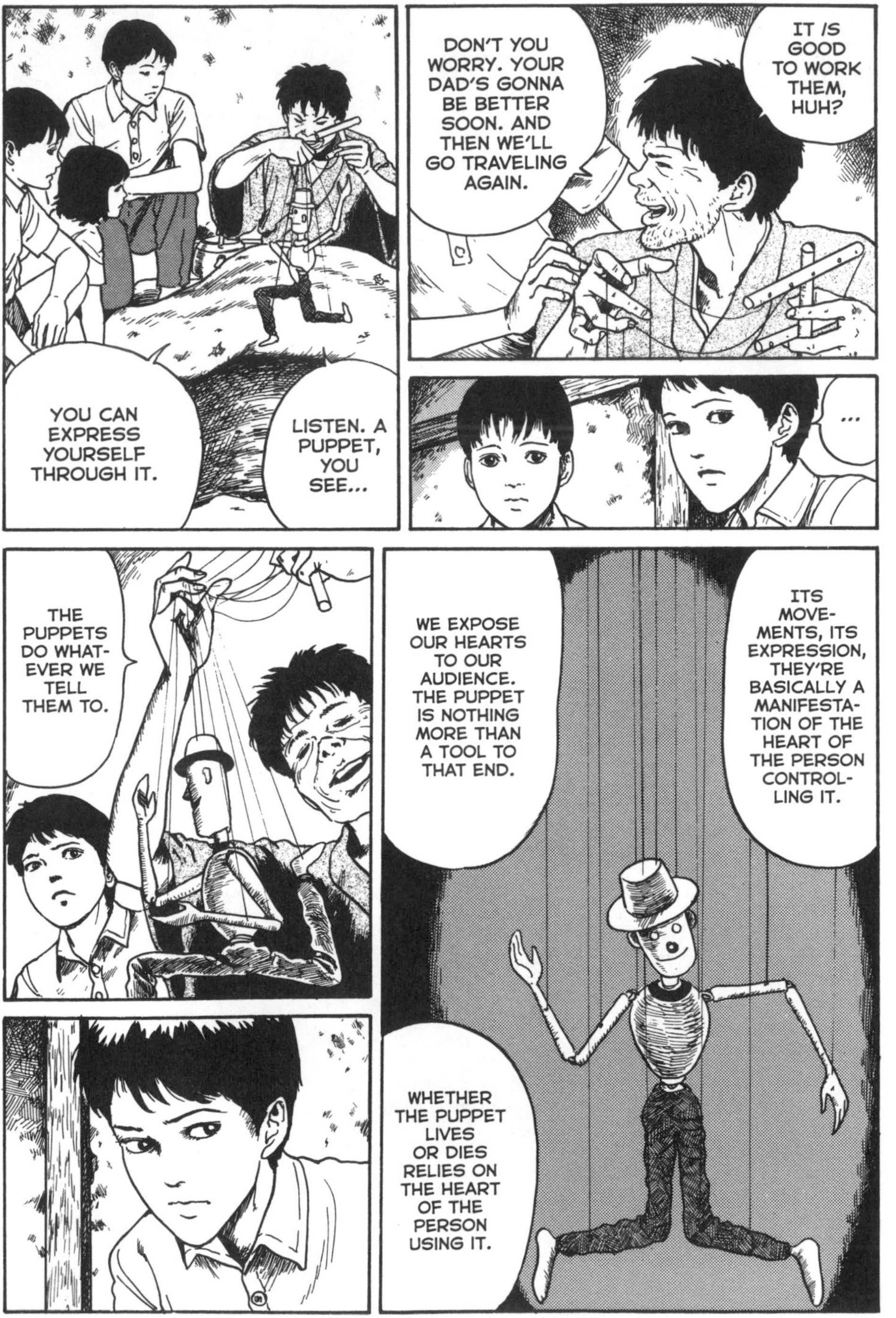
IT IS GOOD TO WORK THEM, HUH?
DON'T YOU WORRY. YOUR DAD'S GONNA BE BETTER SOON. AND THEN WE'LL GO TRAVELING AGAIN.
...
LISTEN. A PUPPET, YOU SEE...
YOU CAN EXPRESS YOURSELF THROUGH IT.
ITS MOVE-MENTS, ITS EXPRESSION, THEY'RE BASICALLY A MANIFESTA-TION OF THE HEART OF THE PERSON CONTROL-LING IT.
WE EXPOSE OUR HEARTS TO OUR AUDIENCE. THE PUPPET IS NOTHING MORE THAN A TOOL TO THAT END.
WHETHER THE PUPPET LIVES OR DIES RELIES ON THE HEART OF THE PERSON USING IT.
THE PUPPETS DO WHAT-EVER WE TELL THEM TO.

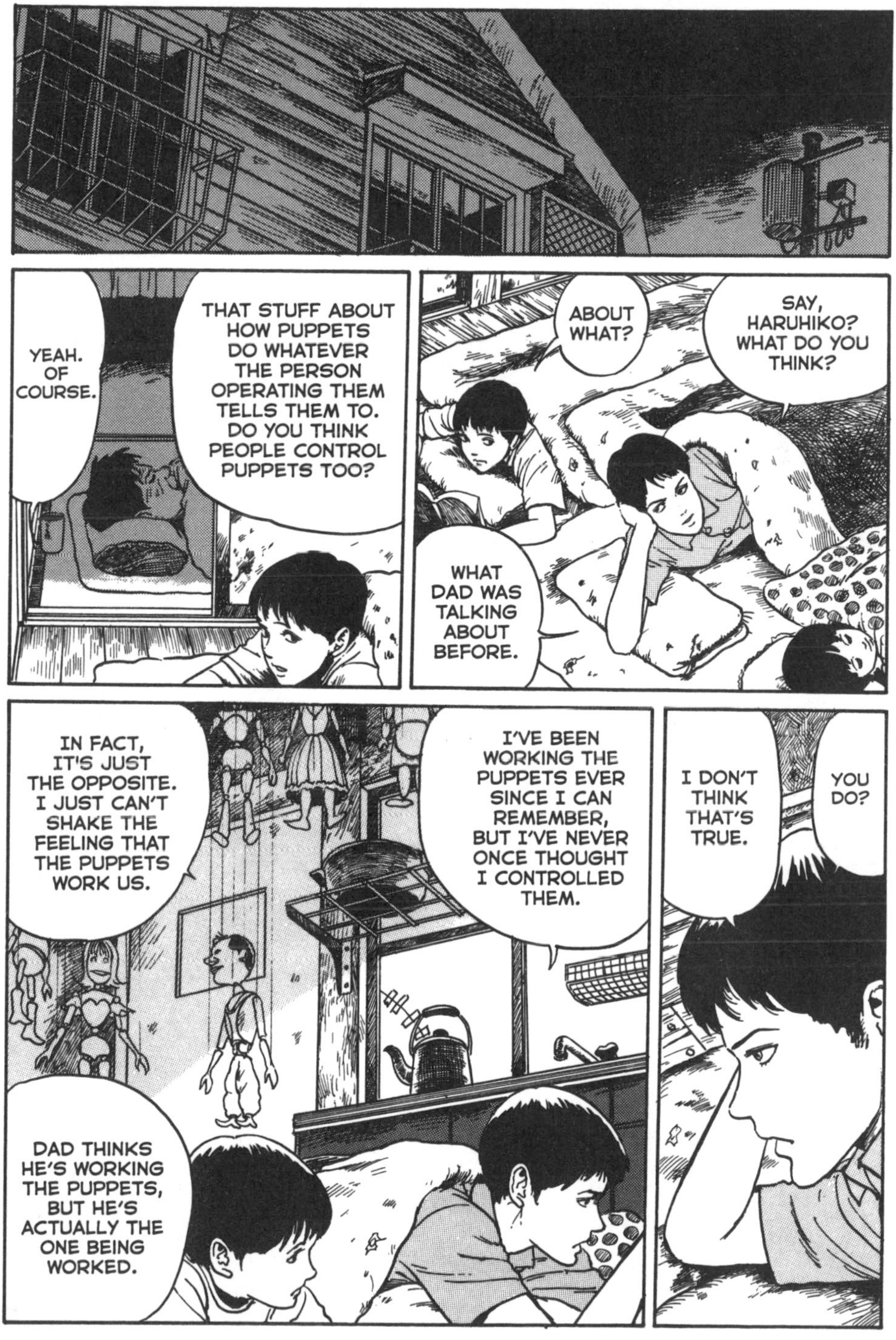
SAY, HARUHIKO? WHAT DO YOU THINK?
ABOUT WHAT?
WHAT DAD WAS TALKING ABOUT BEFORE.
THAT STUFF ABOUT HOW PUPPETS DO WHATEVER THE PERSON OPERATING THEM TELLS THEM TO. DO YOU THINK PEOPLE CONTROL PUPPETS TOO?
YEAH. OF COURSE.
YOU DO?
I DON'T THINK THAT'S TRUE.
I'VE BEEN WORKING THE PUPPETS EVER SINCE I CAN REMEMBER, BUT I'VE NEVER ONCE THOUGHT I CONTROLLED THEM.
IN FACT, IT'S JUST THE OPPOSITE. I JUST CAN'T SHAKE THE FEELING THAT THE PUPPETS WORK US.
DAD THINKS HE'S WORKING THE PUPPETS, BUT HE'S ACTUALLY THE ONE BEING WORKED.

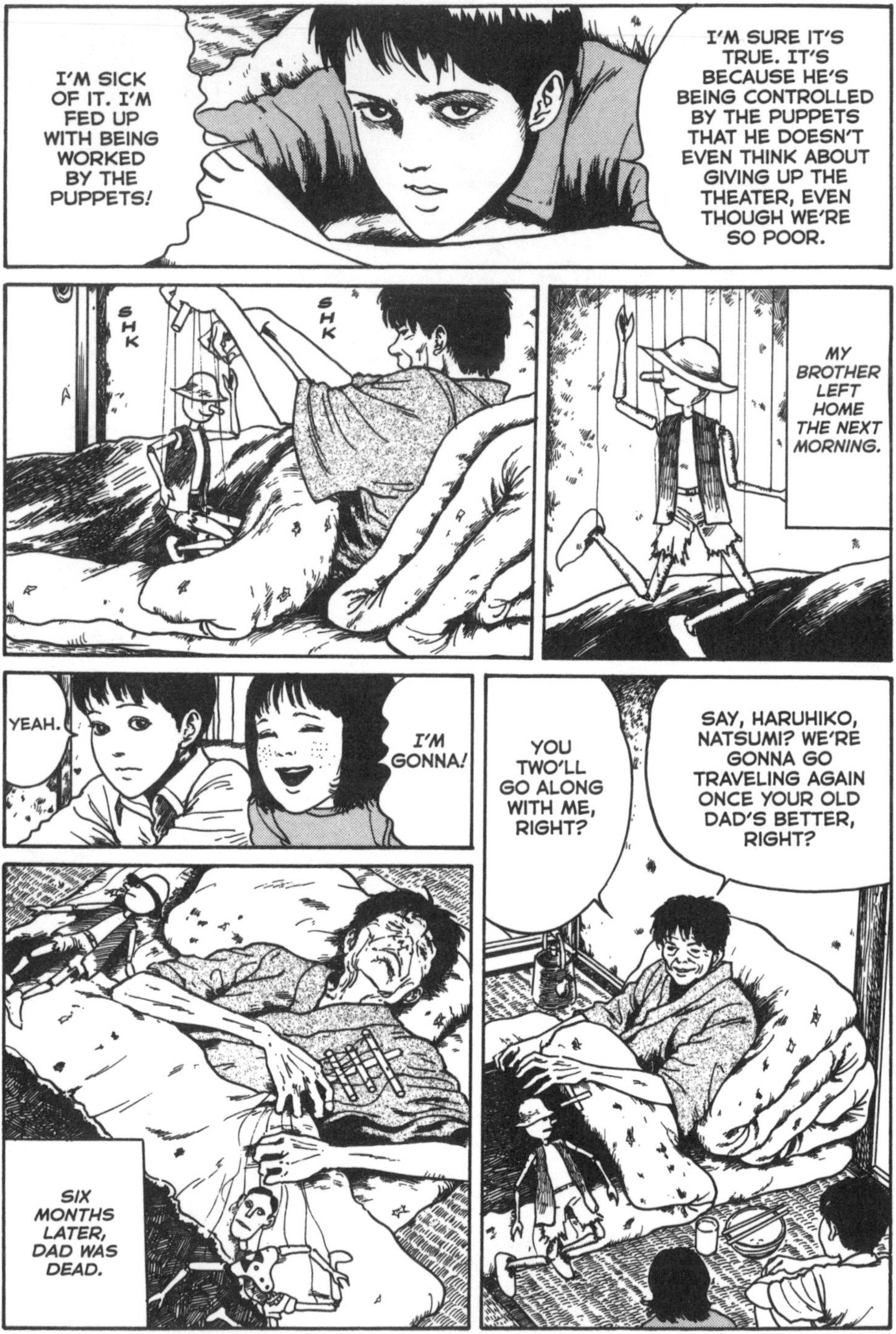
I'M SURE IT'S TRUE. IT'S BECAUSE HE'S BEING CONTROLLED BY THE PUPPETS THAT HE DOESN'T EVEN THINK ABOUT GIVING UP THE THEATER, EVEN THOUGH WE'RE SO POOR.
I'M SICK OF IT. I'M FED UP WITH BEING WORKED BY THE PUPPETS!
MY BROTHER LEFT HOME THE NEXT MORNING.
SHK
SHK
SAY, HARUHIKO, NATSUMI? WE'RE GONNA GO TRAVELING AGAIN ONCE YOUR OLD DAD'S BETTER, RIGHT?
YOU TWO'LL GO ALONG WITH ME, RIGHT?
I'M GONNA!
YEAH.
SIX MONTHS LATER, DAD WAS DEAD.

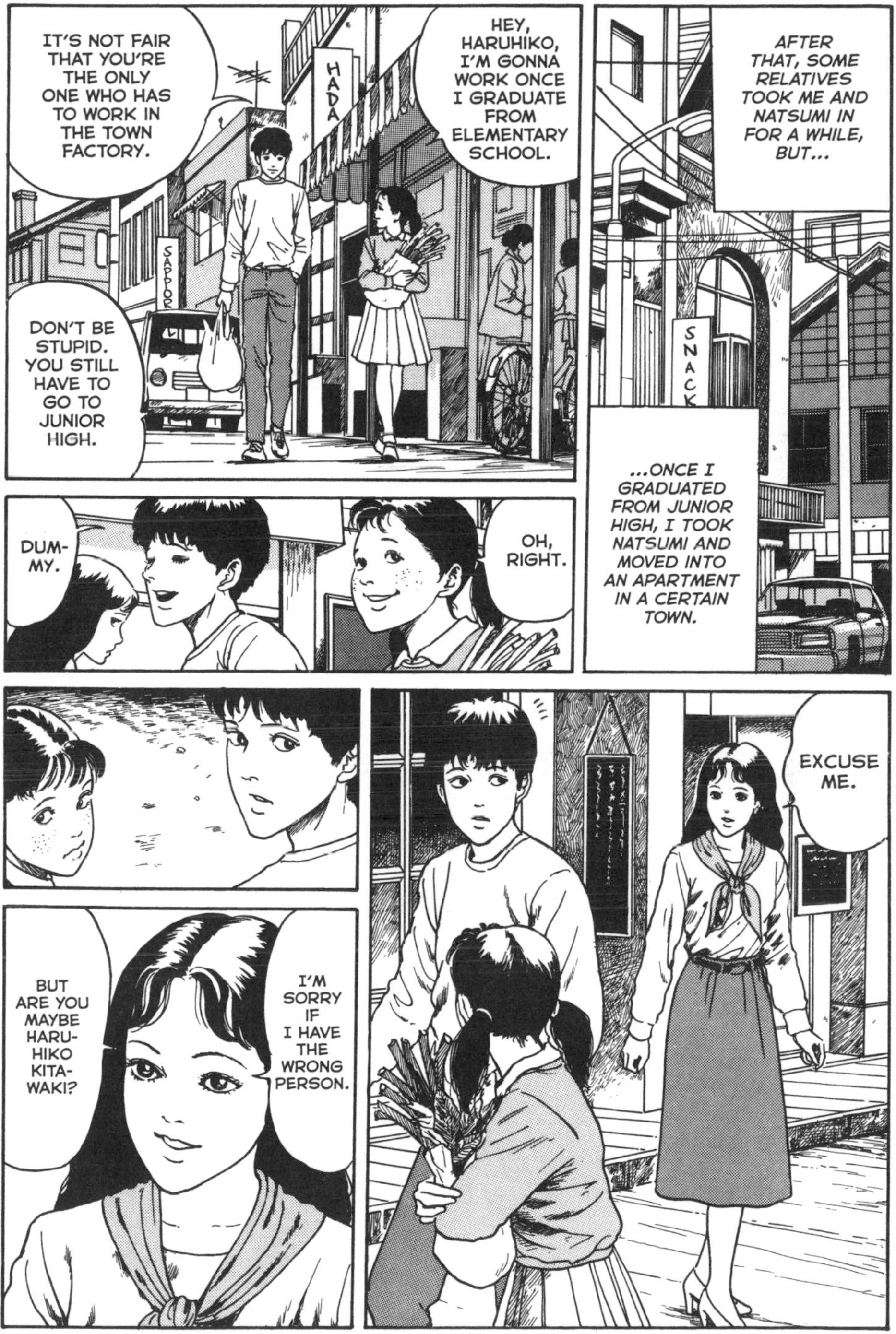
AFTER THAT, SOME RELATIVES TOOK ME AND NATSUMI IN FOR A WHILE, BUT...
SNACK
...ONCE I GRADUATED FROM JUNIOR HIGH, I TOOK NATSUMI AND MOVED INTO AN APARTMENT IN A CERTAIN TOWN.
HEY, HARUHIKO, I'M GONNA WORK ONCE I GRADUATE FROM ELEMENTARY SCHOOL.
HADA
IT'S NOT FAIR THAT YOU'RE THE ONLY ONE WHO HAS TO WORK IN THE TOWN FACTORY.
DON'T BE STUPID. YOU STILL HAVE TO GO TO JUNIOR HIGH.
OH, RIGHT.
DUM-MY.
EXCUSE ME.
I'M SORRY IF I HAVE THE WRONG PERSON.
BUT ARE YOU MAYBE HARU-HIKO KITA-WAKI?

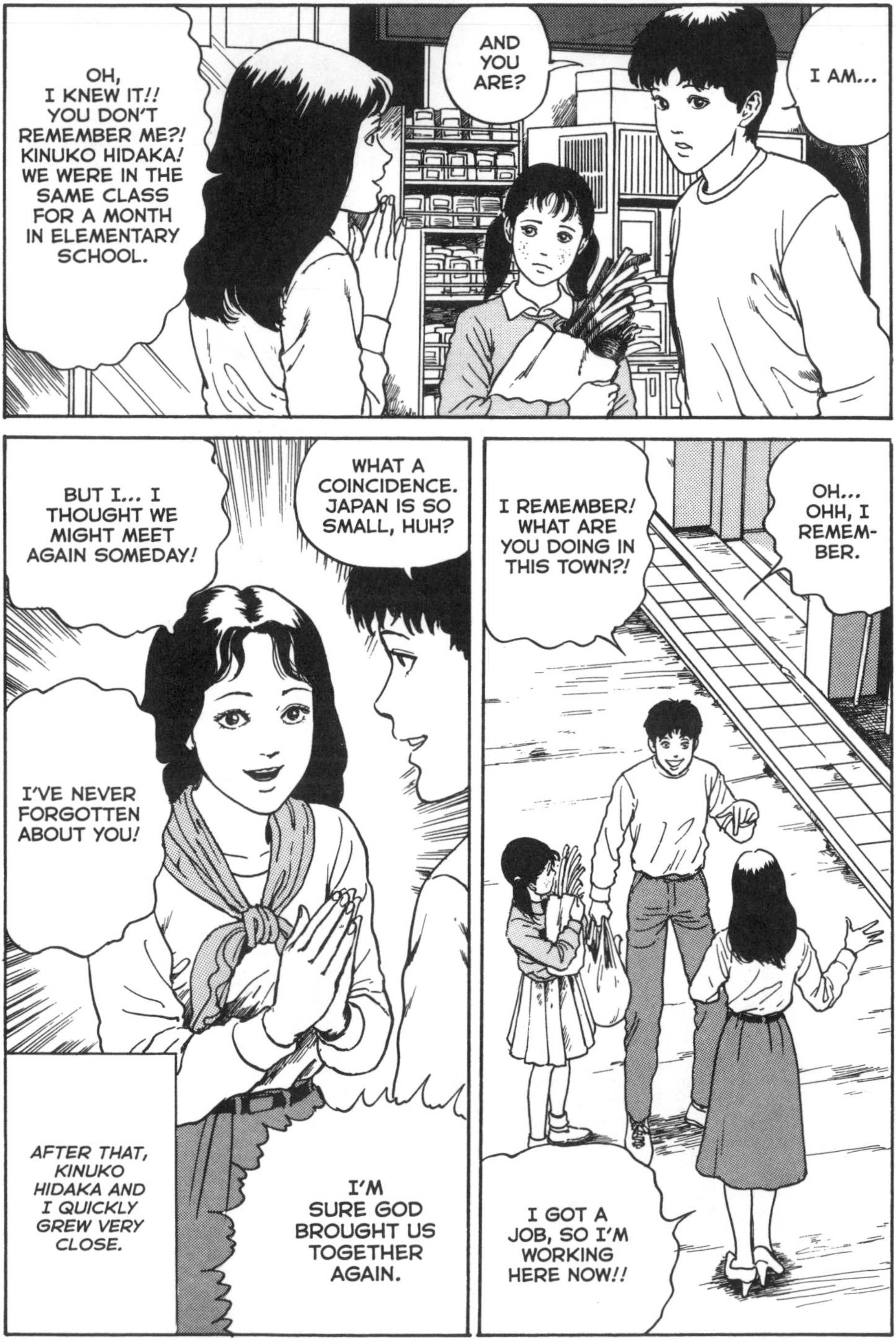
I AM...
AND YOU ARE?
OH, I KNEW IT!! YOU DON'T REMEMBER ME?! KINUKO HIDAKA! WE WERE IN THE SAME CLASS FOR A MONTH IN ELEMENTARY SCHOOL.
OH... OHH, I REMEMBER.
I REMEMBER! WHAT ARE YOU DOING IN THIS TOWN?!
I GOT A JOB, SO I'M WORKING HERE NOW!!
WHAT A COINCIDENCE. JAPAN IS SO SMALL, HUH?
BUT I... I THOUGHT WE MIGHT MEET AGAIN SOMEDAY!
I'VE NEVER FORGOTTEN ABOUT YOU!
I'M SURE GOD BROUGHT US TOGETHER AGAIN.
AFTER THAT, KINUKO HIDAKA AND I QUICKLY GREW VERY CLOSE.

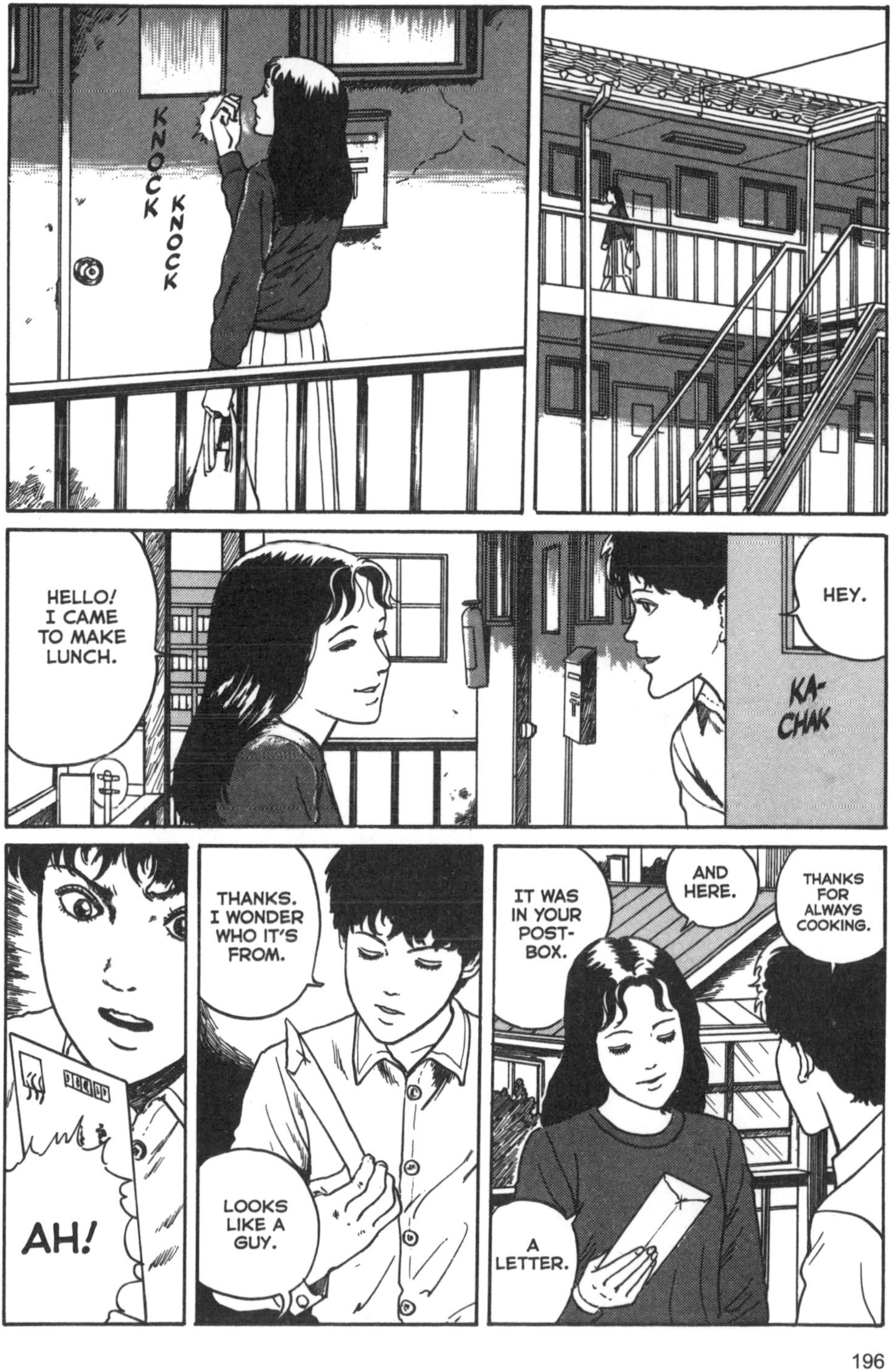
KNOCK KNOCK
HEY.
KA-CHAK
HELLO! I CAME TO MAKE LUNCH.
THANKS FOR ALWAYS COOKING.
AND HERE.
IT WAS IN YOUR POST-BOX.
A LETTER.
THANKS. I WONDER WHO IT'S FROM.
LOOKS LIKE A GUY.
AH!

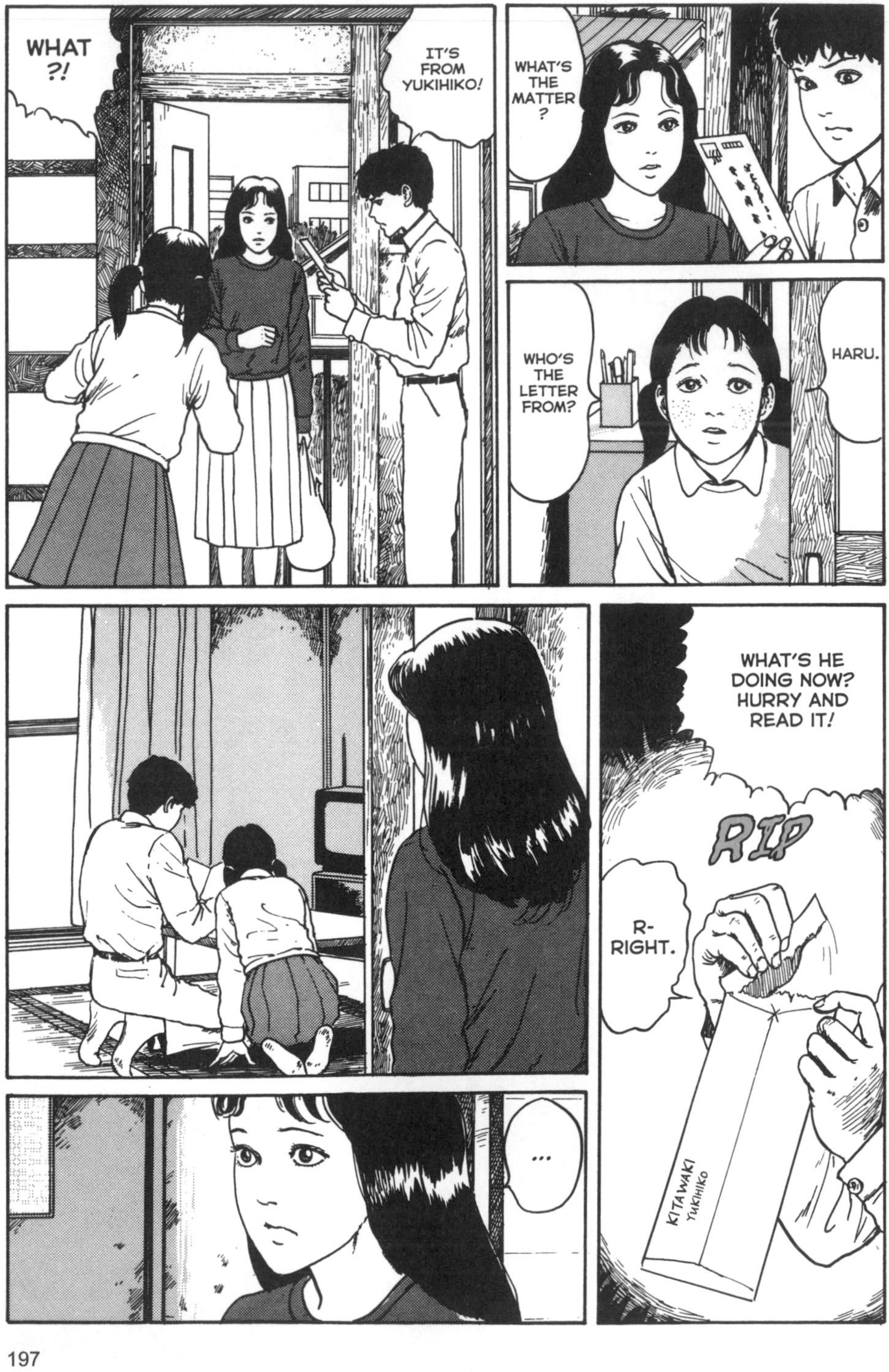
WHAT'S THE MATTER?
HARU.
WHO'S THE LETTER FROM?
IT'S FROM YUKIHIKO!
WHAT ?!
WHAT'S HE DOING NOW? HURRY AND READ IT!
RIP
R-RIGHT.
KITAWAKI YUKIHIKO
...

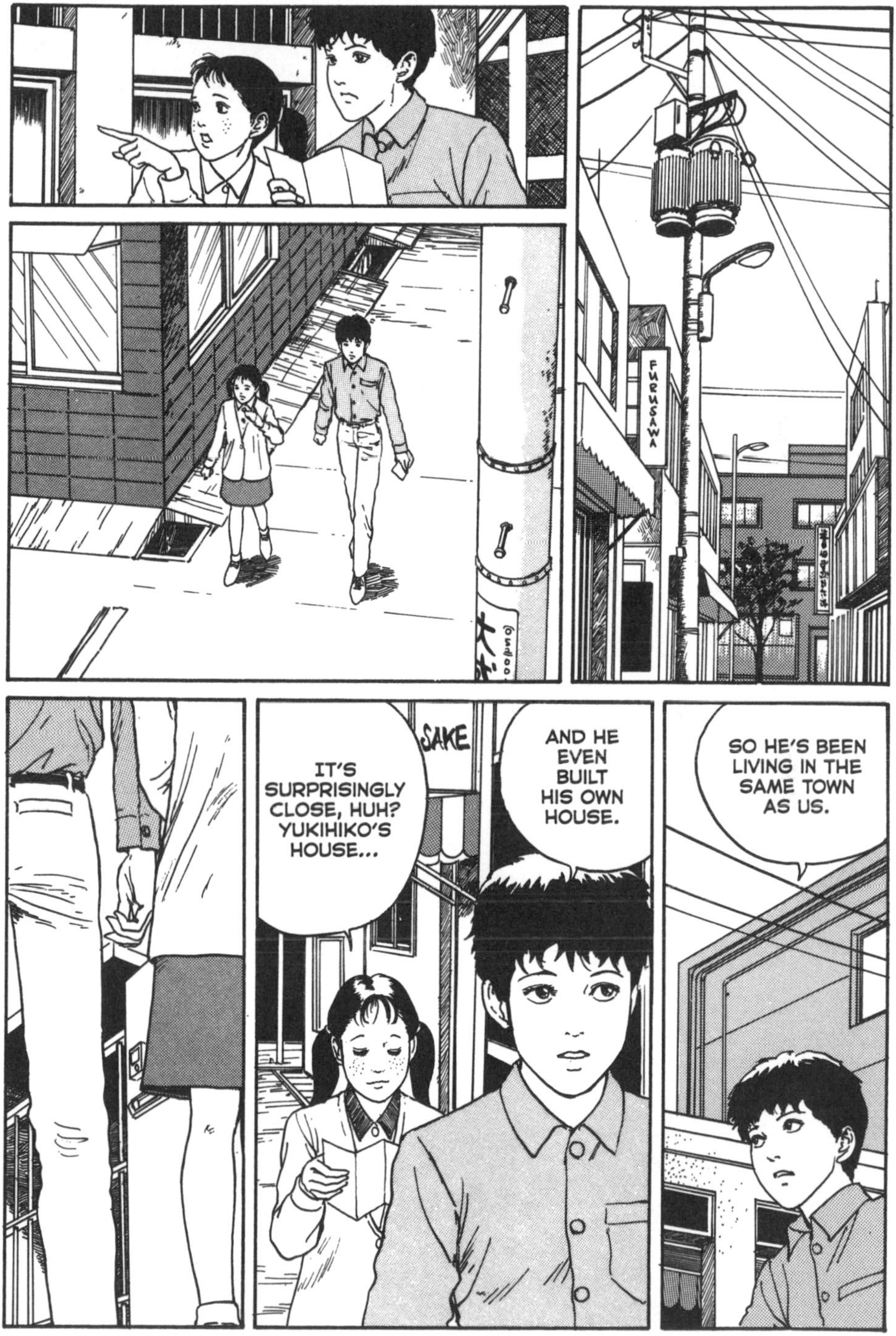
FURUSAWA
SO HE'S BEEN LIVING IN THE SAME TOWN AS US.
SAKE
AND HE EVEN BUILT HIS OWN HOUSE.
IT'S SURPRISINGLY CLOSE, HUH? YUKIHIKO'S HOUSE...

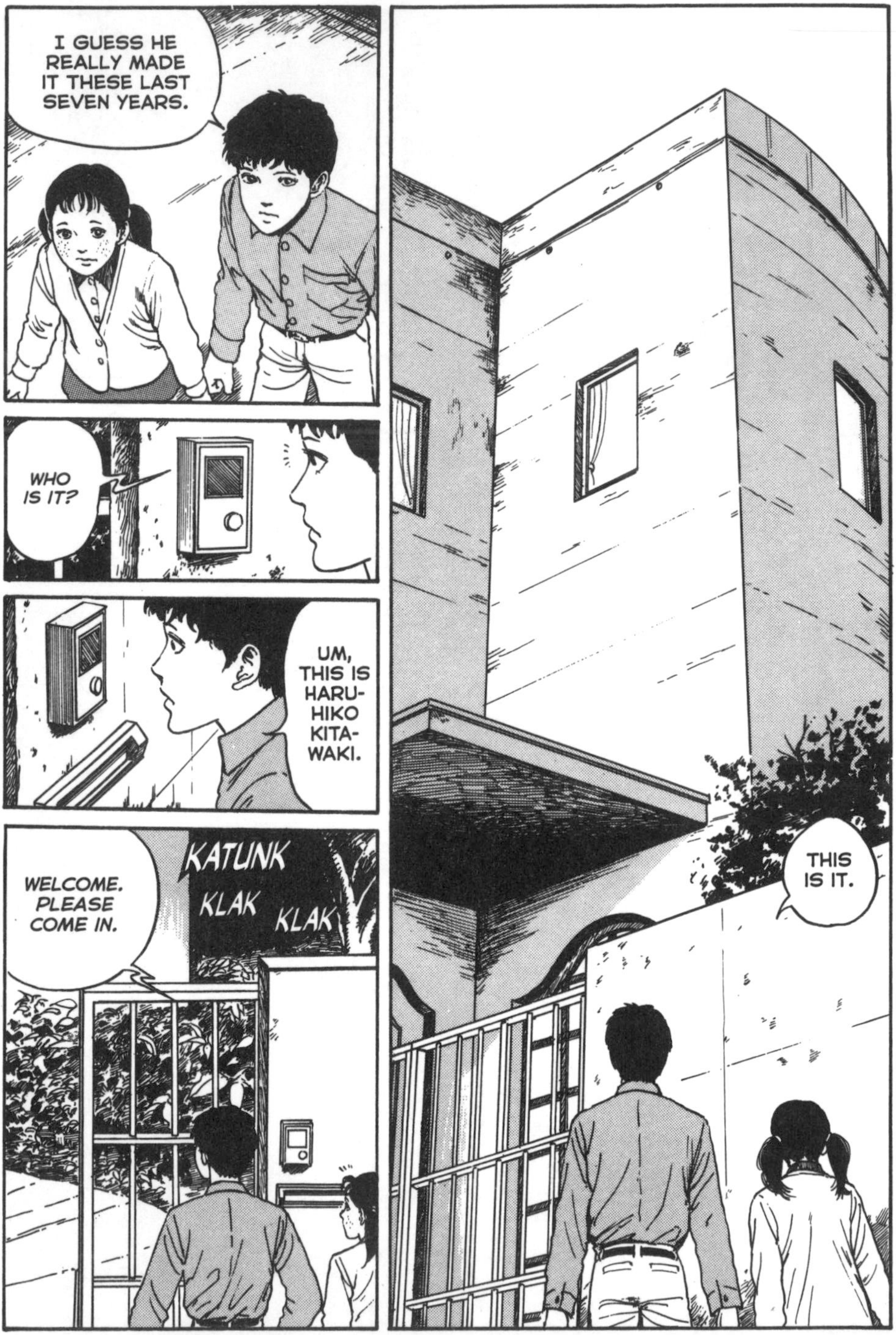
THIS IS IT.
I GUESS HE REALLY MADE IT THESE LAST SEVEN YEARS.
WHO IS IT?
UM, THIS IS HARUHIKO KITAWAKI.
KATUNK
KLAK KLAK
WELCOME. PLEASE COME IN.

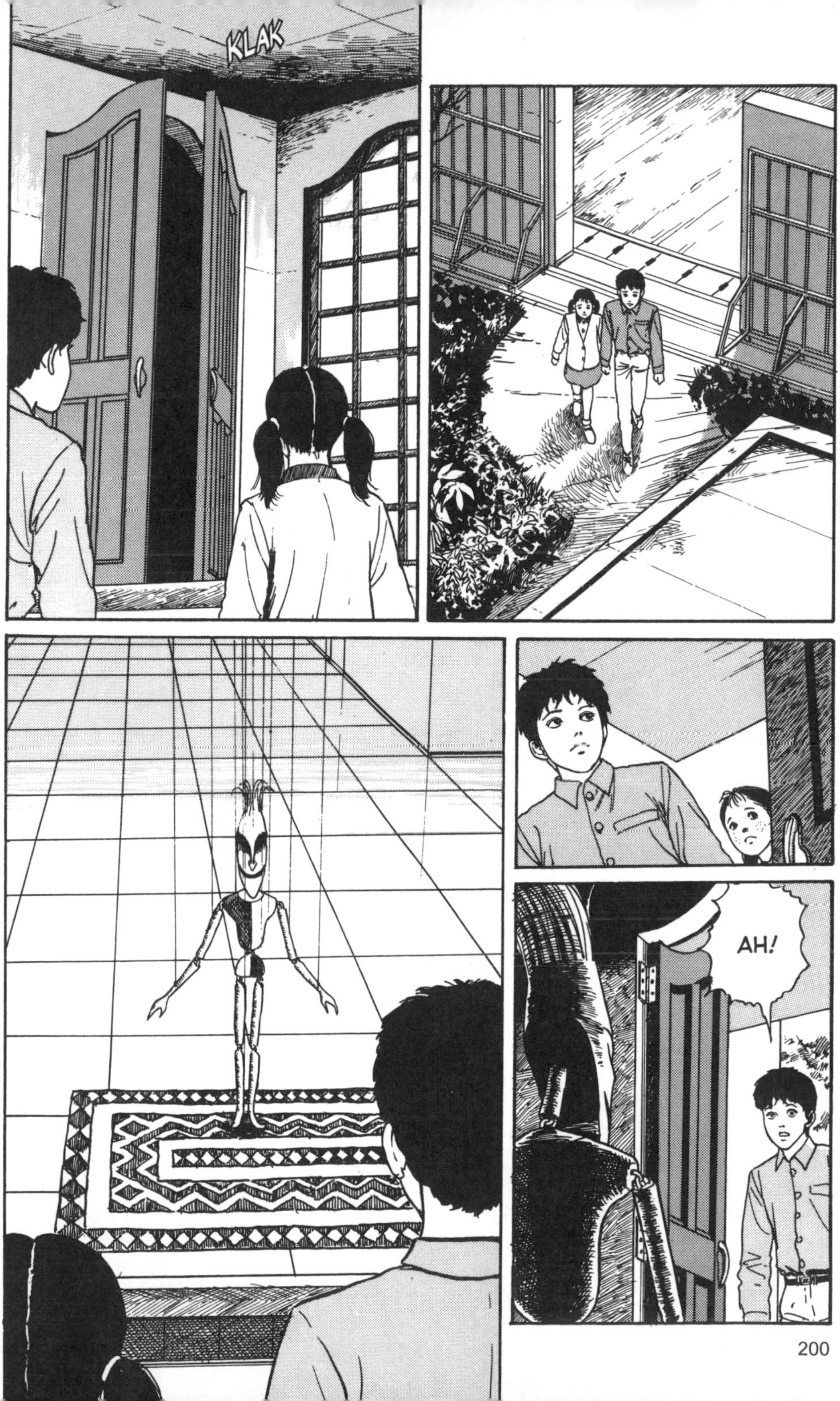
KLAK
AH!

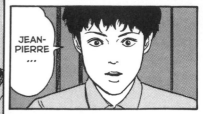
JEAN-PIERRE ...

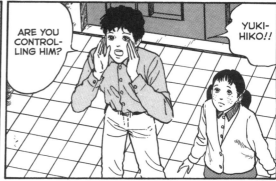

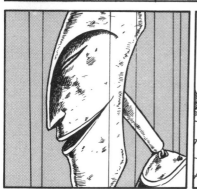

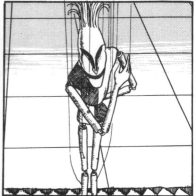
ARE YOU CONTROL-LING HIM?

YUKI-HIKO!!

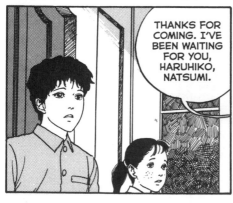
THANKS FOR COMING. I'VE BEEN WAITING FOR YOU, HARUHIKO, NATSUMI.

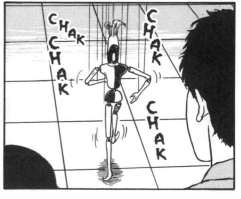
CHAK CHAK CHAK CHAK CHAK

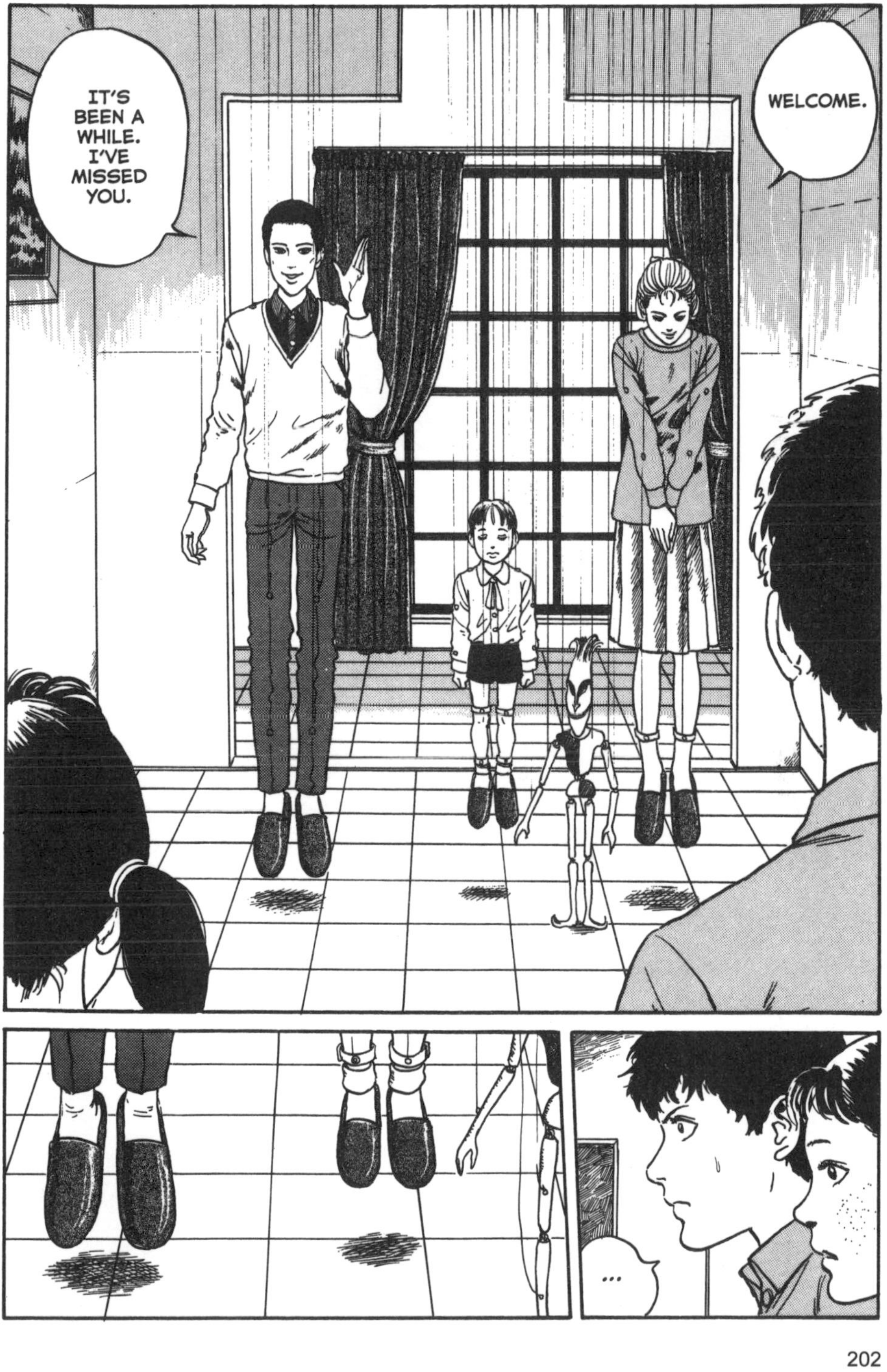
WELCOME.
IT'S BEEN A WHILE. I'VE MISSED YOU.
...

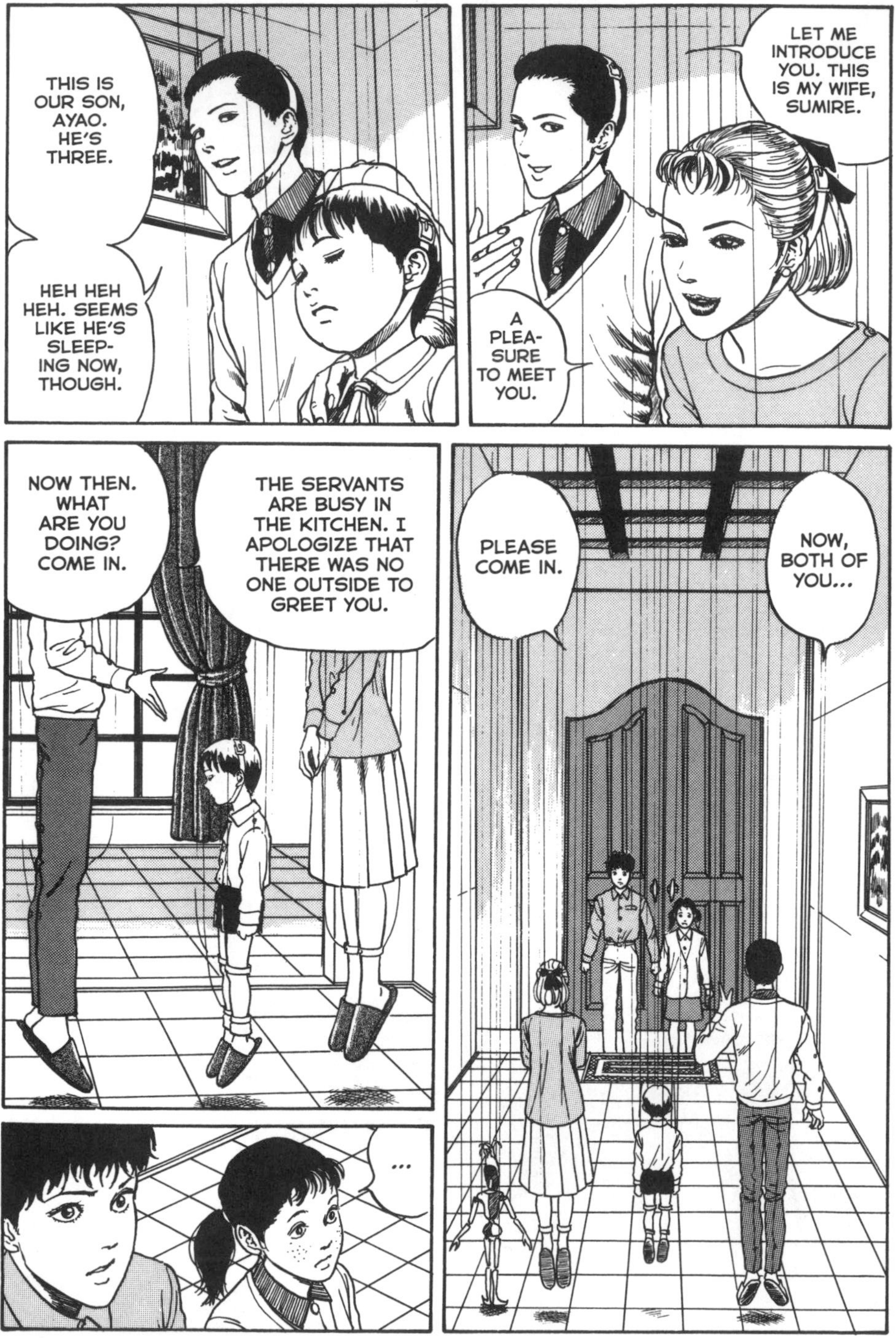
LET ME INTRODUCE YOU. THIS IS MY WIFE, SUMIRE.
A PLEASURE TO MEET YOU.
THIS IS OUR SON, AYAO. HE'S THREE.
HEH HEH HEH. SEEMS LIKE HE'S SLEEPING NOW, THOUGH.
NOW, BOTH OF YOU...
PLEASE COME IN.
THE SERVANTS ARE BUSY IN THE KITCHEN. I APOLOGIZE THAT THERE WAS NO ONE OUTSIDE TO GREET YOU.
NOW THEN. WHAT ARE YOU DOING? COME IN.
...

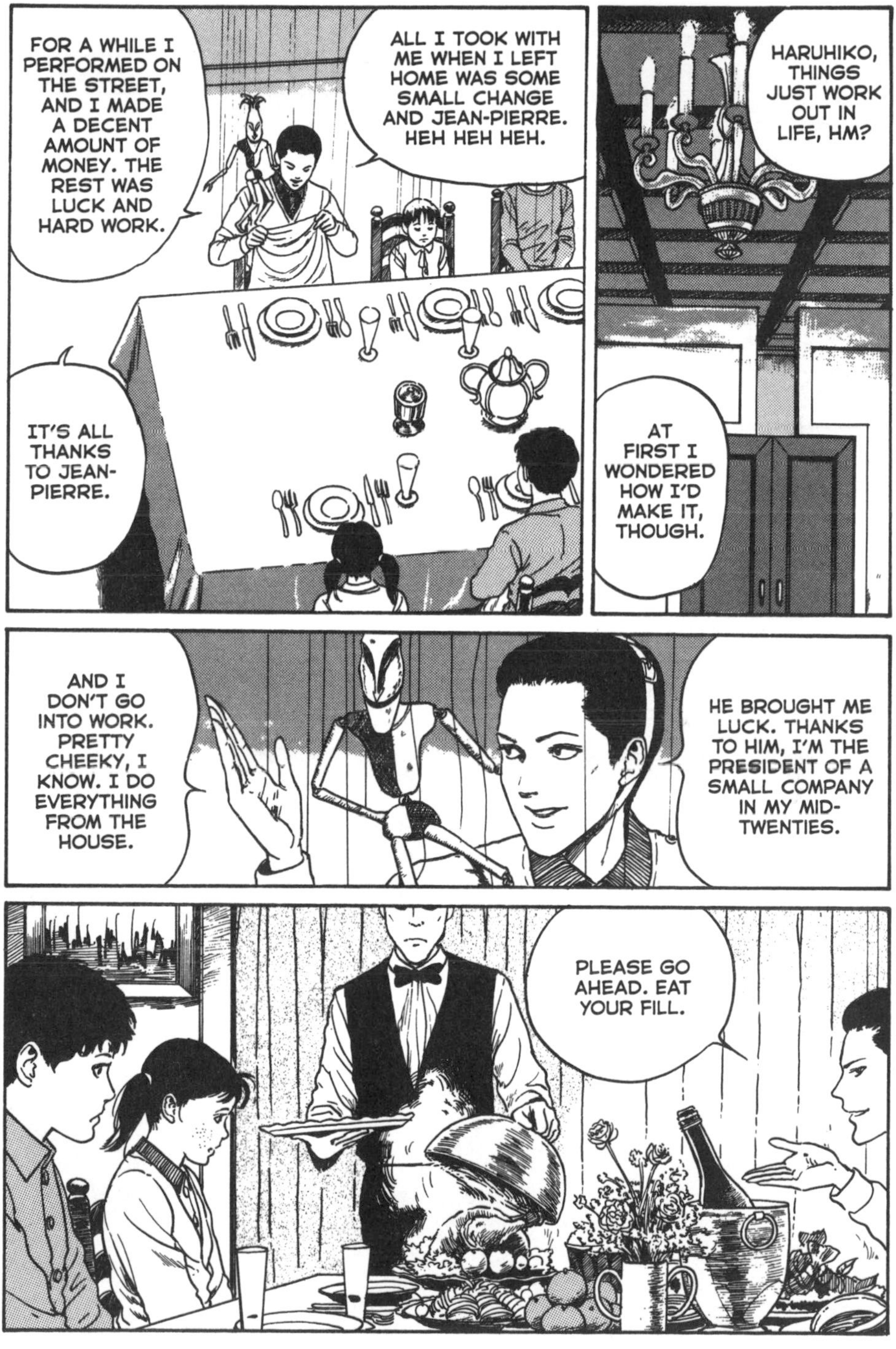
HARUHIKO, THINGS JUST WORK OUT IN LIFE, HM?
AT FIRST I WONDERED HOW I'D MAKE IT, THOUGH.
ALL I TOOK WITH ME WHEN I LEFT HOME WAS SOME SMALL CHANGE AND JEAN-PIERRE. HEH HEH HEH.
FOR A WHILE I PERFORMED ON THE STREET, AND I MADE A DECENT AMOUNT OF MONEY. THE REST WAS LUCK AND HARD WORK.
IT'S ALL THANKS TO JEAN-PIERRE.
HE BROUGHT ME LUCK. THANKS TO HIM, I'M THE PRESIDENT OF A SMALL COMPANY IN MY MID-TWENTIES.
AND I DON'T GO INTO WORK. PRETTY CHEEKY, I KNOW. I DO EVERYTHING FROM THE HOUSE.
PLEASE GO AHEAD. EAT YOUR FILL.

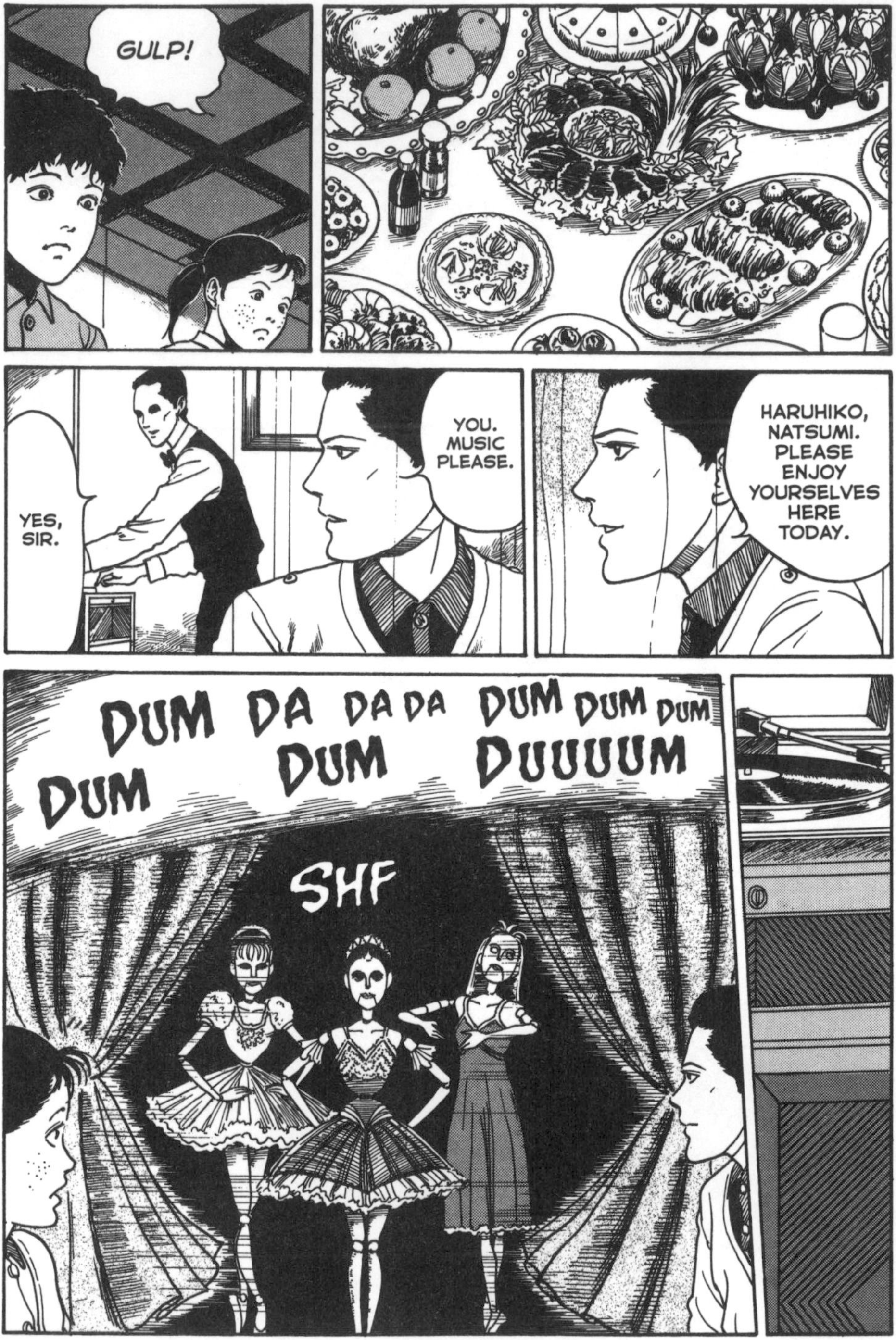
GULP!
HARUHIKO, NATSUMI. PLEASE ENJOY YOURSELVES HERE TODAY.
YOU. MUSIC PLEASE.
YES, SIR.
DUM DA DA DA DUM DUM DUM
DUM DUM DUUUUM
SHF

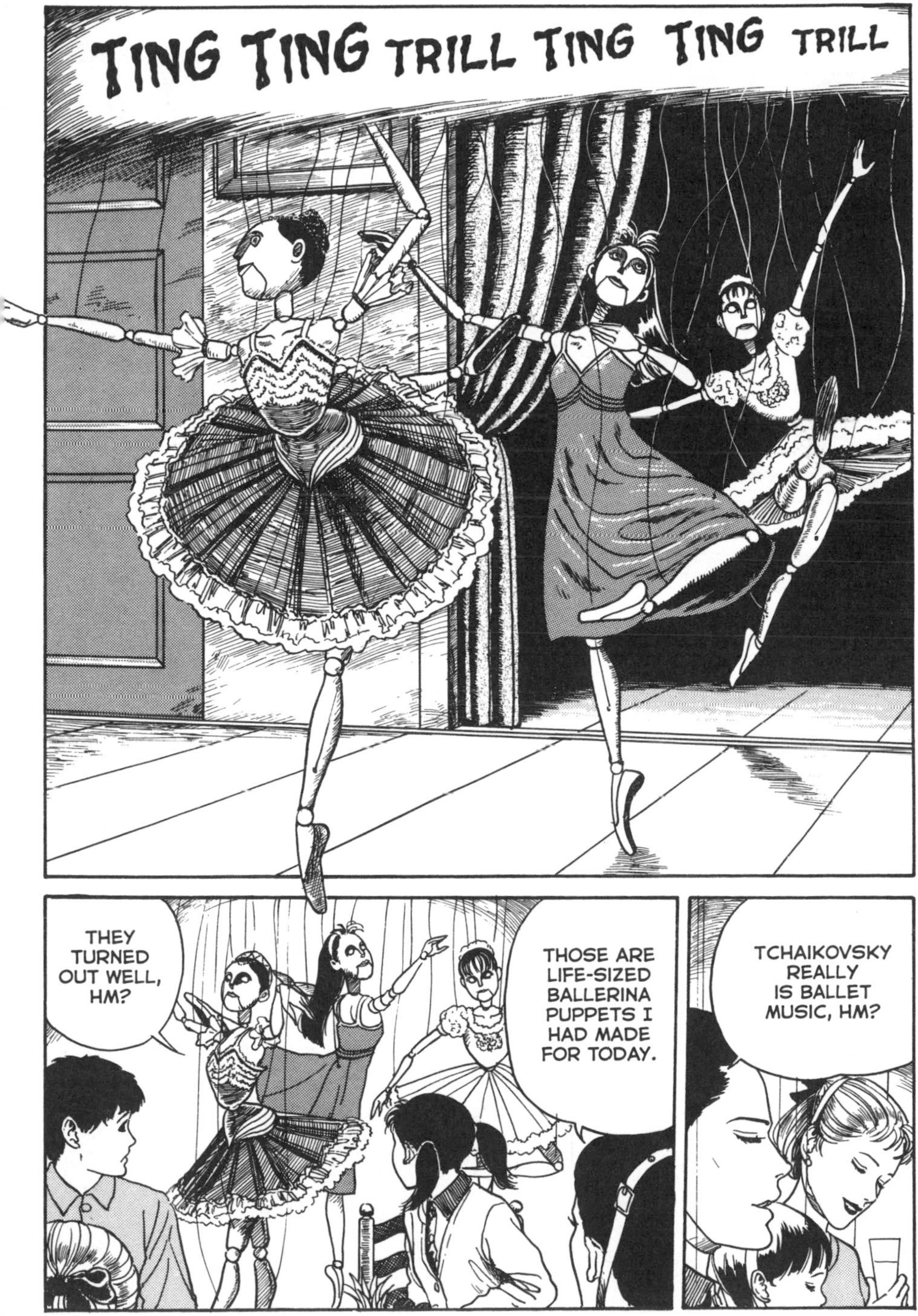
TING TING TRILL TING TING TRILL
TCHAIKOVSKY REALLY IS BALLET MUSIC, HM?
THOSE ARE LIFE-SIZED BALLERINA PUPPETS I HAD MADE FOR TODAY.
THEY TURNED OUT WELL, HM?

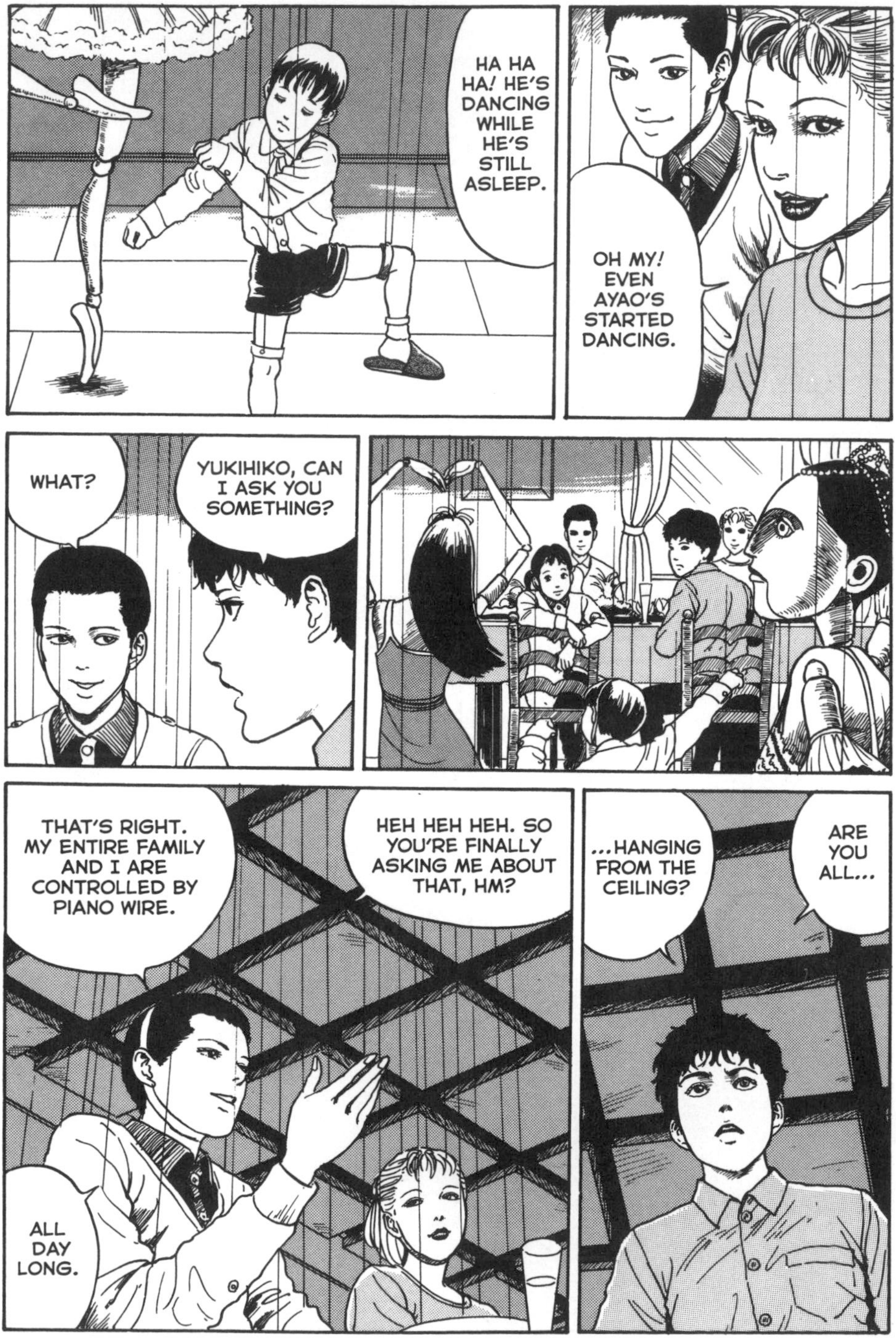
OH MY! EVEN AYAO'S STARTED DANCING.
HA HA HA! HE'S DANCING WHILE HE'S STILL ASLEEP.
YUKIHIKO, CAN I ASK YOU SOMETHING?
WHAT?
ARE YOU ALL...
...HANGING FROM THE CEILING?
HEH HEH HEH. SO YOU'RE FINALLY ASKING ME ABOUT THAT, HM?
THAT'S RIGHT. MY ENTIRE FAMILY AND I ARE CONTROLLED BY PIANO WIRE.
ALL DAY LONG.

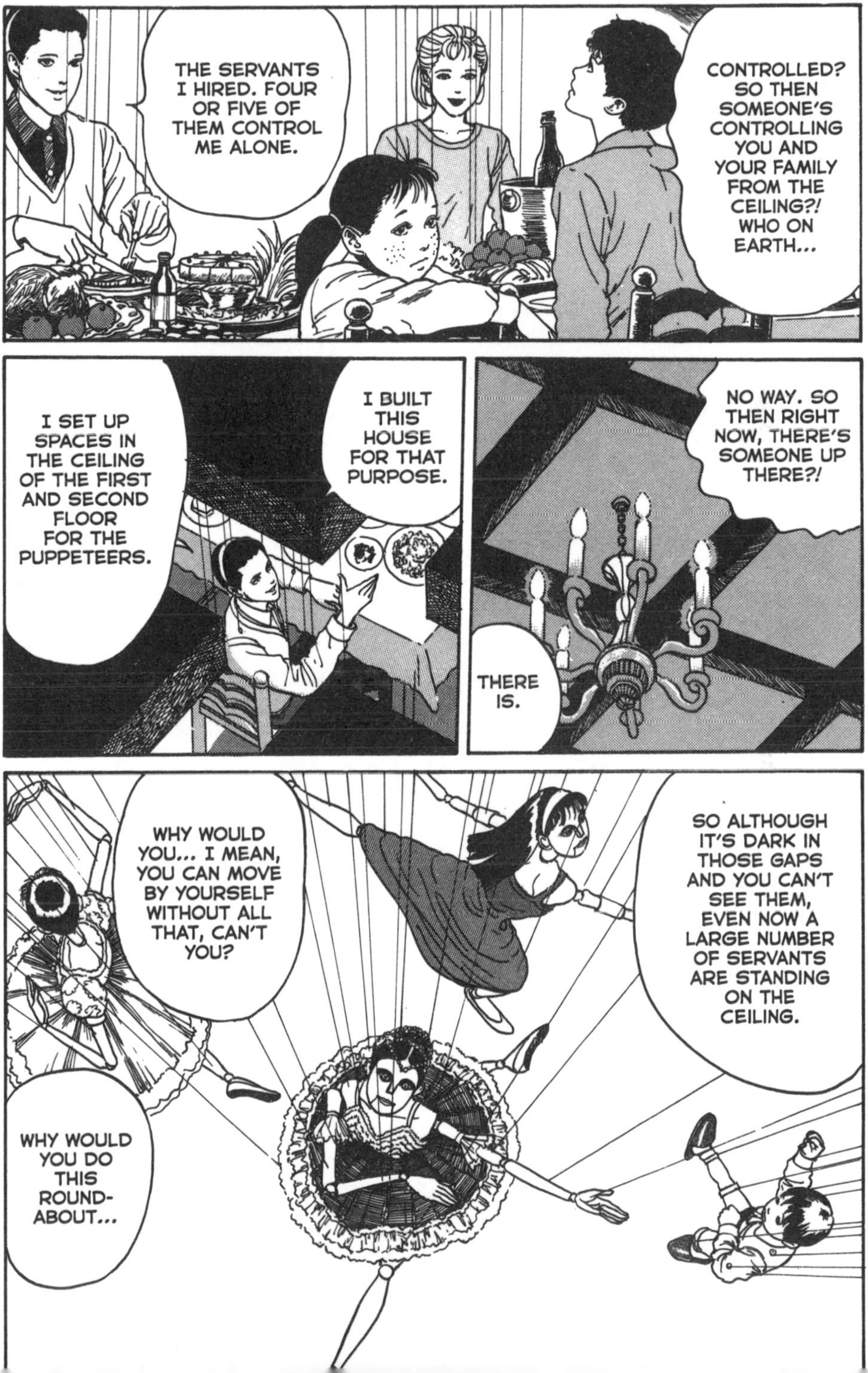
CONTROLLED? SO THEN SOMEONE'S CONTROLLING YOU AND YOUR FAMILY FROM THE CEILING?! WHO ON EARTH...
THE SERVANTS I HIRED. FOUR OR FIVE OF THEM CONTROL ME ALONE.
NO WAY. SO THEN RIGHT NOW, THERE'S SOMEONE UP THERE?!
THERE IS.
I BUILT THIS HOUSE FOR THAT PURPOSE.
I SET UP SPACES IN THE CEILING OF THE FIRST AND SECOND FLOOR FOR THE PUPPETEERS.
SO ALTHOUGH IT'S DARK IN THOSE GAPS AND YOU CAN'T SEE THEM, EVEN NOW A LARGE NUMBER OF SERVANTS ARE STANDING ON THE CEILING.
WHY WOULD YOU... I MEAN, YOU CAN MOVE BY YOURSELF WITHOUT ALL THAT, CAN'T YOU?
WHY WOULD YOU DO THIS ROUND-ABOUT...

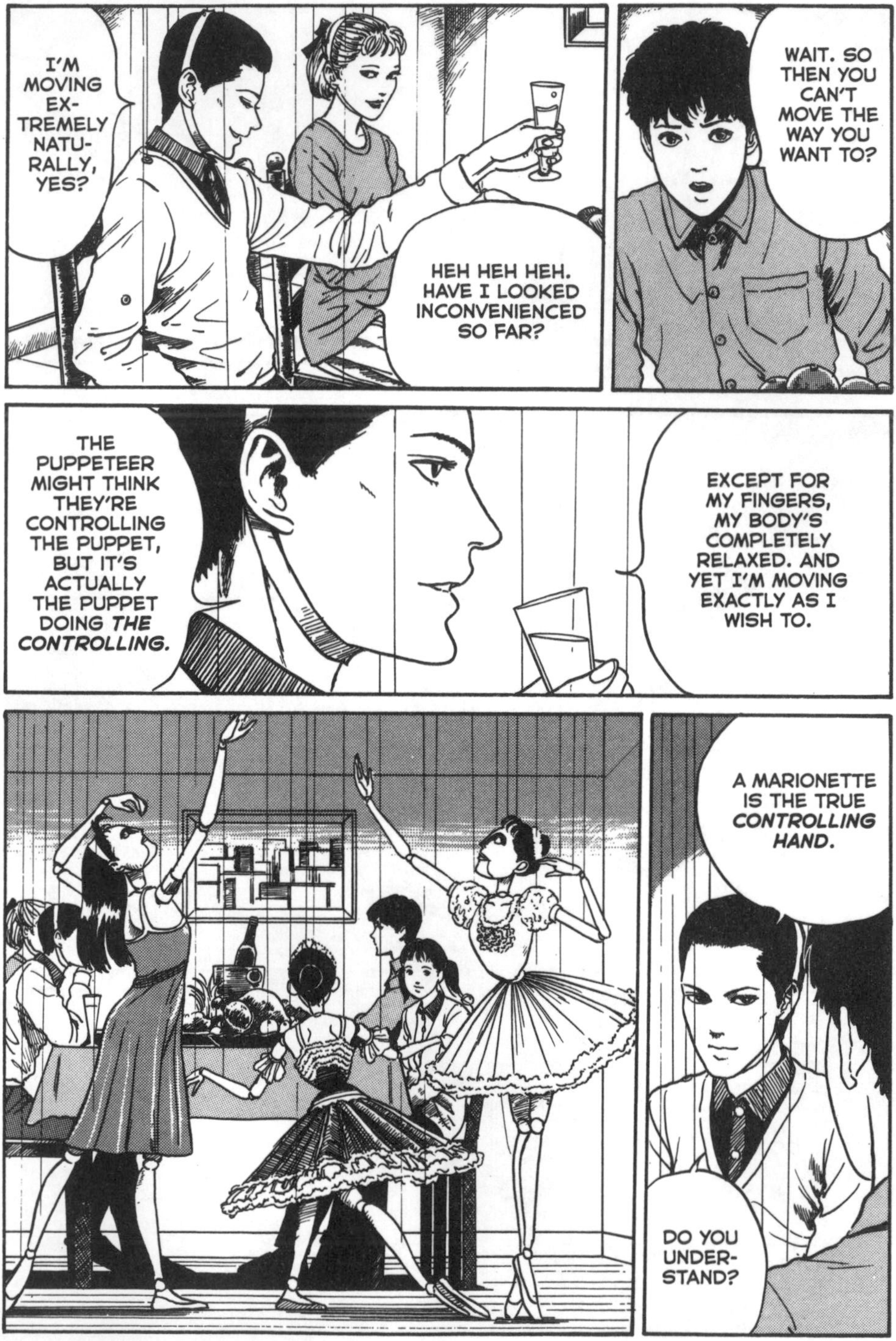
WAIT. SO THEN YOU CAN'T MOVE THE WAY YOU WANT TO?
HEH HEH HEH. HAVE I LOOKED INCONVENIENCED SO FAR?
I'M MOVING EX-TREMELY NATU-RALLY, YES?
EXCEPT FOR MY FINGERS, MY BODY'S COMPLETELY RELAXED. AND YET I'M MOVING EXACTLY AS I WISH TO.
THE PUPPETEER MIGHT THINK THEY'RE CONTROLLING THE PUPPET, BUT IT'S ACTUALLY THE PUPPET DOING *THE CONTROLLING.*
A MARIONETTE IS THE TRUE *CONTROLLING HAND.*
DO YOU UNDER-STAND?

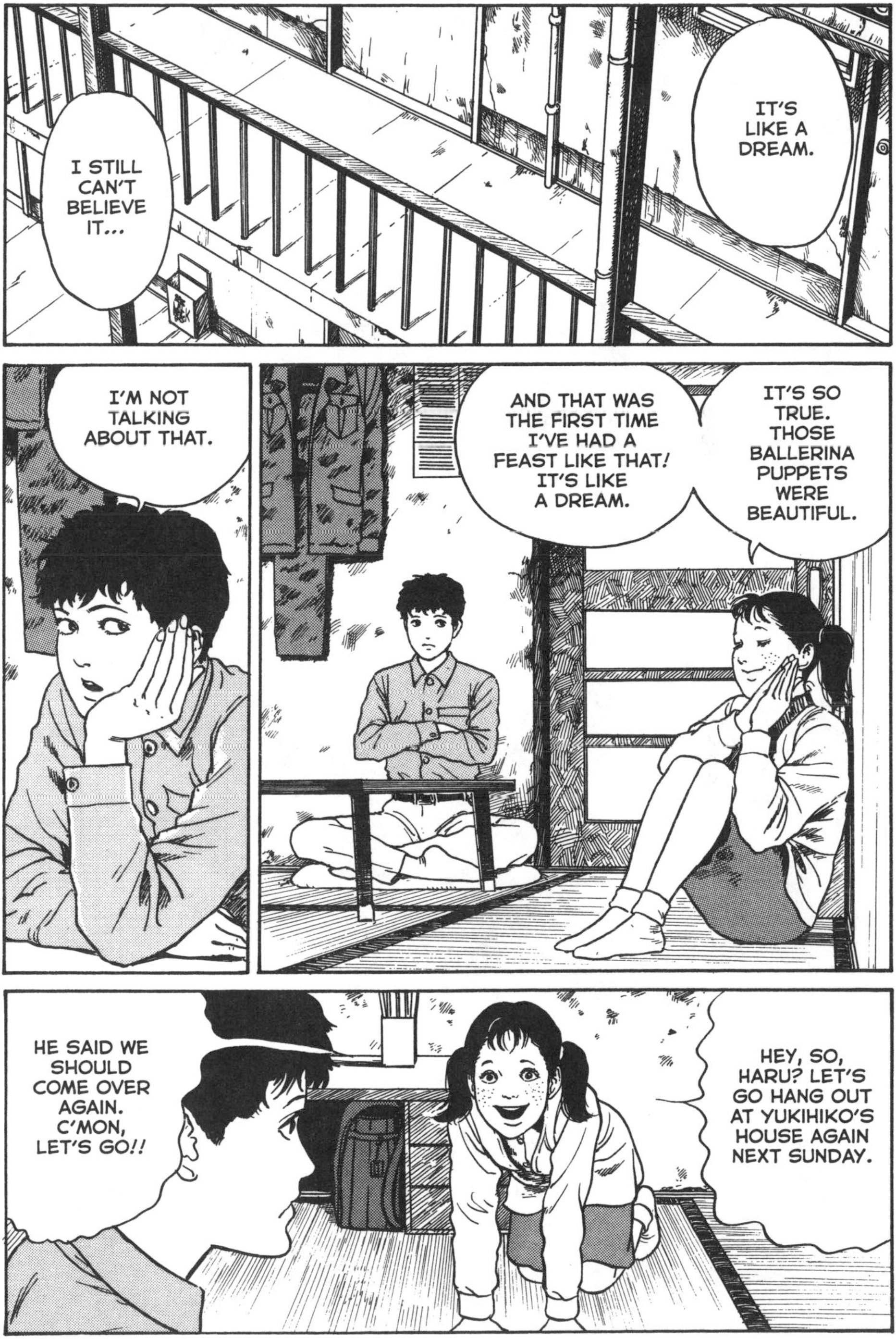
IT'S LIKE A DREAM.
I STILL CAN'T BELIEVE IT...
IT'S SO TRUE. THOSE BALLERINA PUPPETS WERE BEAUTIFUL.
AND THAT WAS THE FIRST TIME I'VE HAD A FEAST LIKE THAT! IT'S LIKE A DREAM.
I'M NOT TALKING ABOUT THAT.
HEY, SO, HARU? LET'S GO HANG OUT AT YUKIHIKO'S HOUSE AGAIN NEXT SUNDAY.
HE SAID WE SHOULD COME OVER AGAIN. C'MON, LET'S GO!!

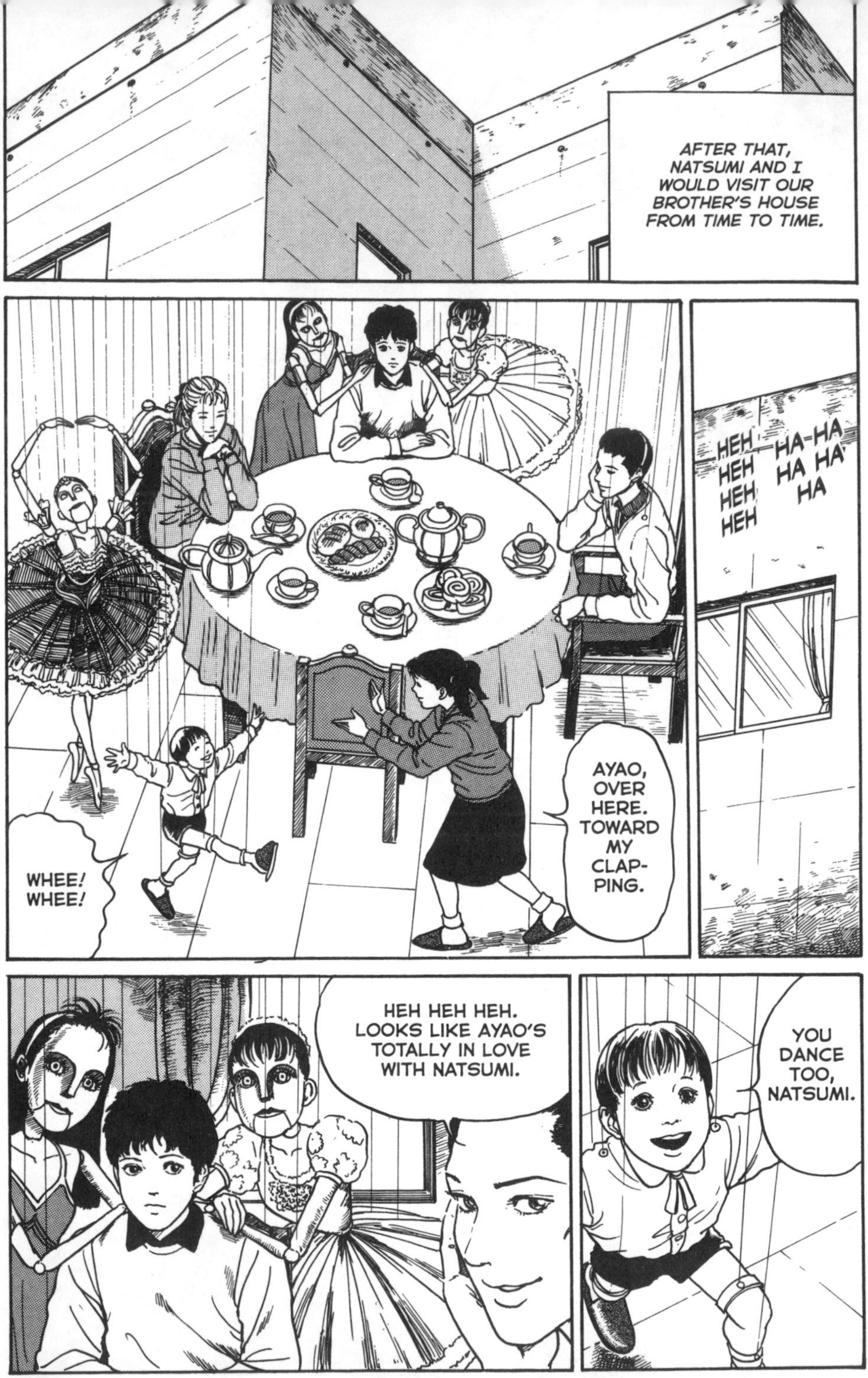
AFTER THAT, NATSUMI AND I WOULD VISIT OUR BROTHER'S HOUSE FROM TIME TO TIME.
HA-HA HA HA HA
HEH HEH HEH HEH
AYAO, OVER HERE. TOWARD MY CLAP-PING.
WHEE! WHEE!
YOU DANCE TOO, NATSUMI.
HEH HEH HEH. LOOKS LIKE AYAO'S TOTALLY IN LOVE WITH NATSUMI.

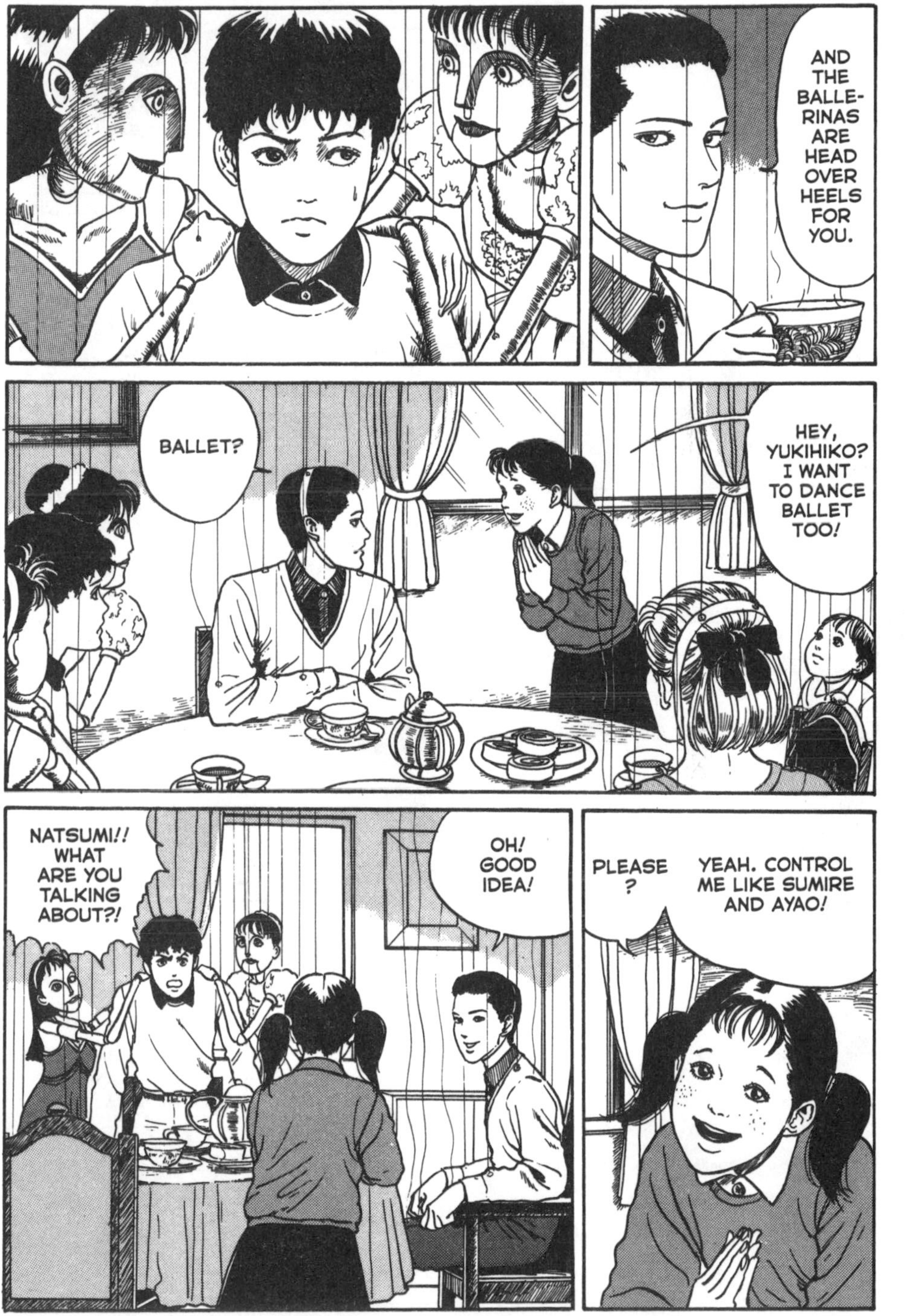
AND THE BALLERINAS ARE HEAD OVER HEELS FOR YOU.
HEY, YUKIHIKO? I WANT TO DANCE BALLET TOO!
BALLET?
YEAH. CONTROL ME LIKE SUMIRE AND AYAO!
PLEASE ?
OH! GOOD IDEA!
NATSUMI!! WHAT ARE YOU TALKING ABOUT?!

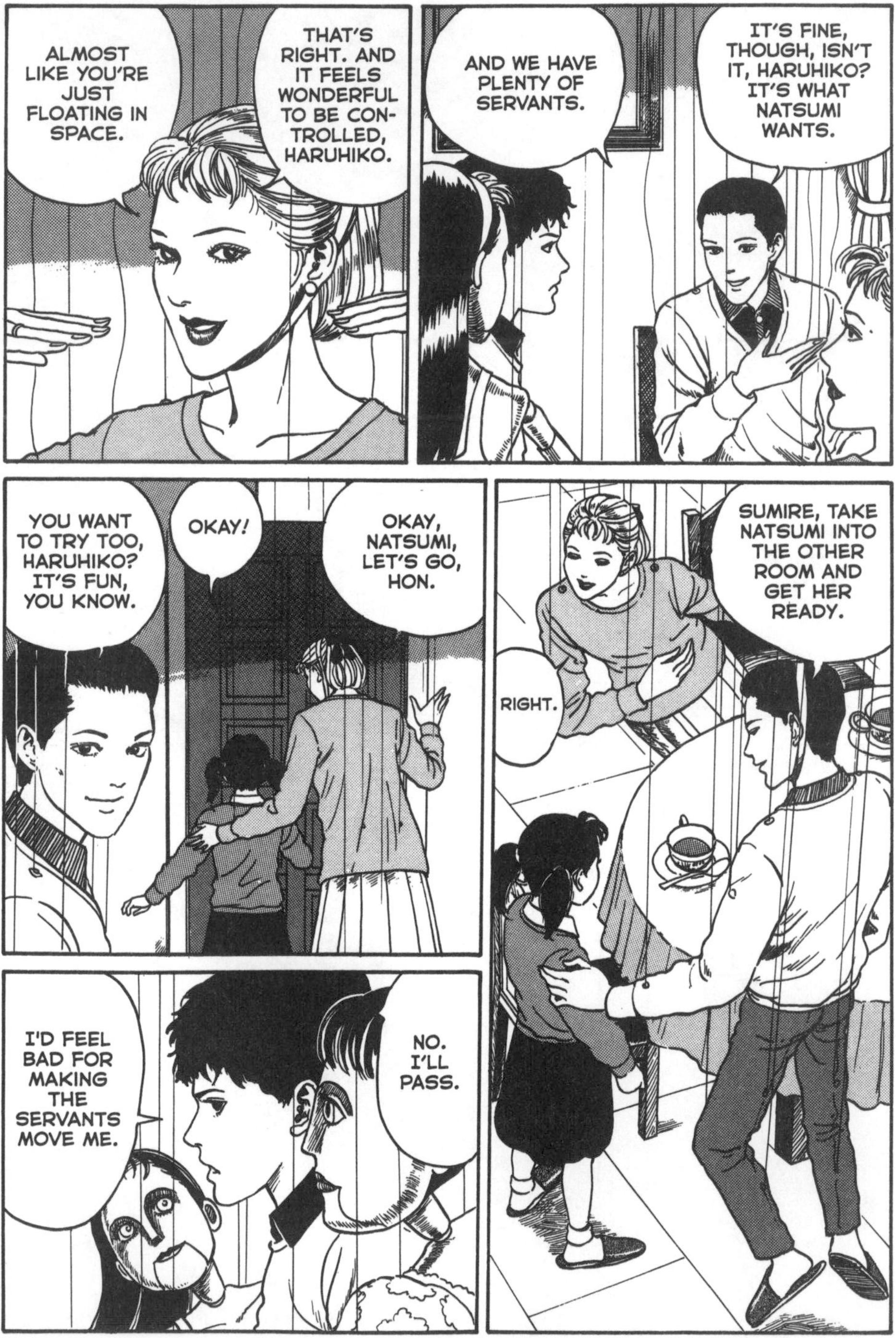
IT'S FINE, THOUGH, ISN'T IT, HARUHIKO? IT'S WHAT NATSUMI WANTS.
AND WE HAVE PLENTY OF SERVANTS.
THAT'S RIGHT. AND IT FEELS WONDERFUL TO BE CONTROLLED, HARUHIKO.
ALMOST LIKE YOU'RE JUST FLOATING IN SPACE.
SUMIRE, TAKE NATSUMI INTO THE OTHER ROOM AND GET HER READY.
RIGHT.
OKAY, NATSUMI, LET'S GO, HON.
OKAY!
YOU WANT TO TRY TOO, HARUHIKO? IT'S FUN, YOU KNOW.
NO. I'LL PASS.
I'D FEEL BAD FOR MAKING THE SERVANTS MOVE ME.

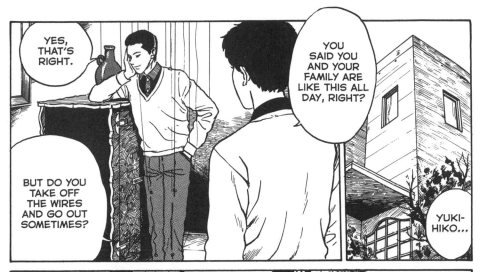

YUKI-HIKO...
YOU SAID YOU AND YOUR FAMILY ARE LIKE THIS ALL DAY, RIGHT?
YES, THAT'S RIGHT.
BUT DO YOU TAKE OFF THE WIRES AND GO OUT SOMETIMES?
NO. IN THE TWO YEARS OR SO SINCE I BUILT THIS HOUSE, HIRED THE SERVANTS AND BEGAN LIVING THIS WAY...
...I HAVEN'T MOVED MY BODY MYSELF.
YUKIHIKO... THAT CAN'T BE GOOD, CAN IT?
I MEAN, ASTRONAUTS, WHEN THEY'RE WEIGHTLESS FOR LONG PERIODS, THEY DO STRENGTH TRAINING AND STUFF.
IF YOU DON'T USE YOUR MUSCLES, THEY GRADUALLY DETERIORATE.
PRETTY SOON YOU WON'T BE ABLE TO STAND UP ON YOUR OWN. AND THEN WHAT WILL YOU DO? I MEAN, THE SERVANTS WON'T NECESSARILY BE HERE FOREVER.
HEH HEH HEH.
NO NEED TO WORRY ABOUT THAT.

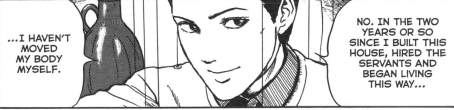

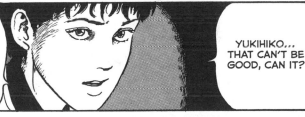

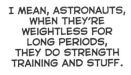

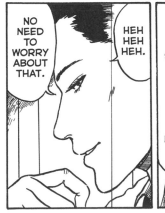

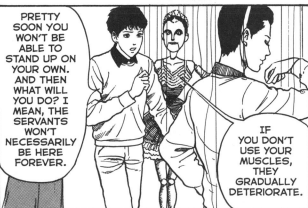

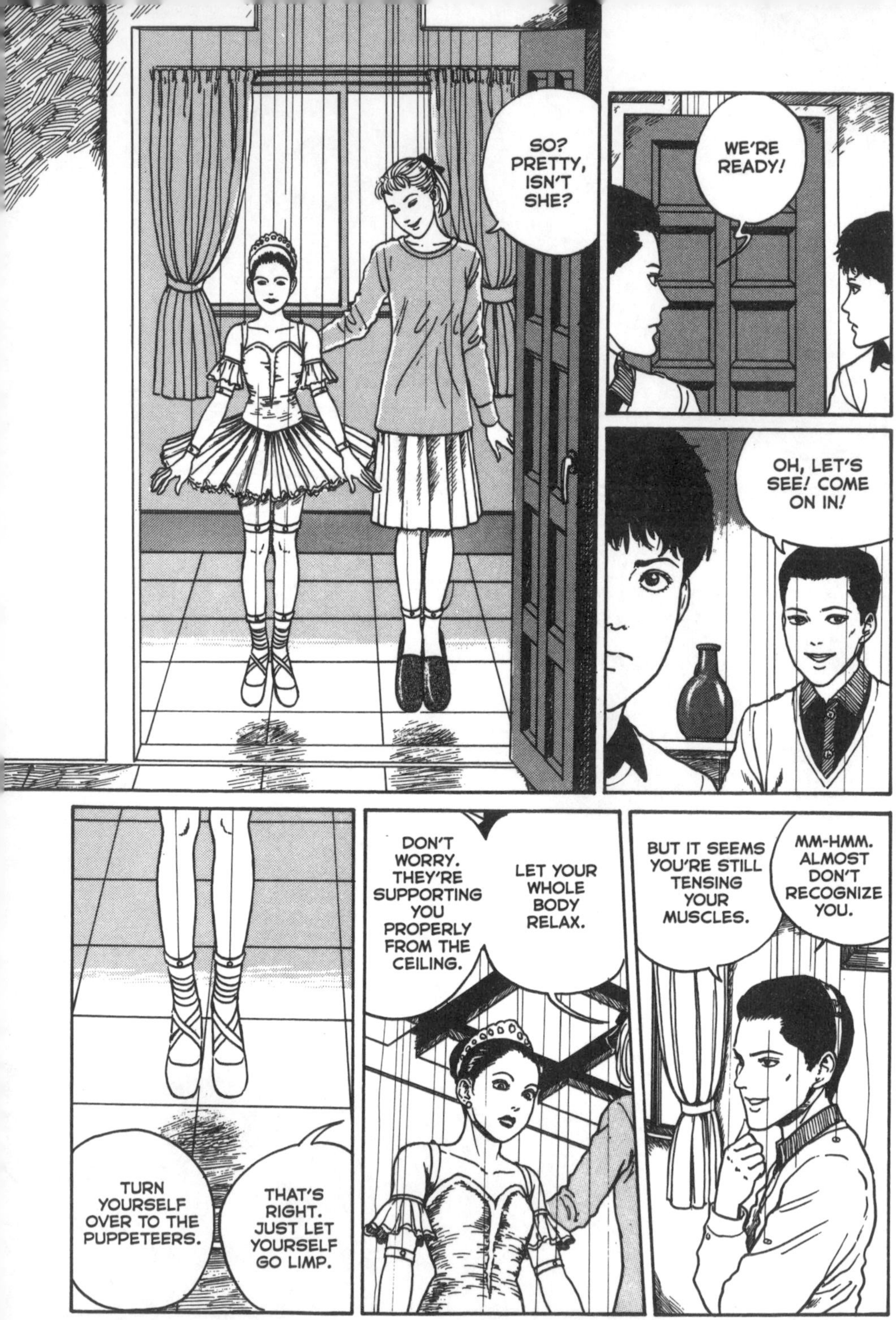
WE'RE READY!
OH, LET'S SEE! COME ON IN!
SO? PRETTY, ISN'T SHE?
MM-HMM. ALMOST DON'T RECOGNIZE YOU.
BUT IT SEEMS YOU'RE STILL TENSING YOUR MUSCLES.
LET YOUR WHOLE BODY RELAX.
DON'T WORRY. THEY'RE SUPPORTING YOU PROPERLY FROM THE CEILING.
THAT'S RIGHT. JUST LET YOURSELF GO LIMP.
TURN YOURSELF OVER TO THE PUPPETEERS.

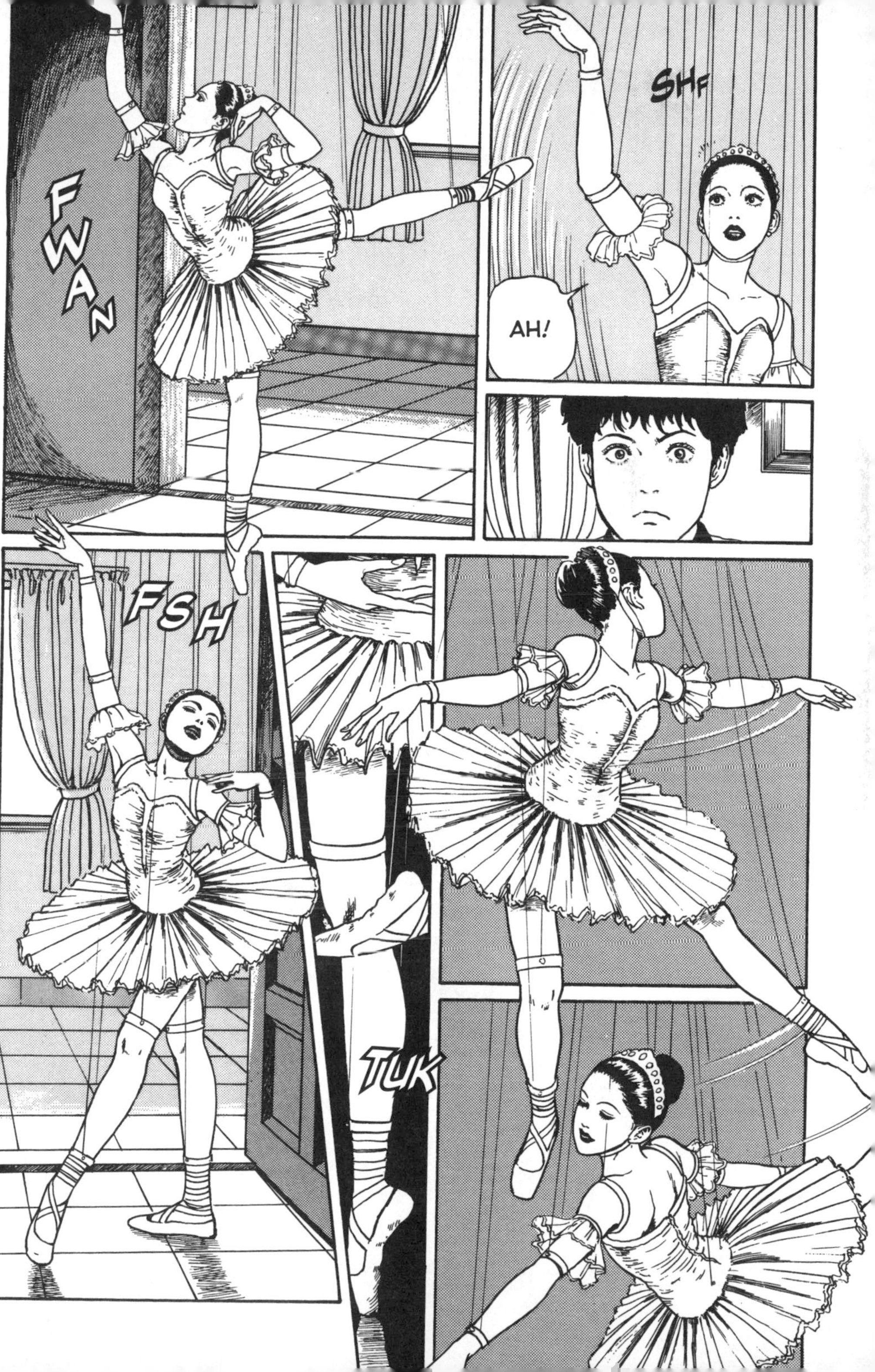
SHF
AH!
FWAN
TUK
FSH

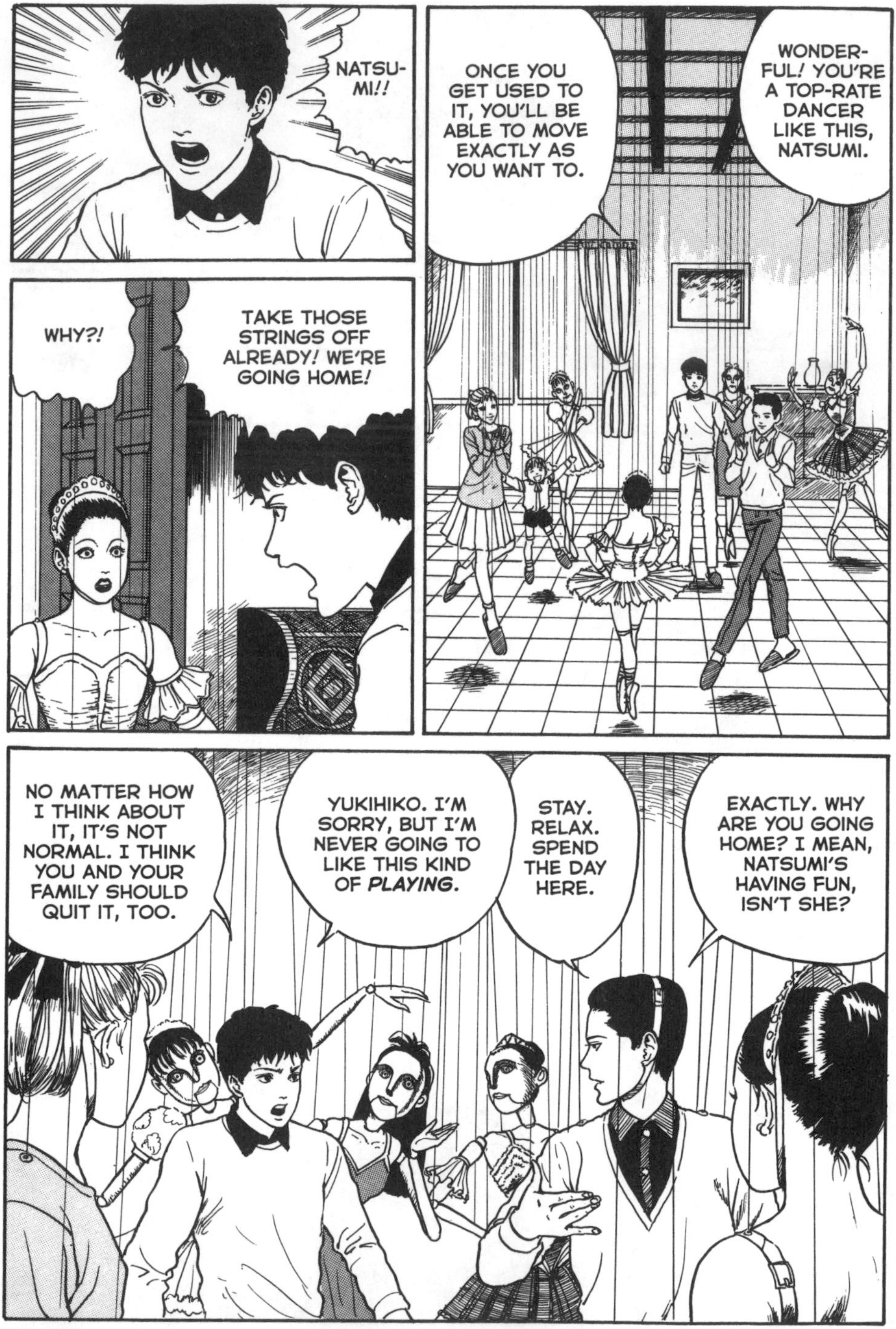
WONDER-FUL! YOU'RE A TOP-RATE DANCER LIKE THIS, NATSUMI.
ONCE YOU GET USED TO IT, YOU'LL BE ABLE TO MOVE EXACTLY AS YOU WANT TO.
NATSU-MI!!
TAKE THOSE STRINGS OFF ALREADY! WE'RE GOING HOME!
WHY?!
EXACTLY. WHY ARE YOU GOING HOME? I MEAN, NATSUMI'S HAVING FUN, ISN'T SHE?
STAY. RELAX. SPEND THE DAY HERE.
YUKIHIKO. I'M SORRY, BUT I'M NEVER GOING TO LIKE THIS KIND OF ***PLAYING***.
NO MATTER HOW I THINK ABOUT IT, IT'S NOT NORMAL. I THINK YOU AND YOUR FAMILY SHOULD QUIT IT, TOO.

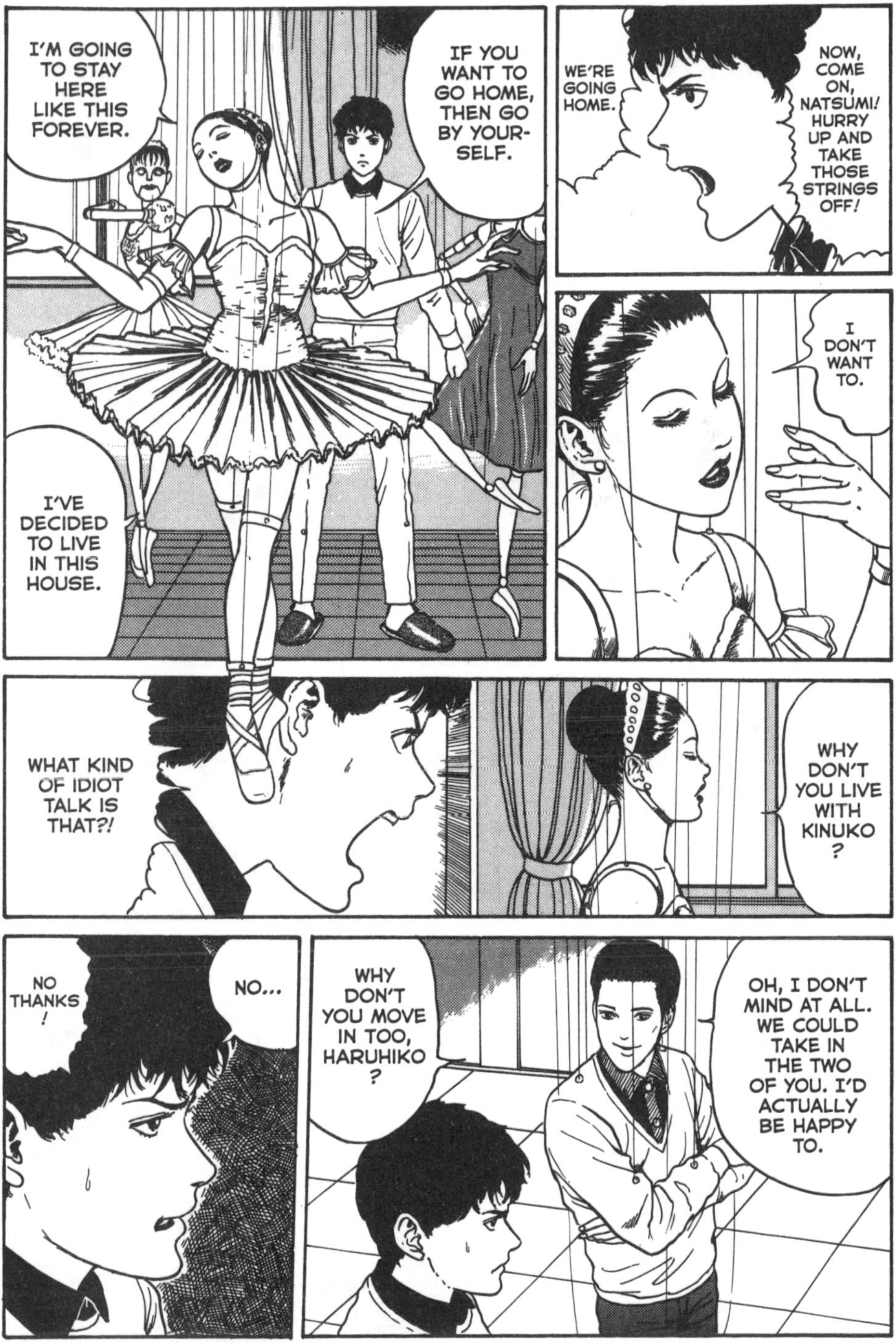
NOW, COME ON, NATSUMI! HURRY UP AND TAKE THOSE STRINGS OFF!
WE'RE GOING HOME.
I DON'T WANT TO.
IF YOU WANT TO GO HOME, THEN GO BY YOUR-SELF.
I'M GOING TO STAY HERE LIKE THIS FOREVER.
I'VE DECIDED TO LIVE IN THIS HOUSE.
WHY DON'T YOU LIVE WITH KINUKO?
WHAT KIND OF IDIOT TALK IS THAT?!
OH, I DON'T MIND AT ALL. WE COULD TAKE IN THE TWO OF YOU. I'D ACTUALLY BE HAPPY TO.
WHY DON'T YOU MOVE IN TOO, HARUHIKO?
NO...
NO THANKS!

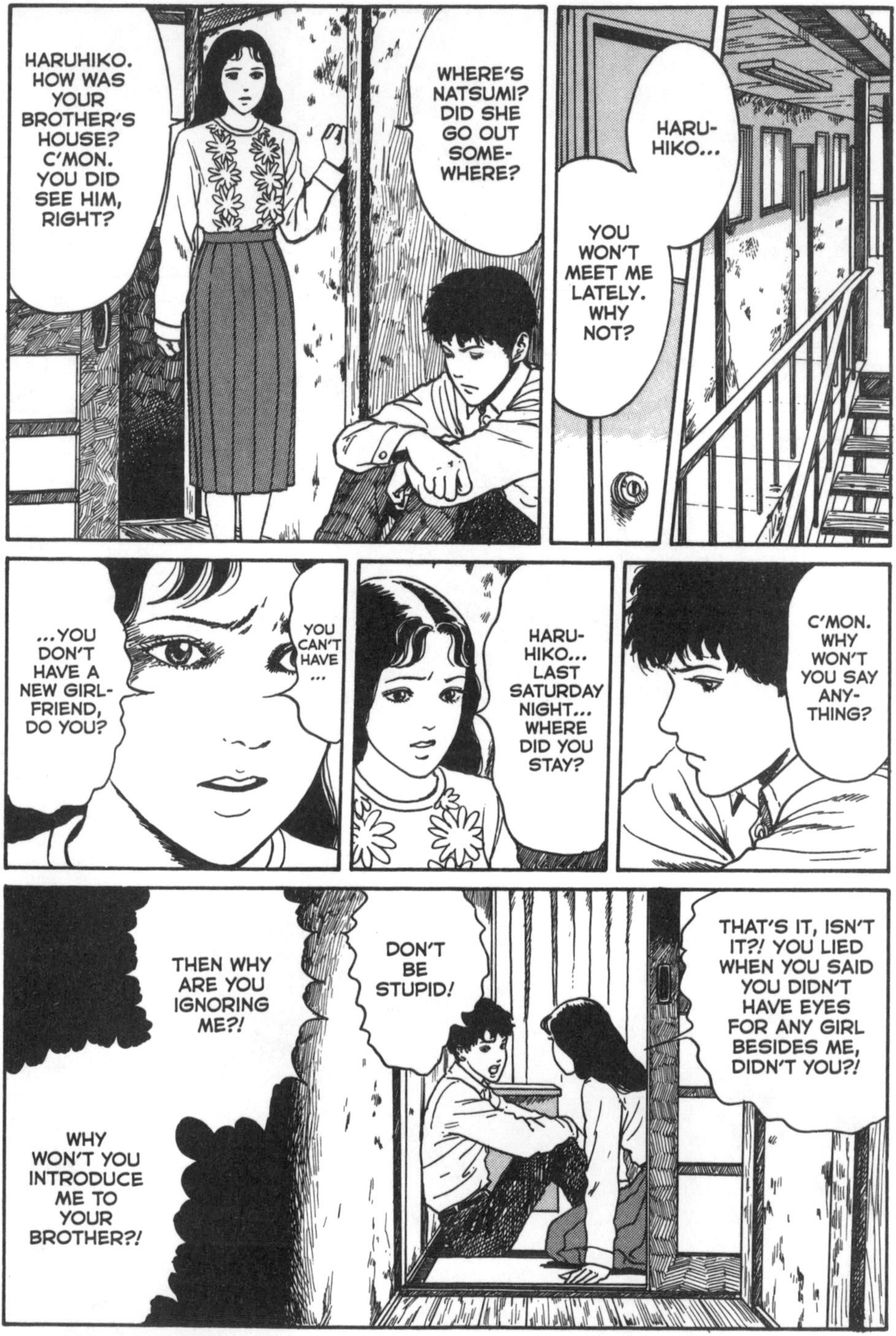
HARU-HIKO...
YOU WON'T MEET ME LATELY. WHY NOT?
WHERE'S NATSUMI? DID SHE GO OUT SOME-WHERE?
HARUHIKO. HOW WAS YOUR BROTHER'S HOUSE? C'MON. YOU DID SEE HIM, RIGHT?
C'MON. WHY WON'T YOU SAY ANY-THING?
HARU-HIKO... LAST SATURDAY NIGHT... WHERE DID YOU STAY?
YOU CAN'T HAVE ...
...YOU DON'T HAVE A NEW GIRL-FRIEND, DO YOU?
THAT'S IT, ISN'T IT?! YOU LIED WHEN YOU SAID YOU DIDN'T HAVE EYES FOR ANY GIRL BESIDES ME, DIDN'T YOU?!
DON'T BE STUPID!
THEN WHY ARE YOU IGNORING ME?!
WHY WON'T YOU INTRODUCE ME TO YOUR BROTHER?!

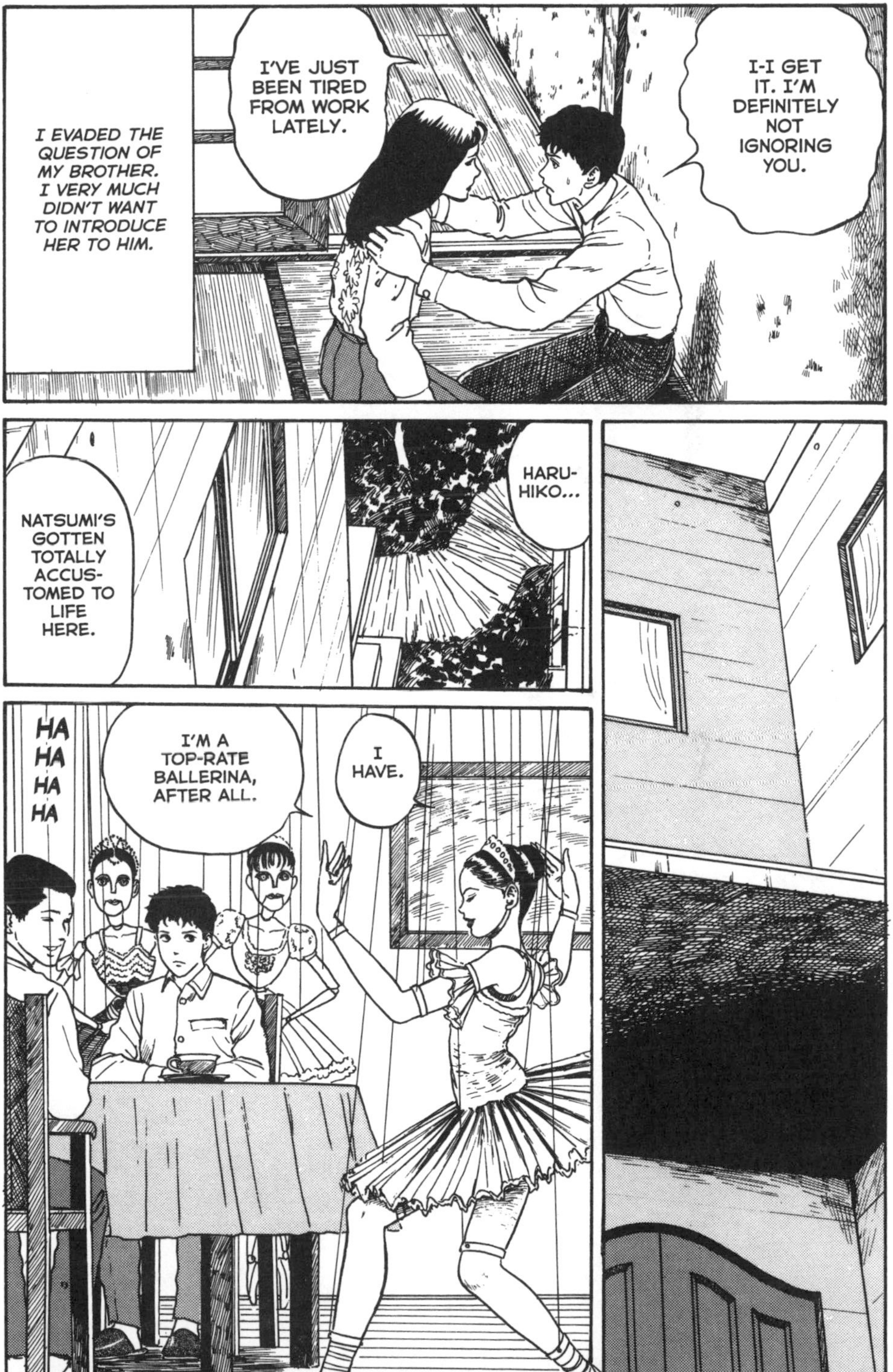
I-I GET IT. I'M DEFINITELY NOT IGNORING YOU.
I'VE JUST BEEN TIRED FROM WORK LATELY.
I EVADED THE QUESTION OF MY BROTHER. I VERY MUCH DIDN'T WANT TO INTRODUCE HER TO HIM.
HARU-HIKO...
NATSUMI'S GOTTEN TOTALLY ACCUS-TOMED TO LIFE HERE.
I HAVE.
I'M A TOP-RATE BALLERINA, AFTER ALL.
HA HA HA HA

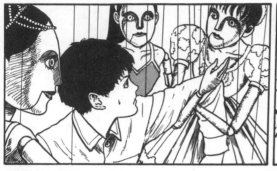

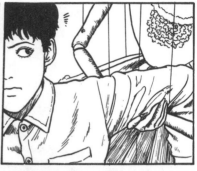

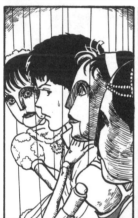

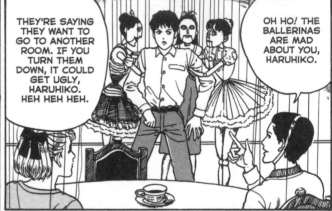

OH HO! THE BALLERINAS ARE MAD ABOUT YOU, HARUHIKO.
THEY'RE SAYING THEY WANT TO GO TO ANOTHER ROOM. IF YOU TURN THEM DOWN, IT COULD GET UGLY, HARUHIKO. HEH HEH HEH.
...
IT'S ALMOST LIKE THEY'RE REALLY ALIVE.
WHAT EXACTLY DO YOU WANT WITH ME?
...I ASK, BUT YOU CAN'T TALK.

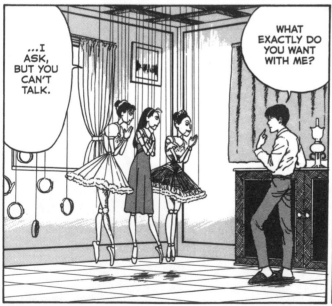

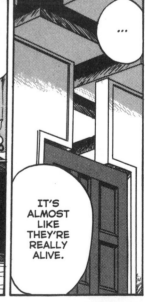

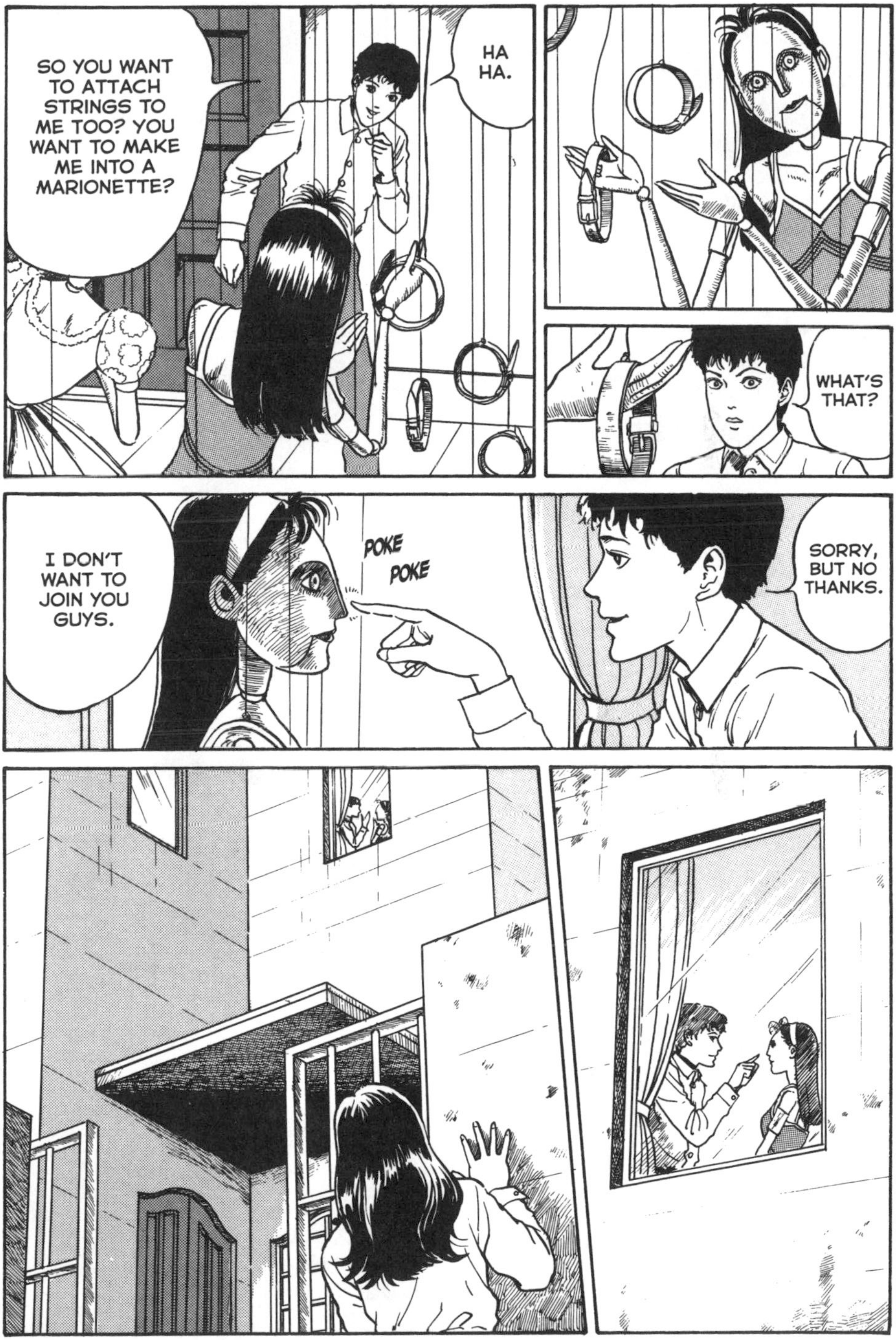
WHAT'S THAT?
HA HA.
SO YOU WANT TO ATTACH STRINGS TO ME TOO? YOU WANT TO MAKE ME INTO A MARIONETTE?
SORRY, BUT NO THANKS.
POKE
POKE
I DON'T WANT TO JOIN YOU GUYS.

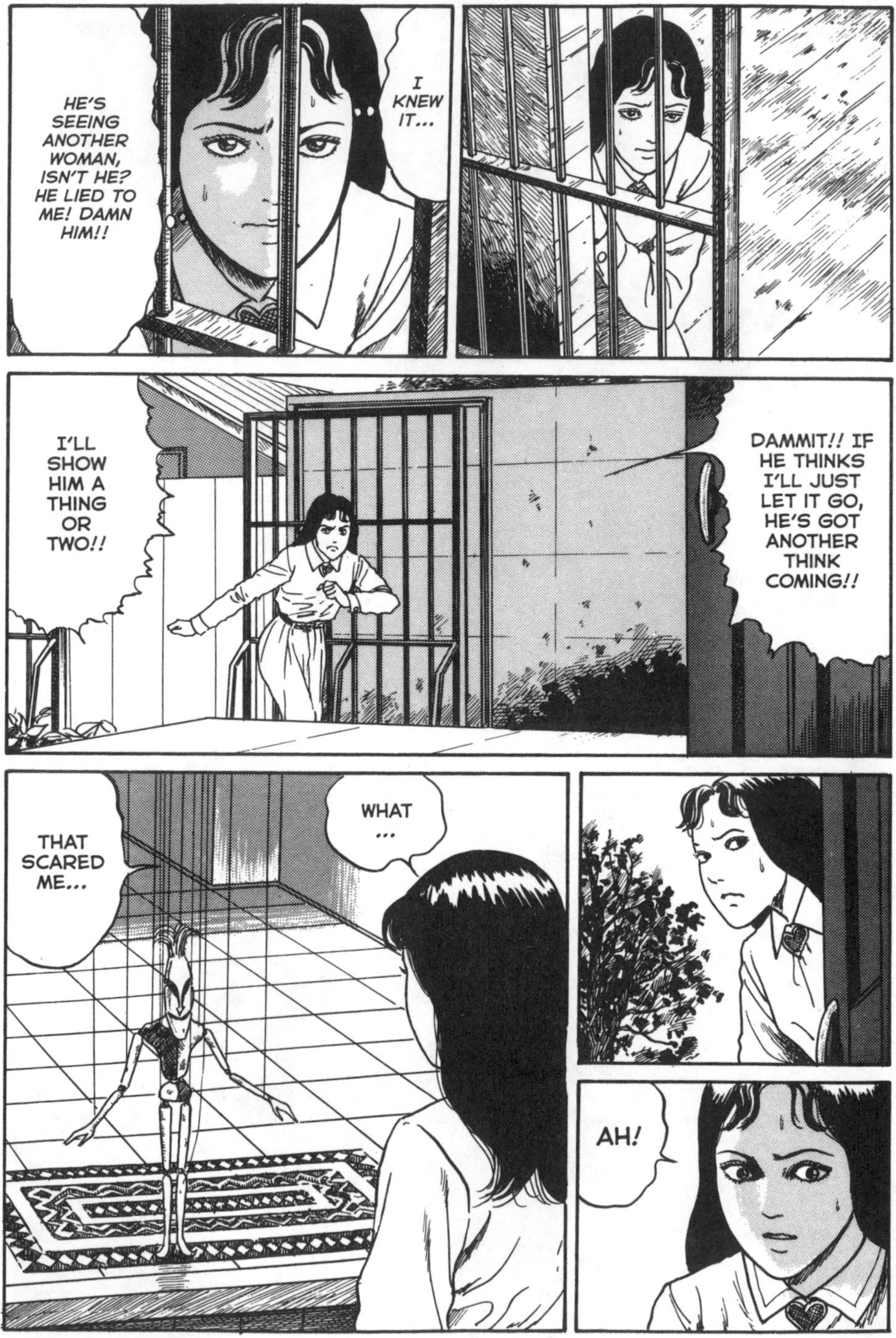
I KNEW IT...
HE'S SEEING ANOTHER WOMAN, ISN'T HE? HE LIED TO ME! DAMN HIM!!
DAMMIT!! IF HE THINKS I'LL JUST LET IT GO, HE'S GOT ANOTHER THINK COMING!!
I'LL SHOW HIM A THING OR TWO!!
AH!
WHAT ...
THAT SCARED ME...

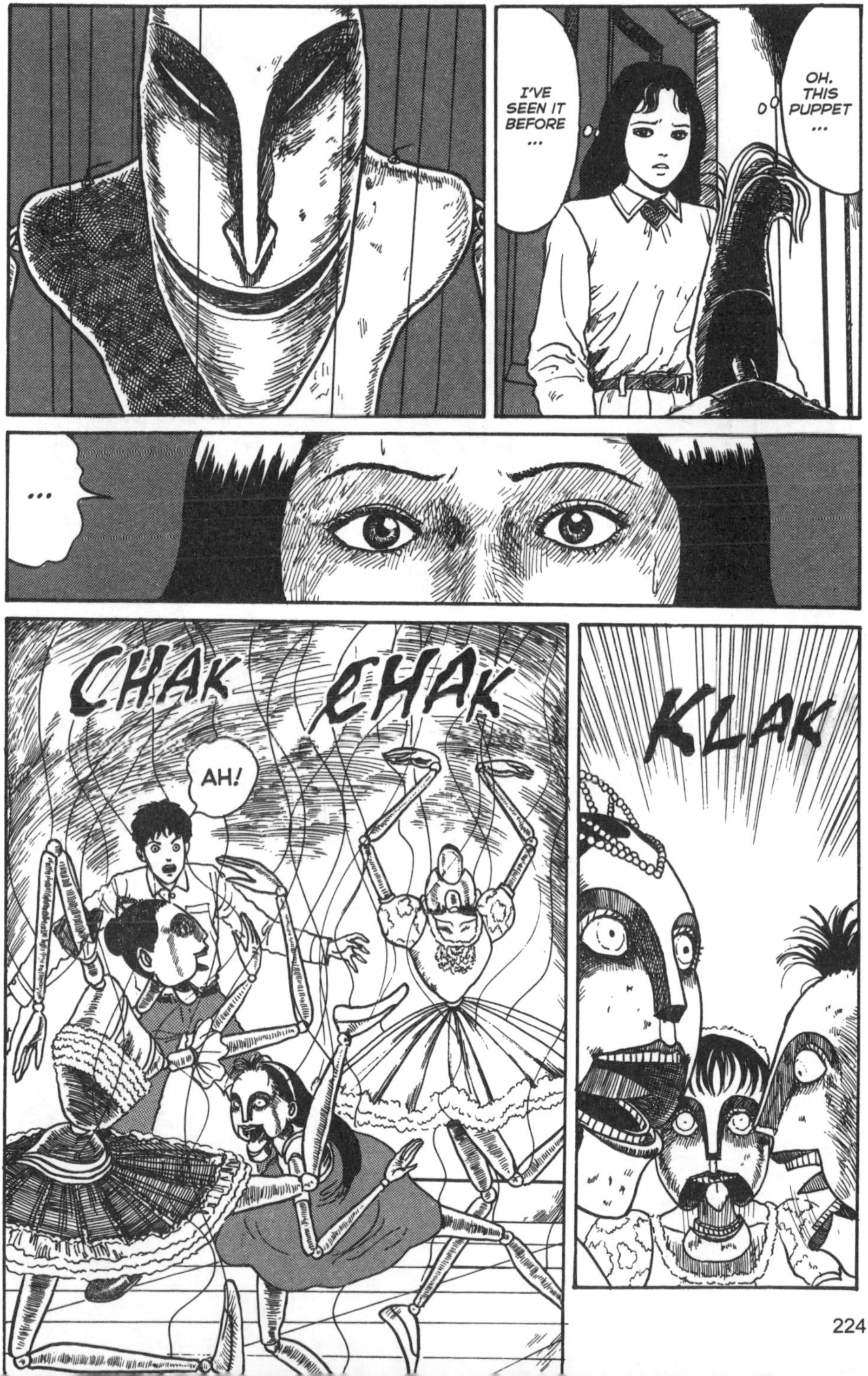
OH. THIS PUPPET ...
I'VE SEEN IT BEFORE ...
...
KLAK
CHAK CHAK
AH!

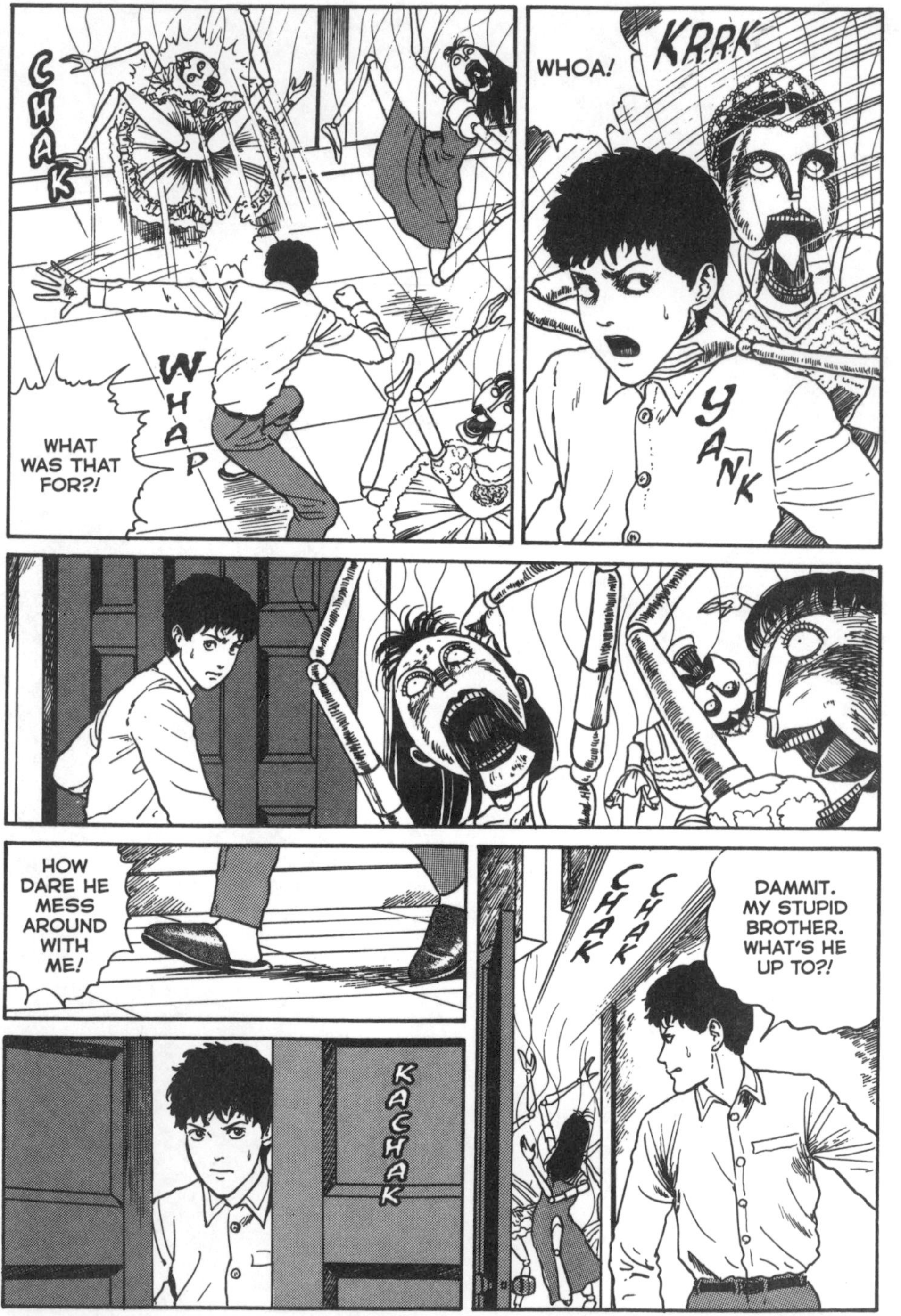
WHOA!
KRRK
YANK
CHAK
WHAP
WHAT WAS THAT FOR?!
CHAK CHAK
DAMMIT. MY STUPID BROTHER. WHAT'S HE UP TO?!
HOW DARE HE MESS AROUND WITH ME!
KACHAK

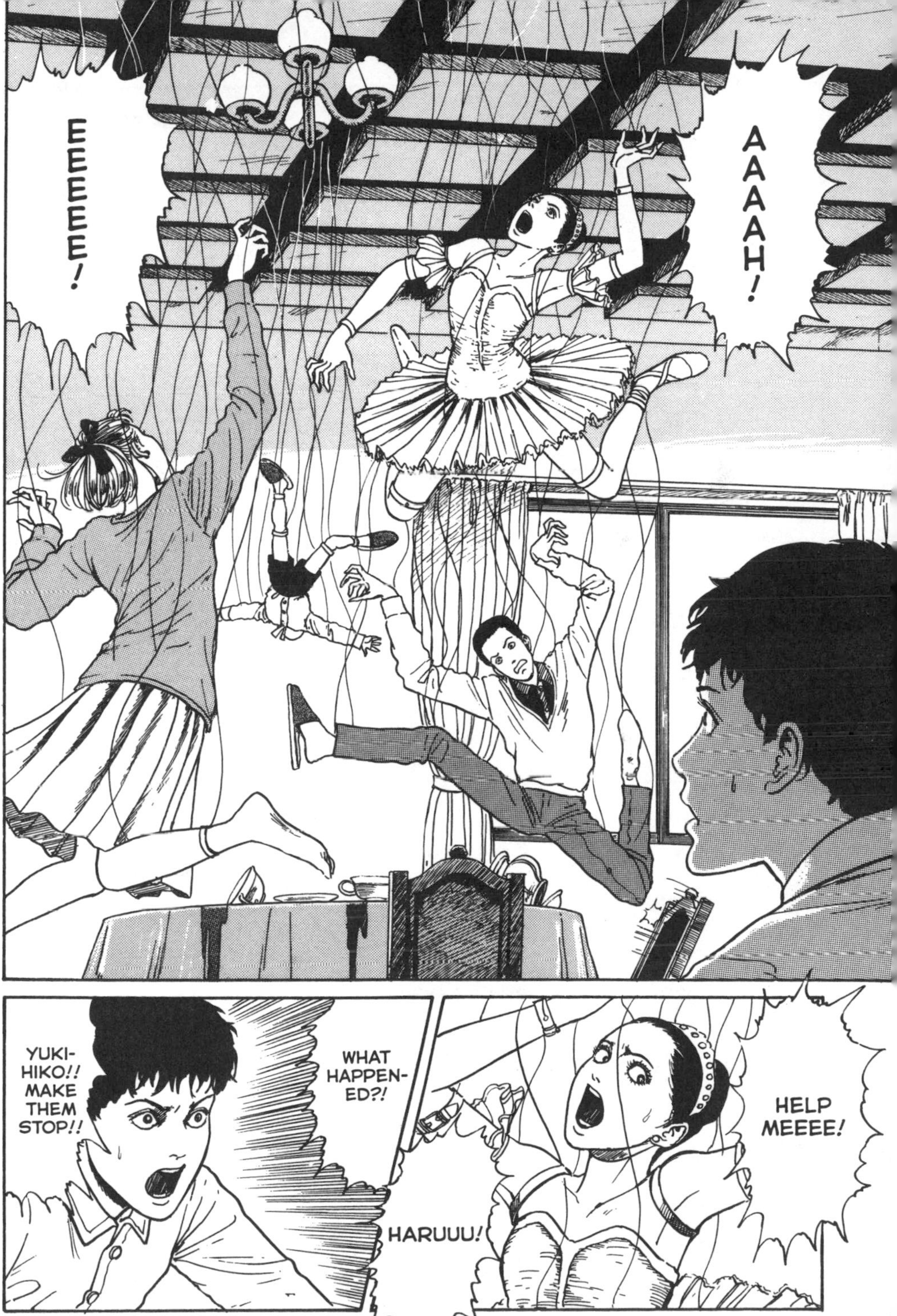
AAAAAH!
EEEEEE!
HELP MEEEE!
HARUUU!
WHAT HAPPEN-ED?!
YUKI-HIKO!! MAKE THEM STOP!!

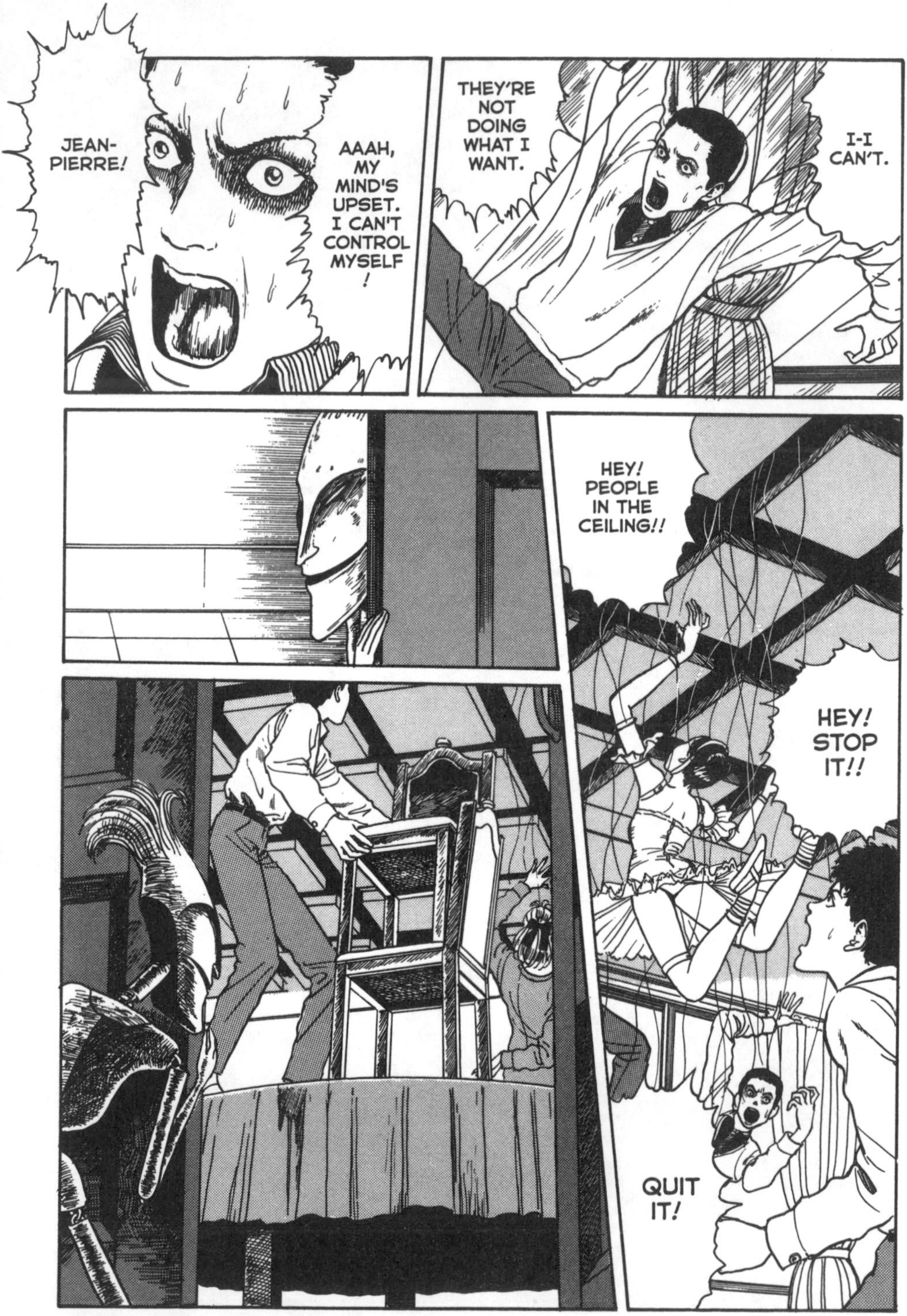
I-I CAN'T.
THEY'RE NOT DOING WHAT I WANT.
AAAH, MY MIND'S UPSET. I CAN'T CONTROL MYSELF!
JEAN-PIERRE!
HEY! PEOPLE IN THE CEILING!!
HEY! STOP IT!!
QUIT IT!

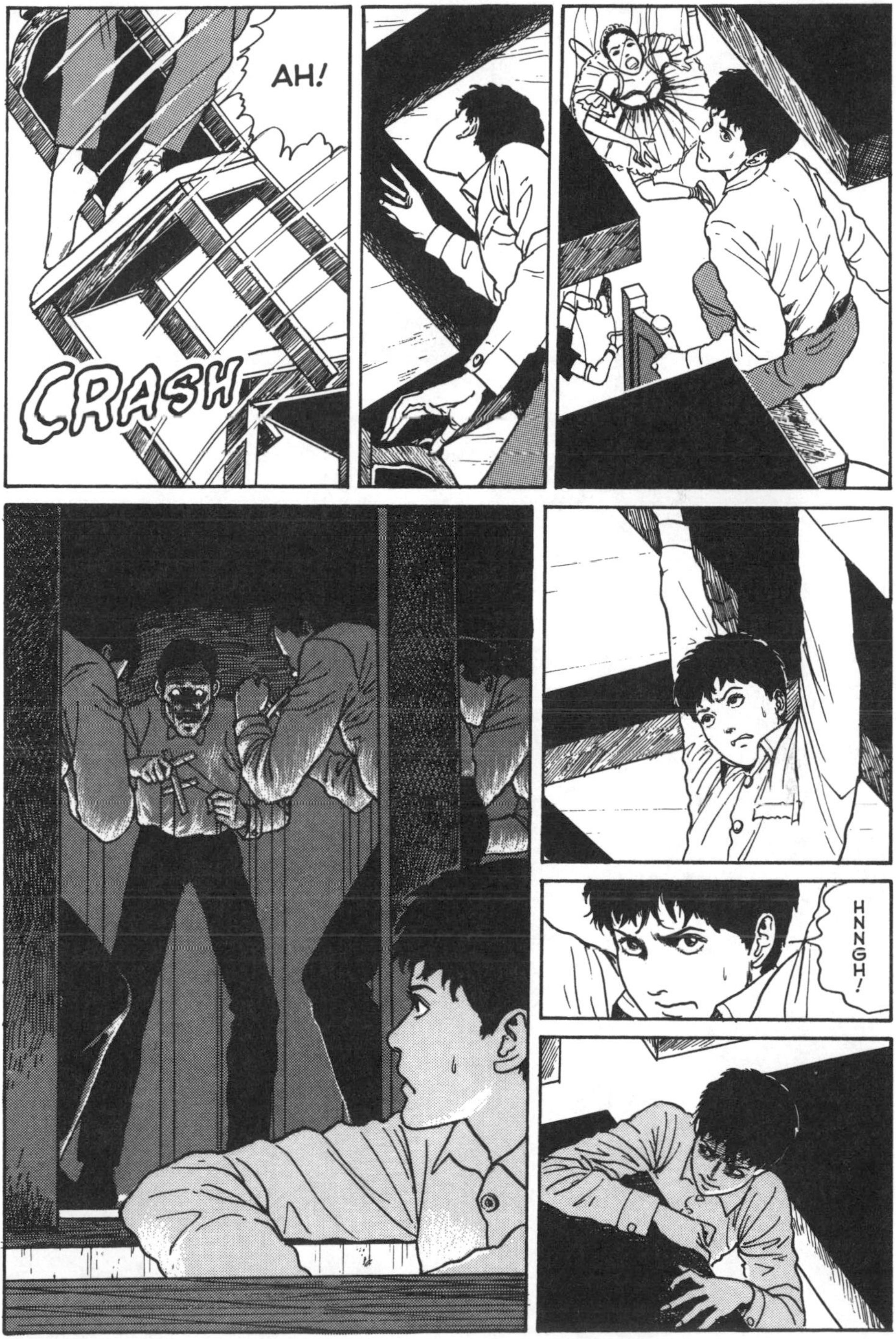
AH!
CRASH
HNNGH!

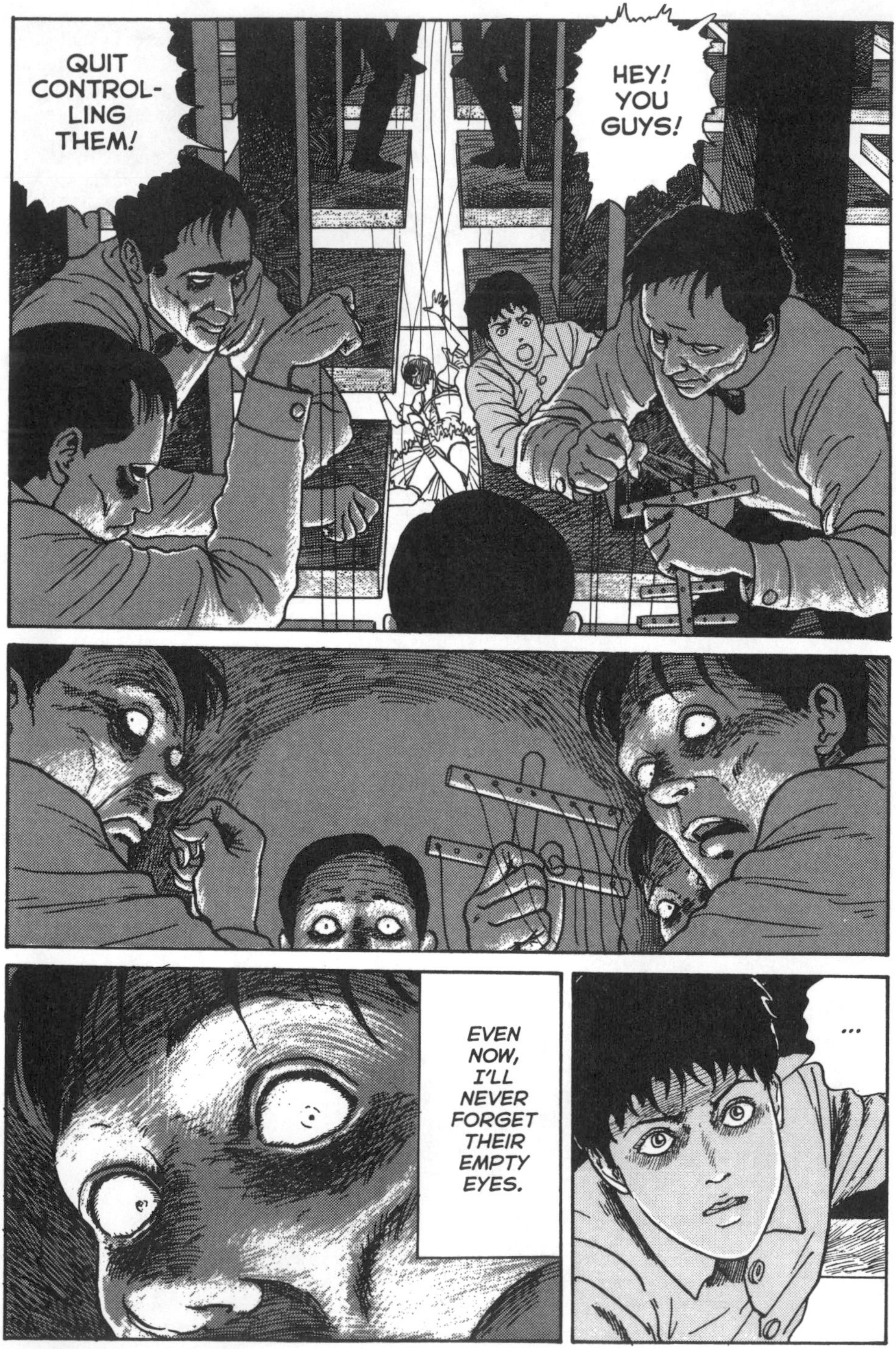
HEY! YOU GUYS!
QUIT CONTROL-LING THEM!
...
EVEN NOW, I'LL NEVER FORGET THEIR EMPTY EYES.

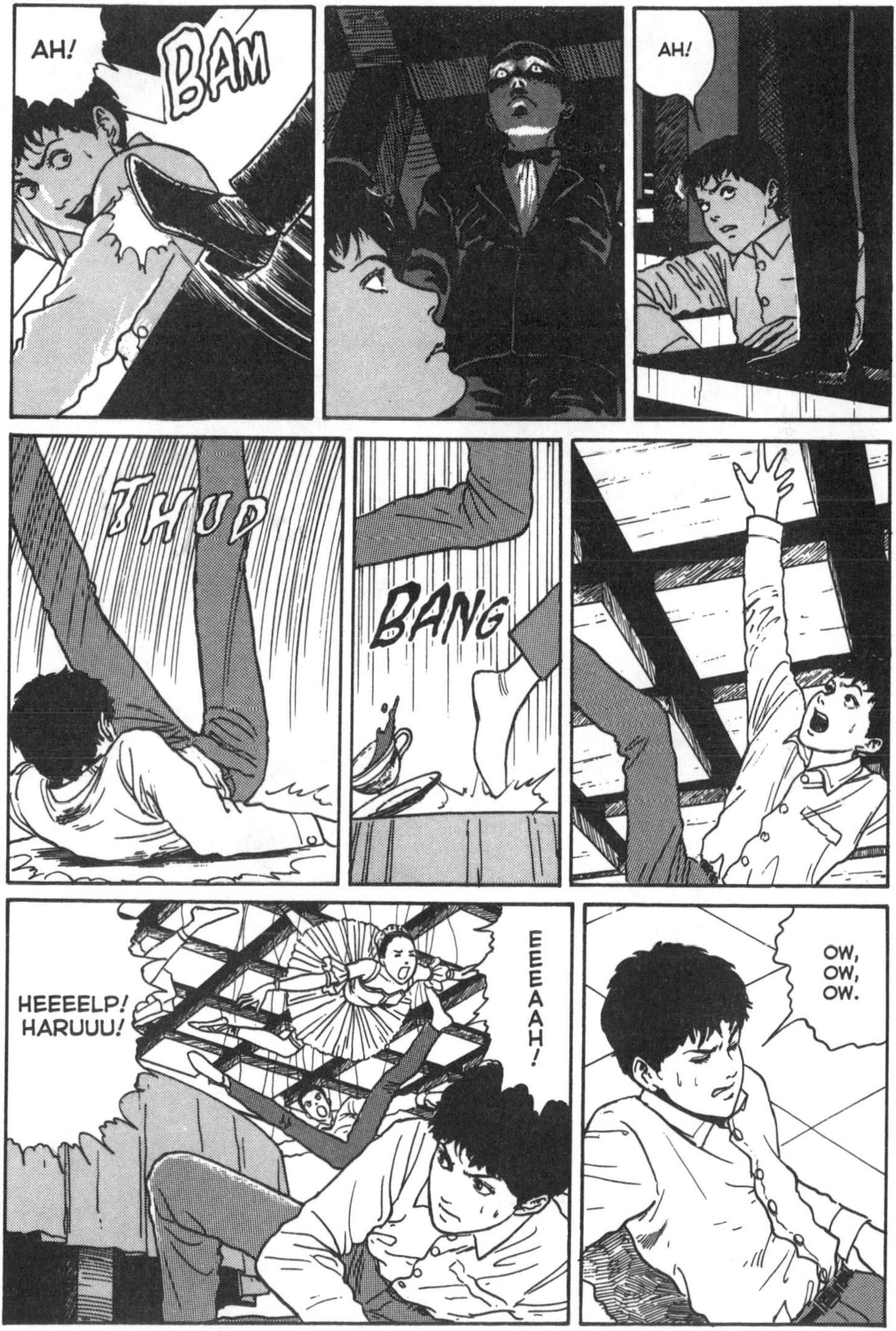
AH!
BAM
AH!
BANG
THUD
OW, OW, OW.
EEEEAAAH!
HEEEELP! HARUUU!

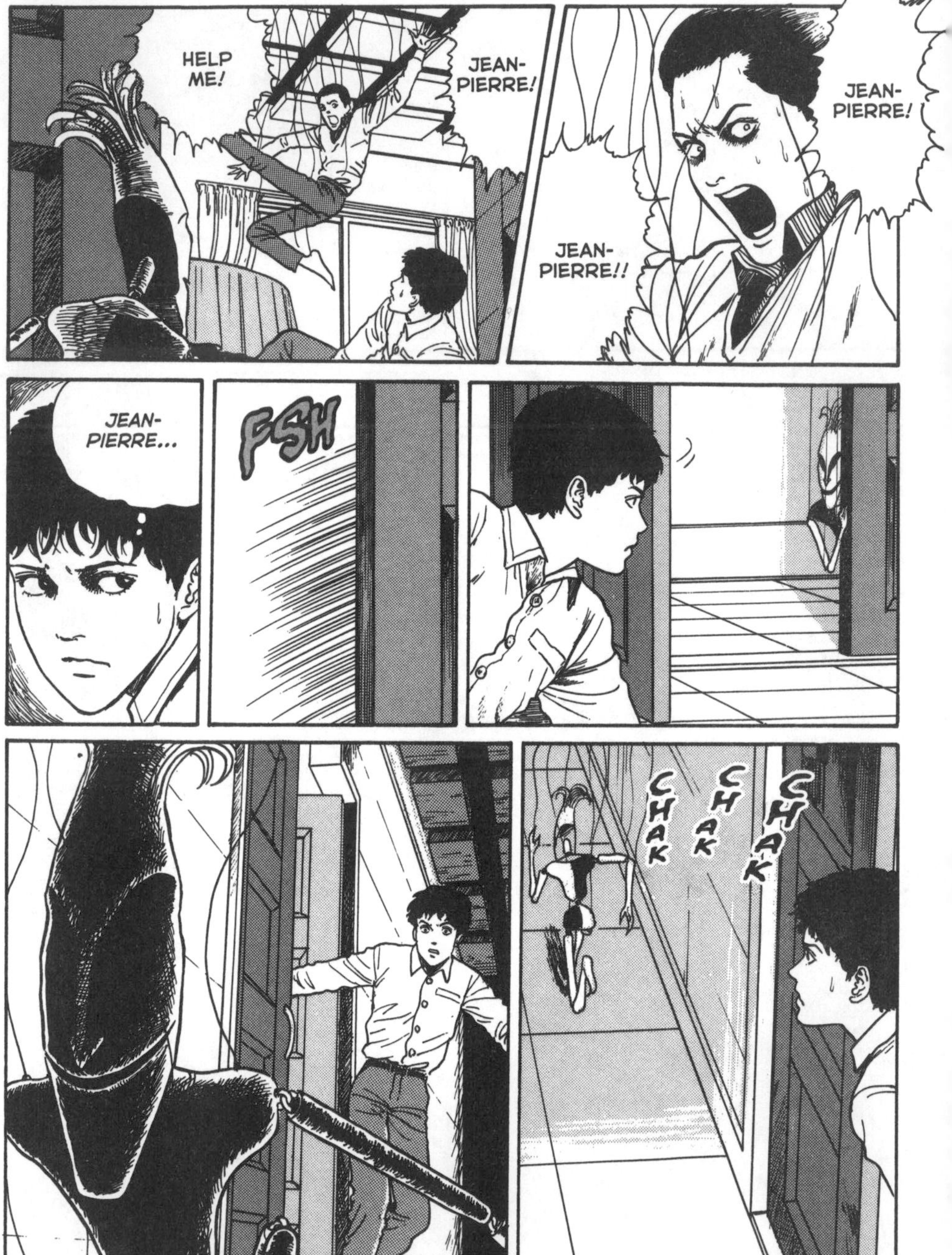

JEAN-PIERRE!
JEAN-PIERRE!!
JEAN-PIERRE!
HELP ME!
FSH
JEAN-PIERRE...
CHAK CHAK CHAK

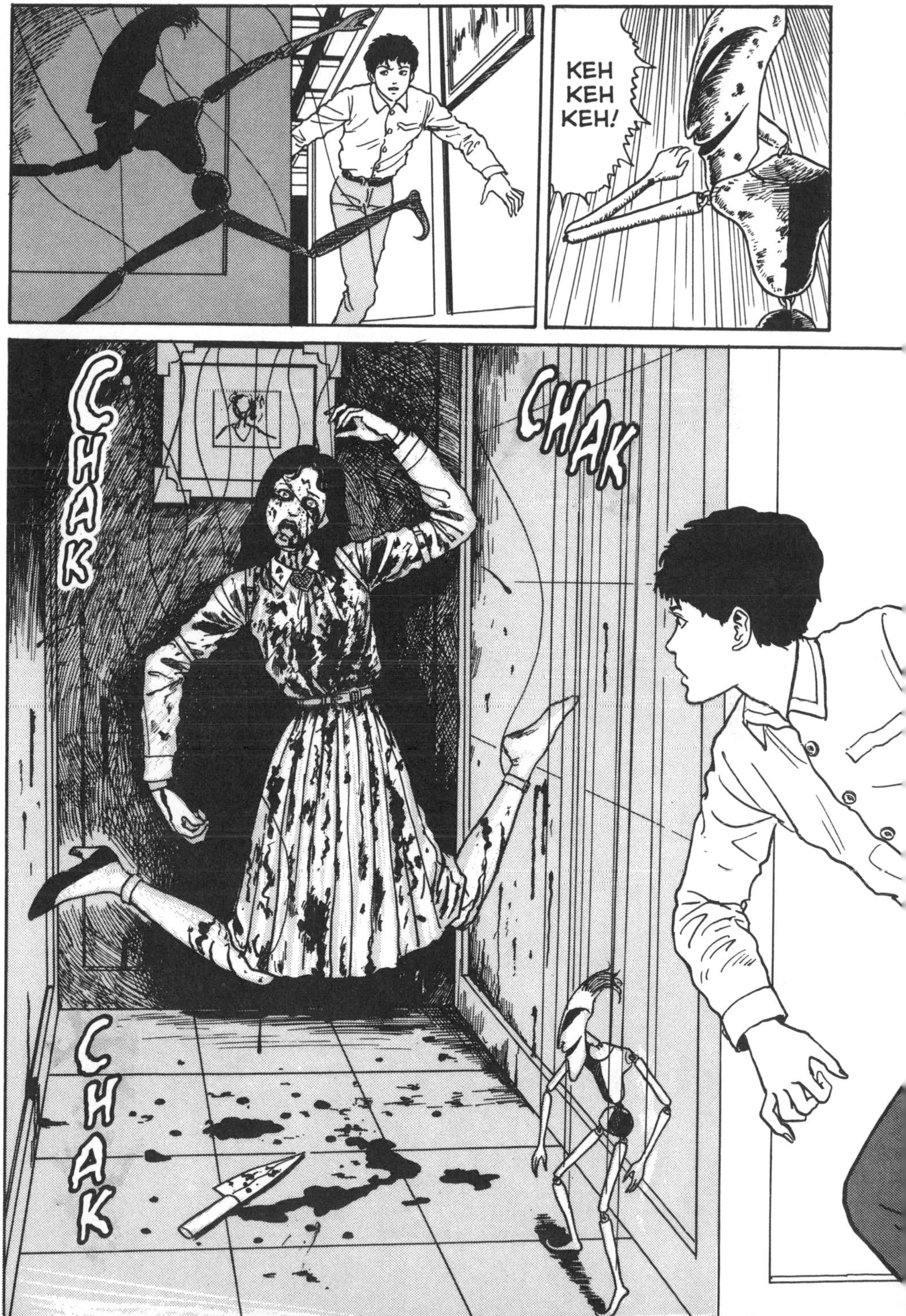
KEH KEH KEH!
CHAK
CHAK
CHAK

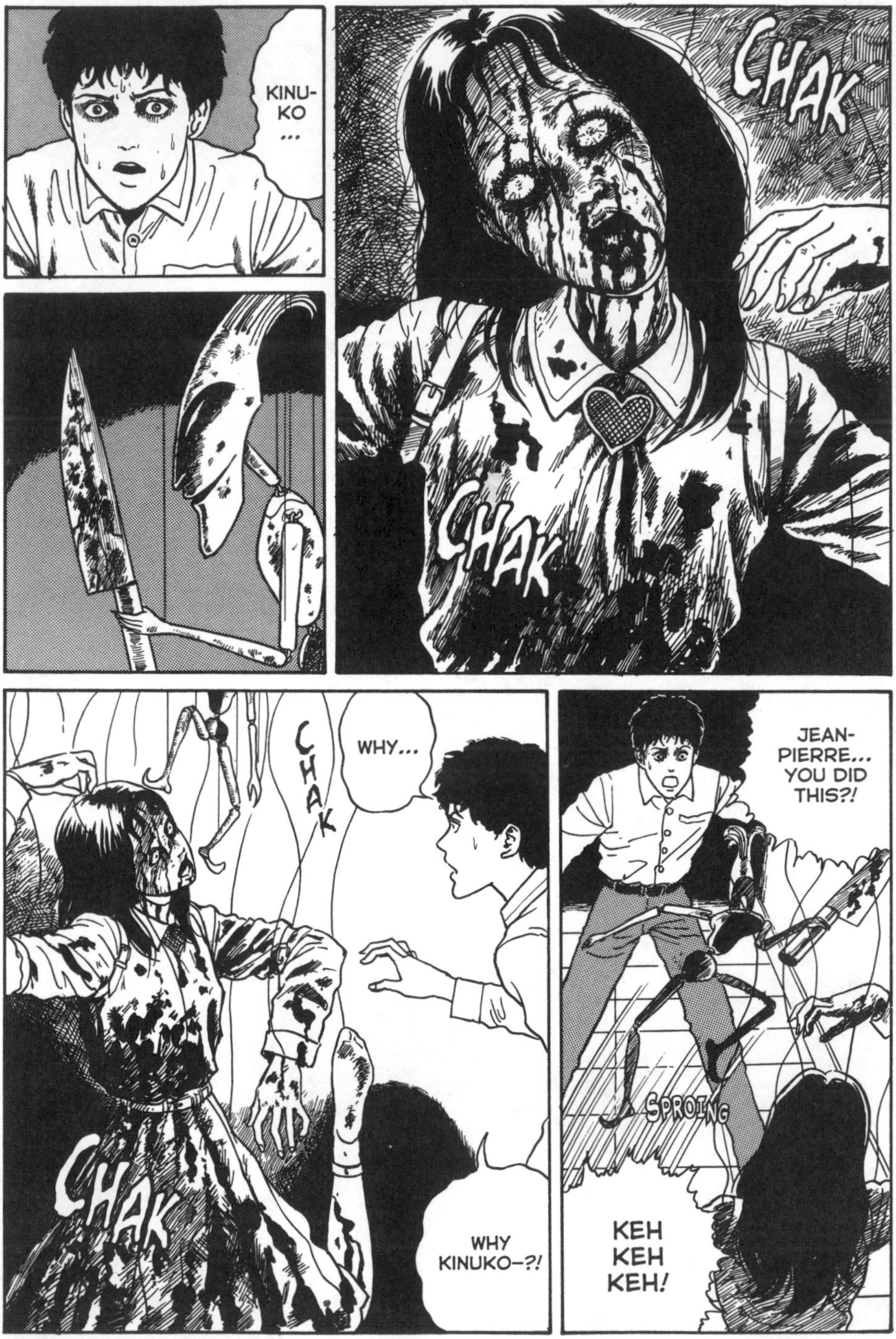
CHAK
CHAK
KINU-
KO
...
JEAN-
PIERRE...
YOU DID
THIS?!
SPROING
KEH
KEH
KEH!
WHY...
CHAK
WHY
KINUKO—?!
CHAK

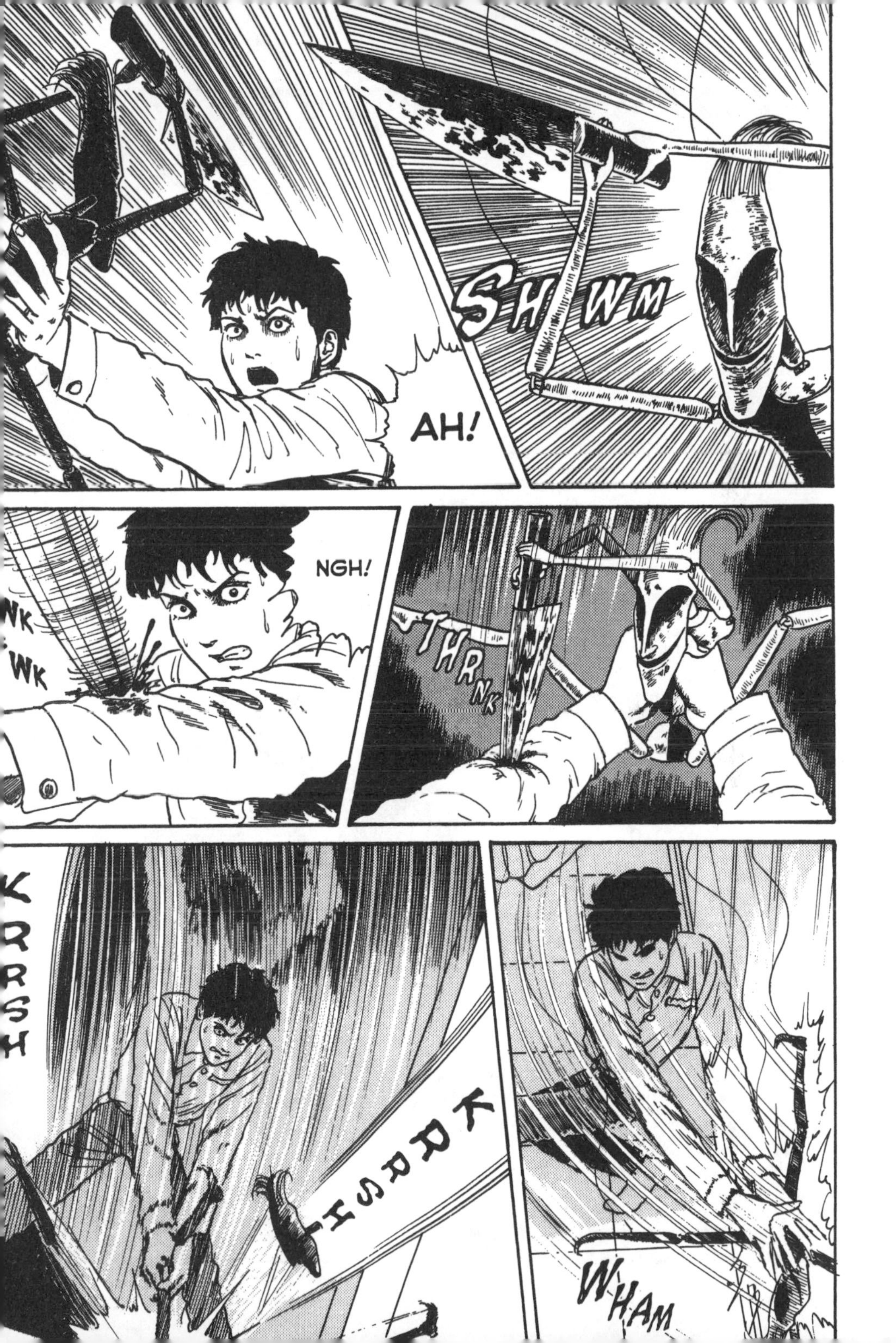
SHWM
AH!
THRNK
NGH!
NK
WK
WHAM
KRRSH
KRRSH

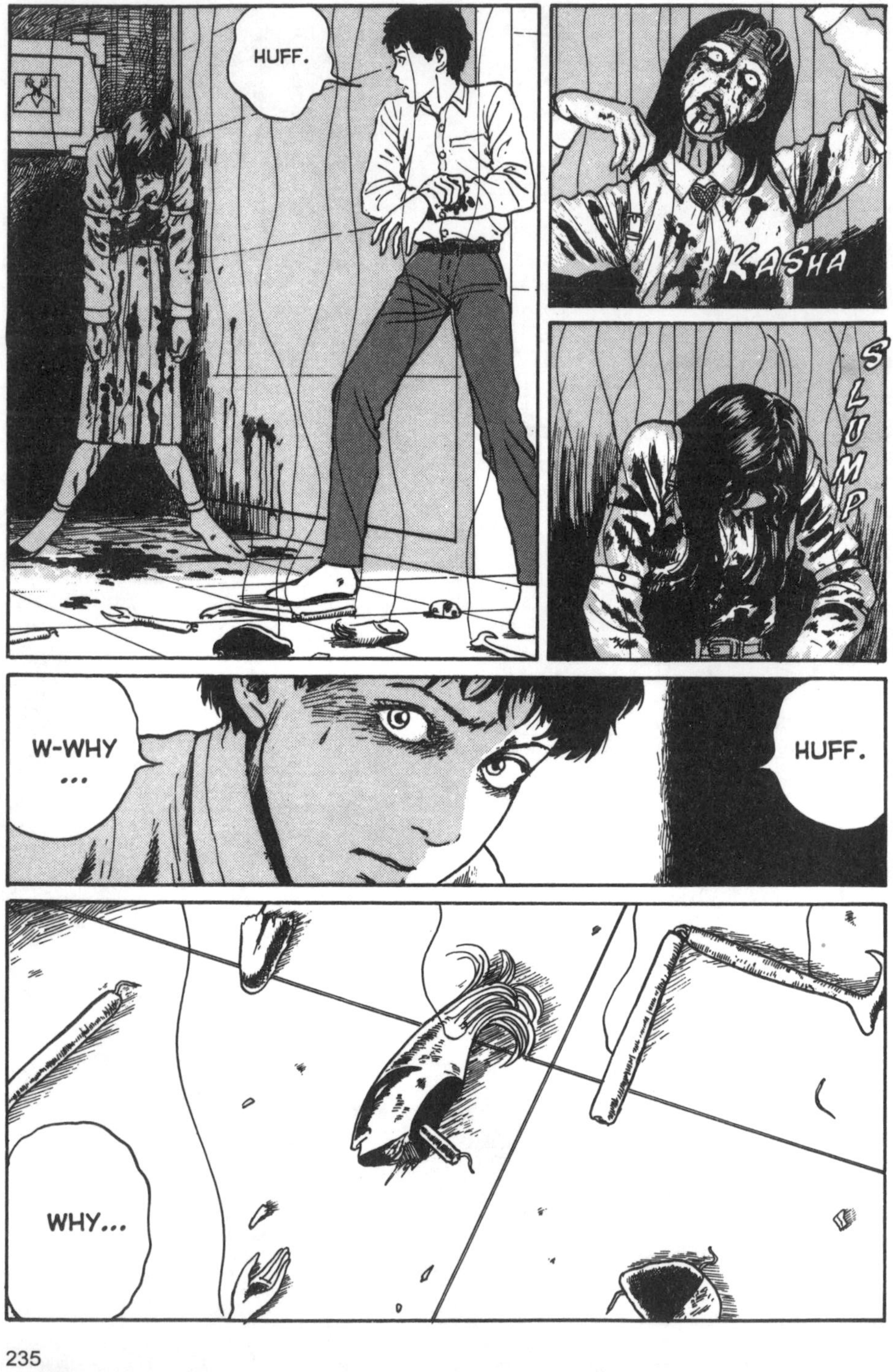
KASHA
SLUMP
HUFF.
HUFF.
W-WHY ...
WHY...

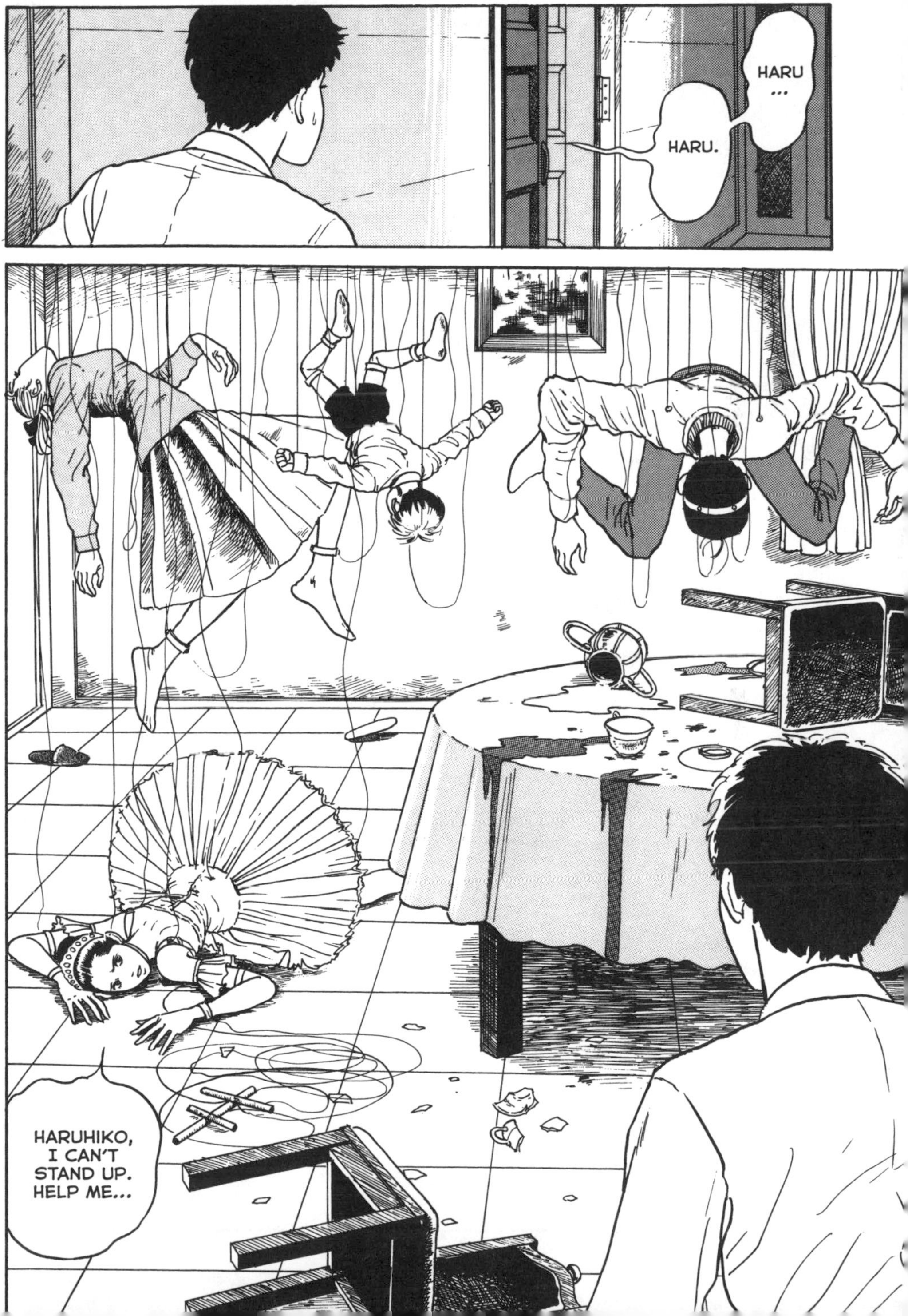
HARU...
HARU.
HARUHIKO, I CAN'T STAND UP. HELP ME...

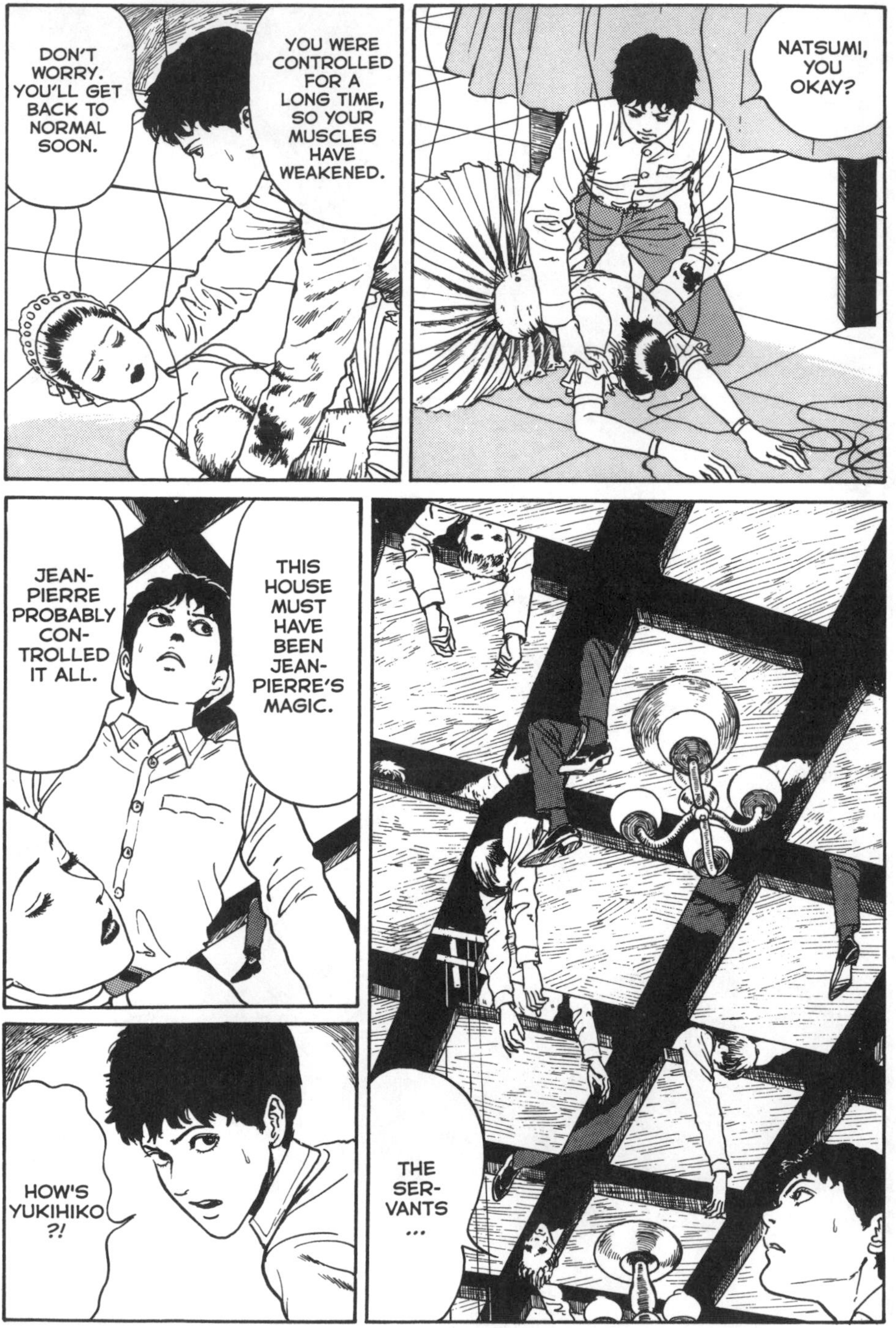
NATSUMI, YOU OKAY?
YOU WERE CONTROLLED FOR A LONG TIME, SO YOUR MUSCLES HAVE WEAKENED.
DON'T WORRY. YOU'LL GET BACK TO NORMAL SOON.
THE SER-VANTS ...
THIS HOUSE MUST HAVE BEEN JEAN-PIERRE'S MAGIC.
JEAN-PIERRE PROBABLY CON-TROLLED IT ALL.
HOW'S YUKIHIKO ?!

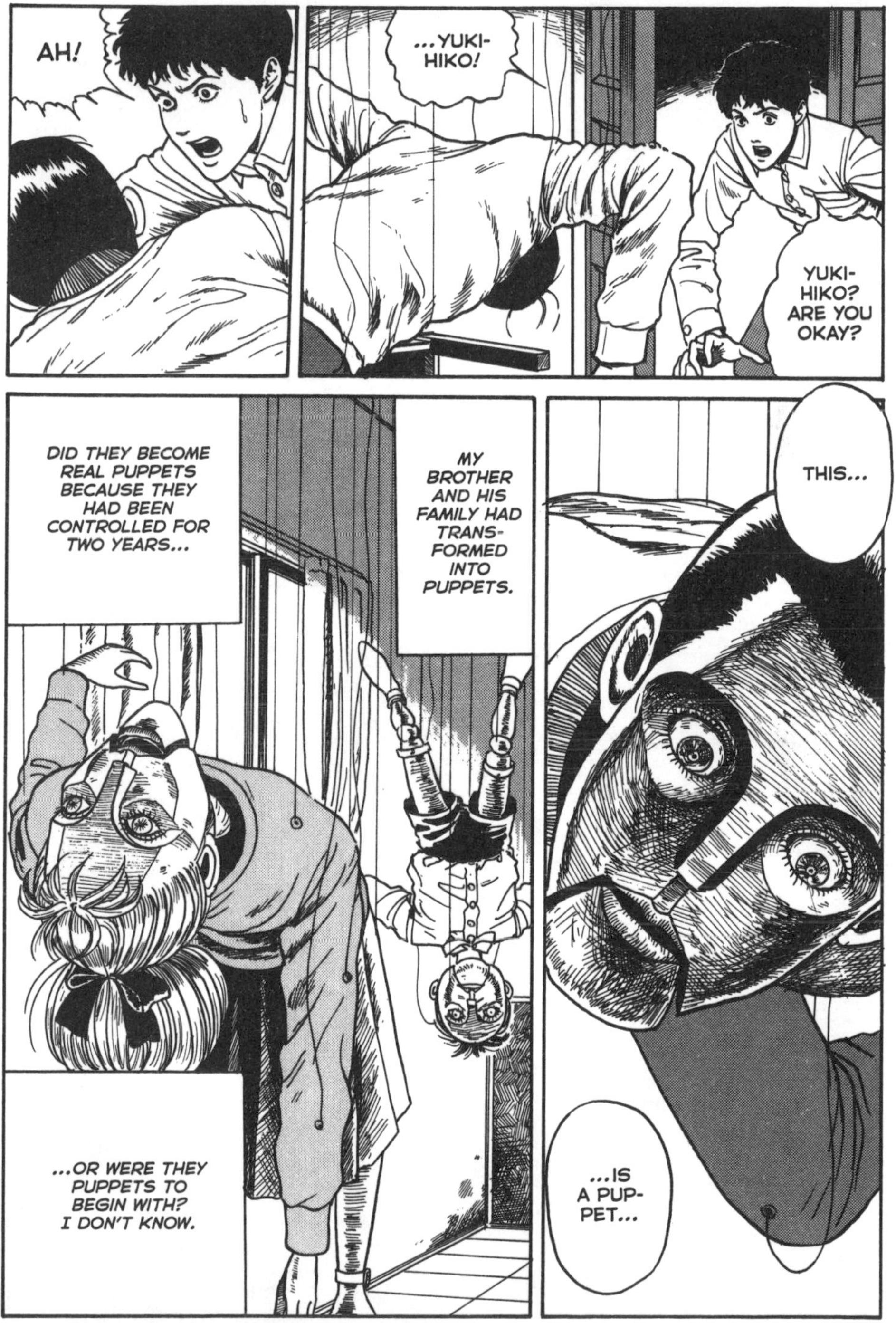
YUKI-HIKO? ARE YOU OKAY?
...YUKI-HIKO!
AH!
THIS...
...IS A PUP-PET...
MY BROTHER AND HIS FAMILY HAD TRANS-FORMED INTO PUPPETS.
DID THEY BECOME REAL PUPPETS BECAUSE THEY HAD BEEN CONTROLLED FOR TWO YEARS...
...OR WERE THEY PUPPETS TO BEGIN WITH? I DON'T KNOW.

MARIONETTE MANSION / END

MARIONETTE MANSION

Manga artists are ascetics. You sit on a chair all day, leaning over your desk, and make the tip of your pen move over the paper of your manga pages. The fact that the page is longer vertically is hateful because you have to lean even farther forward when you're drawing the top panels. Your back and hips shriek in agony. It would be so much better if the page were longer horizontally. No, better still, I'd like to hang my upper body from the ceiling. How lovely would it be to leave my body like that and get the work done? This story came from thoughts like these. Servants would control me from the ceiling. And then I'd be able to get my work done with ease. At the time, I was interested in ballet, and I checked out the Prix de Lausanne, so I included elements of that too.

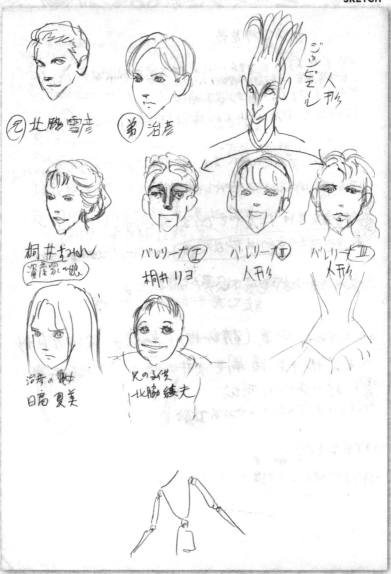

兄 北脇雪彦　　弟 治彦　　ジャンピエール 人形

桐井すみれ
（資産家の娘）

バレリーナ I
桐井リヨ

バレリーナ II
人形

バレリーナ III
人形

治彦の彼女
日高夏美

兄の子供
北脇綾夫

Older brother: Yukihiko Kitawaki　　Younger brother: Haruhiko　　Puppet: Jean-Pierre

Sumire Kirii
Daughter of
a wealthy family

Ballerina I
Riyo Kirii

Ballerina II
Puppet

Ballerina III
Puppet

Haruhiko's girlfriend
Natsumi Hidaka

Older brother's child
Ayao Kitawaki

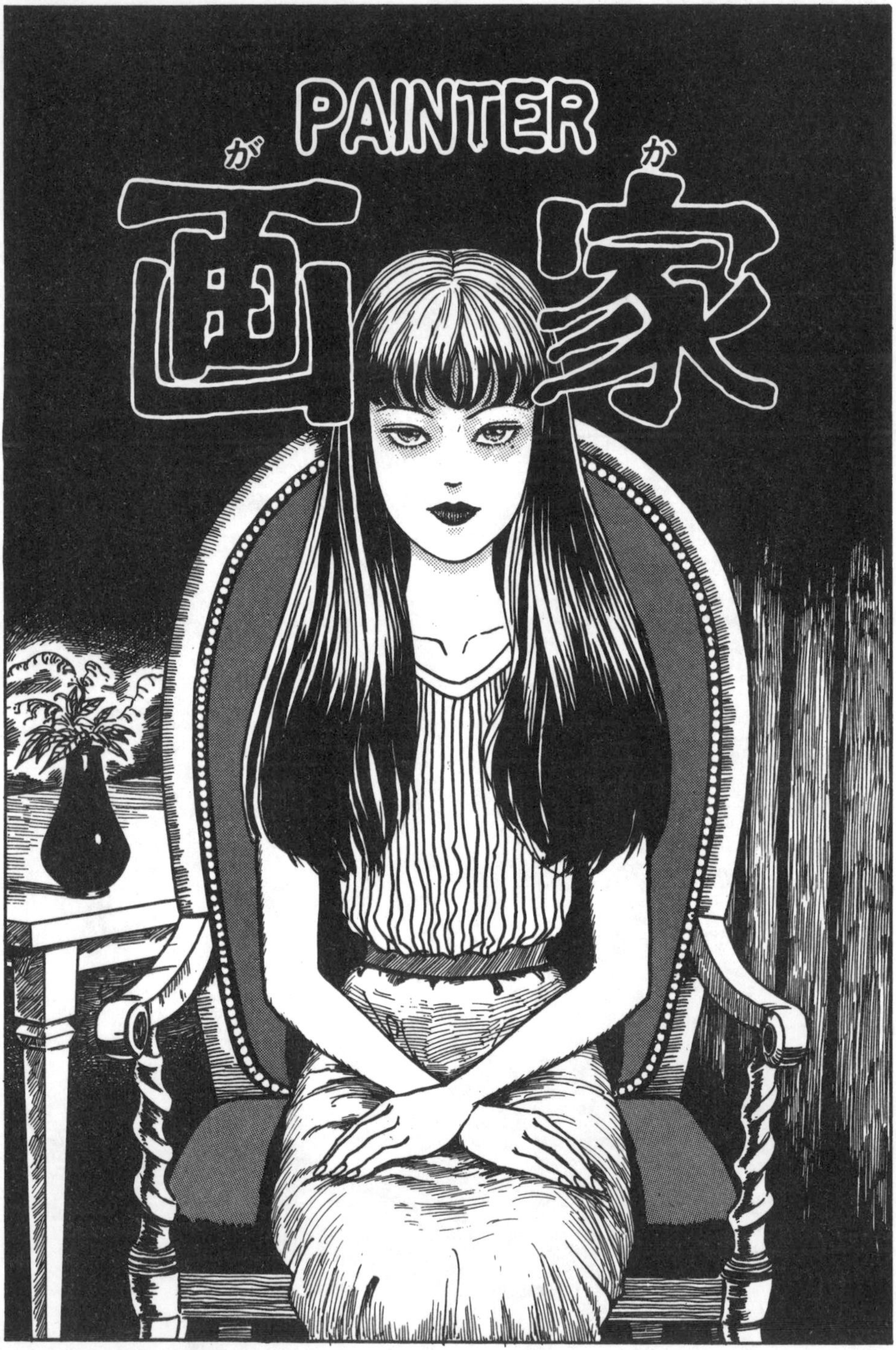
PAINTER
画家
が か

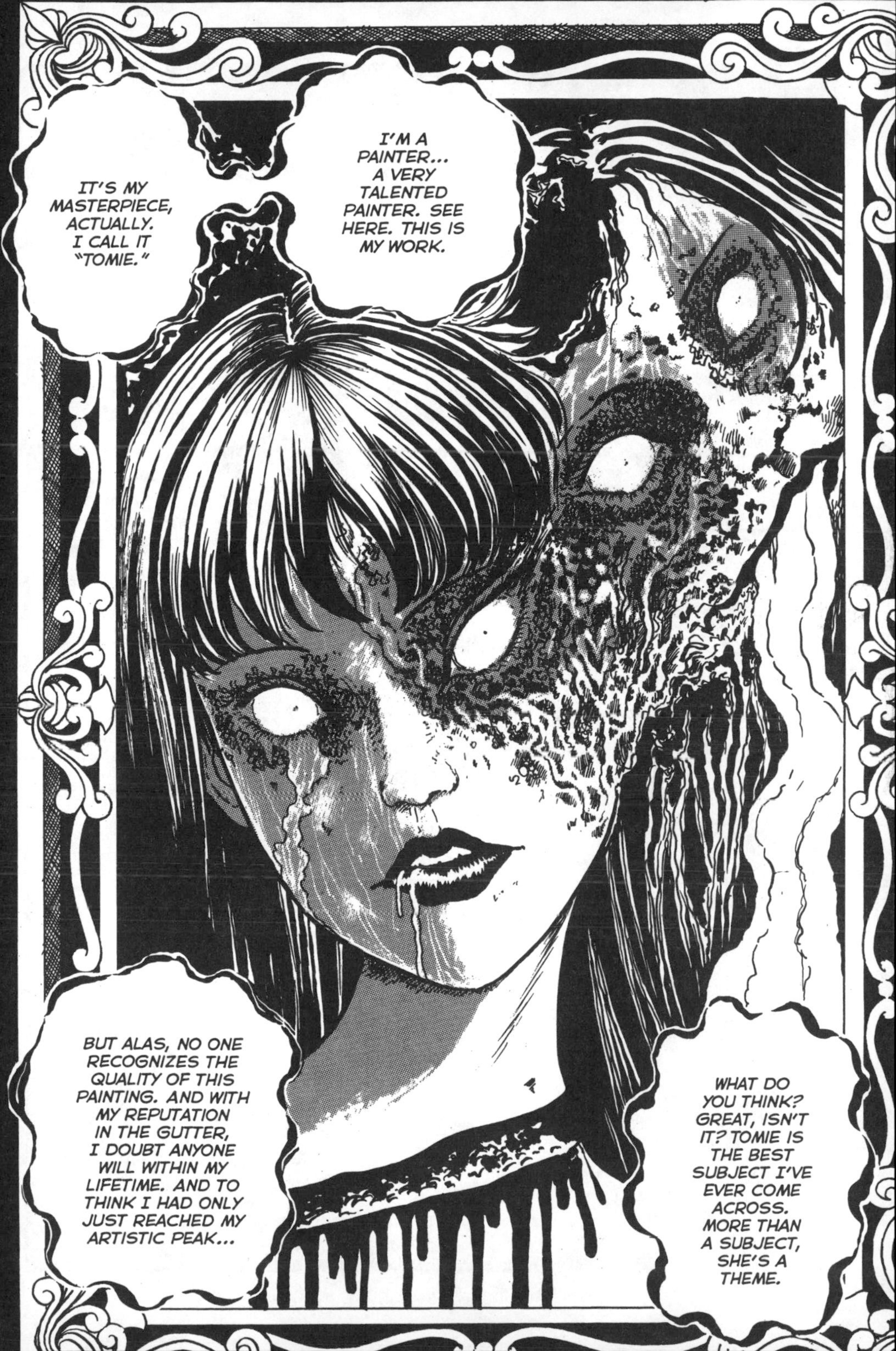
I'M A PAINTER... A VERY TALENTED PAINTER. SEE HERE. THIS IS MY WORK.
IT'S MY MASTERPIECE, ACTUALLY. I CALL IT "TOMIE."
WHAT DO YOU THINK? GREAT, ISN'T IT? TOMIE IS THE BEST SUBJECT I'VE EVER COME ACROSS. MORE THAN A SUBJECT, SHE'S A THEME.
BUT ALAS, NO ONE RECOGNIZES THE QUALITY OF THIS PAINTING. AND WITH MY REPUTATION IN THE GUTTER, I DOUBT ANYONE WILL WITHIN MY LIFETIME. AND TO THINK I HAD ONLY JUST REACHED MY ARTISTIC PEAK...

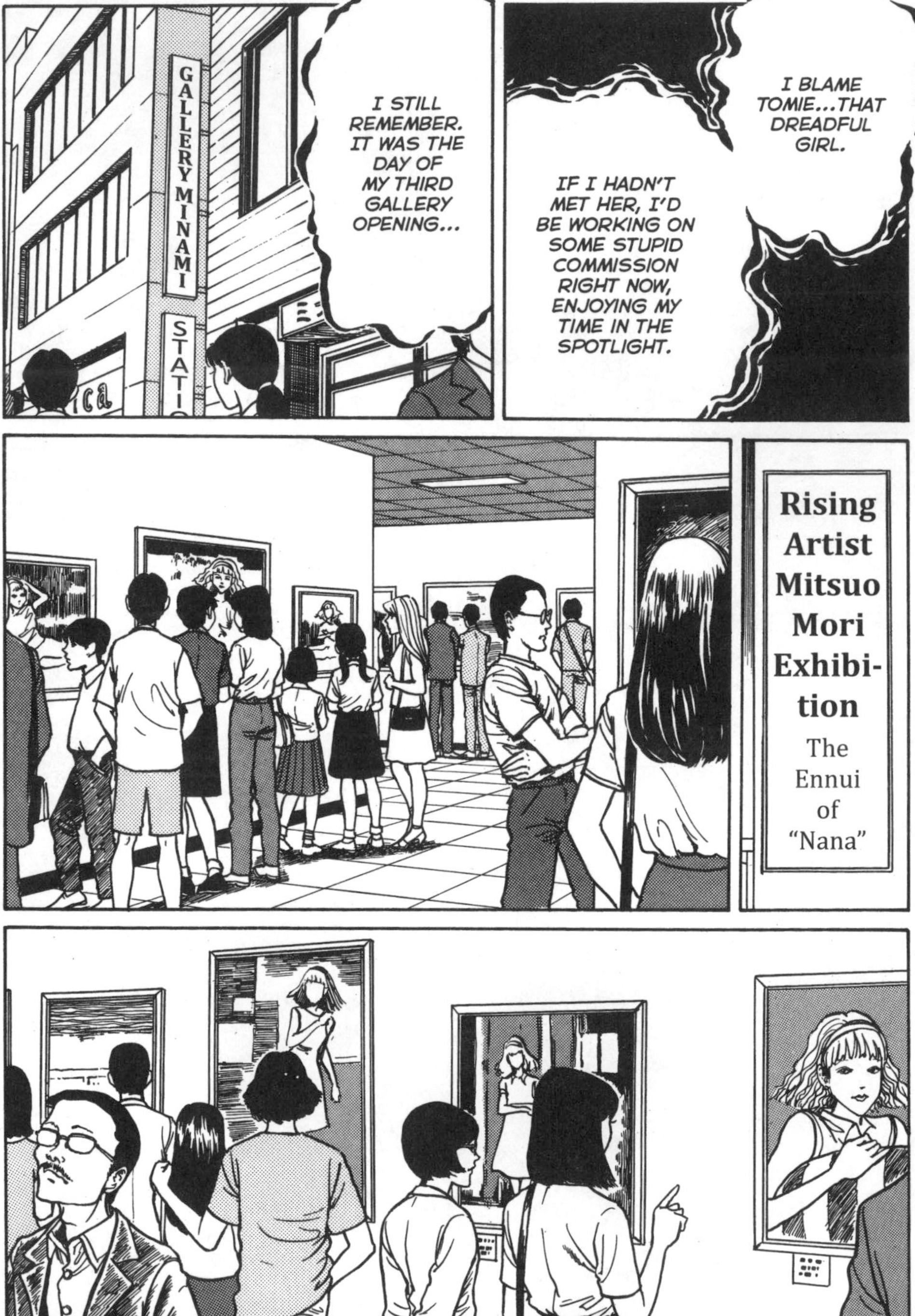
I BLAME TOMIE...THAT DREADFUL GIRL.
IF I HADN'T MET HER, I'D BE WORKING ON SOME STUPID COMMISSION RIGHT NOW, ENJOYING MY TIME IN THE SPOTLIGHT.
I STILL REMEMBER. IT WAS THE DAY OF MY THIRD GALLERY OPENING...
GALLERY MINAMI
STATI
Rising Artist Mitsuo Mori Exhibition
The Ennui of "Nana"

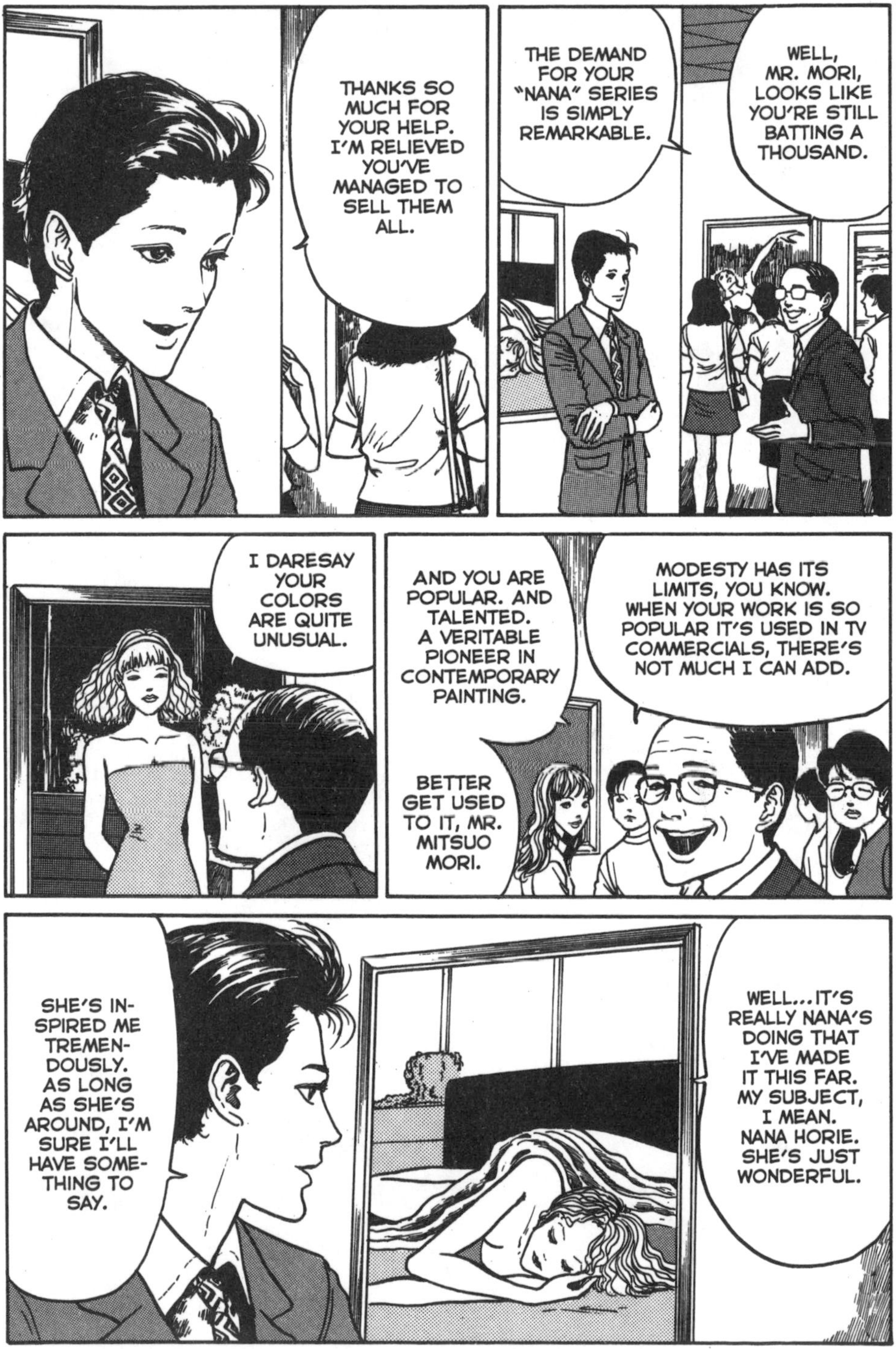
WELL, MR. MORI, LOOKS LIKE YOU'RE STILL BATTING A THOUSAND.
THE DEMAND FOR YOUR "NANA" SERIES IS SIMPLY REMARKABLE.
THANKS SO MUCH FOR YOUR HELP. I'M RELIEVED YOU'VE MANAGED TO SELL THEM ALL.
MODESTY HAS ITS LIMITS, YOU KNOW. WHEN YOUR WORK IS SO POPULAR IT'S USED IN TV COMMERCIALS, THERE'S NOT MUCH I CAN ADD.
AND YOU ARE POPULAR. AND TALENTED. A VERITABLE PIONEER IN CONTEMPORARY PAINTING.
BETTER GET USED TO IT, MR. MITSUO MORI.
I DARESAY YOUR COLORS ARE QUITE UNUSUAL.
WELL...IT'S REALLY NANA'S DOING THAT I'VE MADE IT THIS FAR. MY SUBJECT, I MEAN. NANA HORIE. SHE'S JUST WONDERFUL.
SHE'S IN-SPIRED ME TREMEN-DOUSLY. AS LONG AS SHE'S AROUND, I'M SURE I'LL HAVE SOME-THING TO SAY.

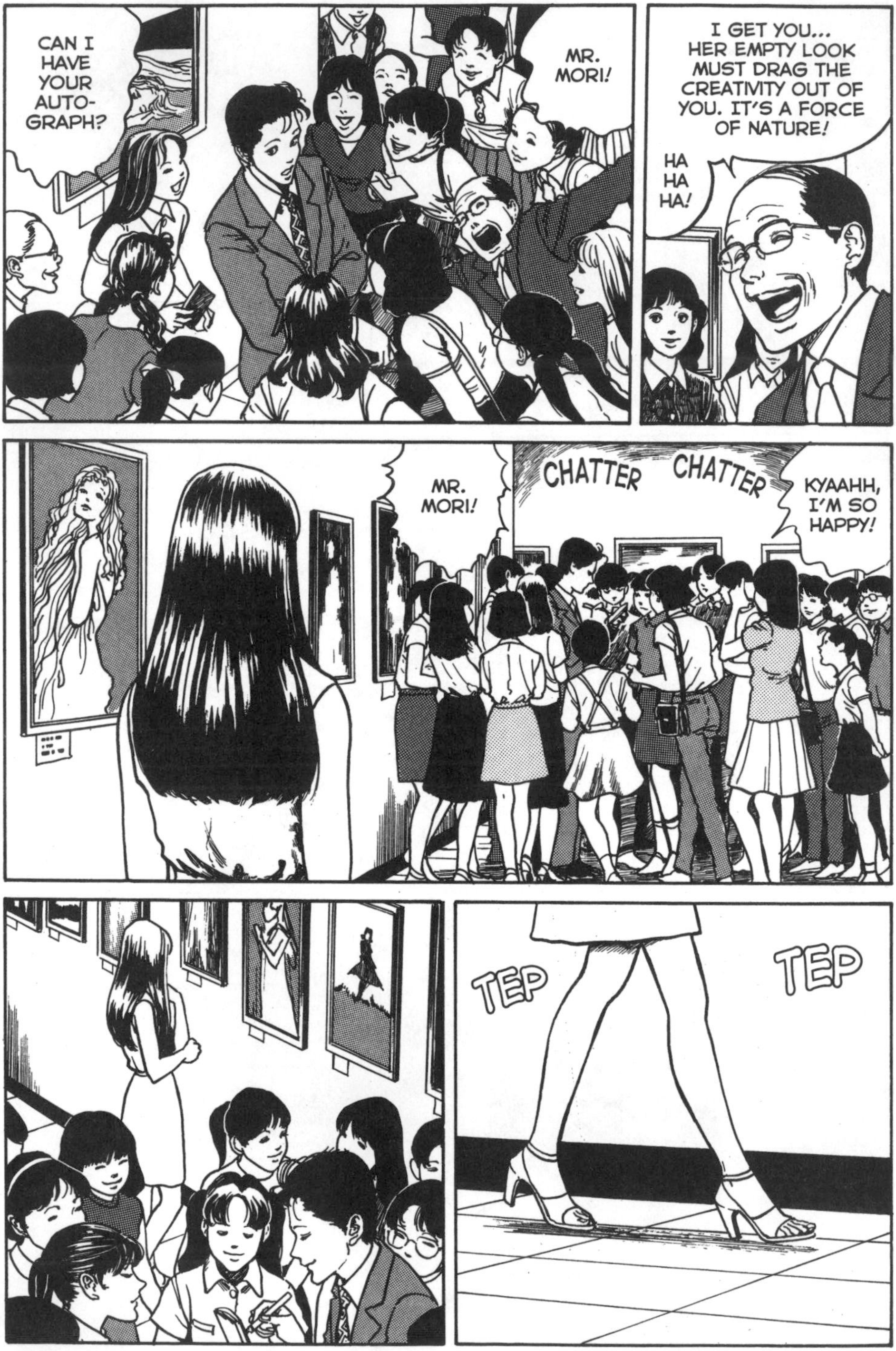
I GET YOU... HER EMPTY LOOK MUST DRAG THE CREATIVITY OUT OF YOU. IT'S A FORCE OF NATURE!
HA HA HA!
MR. MORI!
CAN I HAVE YOUR AUTO-GRAPH?
KYAAHH, I'M SO HAPPY!
CHATTER CHATTER
MR. MORI!
TEP TEP

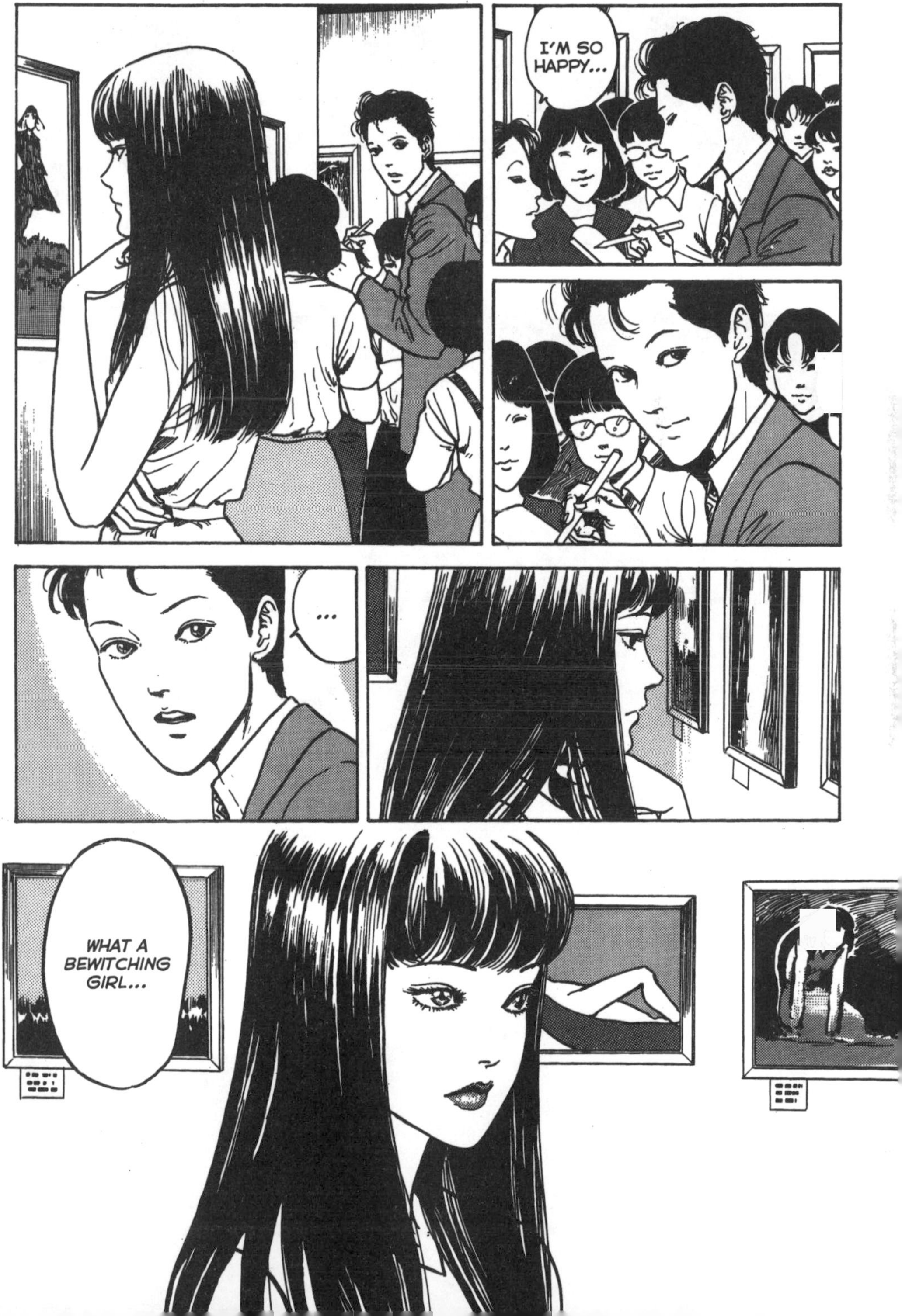
I'M SO HAPPY...
...
WHAT A BEWITCHING GIRL...

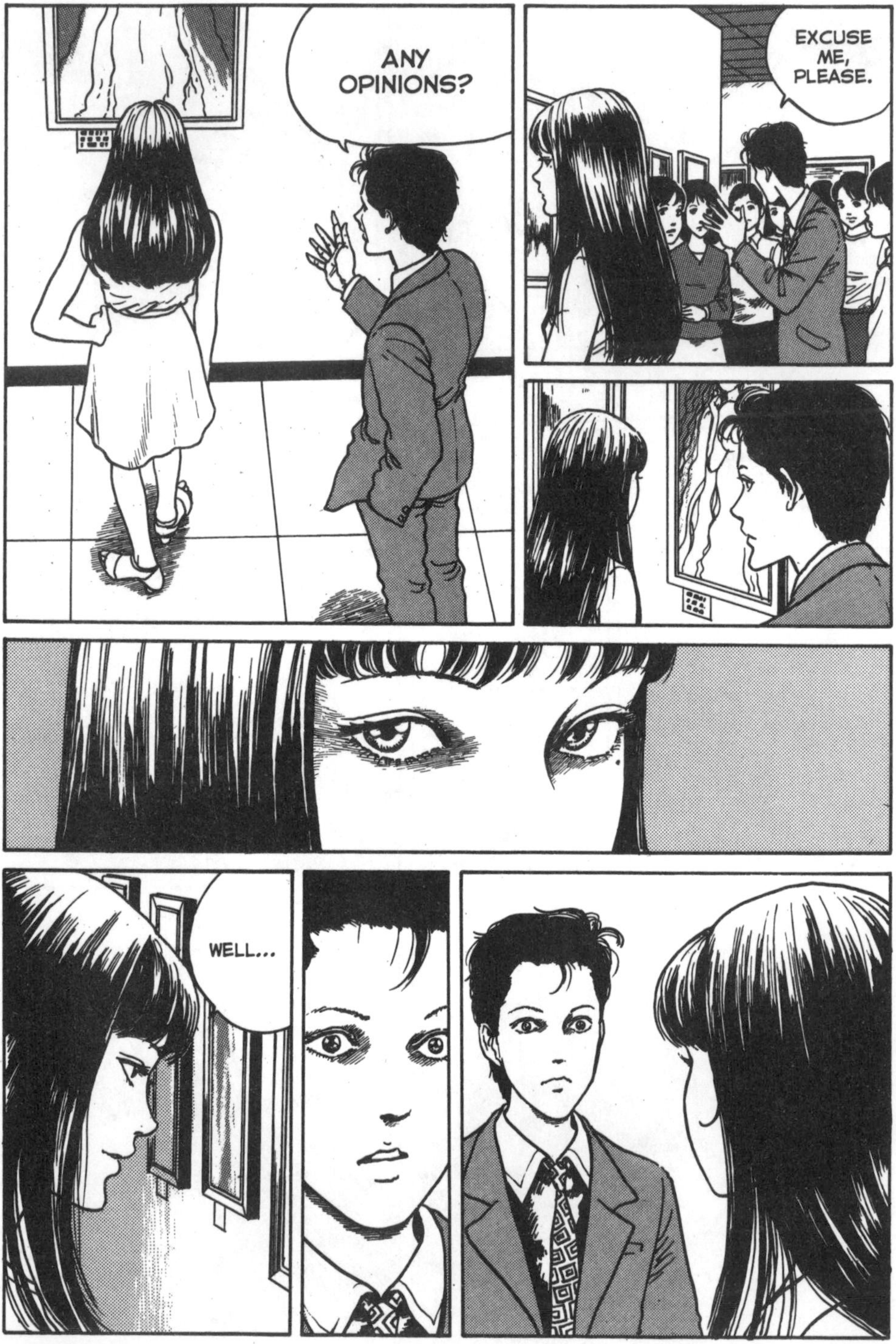
EXCUSE ME, PLEASE.
ANY OPINIONS?
WELL...

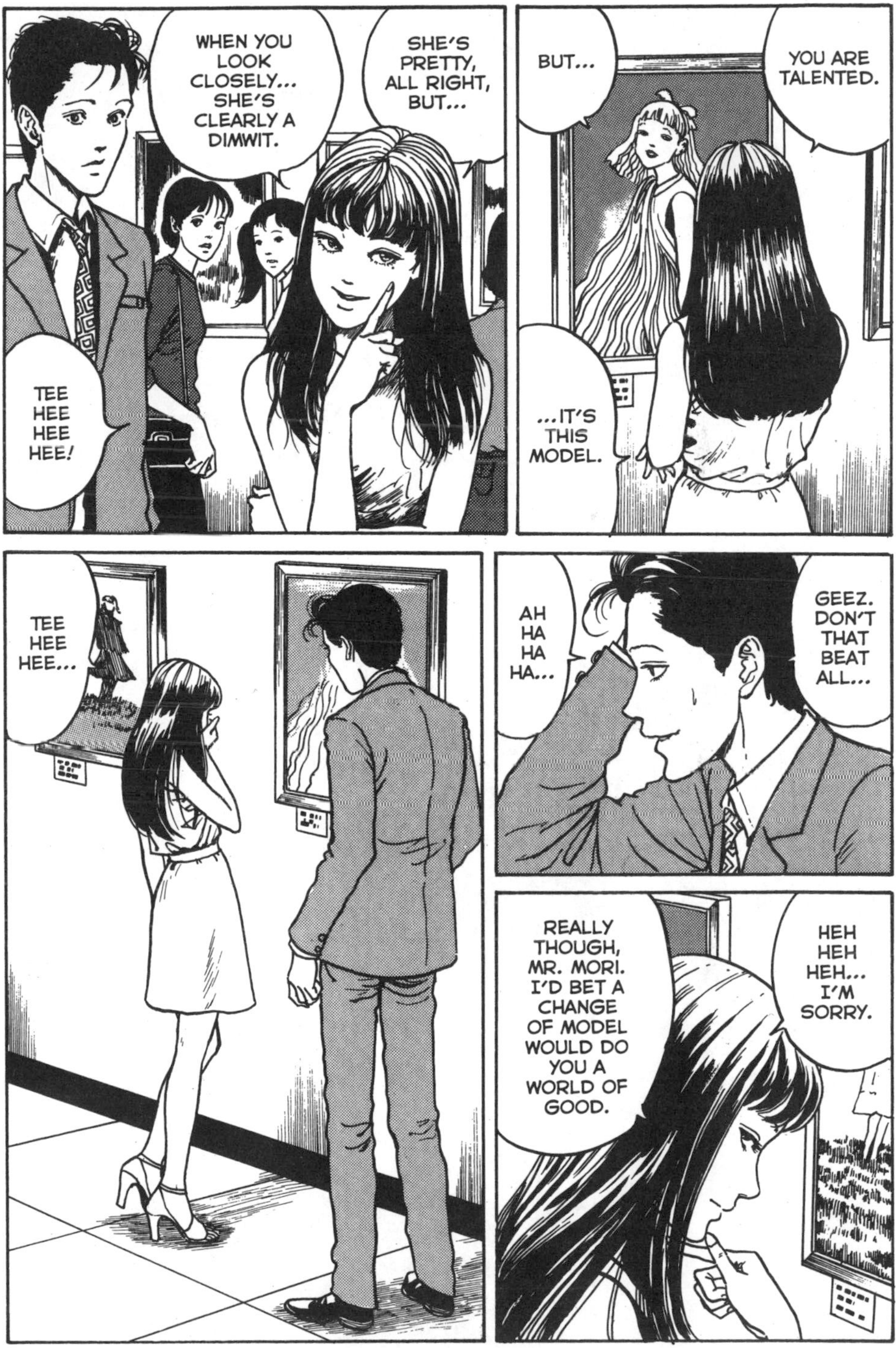
YOU ARE TALENTED.
BUT...
...IT'S THIS MODEL.
SHE'S PRETTY, ALL RIGHT, BUT...
WHEN YOU LOOK CLOSELY... SHE'S CLEARLY A DIMWIT.
TEE HEE HEE HEE!
GEEZ. DON'T THAT BEAT ALL...
AH HA HA HA...
HEH HEH HEH... I'M SORRY.
REALLY THOUGH, MR. MORI. I'D BET A CHANGE OF MODEL WOULD DO YOU A WORLD OF GOOD.
TEE HEE HEE...

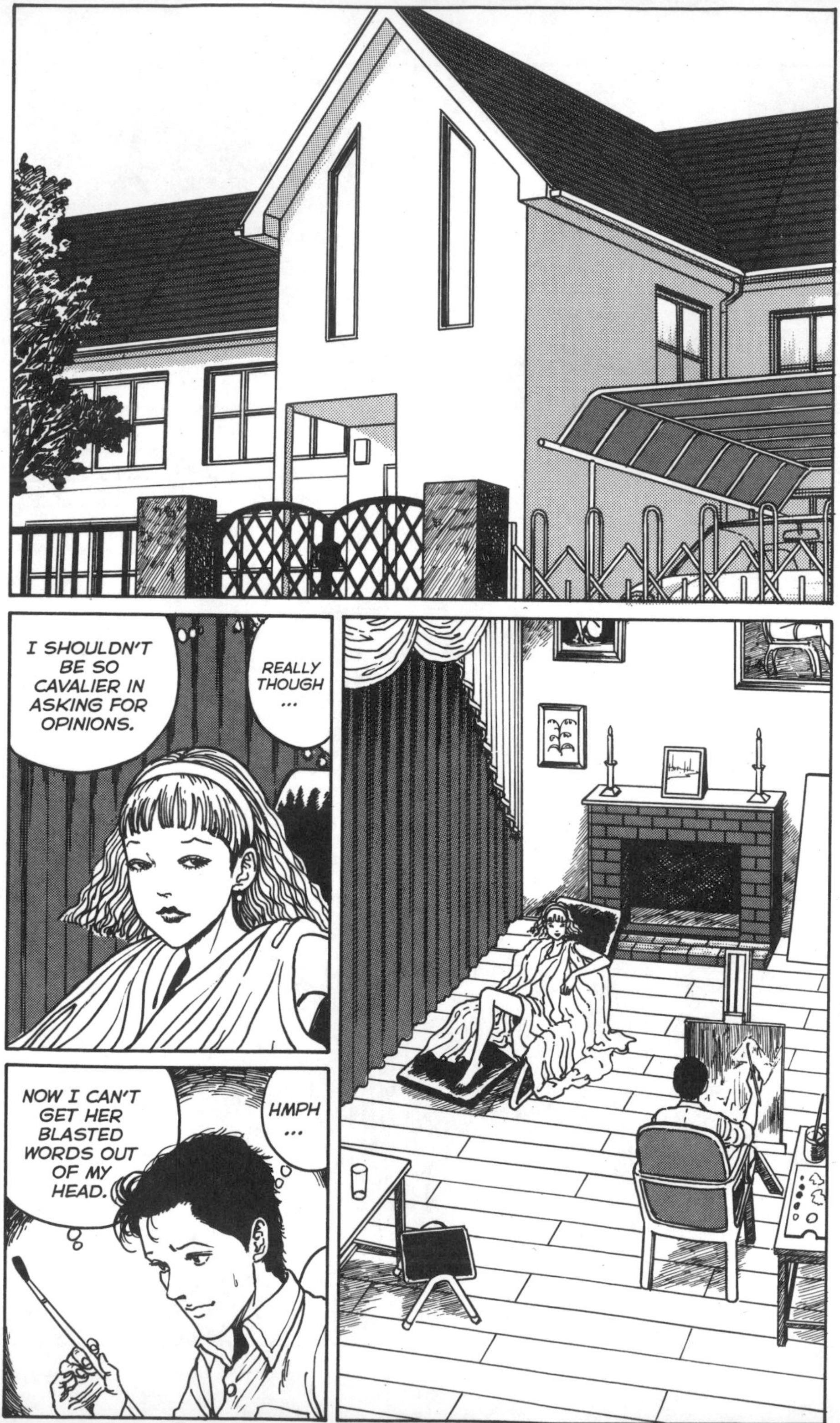
REALLY THOUGH ...
I SHOULDN'T BE SO CAVALIER IN ASKING FOR OPINIONS.
HMPH ...
NOW I CAN'T GET HER BLASTED WORDS OUT OF MY HEAD.

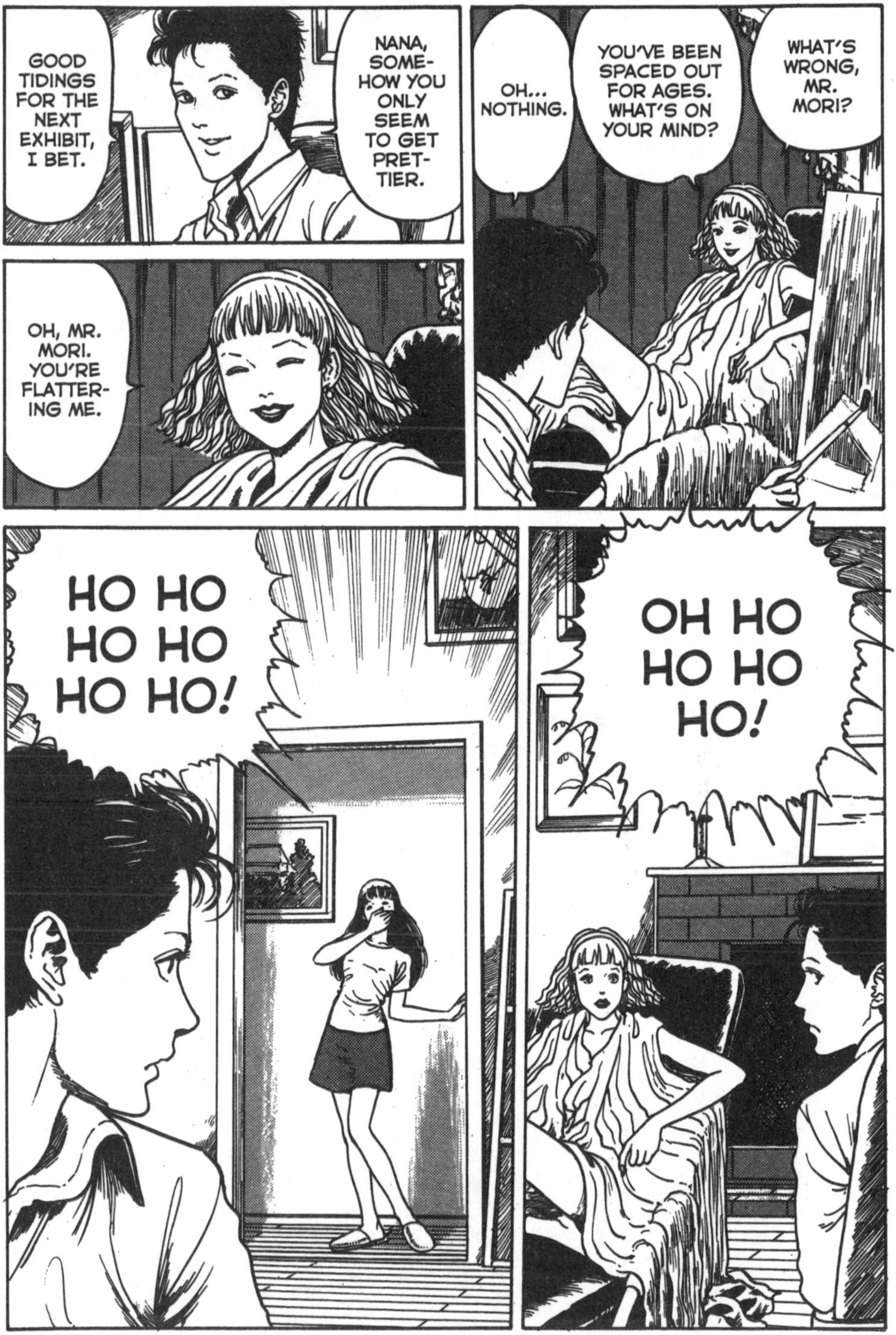
WHAT'S WRONG, MR. MORI?
YOU'VE BEEN SPACED OUT FOR AGES. WHAT'S ON YOUR MIND?
OH... NOTHING.
NANA, SOMEHOW YOU ONLY SEEM TO GET PRETTIER.
GOOD TIDINGS FOR THE NEXT EXHIBIT, I BET.
OH, MR. MORI. YOU'RE FLATTERING ME.
OH HO HO HO HO!
HO HO HO HO HO HO!

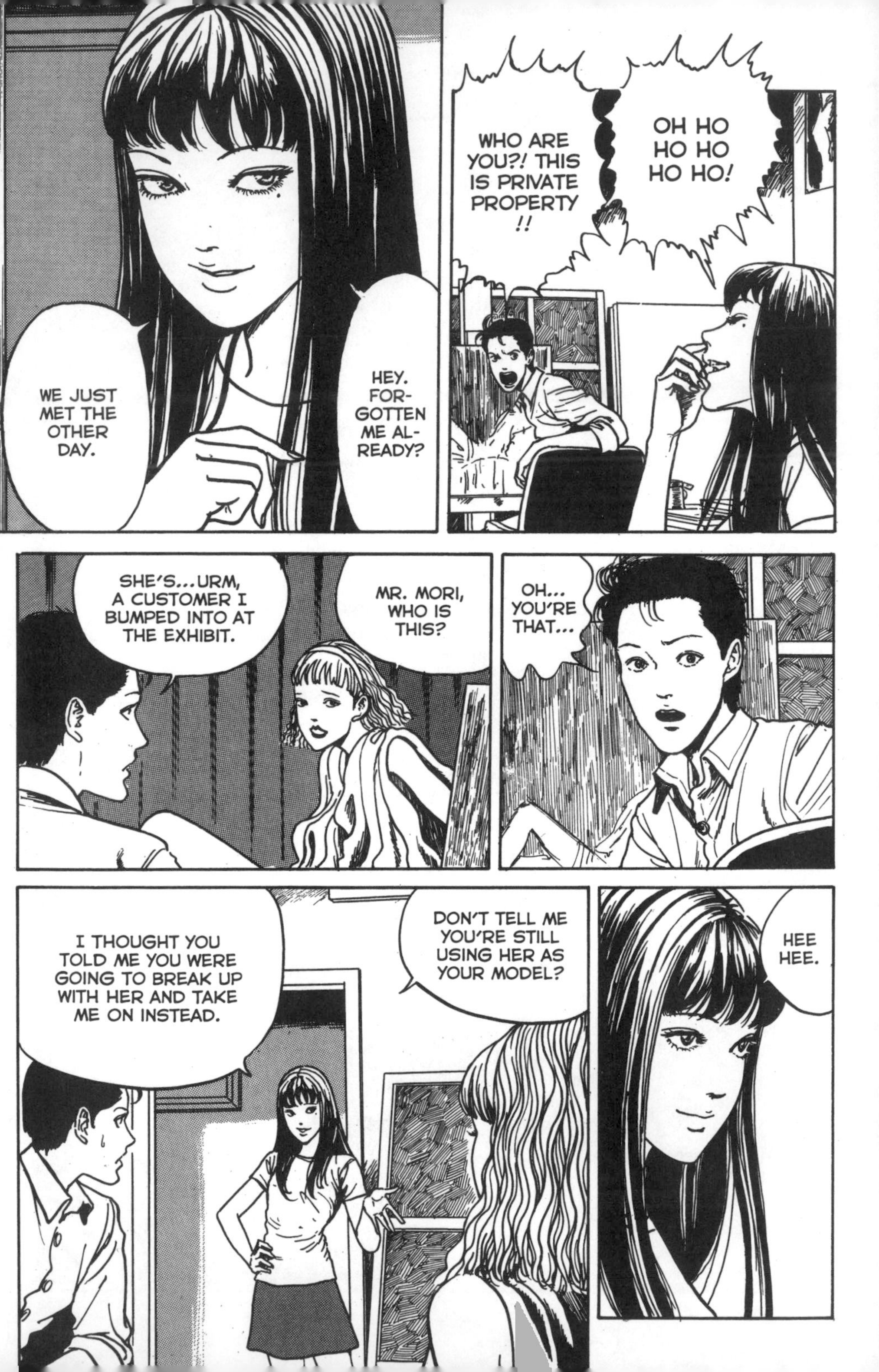
OH HO HO HO HO HO!
WHO ARE YOU?! THIS IS PRIVATE PROPERTY !!
HEY. FOR-GOTTEN ME AL-READY?
WE JUST MET THE OTHER DAY.
OH... YOU'RE THAT...
MR. MORI, WHO IS THIS?
SHE'S...URM, A CUSTOMER I BUMPED INTO AT THE EXHIBIT.
HEE HEE.
DON'T TELL ME YOU'RE STILL USING HER AS YOUR MODEL?
I THOUGHT YOU TOLD ME YOU WERE GOING TO BREAK UP WITH HER AND TAKE ME ON INSTEAD.

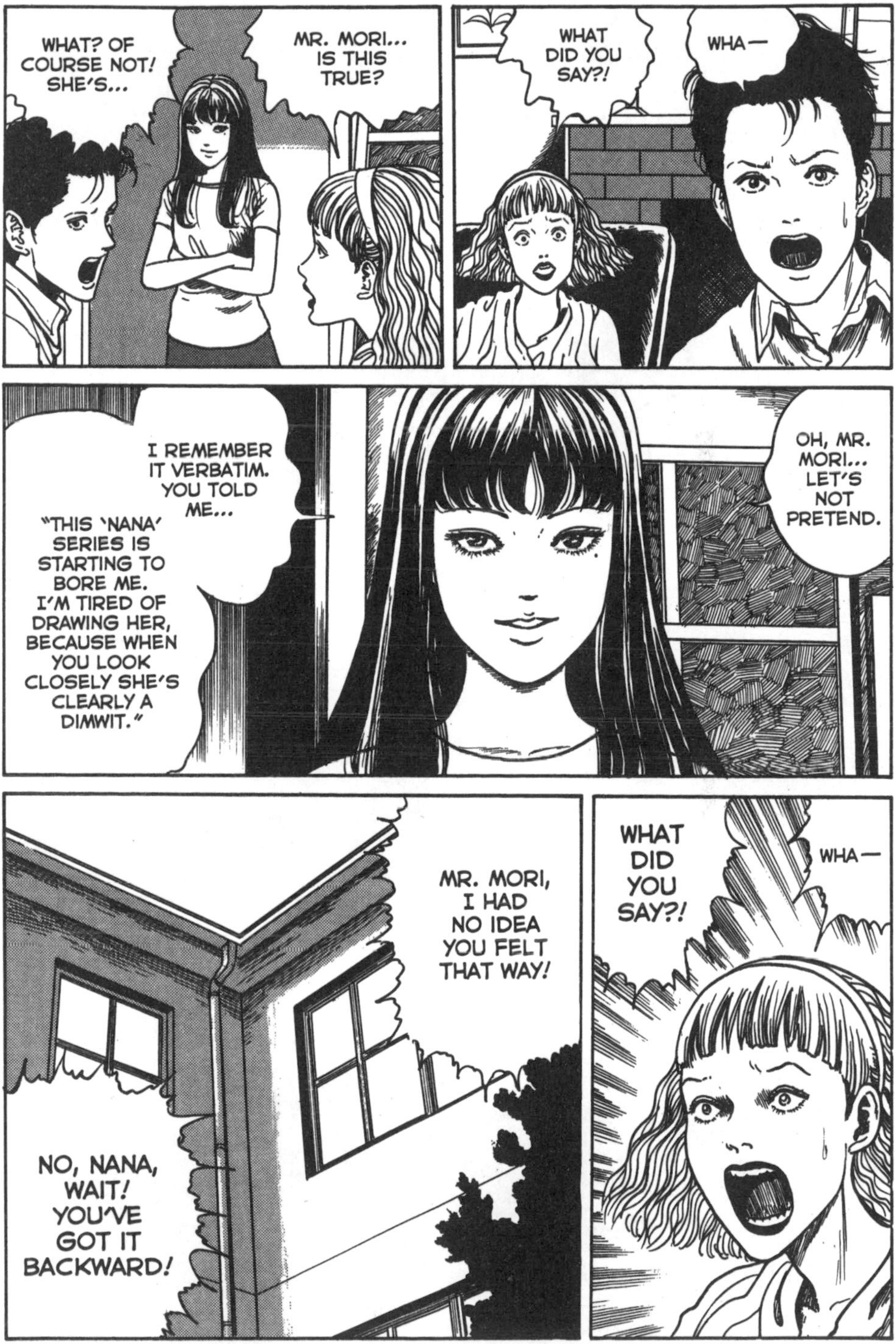
WHA—
WHAT DID YOU SAY?!
MR. MORI... IS THIS TRUE?
WHAT? OF COURSE NOT! SHE'S...
OH, MR. MORI... LET'S NOT PRETEND.
I REMEMBER IT VERBATIM. YOU TOLD ME...
"THIS 'NANA' SERIES IS STARTING TO BORE ME. I'M TIRED OF DRAWING HER, BECAUSE WHEN YOU LOOK CLOSELY SHE'S CLEARLY A DIMWIT."
WHA—
WHAT DID YOU SAY?!
MR. MORI, I HAD NO IDEA YOU FELT THAT WAY!
NO, NANA, WAIT! YOU'VE GOT IT BACKWARD!

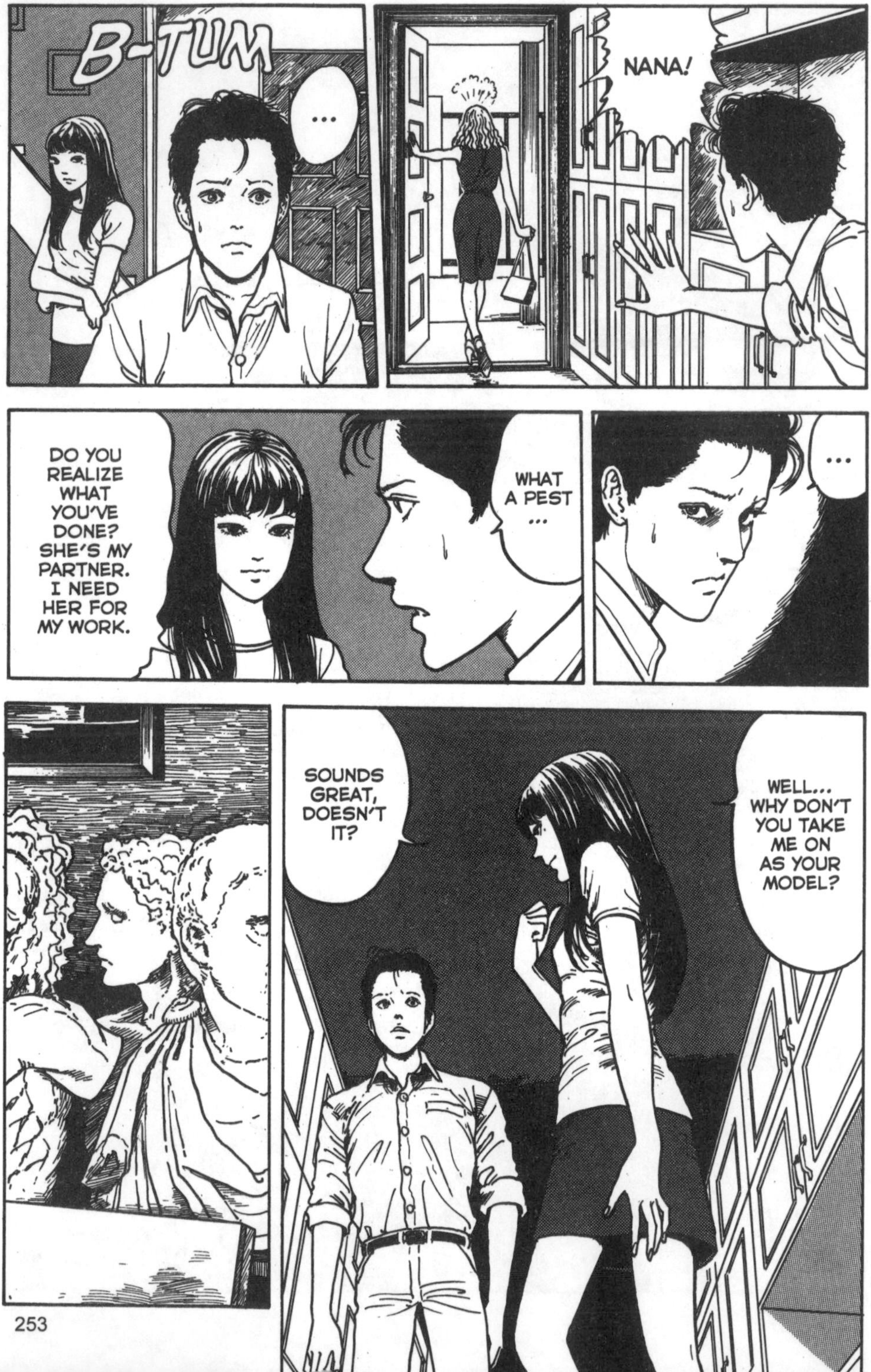
NANA!
B-TUM
...
...
WHAT A PEST ...
DO YOU REALIZE WHAT YOU'VE DONE? SHE'S MY PARTNER. I NEED HER FOR MY WORK.
WELL... WHY DON'T YOU TAKE ME ON AS YOUR MODEL?
SOUNDS GREAT, DOESN'T IT?

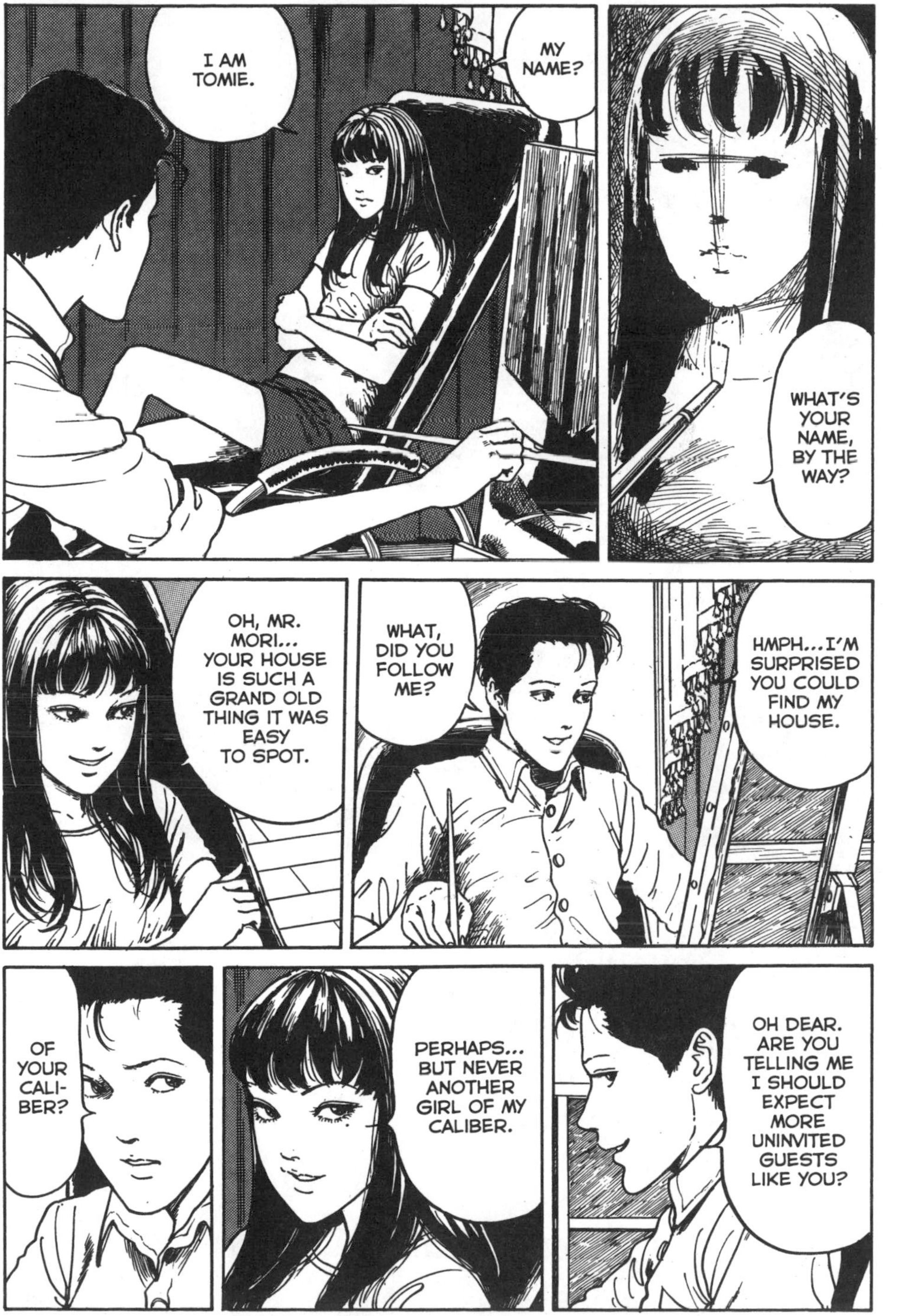
WHAT'S YOUR NAME, BY THE WAY?
MY NAME?
I AM TOMIE.
HMPH...I'M SURPRISED YOU COULD FIND MY HOUSE.
WHAT, DID YOU FOLLOW ME?
OH, MR. MORI... YOUR HOUSE IS SUCH A GRAND OLD THING IT WAS EASY TO SPOT.
OH DEAR. ARE YOU TELLING ME I SHOULD EXPECT MORE UNINVITED GUESTS LIKE YOU?
PERHAPS... BUT NEVER ANOTHER GIRL OF MY CALIBER.
OF YOUR CALI-BER?

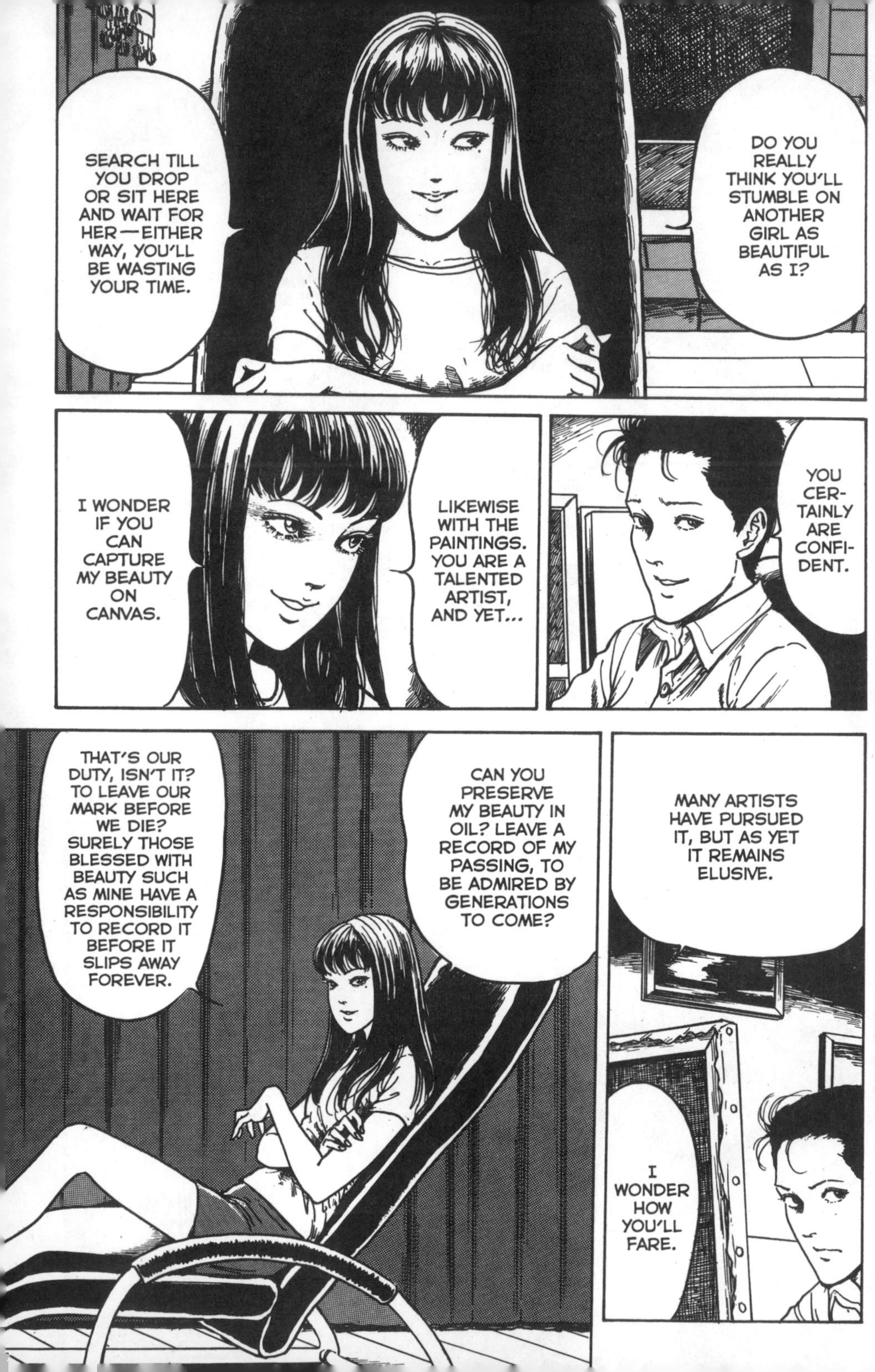
DO YOU REALLY THINK YOU'LL STUMBLE ON ANOTHER GIRL AS BEAUTIFUL AS I?
SEARCH TILL YOU DROP OR SIT HERE AND WAIT FOR HER—EITHER WAY, YOU'LL BE WASTING YOUR TIME.
YOU CERTAINLY ARE CONFIDENT.
LIKEWISE WITH THE PAINTINGS. YOU ARE A TALENTED ARTIST, AND YET...
I WONDER IF YOU CAN CAPTURE MY BEAUTY ON CANVAS.
MANY ARTISTS HAVE PURSUED IT, BUT AS YET IT REMAINS ELUSIVE.
I WONDER HOW YOU'LL FARE.
CAN YOU PRESERVE MY BEAUTY IN OIL? LEAVE A RECORD OF MY PASSING, TO BE ADMIRED BY GENERATIONS TO COME?
THAT'S OUR DUTY, ISN'T IT? TO LEAVE OUR MARK BEFORE WE DIE? SURELY THOSE BLESSED WITH BEAUTY SUCH AS MINE HAVE A RESPONSIBILITY TO RECORD IT BEFORE IT SLIPS AWAY FOREVER.

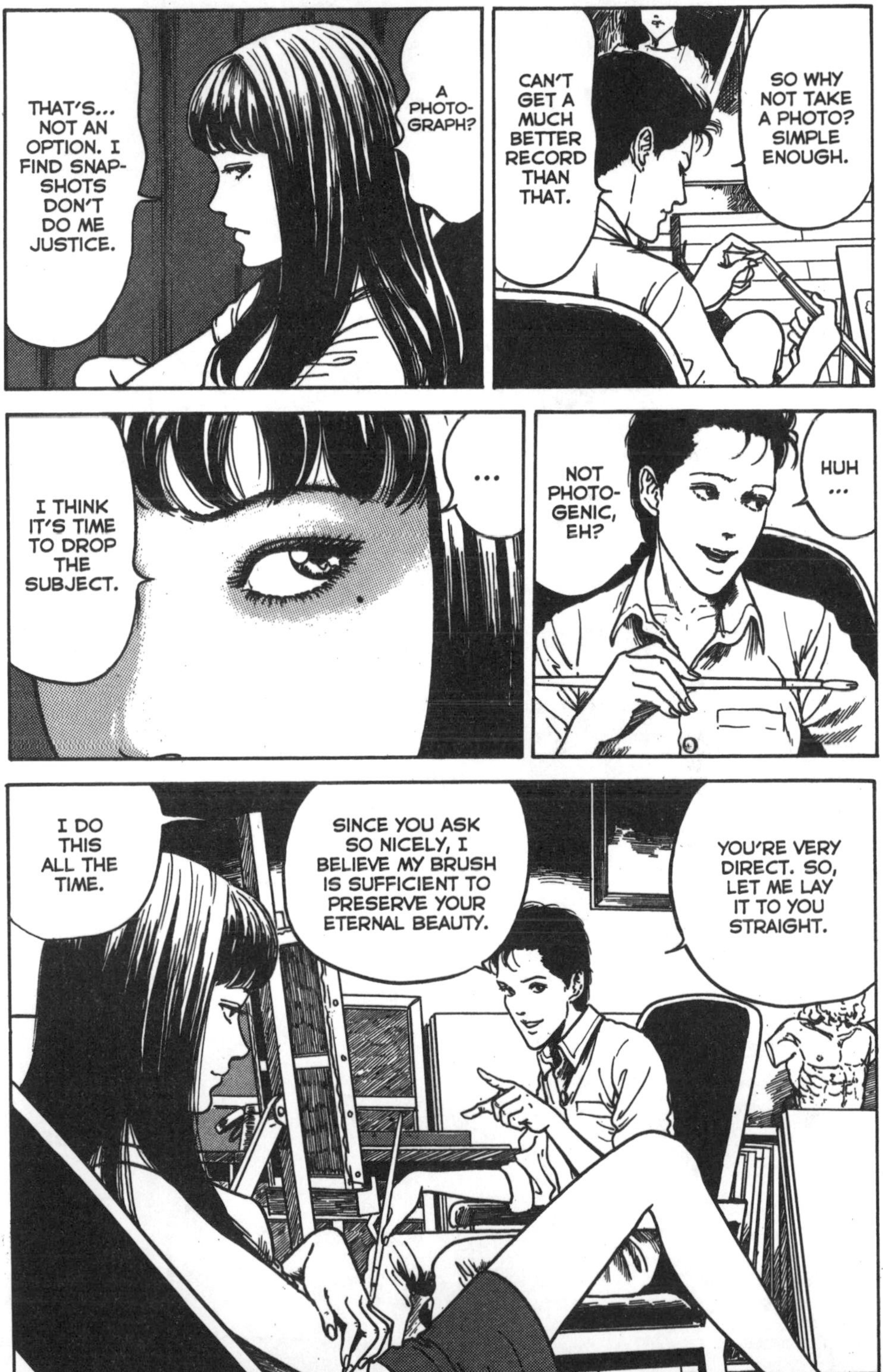
SO WHY NOT TAKE A PHOTO? SIMPLE ENOUGH.
CAN'T GET A MUCH BETTER RECORD THAN THAT.
A PHOTOGRAPH?
THAT'S... NOT AN OPTION. I FIND SNAPSHOTS DON'T DO ME JUSTICE.
HUH ...
NOT PHOTOGENIC, EH?
...
I THINK IT'S TIME TO DROP THE SUBJECT.
YOU'RE VERY DIRECT. SO, LET ME LAY IT TO YOU STRAIGHT.
SINCE YOU ASK SO NICELY, I BELIEVE MY BRUSH IS SUFFICIENT TO PRESERVE YOUR ETERNAL BEAUTY.
I DO THIS ALL THE TIME.

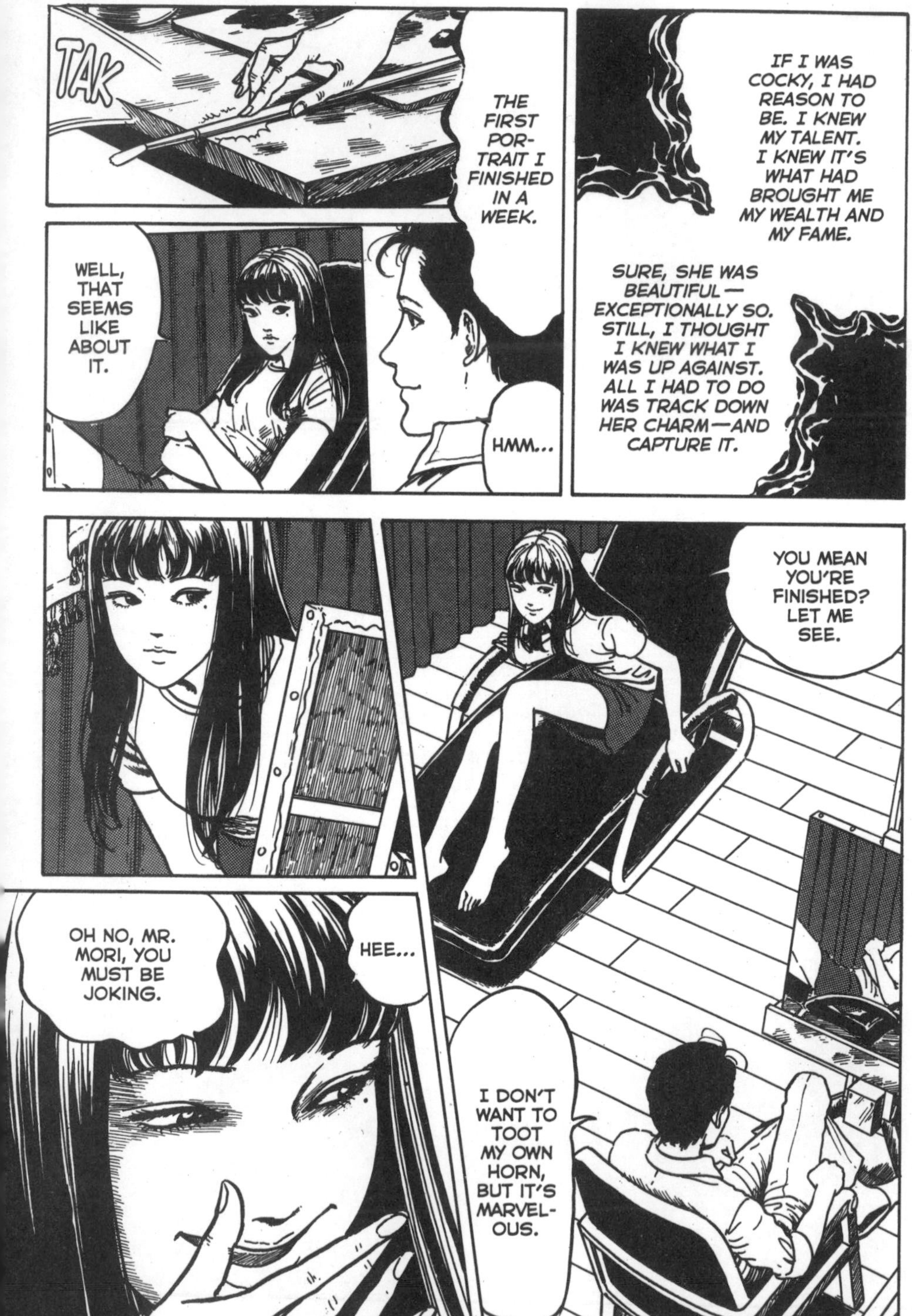
IF I WAS COCKY, I HAD REASON TO BE. I KNEW MY TALENT. I KNEW IT'S WHAT HAD BROUGHT ME MY WEALTH AND MY FAME.
SURE, SHE WAS BEAUTIFUL— EXCEPTIONALLY SO. STILL, I THOUGHT I KNEW WHAT I WAS UP AGAINST. ALL I HAD TO DO WAS TRACK DOWN HER CHARM—AND CAPTURE IT.
THE FIRST POR-TRAIT I FINISHED IN A WEEK.
TAK
HMM...
WELL, THAT SEEMS LIKE ABOUT IT.
YOU MEAN YOU'RE FINISHED? LET ME SEE.
I DON'T WANT TO TOOT MY OWN HORN, BUT IT'S MARVEL-OUS.
HEE...
OH NO, MR. MORI, YOU MUST BE JOKING.

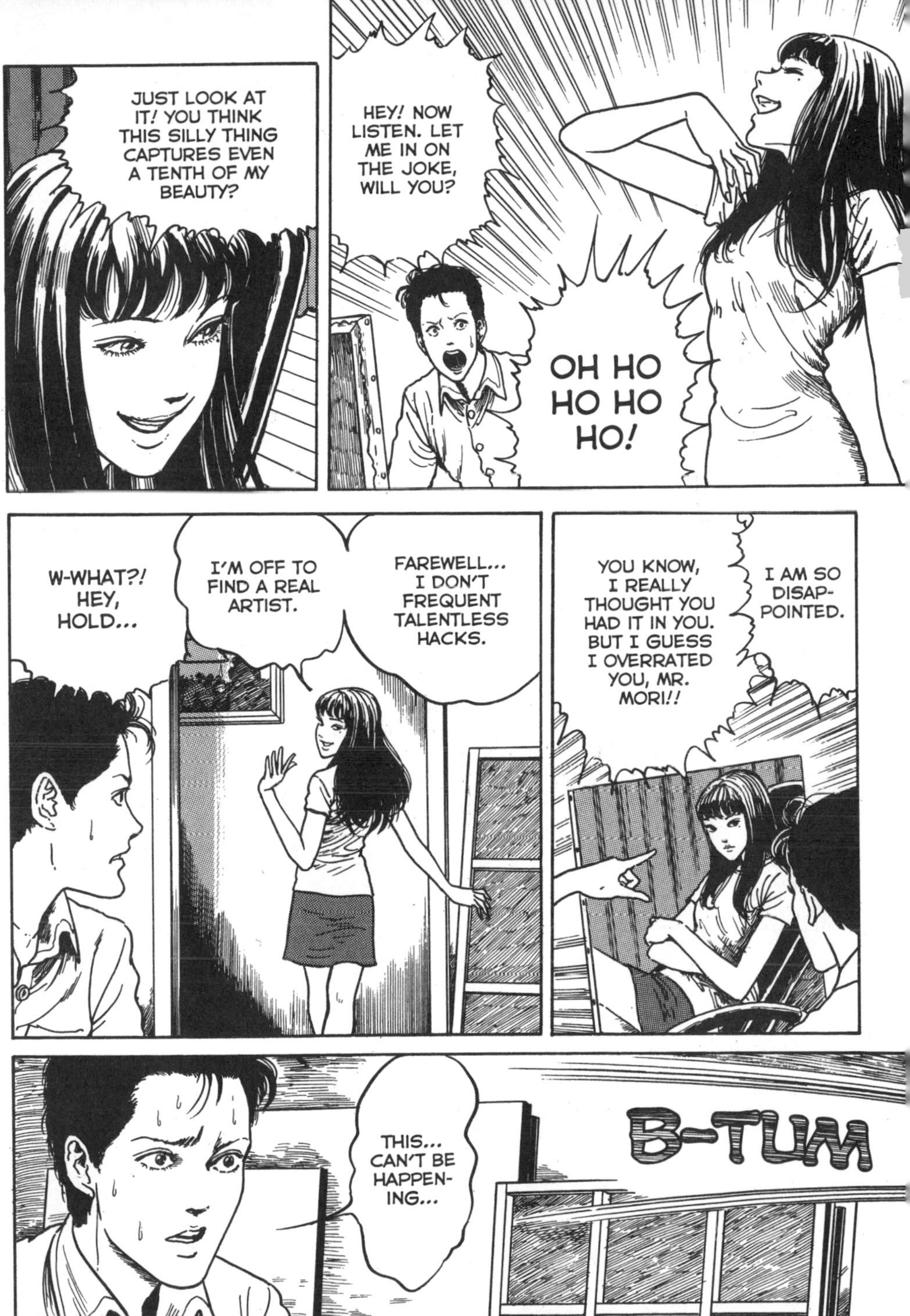
HEY! NOW LISTEN. LET ME IN ON THE JOKE, WILL YOU?
OH HO HO HO HO!
JUST LOOK AT IT! YOU THINK THIS SILLY THING CAPTURES EVEN A TENTH OF MY BEAUTY?
I AM SO DISAPPOINTED.
YOU KNOW, I REALLY THOUGHT YOU HAD IT IN YOU. BUT I GUESS I OVERRATED YOU, MR. MORI!!
FAREWELL... I DON'T FREQUENT TALENTLESS HACKS.
I'M OFF TO FIND A REAL ARTIST.
W-WHAT?! HEY, HOLD...
B-TUM
THIS... CAN'T BE HAPPENING...

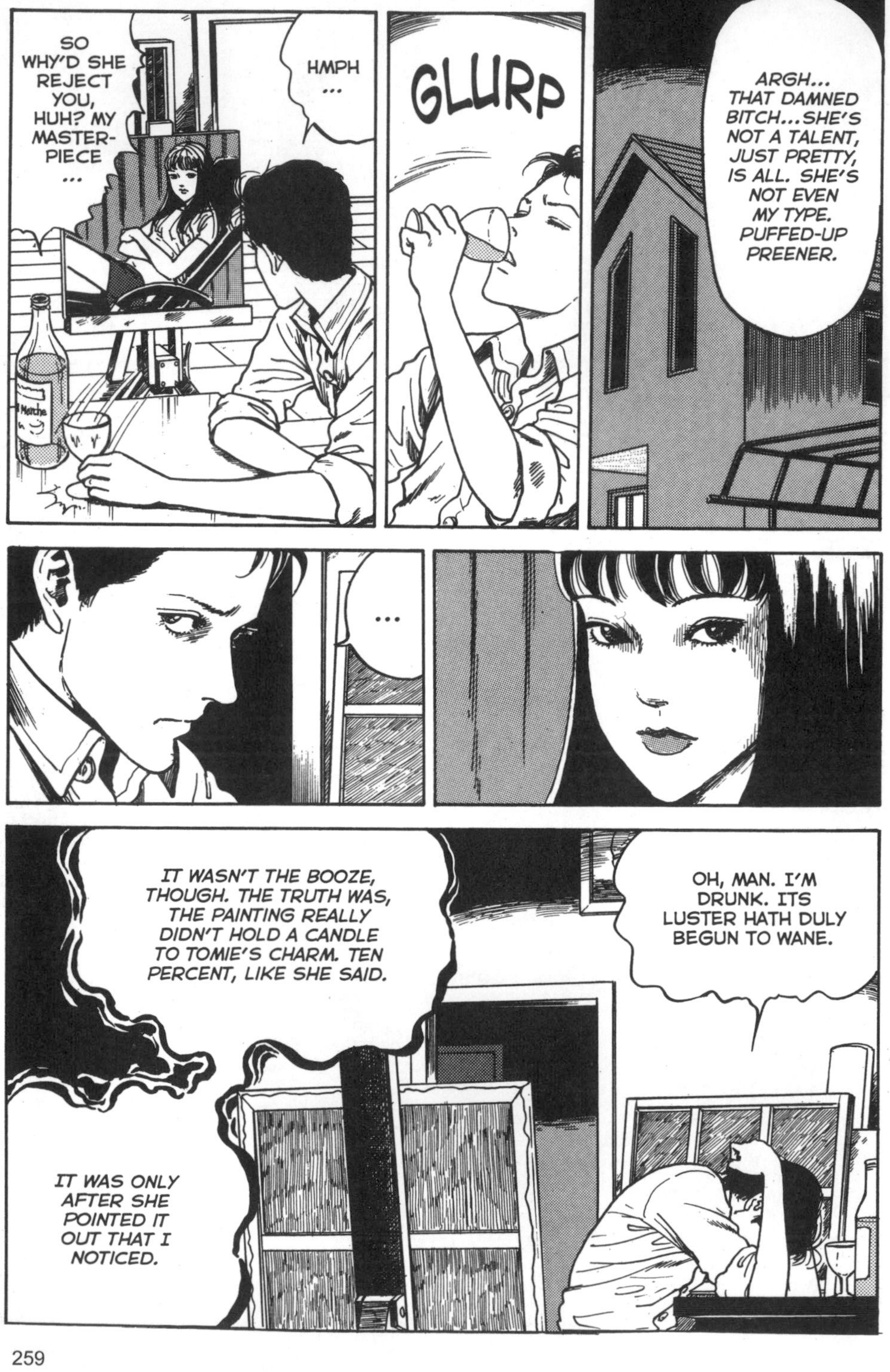
ARGH... THAT DAMNED BITCH...SHE'S NOT A TALENT, JUST PRETTY, IS ALL. SHE'S NOT EVEN MY TYPE. PUFFED-UP PREENER.
GLURP
HMPH ...
SO WHY'D SHE REJECT YOU, HUH? MY MASTER-PIECE ...
...
OH, MAN. I'M DRUNK. ITS LUSTER HATH DULY BEGUN TO WANE.
IT WASN'T THE BOOZE, THOUGH. THE TRUTH WAS, THE PAINTING REALLY DIDN'T HOLD A CANDLE TO TOMIE'S CHARM. TEN PERCENT, LIKE SHE SAID.
IT WAS ONLY AFTER SHE POINTED IT OUT THAT I NOTICED.

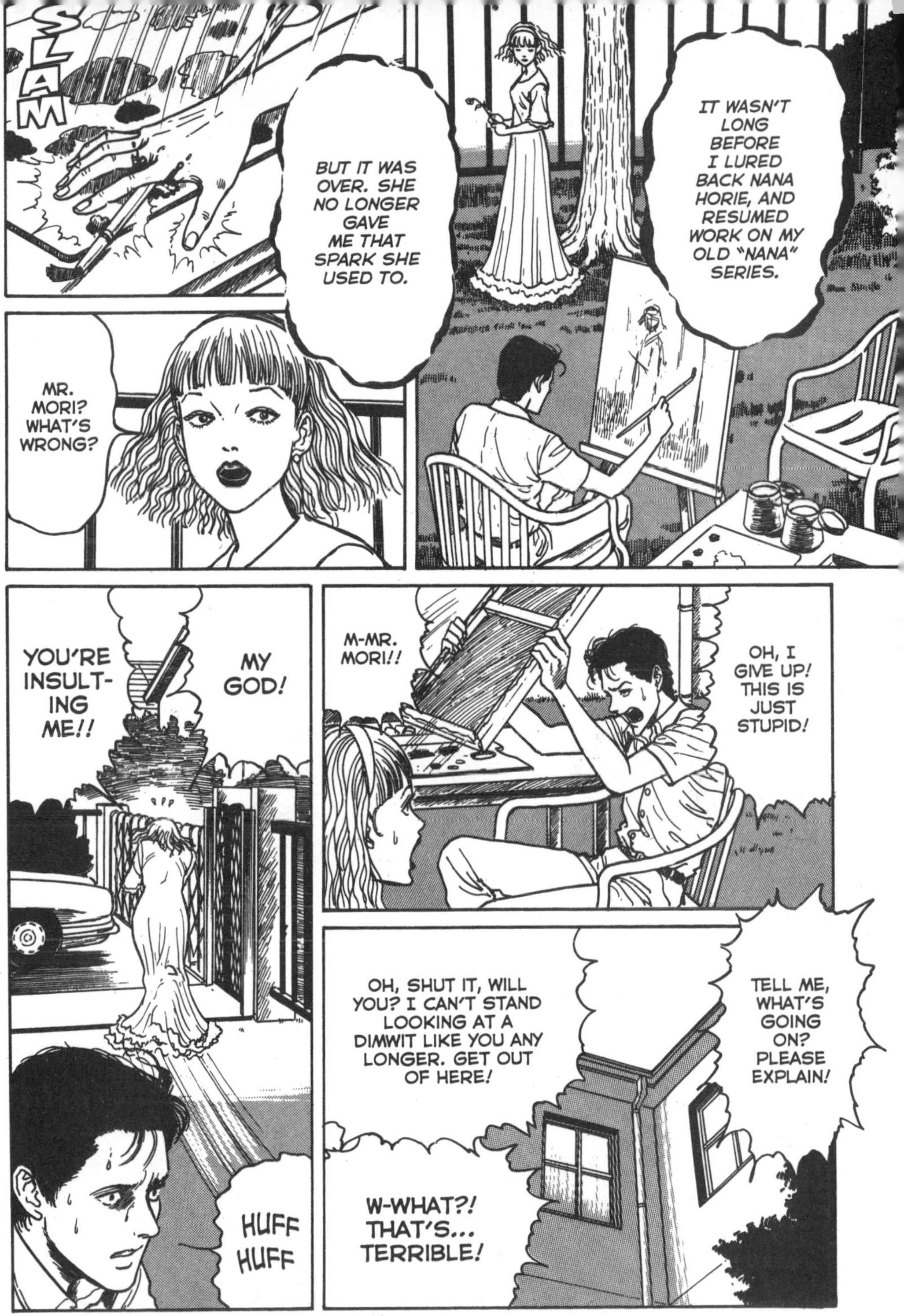
IT WASN'T LONG BEFORE I LURED BACK NANA HORIE, AND RESUMED WORK ON MY OLD "NANA" SERIES.
BUT IT WAS OVER. SHE NO LONGER GAVE ME THAT SPARK SHE USED TO.
SLAM
MR. MORI? WHAT'S WRONG?
OH, I GIVE UP! THIS IS JUST STUPID!
M-MR. MORI!!
TELL ME, WHAT'S GOING ON? PLEASE EXPLAIN!
OH, SHUT IT, WILL YOU? I CAN'T STAND LOOKING AT A DIMWIT LIKE YOU ANY LONGER. GET OUT OF HERE!
W-WHAT?! THAT'S... TERRIBLE!
MY GOD!
YOU'RE INSULTING ME!!
HUFF HUFF

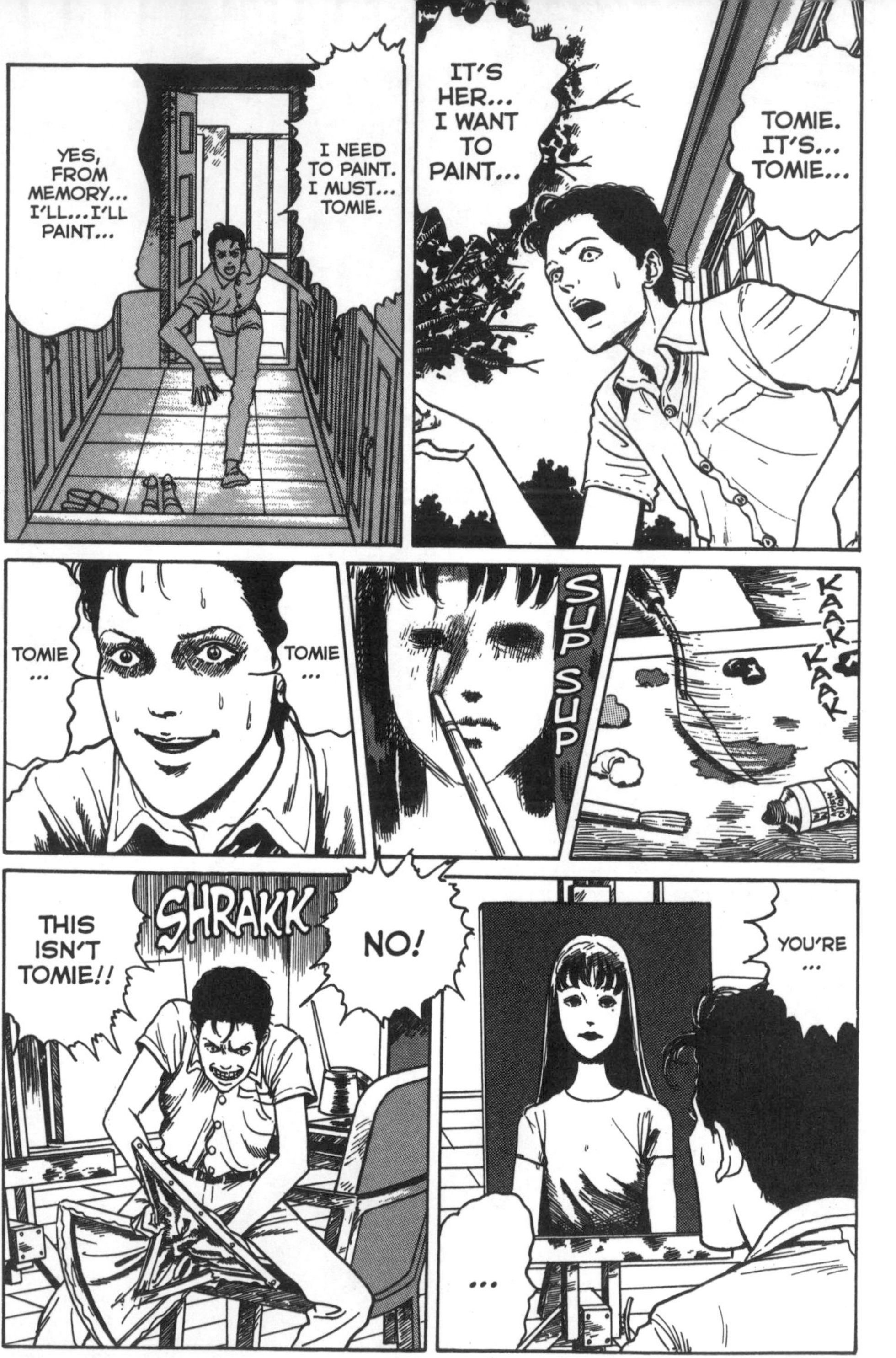
TOMIE. IT'S... TOMIE...
IT'S HER... I WANT TO PAINT...
I NEED TO PAINT. I MUST... TOMIE.
YES, FROM MEMORY... I'LL...I'LL PAINT...
KAAK KAAK
SUP SUP
TOMIE ...
TOMIE ...
YOU'RE ...
...
NO!
SHRAKK
THIS ISN'T TOMIE!!

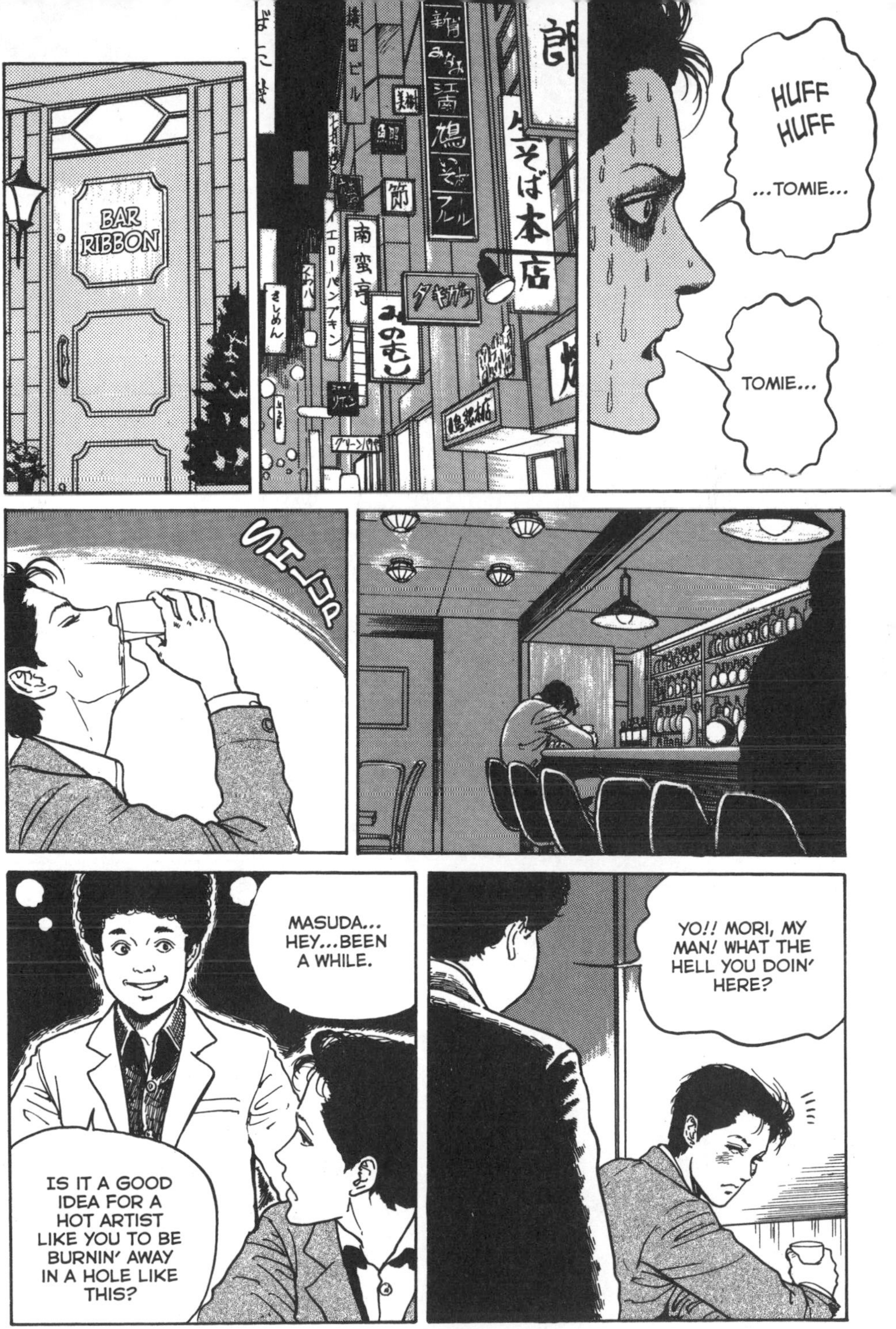
HUFF HUFF
...TOMIE...
TOMIE...
BAR RIBBON
GULP
YO!! MORI, MY MAN! WHAT THE HELL YOU DOIN' HERE?
MASUDA... HEY...BEEN A WHILE.
IS IT A GOOD IDEA FOR A HOT ARTIST LIKE YOU TO BE BURNIN' AWAY IN A HOLE LIKE THIS?

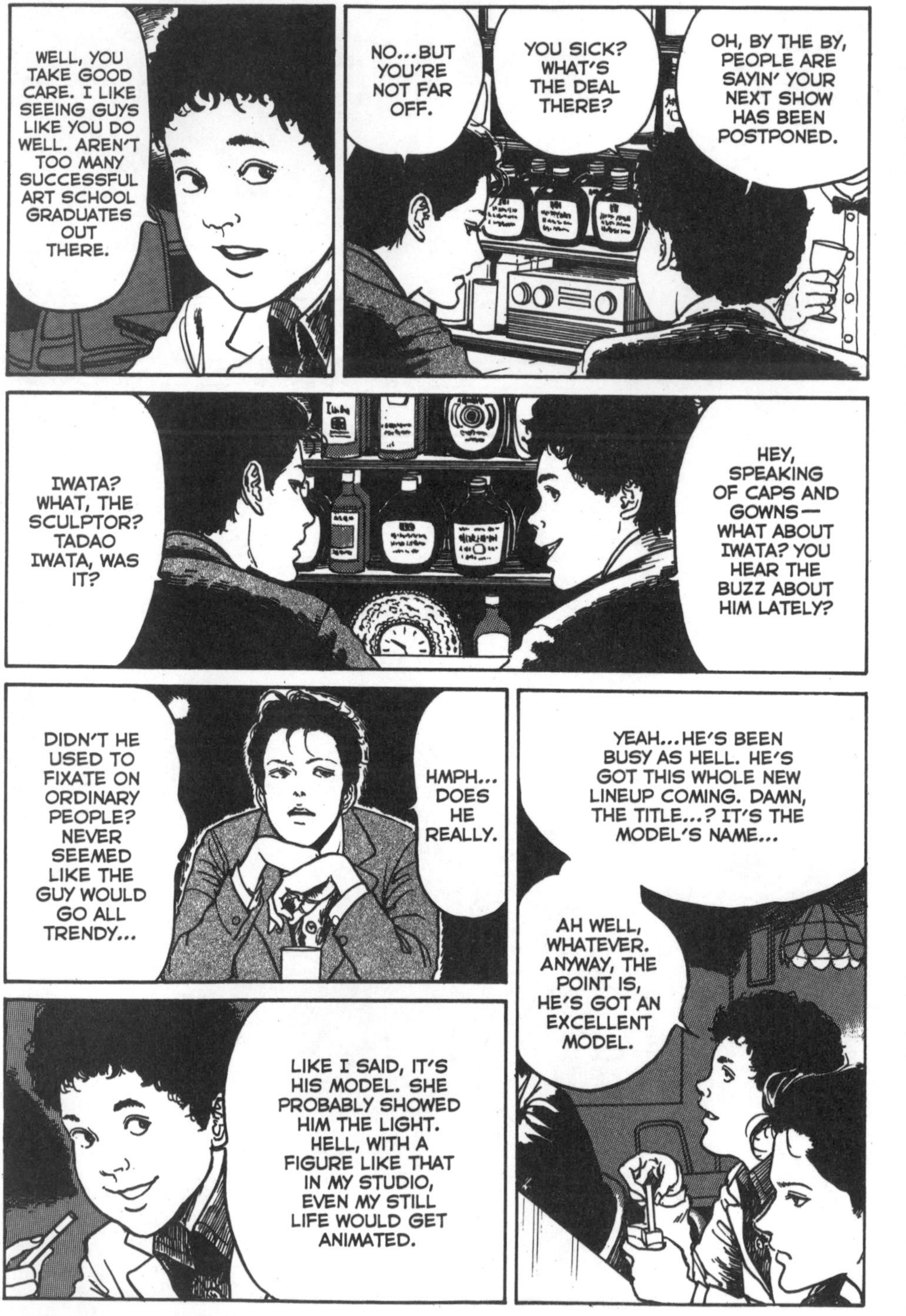
OH, BY THE BY, PEOPLE ARE SAYIN' YOUR NEXT SHOW HAS BEEN POSTPONED.
YOU SICK? WHAT'S THE DEAL THERE?
NO...BUT YOU'RE NOT FAR OFF.
WELL, YOU TAKE GOOD CARE. I LIKE SEEING GUYS LIKE YOU DO WELL. AREN'T TOO MANY SUCCESSFUL ART SCHOOL GRADUATES OUT THERE.
HEY, SPEAKING OF CAPS AND GOWNS—WHAT ABOUT IWATA? YOU HEAR THE BUZZ ABOUT HIM LATELY?
IWATA? WHAT, THE SCULPTOR? TADAO IWATA, WAS IT?
YEAH...HE'S BEEN BUSY AS HELL. HE'S GOT THIS WHOLE NEW LINEUP COMING. DAMN, THE TITLE...? IT'S THE MODEL'S NAME...
AH WELL, WHATEVER. ANYWAY, THE POINT IS, HE'S GOT AN EXCELLENT MODEL.
HMPH... DOES HE REALLY.
DIDN'T HE USED TO FIXATE ON ORDINARY PEOPLE? NEVER SEEMED LIKE THE GUY WOULD GO ALL TRENDY...
LIKE I SAID, IT'S HIS MODEL. SHE PROBABLY SHOWED HIM THE LIGHT. HELL, WITH A FIGURE LIKE THAT IN MY STUDIO, EVEN MY STILL LIFE WOULD GET ANIMATED.

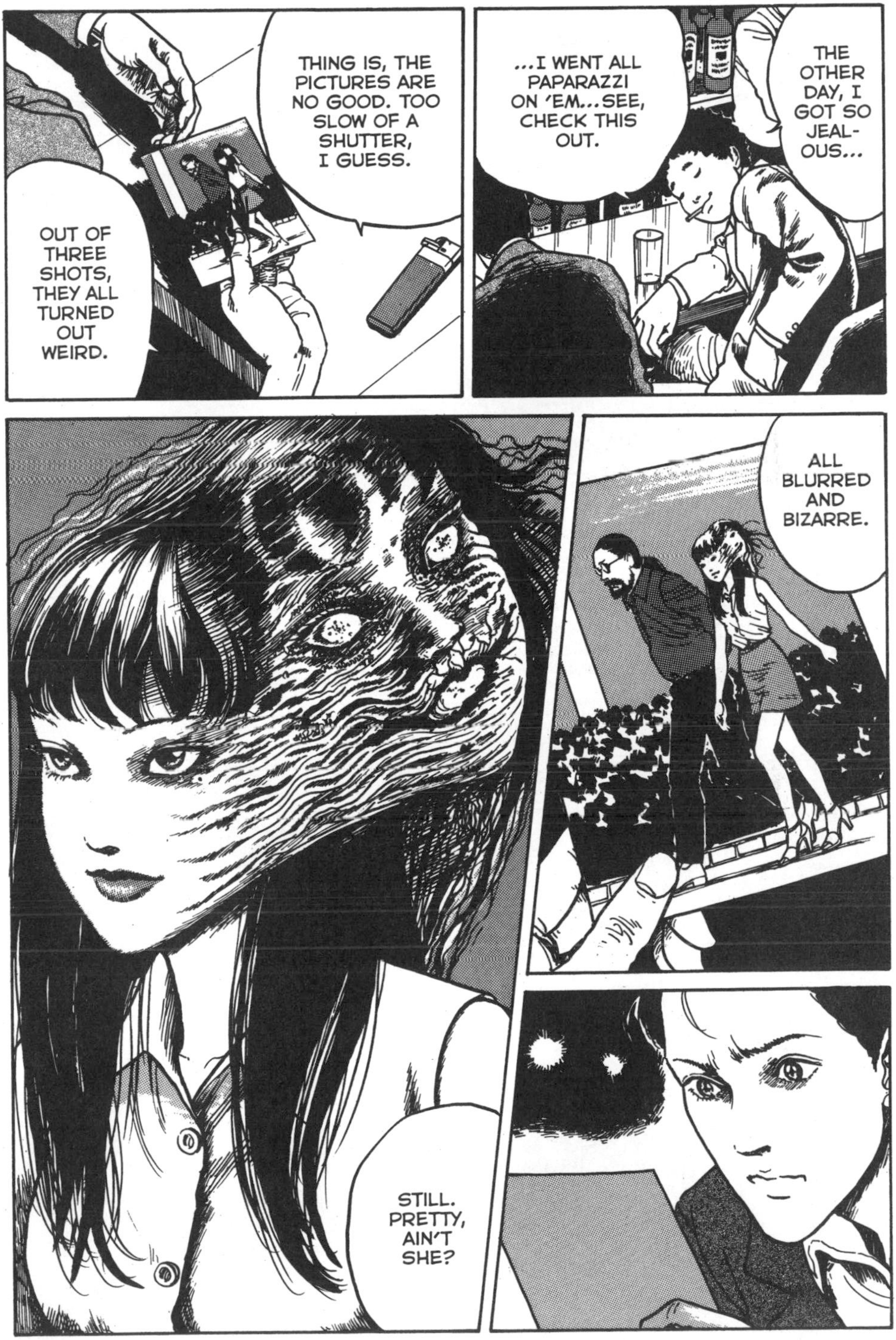
THE OTHER DAY, I GOT SO JEALOUS...
...I WENT ALL PAPARAZZI ON 'EM...SEE, CHECK THIS OUT.
THING IS, THE PICTURES ARE NO GOOD. TOO SLOW OF A SHUTTER, I GUESS.
OUT OF THREE SHOTS, THEY ALL TURNED OUT WEIRD.
ALL BLURRED AND BIZARRE.
STILL. PRETTY, AIN'T SHE?

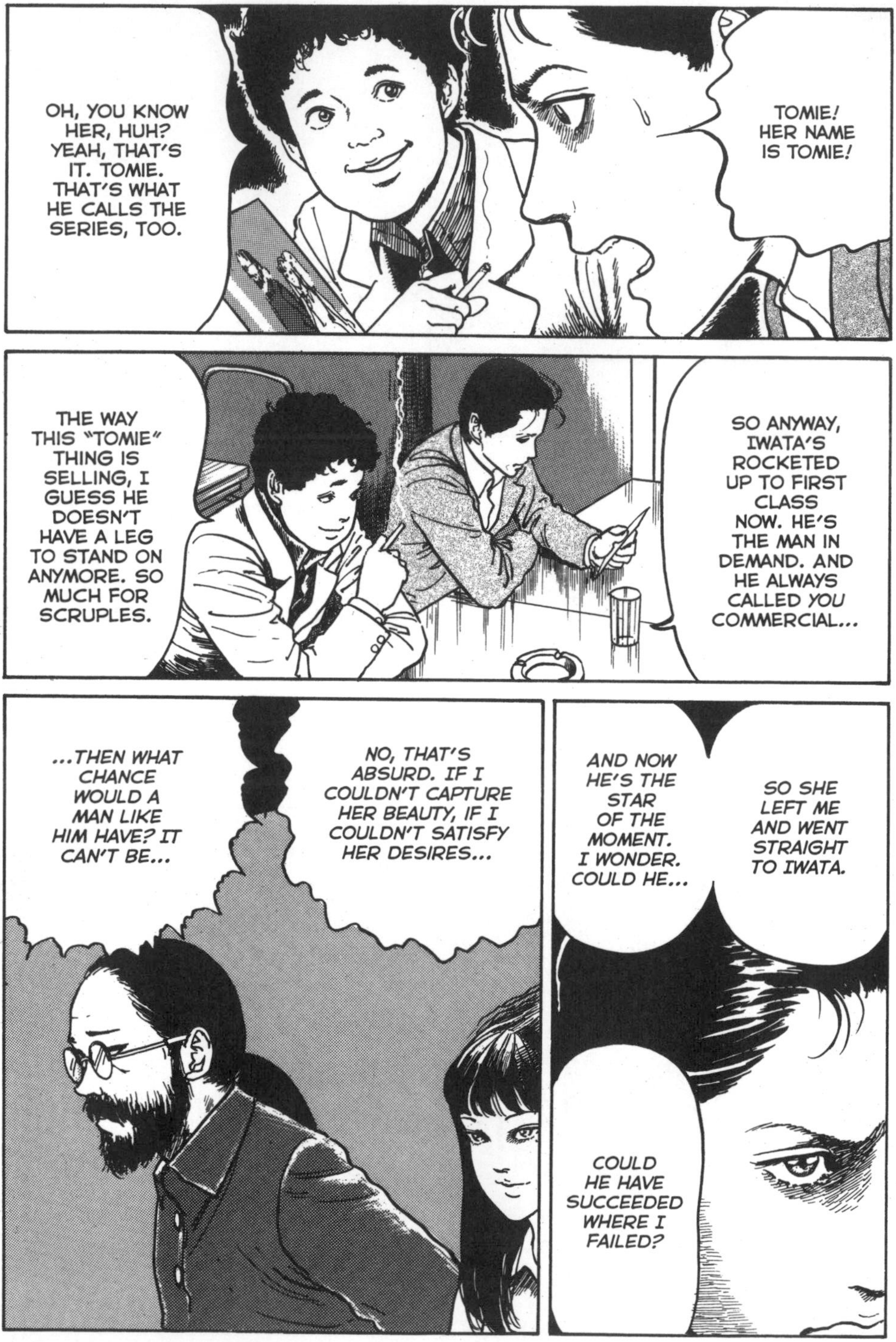
TOMIE! HER NAME IS TOMIE!
OH, YOU KNOW HER, HUH? YEAH, THAT'S IT. TOMIE. THAT'S WHAT HE CALLS THE SERIES, TOO.
SO ANYWAY, IWATA'S ROCKETED UP TO FIRST CLASS NOW. HE'S THE MAN IN DEMAND. AND HE ALWAYS CALLED *YOU* COMMERCIAL...
THE WAY THIS "TOMIE" THING IS SELLING, I GUESS HE DOESN'T HAVE A LEG TO STAND ON ANYMORE. SO MUCH FOR SCRUPLES.
SO SHE LEFT ME AND WENT STRAIGHT TO IWATA.
AND NOW HE'S THE STAR OF THE MOMENT. I WONDER. COULD HE...
COULD HE HAVE SUCCEEDED WHERE I FAILED?
NO, THAT'S ABSURD. IF I COULDN'T CAPTURE HER BEAUTY, IF I COULDN'T SATISFY HER DESIRES...
...THEN WHAT CHANCE WOULD A MAN LIKE HIM HAVE? IT CAN'T BE...

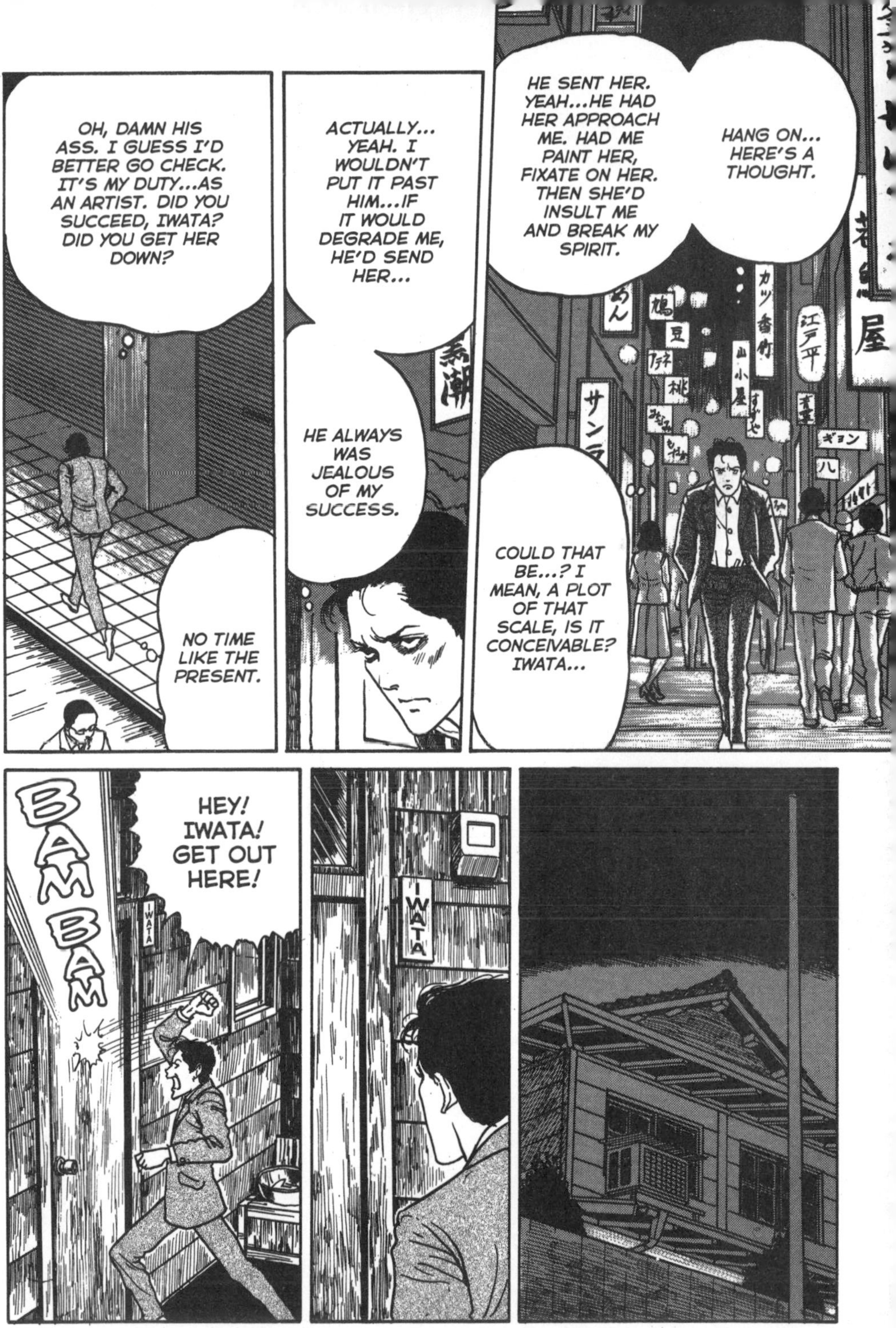
HANG ON... HERE'S A THOUGHT.
HE SENT HER. YEAH...HE HAD HER APPROACH ME. HAD ME PAINT HER, FIXATE ON HER. THEN SHE'D INSULT ME AND BREAK MY SPIRIT.
COULD THAT BE...? I MEAN, A PLOT OF THAT SCALE, IS IT CONCEIVABLE? IWATA...
ACTUALLY... YEAH. I WOULDN'T PUT IT PAST HIM...IF IT WOULD DEGRADE ME, HE'D SEND HER...
HE ALWAYS WAS JEALOUS OF MY SUCCESS.
OH, DAMN HIS ASS. I GUESS I'D BETTER GO CHECK. IT'S MY DUTY...AS AN ARTIST. DID YOU SUCCEED, IWATA? DID YOU GET HER DOWN?
NO TIME LIKE THE PRESENT.
IWATA
HEY! IWATA! GET OUT HERE!
BAM BAM
IWATA

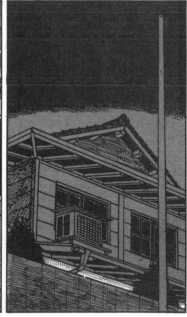

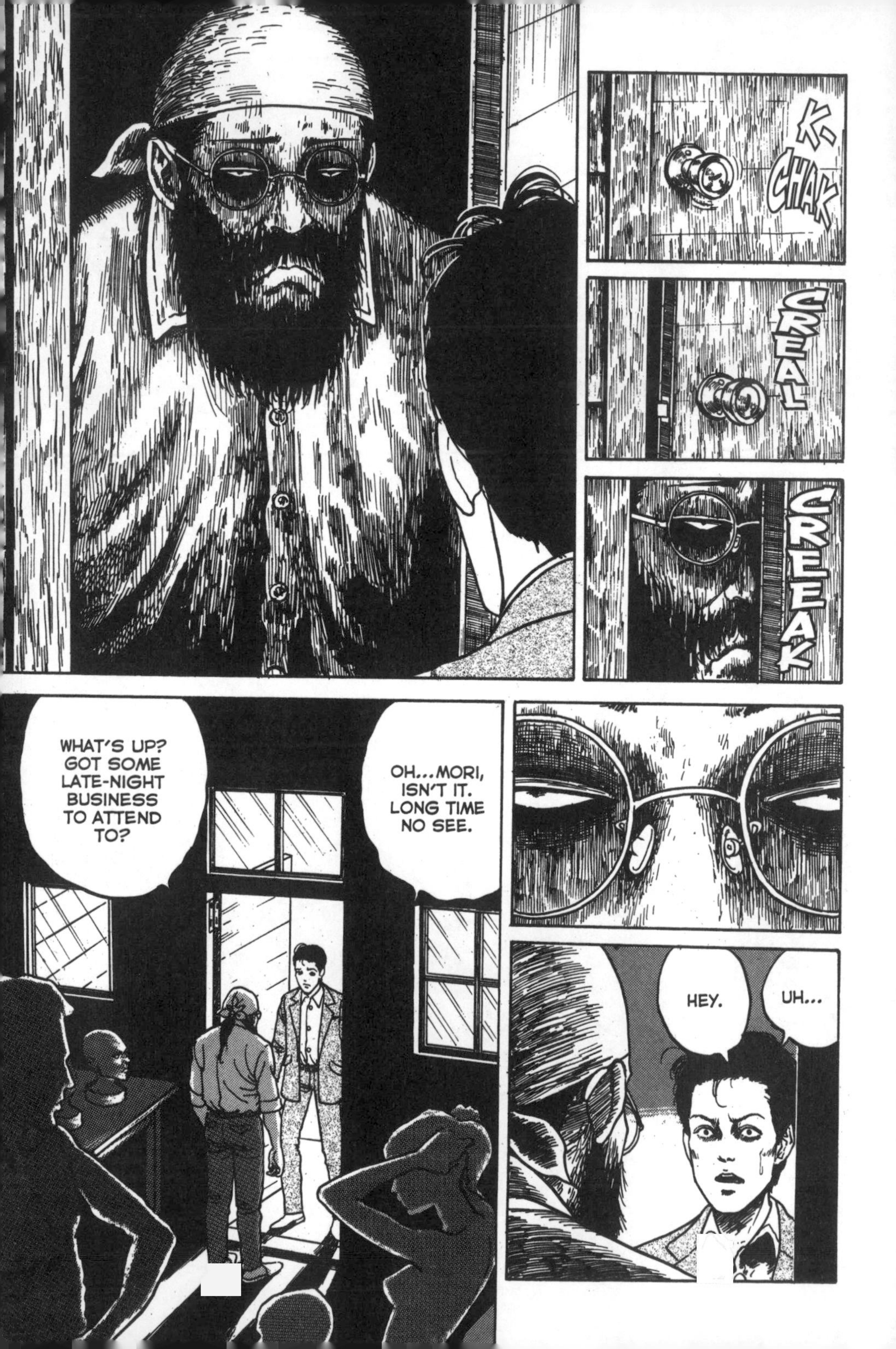
K-CHAK
CREAK
CREEAK
UH...
HEY.
OH...MORI, ISN'T IT. LONG TIME NO SEE.
WHAT'S UP? GOT SOME LATE-NIGHT BUSINESS TO ATTEND TO?

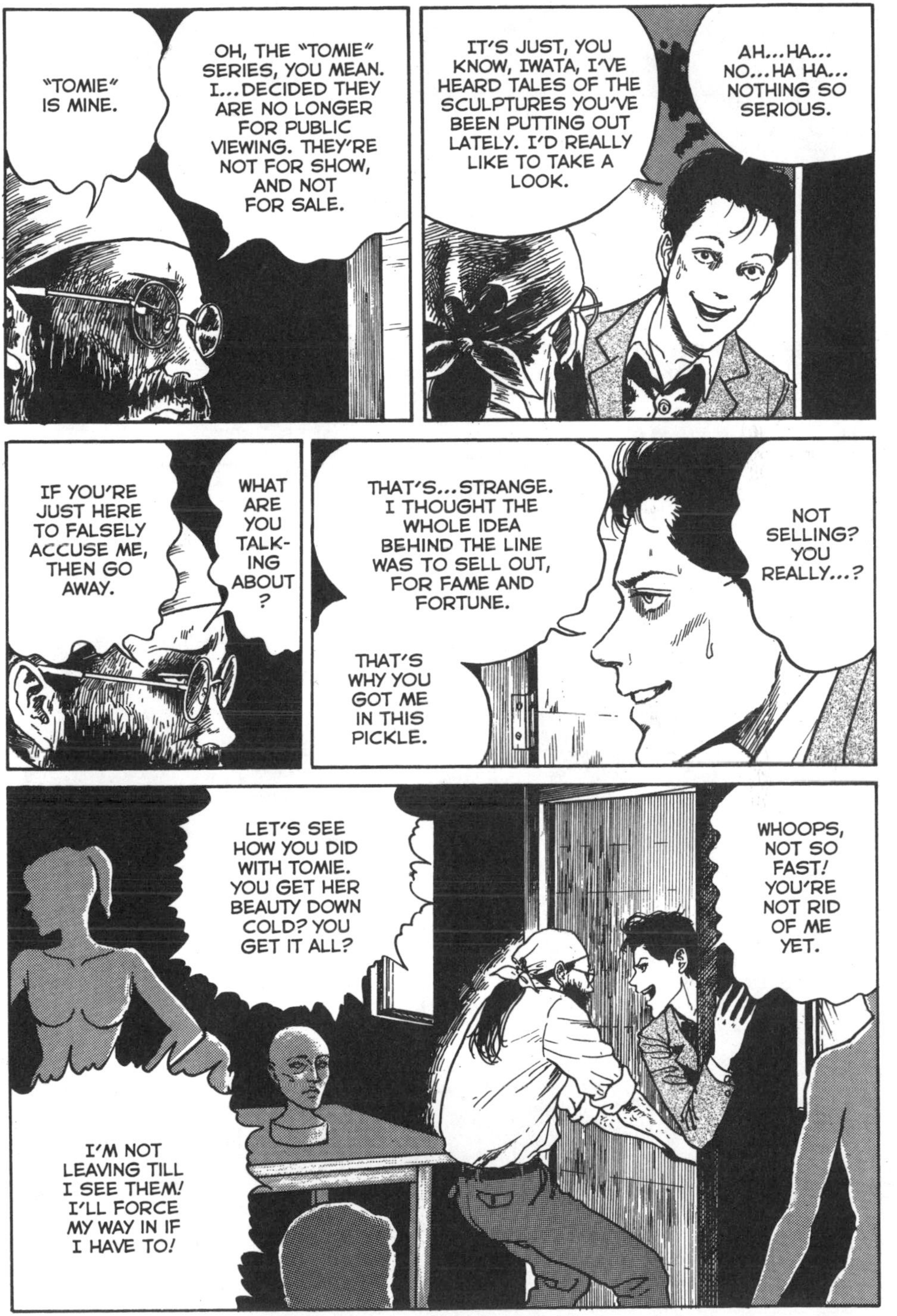
AH...HA... NO...HA HA... NOTHING SO SERIOUS.
IT'S JUST, YOU KNOW, IWATA, I'VE HEARD TALES OF THE SCULPTURES YOU'VE BEEN PUTTING OUT LATELY. I'D REALLY LIKE TO TAKE A LOOK.
OH, THE "TOMIE" SERIES, YOU MEAN. I...DECIDED THEY ARE NO LONGER FOR PUBLIC VIEWING. THEY'RE NOT FOR SHOW, AND NOT FOR SALE.
"TOMIE" IS MINE.
NOT SELLING? YOU REALLY...?
THAT'S...STRANGE. I THOUGHT THE WHOLE IDEA BEHIND THE LINE WAS TO SELL OUT, FOR FAME AND FORTUNE.
THAT'S WHY YOU GOT ME IN THIS PICKLE.
WHAT ARE YOU TALK-ING ABOUT?
IF YOU'RE JUST HERE TO FALSELY ACCUSE ME, THEN GO AWAY.
WHOOPS, NOT SO FAST! YOU'RE NOT RID OF ME YET.
LET'S SEE HOW YOU DID WITH TOMIE. YOU GET HER BEAUTY DOWN COLD? YOU GET IT ALL?
I'M NOT LEAVING TILL I SEE THEM! I'LL FORCE MY WAY IN IF I HAVE TO!

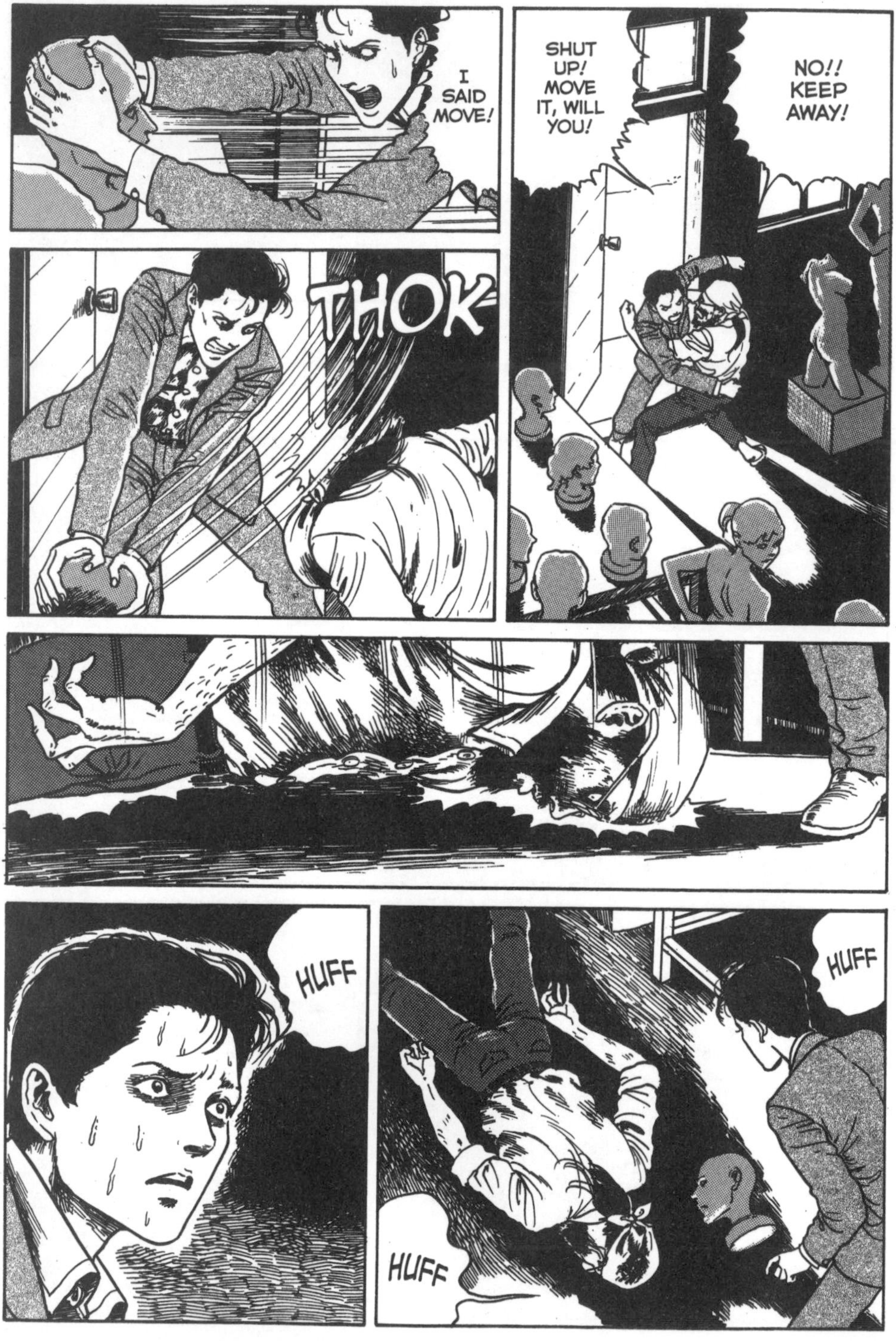
NO!! KEEP AWAY!
SHUT UP! MOVE IT, WILL YOU!
I SAID MOVE!
THOK
HUFF
HUFF
HUFF

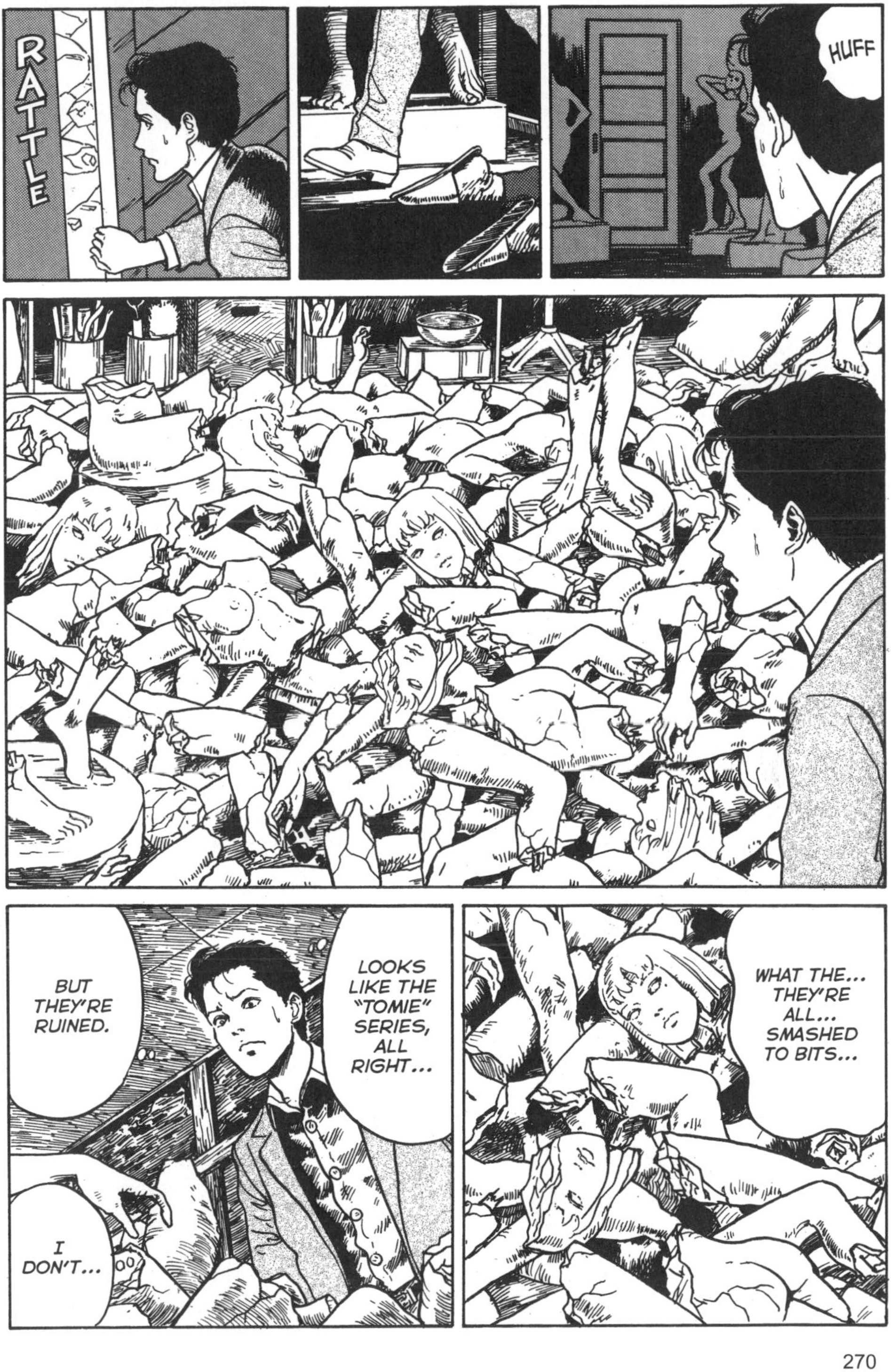
HUFF
RATTLE
WHAT THE... THEY'RE ALL... SMASHED TO BITS...
LOOKS LIKE THE "TOMIE" SERIES, ALL RIGHT...
BUT THEY'RE RUINED.
I DON'T...

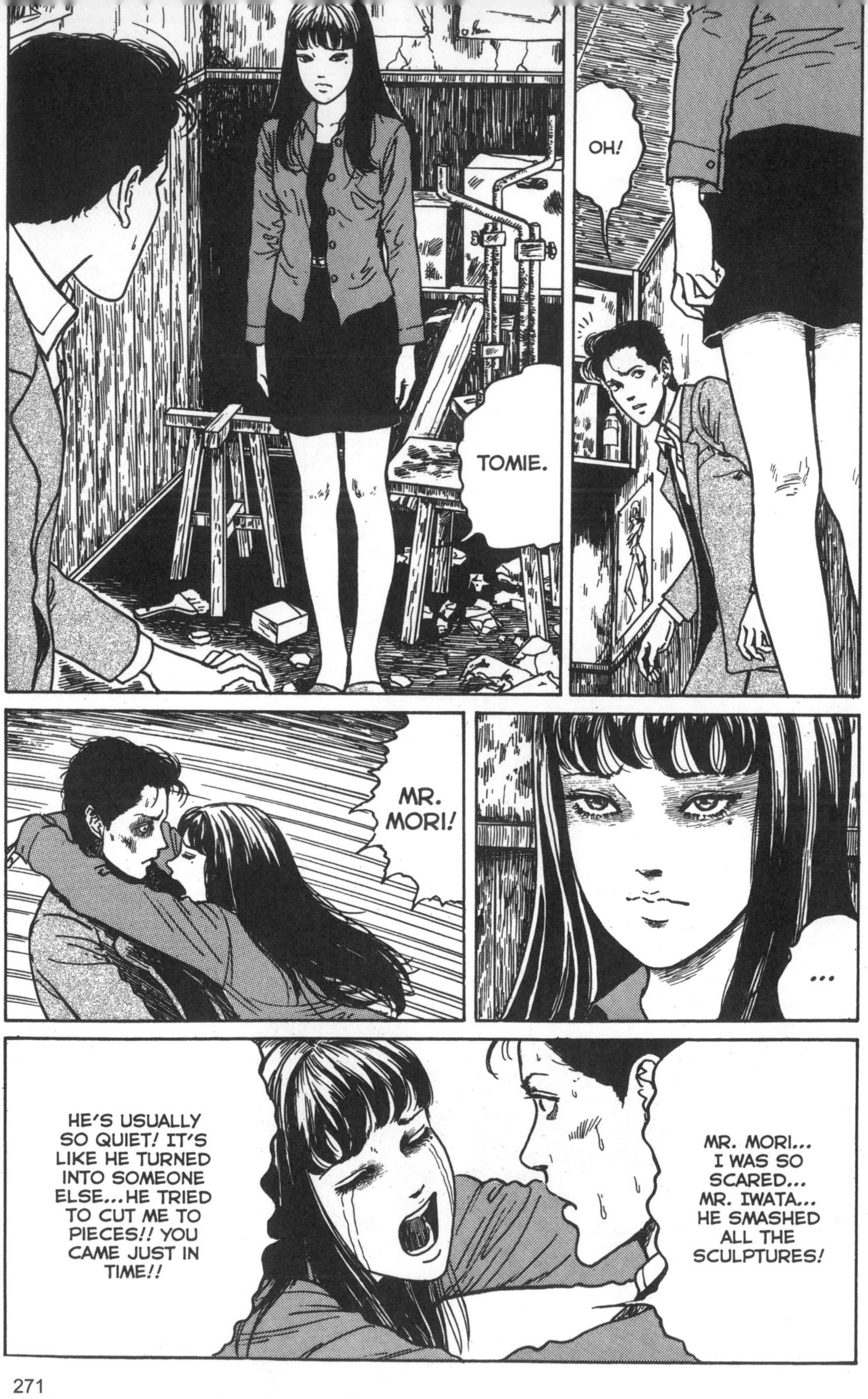
OH!
TOMIE.
...
MR. MORI!
MR. MORI... I WAS SO SCARED... MR. IWATA... HE SMASHED ALL THE SCULPTURES!
HE'S USUALLY SO QUIET! IT'S LIKE HE TURNED INTO SOMEONE ELSE...HE TRIED TO CUT ME TO PIECES!! YOU CAME JUST IN TIME!!

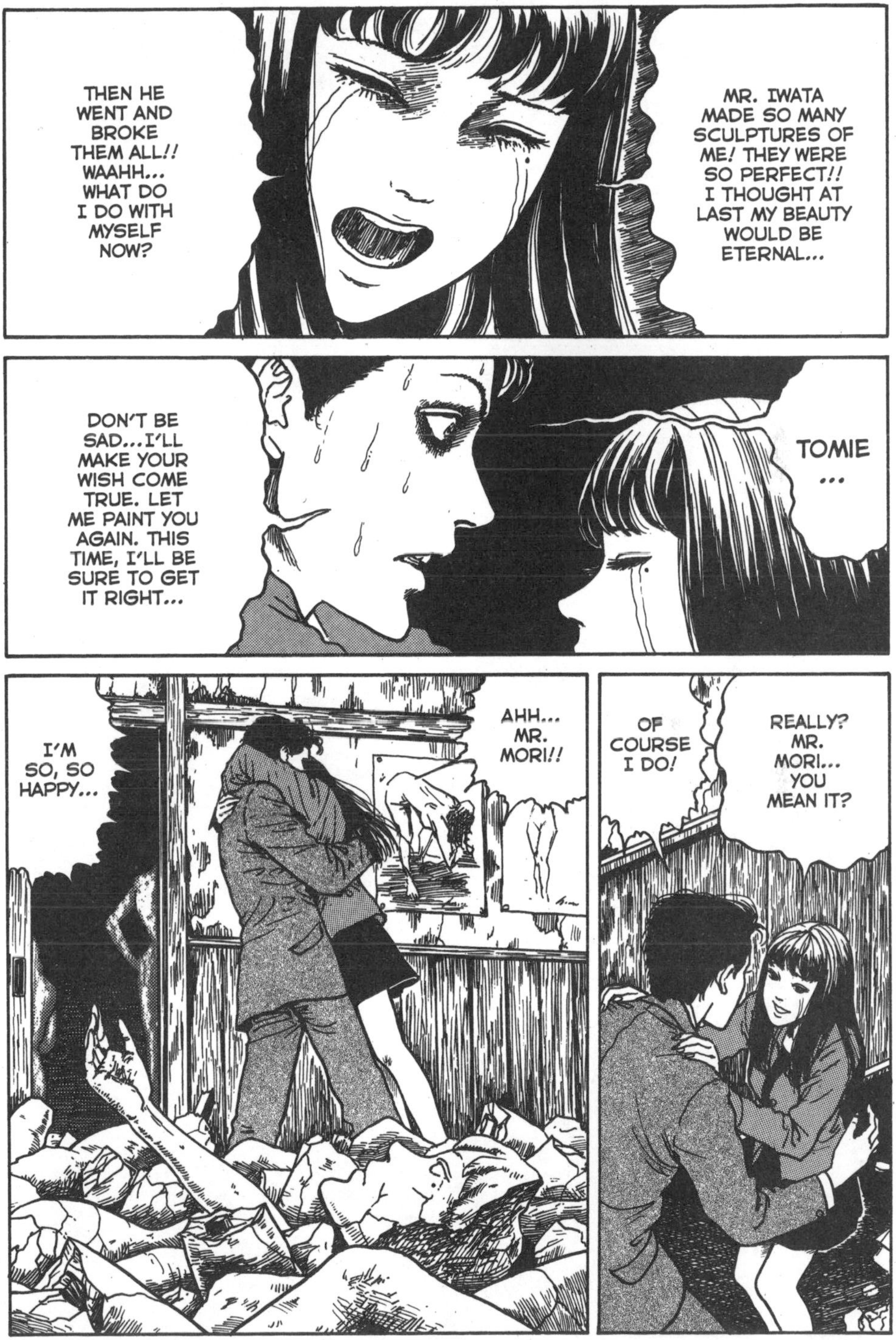
MR. IWATA MADE SO MANY SCULPTURES OF ME! THEY WERE SO PERFECT!! I THOUGHT AT LAST MY BEAUTY WOULD BE ETERNAL...
THEN HE WENT AND BROKE THEM ALL!! WAAHH... WHAT DO I DO WITH MYSELF NOW?
TOMIE ...
DON'T BE SAD...I'LL MAKE YOUR WISH COME TRUE. LET ME PAINT YOU AGAIN. THIS TIME, I'LL BE SURE TO GET IT RIGHT...
REALLY? MR. MORI... YOU MEAN IT?
OF COURSE I DO!
AHH... MR. MORI!!
I'M SO, SO HAPPY...

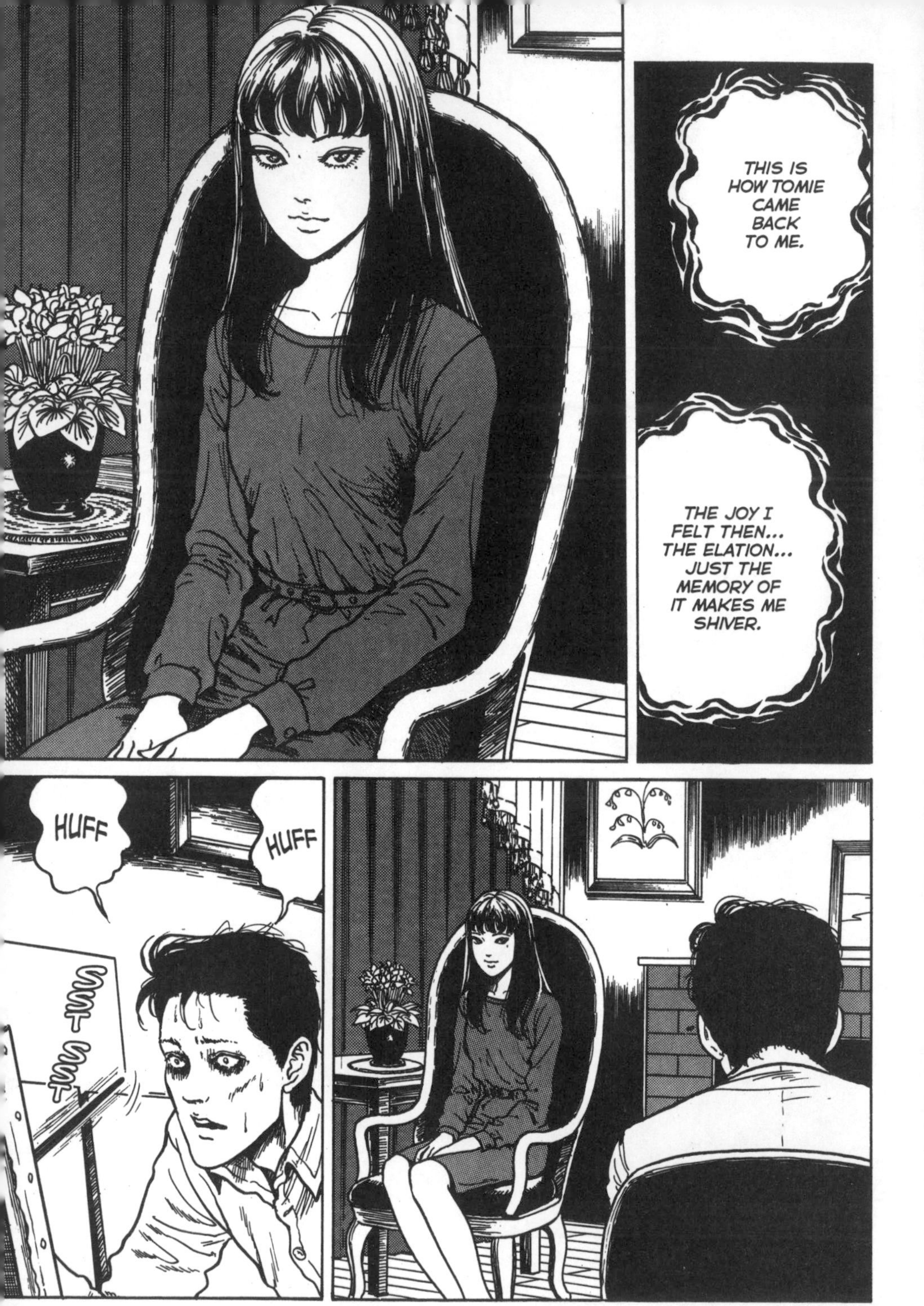
THIS IS HOW TOMIE CAME BACK TO ME.
THE JOY I FELT THEN... THE ELATION... JUST THE MEMORY OF IT MAKES ME SHIVER.
HUFF
HUFF
SST SST

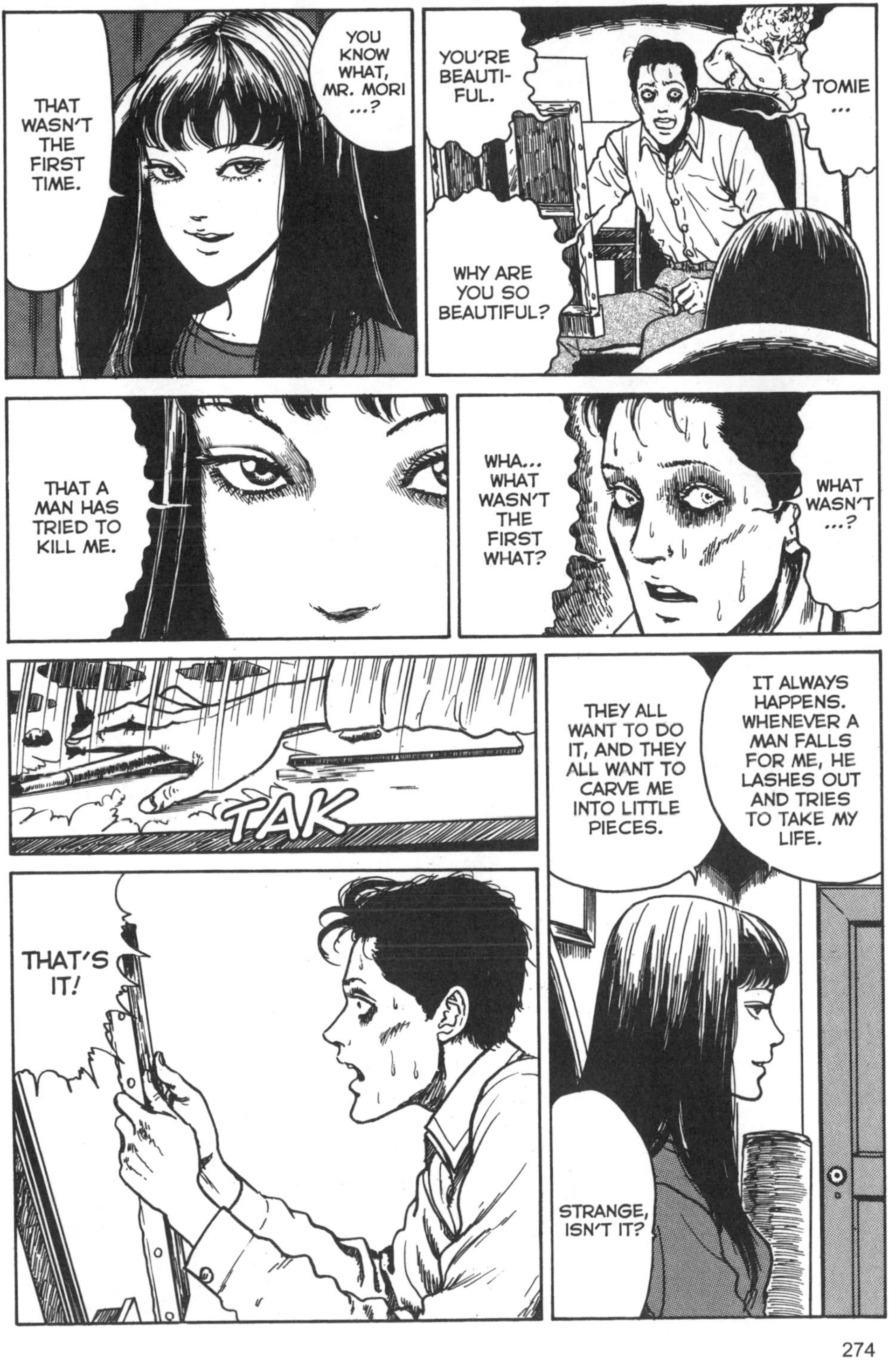
TOMIE ...
YOU'RE BEAUTI-FUL.
WHY ARE YOU SO BEAUTIFUL?
YOU KNOW WHAT, MR. MORI ...?
THAT WASN'T THE FIRST TIME.
WHAT WASN'T ...?
WHA... WHAT WASN'T THE FIRST WHAT?
THAT A MAN HAS TRIED TO KILL ME.
IT ALWAYS HAPPENS. WHENEVER A MAN FALLS FOR ME, HE LASHES OUT AND TRIES TO TAKE MY LIFE.
THEY ALL WANT TO DO IT, AND THEY ALL WANT TO CARVE ME INTO LITTLE PIECES.
STRANGE, ISN'T IT?
TAK
THAT'S IT!

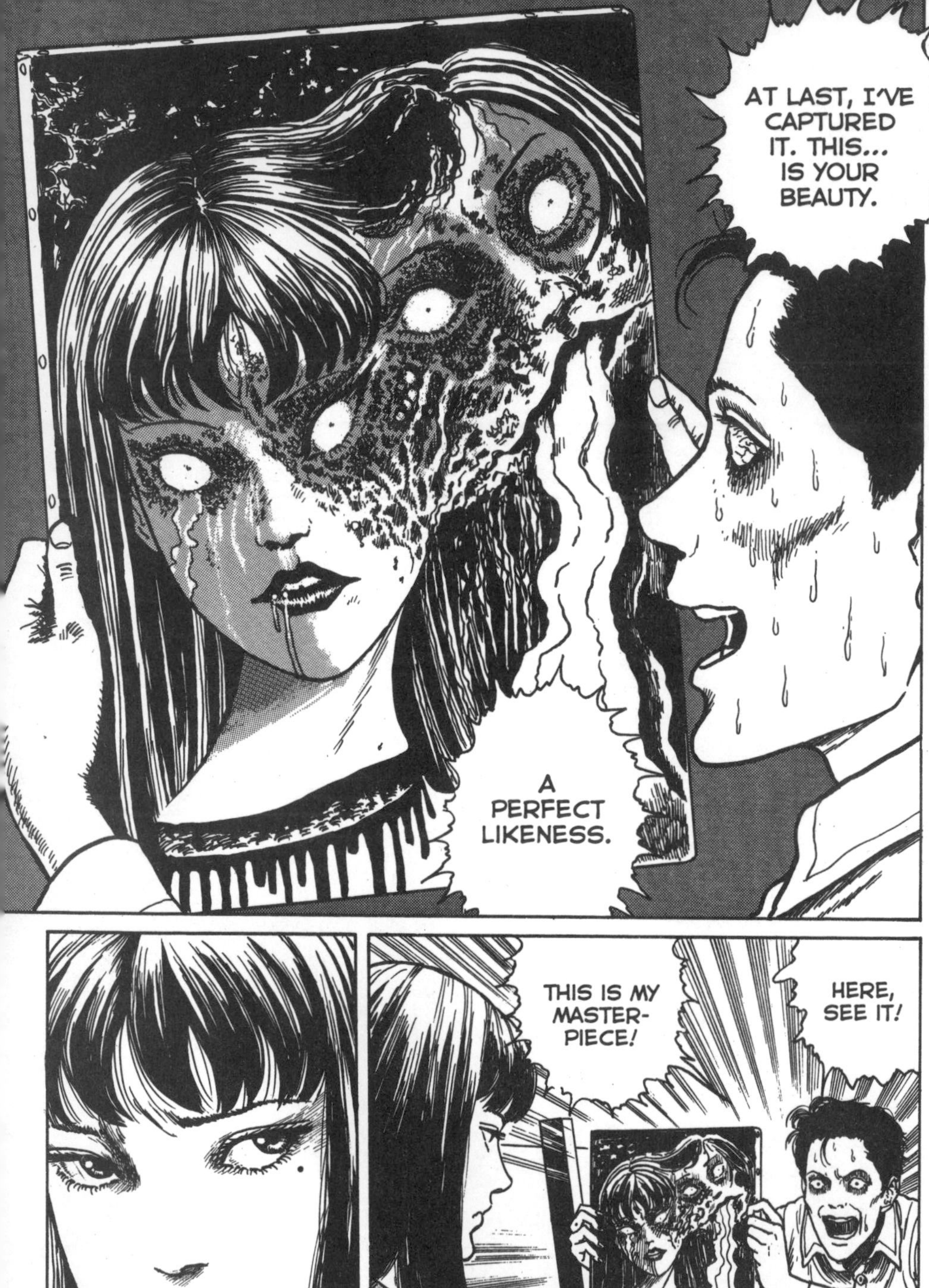
AT LAST, I'VE CAPTURED IT. THIS... IS YOUR BEAUTY.
A PERFECT LIKENESS.
HERE, SEE IT!
THIS IS MY MASTER-PIECE!

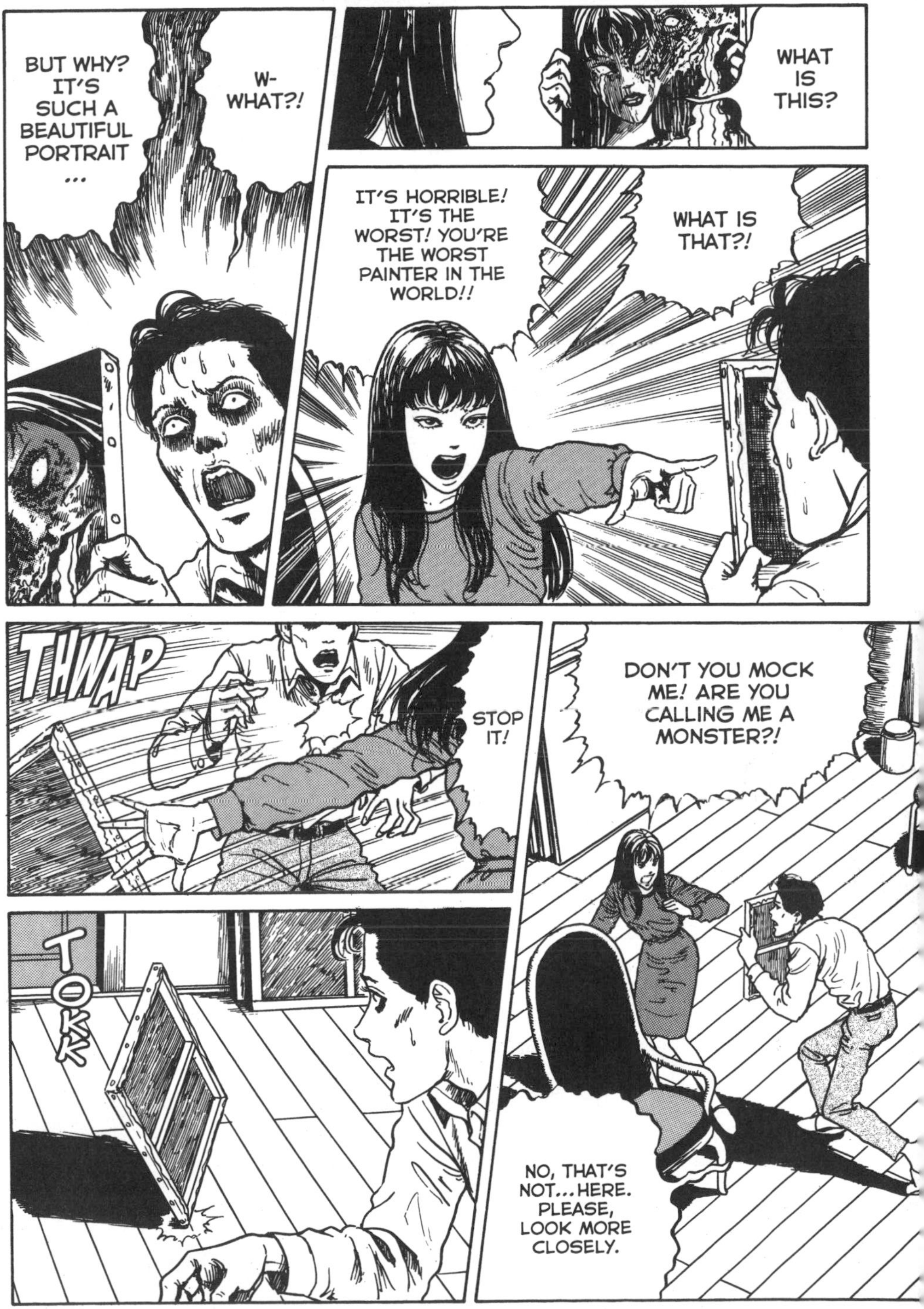
WHAT IS THIS?
WHAT IS THAT?!
IT'S HORRIBLE! IT'S THE WORST! YOU'RE THE WORST PAINTER IN THE WORLD!!
W- WHAT?!
BUT WHY? IT'S SUCH A BEAUTIFUL PORTRAIT...
DON'T YOU MOCK ME! ARE YOU CALLING ME A MONSTER?!
NO, THAT'S NOT...HERE. PLEASE, LOOK MORE CLOSELY.
STOP IT!
THWAP
TOKK

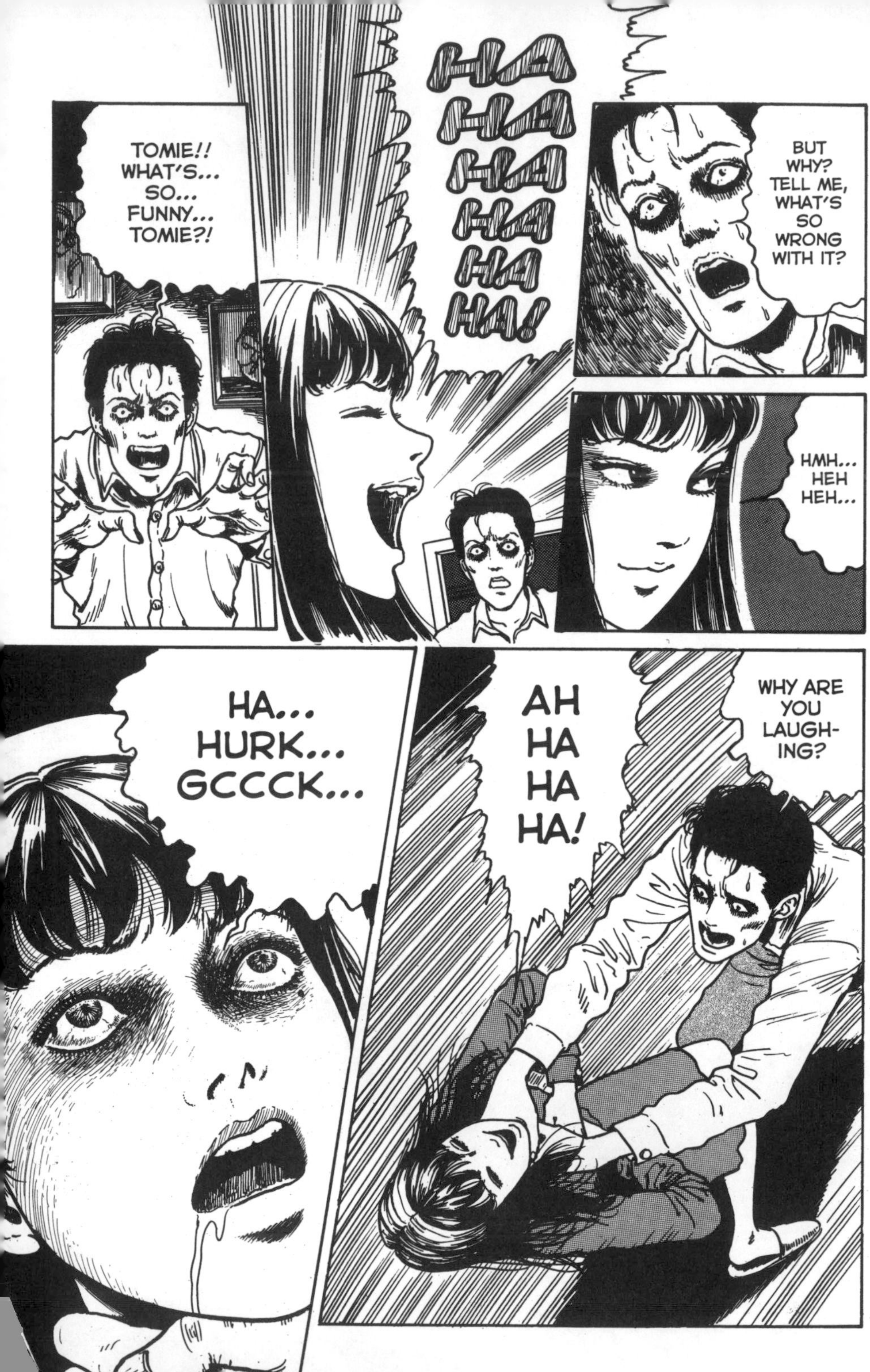
BUT WHY? TELL ME, WHAT'S SO WRONG WITH IT?
HMH... HEH HEH...
HA HA HA HA HA HA!
TOMIE!! WHAT'S... SO... FUNNY... TOMIE?!
WHY ARE YOU LAUGH-ING?
AH HA HA HA!
HA... HURK... GCCCK...

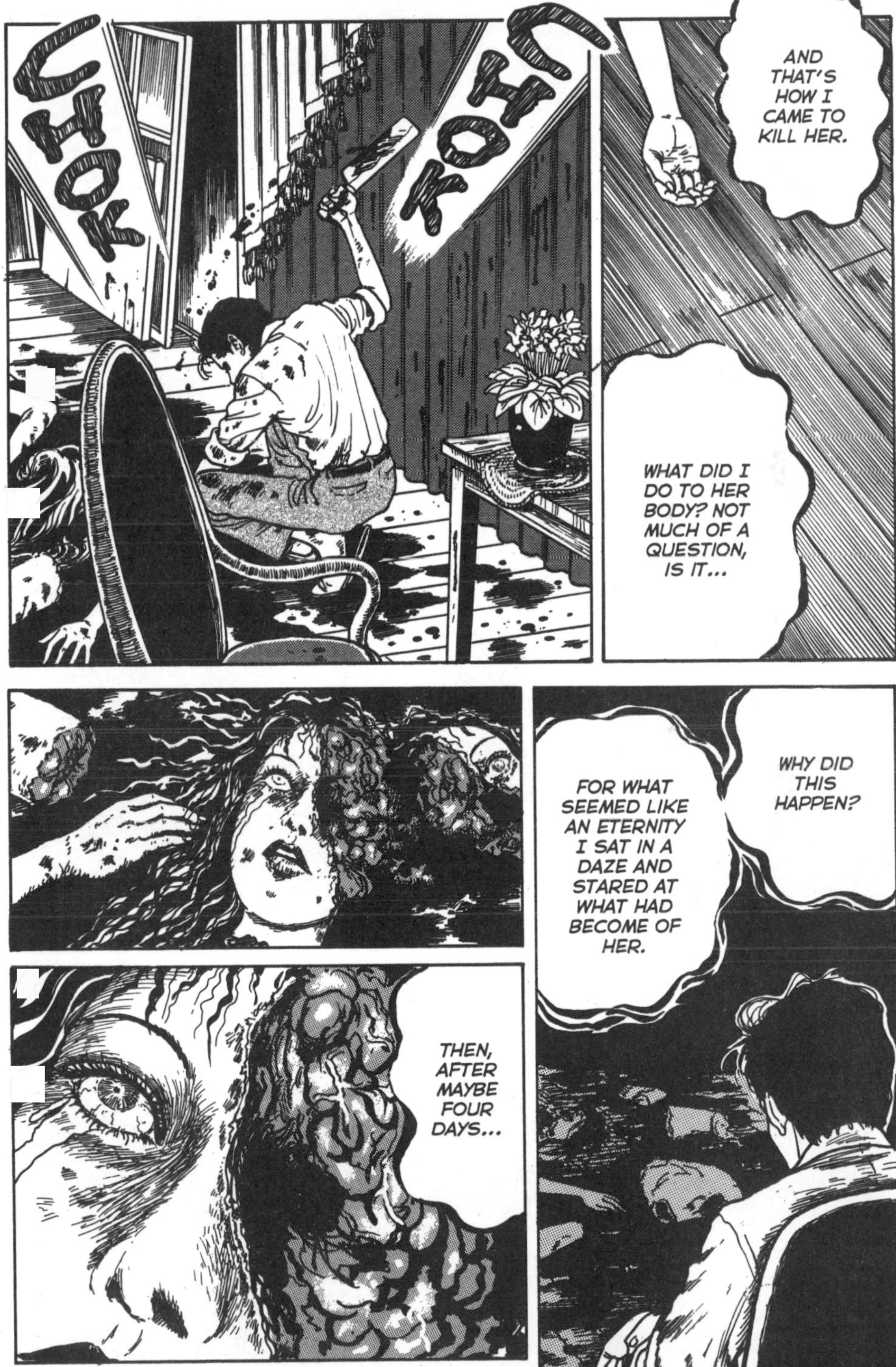
AND THAT'S HOW I CAME TO KILL HER.
WHAT DID I DO TO HER BODY? NOT MUCH OF A QUESTION, IS IT...
CHOK
CHOK
WHY DID THIS HAPPEN?
FOR WHAT SEEMED LIKE AN ETERNITY I SAT IN A DAZE AND STARED AT WHAT HAD BECOME OF HER.
THEN, AFTER MAYBE FOUR DAYS...

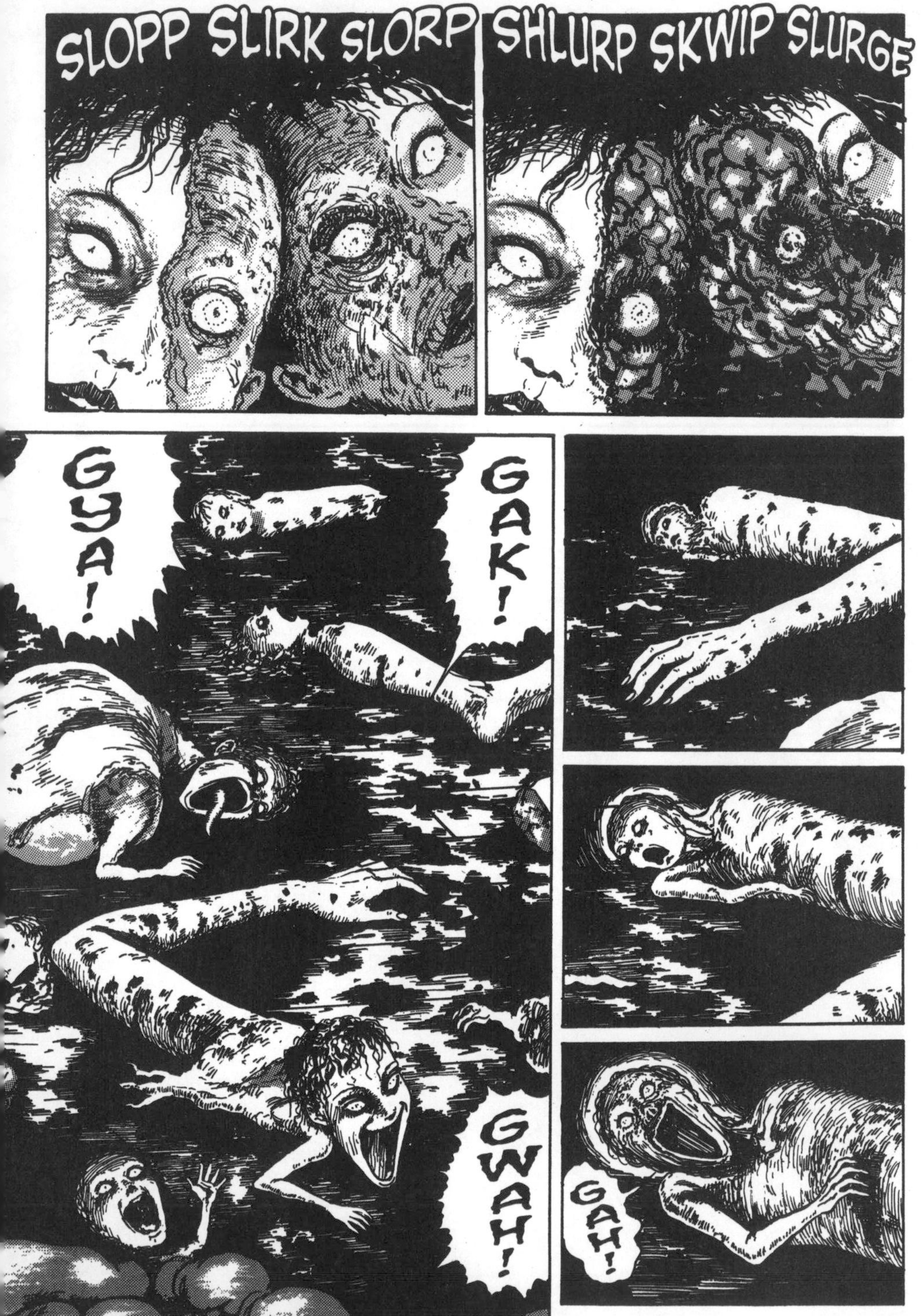
SHLURP SKWIP SLURGE
SLOPP SLIRK SLORP
GAH!
GAK!
GYA!
GWAH!

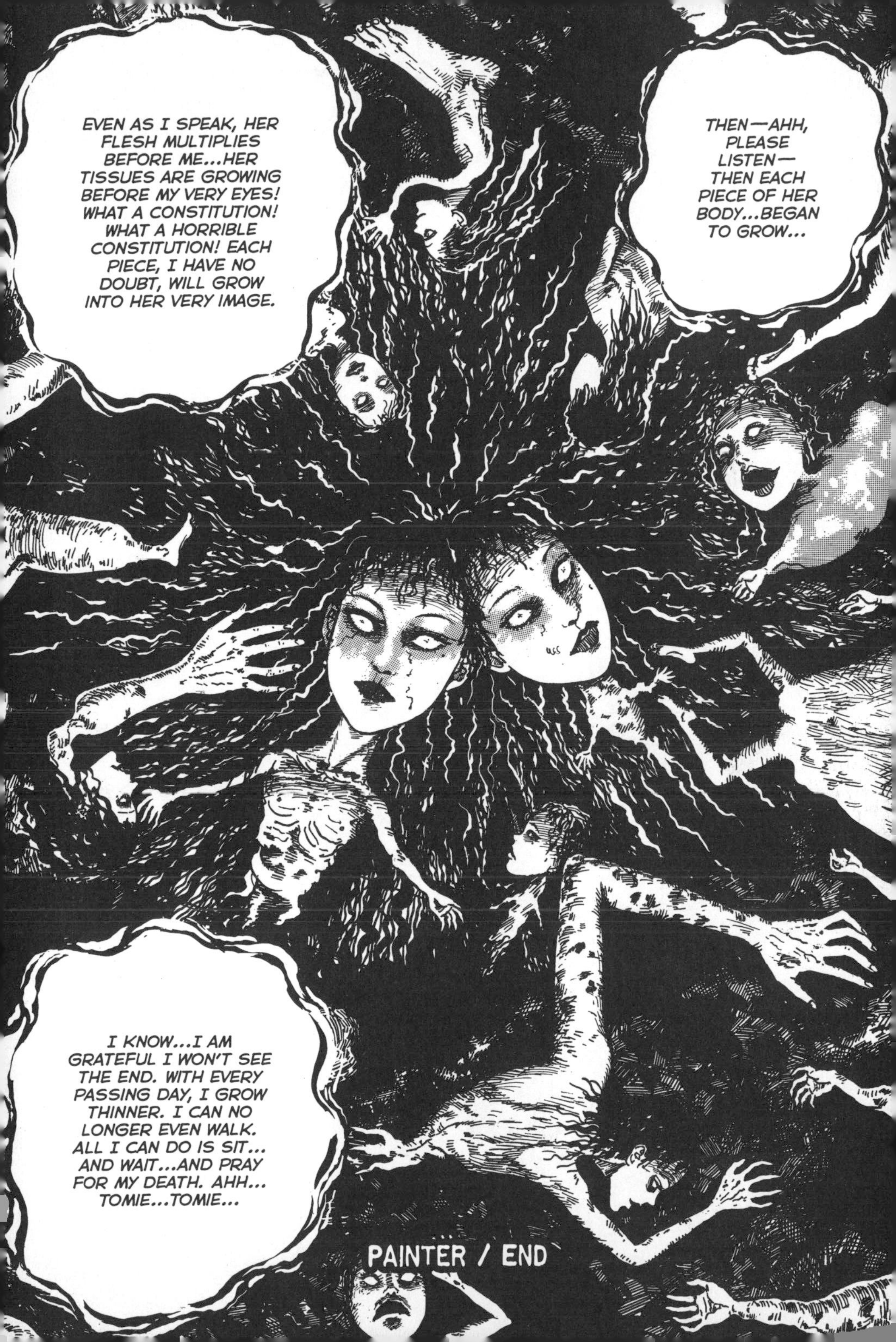
THEN—AHH, PLEASE LISTEN—THEN EACH PIECE OF HER BODY...BEGAN TO GROW...
EVEN AS I SPEAK, HER FLESH MULTIPLIES BEFORE ME...HER TISSUES ARE GROWING BEFORE MY VERY EYES! WHAT A CONSTITUTION! WHAT A HORRIBLE CONSTITUTION! EACH PIECE, I HAVE NO DOUBT, WILL GROW INTO HER VERY IMAGE.
I KNOW...I AM GRATEFUL I WON'T SEE THE END. WITH EVERY PASSING DAY, I GROW THINNER. I CAN NO LONGER EVEN WALK. ALL I CAN DO IS SIT... AND WAIT...AND PRAY FOR MY DEATH. AHH... TOMIE...TOMIE...
PAINTER / END

PAINTER

I drew the *Tomie* series intermittently after her initial appearance, but then my editor Harada-san asked me if I wouldn't try focusing on it. "Painter" is the first chapter of that series. Tomie wants to record her beautiful form, but for some reason, she is shown as a horrible monster in photos. So she decides to have herself immortalized in painting and sculpture...is the idea. Given that this was the first chapter in a new series, I devoted myself to clearly expressing Tomie's characteristics. I remember working really hard to make her as beautiful as possible.

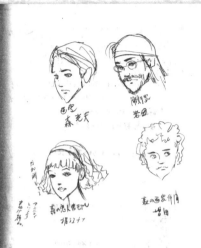

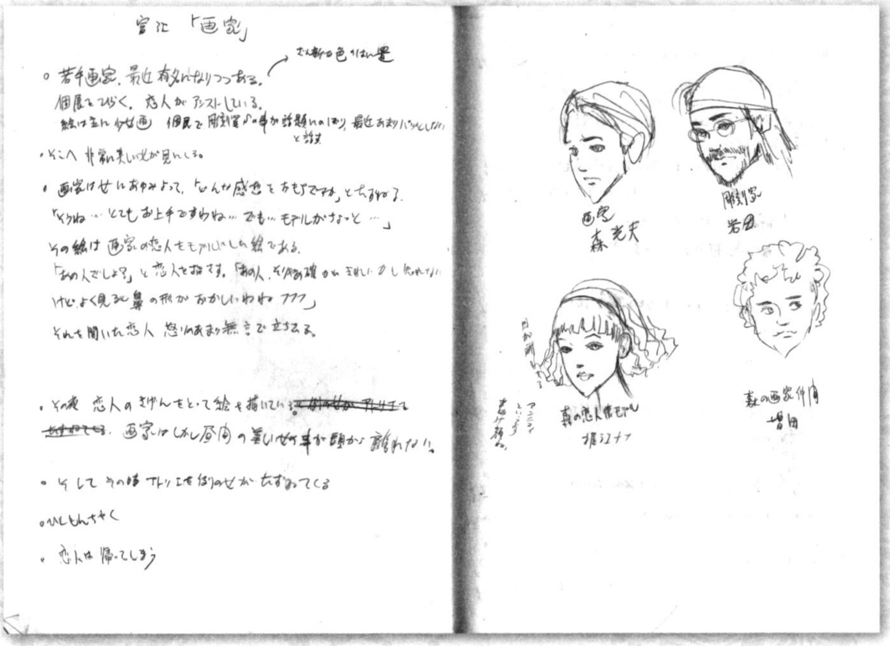

[Left page]
Tomie: Painter

- *A young painter. He's recently been getting recognition. → Novel use of color*
  Has an exhibit. His girlfriend is helping him.
  Paintings are mostly of girls. At the exhibition, conversation turns to the sculptor S, with people saying he's been pretty unimpressive lately.

- *Then an extremely beautiful girl comes to take a look.*
  The painter walks over to her and asks, "What do you think of the work?"
  "Right, it's really very good. ...But the model's a little..."
  The painting is one the painter's girlfriend modeled for.
  "That's her, isn't it?" She points at his girlfriend. "She might have a pretty face, but if you look closely, you can see the shape of her nose is a little strange. Hee hee hee."
  Hearing this, the girlfriend stands stock still, mute with rage.

- *That evening, the painter paints the girlfriend to appease her.*
  He can't get the beautiful girl from that day out of his head.

- *And then, at that moment, the girl herself visits his studio.*

- *A quarrel.*

- *The girlfriend leaves.*

[Right page]
Painter: Mitsuo Mori

Sculptor: Iwata

Mori's girlfriend/model
Nana Horie
Eyes are far apart.
"A face that's less ennui
and more idiot, hm?"

Mori's colleague
Masuda

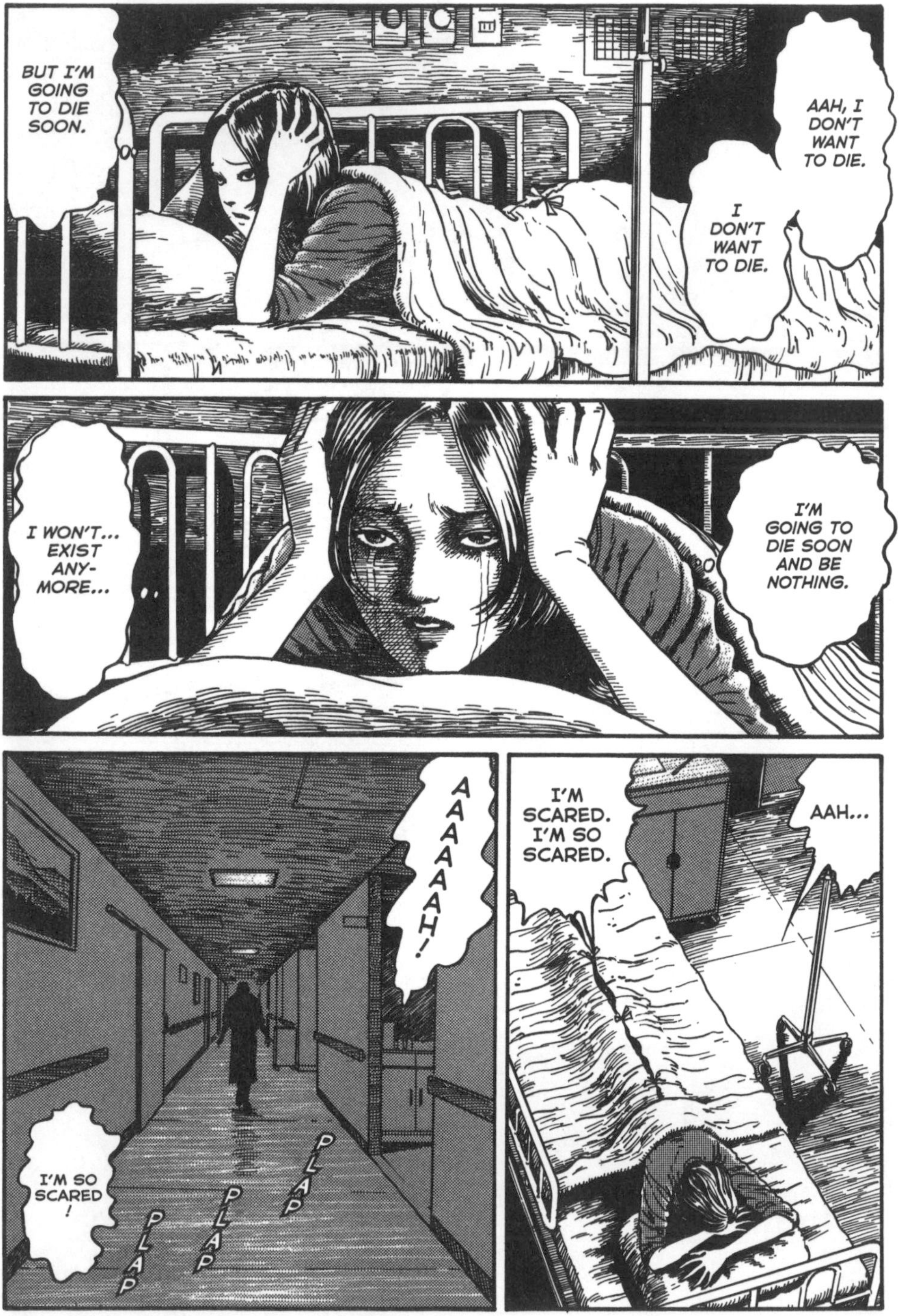
AAH, I DON'T WANT TO DIE.
I DON'T WANT TO DIE.
BUT I'M GOING TO DIE SOON.
I'M GOING TO DIE SOON AND BE NOTHING.
I WON'T... EXIST ANYMORE...
AAH...
I'M SCARED. I'M SO SCARED.
AAAAAAAH!
I'M SO SCARED!
PLAP
PLAP
PLAP

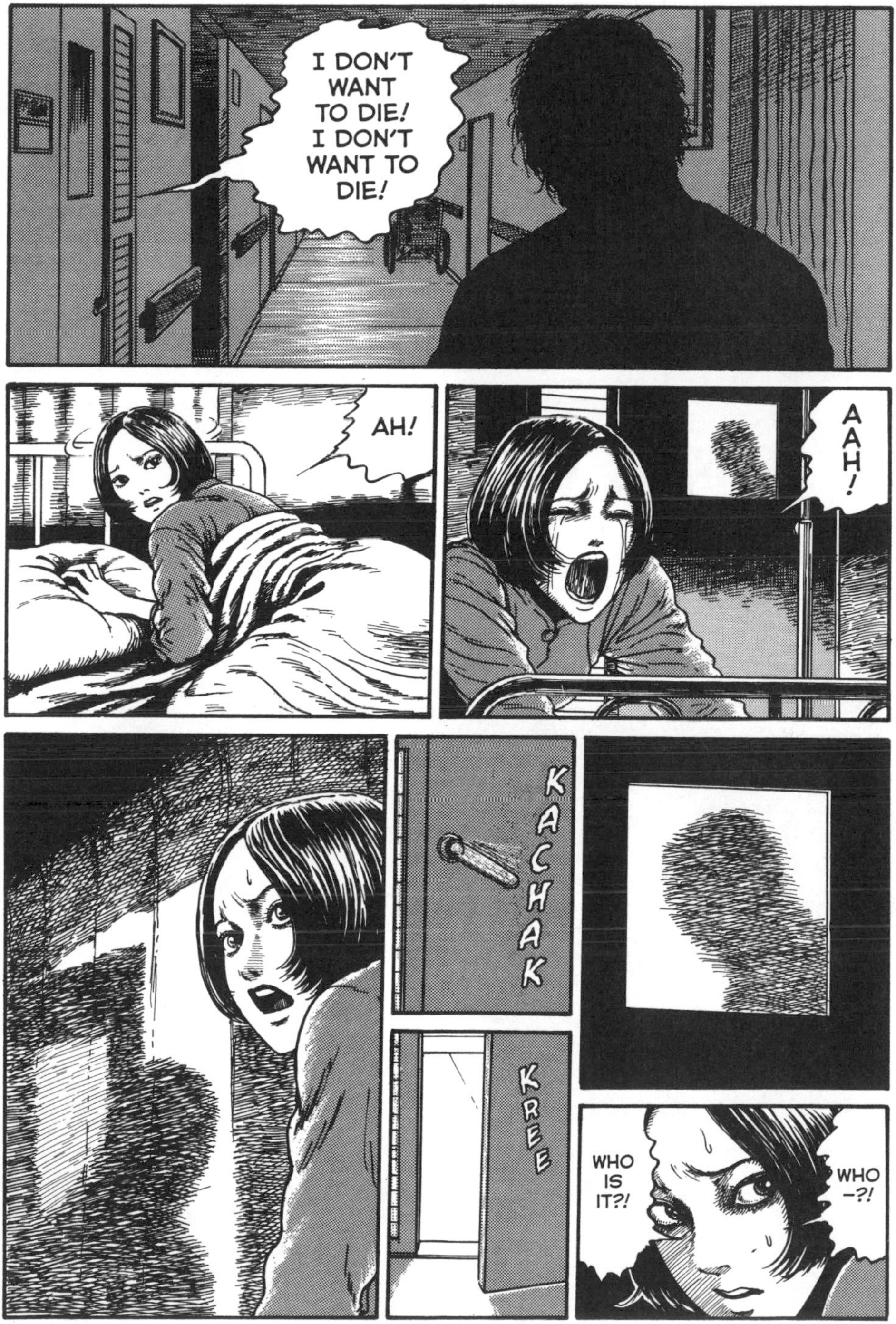
I DON'T WANT TO DIE! I DON'T WANT TO DIE!
AAH!
AH!
WHO —?!
WHO IS IT?!
KACHAK
KREE

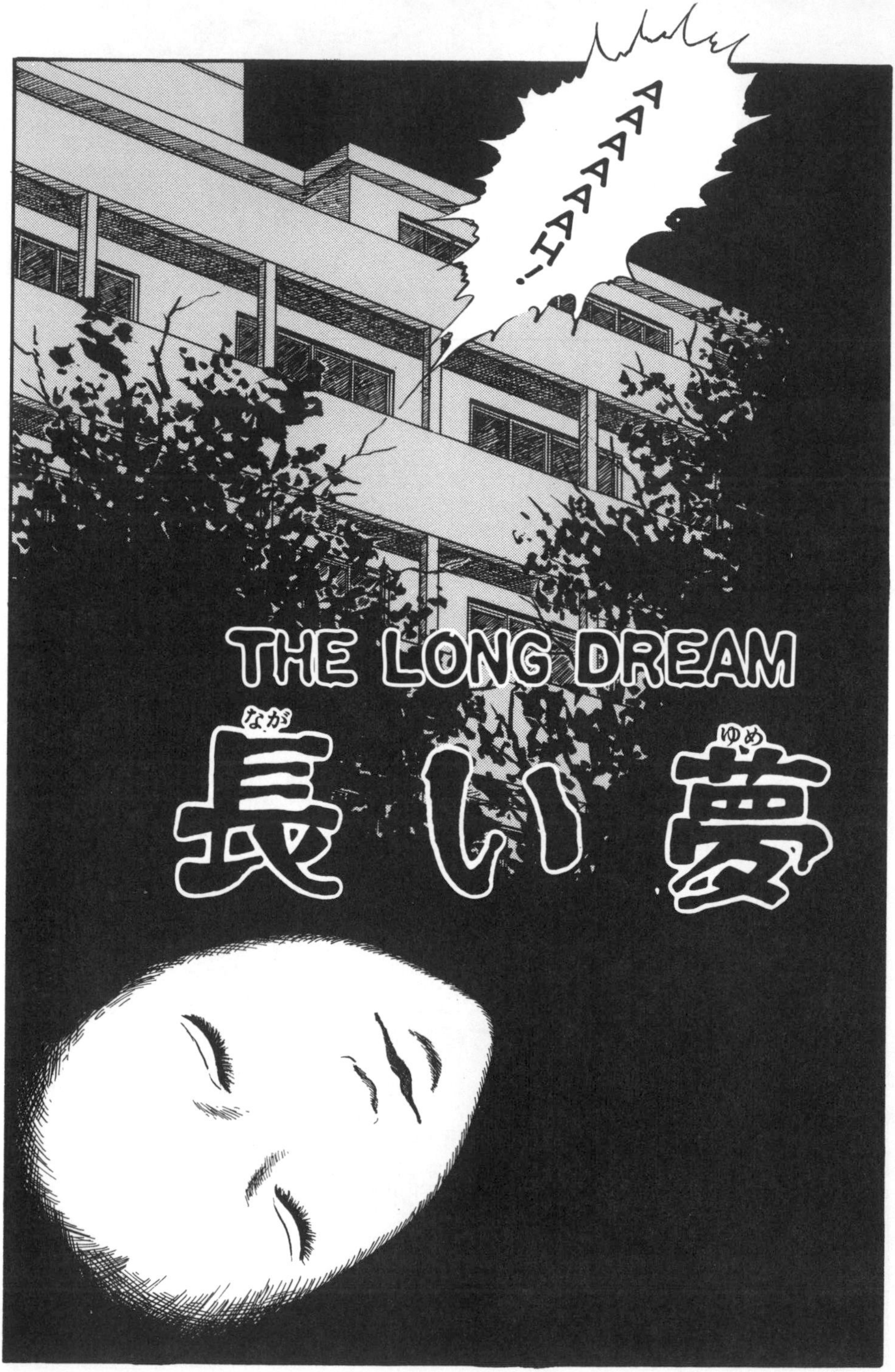
AAAAAAH!
THE LONG DREAM
長い夢

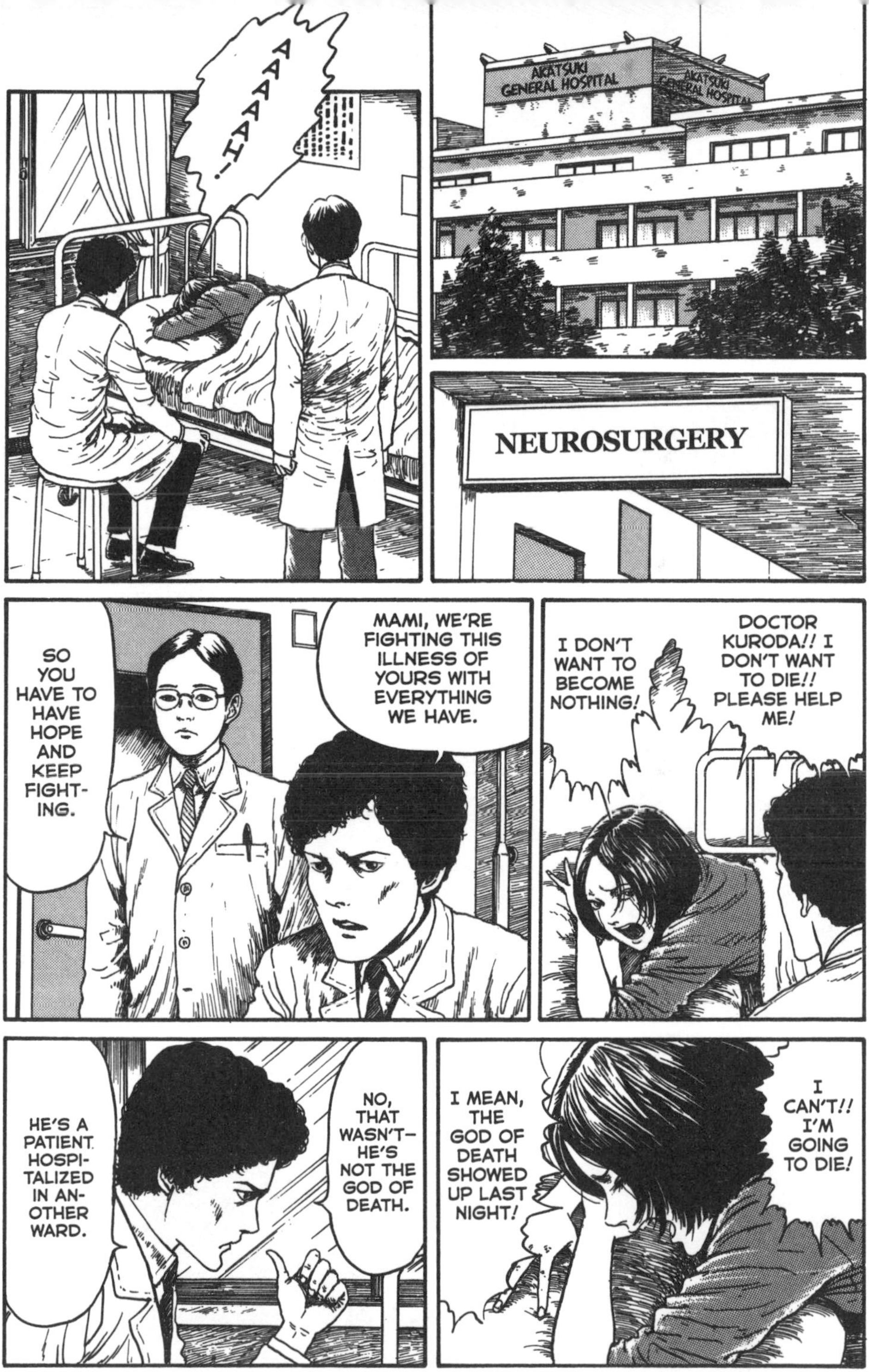
AKATSUKI GENERAL HOSPITAL
AKATSUKI GENERAL HOSPITAL
NEUROSURGERY
AAAAAH!!
DOCTOR KURODA!! I DON'T WANT TO DIE!! PLEASE HELP ME!
I DON'T WANT TO BECOME NOTHING!
MAMI, WE'RE FIGHTING THIS ILLNESS OF YOURS WITH EVERYTHING WE HAVE.
SO YOU HAVE TO HAVE HOPE AND KEEP FIGHT-ING.
I CAN'T!! I'M GOING TO DIE!
I MEAN, THE GOD OF DEATH SHOWED UP LAST NIGHT!
NO, THAT WASN'T— HE'S NOT THE GOD OF DEATH.
HE'S A PATIENT. HOSPI-TALIZED IN AN-OTHER WARD.

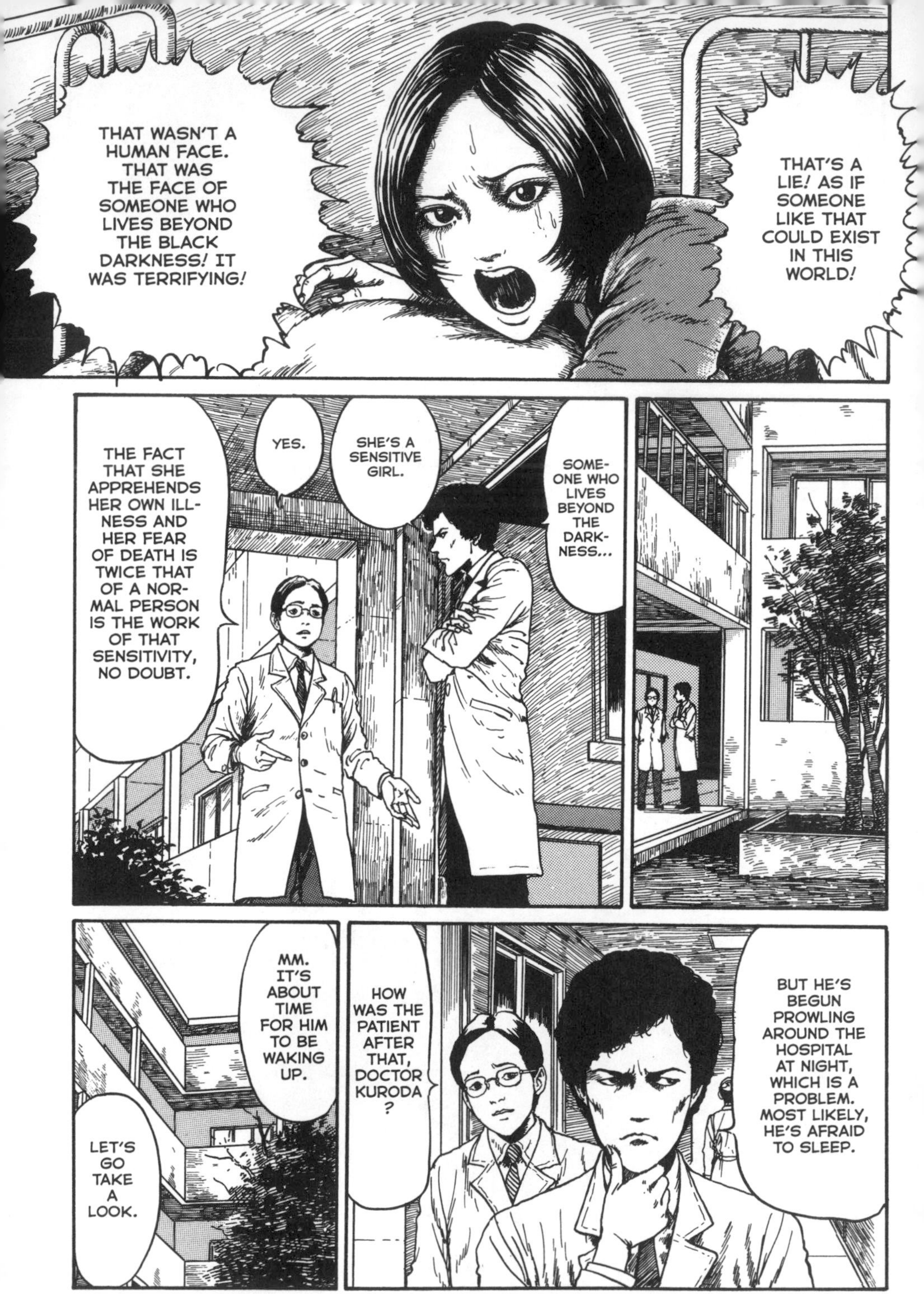
THAT'S A LIE! AS IF SOMEONE LIKE THAT COULD EXIST IN THIS WORLD!
THAT WASN'T A HUMAN FACE. THAT WAS THE FACE OF SOMEONE WHO LIVES BEYOND THE BLACK DARKNESS! IT WAS TERRIFYING!
SOME-ONE WHO LIVES BEYOND THE DARK-NESS...
SHE'S A SENSITIVE GIRL.
YES.
THE FACT THAT SHE APPREHENDS HER OWN ILL-NESS AND HER FEAR OF DEATH IS TWICE THAT OF A NOR-MAL PERSON IS THE WORK OF THAT SENSITIVITY, NO DOUBT.
BUT HE'S BEGUN PROWLING AROUND THE HOSPITAL AT NIGHT, WHICH IS A PROBLEM. MOST LIKELY, HE'S AFRAID TO SLEEP.
HOW WAS THE PATIENT AFTER THAT, DOCTOR KURODA?
MM. IT'S ABOUT TIME FOR HIM TO BE WAKING UP.
LET'S GO TAKE A LOOK.

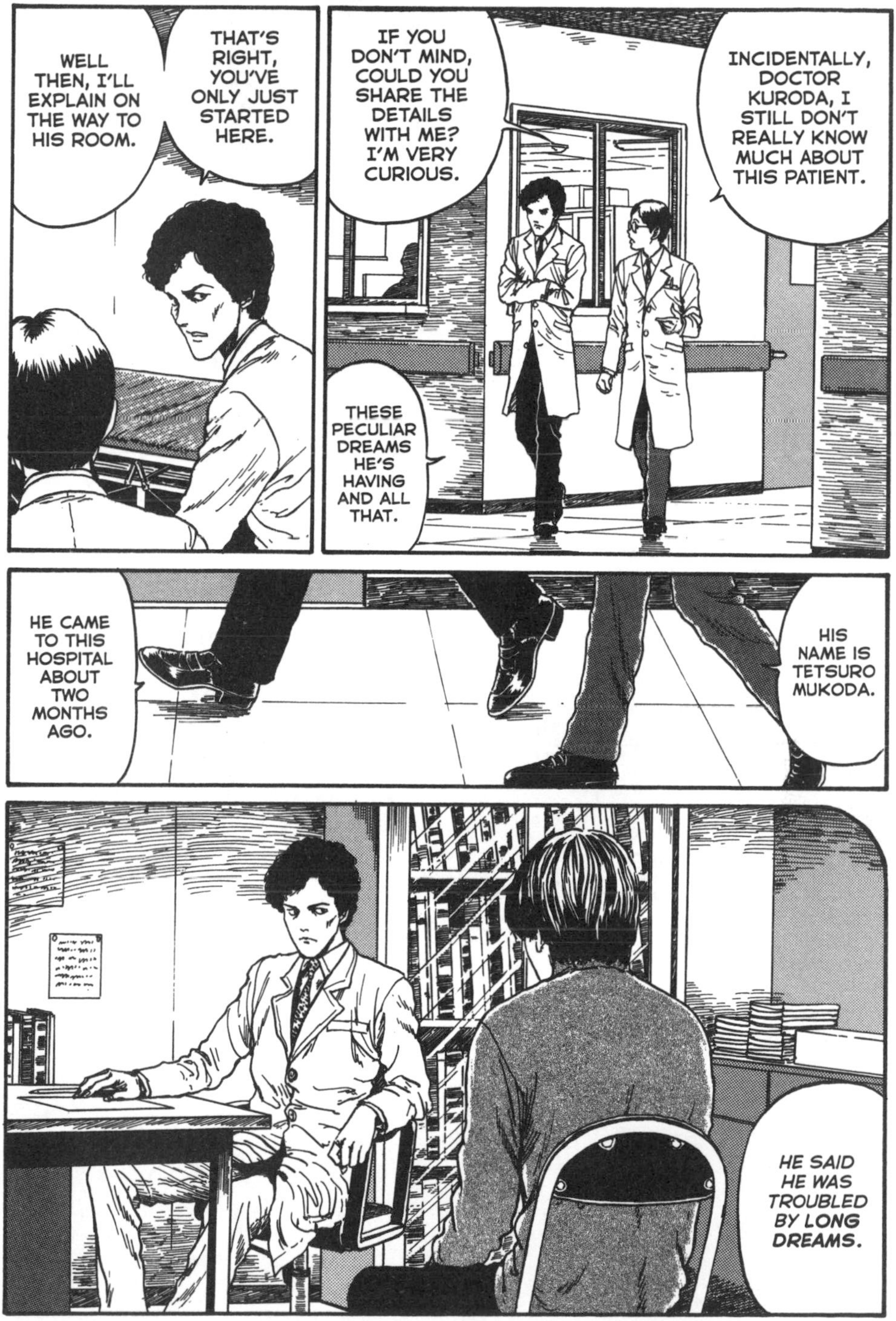
INCIDENTALLY, DOCTOR KURODA, I STILL DON'T REALLY KNOW MUCH ABOUT THIS PATIENT.
IF YOU DON'T MIND, COULD YOU SHARE THE DETAILS WITH ME? I'M VERY CURIOUS.
THESE PECULIAR DREAMS HE'S HAVING AND ALL THAT.
THAT'S RIGHT, YOU'VE ONLY JUST STARTED HERE.
WELL THEN, I'LL EXPLAIN ON THE WAY TO HIS ROOM.
HIS NAME IS TETSURO MUKODA.
HE CAME TO THIS HOSPITAL ABOUT TWO MONTHS AGO.
HE SAID HE WAS TROUBLED BY ***LONG DREAMS***.

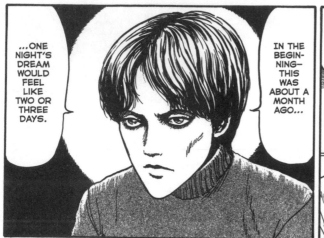

OH, LONG DREAMS ...
HOW LONG DO THEY FEEL, EXACTLY?
IN THE BEGINNING— THIS WAS ABOUT A MONTH AGO...
...ONE NIGHT'S DREAM WOULD FEEL LIKE TWO OR THREE DAYS.
I SEE.
SO YOU MEAN IT FELT LONG ONCE YOU WOKE UP?
NO. IT FELT LONG IN THE DREAM.
VERY CLEAR-LY.
AT FIRST I THOUGHT IT WAS ALL IN MY HEAD.
BUT THE DREAMS GRADUALLY GOT LONGER WITH EACH PASSING DAY.
AND THAT WOULD BE FINE IF THEY WERE ALL GOOD DREAMS, BUT MANY ARE NIGHTMARES.
THEY GET MORE AND MORE UNPLEASANT AND UGLY.

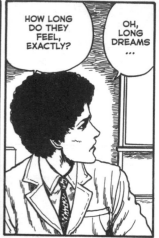

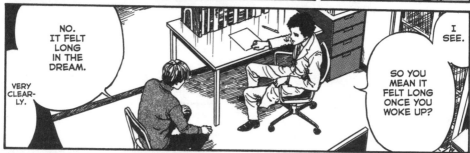

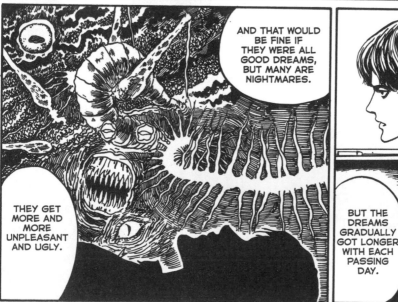

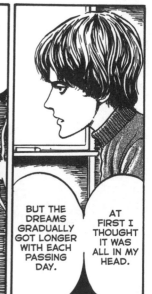

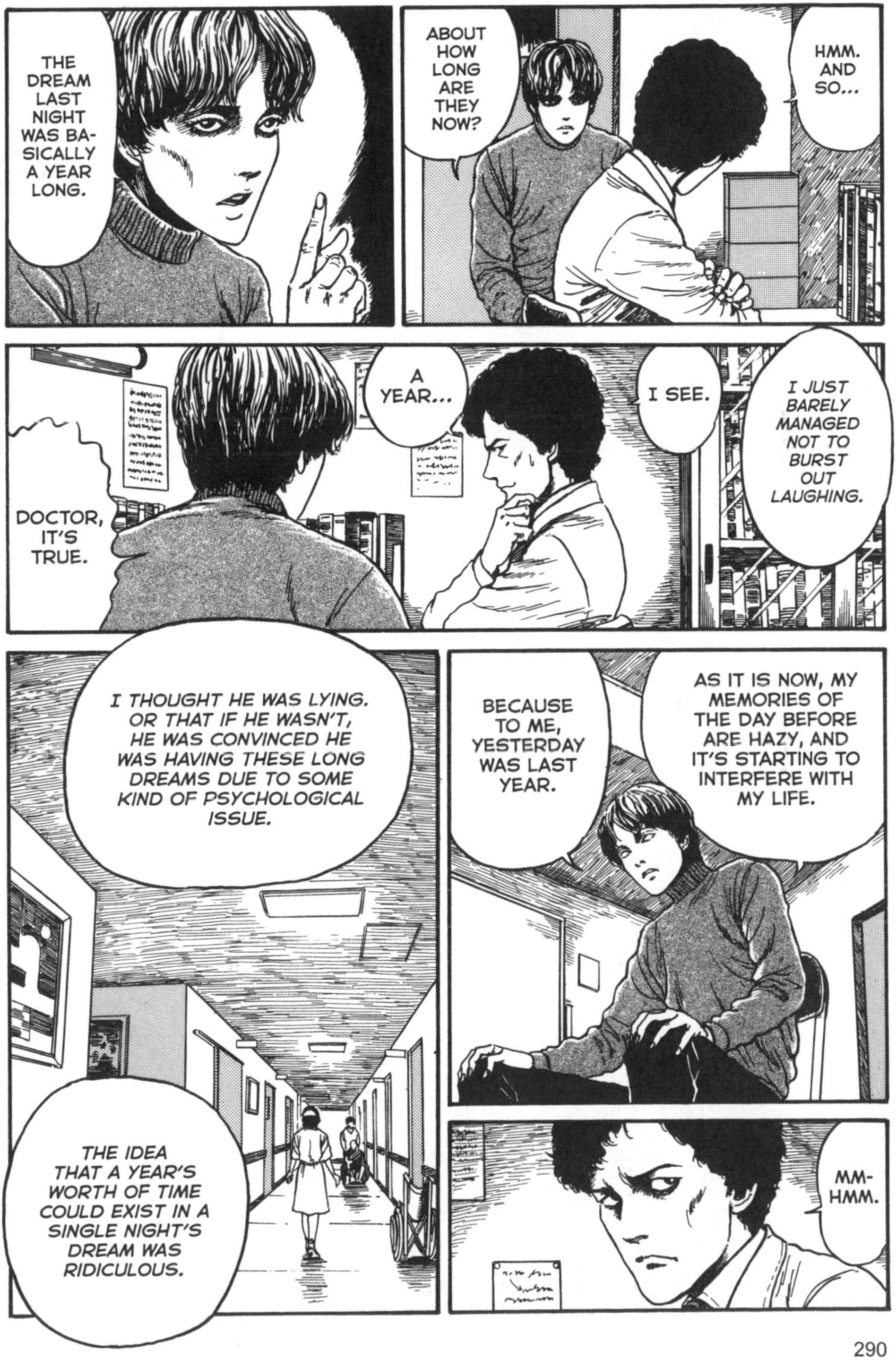
HMM. AND SO...
ABOUT HOW LONG ARE THEY NOW?
THE DREAM LAST NIGHT WAS BASICALLY A YEAR LONG.
I JUST BARELY MANAGED NOT TO BURST OUT LAUGHING.
I SEE.
A YEAR...
DOCTOR, IT'S TRUE.
AS IT IS NOW, MY MEMORIES OF THE DAY BEFORE ARE HAZY, AND IT'S STARTING TO INTERFERE WITH MY LIFE.
BECAUSE TO ME, YESTERDAY WAS LAST YEAR.
MM-HMM.
I THOUGHT HE WAS LYING. OR THAT IF HE WASN'T, HE WAS CONVINCED HE WAS HAVING THESE LONG DREAMS DUE TO SOME KIND OF PSYCHOLOGICAL ISSUE.
THE IDEA THAT A YEAR'S WORTH OF TIME COULD EXIST IN A SINGLE NIGHT'S DREAM WAS RIDICULOUS.

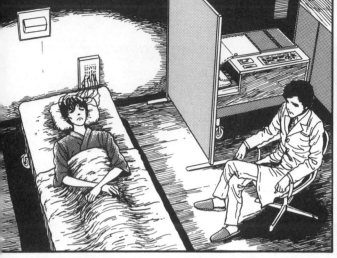

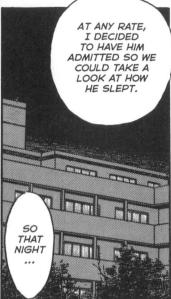

AT ANY RATE, I DECIDED TO HAVE HIM ADMITTED SO WE COULD TAKE A LOOK AT HOW HE SLEPT.

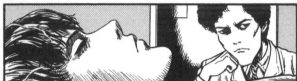

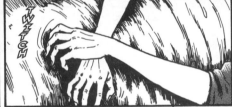

SO THAT NIGHT ...

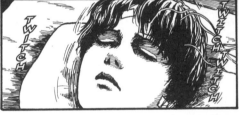

TWITCH TWITCH TWITCH TWITCH

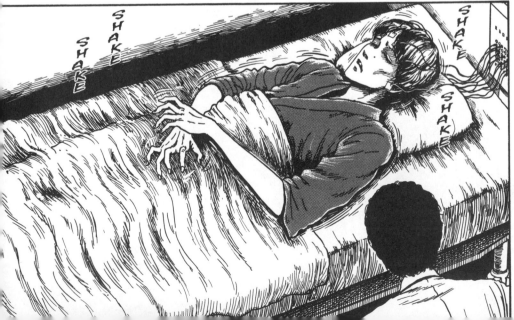

SHAKE SHAKE SHAKE SHAKE SHAKE

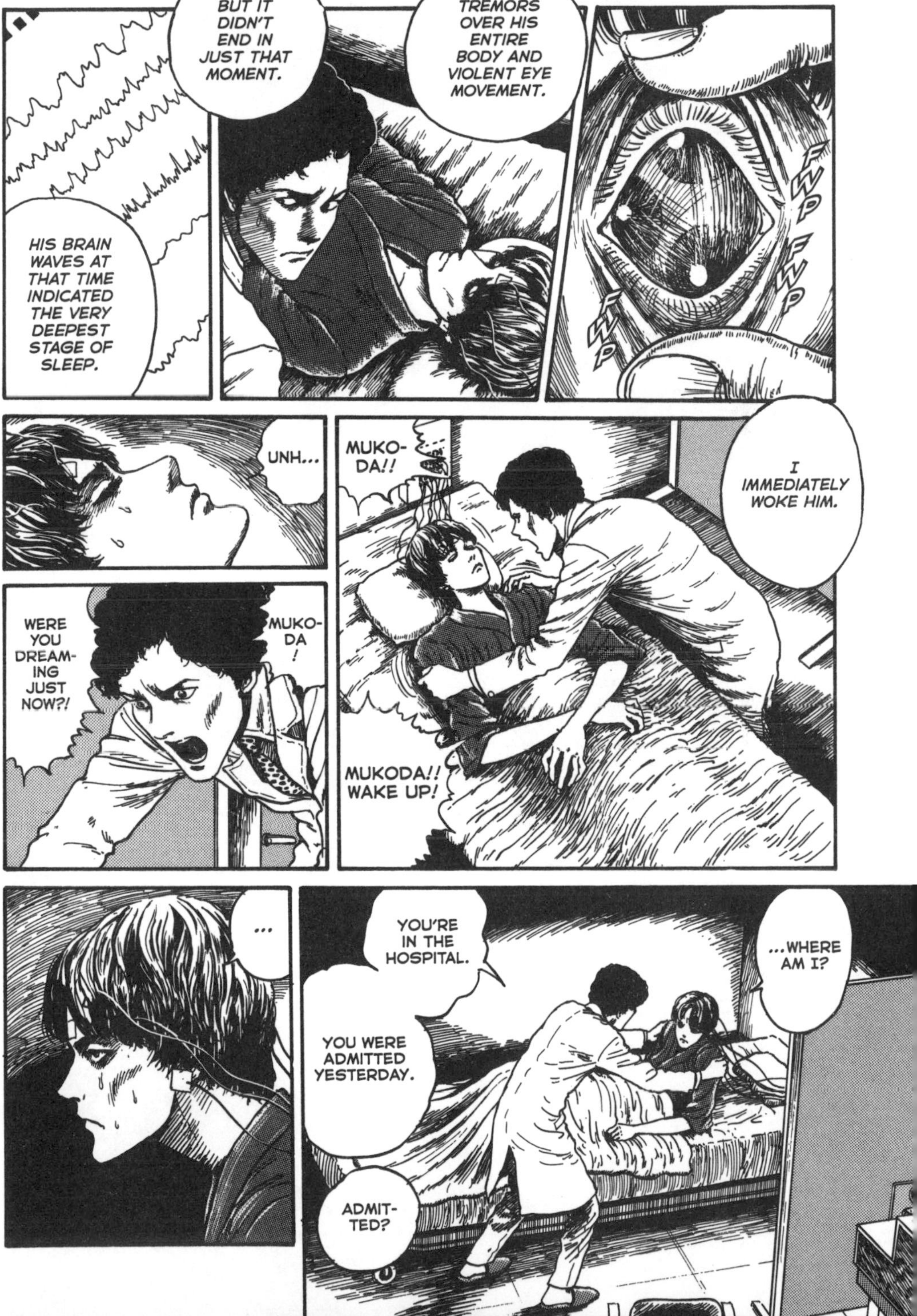
FWP
FWP
FWP
TREMORS OVER HIS ENTIRE BODY AND VIOLENT EYE MOVEMENT.
BUT IT DIDN'T END IN JUST THAT MOMENT.
HIS BRAIN WAVES AT THAT TIME INDICATED THE VERY DEEPEST STAGE OF SLEEP.
I IMMEDIATELY WOKE HIM.
MUKODA!!
MUKODA!! WAKE UP!
UNH...
MUKODA!
WERE YOU DREAMING JUST NOW?!
...WHERE AM I?
YOU'RE IN THE HOSPITAL.
YOU WERE ADMITTED YESTERDAY.
ADMITTED?
...

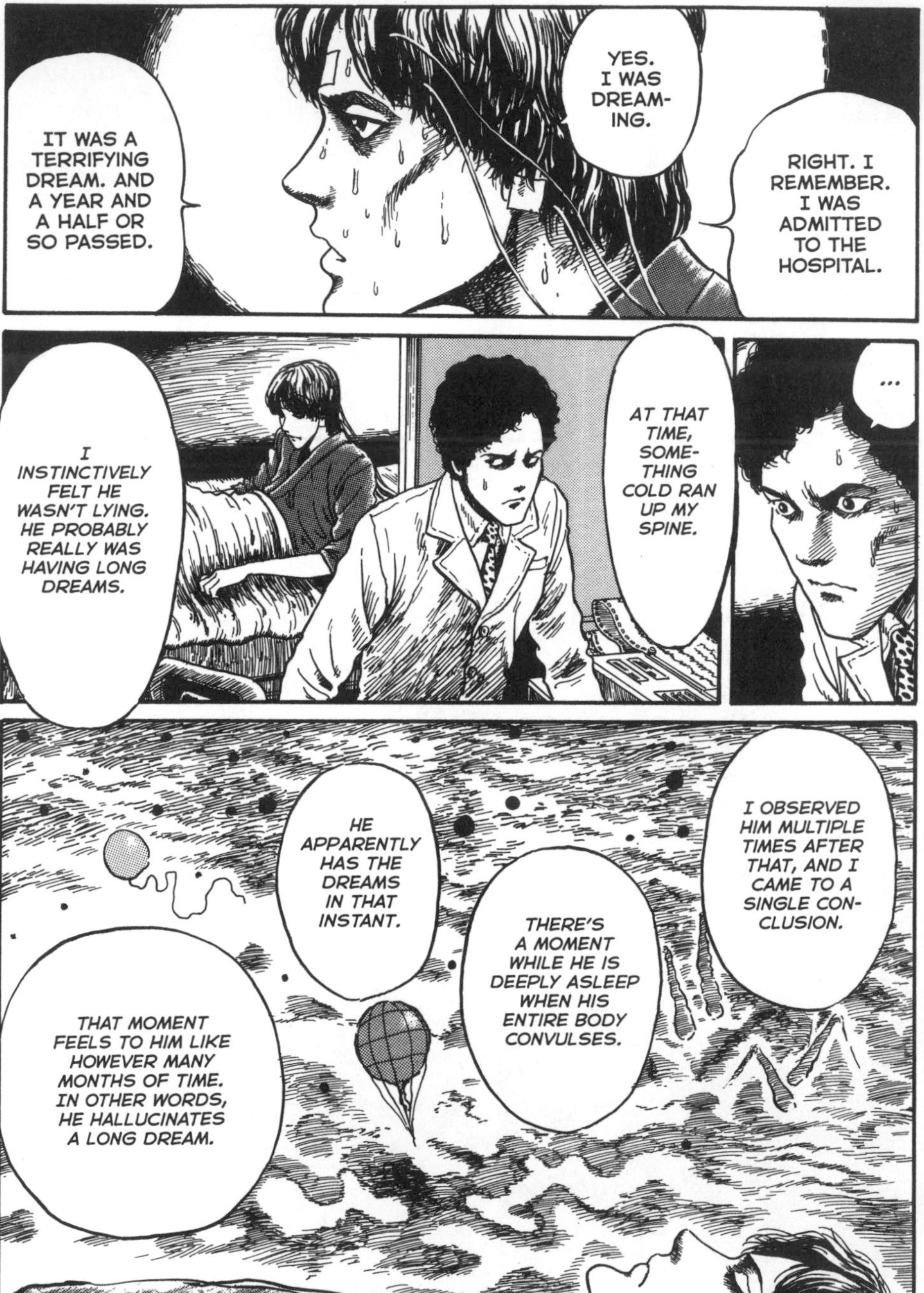
RIGHT. I REMEMBER. I WAS ADMITTED TO THE HOSPITAL.
YES. I WAS DREAM-ING.
IT WAS A TERRIFYING DREAM. AND A YEAR AND A HALF OR SO PASSED.
...
AT THAT TIME, SOME-THING COLD RAN UP MY SPINE.
I INSTINCTIVELY FELT HE WASN'T LYING. HE PROBABLY REALLY WAS HAVING LONG DREAMS.
I OBSERVED HIM MULTIPLE TIMES AFTER THAT, AND I CAME TO A SINGLE CON-CLUSION.
THERE'S A MOMENT WHILE HE IS DEEPLY ASLEEP WHEN HIS ENTIRE BODY CONVULSES.
HE APPARENTLY HAS THE DREAMS IN THAT INSTANT.
THAT MOMENT FEELS TO HIM LIKE HOWEVER MANY MONTHS OF TIME. IN OTHER WORDS, HE HALLUCINATES A LONG DREAM.

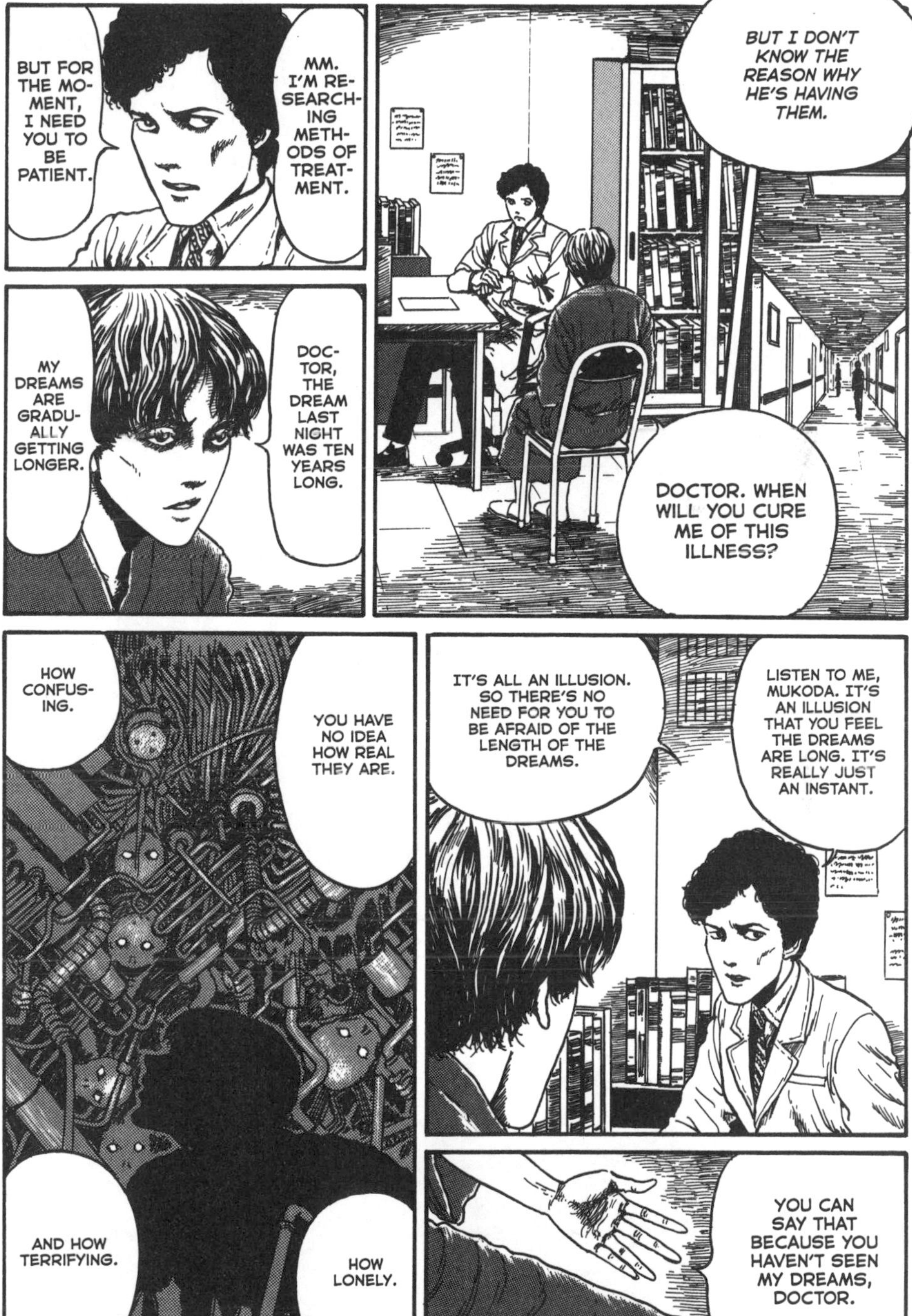
BUT I DON'T KNOW THE REASON WHY HE'S HAVING THEM.
DOCTOR. WHEN WILL YOU CURE ME OF THIS ILLNESS?
MM. I'M RE-SEARCH-ING METH-ODS OF TREAT-MENT.
BUT FOR THE MO-MENT, I NEED YOU TO BE PATIENT.
DOC-TOR, THE DREAM LAST NIGHT WAS TEN YEARS LONG.
MY DREAMS ARE GRADU-ALLY GETTING LONGER.
LISTEN TO ME, MUKODA. IT'S AN ILLUSION THAT YOU FEEL THE DREAMS ARE LONG. IT'S REALLY JUST AN INSTANT.
IT'S ALL AN ILLUSION. SO THERE'S NO NEED FOR YOU TO BE AFRAID OF THE LENGTH OF THE DREAMS.
YOU CAN SAY THAT BECAUSE YOU HAVEN'T SEEN MY DREAMS, DOCTOR.
YOU HAVE NO IDEA HOW REAL THEY ARE.
HOW CONFUS-ING.
HOW LONELY.
AND HOW TERRIFYING.

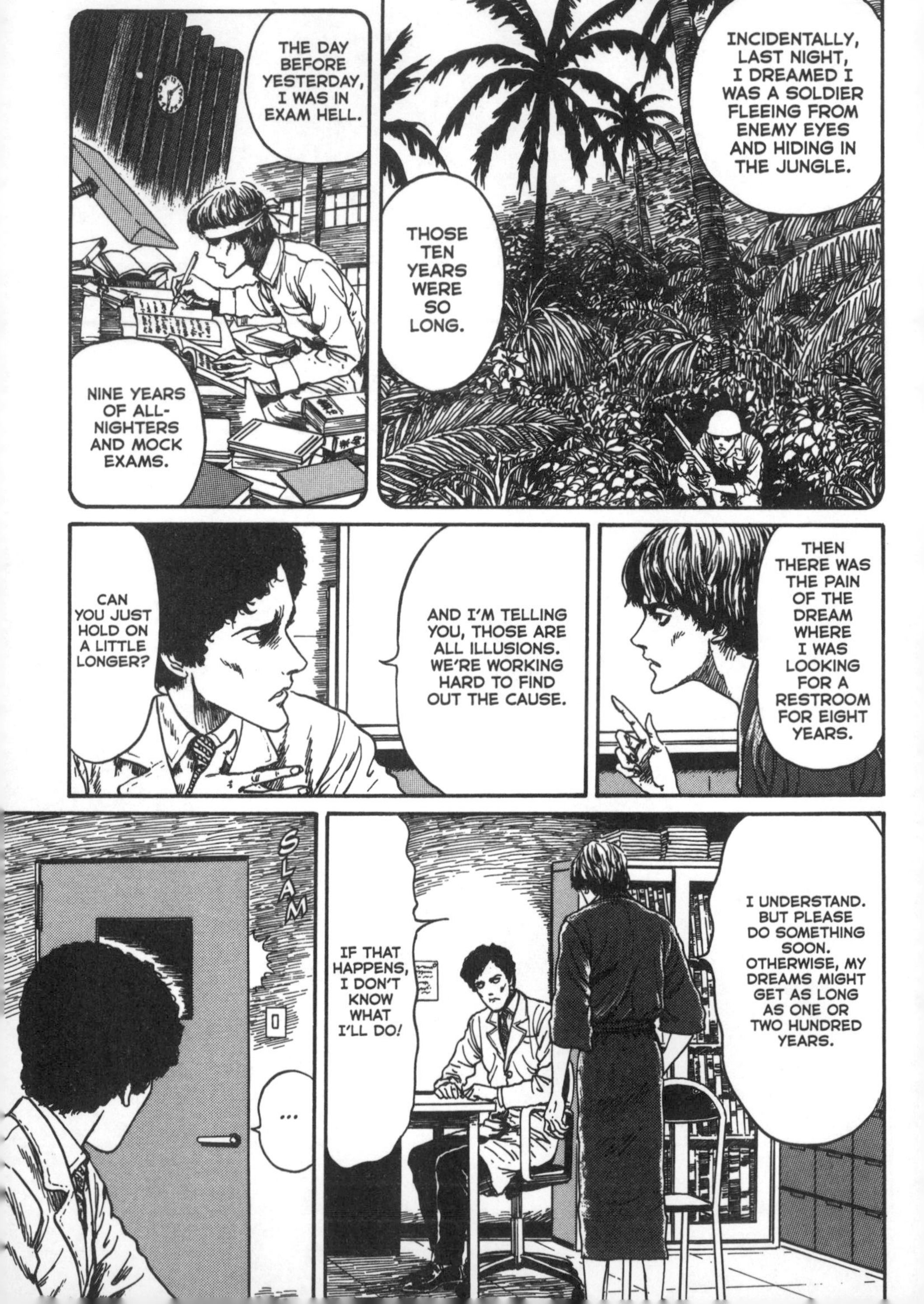
INCIDENTALLY, LAST NIGHT, I DREAMED I WAS A SOLDIER FLEEING FROM ENEMY EYES AND HIDING IN THE JUNGLE.
THOSE TEN YEARS WERE SO LONG.
THE DAY BEFORE YESTERDAY, I WAS IN EXAM HELL.
NINE YEARS OF ALL-NIGHTERS AND MOCK EXAMS.
THEN THERE WAS THE PAIN OF THE DREAM WHERE I WAS LOOKING FOR A RESTROOM FOR EIGHT YEARS.
AND I'M TELLING YOU, THOSE ARE ALL ILLUSIONS. WE'RE WORKING HARD TO FIND OUT THE CAUSE.
CAN YOU JUST HOLD ON A LITTLE LONGER?
I UNDERSTAND. BUT PLEASE DO SOMETHING SOON. OTHERWISE, MY DREAMS MIGHT GET AS LONG AS ONE OR TWO HUNDRED YEARS.
IF THAT HAPPENS, I DON'T KNOW WHAT I'LL DO!
SLAM
...

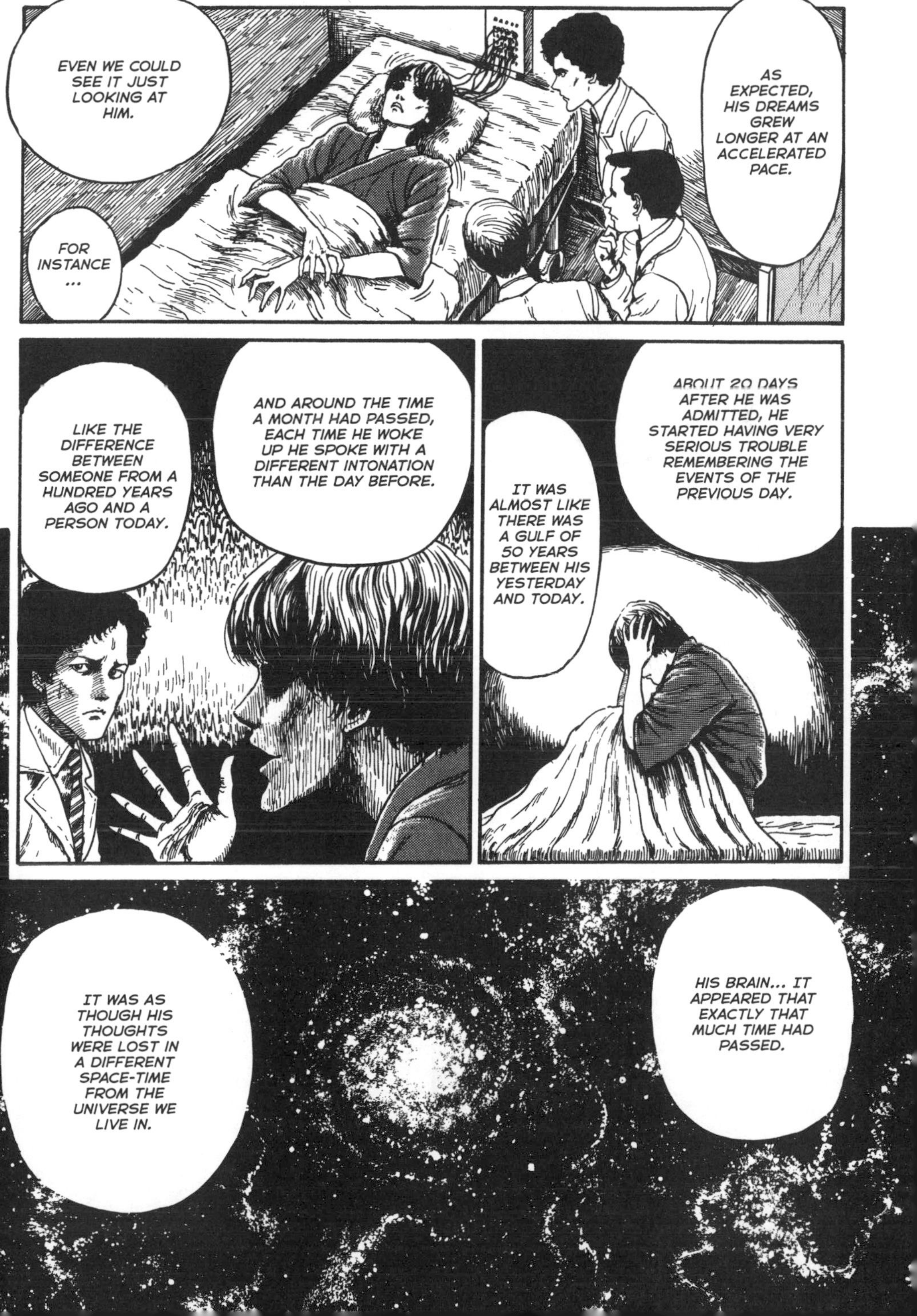
AS EXPECTED, HIS DREAMS GREW LONGER AT AN ACCELERATED PACE.
EVEN WE COULD SEE IT JUST LOOKING AT HIM.
FOR INSTANCE ...
ABOUT 20 DAYS AFTER HE WAS ADMITTED, HE STARTED HAVING VERY SERIOUS TROUBLE REMEMBERING THE EVENTS OF THE PREVIOUS DAY.
IT WAS ALMOST LIKE THERE WAS A GULF OF 50 YEARS BETWEEN HIS YESTERDAY AND TODAY.
AND AROUND THE TIME A MONTH HAD PASSED, EACH TIME HE WOKE UP HE SPOKE WITH A DIFFERENT INTONATION THAN THE DAY BEFORE.
LIKE THE DIFFERENCE BETWEEN SOMEONE FROM A HUNDRED YEARS AGO AND A PERSON TODAY.
HIS BRAIN... IT APPEARED THAT EXACTLY THAT MUCH TIME HAD PASSED.
IT WAS AS THOUGH HIS THOUGHTS WERE LOST IN A DIFFERENT SPACE-TIME FROM THE UNIVERSE WE LIVE IN.

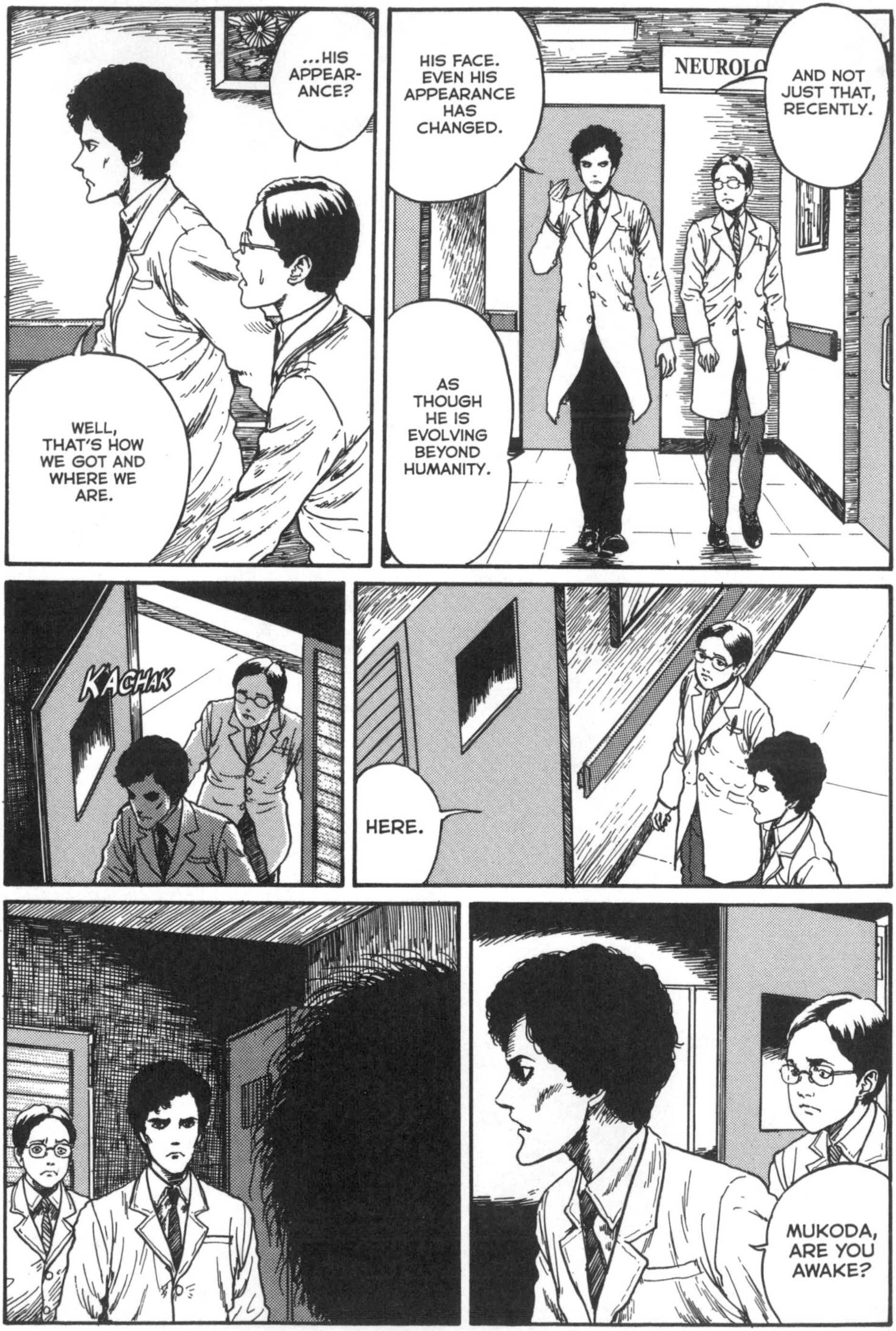
NEUROLO
AND NOT JUST THAT, RECENTLY.
HIS FACE. EVEN HIS APPEARANCE HAS CHANGED.
AS THOUGH HE IS EVOLVING BEYOND HUMANITY.
...HIS APPEARANCE?
WELL, THAT'S HOW WE GOT AND WHERE WE ARE.
HERE.
KACHAK
MUKODA, ARE YOU AWAKE?

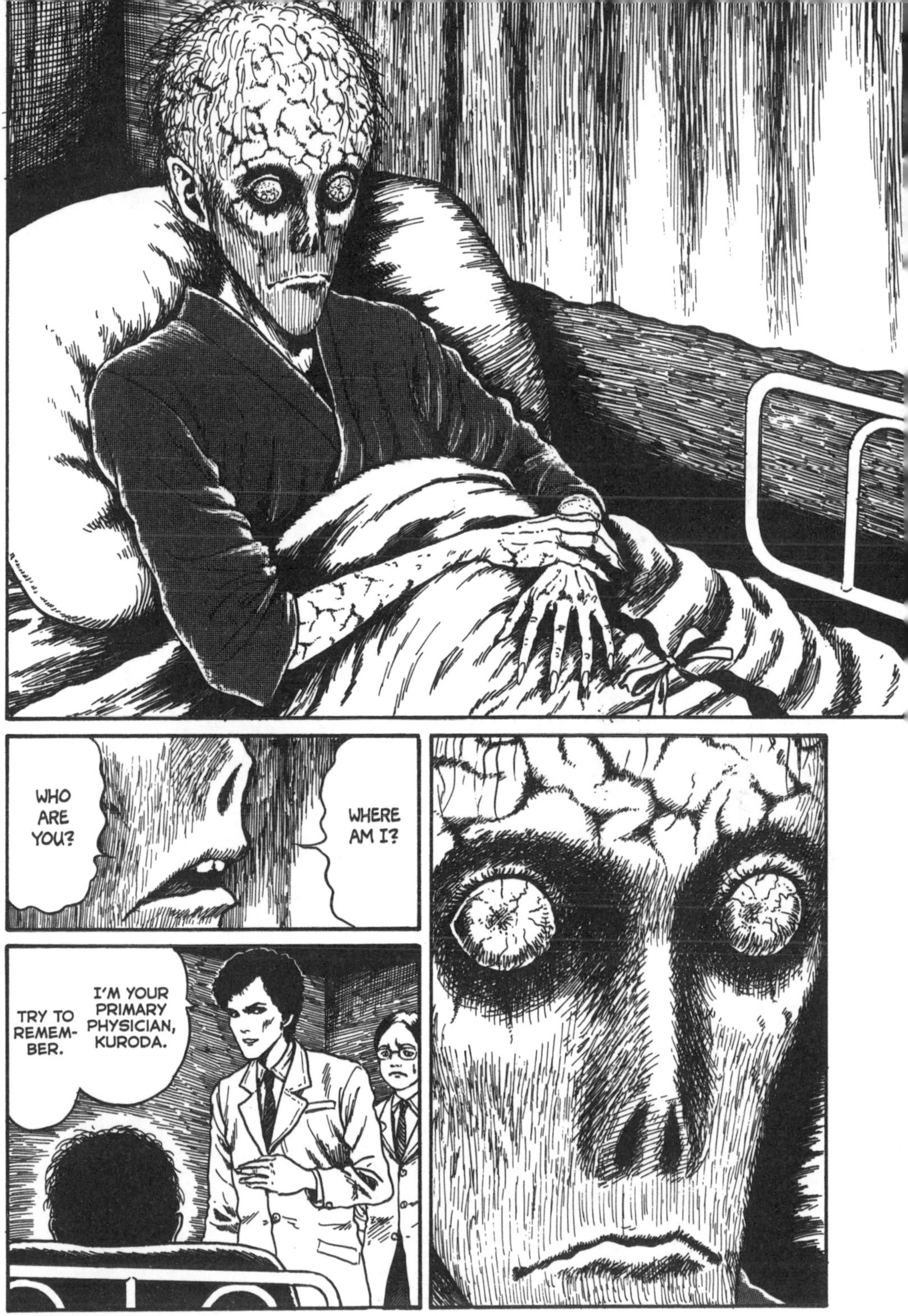
WHERE AM I?
WHO ARE YOU?
I'M YOUR PRIMARY PHYSICIAN, KURODA.
TRY TO REMEM-BER.

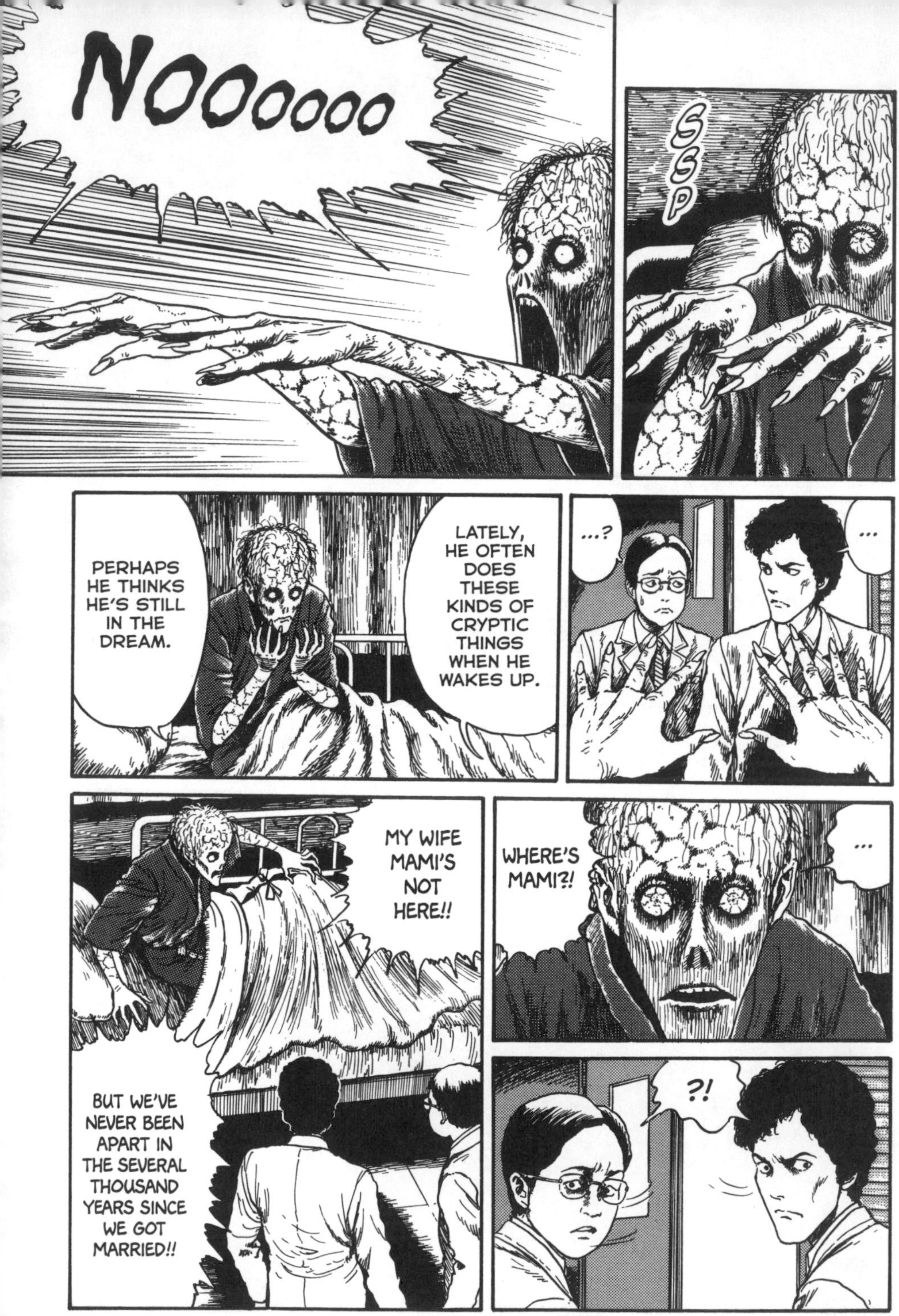
SSP
NOOOOOO
...
...?
LATELY, HE OFTEN DOES THESE KINDS OF CRYPTIC THINGS WHEN HE WAKES UP.
PERHAPS HE THINKS HE'S STILL IN THE DREAM.
...
WHERE'S MAMI?!
?!
MY WIFE MAMI'S NOT HERE!!
BUT WE'VE NEVER BEEN APART IN THE SEVERAL THOUSAND YEARS SINCE WE GOT MARRIED!!

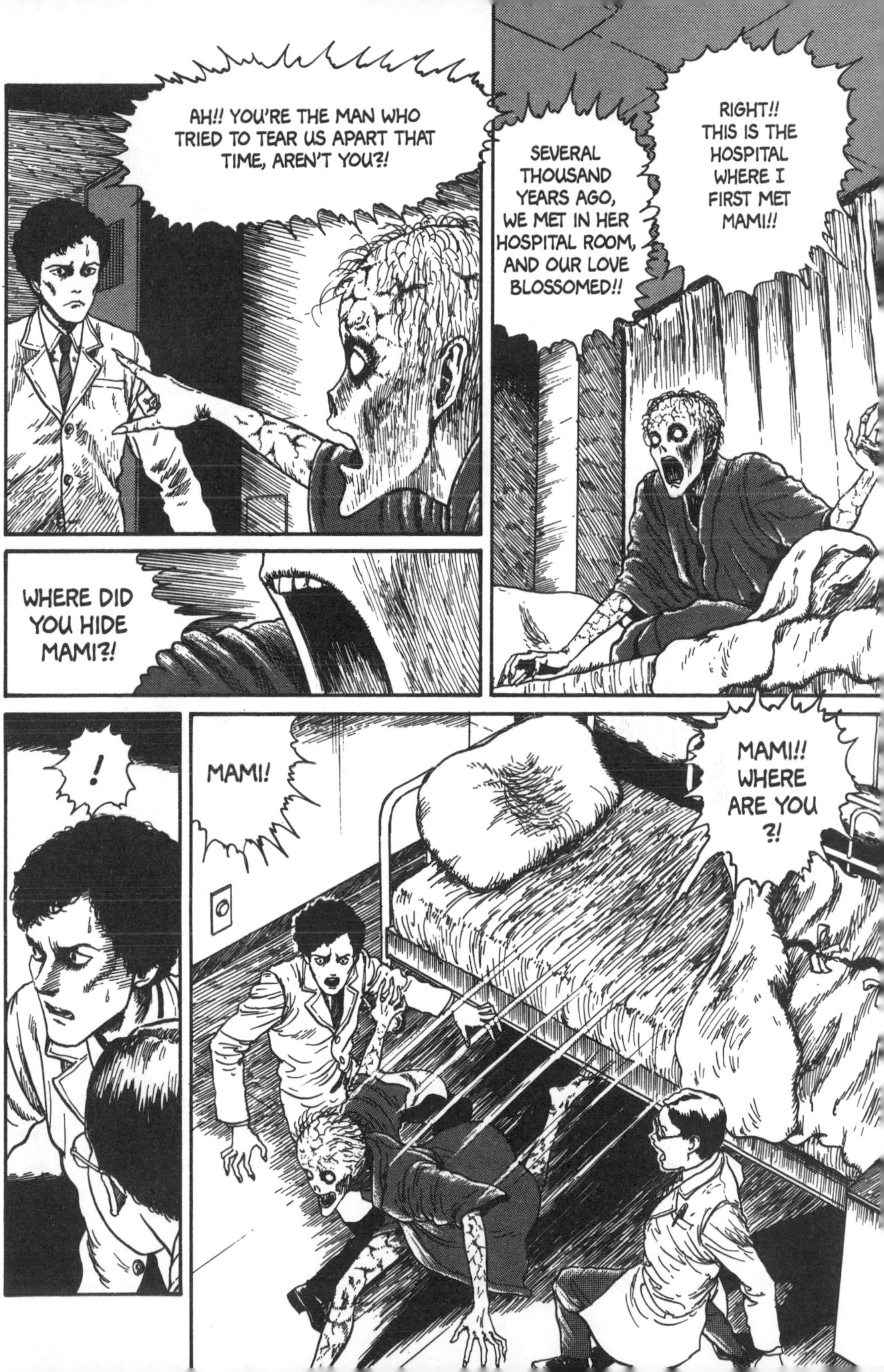
RIGHT!! THIS IS THE HOSPITAL WHERE I FIRST MET MAMI!!
SEVERAL THOUSAND YEARS AGO, WE MET IN HER HOSPITAL ROOM, AND OUR LOVE BLOSSOMED!!
AH!! YOU'RE THE MAN WHO TRIED TO TEAR US APART THAT TIME, AREN'T YOU?!
WHERE DID YOU HIDE MAMI?!
MAMI!! WHERE ARE YOU ?!
MAMI!
!

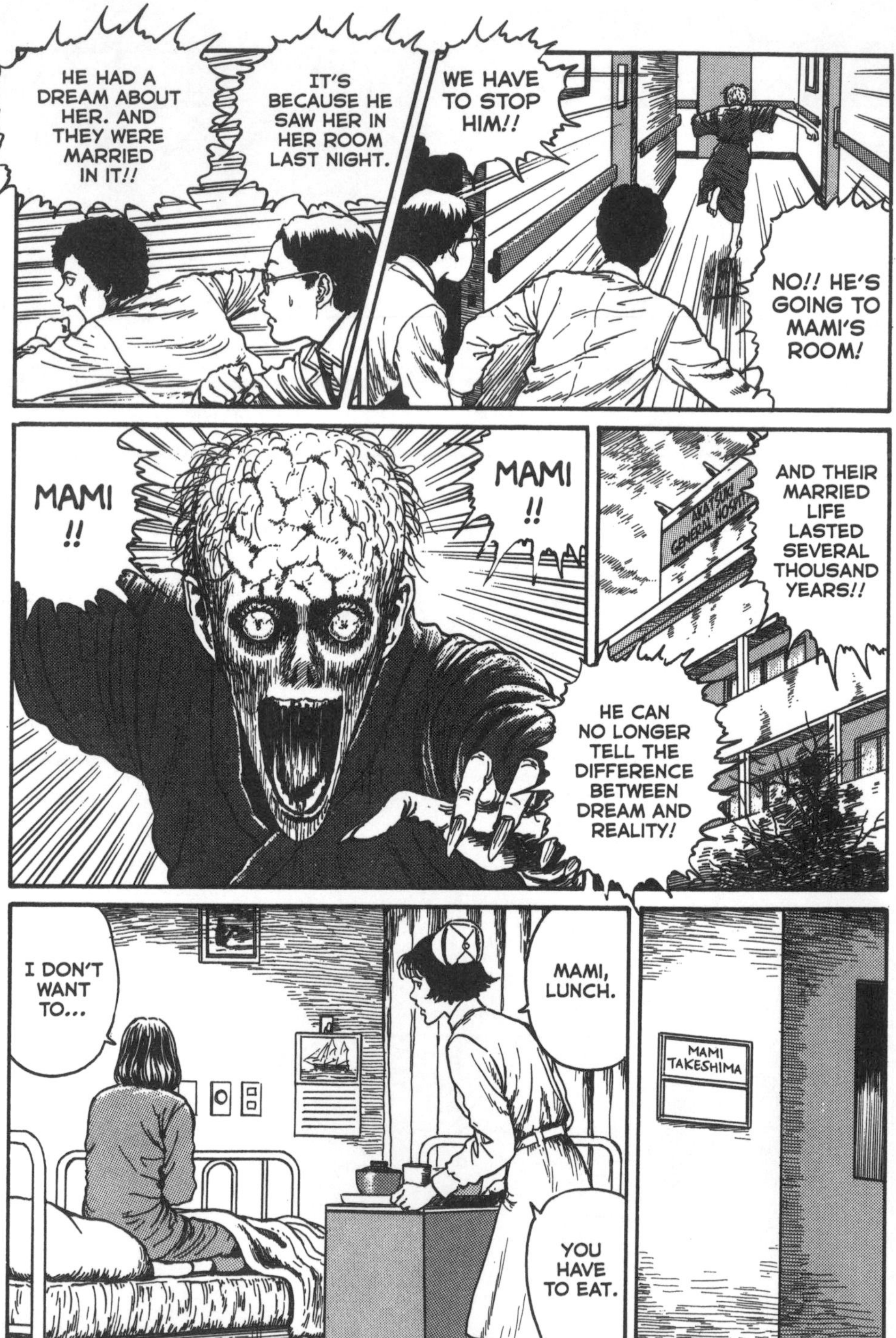
WE HAVE TO STOP HIM!!
NO!! HE'S GOING TO MAMI'S ROOM!
IT'S BECAUSE HE SAW HER IN HER ROOM LAST NIGHT.
HE HAD A DREAM ABOUT HER. AND THEY WERE MARRIED IN IT!!
AND THEIR MARRIED LIFE LASTED SEVERAL THOUSAND YEARS!!
HE CAN NO LONGER TELL THE DIFFERENCE BETWEEN DREAM AND REALITY!
MAMI !!
MAMI !!
MAMI TAKESHIMA
MAMI, LUNCH.
I DON'T WANT TO...
YOU HAVE TO EAT.

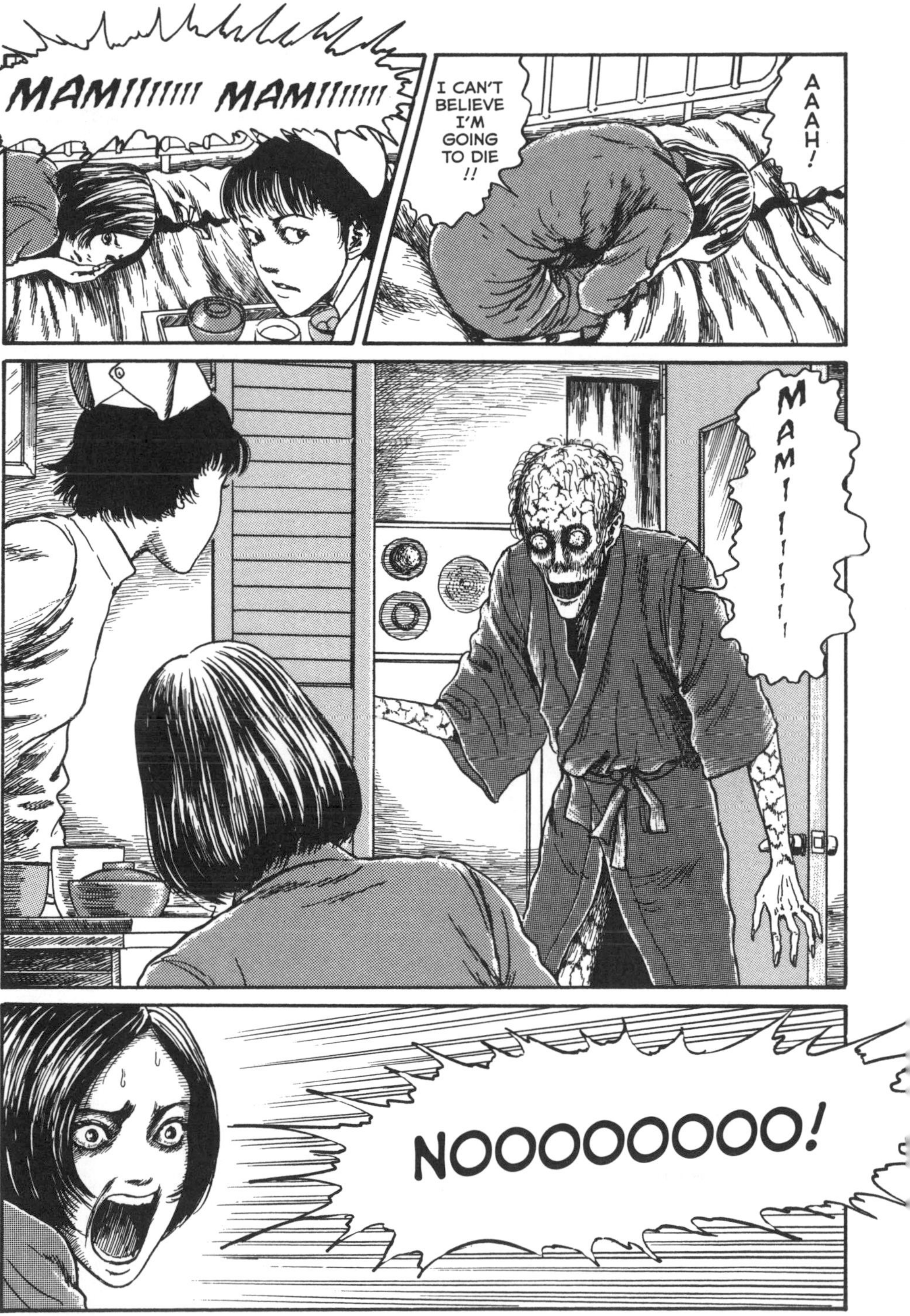
AAAH!
I CAN'T BELIEVE I'M GOING TO DIE!!
MAMI!!!!!! MAMI!!!!!!
MAMI!!!!!!
NOOOOOOOOO!

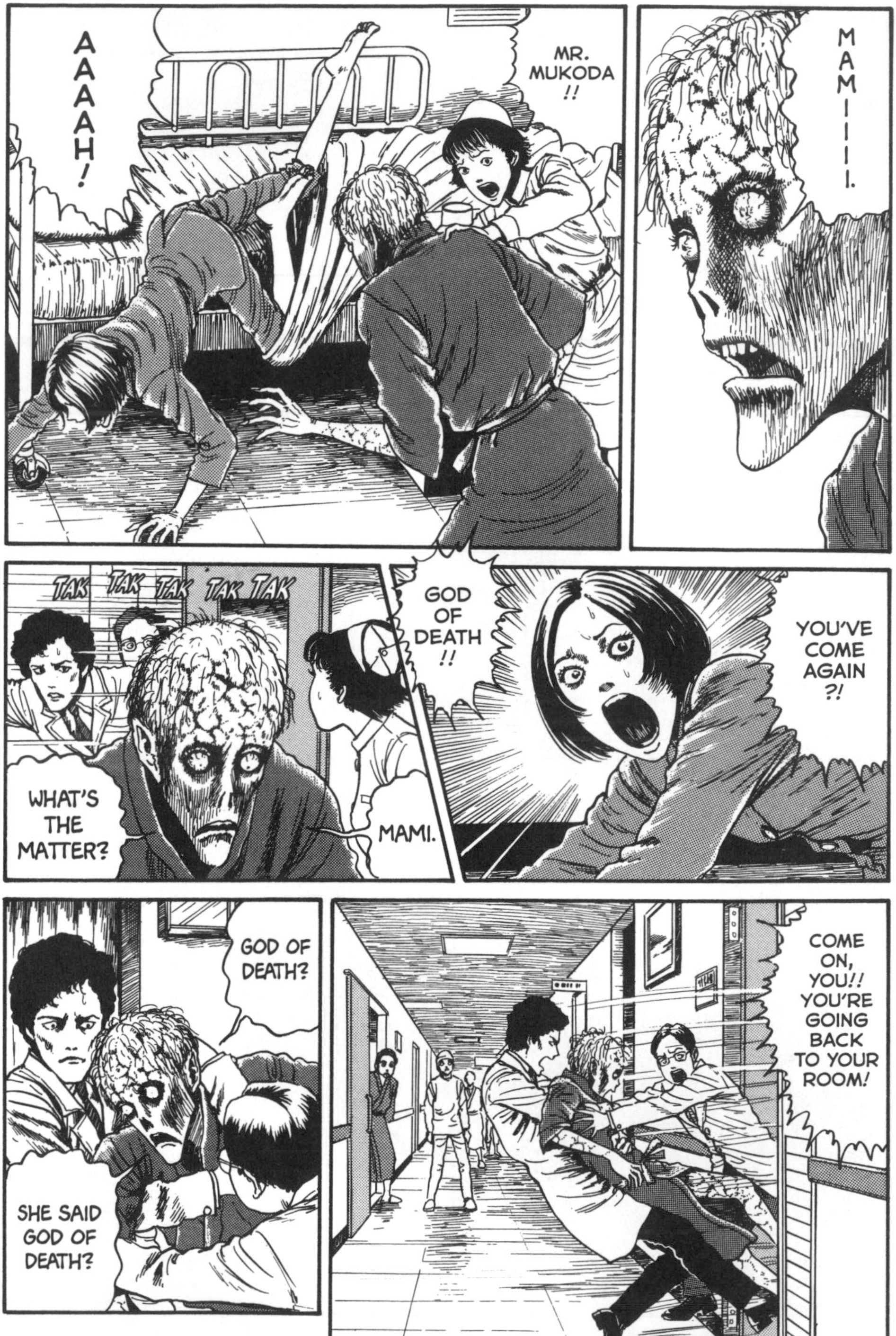

MAMIIII.
MR. MUKODA!!
AAAAAH!
GOD OF DEATH!!
YOU'VE COME AGAIN?!
TAK TAK TAK TAK TAK
MAMI.
WHAT'S THE MATTER?
COME ON, YOU!! YOU'RE GOING BACK TO YOUR ROOM!
GOD OF DEATH?
SHE SAID GOD OF DEATH?

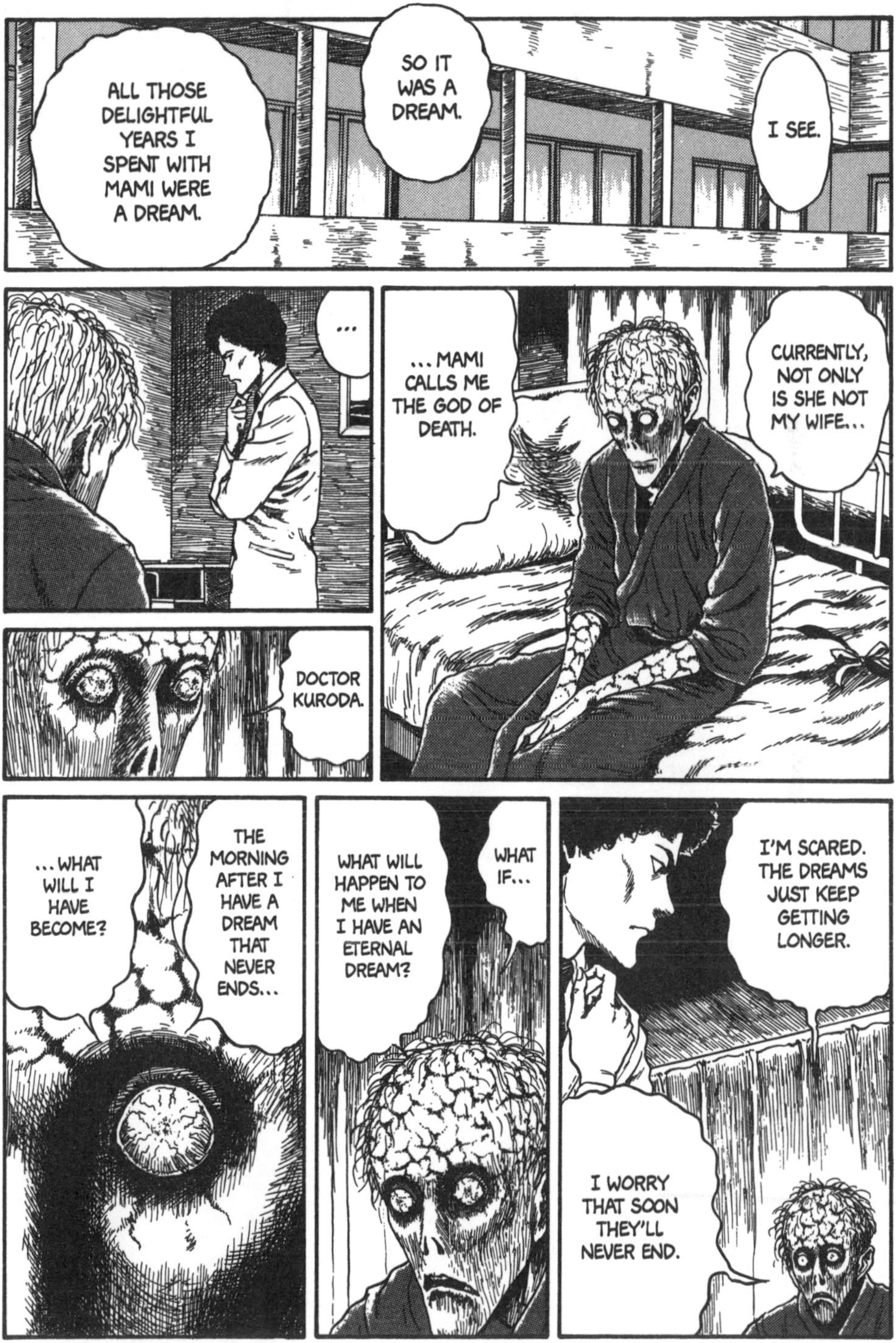
I SEE.
SO IT WAS A DREAM.
ALL THOSE DELIGHTFUL YEARS I SPENT WITH MAMI WERE A DREAM.
CURRENTLY, NOT ONLY IS SHE NOT MY WIFE...
...MAMI CALLS ME THE GOD OF DEATH.
...
DOCTOR KURODA.
I'M SCARED. THE DREAMS JUST KEEP GETTING LONGER.
I WORRY THAT SOON THEY'LL NEVER END.
WHAT IF...
WHAT WILL HAPPEN TO ME WHEN I HAVE AN ETERNAL DREAM?
THE MORNING AFTER I HAVE A DREAM THAT NEVER ENDS...
...WHAT WILL I HAVE BECOME?

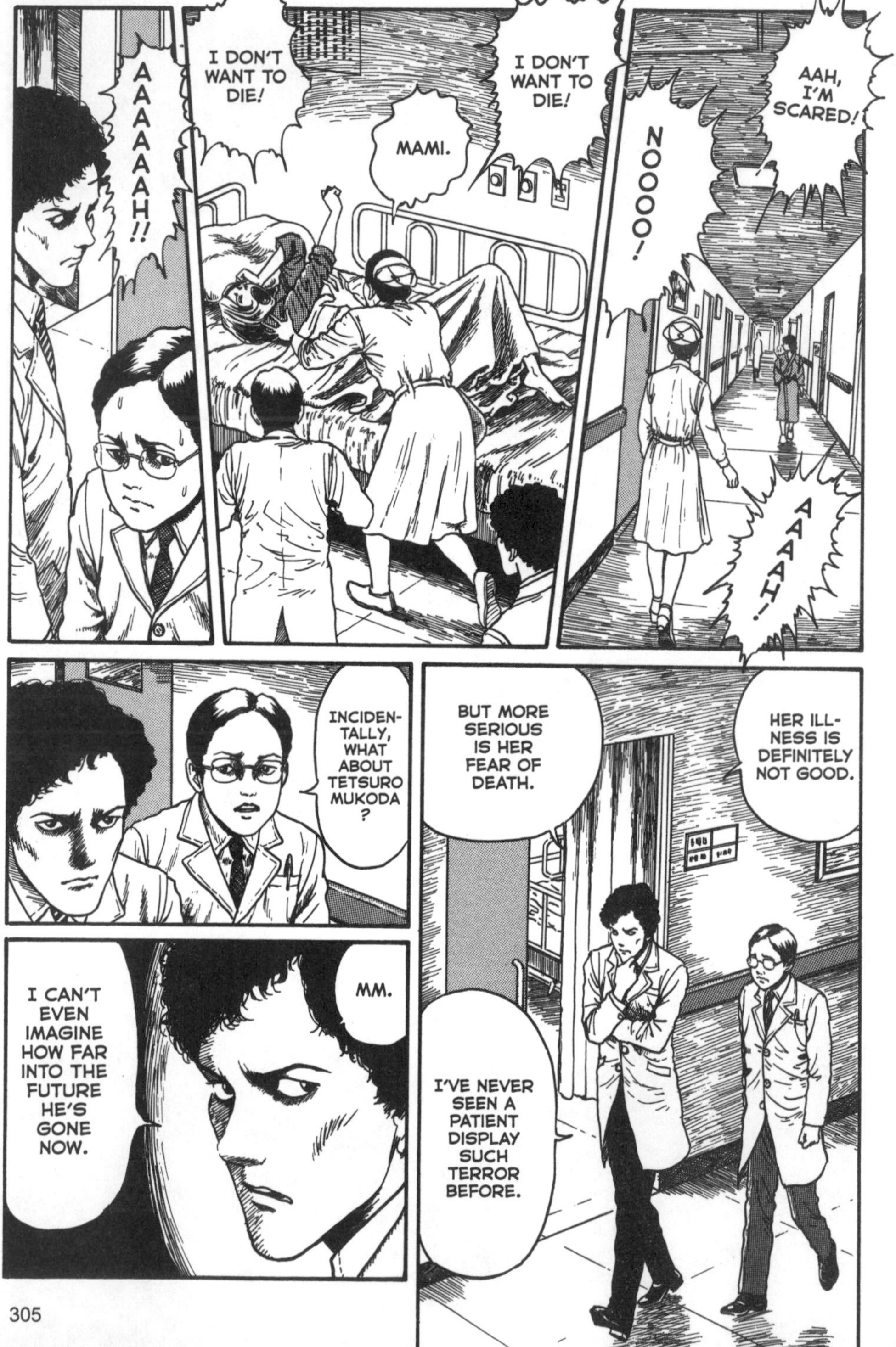
AAH, I'M SCARED!
NOOOO!
AAAAH!
I DON'T WANT TO DIE!
I DON'T WANT TO DIE!
MAMI.
AAAAAAAH!!
HER ILLNESS IS DEFINITELY NOT GOOD.
BUT MORE SERIOUS IS HER FEAR OF DEATH.
I'VE NEVER SEEN A PATIENT DISPLAY SUCH TERROR BEFORE.
INCIDENTALLY, WHAT ABOUT TETSURO MUKODA?
MM.
I CAN'T EVEN IMAGINE HOW FAR INTO THE FUTURE HE'S GONE NOW.

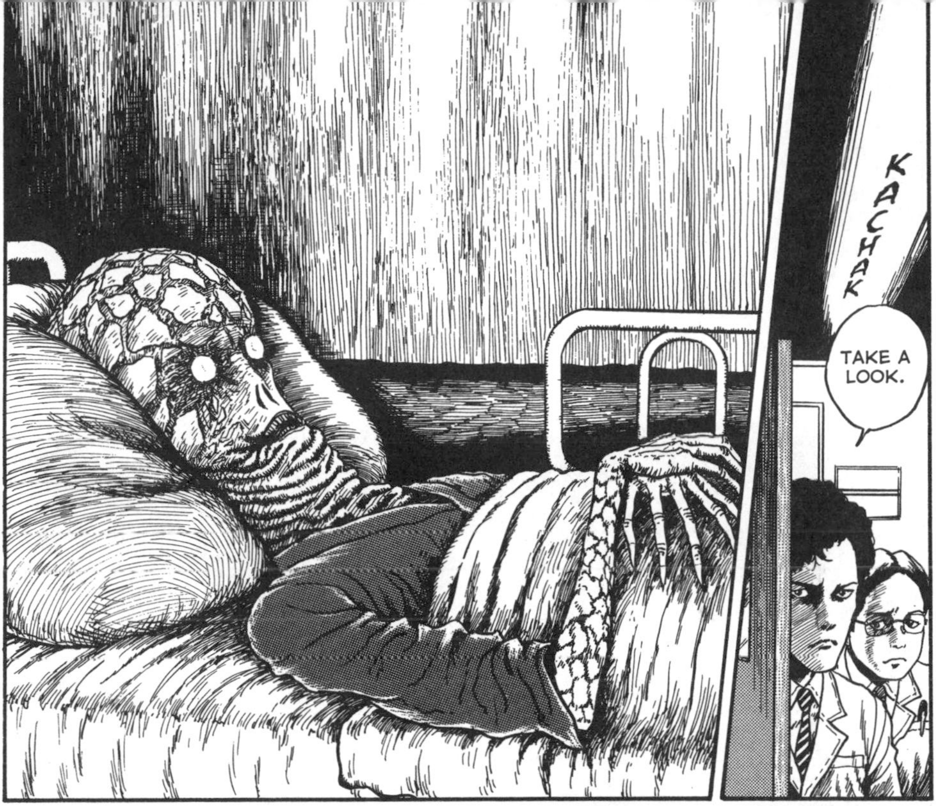
KACHAK
TAKE A LOOK.
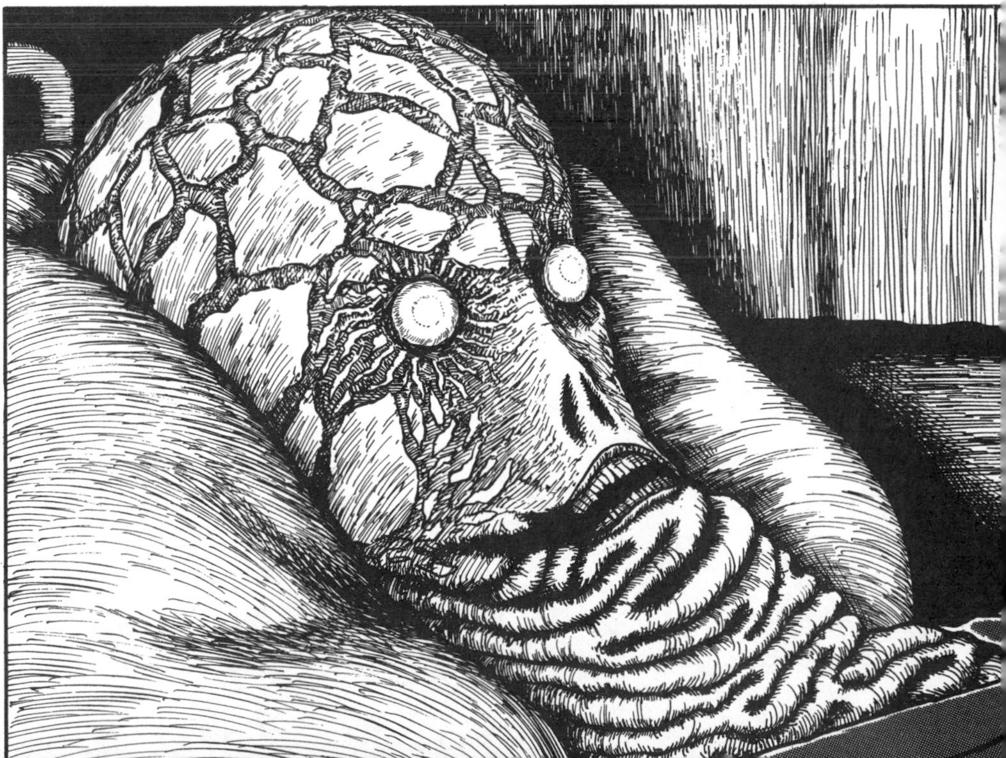

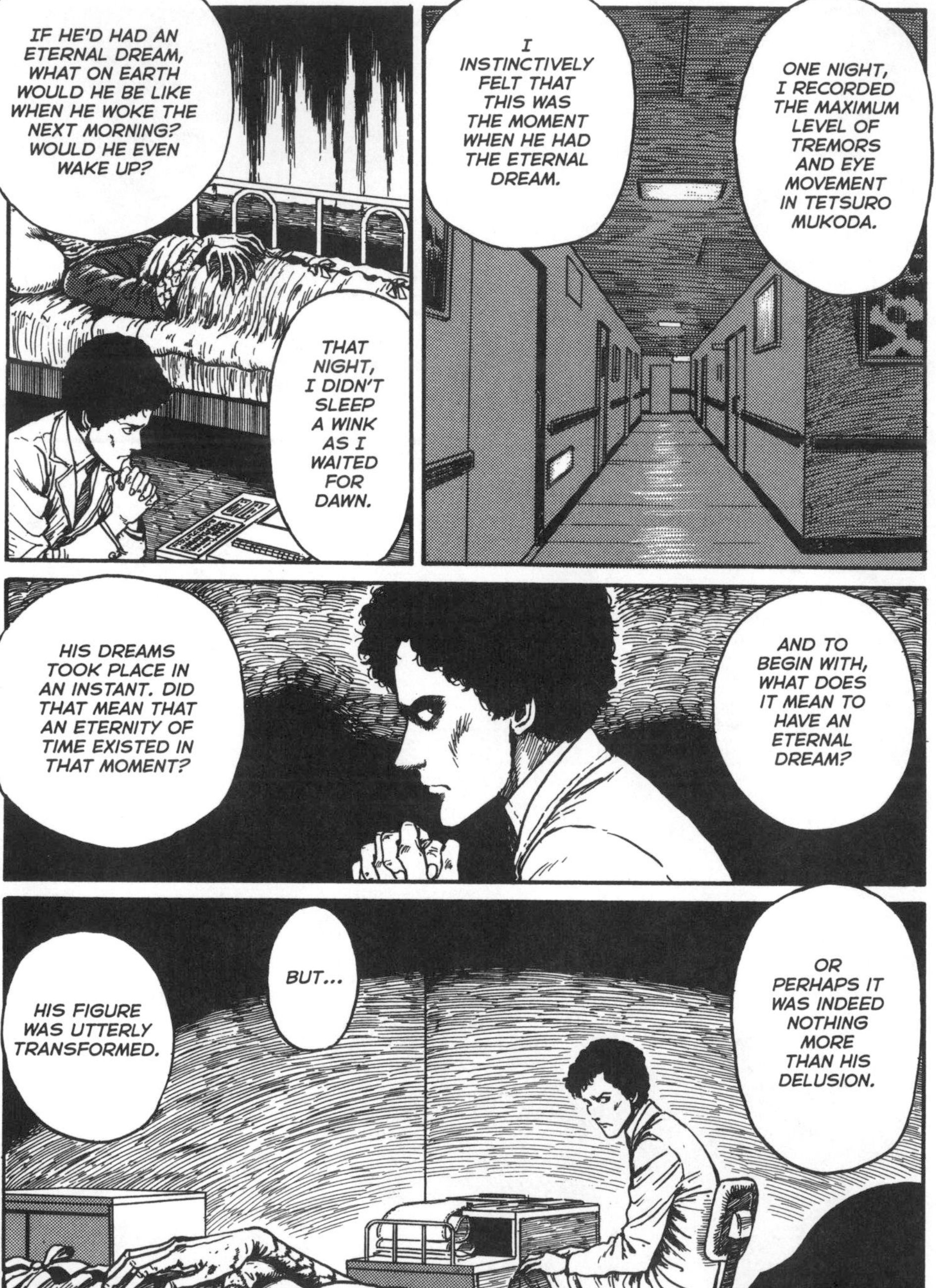
ONE NIGHT, I RECORDED THE MAXIMUM LEVEL OF TREMORS AND EYE MOVEMENT IN TETSURO MUKODA.
I INSTINCTIVELY FELT THAT THIS WAS THE MOMENT WHEN HE HAD THE ETERNAL DREAM.
THAT NIGHT, I DIDN'T SLEEP A WINK AS I WAITED FOR DAWN.
IF HE'D HAD AN ETERNAL DREAM, WHAT ON EARTH WOULD HE BE LIKE WHEN HE WOKE THE NEXT MORNING? WOULD HE EVEN WAKE UP?
AND TO BEGIN WITH, WHAT DOES IT MEAN TO HAVE AN ETERNAL DREAM?
HIS DREAMS TOOK PLACE IN AN INSTANT. DID THAT MEAN THAT AN ETERNITY OF TIME EXISTED IN THAT MOMENT?
OR PERHAPS IT WAS INDEED NOTHING MORE THAN HIS DELUSION.
BUT...
HIS FIGURE WAS UTTERLY TRANSFORMED.

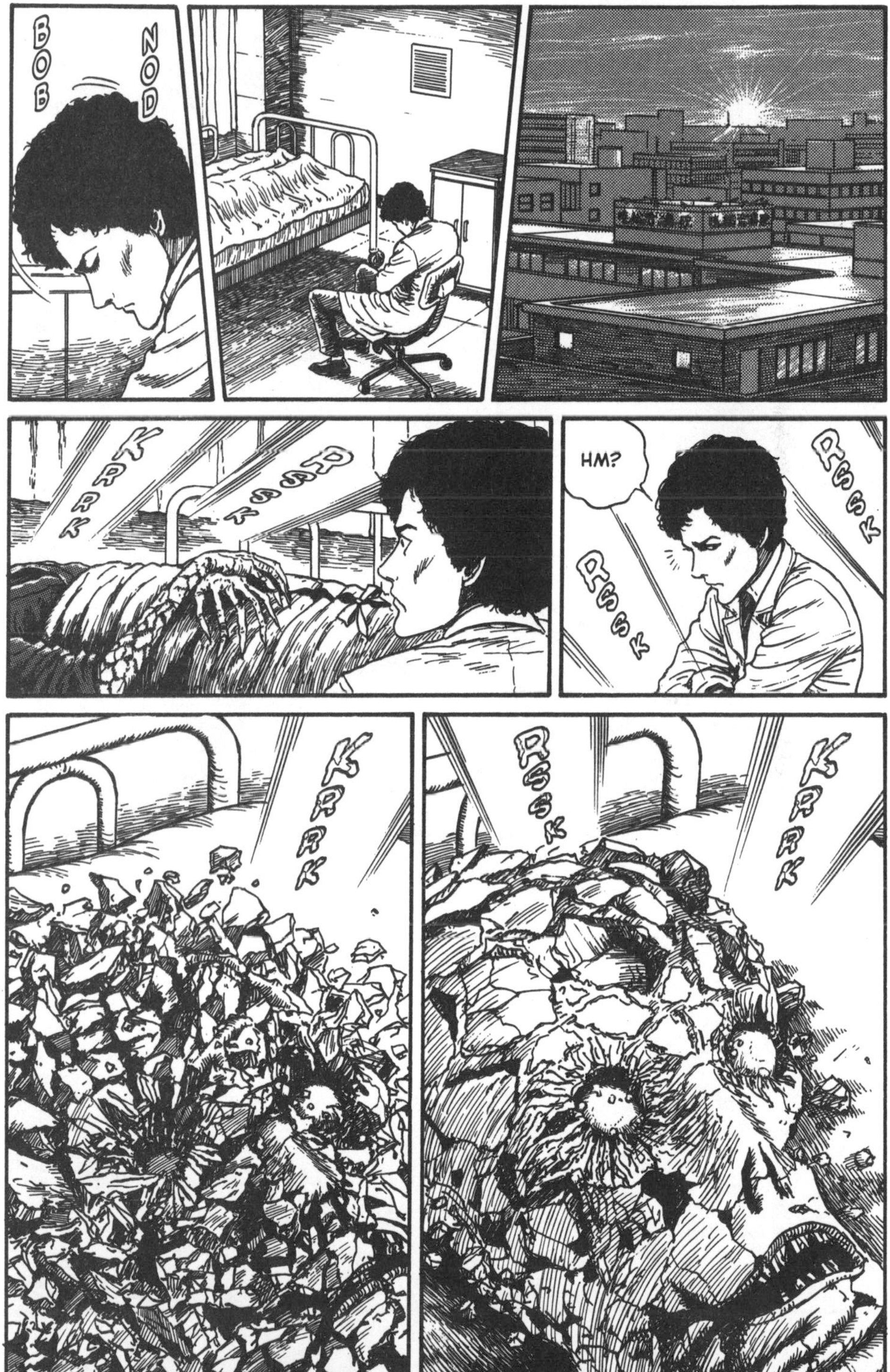
NOD
BOB
RSSK
HM?
RSSK
RSSK
KRRRK
KRRRK
RSSK
KRRRK

KRRK
KRRK
HYOOOO
FWSH
FWSH
FWSH
FWSH

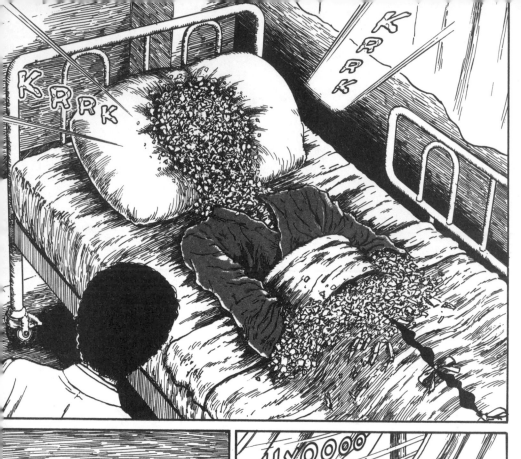

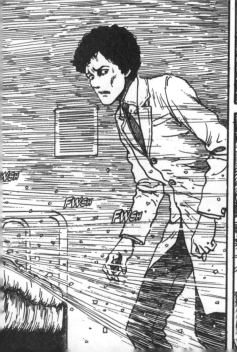

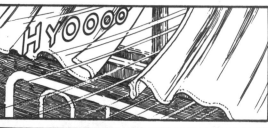

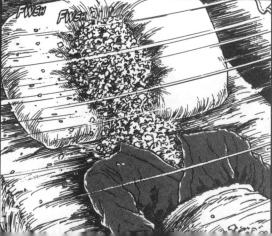

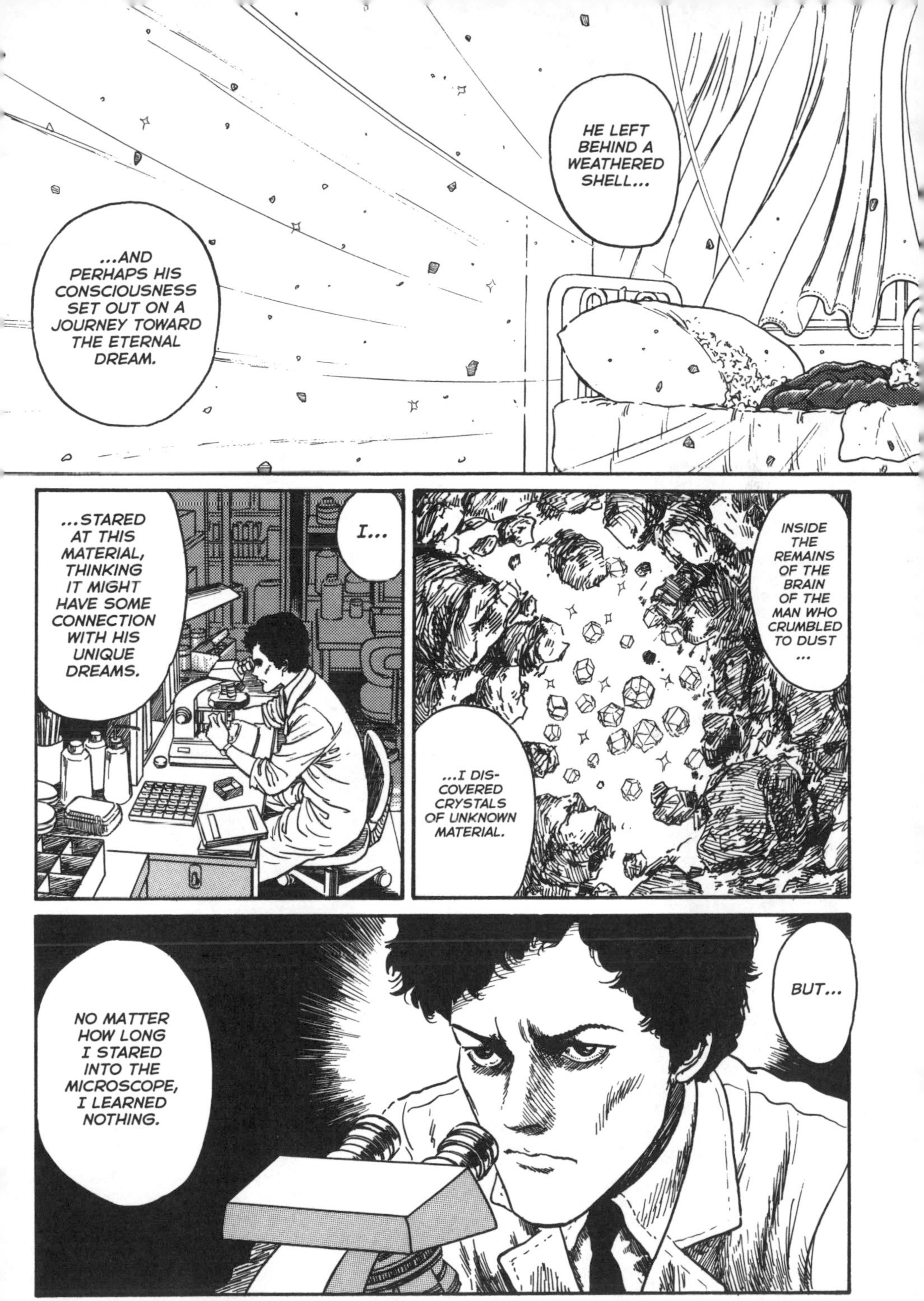
HE LEFT BEHIND A WEATHERED SHELL...
...AND PERHAPS HIS CONSCIOUSNESS SET OUT ON A JOURNEY TOWARD THE ETERNAL DREAM.
INSIDE THE REMAINS OF THE BRAIN OF THE MAN WHO CRUMBLED TO DUST ...
...I DISCOVERED CRYSTALS OF UNKNOWN MATERIAL.
I...
...STARED AT THIS MATERIAL, THINKING IT MIGHT HAVE SOME CONNECTION WITH HIS UNIQUE DREAMS.
BUT...
NO MATTER HOW LONG I STARED INTO THE MICROSCOPE, I LEARNED NOTHING.

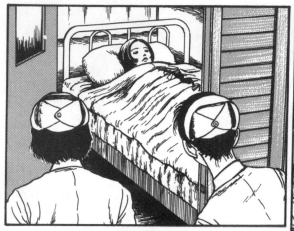

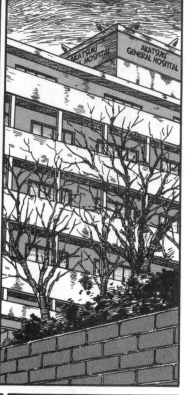

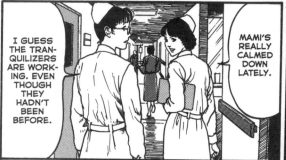

AKATSUKI GENERAL HOSPITAL
MAMI'S REALLY CALMED DOWN LATELY.
I GUESS THE TRANQUILIZERS ARE WORKING. EVEN THOUGH THEY HADN'T BEEN BEFORE.
MAMI, HOW ARE YOU FEELING?
DOCTOR KURODA, ...
I FEEL A LITTLE BETTER TODAY.
HM. YOU DO?

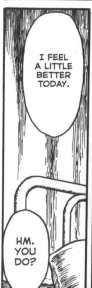

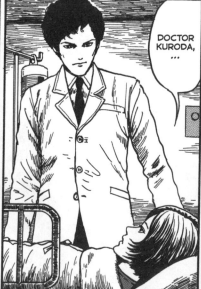

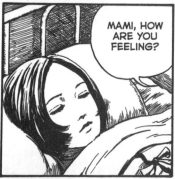

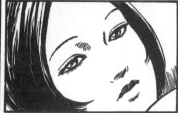

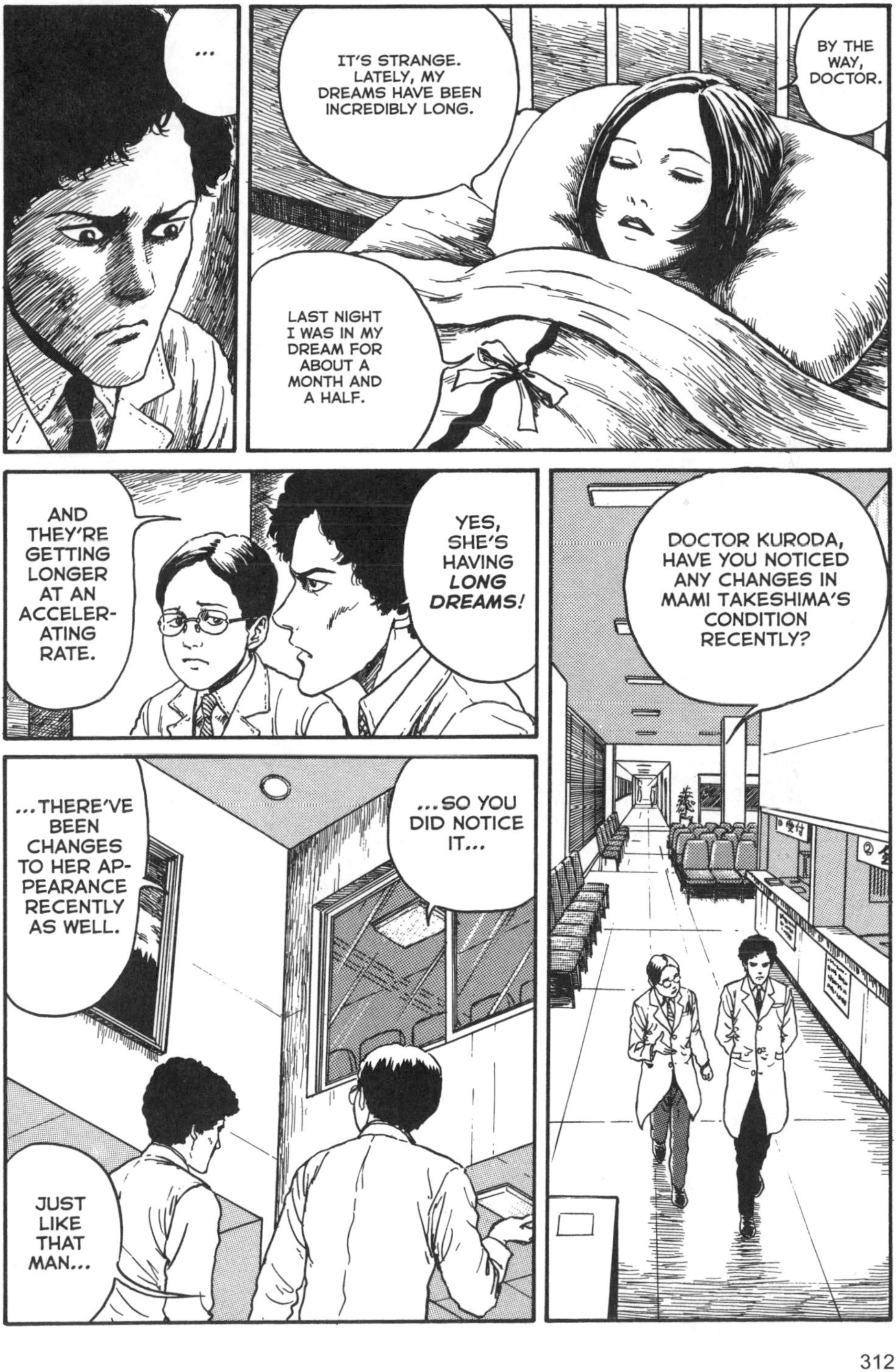
BY THE WAY, DOCTOR.
IT'S STRANGE. LATELY, MY DREAMS HAVE BEEN INCREDIBLY LONG.
LAST NIGHT I WAS IN MY DREAM FOR ABOUT A MONTH AND A HALF.
...
DOCTOR KURODA, HAVE YOU NOTICED ANY CHANGES IN MAMI TAKESHIMA'S CONDITION RECENTLY?
YES, SHE'S HAVING *LONG DREAMS!*
AND THEY'RE GETTING LONGER AT AN ACCELER-ATING RATE.
...SO YOU DID NOTICE IT...
...THERE'VE BEEN CHANGES TO HER AP-PEARANCE RECENTLY AS WELL.
JUST LIKE THAT MAN...

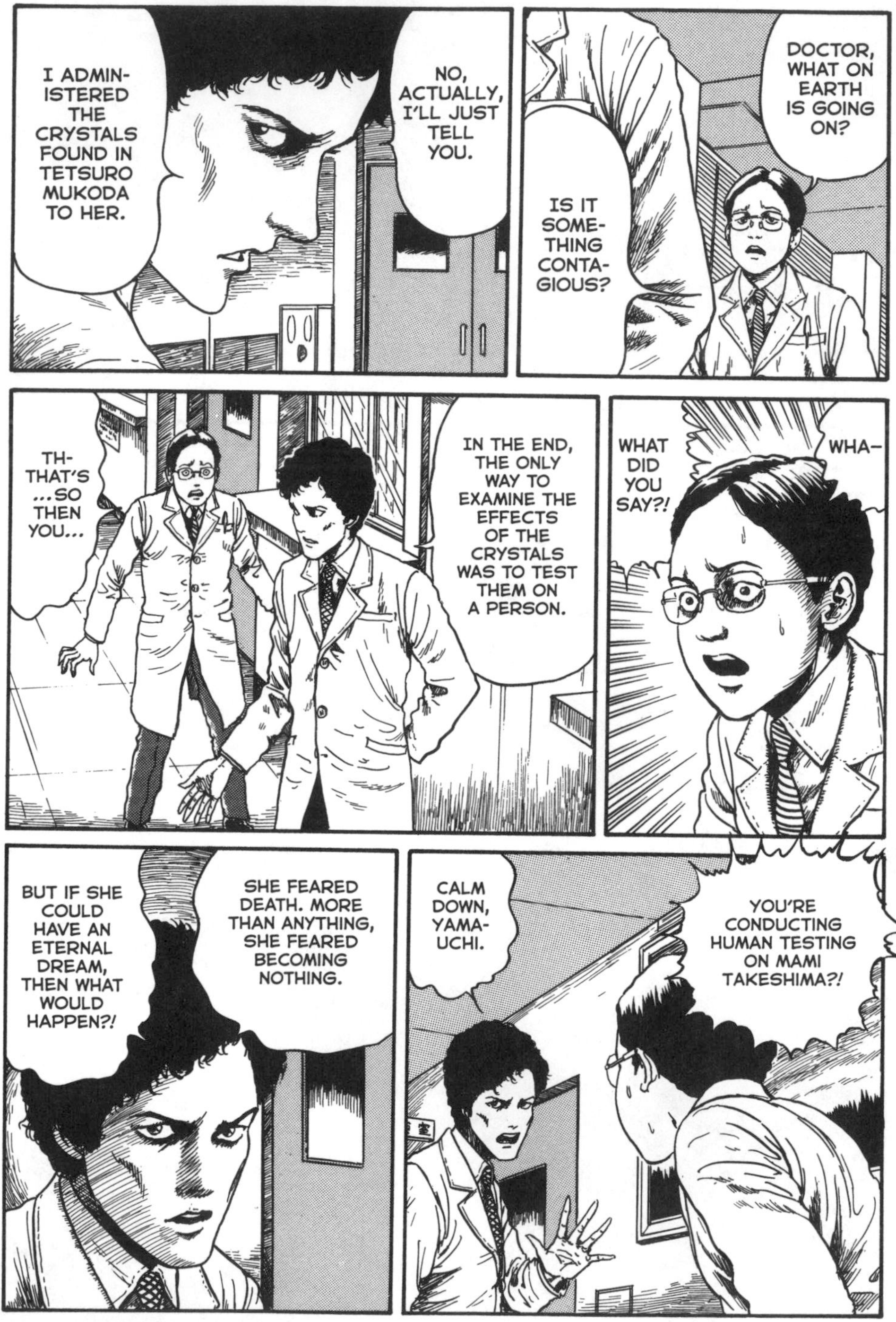
DOCTOR, WHAT ON EARTH IS GOING ON?
IS IT SOMETHING CONTAGIOUS?
NO, ACTUALLY, I'LL JUST TELL YOU.
I ADMINISTERED THE CRYSTALS FOUND IN TETSURO MUKODA TO HER.
WHA-
WHAT DID YOU SAY?!
IN THE END, THE ONLY WAY TO EXAMINE THE EFFECTS OF THE CRYSTALS WAS TO TEST THEM ON A PERSON.
TH-THAT'S ...SO THEN YOU...
YOU'RE CONDUCTING HUMAN TESTING ON MAMI TAKESHIMA?!
CALM DOWN, YAMAUCHI.
SHE FEARED DEATH. MORE THAN ANYTHING, SHE FEARED BECOMING NOTHING.
BUT IF SHE COULD HAVE AN ETERNAL DREAM, THEN WHAT WOULD HAPPEN?!

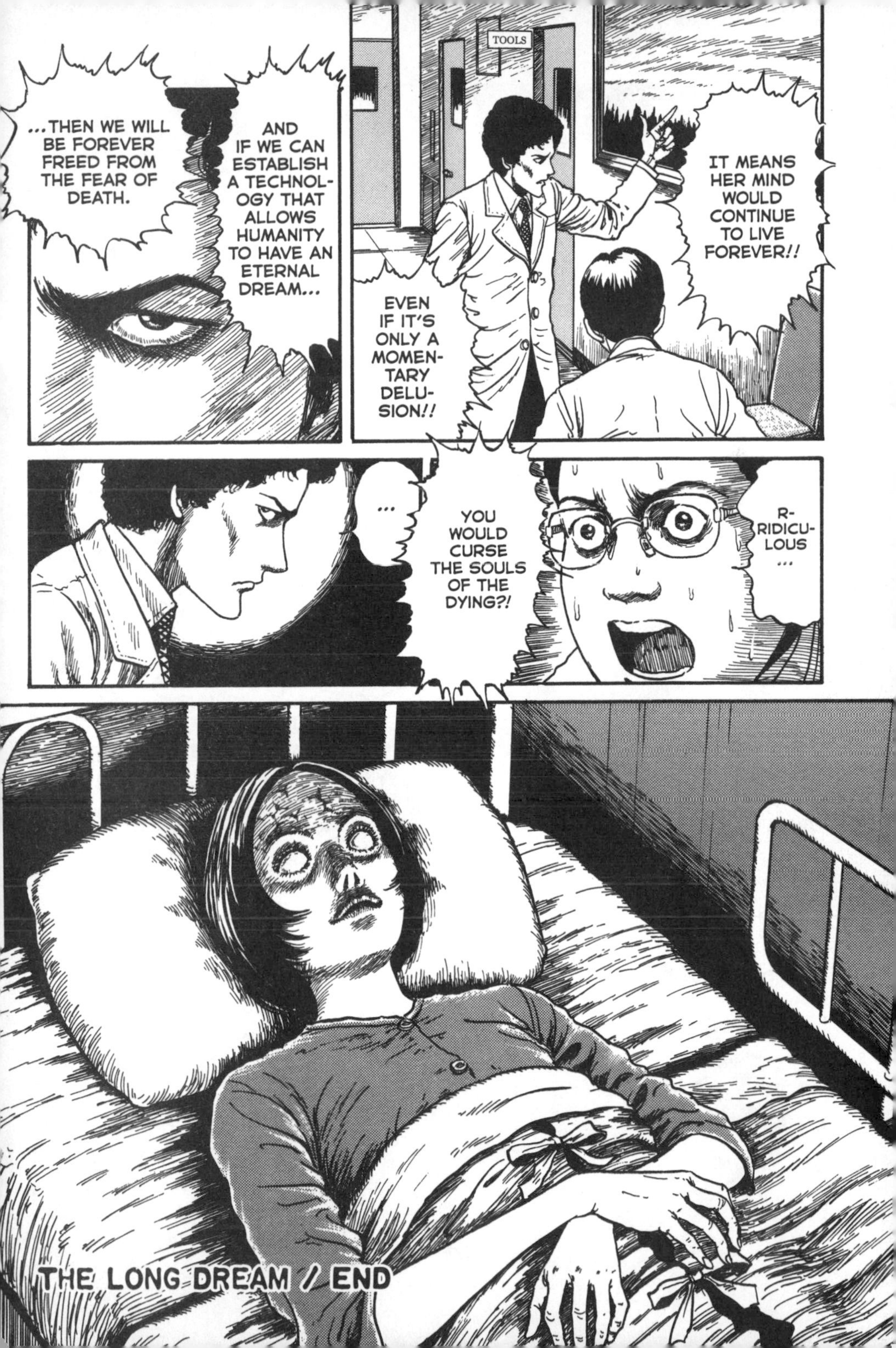
TOOLS
IT MEANS HER MIND WOULD CONTINUE TO LIVE FOREVER!!
EVEN IF IT'S ONLY A MOMENTARY DELUSION!!
AND IF WE CAN ESTABLISH A TECHNOLOGY THAT ALLOWS HUMANITY TO HAVE AN ETERNAL DREAM...
...THEN WE WILL BE FOREVER FREED FROM THE FEAR OF DEATH.
R-RIDICULOUS...
YOU WOULD CURSE THE SOULS OF THE DYING?!
...
THE LONG DREAM / END

THE LONG DREAM

When I was little, my oldest sister once told me this fascinating story she heard from someone. It was the idea that when a person dreams, it's just a moment. That no matter how long the dream might be, objectively, the time you're actually dreaming is a mere instant. I found this interesting, the difference between real time and subjective time, the quantitative (?) strangeness of space and time. With this seed of a story, I wrote half of a novel when I was in junior high or high school. It was about a unique machine that allowed people to have eternal dreams at the moment of death. If you entered a dream right before dying and the dream never ended, wouldn't you have obtained eternal life? That was the idea. I couldn't let it go to waste, so I looked for a chance to reuse it as a horror manga. And then I waited for an opportunity when I had plenty of time, and I drew it. It's thirty pages, but I'm pretty sure it took me two months to do.

The novelist Katsuhiko Takahashi was kind enough to speak very highly of this manga, giving me confidence too. Incidentally, as to the issue of whether or not we have our dreams in an instant, the me of now is of the opinion that we probably don't. And as for whether or not the way we speak changes over a hundred years, I have very little confidence in that.

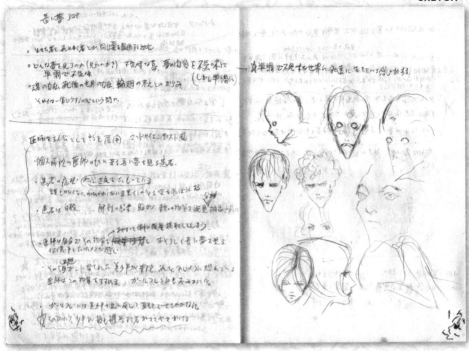

The Long Dream 32P

- Contrast in dosing a living person and a dying person with the same medication
- What kind of dreams do they have? (Did they have?) Creepy dreams, dreams with weird details (but monotonous) → *It feels like they are living forever in a monotonous, creepy world.
- Connection with thinking about the existence of the soul, the existence of a world after death, the cycle of death and rebirth
  The question of what exactly we're supposed to do about these.

Story unfolds with doctor as protagonist. Sort of mad scientist style.
- Patient who's having long dreams comes to the doctor at a private hospital.
- Patient's symptoms. He's just barely hanging onto his sanity.
- He doesn't talk properly. He says words that don't make sense. Tries to fly.
- Patient commits suicide. In the autopsy, foreign substance discovered in his brain, analyzed, extracted, success.

- By accident, the doctor takes a minuscule amount of this substance into his own body. He has terrifying long dreams. Feels as though millions of years have passed.

- Around this time, a beautiful young man comes to the hospital with terminal cancer. He's extremely afraid of death. The doctor recommends this substance. Girlfriend comes to visit.

- Girlfriend whispers in his ear, against wishes of beautiful young man?
  *Instead, the person the young man hates the most starts to whisper.

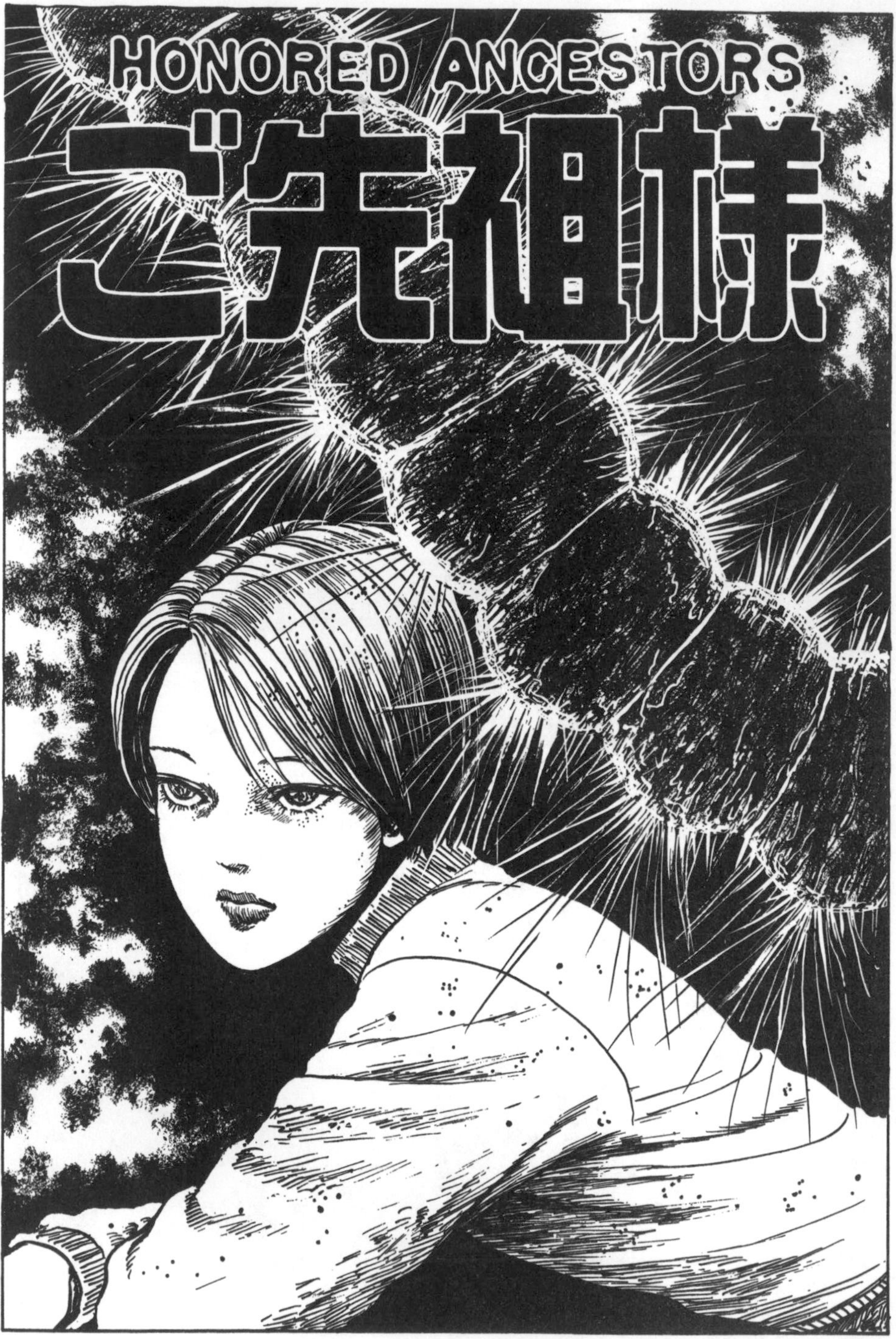
HONORED ANCESTORS
ご先祖様

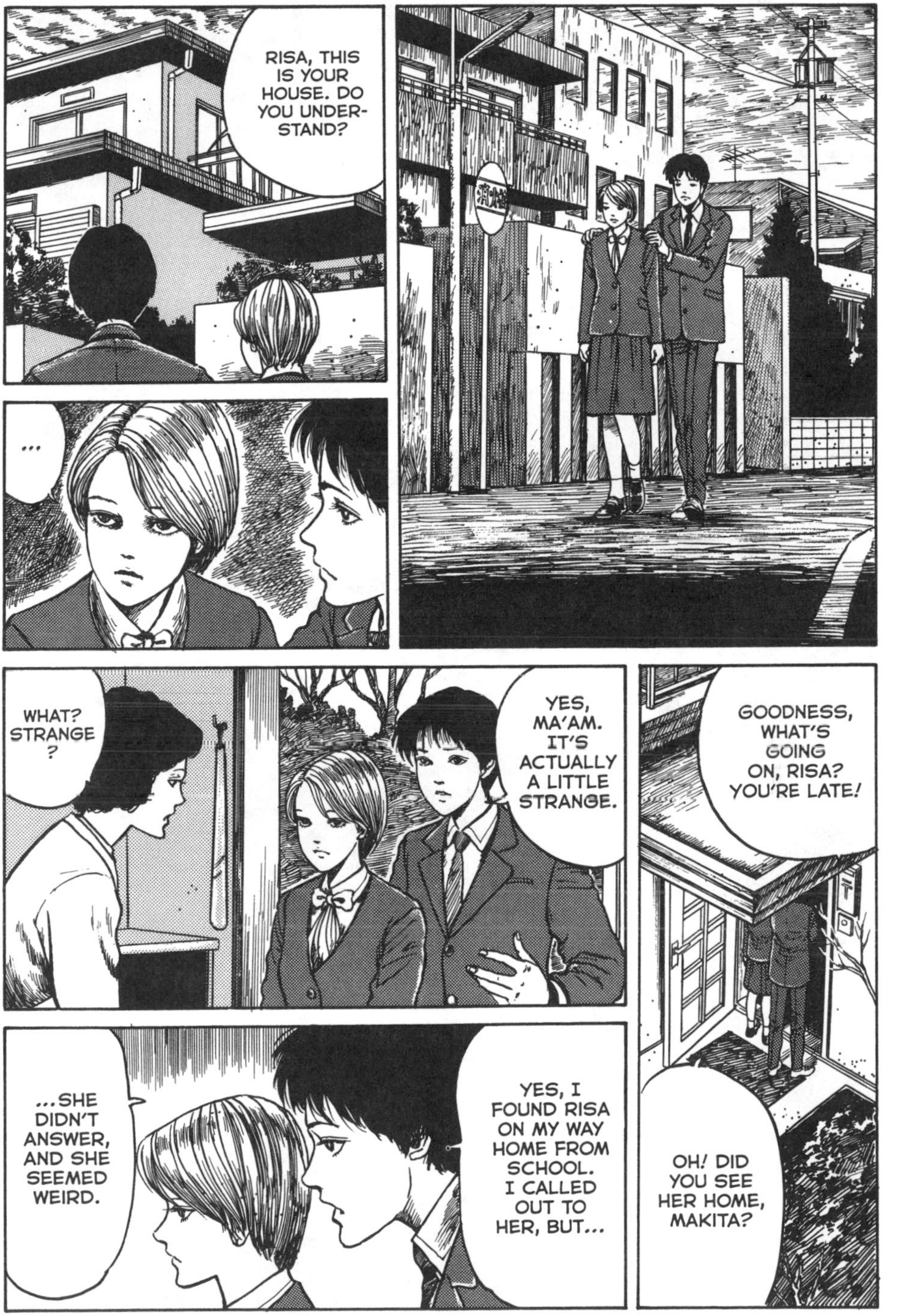
RISA, THIS IS YOUR HOUSE. DO YOU UNDER-STAND?
...
GOODNESS, WHAT'S GOING ON, RISA? YOU'RE LATE!
OH! DID YOU SEE HER HOME, MAKITA?
YES, MA'AM. IT'S ACTUALLY A LITTLE STRANGE.
WHAT? STRANGE?
YES, I FOUND RISA ON MY WAY HOME FROM SCHOOL. I CALLED OUT TO HER, BUT...
...SHE DIDN'T ANSWER, AND SHE SEEMED WEIRD.

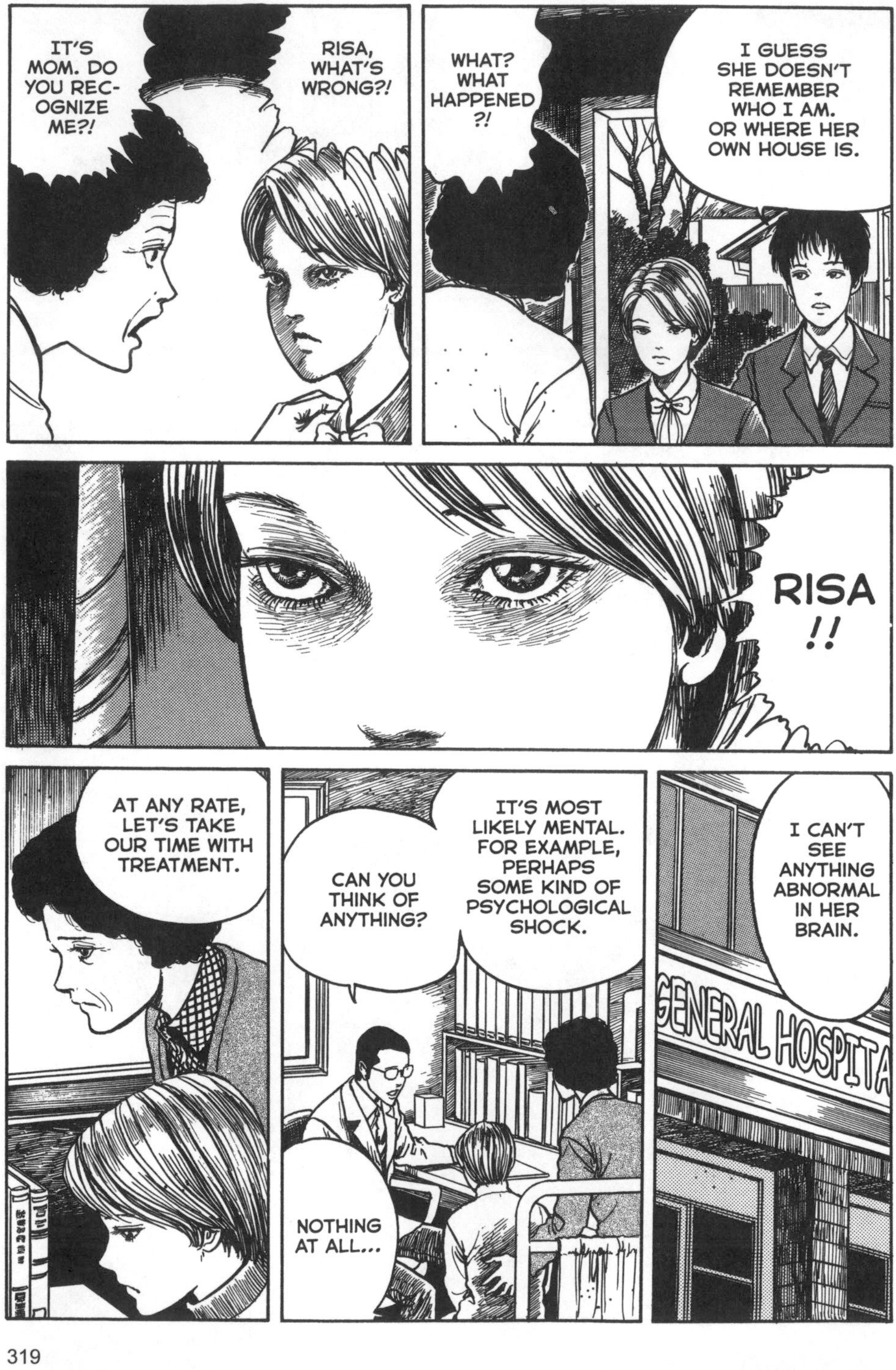
I GUESS SHE DOESN'T REMEMBER WHO I AM. OR WHERE HER OWN HOUSE IS.
WHAT? WHAT HAPPENED ?!
RISA, WHAT'S WRONG?!
IT'S MOM. DO YOU RECOGNIZE ME?!
RISA !!
I CAN'T SEE ANYTHING ABNORMAL IN HER BRAIN.
GENERAL HOSPITA
IT'S MOST LIKELY MENTAL. FOR EXAMPLE, PERHAPS SOME KIND OF PSYCHOLOGICAL SHOCK.
CAN YOU THINK OF ANYTHING?
NOTHING AT ALL...
AT ANY RATE, LET'S TAKE OUR TIME WITH TREATMENT.

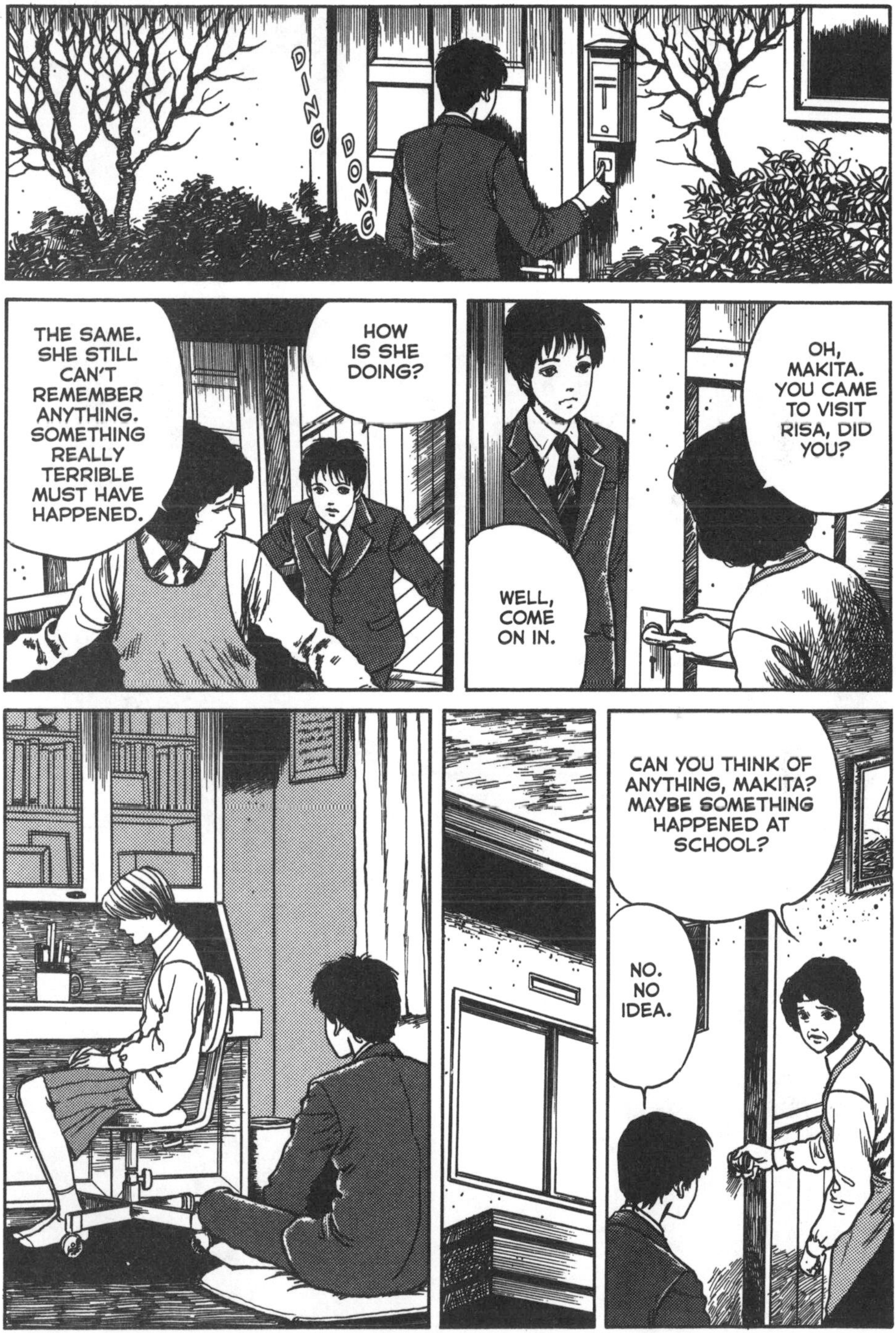
DING
DONG
OH, MAKITA. YOU CAME TO VISIT RISA, DID YOU?
WELL, COME ON IN.
HOW IS SHE DOING?
THE SAME. SHE STILL CAN'T REMEMBER ANYTHING. SOMETHING REALLY TERRIBLE MUST HAVE HAPPENED.
CAN YOU THINK OF ANYTHING, MAKITA? MAYBE SOMETHING HAPPENED AT SCHOOL?
NO. NO IDEA.

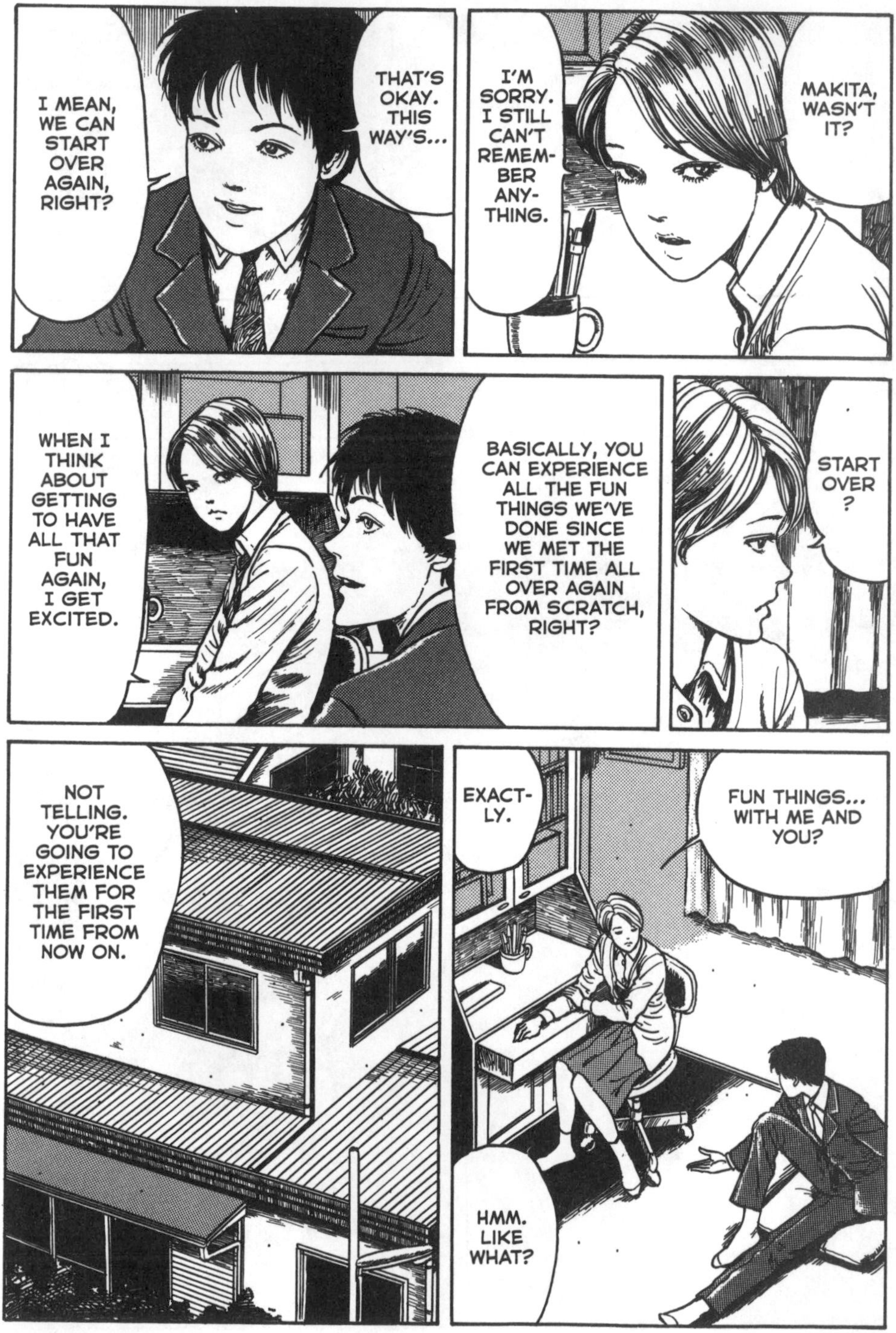
MAKITA, WASN'T IT?
I'M SORRY. I STILL CAN'T REMEMBER ANYTHING.
THAT'S OKAY. THIS WAY'S...
I MEAN, WE CAN START OVER AGAIN, RIGHT?
START OVER?
BASICALLY, YOU CAN EXPERIENCE ALL THE FUN THINGS WE'VE DONE SINCE WE MET THE FIRST TIME ALL OVER AGAIN FROM SCRATCH, RIGHT?
WHEN I THINK ABOUT GETTING TO HAVE ALL THAT FUN AGAIN, I GET EXCITED.
FUN THINGS... WITH ME AND YOU?
EXACTLY.
HMM. LIKE WHAT?
NOT TELLING. YOU'RE GOING TO EXPERIENCE THEM FOR THE FIRST TIME FROM NOW ON.

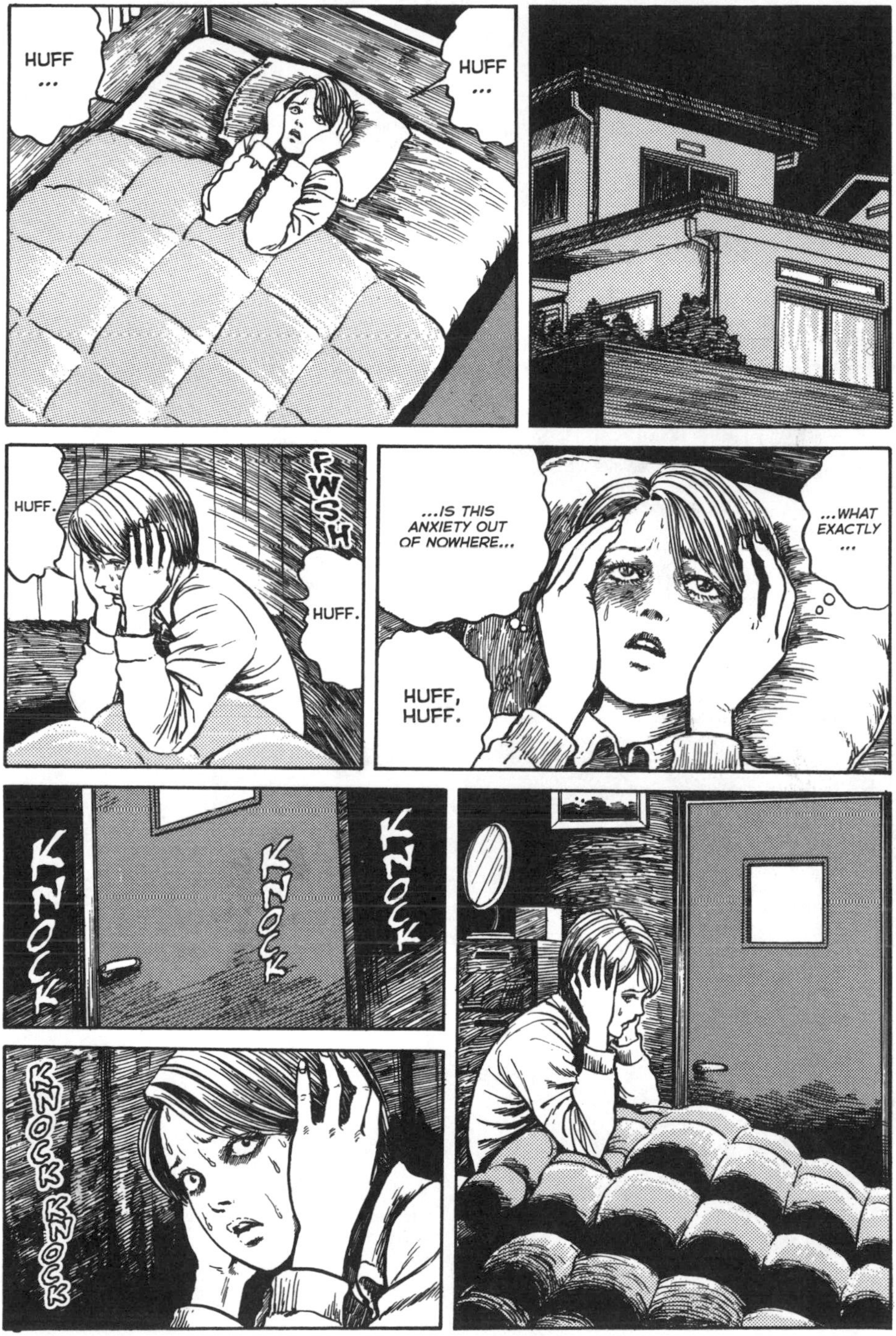
HUFF ...
HUFF ...
...WHAT EXACTLY ...
...IS THIS ANXIETY OUT OF NOWHERE...
HUFF, HUFF.
FWSH
HUFF.
HUFF.
KNOCK
KNOCK
KNOCK
KNOCK KNOCK

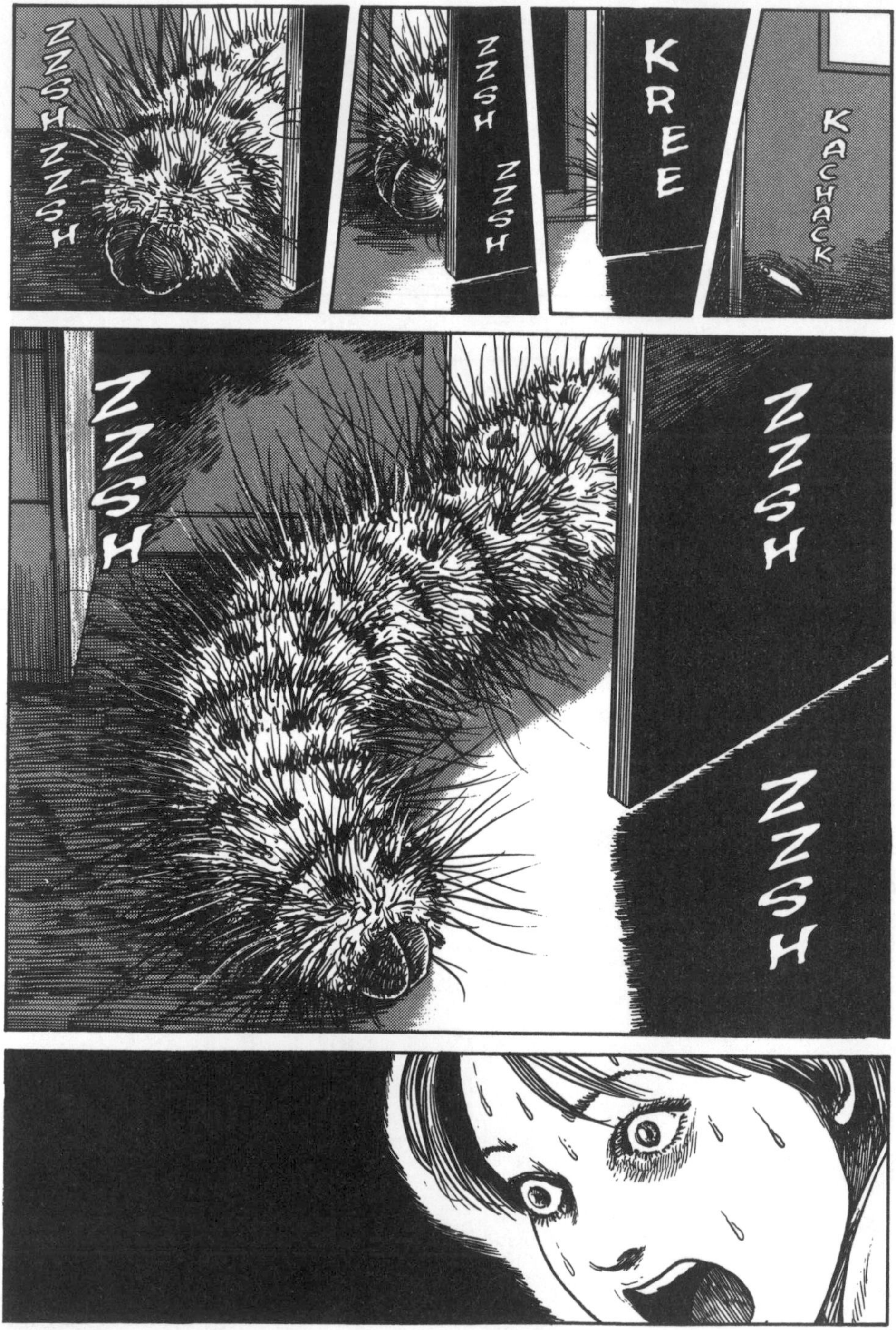
KACHACK
KREE
ZZSH ZZSH
ZZSH ZZSH ZZSH
ZZSH
ZZSH
ZZSH

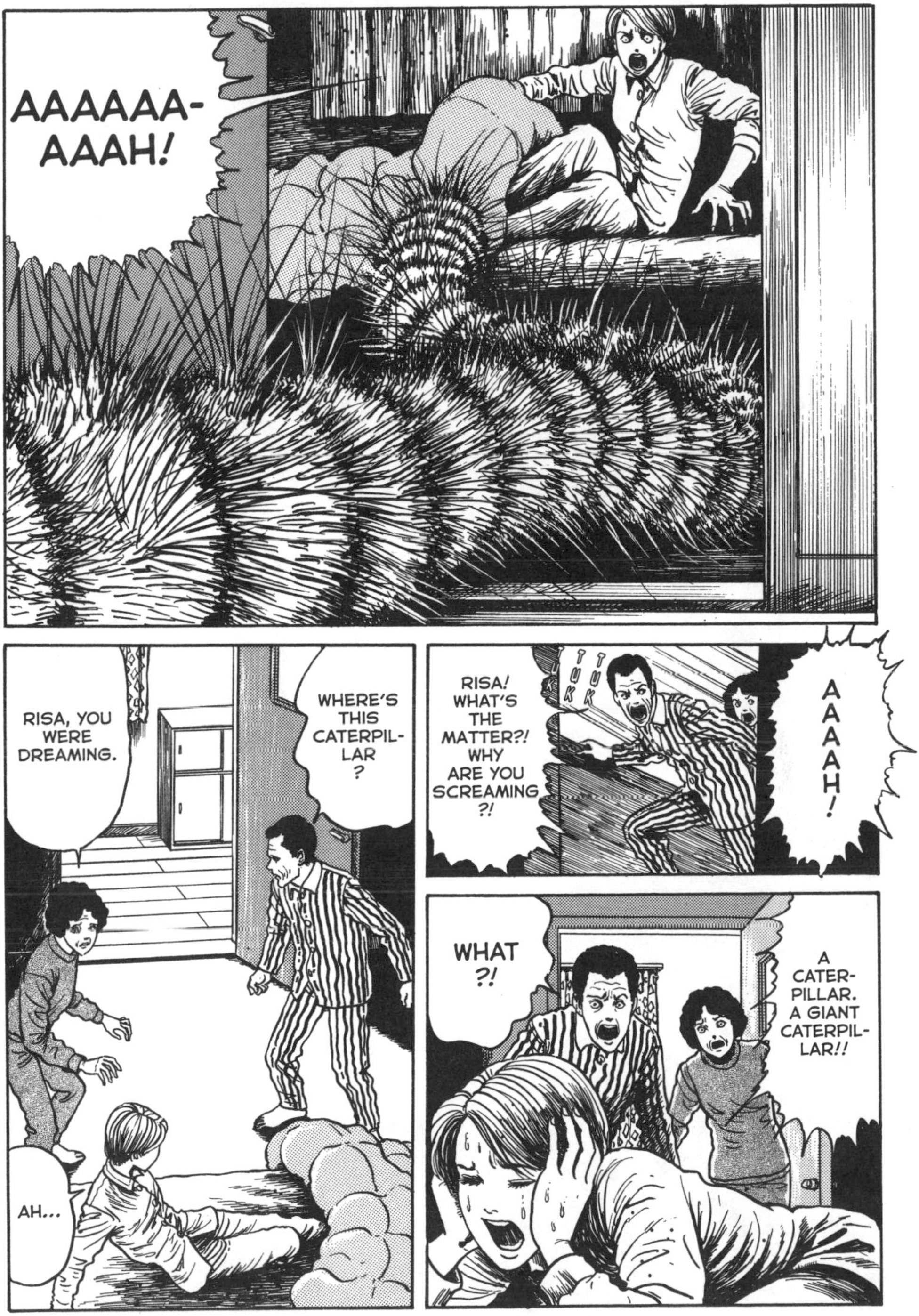
AAAAAA-AAAH!
AAAAH!
TUK TUK
RISA! WHAT'S THE MATTER?! WHY ARE YOU SCREAMING?!
A CATERPILLAR. A GIANT CATERPILLAR!!
WHAT?!
WHERE'S THIS CATERPILLAR?
RISA, YOU WERE DREAMING.
AH...

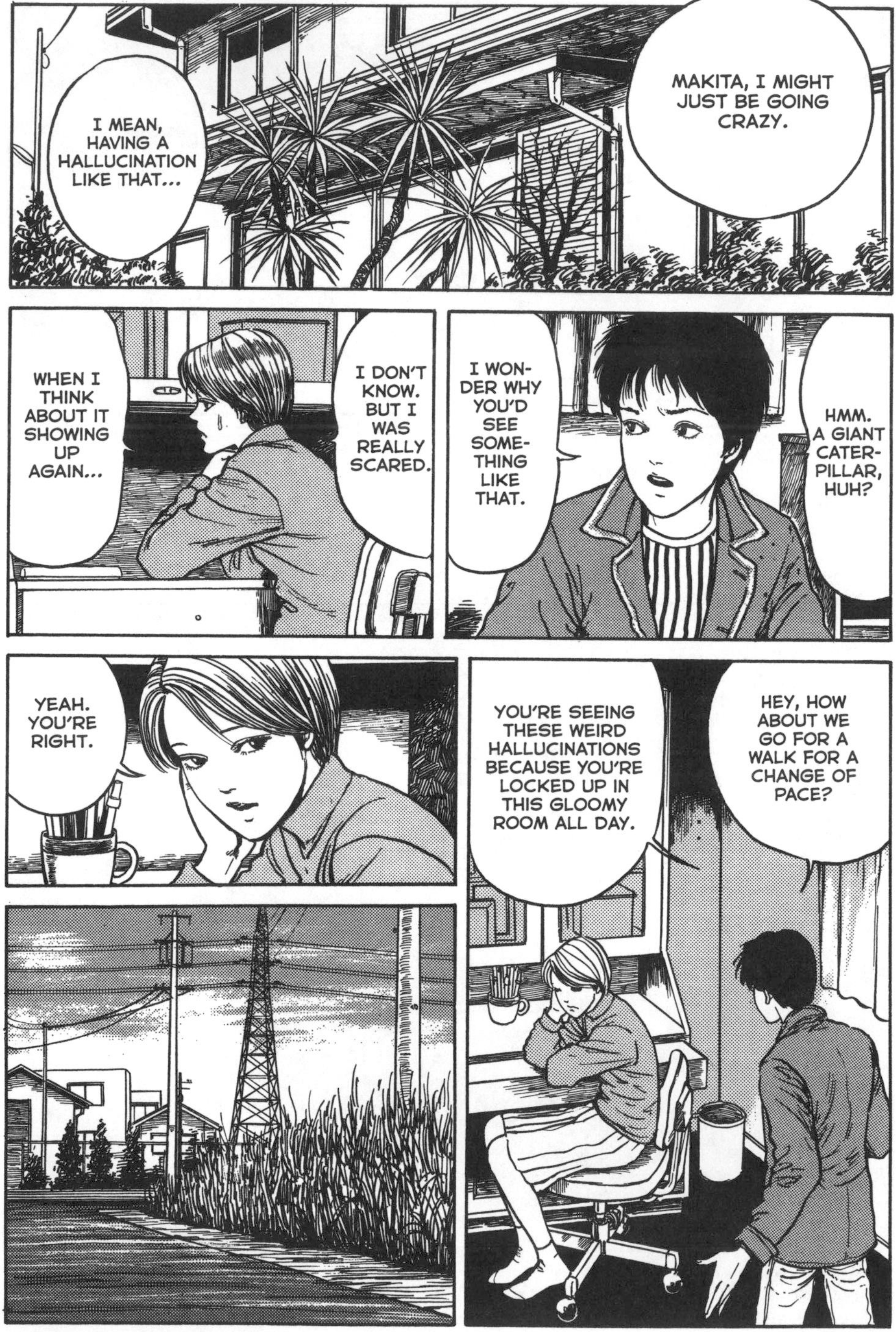

MAKITA, I MIGHT JUST BE GOING CRAZY.
I MEAN, HAVING A HALLUCINATION LIKE THAT...
HMM. A GIANT CATER-PILLAR, HUH?
I WON-DER WHY YOU'D SEE SOME-THING LIKE THAT.
I DON'T KNOW. BUT I WAS REALLY SCARED.
WHEN I THINK ABOUT IT SHOWING UP AGAIN...
HEY, HOW ABOUT WE GO FOR A WALK FOR A CHANGE OF PACE?
YOU'RE SEEING THESE WEIRD HALLUCINATIONS BECAUSE YOU'RE LOCKED UP IN THIS GLOOMY ROOM ALL DAY.
YEAH. YOU'RE RIGHT.

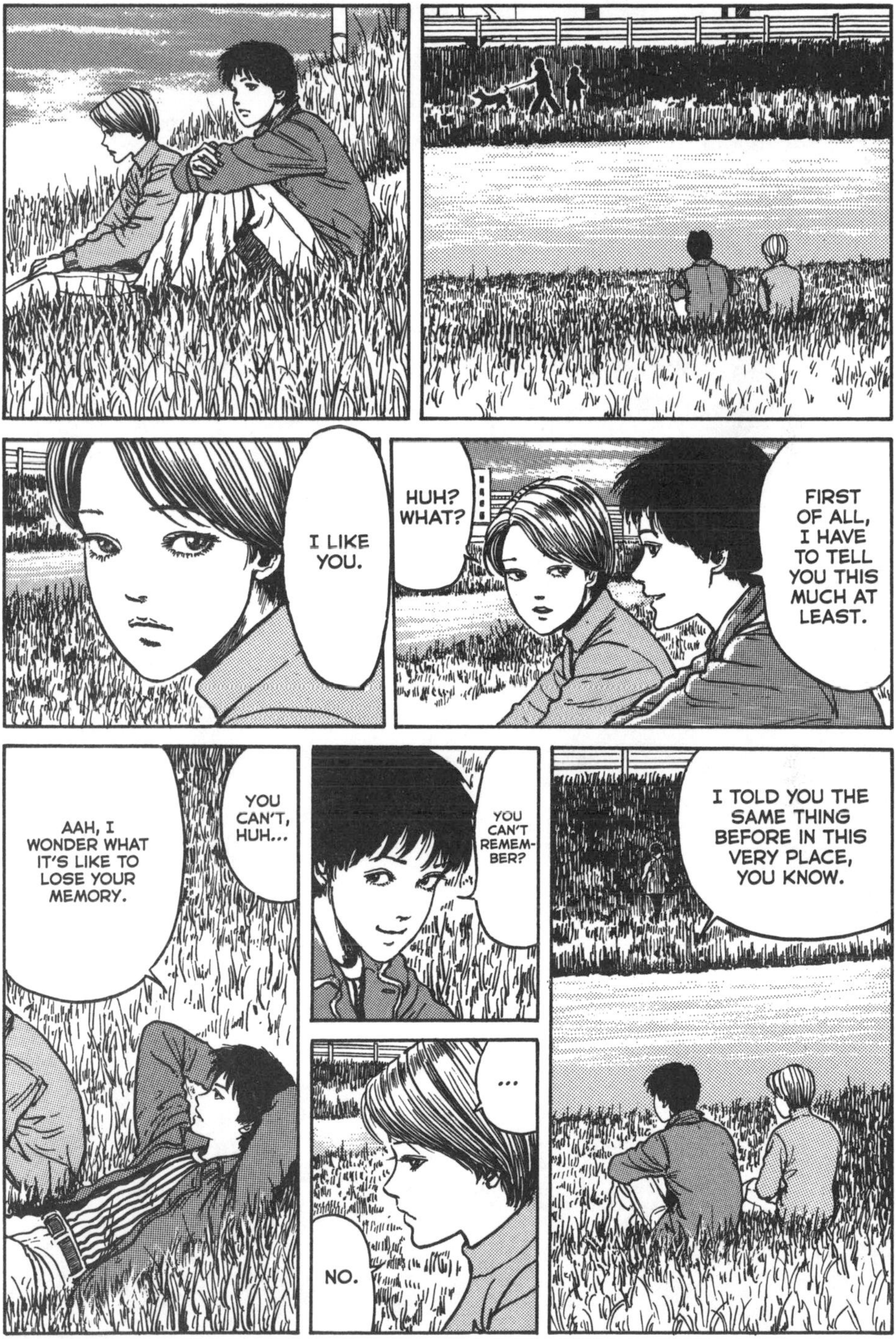
FIRST OF ALL, I HAVE TO TELL YOU THIS MUCH AT LEAST.
HUH? WHAT?
I LIKE YOU.
I TOLD YOU THE SAME THING BEFORE IN THIS VERY PLACE, YOU KNOW.
YOU CAN'T REMEMBER?
...
NO.
YOU CAN'T, HUH...
AAH, I WONDER WHAT IT'S LIKE TO LOSE YOUR MEMORY.

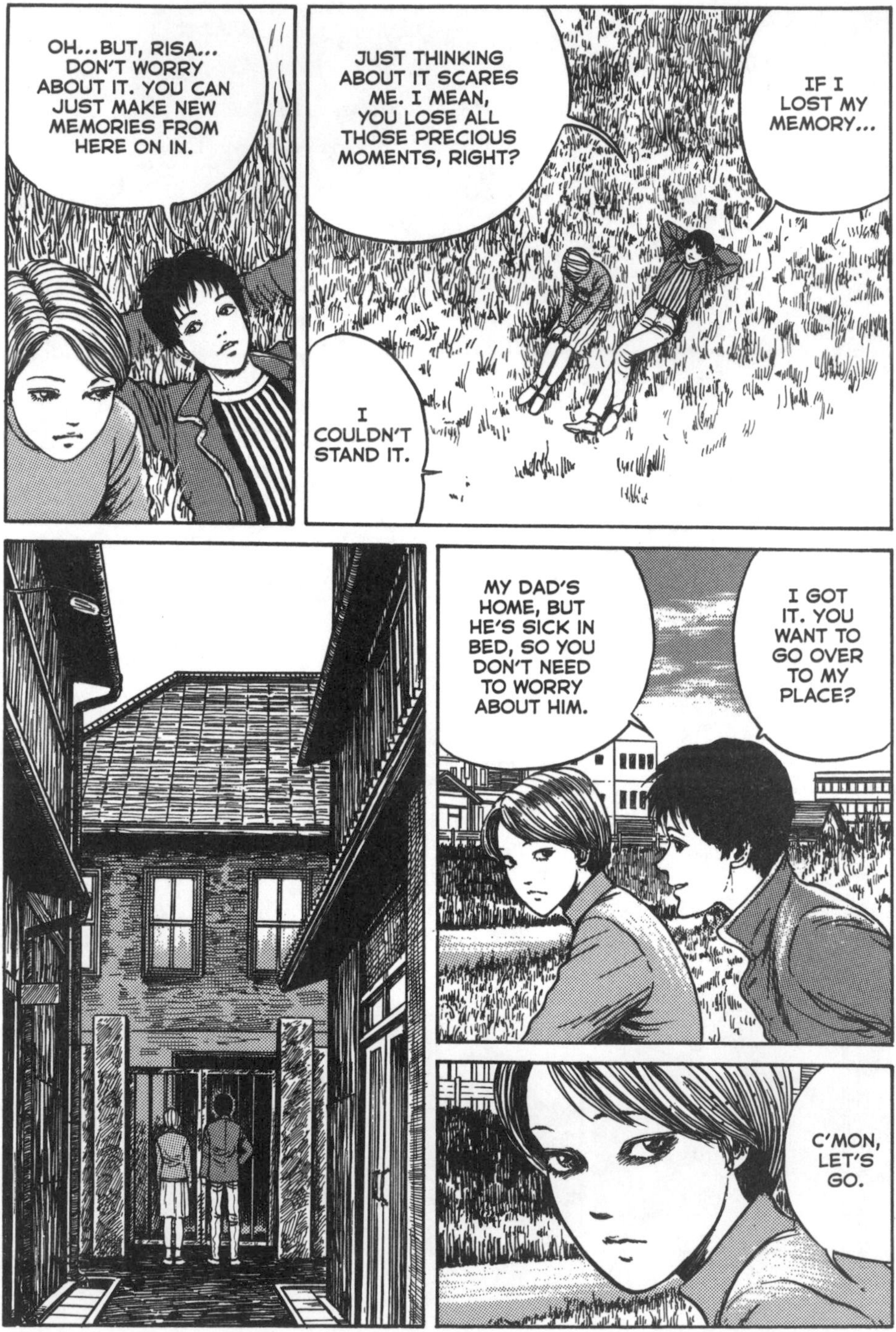
IF I LOST MY MEMORY...
JUST THINKING ABOUT IT SCARES ME. I MEAN, YOU LOSE ALL THOSE PRECIOUS MOMENTS, RIGHT?
I COULDN'T STAND IT.
OH...BUT, RISA... DON'T WORRY ABOUT IT. YOU CAN JUST MAKE NEW MEMORIES FROM HERE ON IN.
I GOT IT. YOU WANT TO GO OVER TO MY PLACE?
MY DAD'S HOME, BUT HE'S SICK IN BED, SO YOU DON'T NEED TO WORRY ABOUT HIM.
C'MON, LET'S GO.

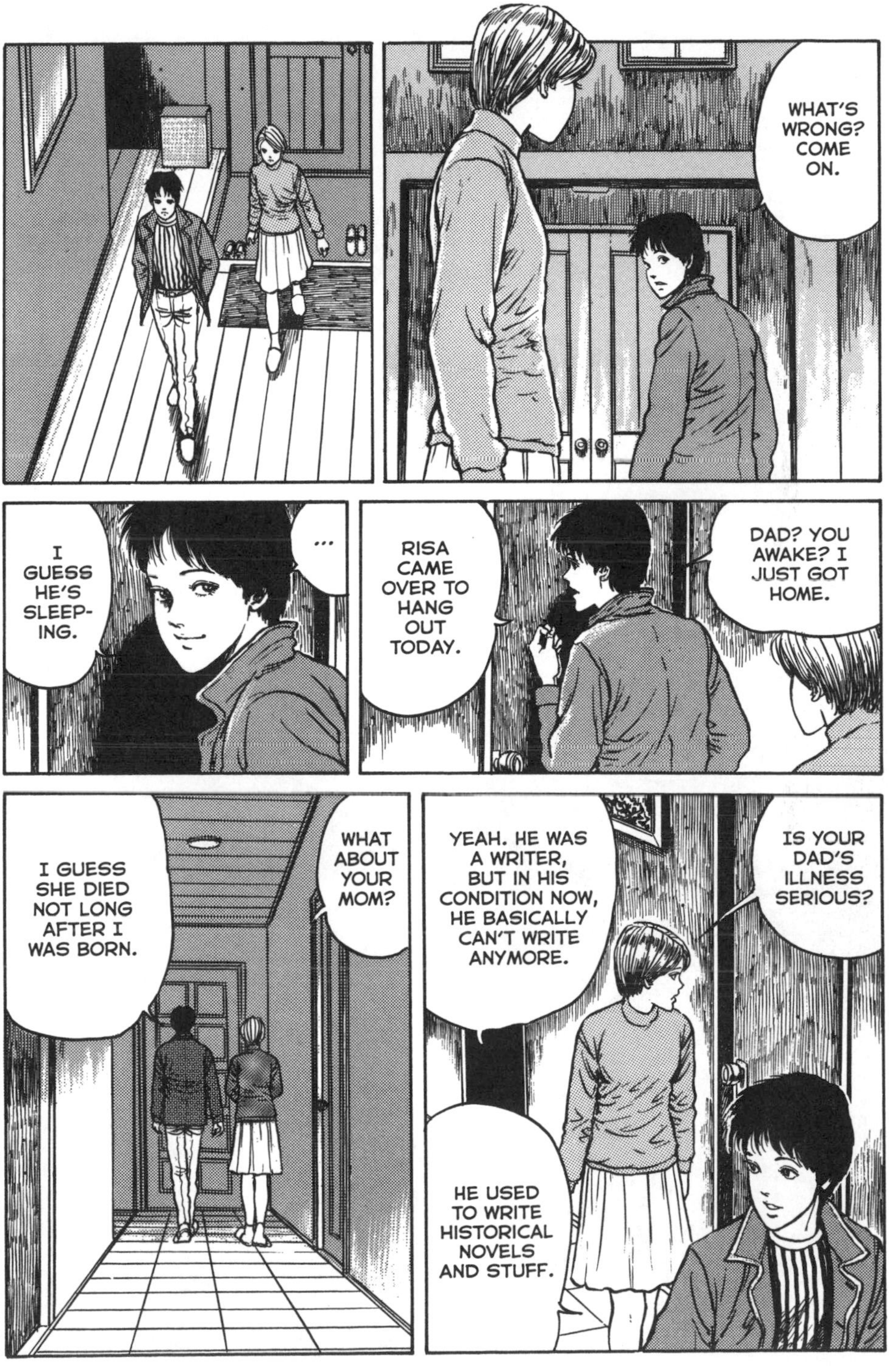
WHAT'S WRONG? COME ON.
DAD? YOU AWAKE? I JUST GOT HOME.
RISA CAME OVER TO HANG OUT TODAY.
...
I GUESS HE'S SLEEP-ING.
IS YOUR DAD'S ILLNESS SERIOUS?
YEAH. HE WAS A WRITER, BUT IN HIS CONDITION NOW, HE BASICALLY CAN'T WRITE ANYMORE.
HE USED TO WRITE HISTORICAL NOVELS AND STUFF.
WHAT ABOUT YOUR MOM?
I GUESS SHE DIED NOT LONG AFTER I WAS BORN.

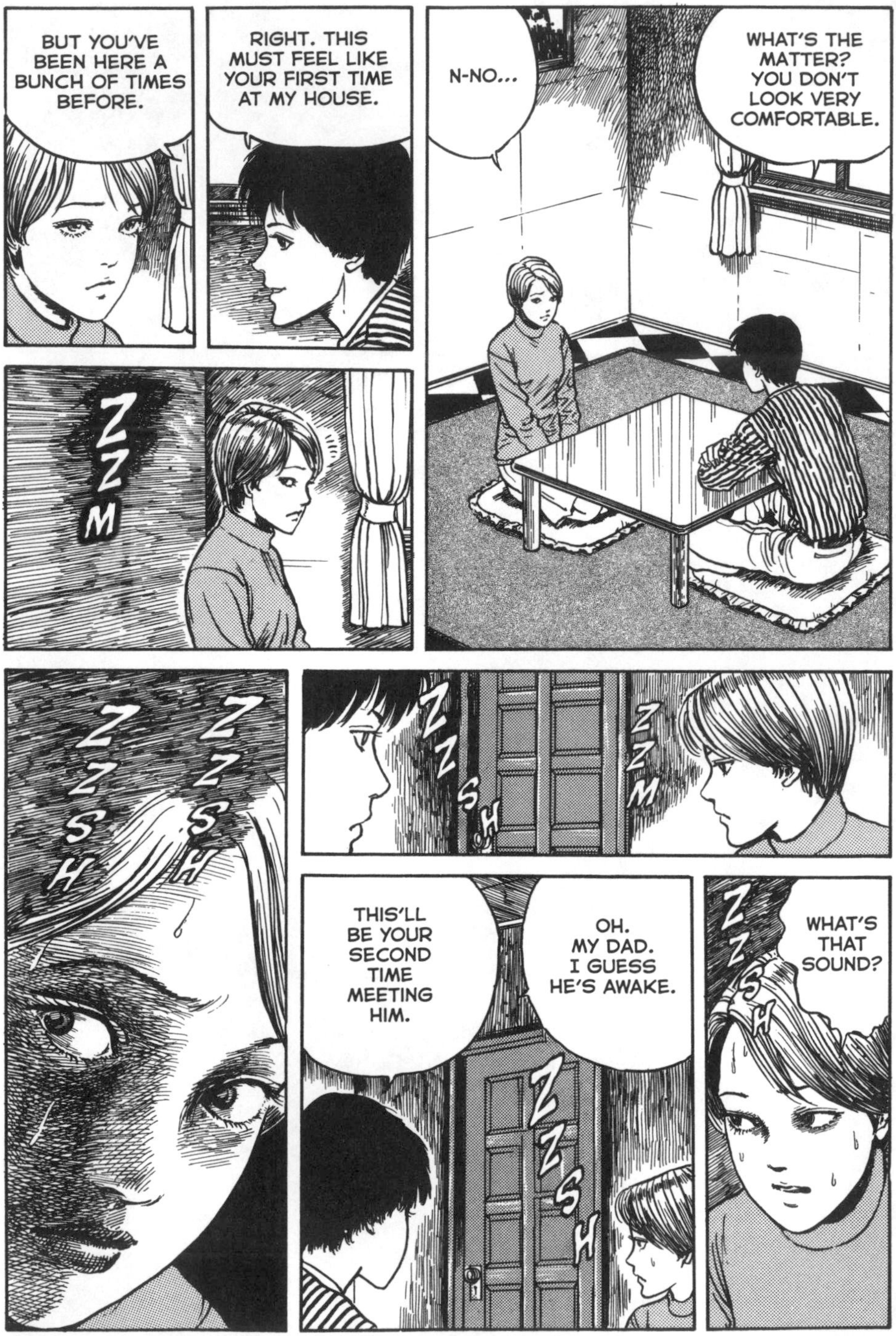
WHAT'S THE MATTER? YOU DON'T LOOK VERY COMFORTABLE.
N-NO...
RIGHT. THIS MUST FEEL LIKE YOUR FIRST TIME AT MY HOUSE.
BUT YOU'VE BEEN HERE A BUNCH OF TIMES BEFORE.
ZZM
ZZM
ZZSH
WHAT'S THAT SOUND?
ZZSH
OH. MY DAD. I GUESS HE'S AWAKE.
THIS'LL BE YOUR SECOND TIME MEETING HIM.
ZZSH
ZZSH
ZZSH

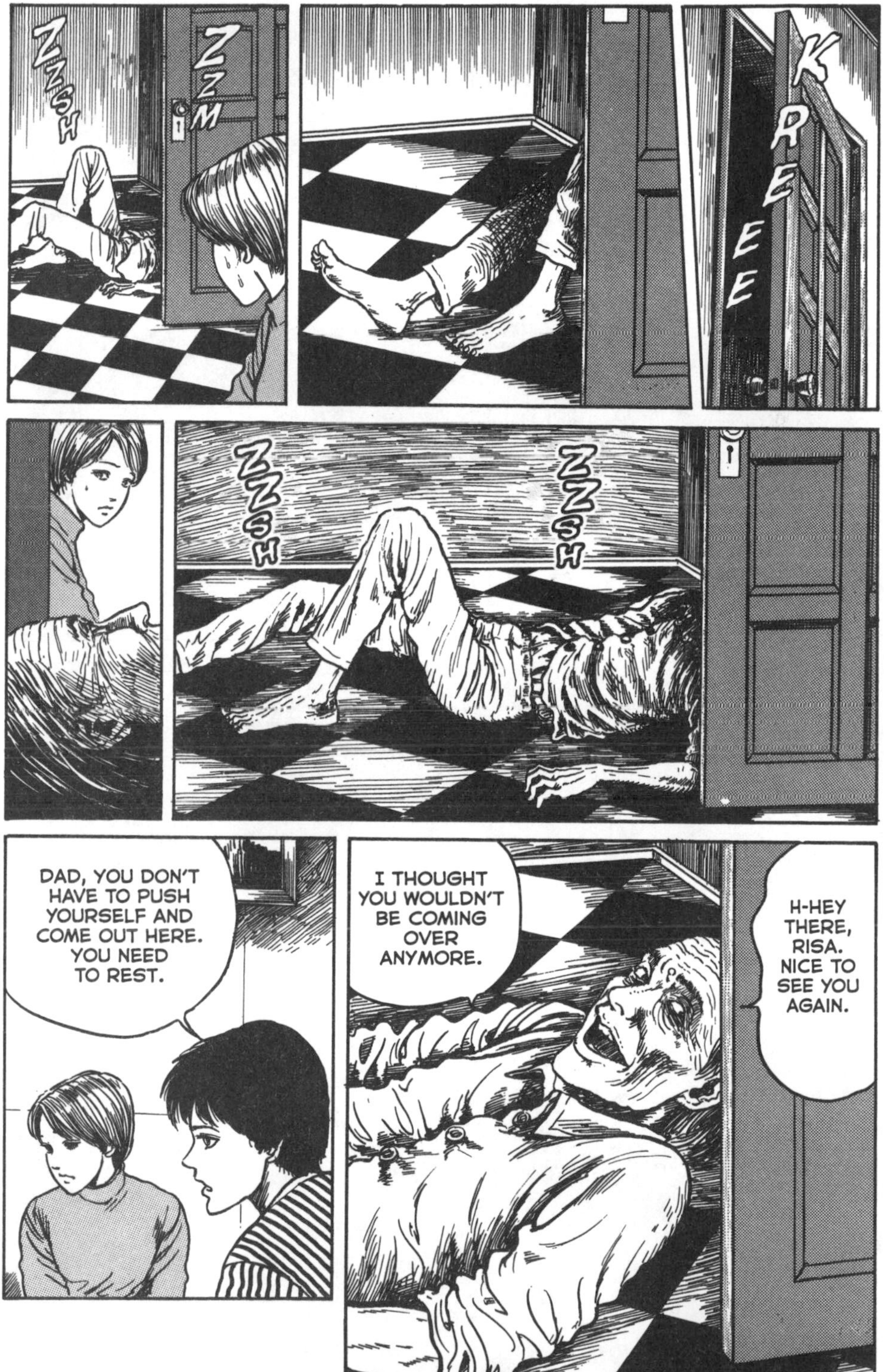
KREEEE
ZZM
ZZSH
ZZSH
ZZSH
H-HEY THERE, RISA. NICE TO SEE YOU AGAIN.
I THOUGHT YOU WOULDN'T BE COMING OVER ANYMORE.
DAD, YOU DON'T HAVE TO PUSH YOURSELF AND COME OUT HERE. YOU NEED TO REST.

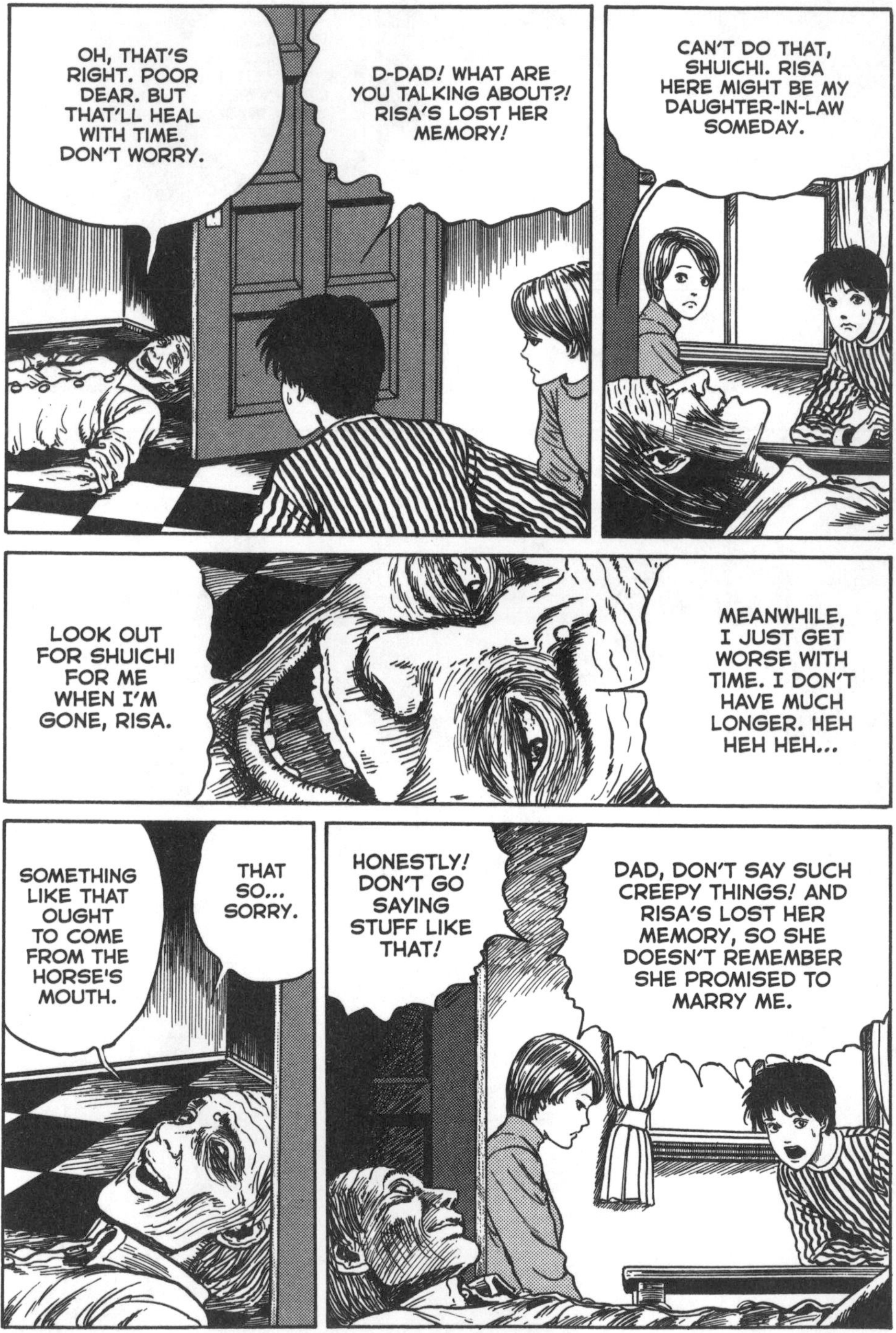
CAN'T DO THAT, SHUICHI. RISA HERE MIGHT BE MY DAUGHTER-IN-LAW SOMEDAY.
D-DAD! WHAT ARE YOU TALKING ABOUT?! RISA'S LOST HER MEMORY!
OH, THAT'S RIGHT. POOR DEAR. BUT THAT'LL HEAL WITH TIME. DON'T WORRY.
MEANWHILE, I JUST GET WORSE WITH TIME. I DON'T HAVE MUCH LONGER. HEH HEH HEH...
LOOK OUT FOR SHUICHI FOR ME WHEN I'M GONE, RISA.
DAD, DON'T SAY SUCH CREEPY THINGS! AND RISA'S LOST HER MEMORY, SO SHE DOESN'T REMEMBER SHE PROMISED TO MARRY ME.
HONESTLY! DON'T GO SAYING STUFF LIKE THAT!
THAT SO... SORRY.
SOMETHING LIKE THAT OUGHT TO COME FROM THE HORSE'S MOUTH.

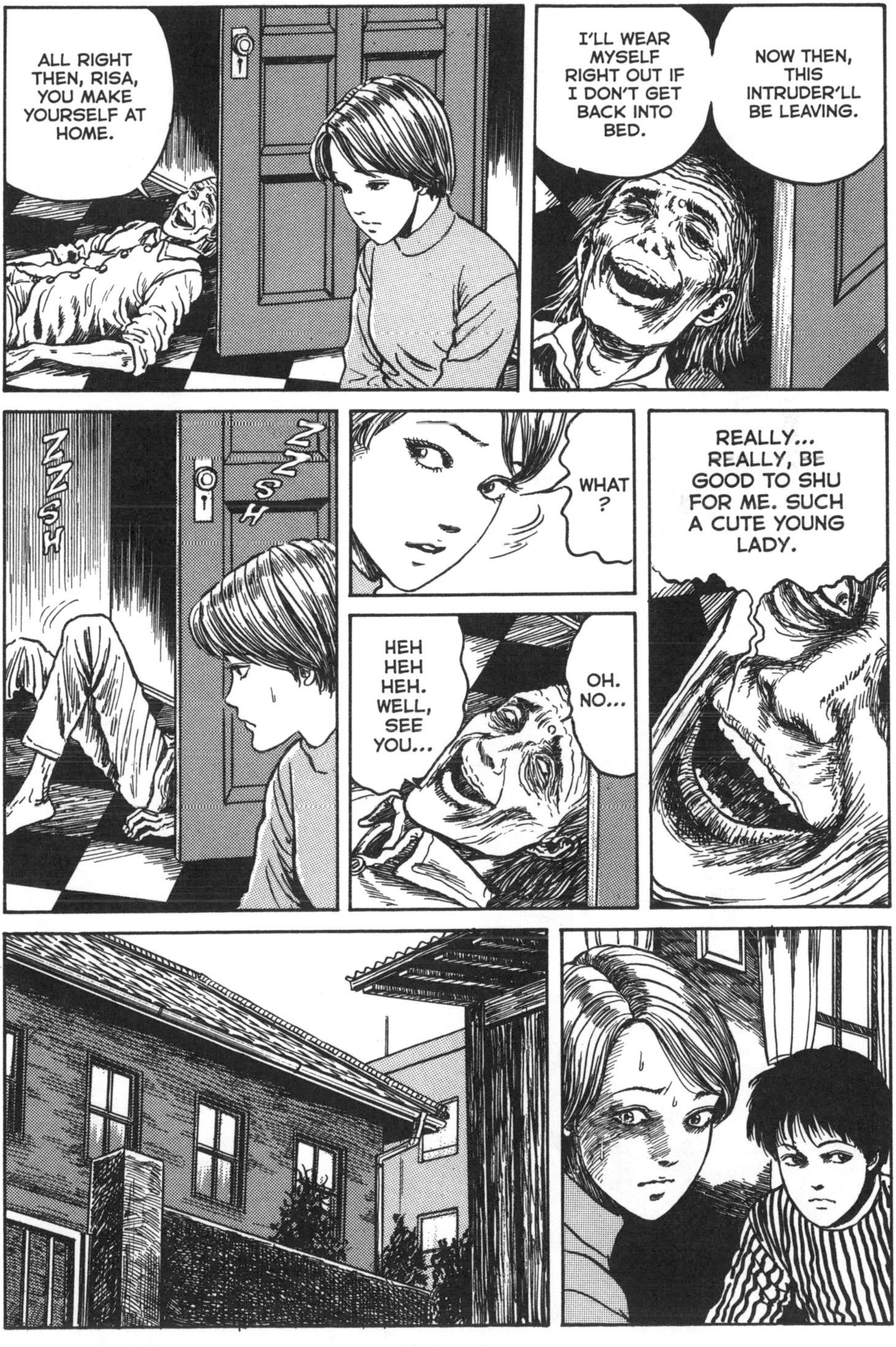
NOW THEN, THIS INTRUDER'LL BE LEAVING.
I'LL WEAR MYSELF RIGHT OUT IF I DON'T GET BACK INTO BED.
ALL RIGHT THEN, RISA, YOU MAKE YOURSELF AT HOME.
REALLY... REALLY, BE GOOD TO SHU FOR ME. SUCH A CUTE YOUNG LADY.
WHAT?
OH. NO...
HEH HEH HEH. WELL, SEE YOU...
ZZSH
ZZSH

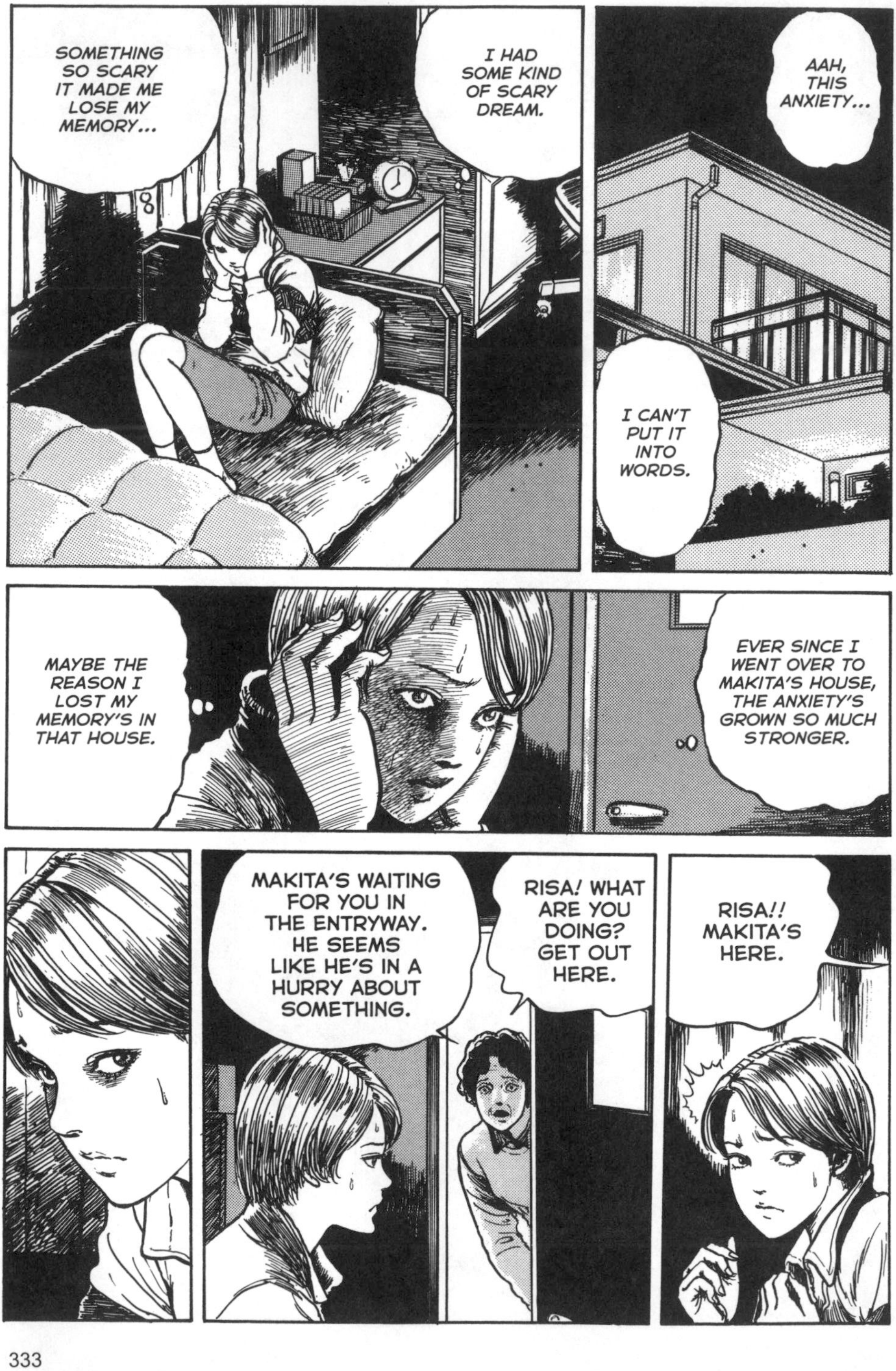
AAH, THIS ANXIETY...
I CAN'T PUT IT INTO WORDS.
I HAD SOME KIND OF SCARY DREAM.
SOMETHING SO SCARY IT MADE ME LOSE MY MEMORY...
EVER SINCE I WENT OVER TO MAKITA'S HOUSE, THE ANXIETY'S GROWN SO MUCH STRONGER.
MAYBE THE REASON I LOST MY MEMORY'S IN THAT HOUSE.
RISA!! MAKITA'S HERE.
RISA! WHAT ARE YOU DOING? GET OUT HERE.
MAKITA'S WAITING FOR YOU IN THE ENTRYWAY. HE SEEMS LIKE HE'S IN A HURRY ABOUT SOMETHING.

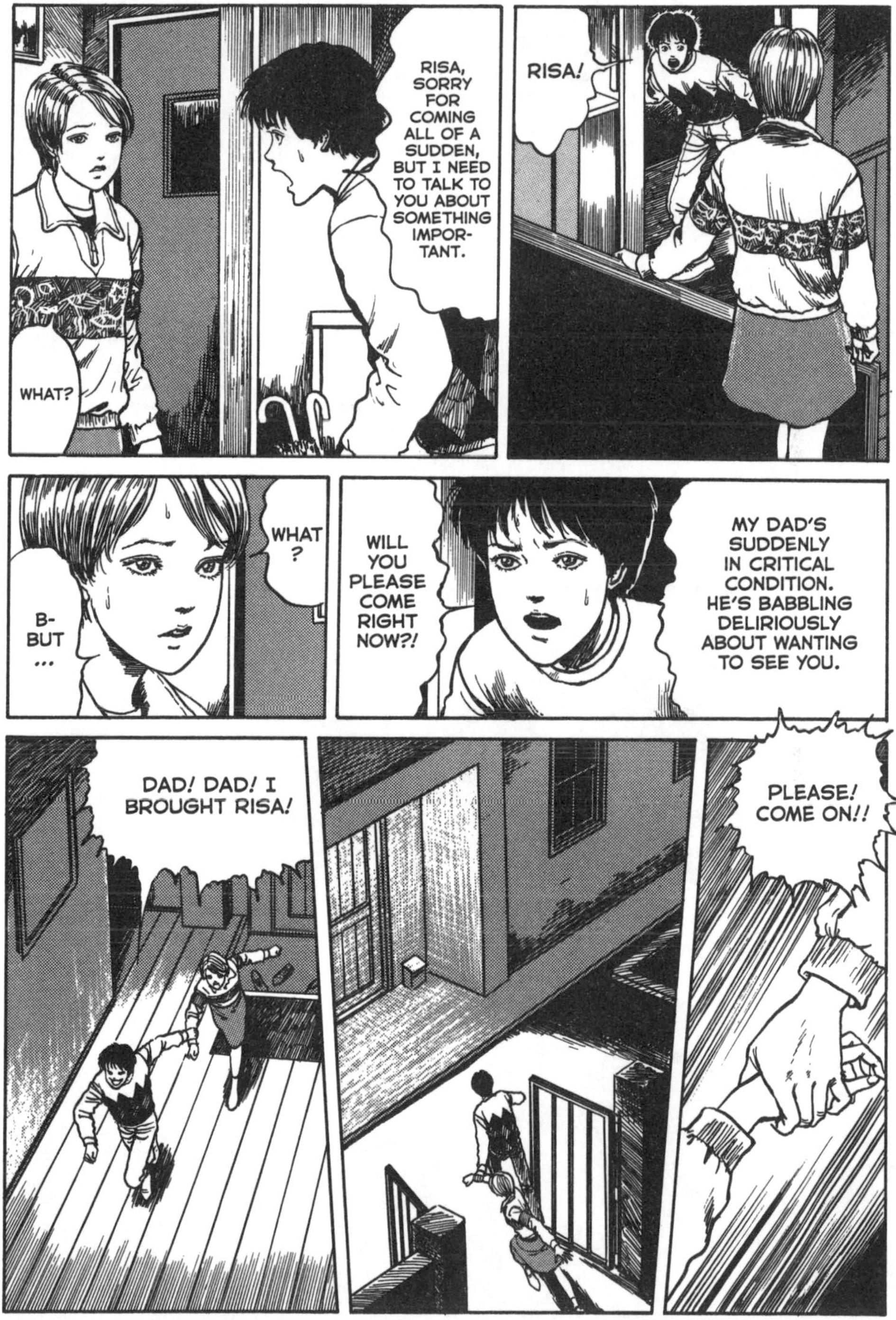
RISA!
RISA, SORRY FOR COMING ALL OF A SUDDEN, BUT I NEED TO TALK TO YOU ABOUT SOMETHING IMPORTANT.
WHAT?
MY DAD'S SUDDENLY IN CRITICAL CONDITION. HE'S BABBLING DELIRIOUSLY ABOUT WANTING TO SEE YOU.
WILL YOU PLEASE COME RIGHT NOW?!
WHAT?
B-BUT...
PLEASE! COME ON!!
DAD! DAD! I BROUGHT RISA!

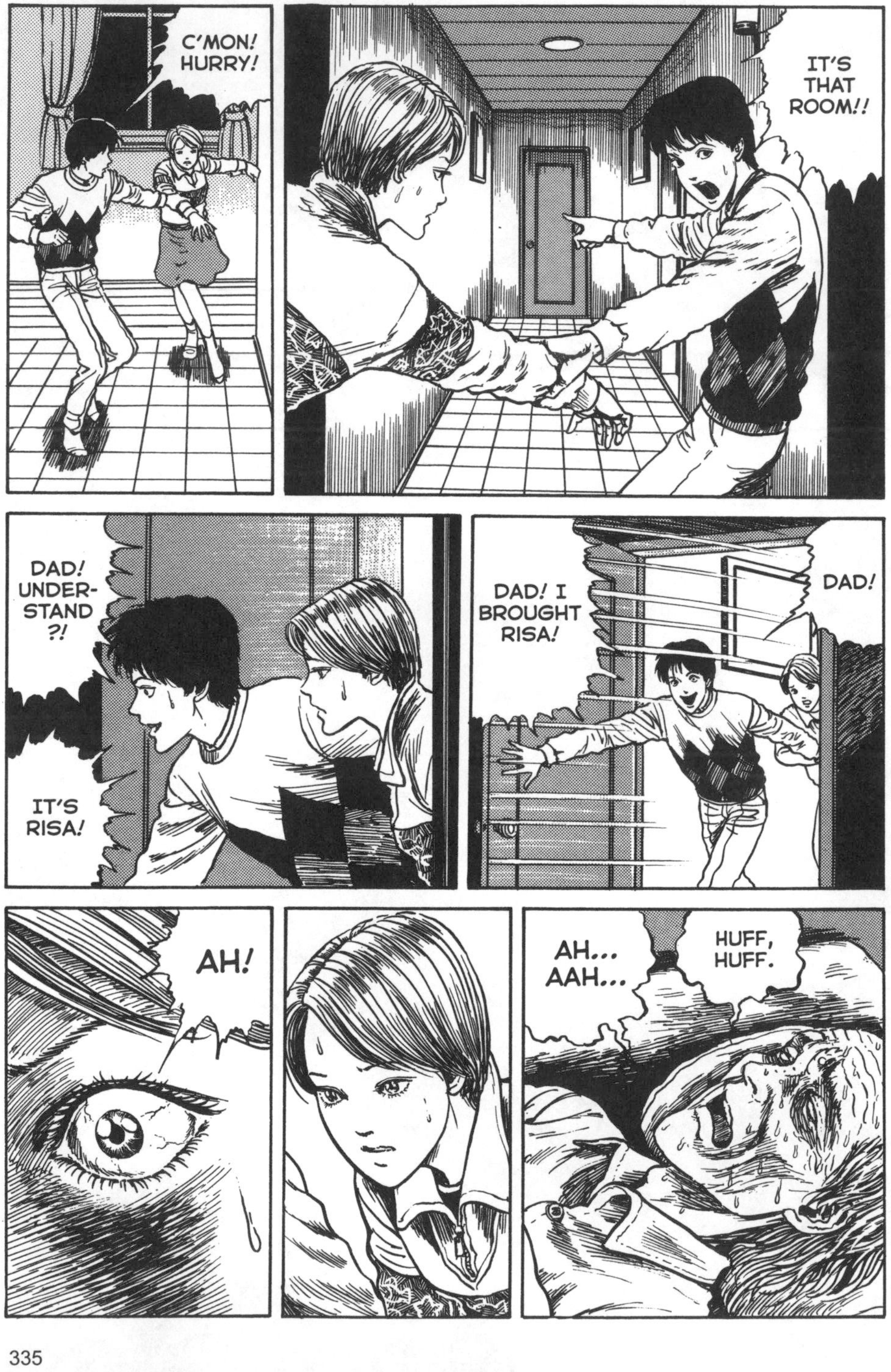
IT'S THAT ROOM!!
C'MON! HURRY!
DAD!
DAD! I BROUGHT RISA!
DAD! UNDER-STAND?!
IT'S RISA!
HUFF, HUFF.
AH... AAH...
AH!

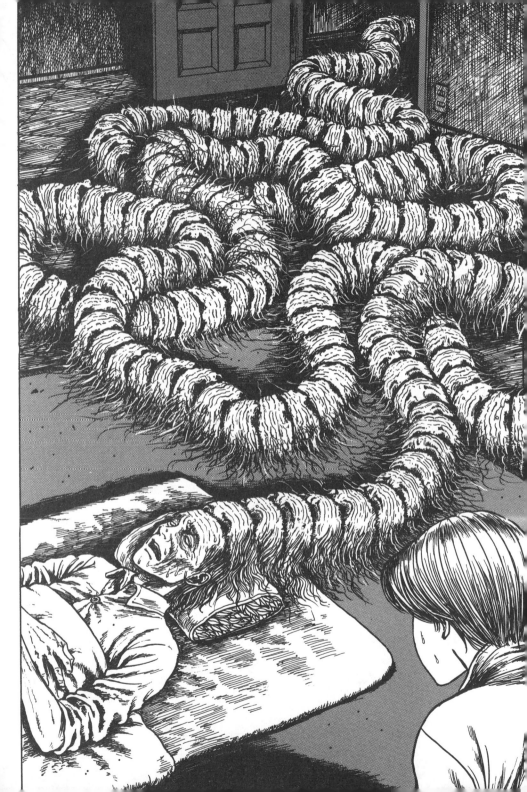

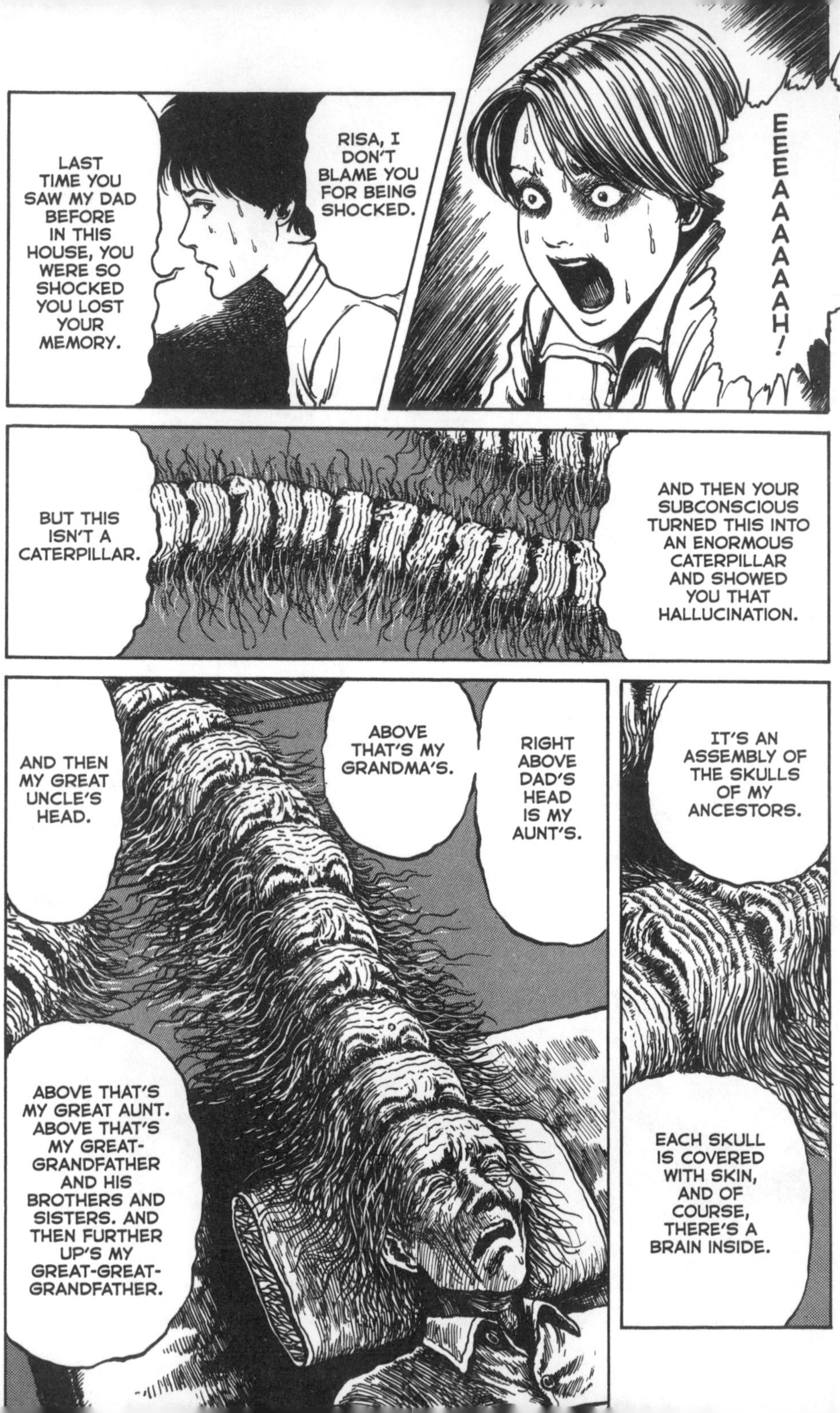
EEEAAAAAAAH!
RISA, I DON'T BLAME YOU FOR BEING SHOCKED.
LAST TIME YOU SAW MY DAD BEFORE IN THIS HOUSE, YOU WERE SO SHOCKED YOU LOST YOUR MEMORY.
AND THEN YOUR SUBCONSCIOUS TURNED THIS INTO AN ENORMOUS CATERPILLAR AND SHOWED YOU THAT HALLUCINATION.
BUT THIS ISN'T A CATERPILLAR.
IT'S AN ASSEMBLY OF THE SKULLS OF MY ANCESTORS.
EACH SKULL IS COVERED WITH SKIN, AND OF COURSE, THERE'S A BRAIN INSIDE.
RIGHT ABOVE DAD'S HEAD IS MY AUNT'S.
ABOVE THAT'S MY GRANDMA'S.
AND THEN MY GREAT UNCLE'S HEAD.
ABOVE THAT'S MY GREAT AUNT. ABOVE THAT'S MY GREAT-GRANDFATHER AND HIS BROTHERS AND SISTERS. AND THEN FURTHER UP'S MY GREAT-GREAT-GRANDFATHER.

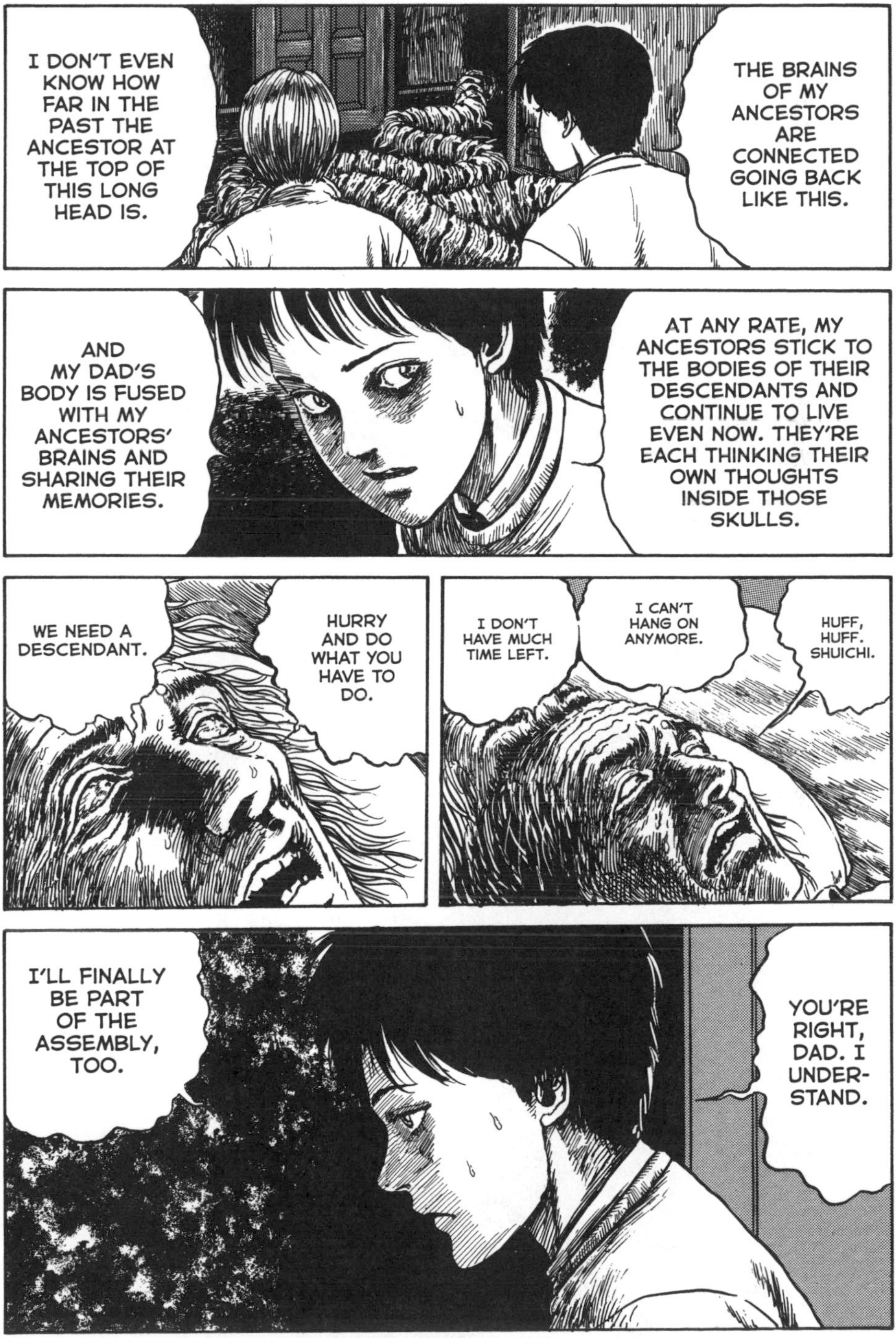
THE BRAINS OF MY ANCESTORS ARE CONNECTED GOING BACK LIKE THIS.
I DON'T EVEN KNOW HOW FAR IN THE PAST THE ANCESTOR AT THE TOP OF THIS LONG HEAD IS.
AT ANY RATE, MY ANCESTORS STICK TO THE BODIES OF THEIR DESCENDANTS AND CONTINUE TO LIVE EVEN NOW. THEY'RE EACH THINKING THEIR OWN THOUGHTS INSIDE THOSE SKULLS.
AND MY DAD'S BODY IS FUSED WITH MY ANCESTORS' BRAINS AND SHARING THEIR MEMORIES.
HUFF, HUFF. SHUICHI.
I CAN'T HANG ON ANYMORE.
I DON'T HAVE MUCH TIME LEFT.
HURRY AND DO WHAT YOU HAVE TO DO.
WE NEED A DESCENDANT.
YOU'RE RIGHT, DAD. I UNDER-STAND.
I'LL FINALLY BE PART OF THE ASSEMBLY, TOO.

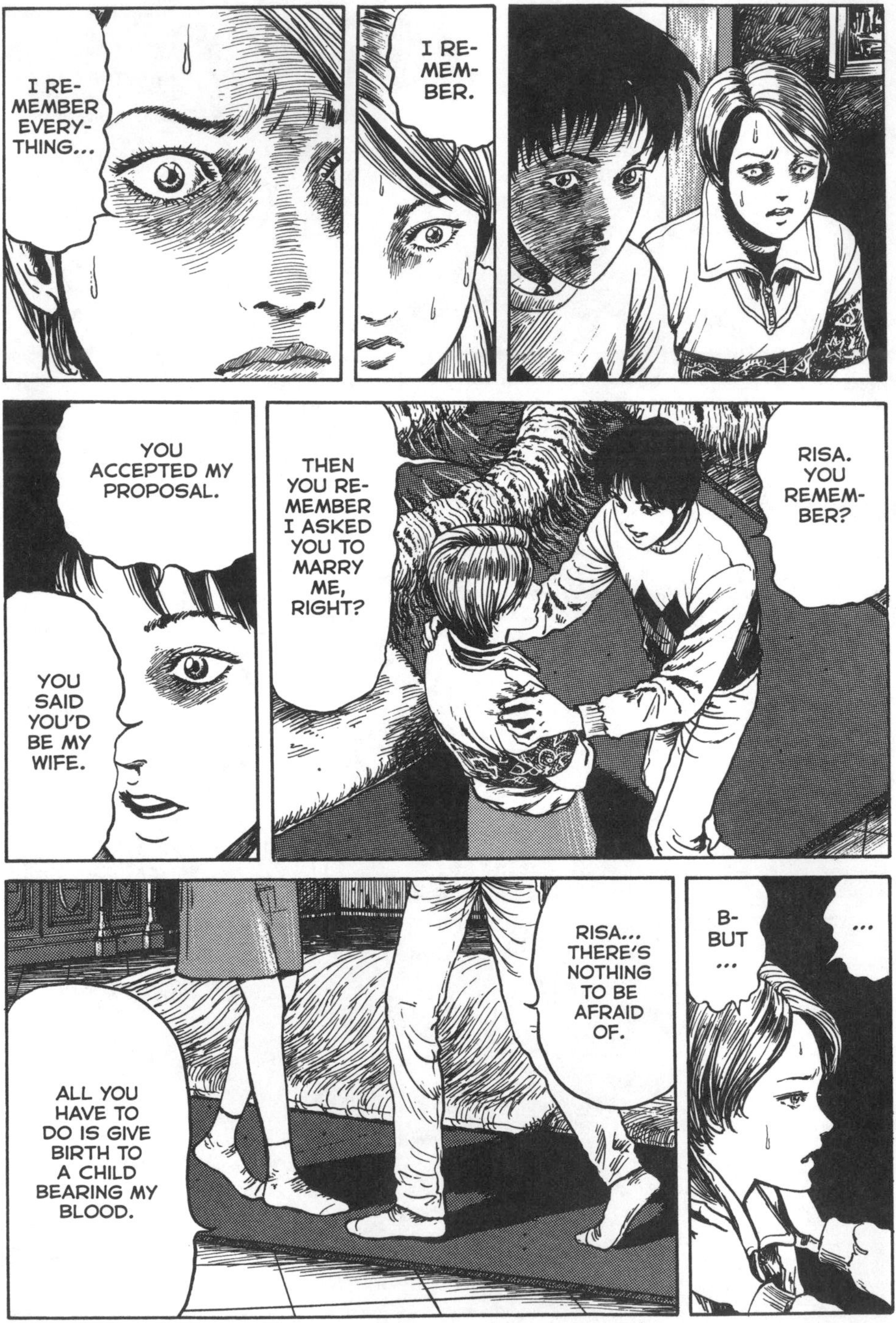
I RE-MEM-BER.
I RE-MEMBER EVERY-THING...
RISA. YOU REMEM-BER?
THEN YOU RE-MEMBER I ASKED YOU TO MARRY ME, RIGHT?
YOU ACCEPTED MY PROPOSAL.
YOU SAID YOU'D BE MY WIFE.
...
B-BUT...
RISA... THERE'S NOTHING TO BE AFRAID OF.
ALL YOU HAVE TO DO IS GIVE BIRTH TO A CHILD BEARING MY BLOOD.

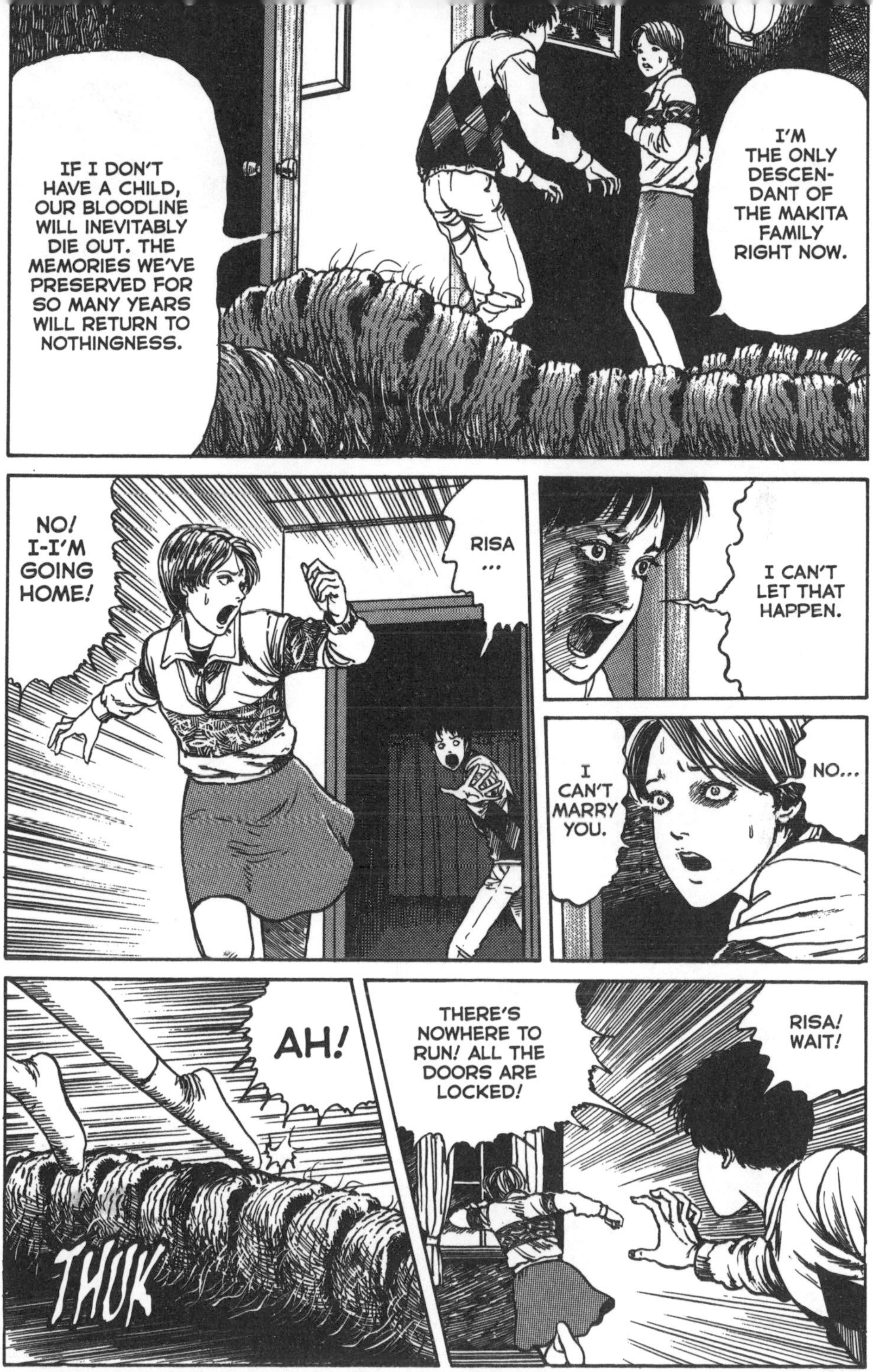

I'M THE ONLY DESCEN-DANT OF THE MAKITA FAMILY RIGHT NOW.
IF I DON'T HAVE A CHILD, OUR BLOODLINE WILL INEVITABLY DIE OUT. THE MEMORIES WE'VE PRESERVED FOR SO MANY YEARS WILL RETURN TO NOTHINGNESS.
I CAN'T LET THAT HAPPEN.
NO...
I CAN'T MARRY YOU.
RISA ...
NO! I-I'M GOING HOME!
RISA! WAIT!
THERE'S NOWHERE TO RUN! ALL THE DOORS ARE LOCKED!
AH!
THUK

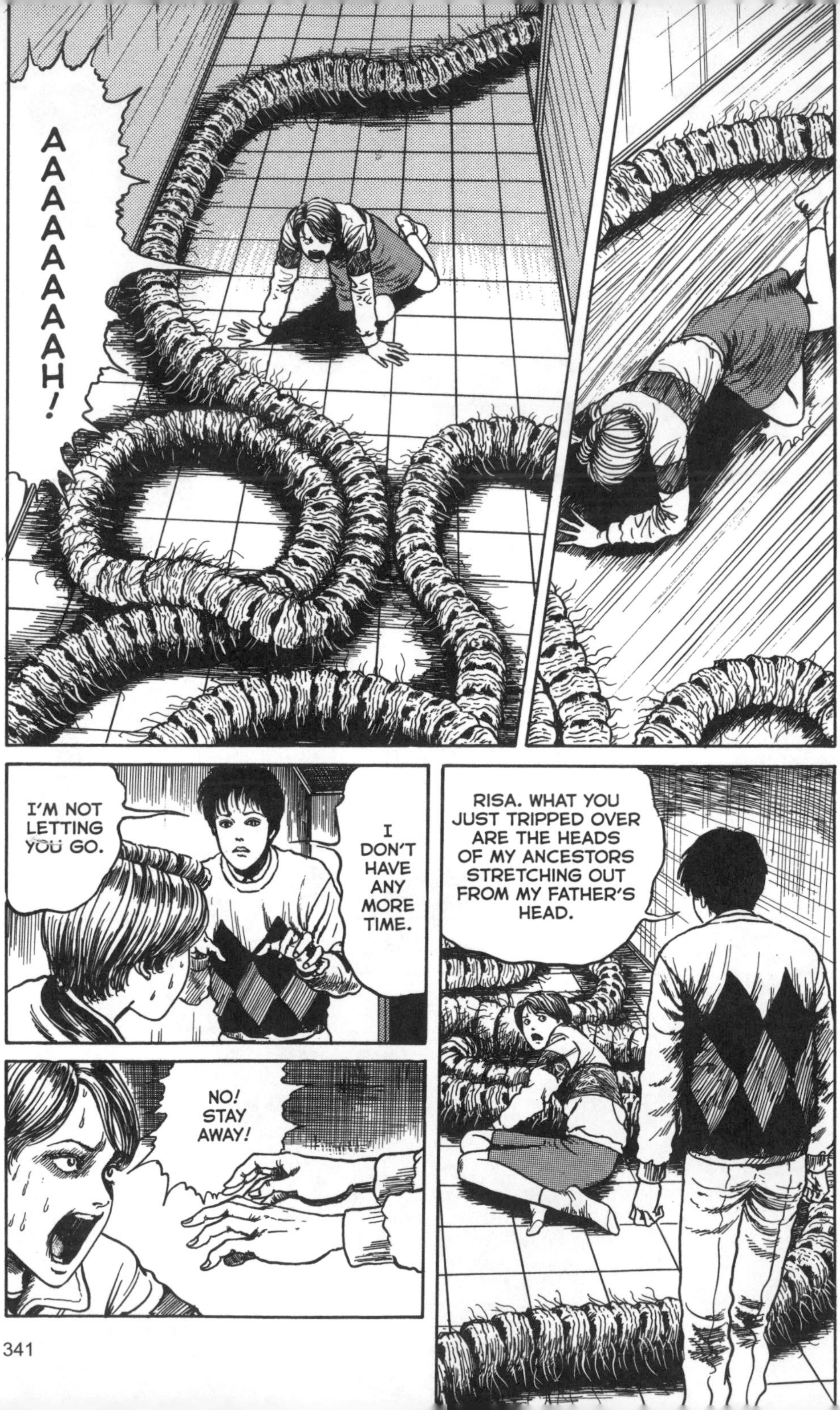
AAAAAAAAH!
RISA. WHAT YOU JUST TRIPPED OVER ARE THE HEADS OF MY ANCESTORS STRETCHING OUT FROM MY FATHER'S HEAD.
I DON'T HAVE ANY MORE TIME.
I'M NOT LETTING YOU GO.
NO! STAY AWAY!

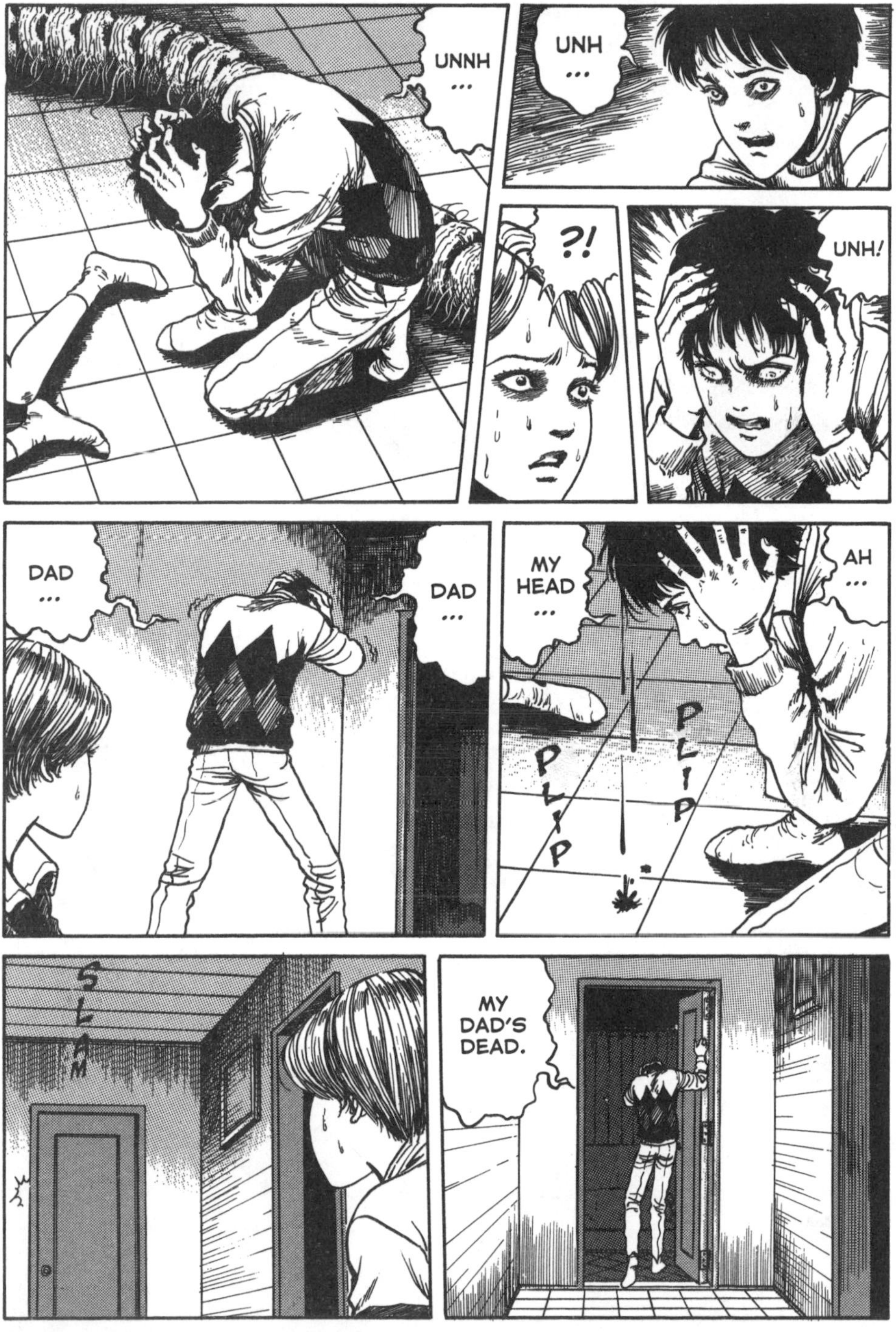
UNH ...
UNH!
?!
UNNH ...
AH ...
MY HEAD ...
PLIP
PLIP
DAD ...
DAD ...
MY DAD'S DEAD.
SLAM

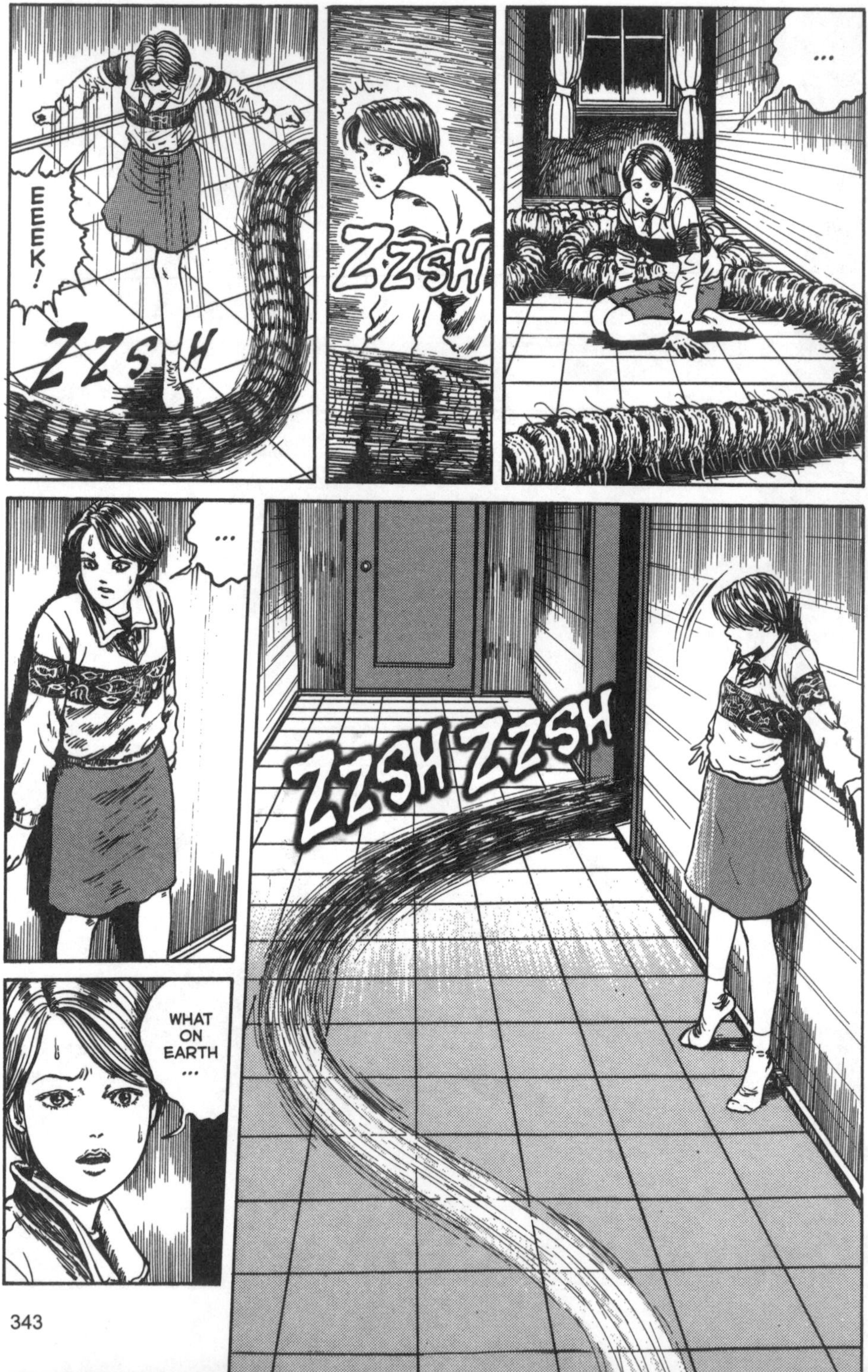
...
ZZSH
EEEK!
ZZSH
ZZSH ZZSH
...
WHAT ON EARTH ...

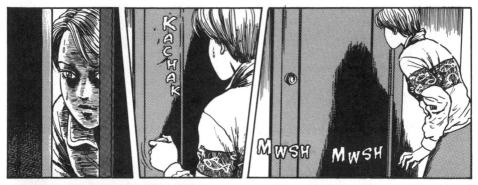

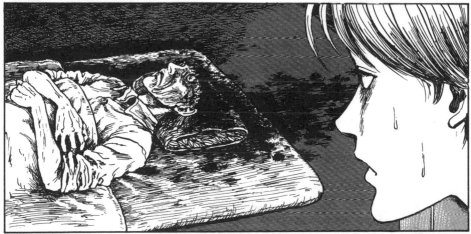

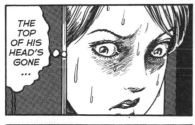

THE
TOP
OF HIS
HEAD'S
GONE
...

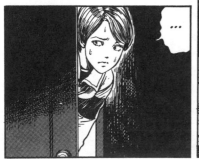

...

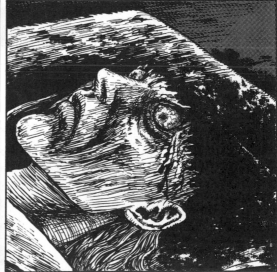

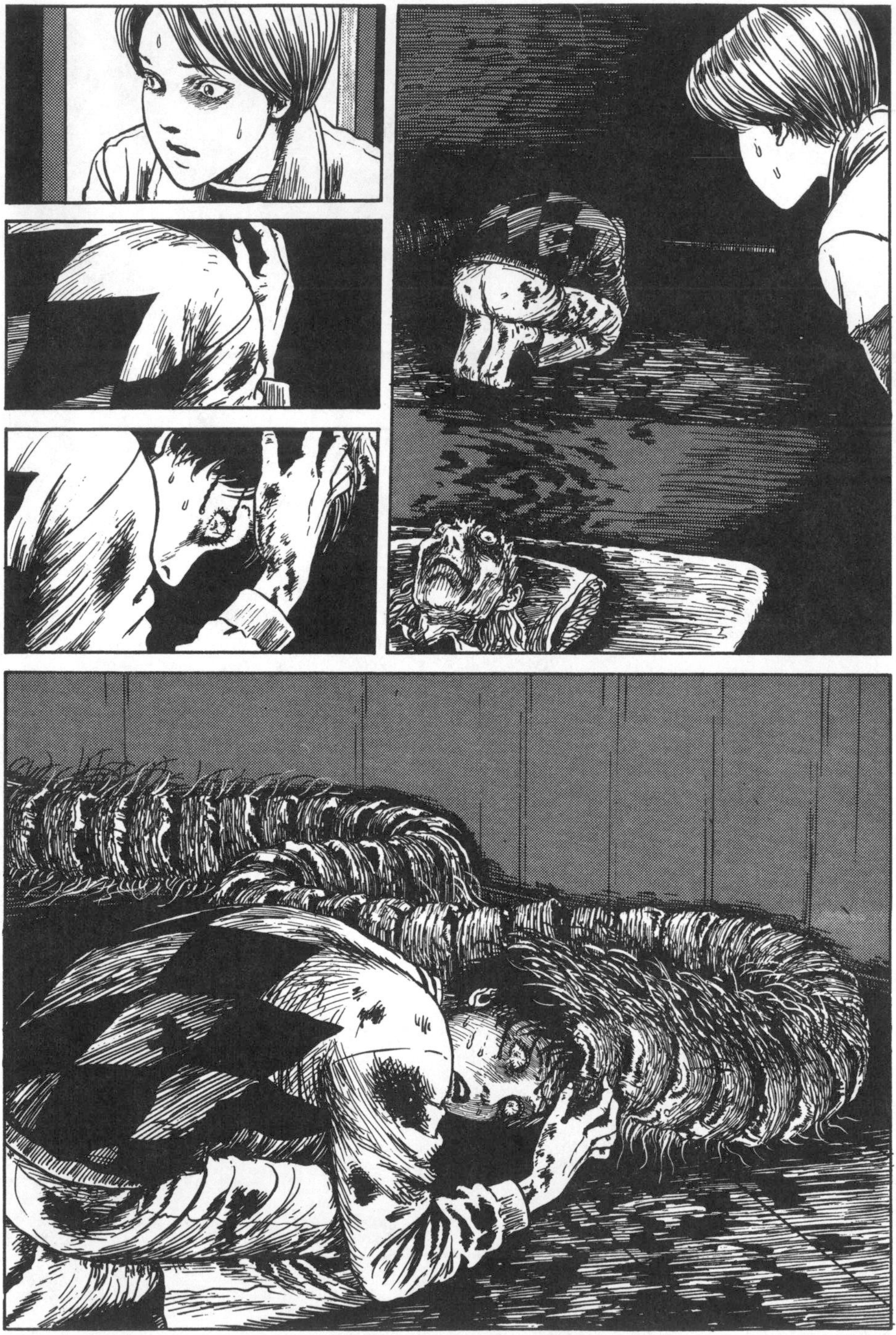

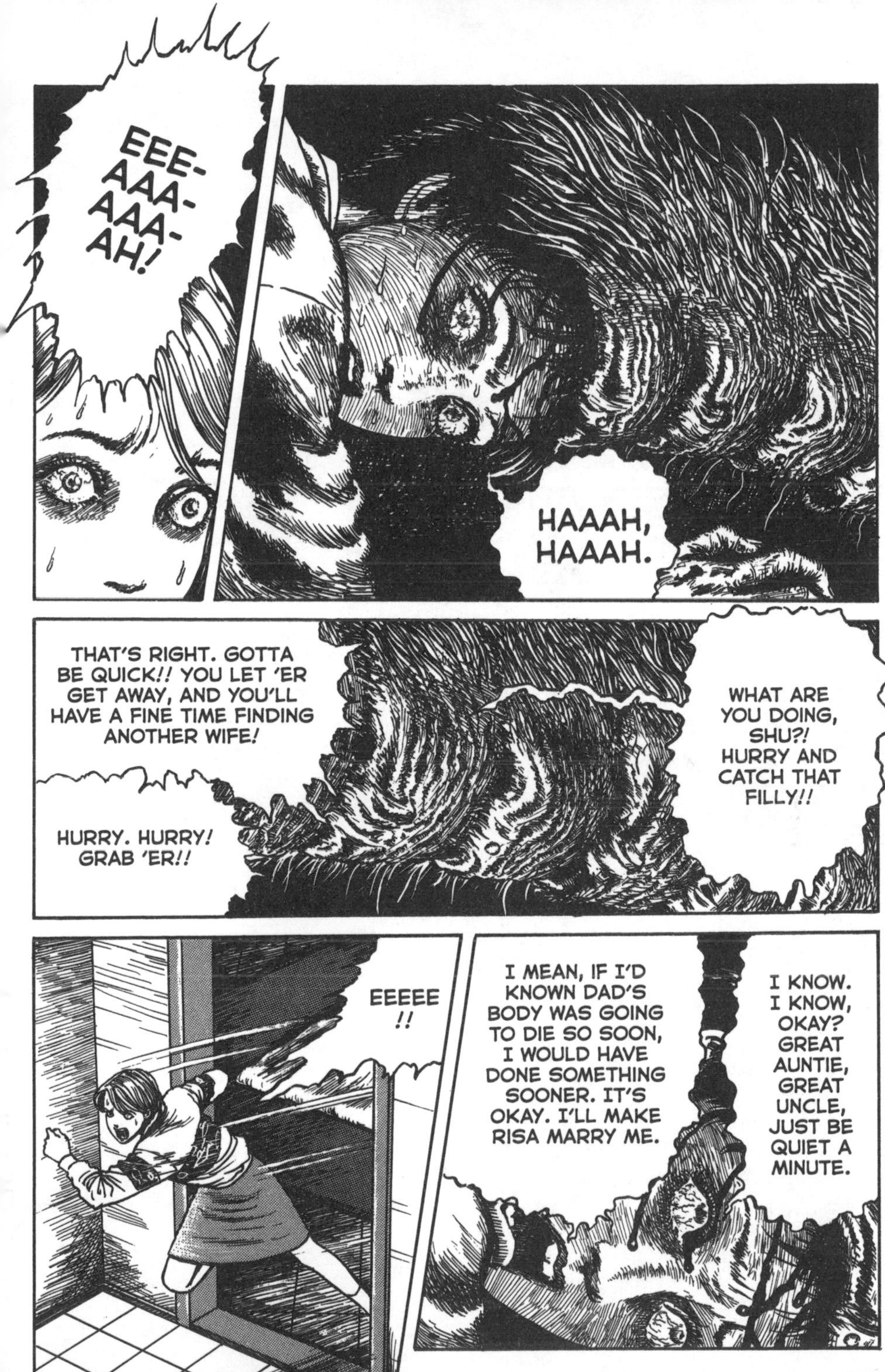
HAAAH, HAAAH.
EEE-AAA-AAA-AH!
WHAT ARE YOU DOING, SHU?! HURRY AND CATCH THAT FILLY!!
THAT'S RIGHT. GOTTA BE QUICK!! YOU LET 'ER GET AWAY, AND YOU'LL HAVE A FINE TIME FINDING ANOTHER WIFE!
HURRY. HURRY! GRAB 'ER!!
I KNOW. I KNOW, OKAY? GREAT AUNTIE, GREAT UNCLE, JUST BE QUIET A MINUTE.
I MEAN, IF I'D KNOWN DAD'S BODY WAS GOING TO DIE SO SOON, I WOULD HAVE DONE SOMETHING SOONER. IT'S OKAY. I'LL MAKE RISA MARRY ME.
EEEEE !!

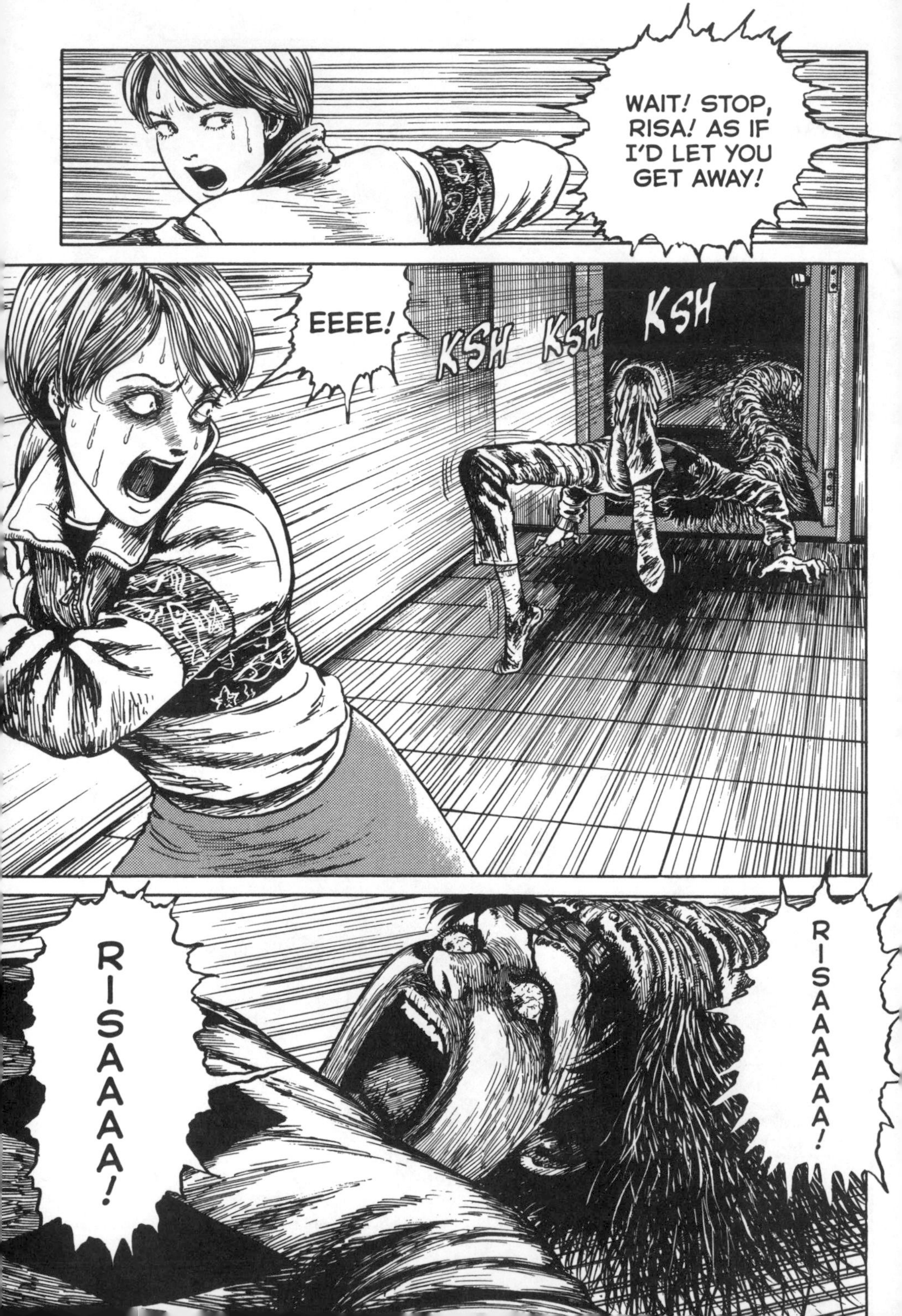
WAIT! STOP, RISA! AS IF I'D LET YOU GET AWAY!
KSH KSH KSH
EEEE!
RISAAAAAA!
RISAAAA!

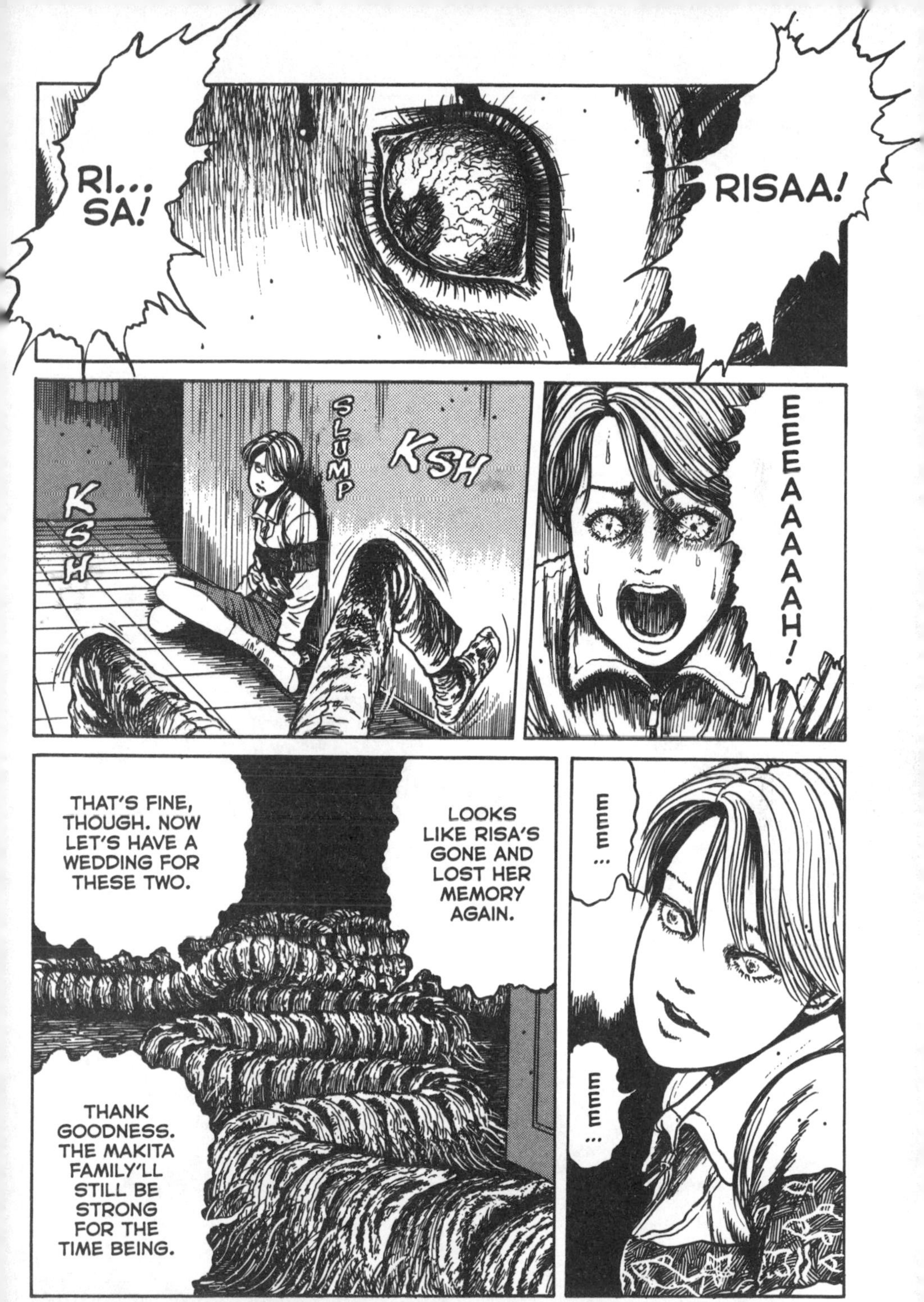
RISAA!
RI... SA!
EEEAAAAAAH!
SLUMP
KSH
KSH
EEE...
EEE...
LOOKS LIKE RISA'S GONE AND LOST HER MEMORY AGAIN.
THAT'S FINE, THOUGH. NOW LET'S HAVE A WEDDING FOR THESE TWO.
THANK GOODNESS. THE MAKITA FAMILY'LL STILL BE STRONG FOR THE TIME BEING.

HONORED ANCESTORS / END

HONORED ANCESTORS

I started with an image of a monster with connected heads. These were the heads of the ancestors, and the ancestors parasitized the bodies of their descendants. When I have this kind of very clear image right from the start, the story is easy to create. All I have to do is think about it inductively moving, toward the image. I used to create like that a lot. As the ideas dry up, a lot of times I'll write the story by forcing some vague image or idea to take shape. In those cases, it really is a lot of work. Lately, it's been nothing but that.

The scene where the descendant carrying all the ancestors is lying on his back running is something I was proud to create, but later when the director's cut of *The Exorcist* was released, I found out there was this thing called the "spider walk," and I was a little disappointed.

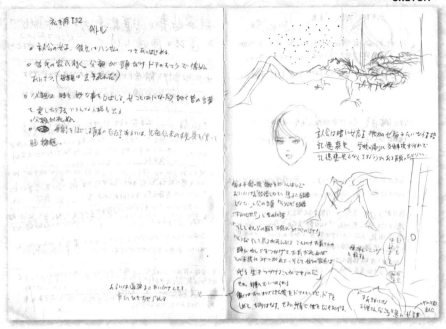

[Left page]

For Nemuki P32

Title

- *Protagonist girl. Handsome boy. They start going out.*
- *They go to his house. His dad greets her, poking just his head out from the other side of the door. (His mother died last year.)*
- *Father sometimes says weird things. He'll start talking like a woman or use words that are ridiculously old. All kinds of personalities show up.*
- *The father dies.*
- *A doctor who carries out an operation? Or a brain transplant using some secret family heirloom tool.*

[Right page]

The protagonist is a gloomy high school girl. Personality like the female version of Oshikiri.

<u>*Amnesia.*</u> *She loses her memory in a traffic accident or something on the way home from school, and after wandering for a while, she arrives at a certain house.*

After the operation, he crawls around on all fours. "Get married. Marry my son," says the father. "A-yup! You gotta get married!," old-fashioned way of speaking.

"An' then our descendant's gotta inherit our brains!"

"And then when my son dies, next, we'll be connected to your head. And when you die, that child will inherit. And then our family can live on through the generations."

She's chased into a small room.

When he comes chasing after her, she slams the door shut and cuts him off. She holds him in her arms in the small room.

↓

Or he chases her out into the road and gets ripped apart by a car.

Calls it strength training.

"Hello, it's nice to meet you."

"My goodness, what a lovely girl" Suddenly talks like a woman → protagonist shivers

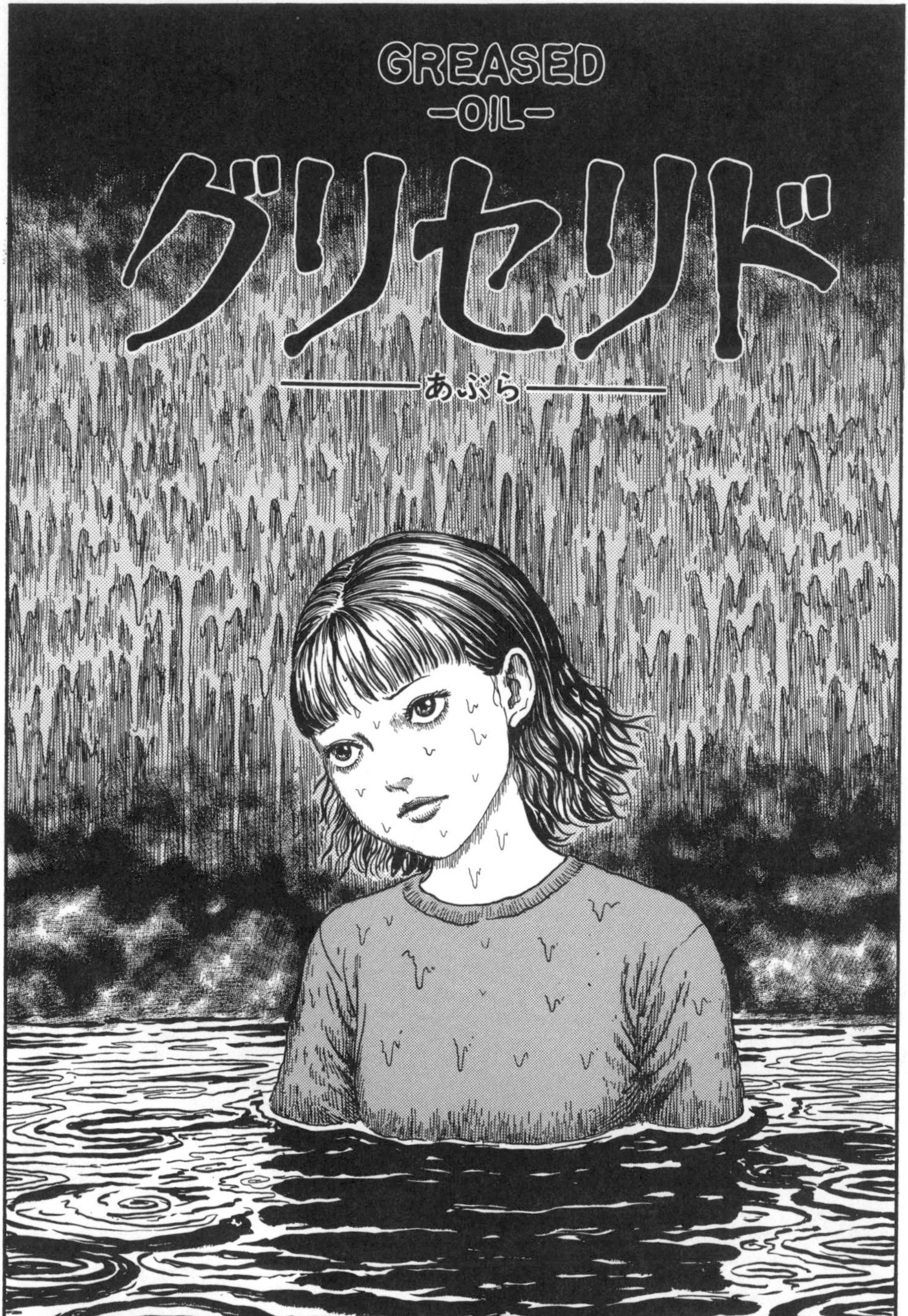
GREASED
-OIL-
グリセリド
あぶら

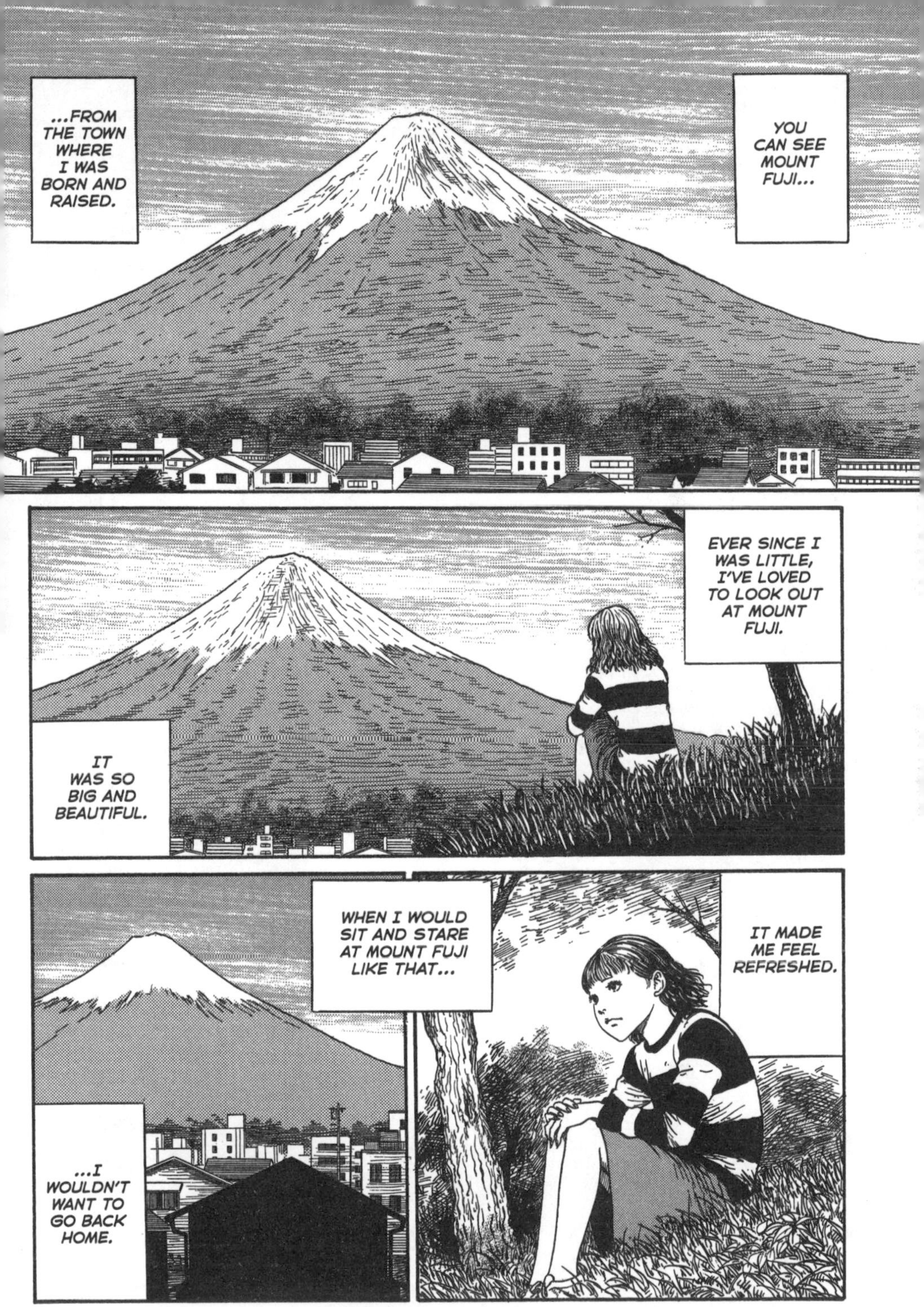
YOU CAN SEE MOUNT FUJI...
...FROM THE TOWN WHERE I WAS BORN AND RAISED.
EVER SINCE I WAS LITTLE, I'VE LOVED TO LOOK OUT AT MOUNT FUJI.
IT WAS SO BIG AND BEAUTIFUL.
WHEN I WOULD SIT AND STARE AT MOUNT FUJI LIKE THAT...
IT MADE ME FEEL REFRESHED.
...I WOULDN'T WANT TO GO BACK HOME.

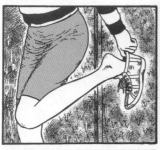

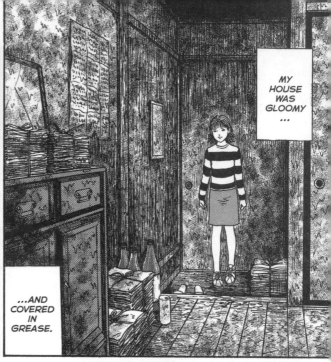

MY HOUSE WAS GLOOMY...

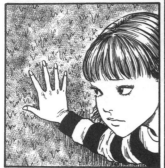

...AND COVERED IN GREASE.

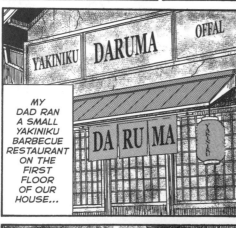

YAKINIKU DARUMA OFFAL

DA RU MA

MY DAD RAN A SMALL YAKINIKU BARBECUE RESTAURANT ON THE FIRST FLOOR OF OUR HOUSE...

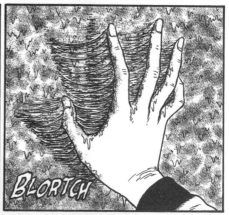

BLORTCH

...BUT THE VENTILATION WAS POOR, AND THE OILY SMOKE...

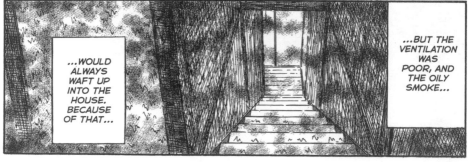

...WOULD ALWAYS WAFT UP INTO THE HOUSE. BECAUSE OF THAT...

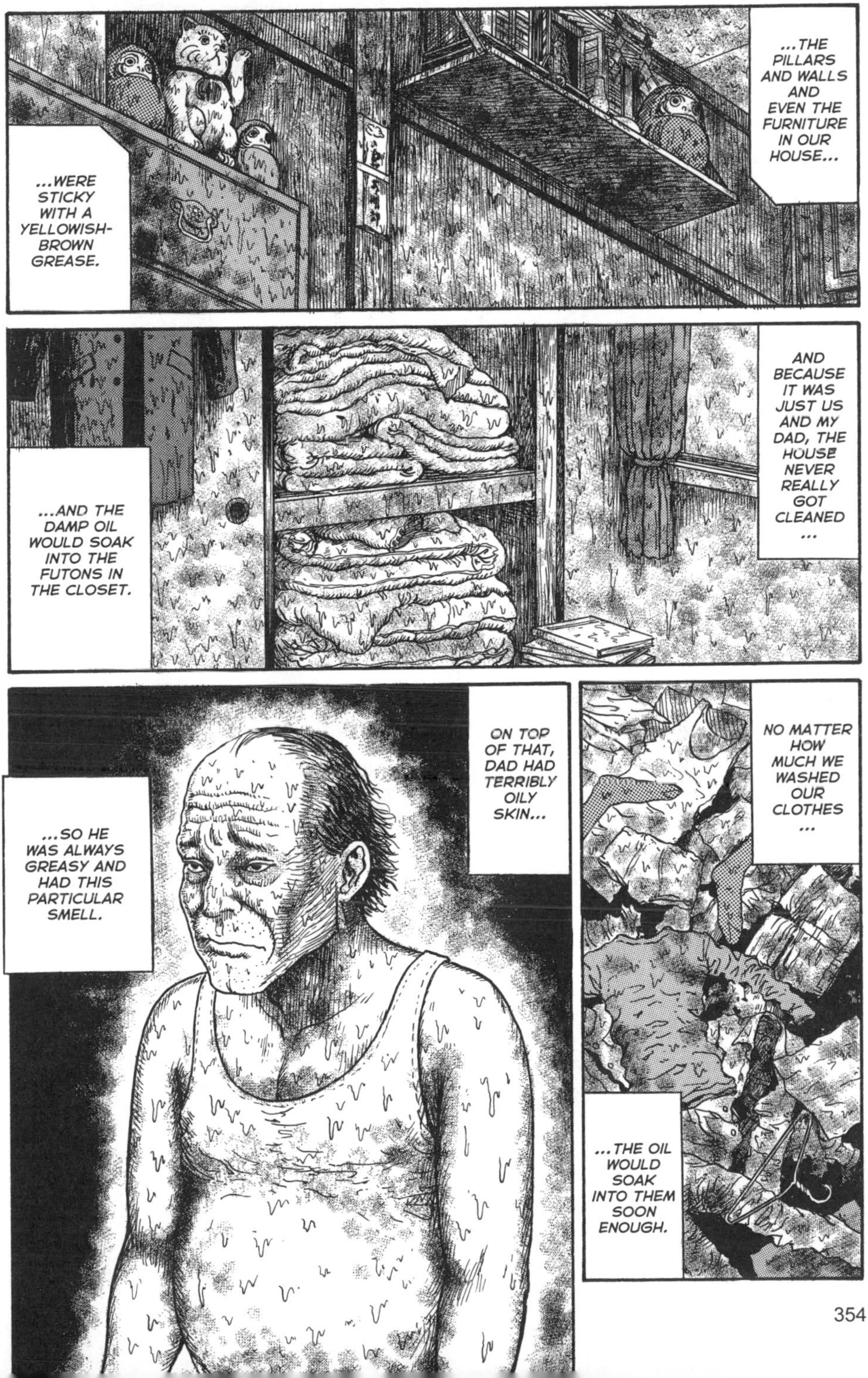
...THE PILLARS AND WALLS AND EVEN THE FURNITURE IN OUR HOUSE...
...WERE STICKY WITH A YELLOWISH-BROWN GREASE.
AND BECAUSE IT WAS JUST US AND MY DAD, THE HOUSE NEVER REALLY GOT CLEANED ...
...AND THE DAMP OIL WOULD SOAK INTO THE FUTONS IN THE CLOSET.
NO MATTER HOW MUCH WE WASHED OUR CLOTHES ...
...THE OIL WOULD SOAK INTO THEM SOON ENOUGH.
ON TOP OF THAT, DAD HAD TERRIBLY OILY SKIN...
...SO HE WAS ALWAYS GREASY AND HAD THIS PARTICULAR SMELL.

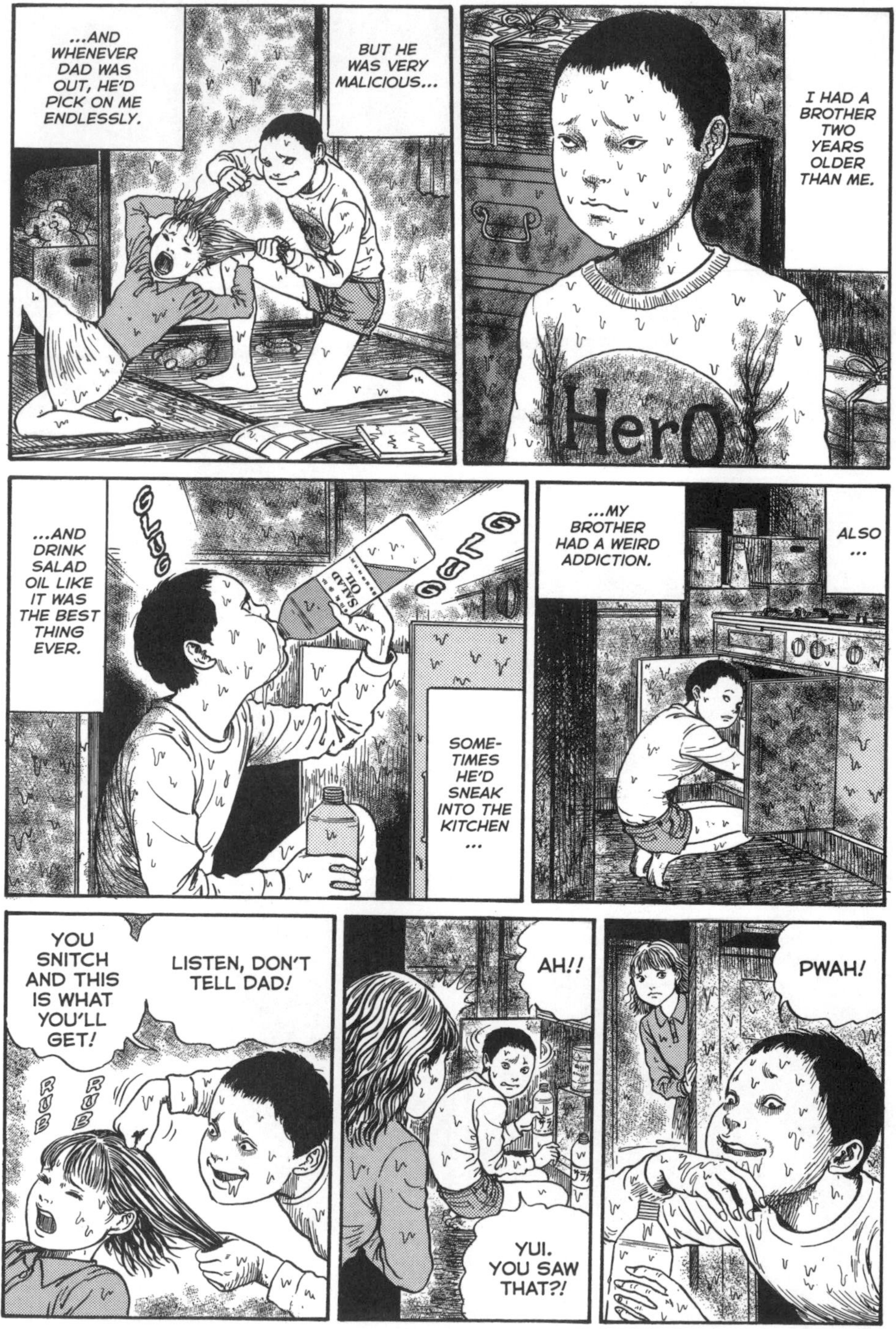
I HAD A BROTHER TWO YEARS OLDER THAN ME.
HerO
BUT HE WAS VERY MALICIOUS...
...AND WHENEVER DAD WAS OUT, HE'D PICK ON ME ENDLESSLY.
ALSO ...
...MY BROTHER HAD A WEIRD ADDICTION.
SOMETIMES HE'D SNEAK INTO THE KITCHEN ...
GLUG
GLUG
SALAD OIL
...AND DRINK SALAD OIL LIKE IT WAS THE BEST THING EVER.
PWAH!
AH!!
YUI. YOU SAW THAT?!
LISTEN, DON'T TELL DAD!
YOU SNITCH AND THIS IS WHAT YOU'LL GET!
RUB
RUB

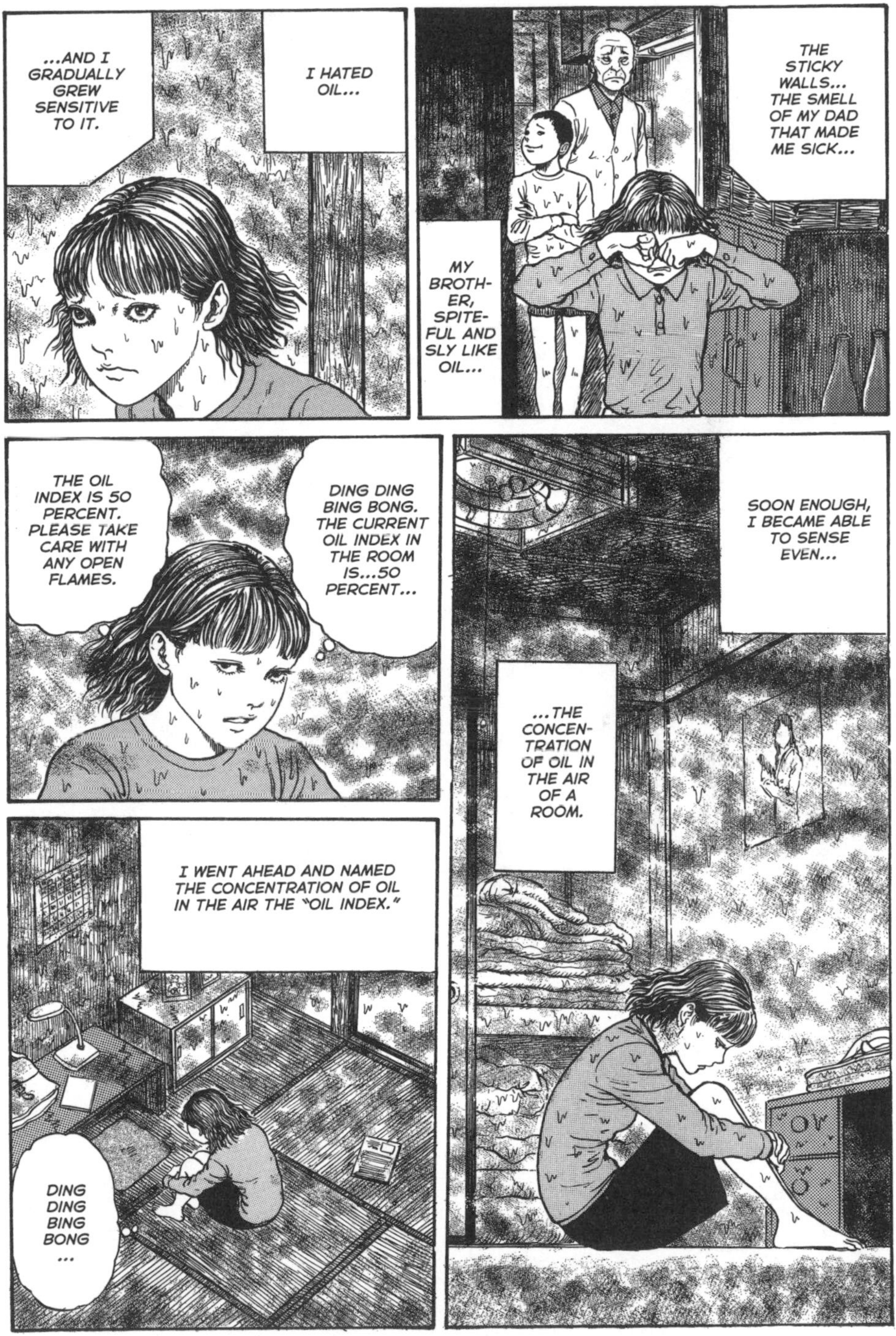
THE STICKY WALLS... THE SMELL OF MY DAD THAT MADE ME SICK...
MY BROTHER, SPITEFUL AND SLY LIKE OIL...
I HATED OIL...
...AND I GRADUALLY GREW SENSITIVE TO IT.
SOON ENOUGH, I BECAME ABLE TO SENSE EVEN...
...THE CONCENTRATION OF OIL IN THE AIR OF A ROOM.
DING DING BING BONG. THE CURRENT OIL INDEX IN THE ROOM IS...50 PERCENT...
THE OIL INDEX IS 50 PERCENT. PLEASE TAKE CARE WITH ANY OPEN FLAMES.
I WENT AHEAD AND NAMED THE CONCENTRATION OF OIL IN THE AIR THE "OIL INDEX."
DING DING BING BONG ...

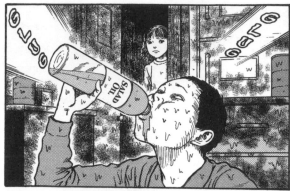
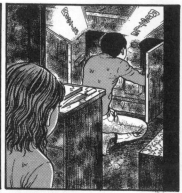

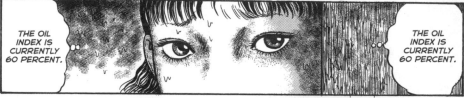

THE OIL INDEX IS CURRENTLY 60 PERCENT.

THE OIL INDEX IS CURRENTLY 60 PERCENT.

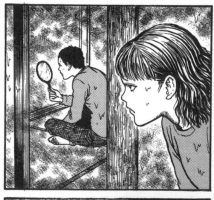

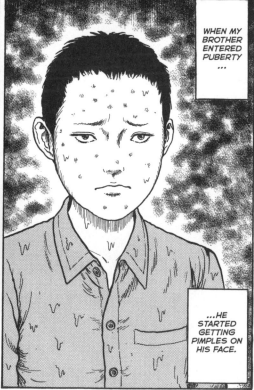

WHEN MY BROTHER ENTERED PUBERTY ...

...HE STARTED GETTING PIMPLES ON HIS FACE.

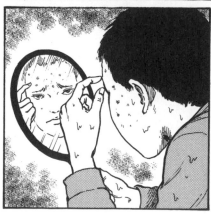

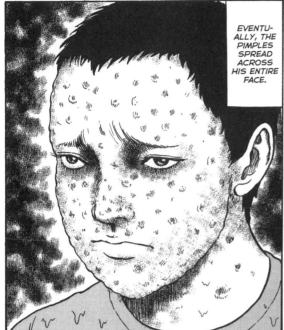

EVENTU-ALLY, THE PIMPLES SPREAD ACROSS HIS ENTIRE FACE.

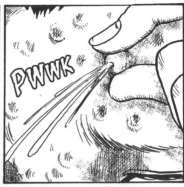

PWWK

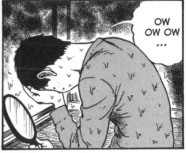

OW OW OW ...

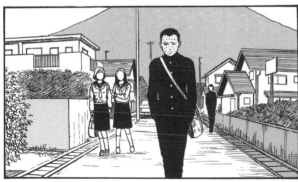

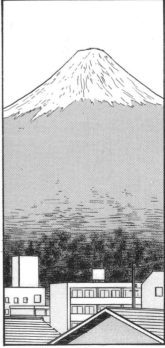

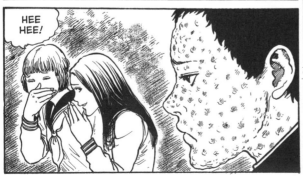

HEE HEE!

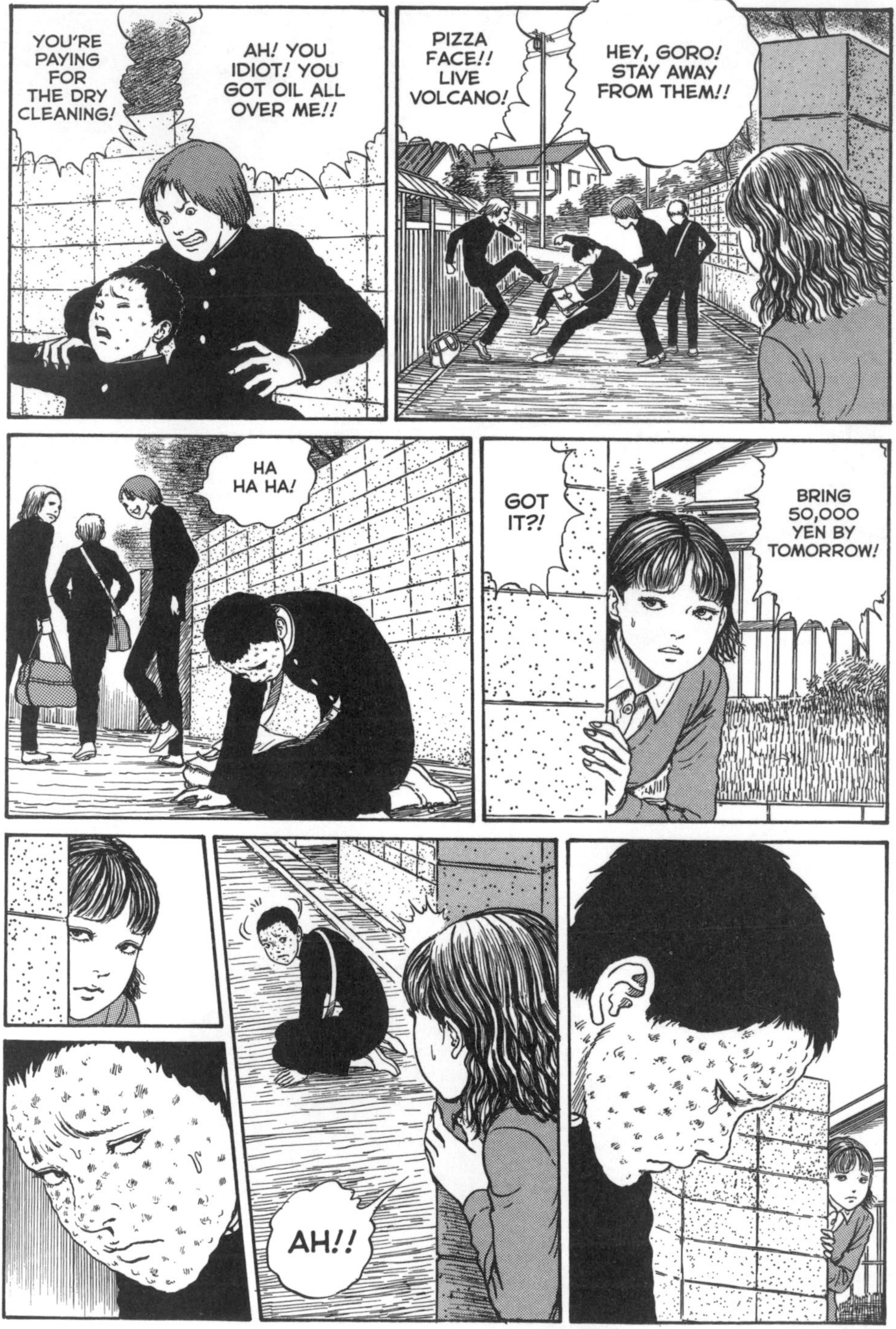
HEY, GORO! STAY AWAY FROM THEM!!
PIZZA FACE!! LIVE VOLCANO!
AH! YOU IDIOT! YOU GOT OIL ALL OVER ME!!
YOU'RE PAYING FOR THE DRY CLEANING!
BRING 50,000 YEN BY TOMORROW!
GOT IT?!
HA HA HA!
AH!!

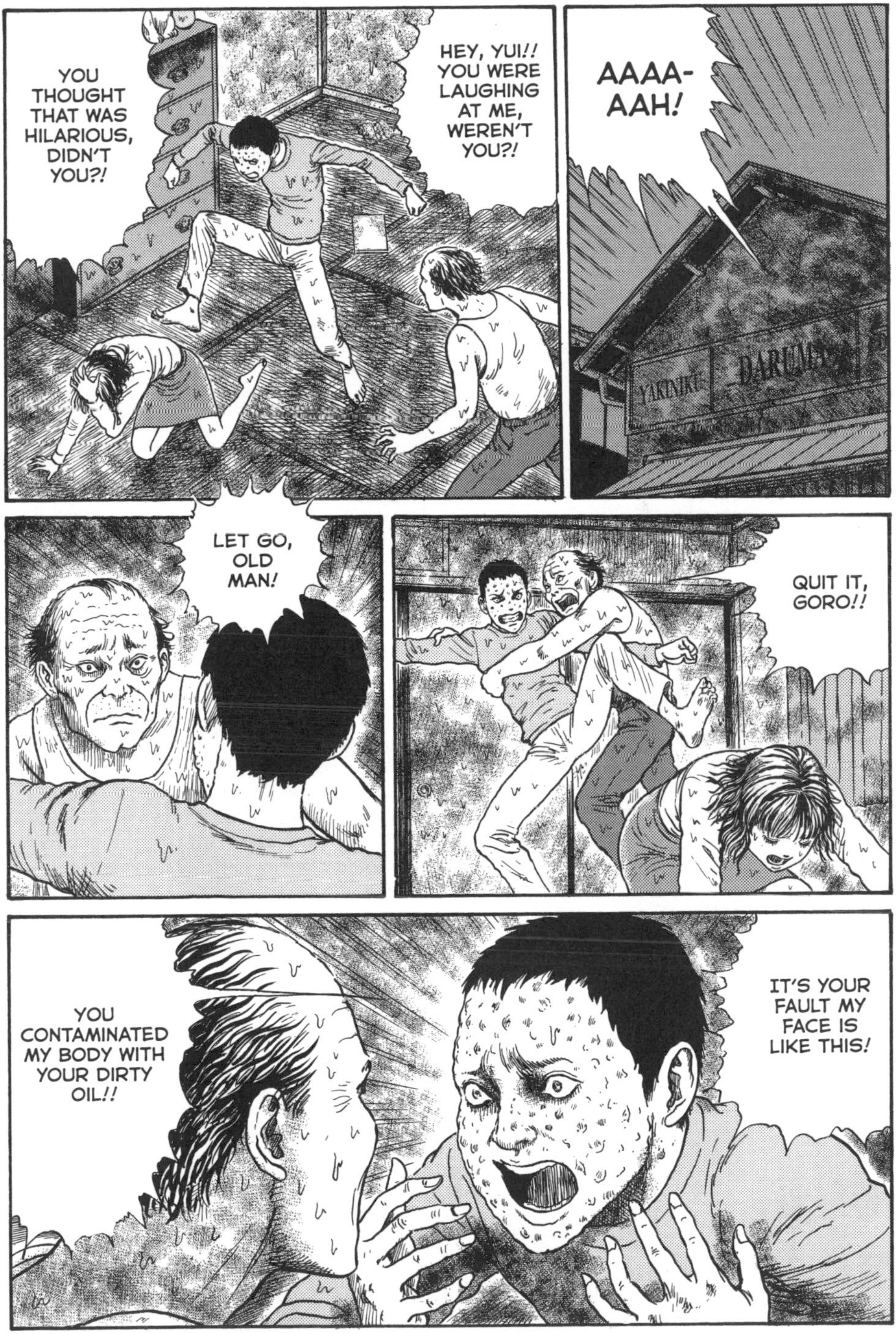
AAAA-AAH!
YAKINIKU
DARUMA
HEY, YUI!! YOU WERE LAUGHING AT ME, WEREN'T YOU?!
YOU THOUGHT THAT WAS HILARIOUS, DIDN'T YOU?!
QUIT IT, GORO!!
LET GO, OLD MAN!
IT'S YOUR FAULT MY FACE IS LIKE THIS!
YOU CONTAMINATED MY BODY WITH YOUR DIRTY OIL!!

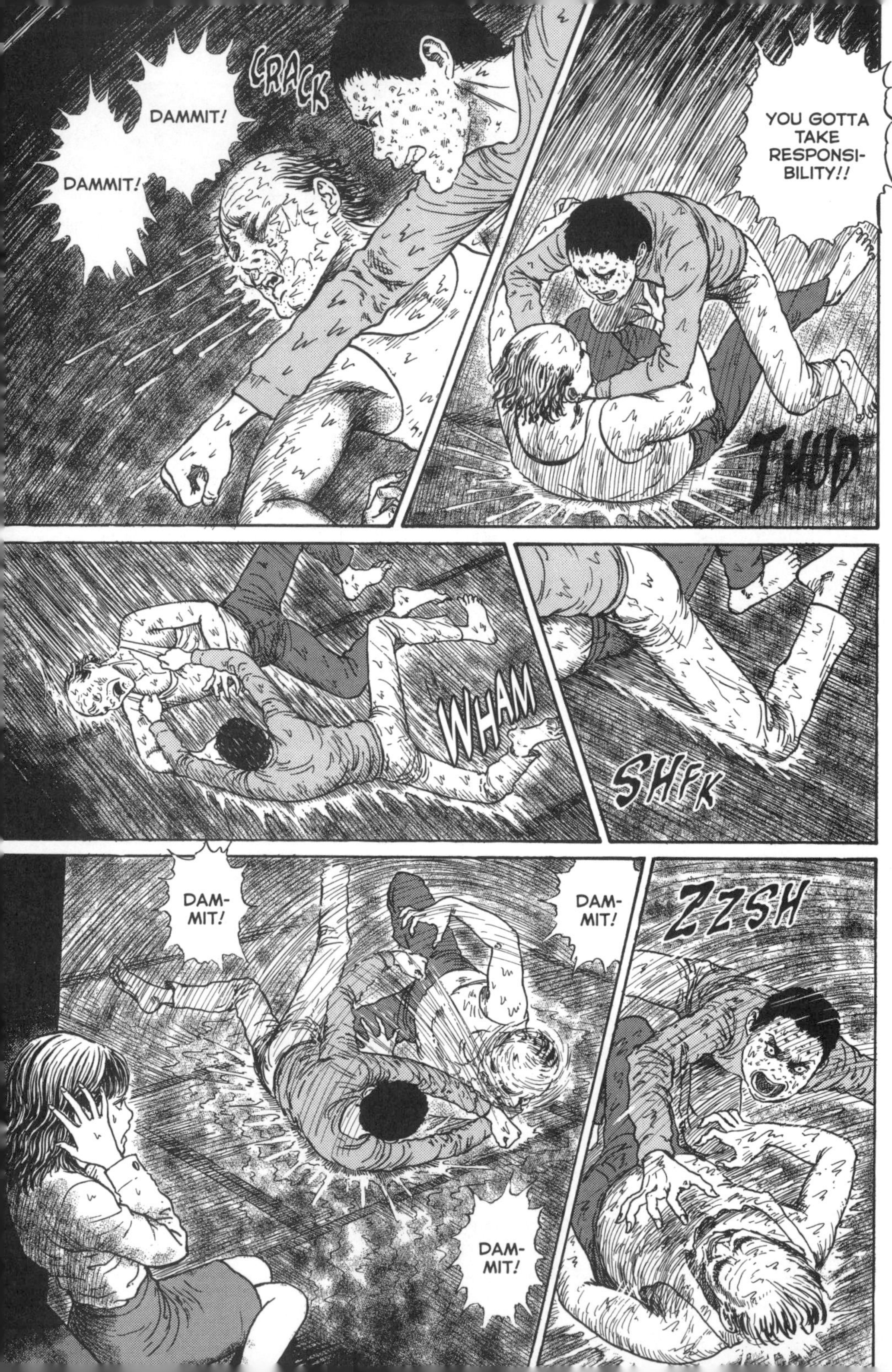
YOU GOTTA TAKE RESPONSI-BILITY!!
THUD
CRACK
DAMMIT!
DAMMIT!
SHFK
WHAM
ZZSH
DAM-MIT!
DAM-MIT!
DAM-MIT!

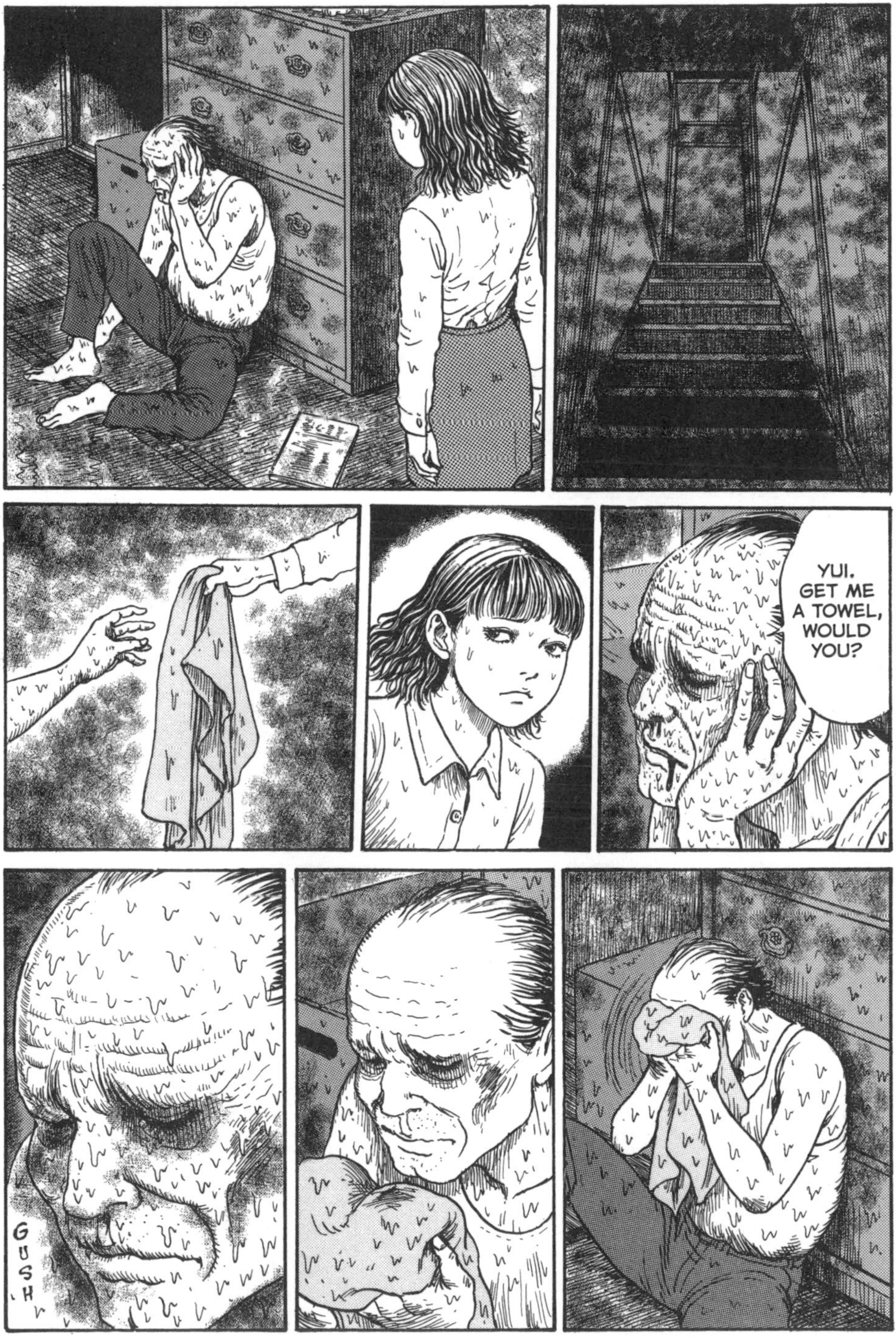
YUI. GET ME A TOWEL, WOULD YOU?
GUSH

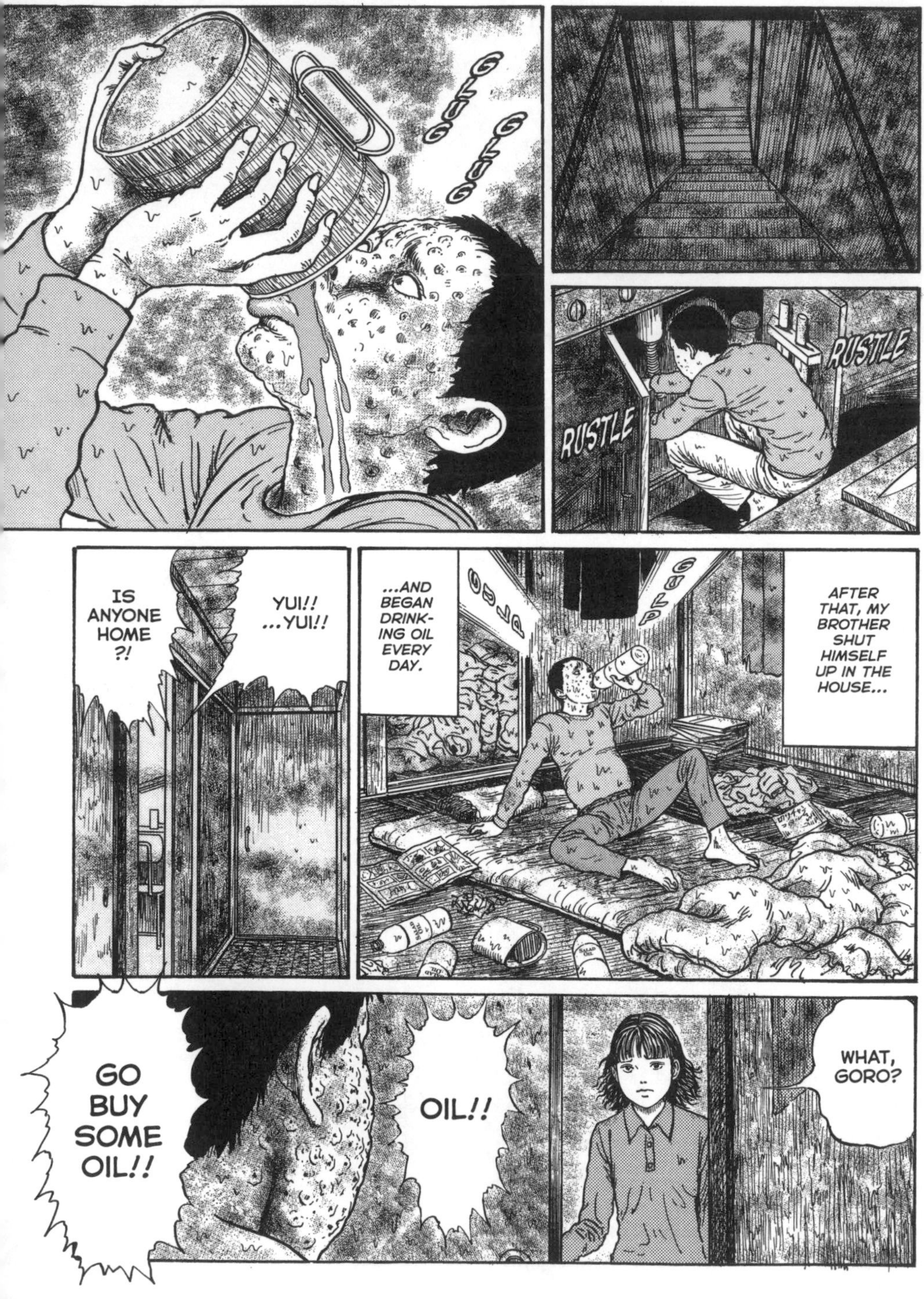
RUSTLE
RUSTLE
GLUG GLUG
AFTER THAT, MY BROTHER SHUT HIMSELF UP IN THE HOUSE...
...AND BEGAN DRINKING OIL EVERY DAY.
YUI!! ...YUI!!
IS ANYONE HOME?!
WHAT, GORO?
OIL!!
GO BUY SOME OIL!!

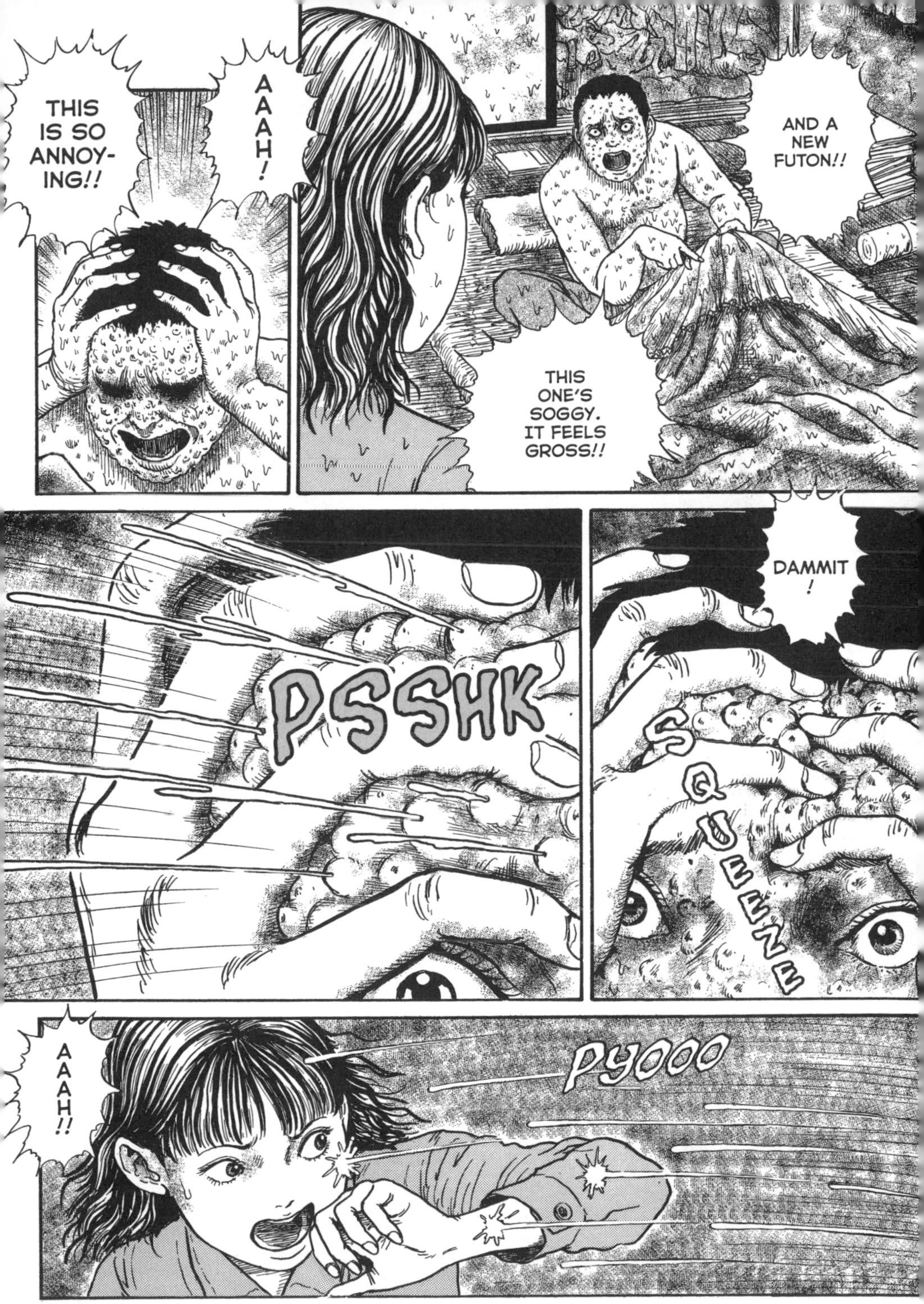
AND A NEW FUTON!!
THIS ONE'S SOGGY. IT FEELS GROSS!!
AAAH!
THIS IS SO ANNOY-ING!!
DAMMIT!
SQUEEZE
PSSHK
PYOOO
AAAH!!

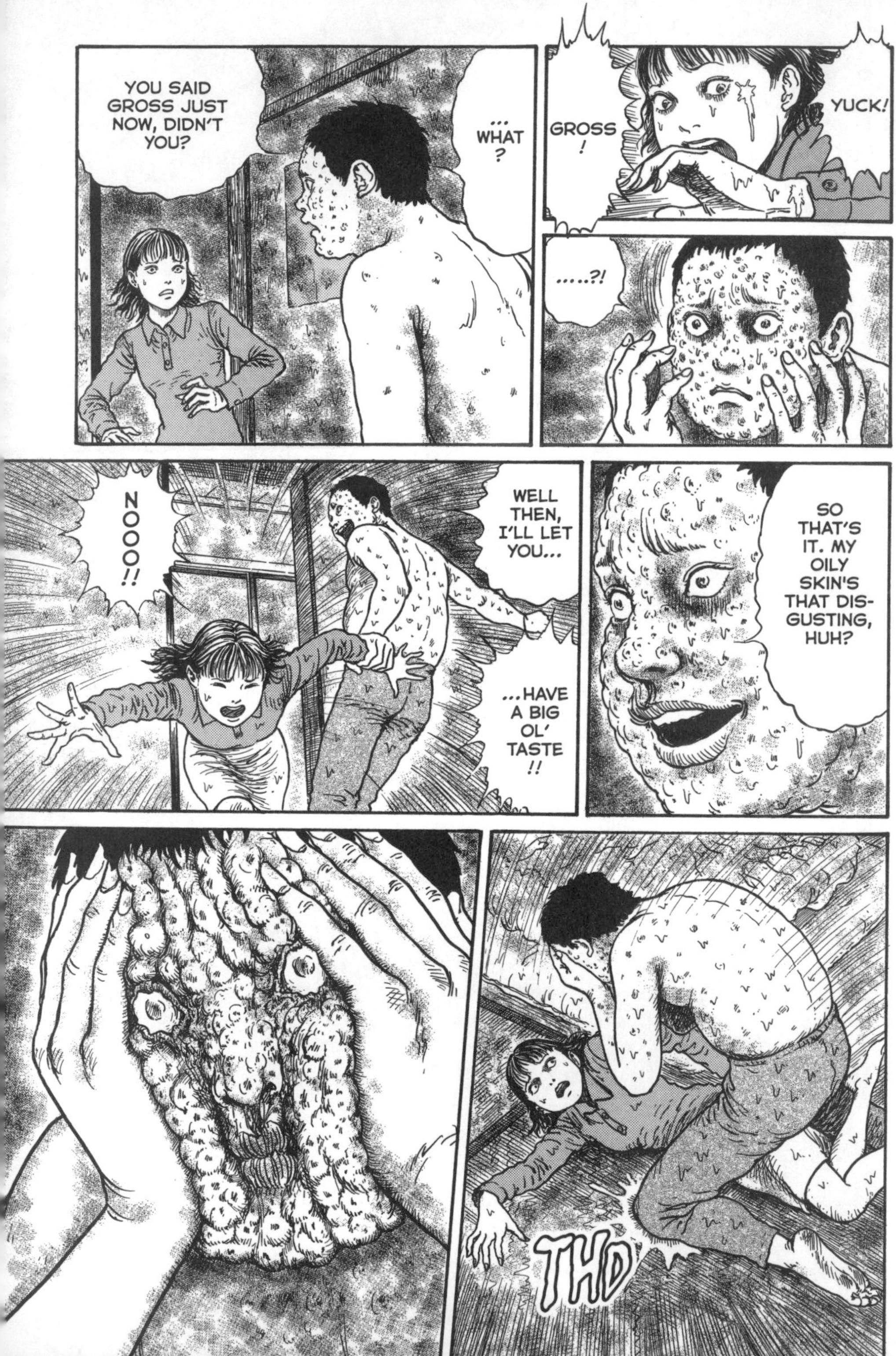
GROSS!
YUCK!
.....?!
...WHAT?
YOU SAID GROSS JUST NOW, DIDN'T YOU?
SO THAT'S IT. MY OILY SKIN'S THAT DIS-GUSTING, HUH?
WELL THEN, I'LL LET YOU...
...HAVE A BIG OL' TASTE!!
NOOOO!!
THD

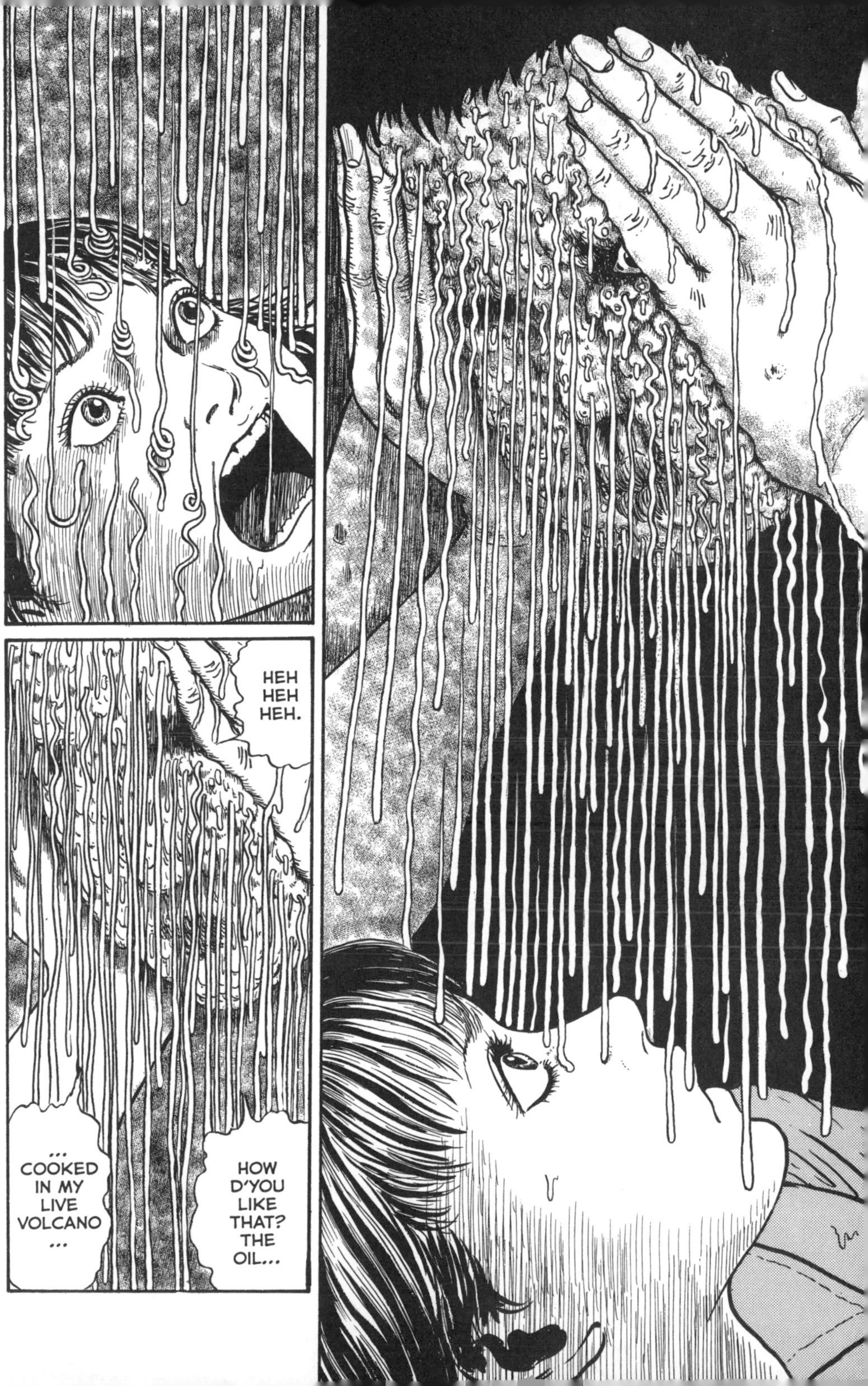
HEH HEH HEH.
HOW D'YOU LIKE THAT? THE OIL...
...COOKED IN MY LIVE VOLCANO...

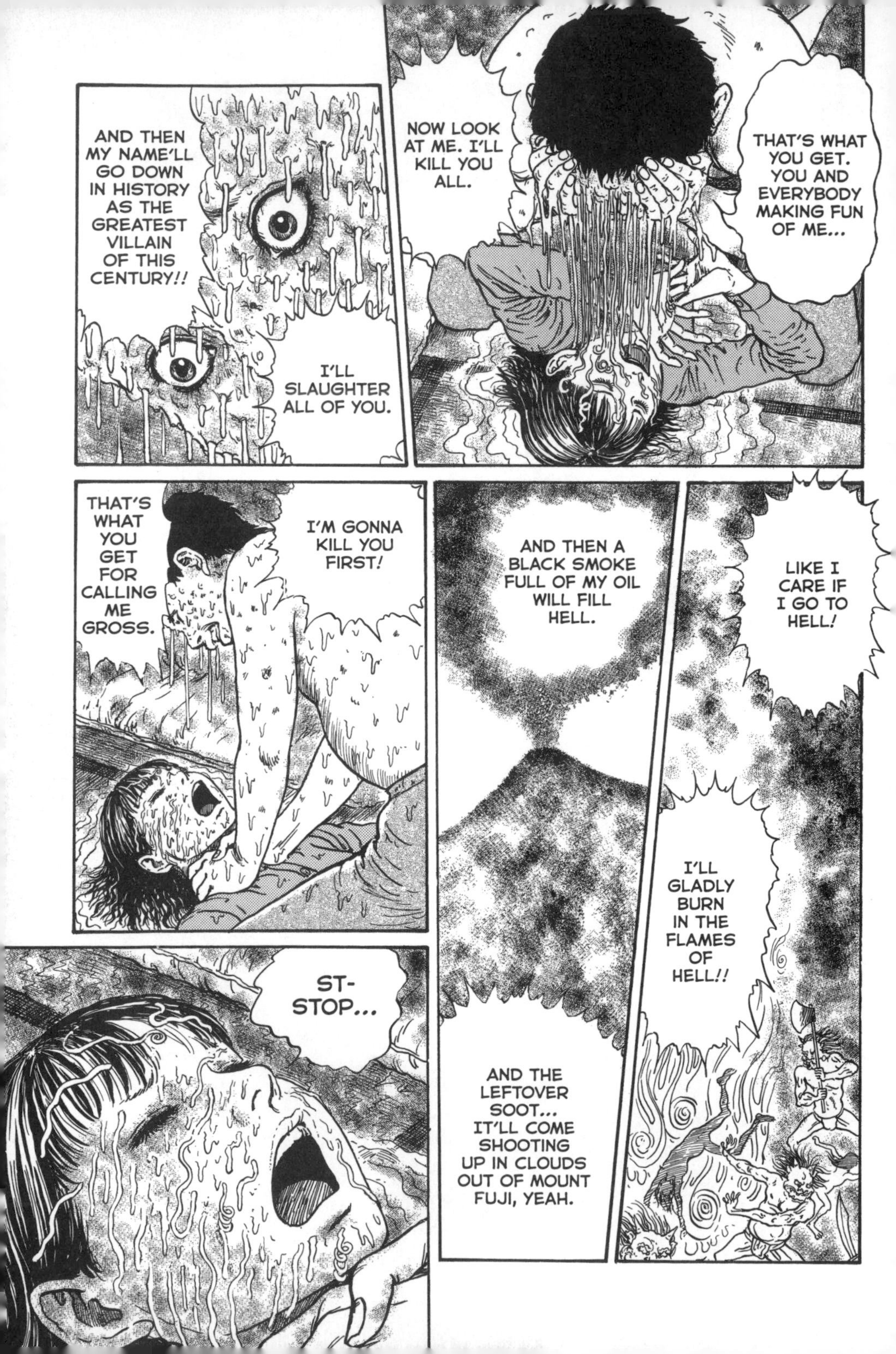

THAT'S WHAT YOU GET. YOU AND EVERYBODY MAKING FUN OF ME...
NOW LOOK AT ME. I'LL KILL YOU ALL.
I'LL SLAUGHTER ALL OF YOU.
AND THEN MY NAME'LL GO DOWN IN HISTORY AS THE GREATEST VILLAIN OF THIS CENTURY!!
LIKE I CARE IF I GO TO HELL!
I'LL GLADLY BURN IN THE FLAMES OF HELL!!
AND THEN A BLACK SMOKE FULL OF MY OIL WILL FILL HELL.
AND THE LEFTOVER SOOT... IT'LL COME SHOOTING UP IN CLOUDS OUT OF MOUNT FUJI, YEAH.
I'M GONNA KILL YOU FIRST!
THAT'S WHAT YOU GET FOR CALLING ME GROSS.
ST-STOP...

CLANG
HAAAH HAAAH.
SORRY, GORO.
FORGIVE ME.
YUI. HELP ME.
GRAB ONE OF HIS LEGS.
ZZSH
ZZSH
YAKINIKU
DARUMA
OFFAL
ZZSH

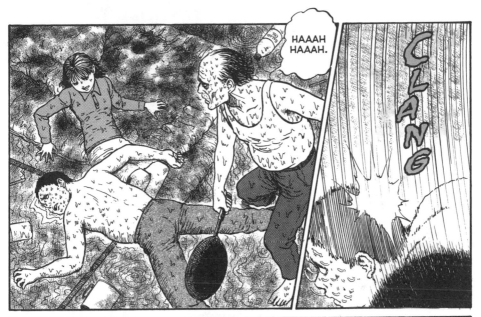

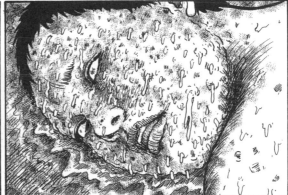

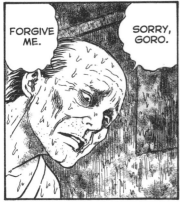

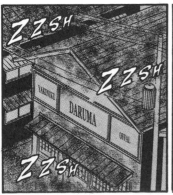

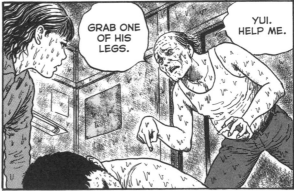

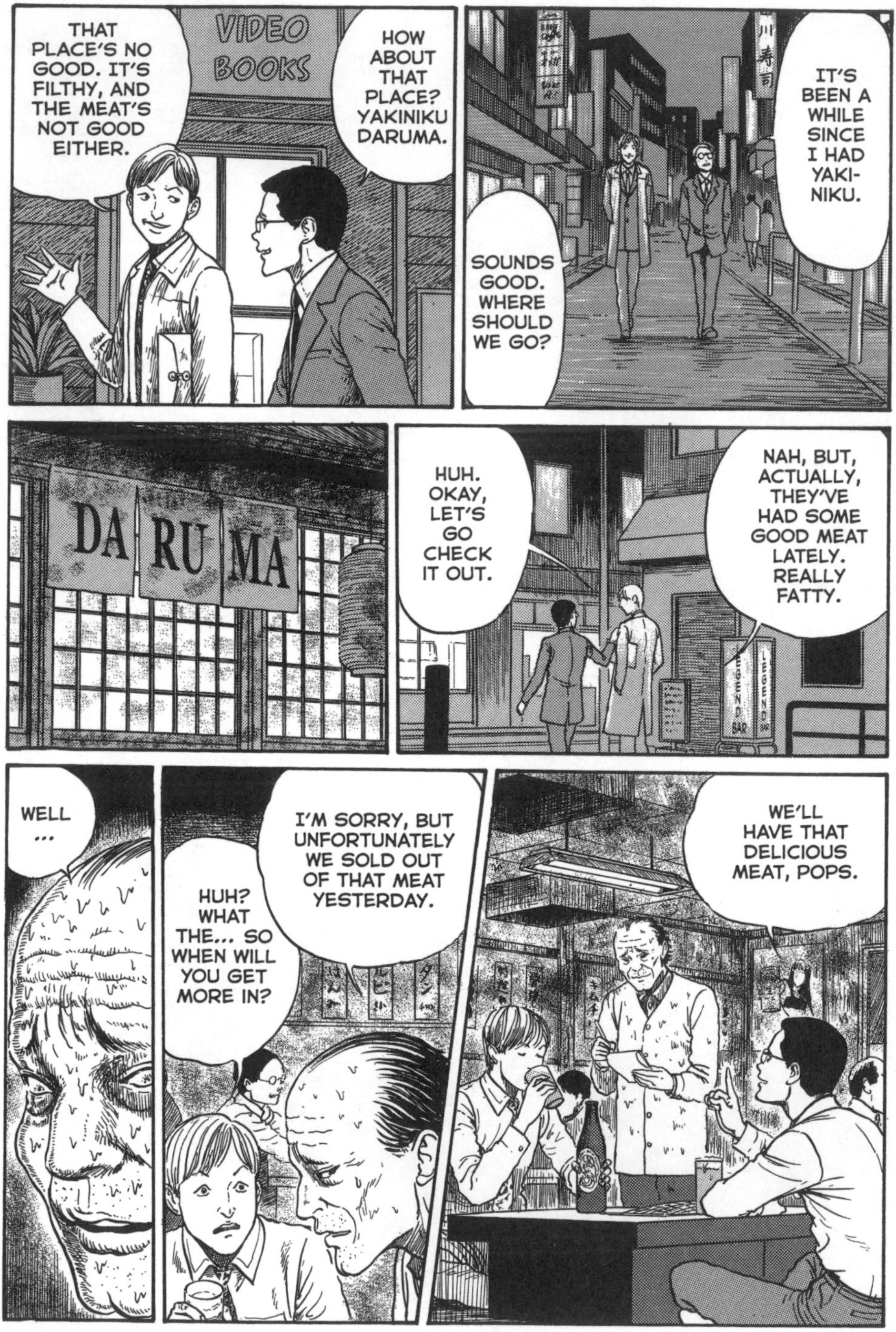
IT'S BEEN A WHILE SINCE I HAD YAKI-NIKU.
SOUNDS GOOD. WHERE SHOULD WE GO?
VIDEO BOOKS
HOW ABOUT THAT PLACE? YAKINIKU DARUMA.
THAT PLACE'S NO GOOD. IT'S FILTHY, AND THE MEAT'S NOT GOOD EITHER.
NAH, BUT, ACTUALLY, THEY'VE HAD SOME GOOD MEAT LATELY. REALLY FATTY.
HUH. OKAY, LET'S GO CHECK IT OUT.
LEGEND BAR
DA RU MA
WE'LL HAVE THAT DELICIOUS MEAT, POPS.
I'M SORRY, BUT UNFORTUNATELY WE SOLD OUT OF THAT MEAT YESTERDAY.
HUH? WHAT THE... SO WHEN WILL YOU GET MORE IN?
WELL ...

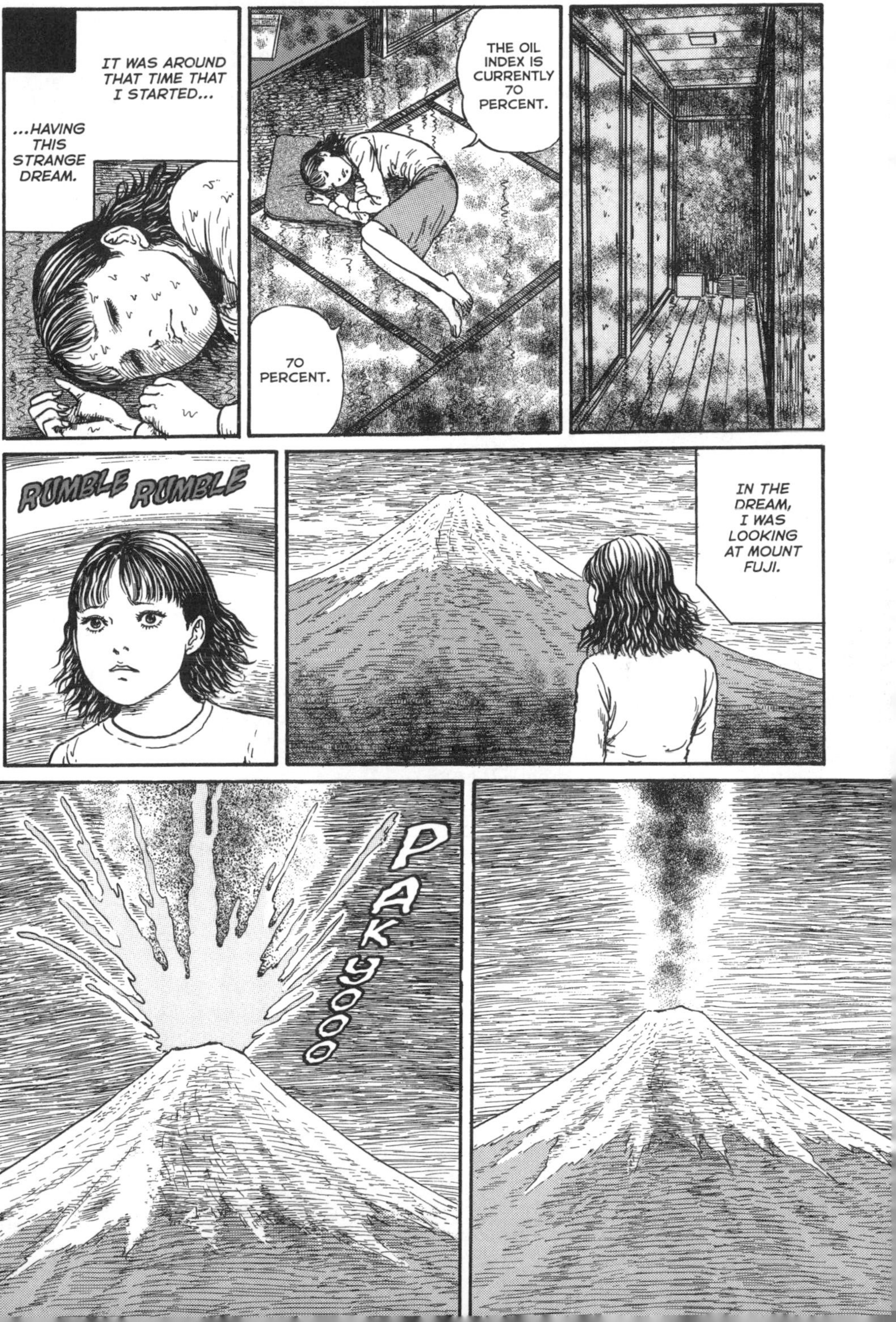
THE OIL INDEX IS CURRENTLY 70 PERCENT.
70 PERCENT.
IT WAS AROUND THAT TIME THAT I STARTED...
...HAVING THIS STRANGE DREAM.
IN THE DREAM, I WAS LOOKING AT MOUNT FUJI.
RUMBLE RUMBLE
PAKYOOO

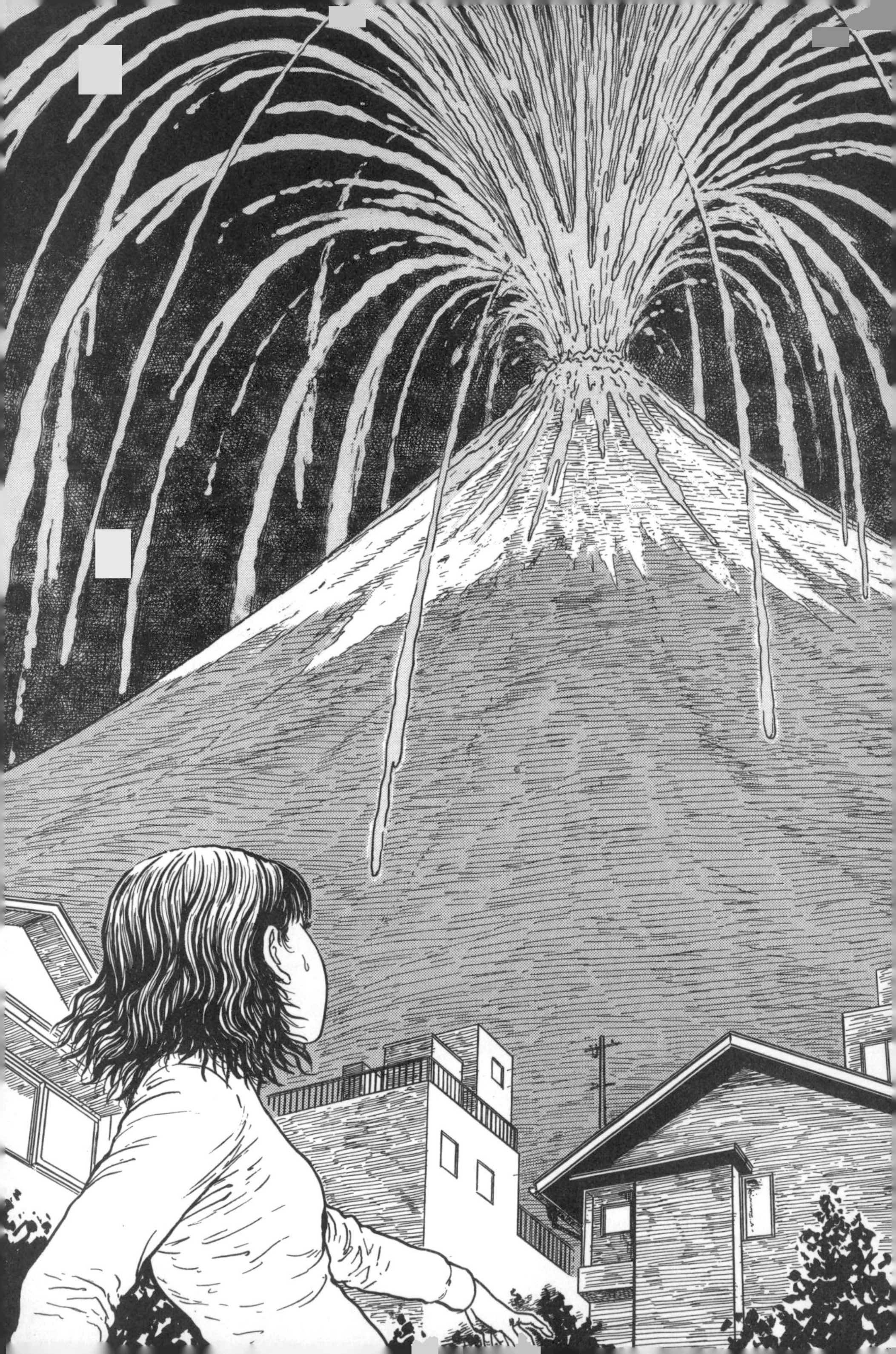

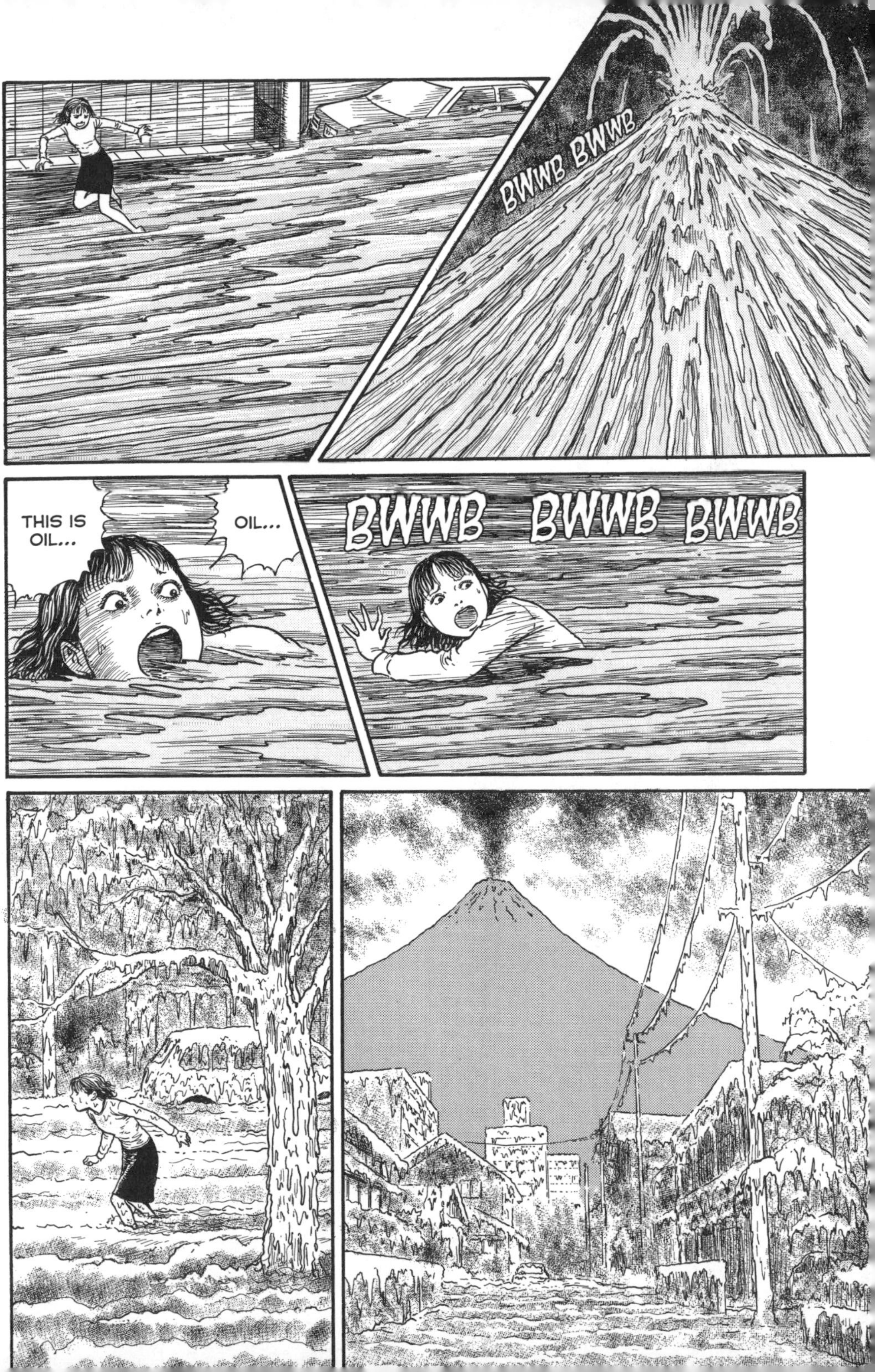
BWWB BWWB
BWWB BWWB BWWB
THIS IS OIL...
OIL...

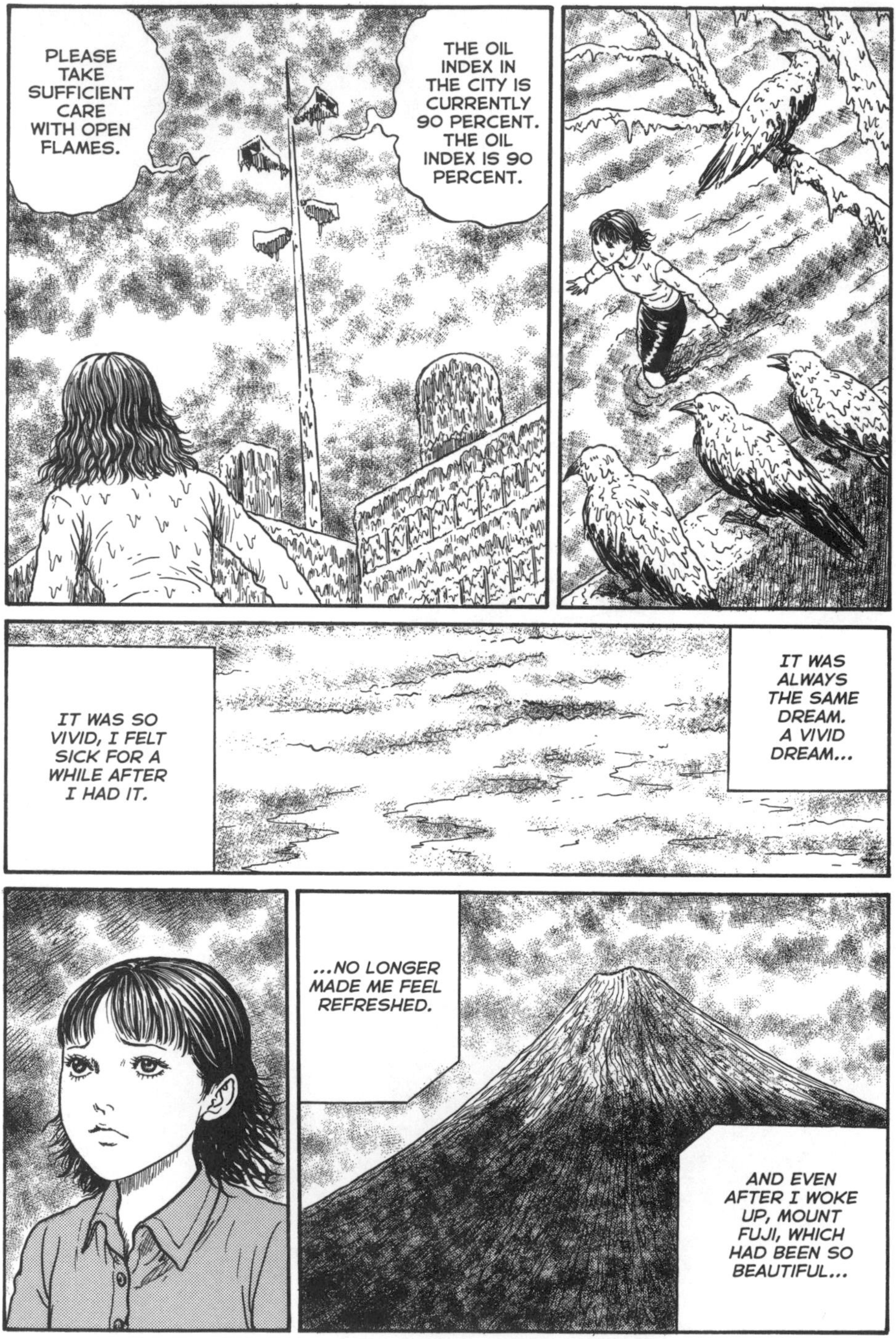
THE OIL INDEX IN THE CITY IS CURRENTLY 90 PERCENT. THE OIL INDEX IS 90 PERCENT.
PLEASE TAKE SUFFICIENT CARE WITH OPEN FLAMES.
IT WAS ALWAYS THE SAME DREAM. A VIVID DREAM...
IT WAS SO VIVID, I FELT SICK FOR A WHILE AFTER I HAD IT.
AND EVEN AFTER I WOKE UP, MOUNT FUJI, WHICH HAD BEEN SO BEAUTIFUL...
...NO LONGER MADE ME FEEL REFRESHED.

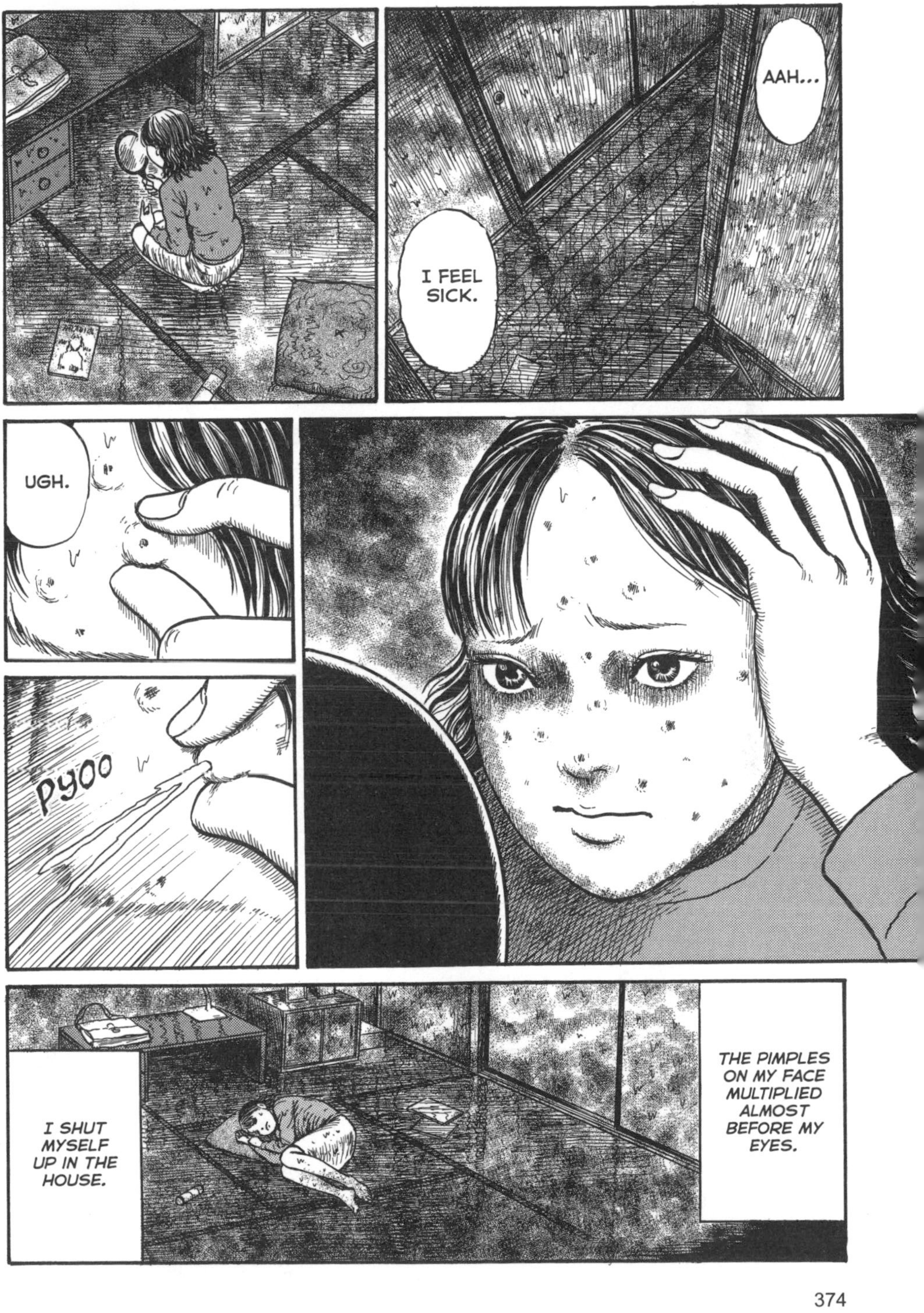
AAH...
I FEEL SICK.
UGH.
PYOO
THE PIMPLES ON MY FACE MULTIPLIED ALMOST BEFORE MY EYES.
I SHUT MYSELF UP IN THE HOUSE.

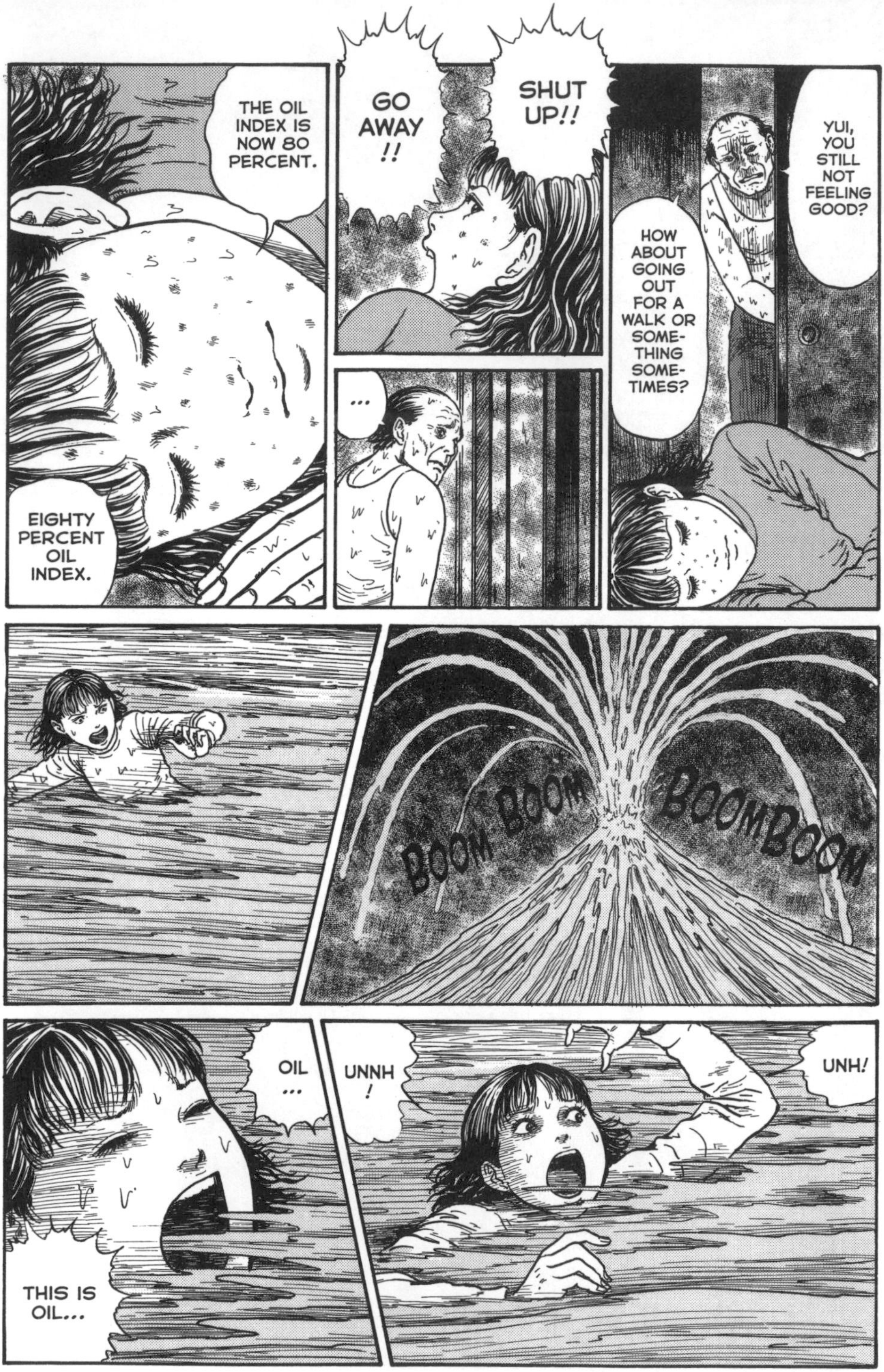
YUI, YOU STILL NOT FEELING GOOD?
HOW ABOUT GOING OUT FOR A WALK OR SOME-THING SOME-TIMES?
SHUT UP!!
GO AWAY!!
...
THE OIL INDEX IS NOW 80 PERCENT.
EIGHTY PERCENT OIL INDEX.
BOOMBOOM
BOOM BOOM
UNH!
UNNH!
OIL...
THIS IS OIL...

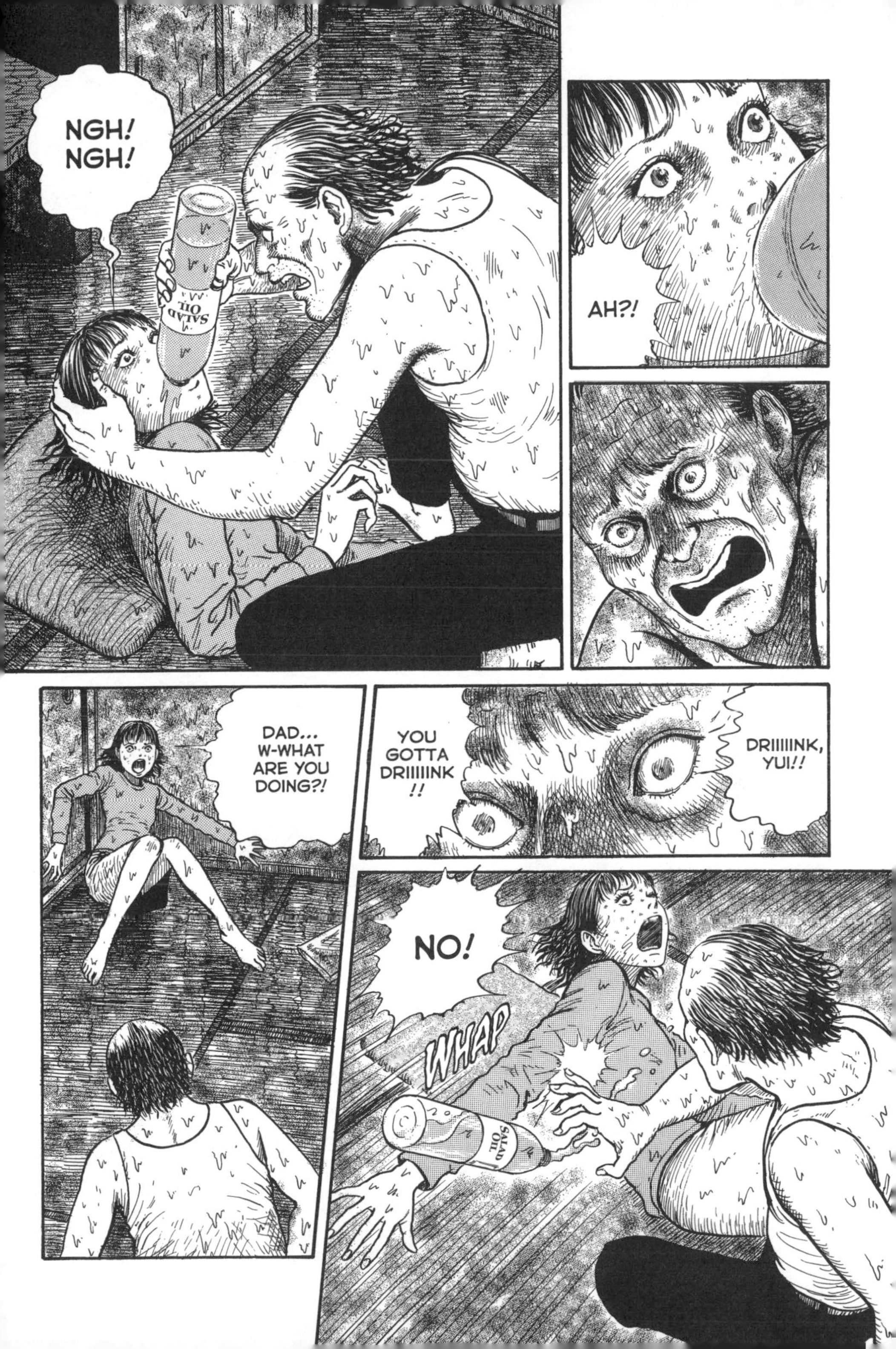
AH?!
NGH! NGH!
SALAD OIL
DRIIIIINK, YUI!!
YOU GOTTA DRIIIIINK!!
NO!
WHAP
SALAD OIL
DAD... W-WHAT ARE YOU DOING?!

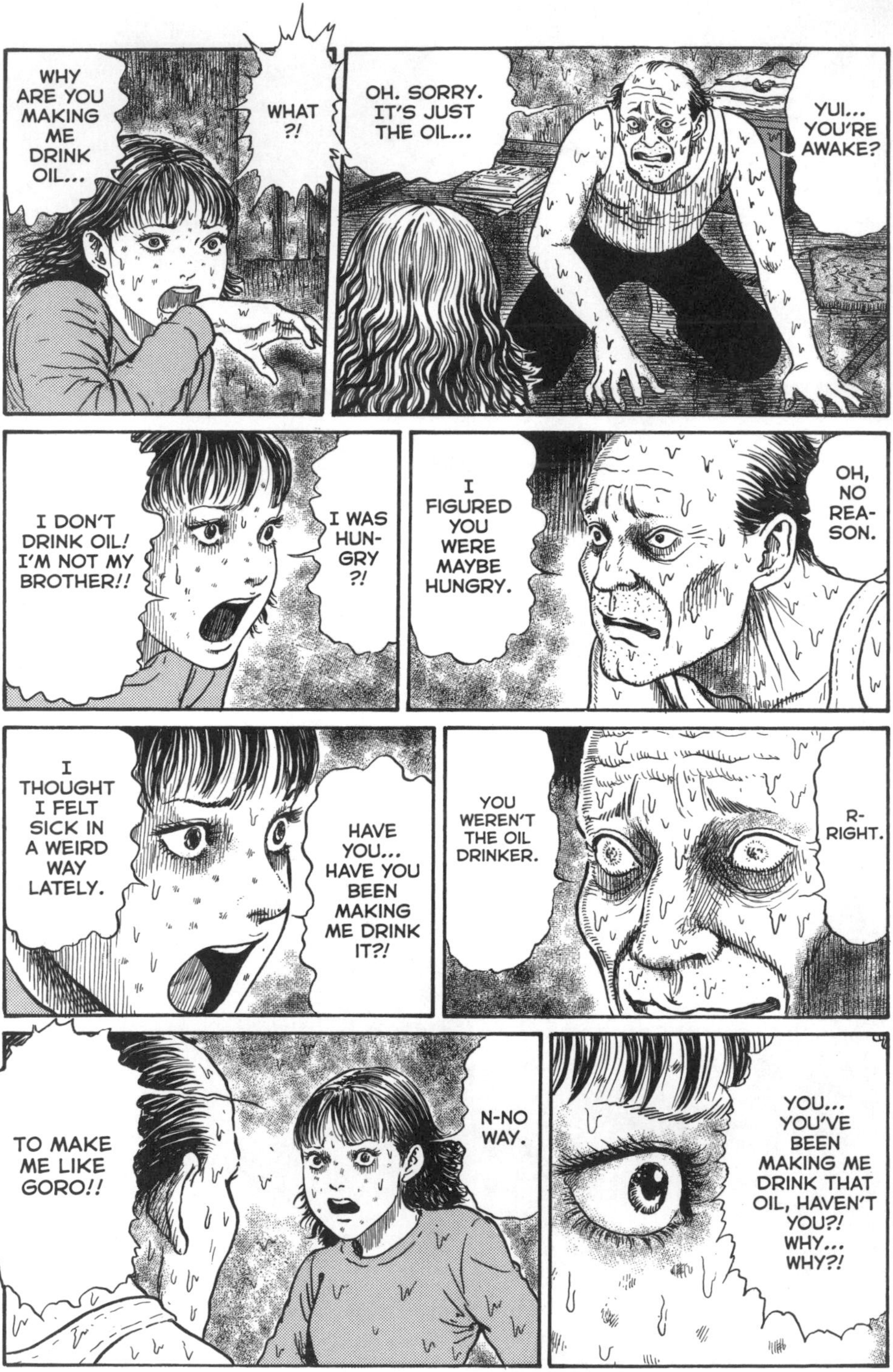
YUI... YOU'RE AWAKE?
OH. SORRY. IT'S JUST THE OIL...
WHAT?!
WHY ARE YOU MAKING ME DRINK OIL...
OH, NO REA-SON.
I FIGURED YOU WERE MAYBE HUNGRY.
I WAS HUN-GRY?!
I DON'T DRINK OIL! I'M NOT MY BROTHER!!
R-RIGHT.
YOU WEREN'T THE OIL DRINKER.
HAVE YOU... HAVE YOU BEEN MAKING ME DRINK IT?!
I THOUGHT I FELT SICK IN A WEIRD WAY LATELY.
YOU... YOU'VE BEEN MAKING ME DRINK THAT OIL, HAVEN'T YOU?! WHY... WHY?!
N-NO WAY.
TO MAKE ME LIKE GORO!!

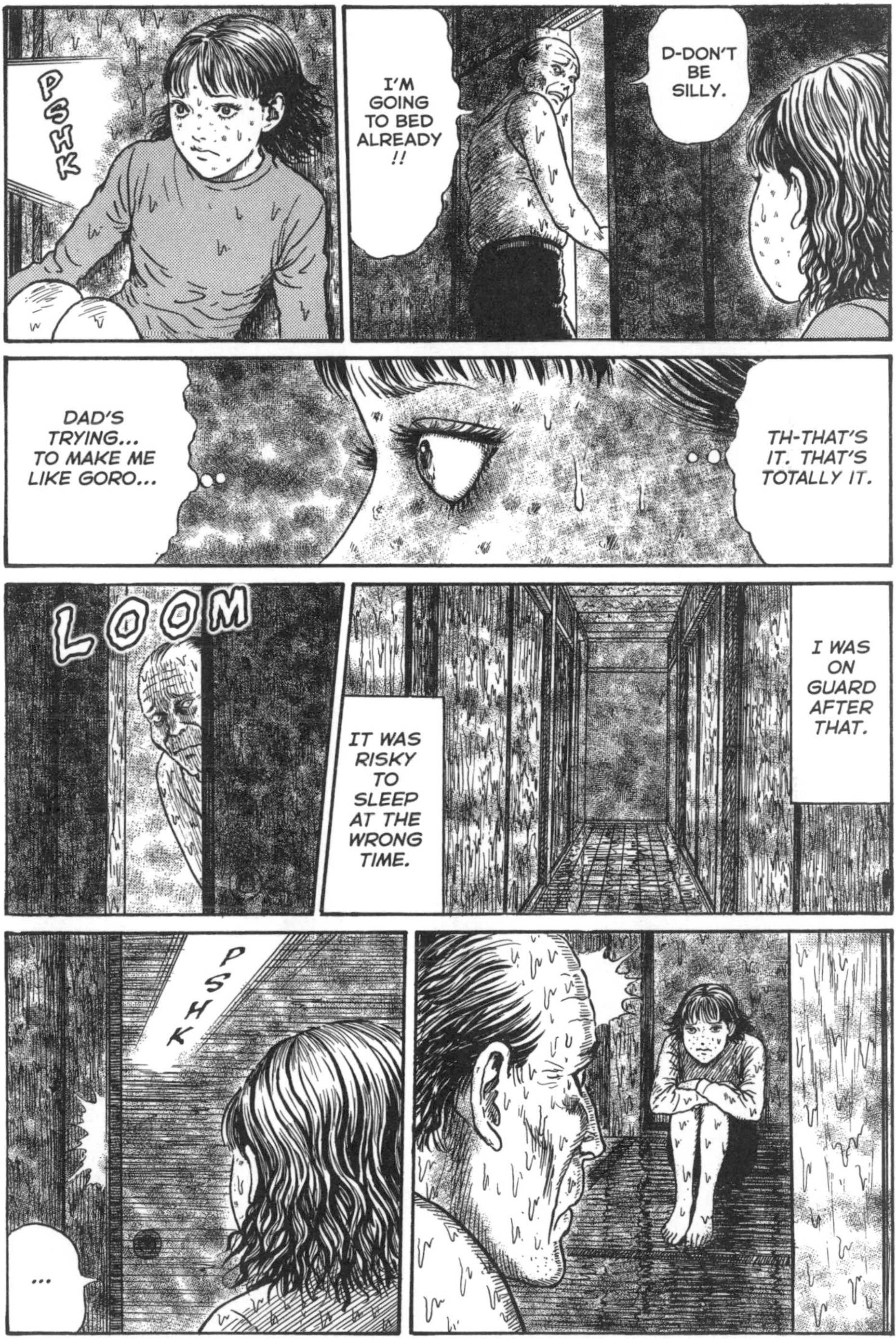
D-DON'T BE SILLY.
I'M GOING TO BED ALREADY!!
PSHK
TH-THAT'S IT. THAT'S TOTALLY IT.
DAD'S TRYING... TO MAKE ME LIKE GORO...
I WAS ON GUARD AFTER THAT.
IT WAS RISKY TO SLEEP AT THE WRONG TIME.
LOOM
PSHK
...

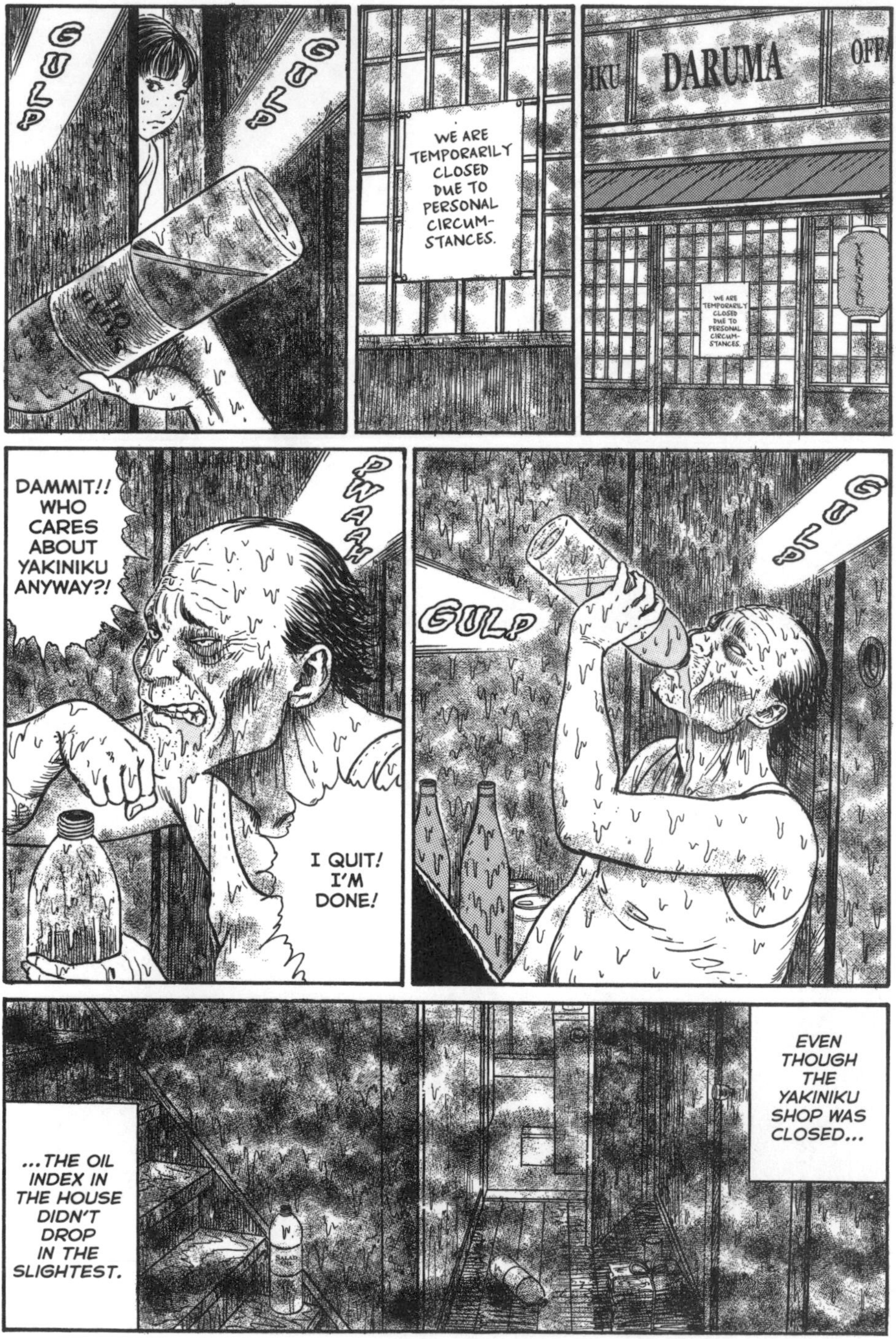

IKU
DARUMA
OFF
WE ARE TEMPORARILY CLOSED DUE TO PERSONAL CIRCUM-STANCES.
WE ARE TEMPORARILY CLOSED DUE TO PERSONAL CIRCUM-STANCES.
GULP
GULP
GULP
GULP
PWAAAH
DAMMIT!! WHO CARES ABOUT YAKINIKU ANYWAY?!
I QUIT! I'M DONE!
EVEN THOUGH THE YAKINIKU SHOP WAS CLOSED...
...THE OIL INDEX IN THE HOUSE DIDN'T DROP IN THE SLIGHTEST.

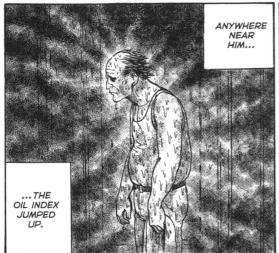

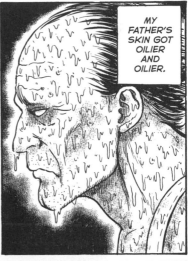

MY FATHER'S SKIN GOT OILIER AND OILIER.
ANYWHERE NEAR HIM...
...THE OIL INDEX JUMPED UP.
AFTER MY FATHER HAD BEEN IN THE BATH, THERE WAS A THICK LAYER OF OIL OVER THE WATER.
AND THE FUTONS IN THE CLOSET WERE EVEN MORE SOAKED THAN EVER WITH OIL..
THE OIL INDEX IN THE HOUSE WAS ALWAYS 90 PERCENT OR HIGHER.
DRIP
DRIP
...AND IT FELL FROM THE CEILING LIKE RAIN.

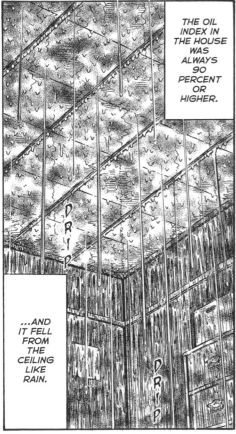

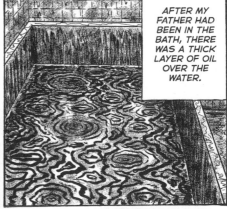

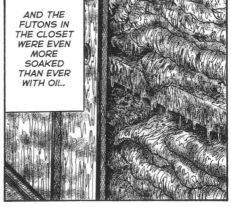

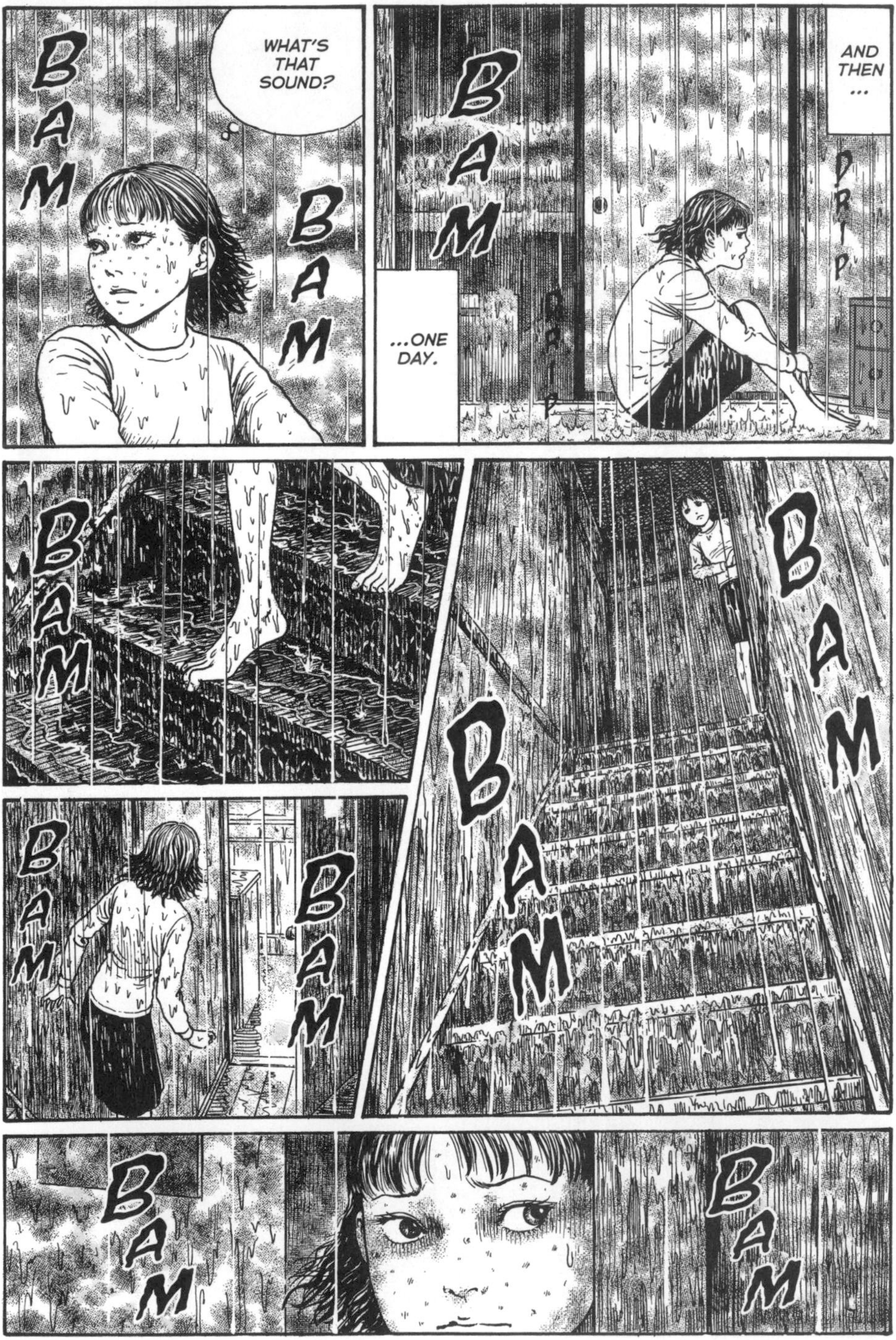

AND THEN ...
DRIP
BAM
DRIP
...ONE DAY.
WHAT'S THAT SOUND?
BAM
BAM
BAM
BAM
BAM
BAM
BAM
BAM
BAM

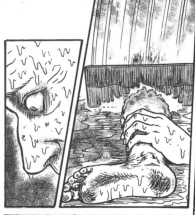

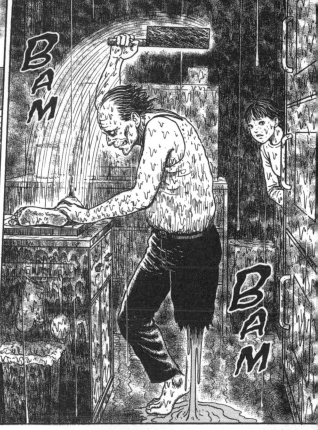

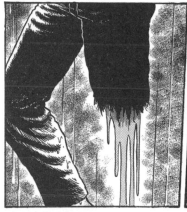

BAM
BAM
WHAT GUSHED OUT FROM MY FATHER'S SEVERED LEG WAS NOT BLOOD, BUT YELLOWISH-BROWN OIL...
THE CURRENT OIL INDEX IS 100 PERCENT.
THE OIL INDEX IS 100 PERCENT ...

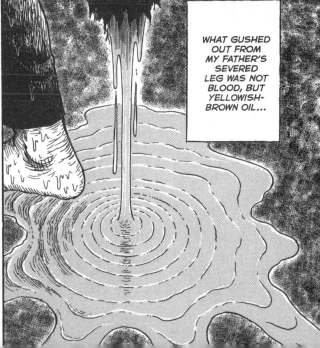

END

AUTHOR COMMENTARY

GREASED

First, I had as an image the unpleasantness of an oil-soaked futon. The dental technician school I went to in Nagoya was a Buddhist corporation, so there was also Buddhist study. I'm pretty sure it was in Mie prefecture, but in any case, we stayed over at this temple for a few days, did *zazen* meditation, and chanted prayers while tapping our *mokugyo* temple blocks. Naturally, we also did the cleaning inside the temple and on the temple grounds, but the most difficult thing was when we would go to sleep at night. The futons they had at the temple hadn't been aired out for who knew how many years, like they were fermenting them inside the humid closets, and they were stained a solid brown from the sweat of Buddhist students, and had wrinkles that were hardened in place. Sleeping on that sticky futon on the hot, humid summer nights was really difficult ascetic practice. I wanted to put that discomfort into a manga.

When I took up oil as my subject, other related things came out. Like pimples. When I was a teenager, I had terrible skin, and I squeezed so much out of the super large pimples on my forehead! So then I thought that if we talk about humidity levels to indicate the amount of moisture in the air, then it would be good if there was also something to indicate the amount of oil in the air. I wish I had been able to come up with a better name than "oil index," but I couldn't.

"Greased" is a collection of unpleasant things, and since I'm sure this will cause significant trouble for all you readers, I decided to wrap up this self-absorbed author commentary while reproaching myself and chanting prayers. Hail to the Lotus Sutra!

当初 油湿度と呼ばれたがやがて
油度と簡略化された.

油度の話　　　油湿度
（湿）

油度という湿度に次ぐ空気の状態.

そこに住む人々は油っこい人々.

植物性. 動物性。石油系.

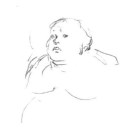

[人間の脂]　深呼吸

　　　　　　　　　さわやかさを切望する人々

油田から新鮮な油が産出. そこで働く労働者.
「本日の油度80%」
　　　　（湿）

街中黄ばんでいる. 壁にさわってみると. ベトッとして　指が壁に
　　　　　　　　　　　　　　　　　　　　　　　　すべらない

コッテリした人々　脂っこい恋. 粘っこく. しつっこく離れない. 一緒にいると
　　　　　　　　　　　　　　　　　　　　　　　　　　　　　心地良い

頑固な人. （頑固な人って甘えてる人なんじゃねえの?）

「本日の油度30%. 本日の油度80%. 本日の油度100%」
　　　　　　　　　　　　　　　　　　　○油度100%で油の雨が降る
日本に大油田発見さる.　動物性油　○火事多発

[5. ふかふかの布団に眠りたい]　　○消化吸収の悪い油 胃もたれ
　　　　　　　　　　　　　　　　　○みにくい吐き出し物
油のぬちっこい壁に 何かが付着. 盛り上がる.
肥満体が増える.（死者が体にとりこまれる）
○油やけ（油脂の酸化分解, 長期貯蔵により黄か色・赤か色. にがみ. 不快臭
[○電家製品がどんどん壊れる]　○セッケンが必需品

A story about an oil (humidity) index
    At first, it's called the oil humidity index, but eventually, it's abbreviated to oil index.
    Oil humidity index

Air quality according to a humidity index called the oil (humidity) index
    The people who live in the town are greasy people.

Vegetable   Animal   Petroleum-related

Human fat   Deep breathing   People who long for freshness

New type of oil produced in oil fields. The people who work there.
    "Today's oil (humidity) index is 80%."

The whole town is yellowed. If you touch the walls, they're sticky and your fingers don't slide down it.

Thick, heavy people. Greasy love, sticky, refuse to leave your side. Feels gross to be with them.
    Stubborn people (Aren't stubborn people spoiled people?)

"Today's oil index is 30%. Today's oil index is 80%. Today's oil index is 100%."
    • *Oil rain falls at an oil index of 100%.*
    • *Frequent fires*

A large oil field is discovered in Japan. Animal oil.

"I want to sleep in a fluffy futon."
    • *Oil hard to digest/breathe, sits in the stomach heavily*
    • *Ugly pimples*

Things get stuck *to the sticky, oily wall and* pile up.
    The number of obese bodies increases. (It's taken into the bodies of the dead.)
    • *Oil burns (Yellowish-brown or reddish-brown due to oxidation/decomposition of oil, long-term storage. Bitter taste, unpleasant smell*
    • *Electrical appliances soon break.*   • *Soap is a must-have.*

BONUS STORY

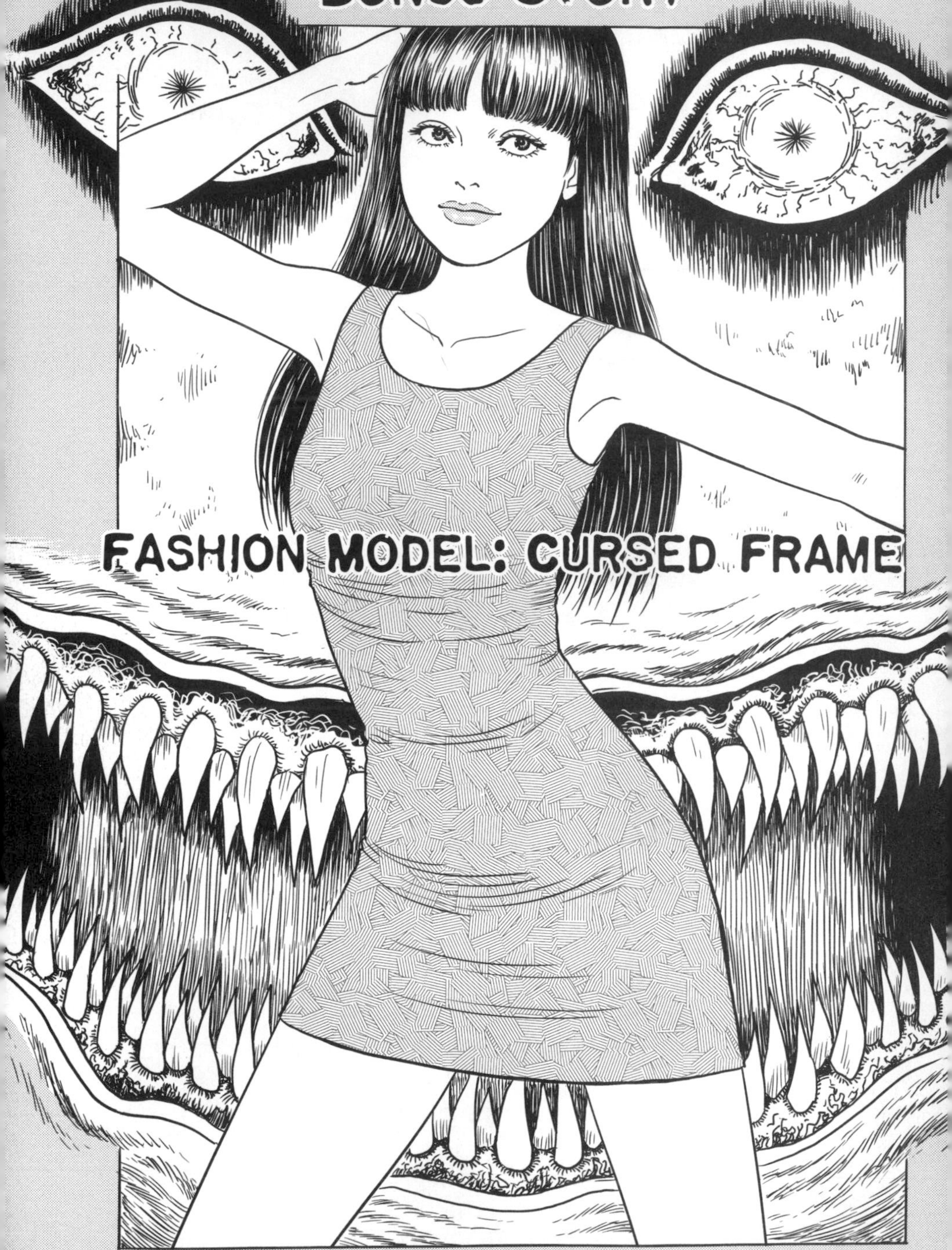
FASHION MODEL: CURSED FRAME

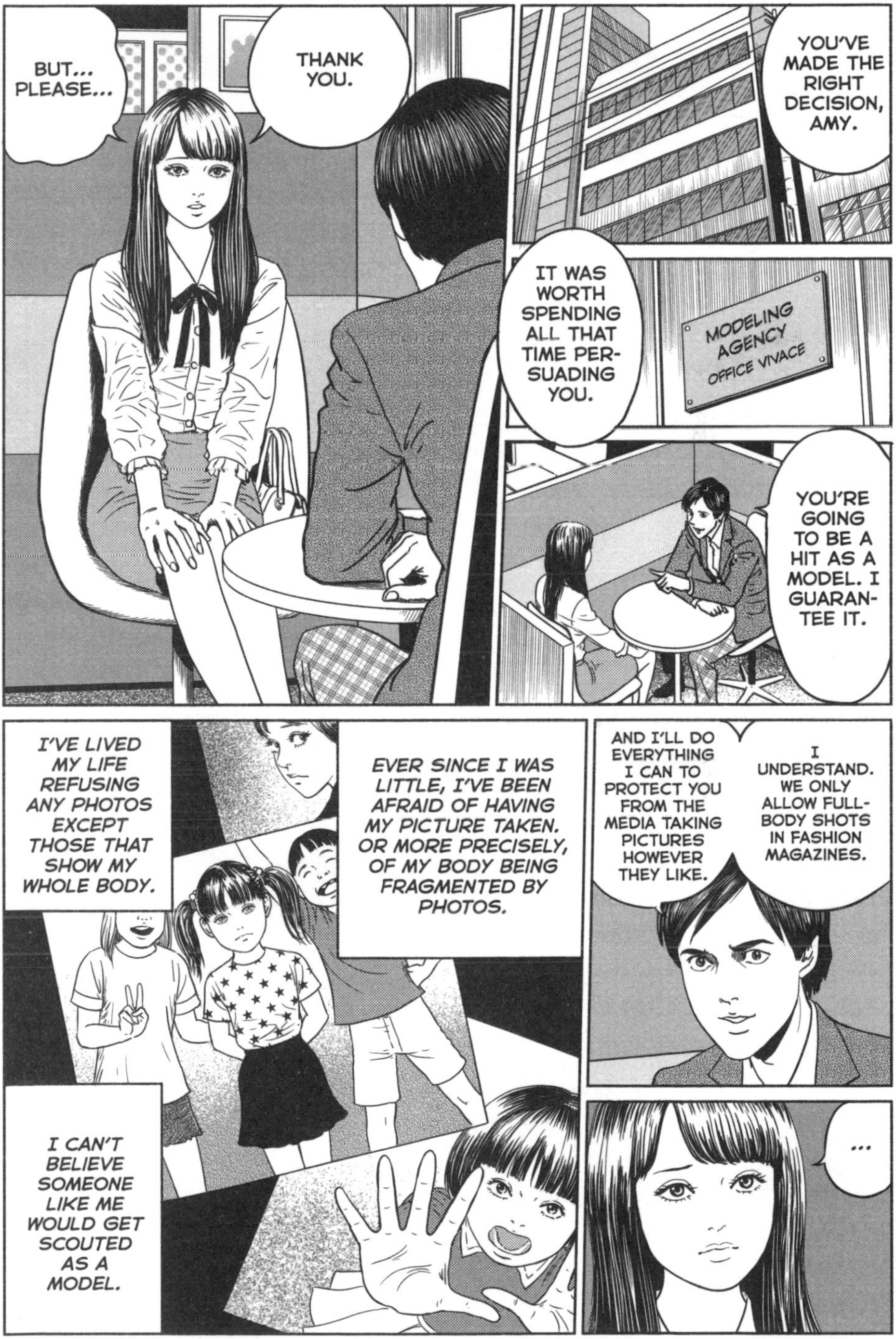
YOU'VE MADE THE RIGHT DECISION, AMY.
IT WAS WORTH SPENDING ALL THAT TIME PERSUADING YOU.
MODELING AGENCY OFFICE VIVACE
YOU'RE GOING TO BE A HIT AS A MODEL. I GUARANTEE IT.
THANK YOU.
BUT... PLEASE...
I UNDERSTAND. WE ONLY ALLOW FULL-BODY SHOTS IN FASHION MAGAZINES.
AND I'LL DO EVERYTHING I CAN TO PROTECT YOU FROM THE MEDIA TAKING PICTURES HOWEVER THEY LIKE.
...
EVER SINCE I WAS LITTLE, I'VE BEEN AFRAID OF HAVING MY PICTURE TAKEN. OR MORE PRECISELY, OF MY BODY BEING FRAGMENTED BY PHOTOS.
I'VE LIVED MY LIFE REFUSING ANY PHOTOS EXCEPT THOSE THAT SHOW MY WHOLE BODY.
I CAN'T BELIEVE SOMEONE LIKE ME WOULD GET SCOUTED AS A MODEL.

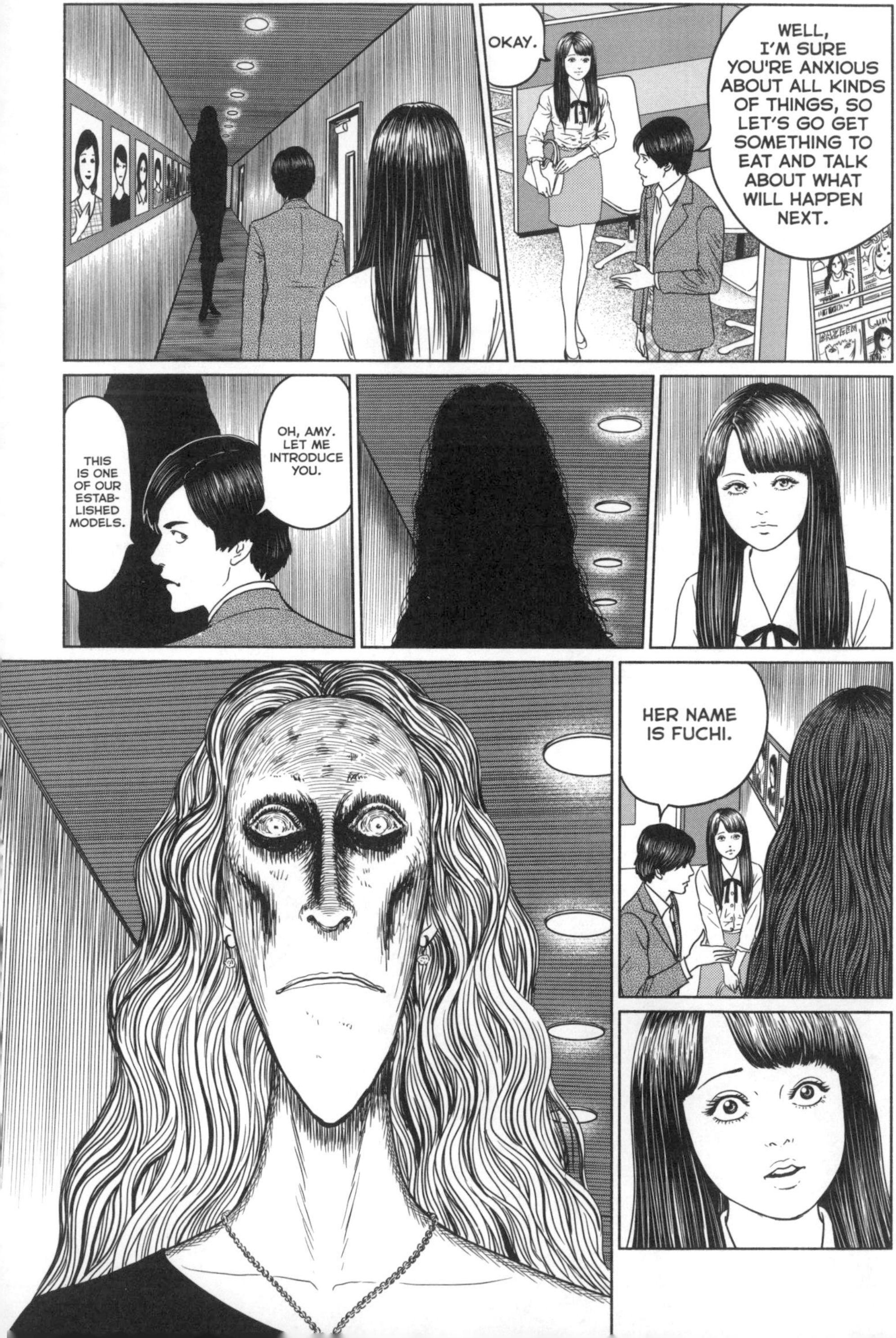
WELL, I'M SURE YOU'RE ANXIOUS ABOUT ALL KINDS OF THINGS, SO LET'S GO GET SOMETHING TO EAT AND TALK ABOUT WHAT WILL HAPPEN NEXT.
OKAY.
OH, AMY. LET ME INTRODUCE YOU.
THIS IS ONE OF OUR ESTAB-LISHED MODELS.
HER NAME IS FUCHI.

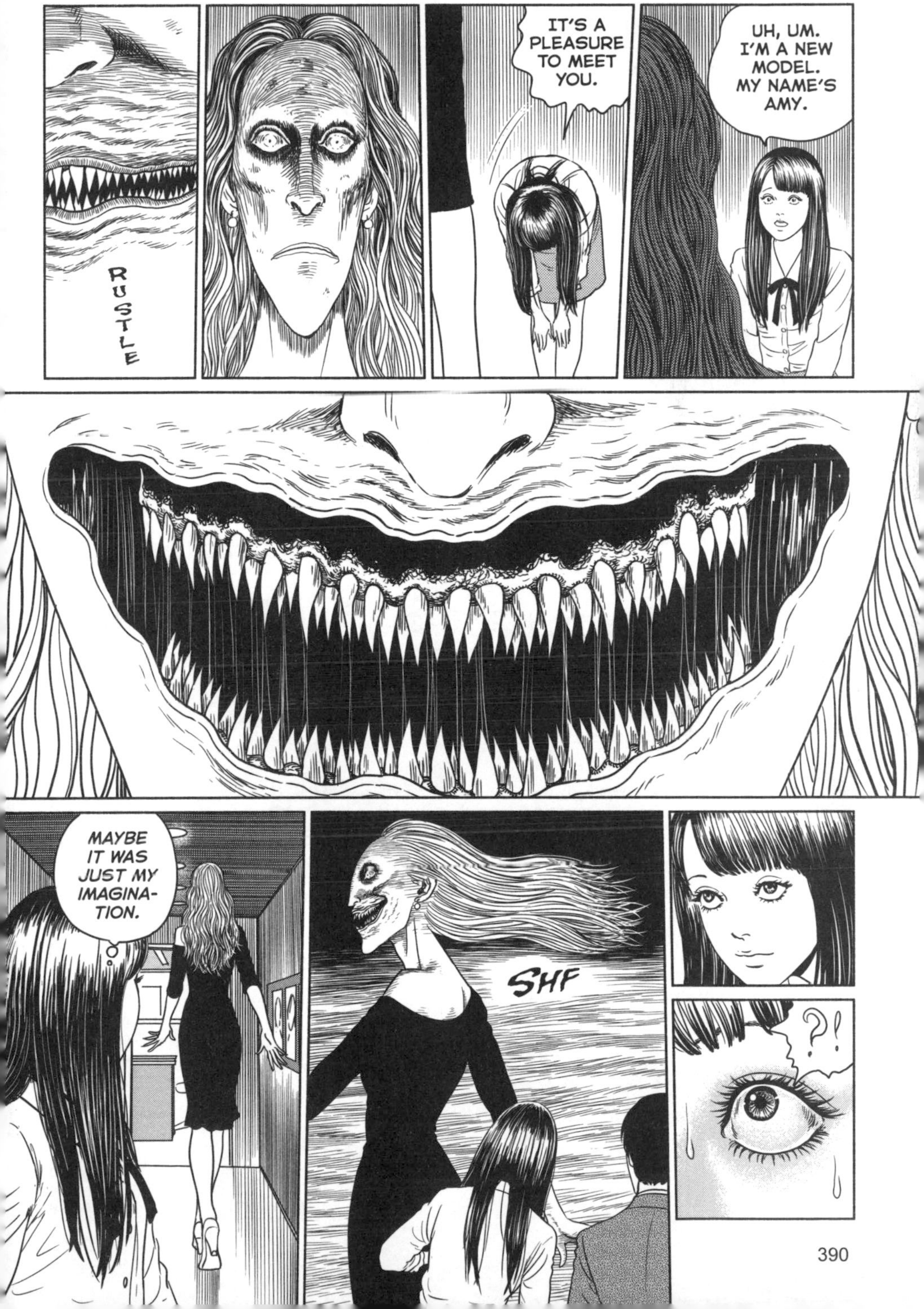

UH, UM. I'M A NEW MODEL. MY NAME'S AMY.
IT'S A PLEASURE TO MEET YOU.
RUSTLE
?!
SHF
MAYBE IT WAS JUST MY IMAGINATION.

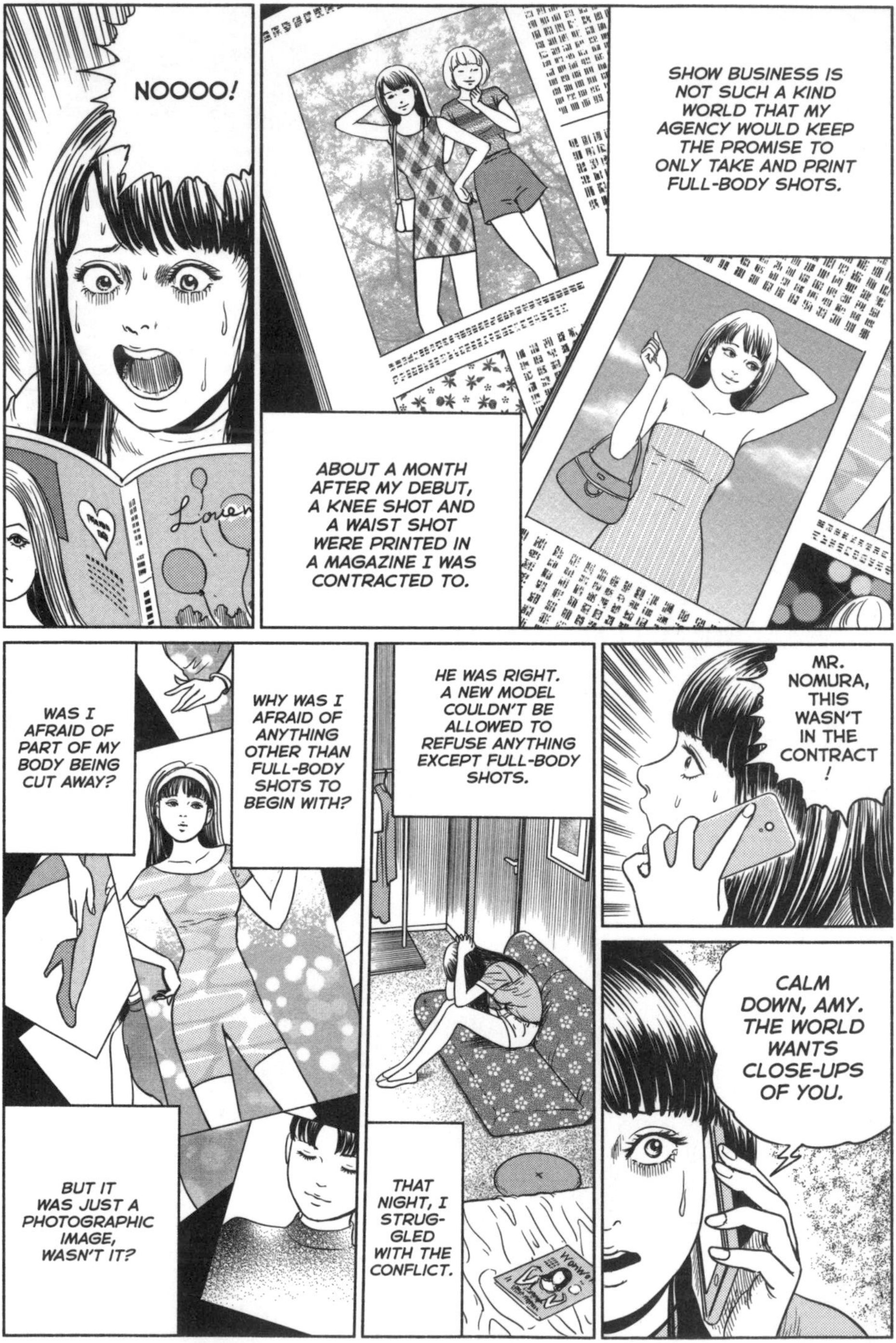
SHOW BUSINESS IS NOT SUCH A KIND WORLD THAT MY AGENCY WOULD KEEP THE PROMISE TO ONLY TAKE AND PRINT FULL-BODY SHOTS.
ABOUT A MONTH AFTER MY DEBUT, A KNEE SHOT AND A WAIST SHOT WERE PRINTED IN A MAGAZINE I WAS CONTRACTED TO.
NOOOO!
MR. NOMURA, THIS WASN'T IN THE CONTRACT!
CALM DOWN, AMY. THE WORLD WANTS CLOSE-UPS OF YOU.
HE WAS RIGHT. A NEW MODEL COULDN'T BE ALLOWED TO REFUSE ANYTHING EXCEPT FULL-BODY SHOTS.
THAT NIGHT, I STRUG-GLED WITH THE CONFLICT.
WHY WAS I AFRAID OF ANYTHING OTHER THAN FULL-BODY SHOTS TO BEGIN WITH?
WAS I AFRAID OF PART OF MY BODY BEING CUT AWAY?
BUT IT WAS JUST A PHOTOGRAPHIC IMAGE, WASN'T IT?

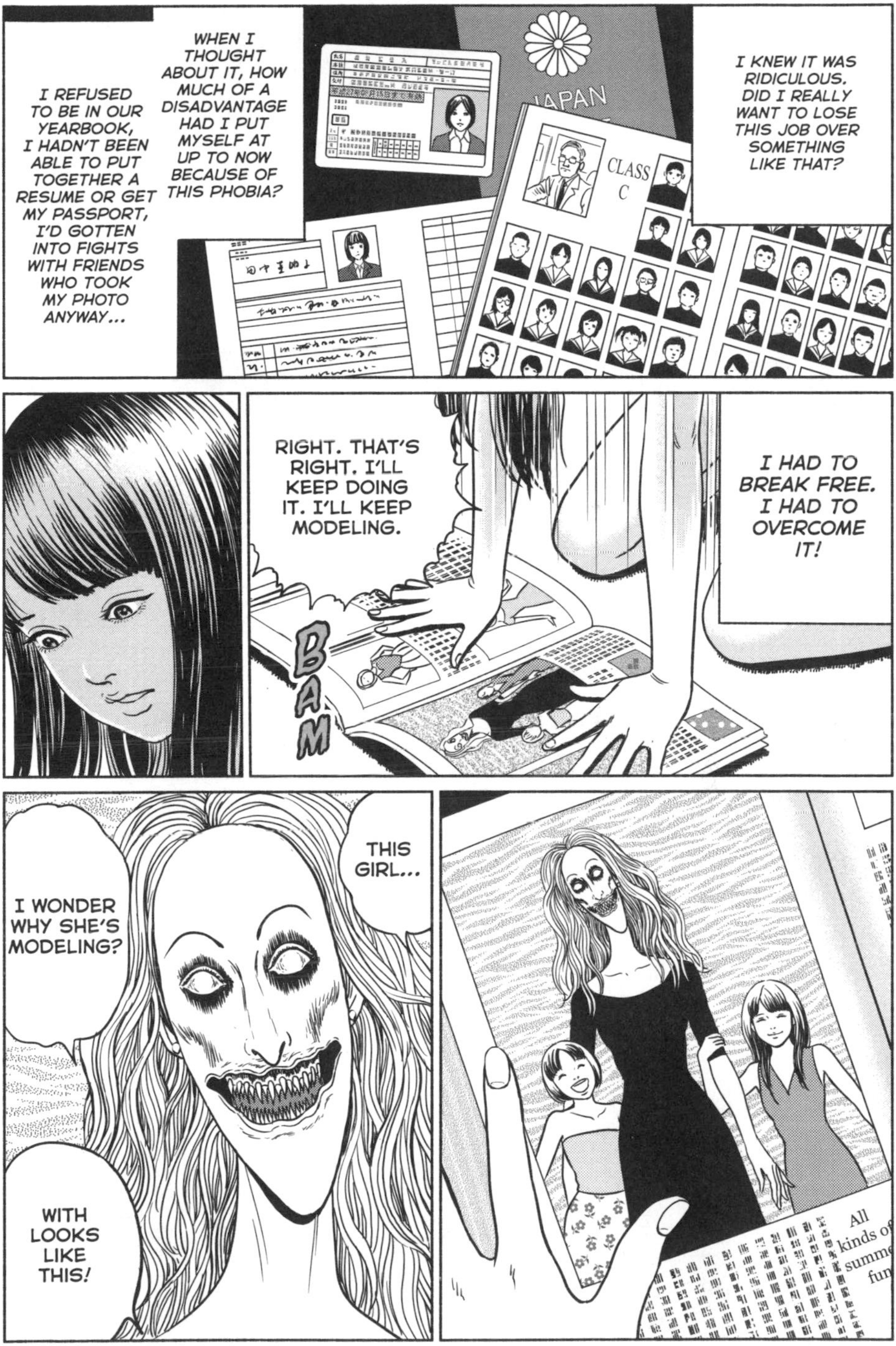
I KNEW IT WAS RIDICULOUS. DID I REALLY WANT TO LOSE THIS JOB OVER SOMETHING LIKE THAT?
CLASS C
JAPAN
WHEN I THOUGHT ABOUT IT, HOW MUCH OF A DISADVANTAGE HAD I PUT MYSELF AT UP TO NOW BECAUSE OF THIS PHOBIA?
I REFUSED TO BE IN OUR YEARBOOK, I HADN'T BEEN ABLE TO PUT TOGETHER A RESUME OR GET MY PASSPORT, I'D GOTTEN INTO FIGHTS WITH FRIENDS WHO TOOK MY PHOTO ANYWAY...
I HAD TO BREAK FREE. I HAD TO OVERCOME IT!
RIGHT. THAT'S RIGHT. I'LL KEEP DOING IT. I'LL KEEP MODELING.
BAM
All kinds of
THIS GIRL...
I WONDER WHY SHE'S MODELING?
WITH LOOKS LIKE THIS!

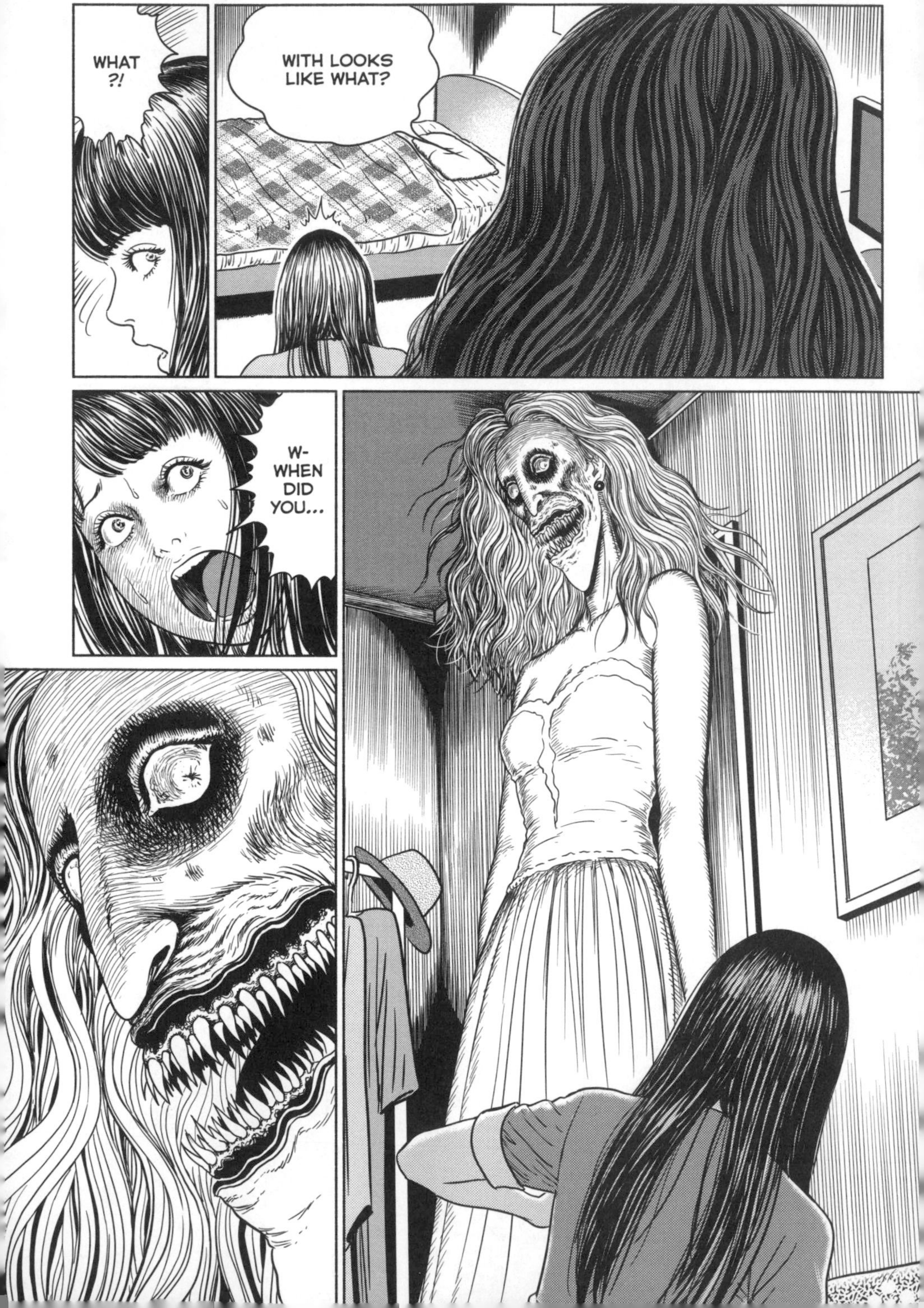
WITH LOOKS LIKE WHAT?
WHAT ?!
W- WHEN DID YOU...

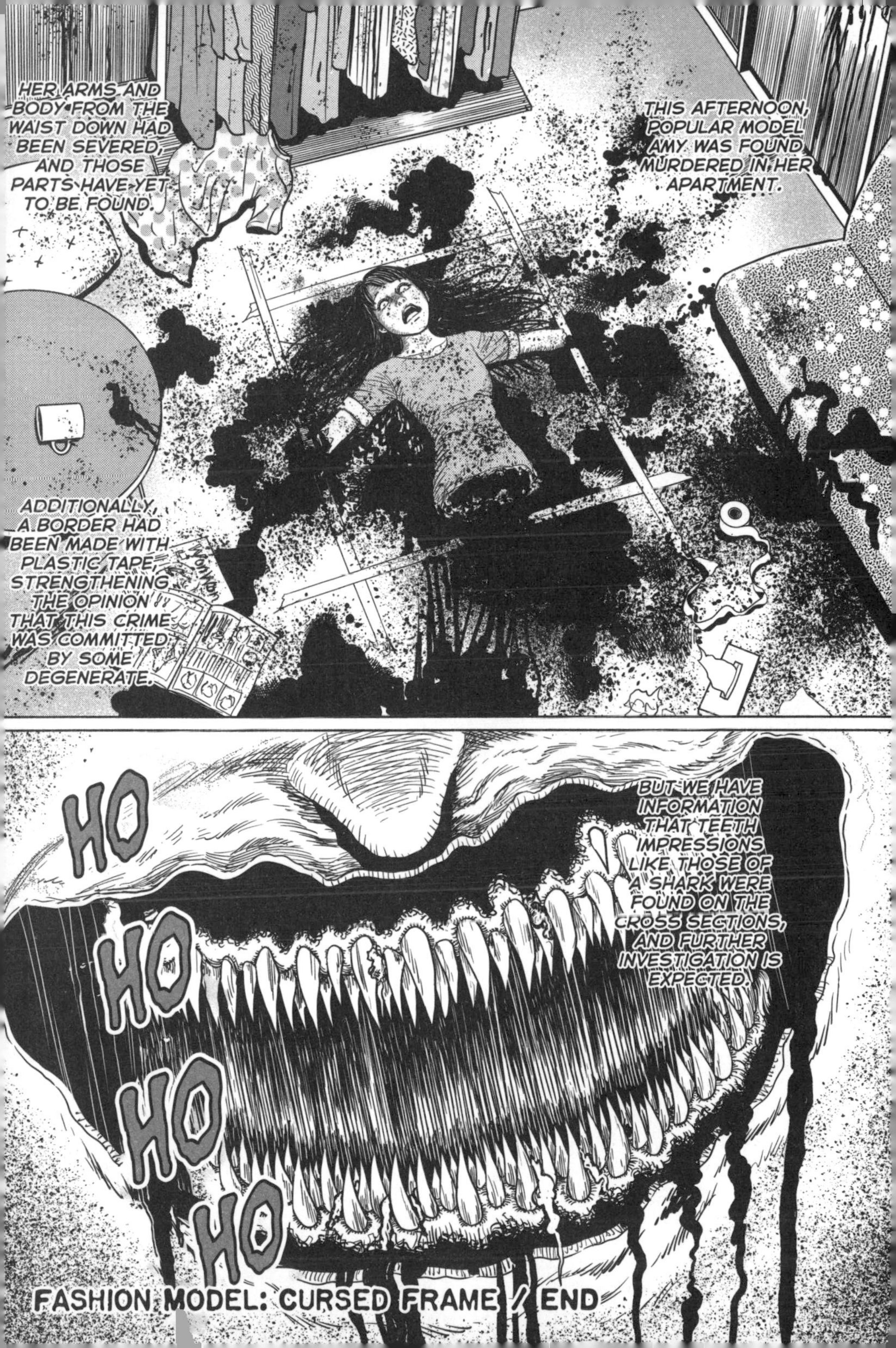
THIS AFTERNOON, POPULAR MODEL AMY WAS FOUND MURDERED IN HER APARTMENT.
HER ARMS AND BODY FROM THE WAIST DOWN HAD BEEN SEVERED, AND THOSE PARTS HAVE YET TO BE FOUND.
ADDITIONALLY, A BORDER HAD BEEN MADE WITH PLASTIC TAPE, STRENGTHENING THE OPINION THAT THIS CRIME WAS COMMITTED BY SOME DEGENERATE.
BUT WE HAVE INFORMATION THAT TEETH IMPRESSIONS LIKE THOSE OF A SHARK WERE FOUND ON THE CROSS SECTIONS, AND FURTHER INVESTIGATION IS EXPECTED.
HO
HO
HO
HO
FASHION MODEL: CURSED FRAME / END

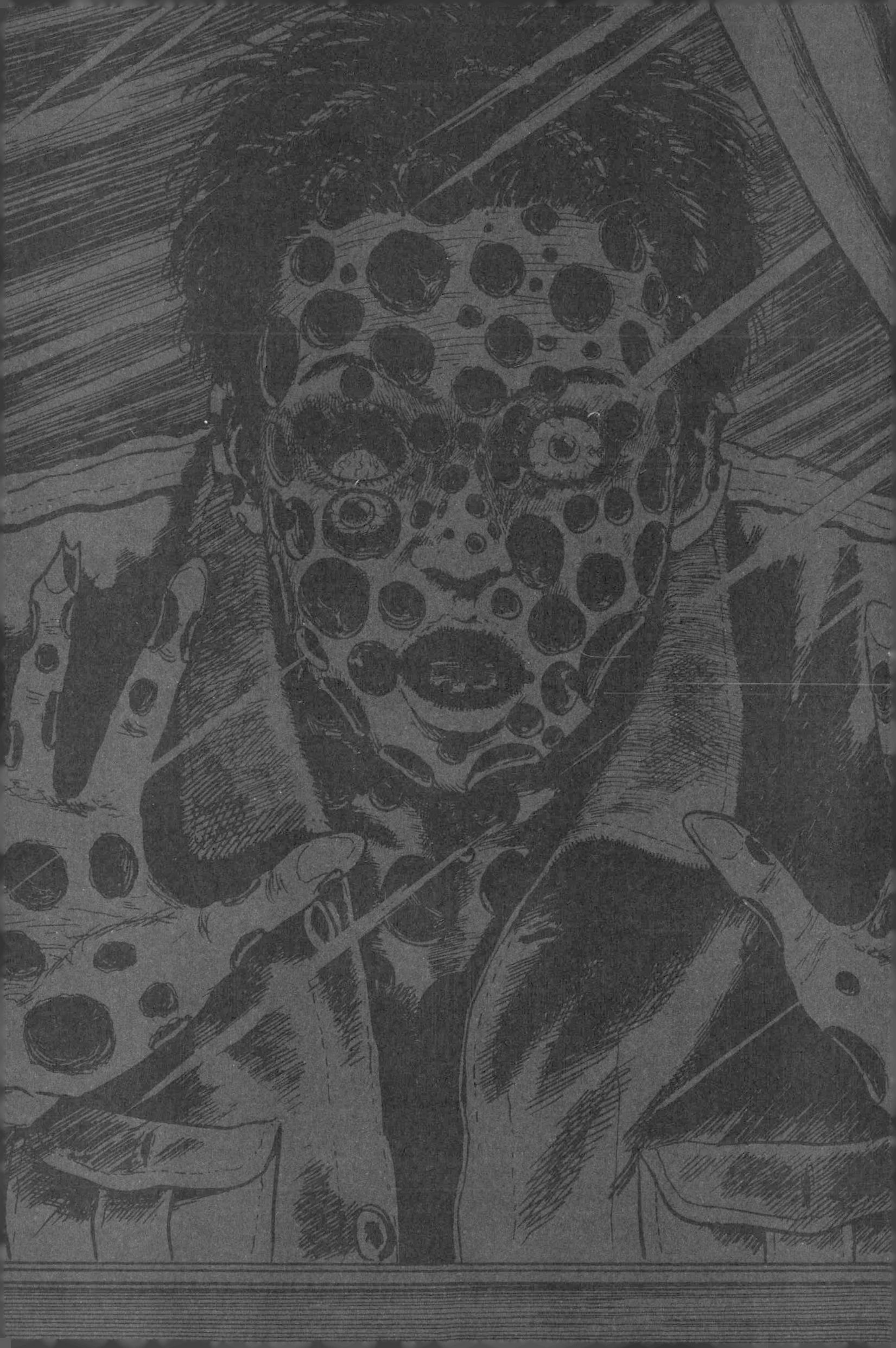

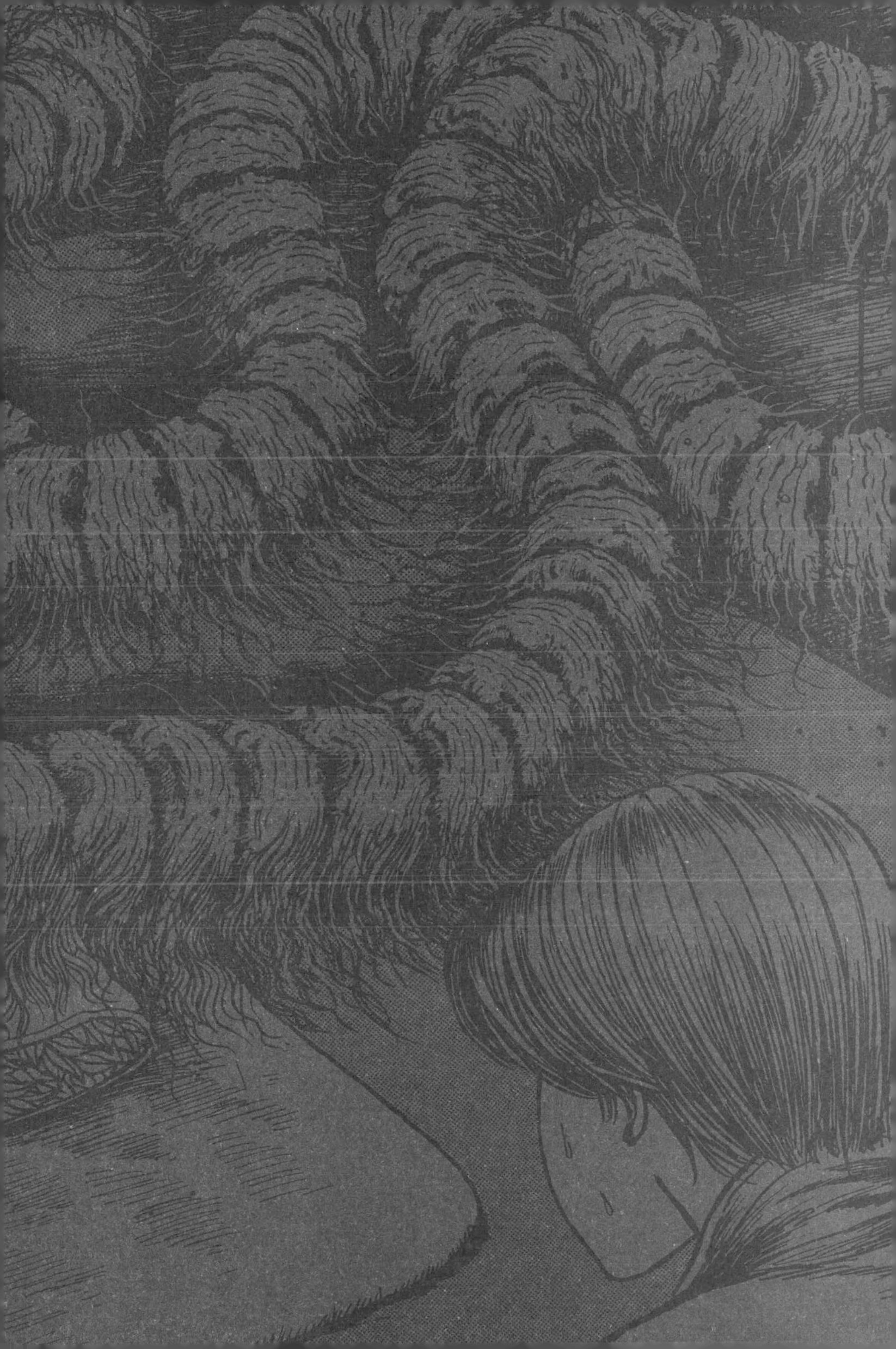

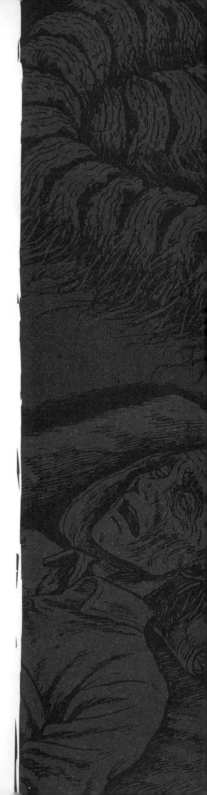

SHIVER: JUNJI ITO SELECTED STORIES
AFTERWORD

So we ended up publishing a selected collection of my stories. I've been drawing manga for nearly thirty years, but I'm actually still very attached to my work. Memories from the times I drew them are stuffed into each and every story.

In putting together the stories for this collection and then writing the commentaries for them, all kinds of things came back to life from the period when I wrote them, so it was a very fun bit of work to do. When writing the commentaries, I wanted to imitate the annotations of his own work that Edogawa Ranpo did, but when I reread my comments, the text seemed really arrogant. Ranpo's seemed so much more humble somehow.

I also included concept sketches, so with my terrible handwriting and all my misspellings, I've apparently decided to show you something truly embarrassing. Please be kind.

Finally, for giving me the opportunity to release this collection, I want to offer my sincerest gratitude to Asahi Shimbun Publications comics editor-in-chief Yusuke Hatanaka, and my editors Mikio Yoshida and Makiko Hara, along with everyone else in the editorial department. And I'd especially like to say how eternally grateful I am to my late editor Toshiyasu Harada, who guided me from the time of my debut when I was basically a rank amateur and sometimes also gave me inspiration.

—Junji Ito
August 4, 2015

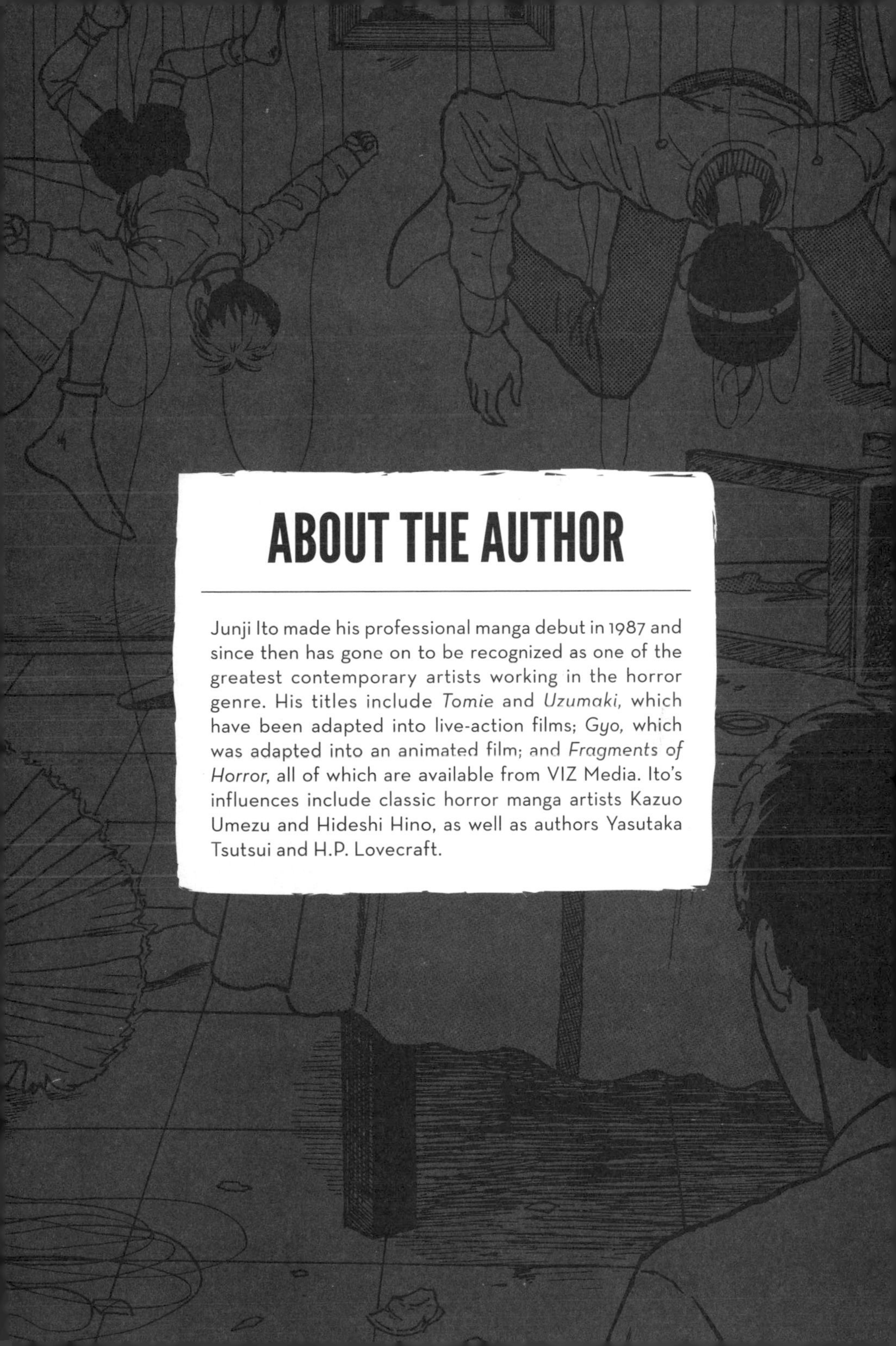

ABOUT THE AUTHOR

Junji Ito made his professional manga debut in 1987 and since then has gone on to be recognized as one of the greatest contemporary artists working in the horror genre. His titles include *Tomie* and *Uzumaki*, which have been adapted into live-action films; *Gyo*, which was adapted into an animated film; and *Fragments of Horror*, all of which are available from VIZ Media. Ito's influences include classic horror manga artists Kazuo Umezu and Hideshi Hino, as well as authors Yasutaka Tsutsui and H.P. Lovecraft.

SHIVER

JUNJI ITO SELECTED STORIES

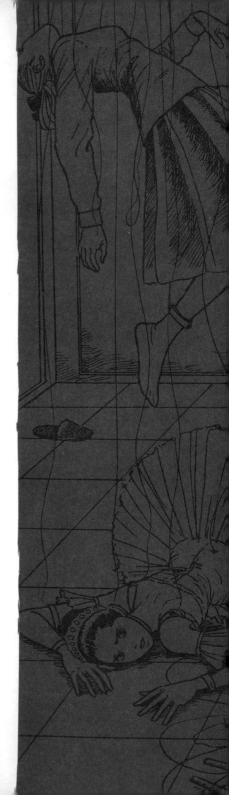

Story & Art by Junji Ito

Ito Junji Jisen Kessakushu
© JI Inc. 2015
Originally published in Japan in 2015 by Asahi Shimbun
Publications Inc., Tokyo. English translation rights arranged
with Asahi Shimbun Publications Inc., Tokyo through
TOHAN CORPORATION, Tokyo.

Translation & Adaptation: Jocelyne Allen
Touch-Up Art & Lettering: James Dashiell

"Painter"
Translation: Naomi Kokubo
Touch-Up Art & Lettering: Eric Erbes

Cover & Graphic Design: Adam Grano
Editor: Masumi Washington

The stories, characters and incidents mentioned in this
publication are entirely fictional.

No portion of this book may be reproduced or transmitted
in any form or by any means without written permission
from the copyright holders.

Printed in the U.S.A.

Published by VIZ Media, LLC
P.O. Box 77010
San Francisco, CA 94107

10 9 8 7 6 5
First printing, December 2017
Fifth printing, October 2020

VIZ SIGNATURE

PARENTAL ADVISORY
SHIVER is rated T+ for Older Teen and is recommended
for ages 16 and up. This volume contains graphic violence
and disturbing themes.

VIZ MEDIA
viz.com

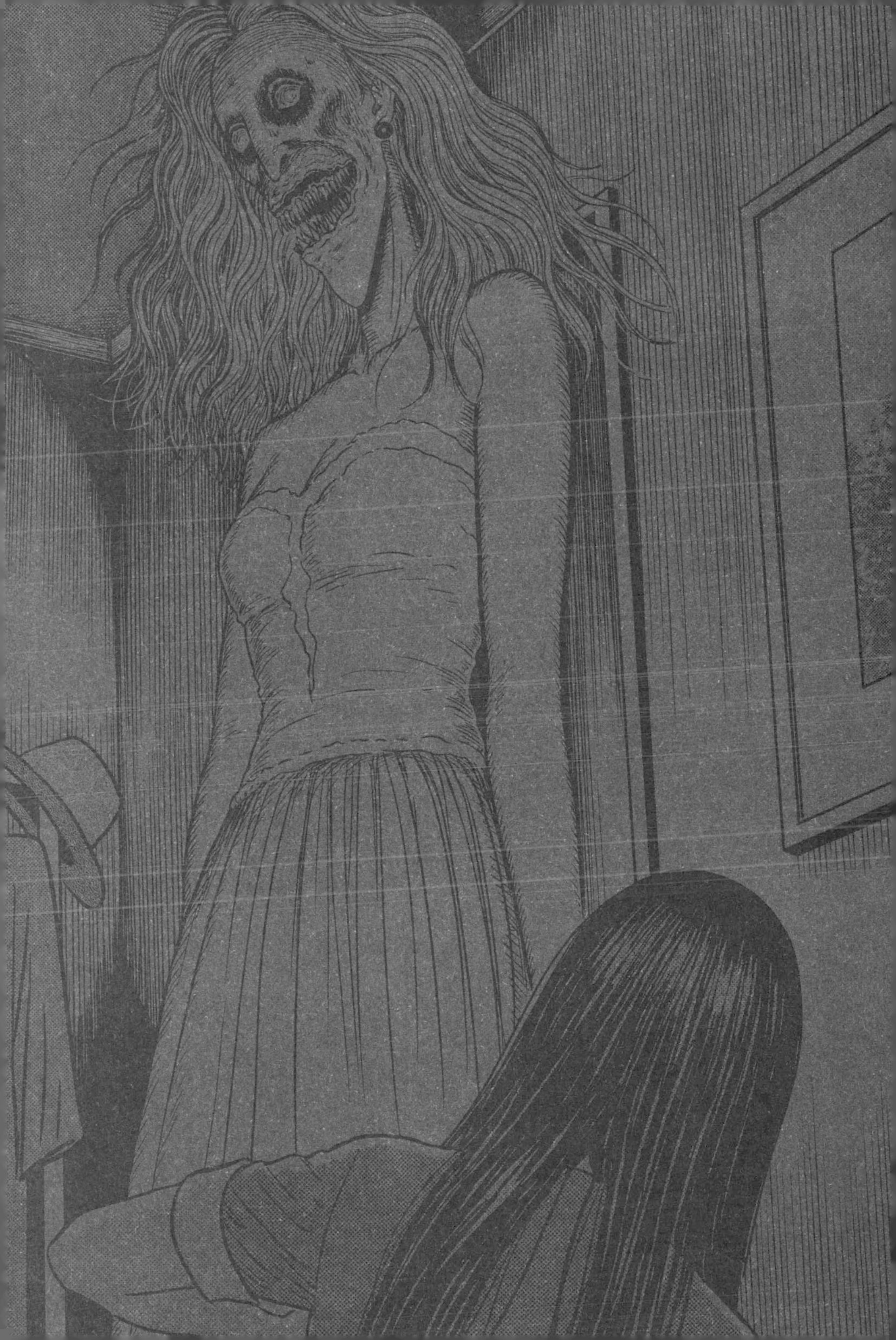

KU-165-601